Urbanism in the Preindustrial World

Urbanism in the Preindustrial World

Cross-Cultural Approaches

Edited by Glenn R. Storey

THE UNIVERSITY OF ALABAMA PRESS

Tuscaloosa

Typeface is AGaramond and Triplex

∞

The paper on which this book is printed meets the minimum requirements of American
National Standard for Information Sciences-Permanence of Paper for Printed Library Materials,
ANSI Z39.48-1984.

Library of Congress Cataloging-in-Publication Data

Urbanism in the preindustrial world : cross-cultural approaches / edited by Glenn R. Storey.
p. cm.
"Originated as an Archaeology Division session for the 95th Meeting of the American
Anthropological Association in Philadelphia, December 1998"—Ack.
Includes bibliographical references and index.
ISBN-13: 978-0-8173-1476-7 (cloth : alk. paper)
ISBN-10: 0-8173-1476-8
ISBN-13: 978-0-8173-5246-2 (pbk. : alk. paper)
ISBN-10: 0-8173-5246-5
1. Cities and towns—History. 2. Urbanization—History. 3. Rural-urban
migration—History. 4. Population—History. I. Storey, Glenn Reed, 1955– II. Title.
HT111.U75 2006
307.76—dc22
2005014490

Glenn and Rebecca Storey dedicate this volume to their father, Reed Karl Storey, an accountant who had the good humor to let two of his children become anthropologists.

DIS MANIBUS SACRUM

R K STOREIO

TABULARIO

AICPA

FASB

VIXIT ANNIS LXXII

MENSIBUS V

DIEBUS XXVI

PATRI PIENTISSIMO

FILIA ET FILIUS INFELICISSIMI

BENE MERENTI FECERUNT

(Sacred to the Gods of the Shades:

To R. K. Storey, Accountant

American Institute of Certified Public Accountants

Financial Accounting Standards Board

He lived 72 years, 5 months, 26 days.

To a most upright father, his daughter and son, most unfortunate in their loss, dedicated this to him because he merited it well.)

Contents

Figures

Tables

Acknowledgments

Urbanism in the Preindustrial World originated as an Archaeology Division session for the 95th meeting of the American Anthropological Association in Philadelphia, December 1998, in accordance with the theme of those meetings, the 200th anniversary of Thomas Malthus's *On Population*. The original invitation came from Elizabeth Brumfiel, to whom we extend our sincerest thanks and appreciation. Her early support and suggestions helped to craft this volume as it has ultimately turned out, reflecting her broad view of how urban populations of the past should be treated by scholars. Don Dumond also deserves special mention for playing a pivotal role in guiding us toward more explicit consideration of city populations in terms of the urban-rural continuum. Although the original theme was the population of cities, the contributions in this volume demonstrate how study of the demographic dimension of cities inevitably evolves into consideration of the question of urbanism itself.

I wish to thank all the chapter authors for their hard work and fine contributions, including those who were involved only with the original conference session. Two anonymous reviewers provided crucial feedback. I wish to thank my two research assistants at the University of Iowa, Katharine Dale and Heather Waddell-Gruber. I would like to express my gratitude to the staff of the University of Alabama Press, but above all my highest praise goes to Judith Knight, for her unfailing support for this project and unending good humor, and to Kathy Swain, for her outstanding and tireless copyediting. A special thanks to Jay Semel and the Office of the Vice President for Research at the University of Iowa for generous financial support of this publication.

Urbanism in the Preindustrial World

Introduction

Urban Demography of the Past

Glenn R. Storey

The contributions in this volume cover only a subset of worldwide preindustrial urbanism. The purpose of the volume is to provide examples of archaeological grappling with the subject of the population of cities before industrialization and to explore how scholars differently conceive and execute their research. Because I am a Romanist cognizant of the large literature on Classical cities, with its different conception and approach to the demography of cities, I have included historians in this discourse (some at the time of the conference and others joining shortly thereafter). Because of my background in Mesoamerican archaeology, I also initially focused on Mesoamerica and the Andes.

Granted the emphasis on the Classical world and the New World, the idea was never to cover every culture or case of preindustrial urbanization; obviously some important regions are left out (e.g., Indus Valley, Iran, central Asia, Moghul India). The most glaring omission is Mesopotamia, although some material on that region appears from the neglected period of the Hellenistic world (Morris, chapter 1) and in Small's cross-cultural discussions (chapter 16). Liu (chapter 9, on Erlitou, the earliest Chinese urban site) compares the processes of urbanization in early China to those in Mesopotamia.

There is compensatory advantage in sampling with a broad brush and opting for greater depth of coverage in a joint venture with our colleagues in history on an ancient metropolis such as Rome (Lo Cascio, chapter 2; Paine and G. Storey, chapter 3; Shaw, chapter 4) and of Teotihuacan (R. Storey, chapter 14, and Gorenflo, chapter 15). This attention to the largest, best-known preindustrial cities is profitably contrasted with exploration of lesser-known cases, which introduce novel processes of urbanization or cityscapes of unusual configuration: early China (Liu, chapter 9), Roman Egypt (Bagnall, chapter 7), Africa (Kusimba, Kusimba, and Agbaje-Williams, chapter 8), precolonial Southeast Asia (Junker, chapter 11), medieval Denmark (Petersen, Boldsen, and Paine, chapter 5), Tiwanaku (Janusek and Blom, chapter 12), and the Maya (Rice, chapter 13). The volume is arranged in four major similar tradition categories, which are only roughly geographical: "The Western Urban Tradition," "Urban Society on the African Continent," "Far Eastern Urbanization," and "Urban Centers of the New World," closing with the brief "Cross-Cultural Synthesis." The volume's "ring composition," beginning and ending with Greece (Morris, chapter 1, and Small, chapter 16), utilizes the ancient Greek concept of the polis, the city-state, to provide a useful framework for study of preindustrial urbanism as a unity of city and hinterland.

As Cowgill (2004:1) pointed out, approaches to cities and urbanism are "often undertheorized," so a volume on cities must begin with the problem of defining *city* and *urbanism*. This problem has spawned a huge literature; no single volume on the subject can provide a comprehensive definition. Although Cowgill (2004:1) prefers not to define urbanism in terms used to define pornography ("we know it when we see it"), something of that definition must be applied because of the continuing legitimate scholarly disagreement on what essential features constitute a city. Hence, in this volume we have implicitly adopted a definition of the city as the following: a kind of physical site that is home to "urban activities" (Cowgill 2004:3), with that site enjoying some (if not universal) consensus that the place in question was in fact a city or urban place *among the scholars who study that place and its cultural setting.* Such a definition is hardly ideal, and as Webster warns (2002:156), we must not simply apply the term *city* to any and every settlement we wish to, but when the majority of investigators find sufficient reason to call a site a city, even though it may not look like a city according to our modern standards, then it should be treated as one.

Students of cities of the past currently conceptualize the issue of urban demography in two major frameworks: (1) population size and density—population *magnitude;* and (2) identification and characterization of the constituent elements of urban populations—population *makeup.* Golden (2000:24) distinguishes *stock* data, raw counts of people, and *flow* data, information on population dynamics such as fertility, mortality, and so on. Makeup extends into the realm of the social, political, and economic factors associated with life in cities (M. L. Smith 2003). In turn, magnitude and makeup are embedded in the demography of the rural-urban continuum of city and hinterland. Table I-1 provides a summary guide to the chapters in this volume and what aspect of population each chiefly addresses.

Western Urbanization

In chapter 1 Ian Morris sees the biggest "super-cities" of the ancient Mediterranean world as all postdating 300 BC, with populations only on the order of 250,000 to 500,000. Morris's terminology of "super-city" recalls that of Marcus (1983:216) who spoke of "hyper-urban" centers for Mesoamerica. Junker (chapter 11, this volume) speaks of "hyperlarge" cities. Southall (1998:49) commented

Table I-1. Subject Guide to Chapters

City and Hinterland		
Magnitude		*Makeup*
Stock	Flow	Social Process
The Western Urban Tradition		
Ch. 1 Morris— Greek World		Ch. 1 Morris— Greek World
Ch. 2 Lo Cascio— Rome	Ch. 2 Lo Cascio— Rome	
	Ch. 3 Paine and G. Storey—Rome	
	Ch. 4 Shaw—Rome, N. Italy, Roman Egypt	Ch. 4 Shaw—Rome, N. Italy, Roman Egypt
	Ch. 5 Petersen, Boldsen, and Paine— Medieval Denmark	Ch. 5 Petersen, Boldsen, and Paine—Medieval Denmark
Ch. 6 Rothschild—New York		Ch. 6 Rothschild—New York
Urban Society on the African Continent		
	Ch. 7 Bagnall—Roman Egypt	Ch. 7 Bagnall—Roman Egypt
Ch. 8 Kusimba, Kusimba,and Agbaje-Williams—Africa		Ch. 8 Kusimba, Kusimba, and Abgaje-Williams—Africa
Far Eastern Egypt Urbanization		
Ch. 9 Liu—Early China		Ch. 9 Liu—Early China
Ch. 10 Nelson— Ancient Korea		Ch. 10 Nelson— Ancient Korea
Ch. 11 Junker—Southeast Asia		Ch. 11 Junker—Southeast Asia
Urban Centers of the New World		
Ch. 12 Janusek and Blom—Andes		Ch. 12 Janusek and Blom—Andes
Ch. 13 Rice—Maya		Ch. 13 Rice—Maya
	Ch. 14 R. Storey—Teotihuacan	Ch. 14 R. Storey—Teotihuacan
Ch. 15 Gorenflo—Teotihuacan		Ch. 15 Gorenflo—Teotihuacan

Continued on the next page

Table I-1. *Continued*

City and Hinterland		
Magnitude		*Makeup*
Stock	Flow	Social Process
	Cross-Cultural Synthesis	
		Ch. 16 Small (Old and New World City and Hinterland)
Ch. 17 Nichols (Themes)	Ch. 17 Nichols (Themes)	Ch. 17 Nichols (Themes)

aptly on this type of city as exemplified by Teotihuacan in Mexico: "The extraordinary size of Teotihuacan, far larger than any other pristine city in the whole world, evokes bafflement and incredulity. It belongs to a qualitatively different dimension of its own." Ancient and modern examples of hyper-urban cities are relatively easy to identify, the *metropoleis* (the correct Greek plural) of this volume. We might call the other main type of city featured in this volume, the *mbanza*, the "hypo-urban" city (a logical step from Marcus's suggestion). And, as Morris demonstrates, many Greek city-states may have had this latter configuration.

By their very definition, Greek cities (and Rome, for that matter) started out as multifocal, coalescing from separate villages into a single city via a process called, in Greek, *synoikismos* ("living together"). The residue of this ancient process is reflected in the names of Greek city-states, which are feminine plural nouns (the gender of the word for village being feminine). Some of the nucleated settlements that result from this process of "village coalescence" are of surprisingly low density in comparison to the hyper-urban type. Such centers can be large, covering tens of square kilometers, with populations of 5,000 and more, but often less. Morris suggests that even in the Classical period, the population of a typical city-state was less than 6,000, many numbering their populations in hundreds rather than thousands; he describes them as "no more than large villages." Morgan and Coulton (1997:92) comment on Sparta that "archaeologically, this pattern of *conurbation* seems more common than not" (my italics). The term "conurbation" for communities at the dawn of urbanization matches the term used currently to describe the settlement patterns of the world's largest megalopolis cities, such as the Boston-Norfolk or Tokyo-Osaka corridors. Neither the term "ancient conurbation" nor "modern conurbation" seems to be properly isomorphic analytically, but the key in retaining them for their respective contexts is the legitimate reflection that such configurations are characterized by alternations of concentrated areas of high population density and zones of empty (or far less densely populated) space. The Greek conurbations have a clear modern counterpart in the smaller cities of the world, especially those in the West, whose particular look we call "suburban," the "dispersed city" type in Canada (Filion et al. 1996).

Morris also introduces the problem of the evidence for assessing ancient city population sizes. He characterizes the process as "unverifiable calculations to reach total populations, but at least establish an order of magnitude." In a nutshell, this summarizes the entire enterprise of "stock" estimation for preindustrial cities, encapsulating both the limitations and the utility of the procedure. This must be attempted because, as emphasized by Nichols (chapter 17), the scale of an ancient city population size is important for determining the character of economic behavior and the ramifications of social structure.

Morris's discussion of population shifts introduces the question of in- and out-migration, which appears often in this volume. Morris suggests that in the transition from the Archaic to the Classical periods, preference for urban living appears to have been a strong motivation for in-migration to the fledgling urban city-states. That raises the possibility that many citizens of the various Greek city-states possessed residences both in the urban center and at their agricultural properties in the countryside. This pattern is ubiquitous in Greco-Roman town foundation and layout; urban and rural land division was a single process assigning each community participant a holding in both places. Roman *centuriation,* laying out rectangular plots in both city and countryside on the same grid, is the best example. That cities were laid out on orthogonal grids, something first seen in Mesopotamia but occurring in Greece from the fourth century BC on in such cities as Olynthos and Priene, illustrates how the occupying of the community space was thought of as a unity. So, in this one chapter, Morris raises many of the issues of importance we will see addressed in the rest of the volume.

It is convenient to treat chapters 2 and 3 as a unity, given the exploration of common goals in trying to assess the population of ancient Rome in both stock and flow dimensions. We arguably have the finest data available (both historical and archaeological) for any ancient city, so it is important to see how far the quality of this data can take us in answering basic questions about the demography of the city. In chapter 3 Paine and I have incorporated ages-at-death data from Roman funerary inscriptions into a statistical model assessing the effects of the Antonine plague (AD 165 with recurrences) on long-term demographic trends for the city of Rome. We believe that the catastrophic mortality profile we find in the epigraphic data may be an indicator of the effects of the Antonine plague.

In chapter 2 Lo Cascio comprehensively and ably offers a powerful challenge to the prevailing conventional wisdom that large cities were "population sinks" subject to an "iron law" of excess deaths over births constituting an "urban graveyard effect," a position that Sallares (2002), Morley (2003), Jongman (2003), and

Scheidel (2003a) strongly support. Paine and I believe that the urban graveyard effect is probably demonstrated in our analysis, and the effect is generally supported both in the chapters of this volume that touch on the question and in Woods (2003). However, Lo Cascio presents a strong argument as to why any extreme form of the "iron law" should be rejected, in line with Woods's (2003:44) admonition that "crude depiction of an urban graveyard effect be replaced by a far more contingent account that is sensitive to the diversity of health environments that may be associated with the clustering of populations in high-density areas." Shaw (chapter 4) adds the important point that the characteristics of the general environment may be most responsible for mortality patterns, even to the point of trumping the significance of the rural versus urban patterns.

Lo Cascio uses Sharlin's (1978, 1981) argument that the effect is exaggerated because historical urban immigration suggests that immigrants die at a higher frequency than native-born city dwellers. Immigration skewers death rates because migrants register their births elsewhere, but their deaths occur in the city to which they have moved. Lo Cascio uses data from early modern Rome (from the seventeenth century on) to argue that immigration increased mortality but that sanitary conditions were probably no worse in Rome than any other city and so not "exclusively responsible" for the decrease in population. Part of the thrust of Lo Cascio's argument is his determination to counteract the "making of an image," singularly negative on Rome's urbanism as depicted in the widely accepted review of Scobie (1986), who painted the imperial city as a hellhole of health disaster. Scobie's argument is vulnerable because (1) his evidence often amounts to literary anecdotes or rhetorical tropes that may well not represent the typical situation, and (2) his rhetoric is full of Victorian moral outrage at the callous neglect of the common people of the city by the Roman authorities that is inappropriately transferred to a period of the ancient world in which such sentiments would rarely have been articulated, even by the most sympathetic elements of the educated population, let alone acted on, and are thus grossly unfair (cf. Laurence 1997 and Scheidel 2003a).

Lo Cascio then takes up the question of Sallares's argument that Rome was subject to hyperendemic malaria for much of antiquity (2002), raising doubts that malaria could have been as all-pervasive a noxious demographic influence as Sallares envisions because the evidence, both literary and archaeological, indicates that Rome and its immediate hinterland were densely occupied and experienced considerable population growth during periods of supposed endemicity. Sallares suggests that the population growth was on farms worked by slaves who were dying from malaria in droves and thus needed constant replacement. But if that were true, there would have been difficulty keeping those properties worked, as well as serious challenges in maintaining the supply of slaves—*something would have to give.* The disjunction between the relatively healthy-looking "physical plant" of Rome and environs and the dire straits of Sallares's malaria requires explanation. An ongoing debate explores whether archaeology can identify the effects of disease, commencing with Duncan-Jones's (1996) attempt to show how the demographic crash of the Antonine plague was reflected in a number of archaeologically relevant dimensions. Scheidel (2002) attempted to provide a similar demonstration for Roman Egypt; however, serious challenges to both scenarios have been offered (Bagnall 2002; Bruun 2003, Greenberg 2003).

Lo Cascio emphasizes that if malaria affected Rome's demographic regime, then it is strictly not the unhealthiness of cities per se that is responsible for this particular urban graveyard effect. Although true, there is a corollary to that argument. Sanitary conditions may not solely be responsible for the urban graveyard effect, but the degree of density favors endemic and pandemic diseases. Lo Cascio characterizes Rome's demographic history as a series of "normal" (some growth) and "crisis" (essentially the same as "catastrophic") conditions. He notes that our data (chapter 3) may be picking up the crisis in the same way that it is possible to determine the fluctuations between growth and crisis in Tuscany in the fifteenth century (Herlihy and Klapisch-Zuber 1985), when there was a crisis event every nine years. In Roman history, Livy reports a disease event about every eight years. Lo Cascio concludes that the population of Rome had periods of stability (and even growth) alternating with periods of crisis when the urban graveyard effect was uppermost. Although I agree with the spirit of that conclusion, Paine and I approach the issue with a difference in emphasis: our model is one of normal mortality punctuated by episodes of crisis/catastrophic mortality, which seem to have been very severe (accepting that some commemoration bias is obviously at work, making the statistics look more extreme than they probably were).

Paine and I argue that the effects of disease may be reflected in our data insofar as that data can be relied on (still at issue), and we also argue that working with a funerary sample, though flawed, is still worth pursuing because it is a direct data set. Model life table analysis aims to fit samples and is not properly used to present general scenarios of probability. Catastrophic mortality from pandemics such as the Antonine plague may be partly responsible for the extremely depressed Roman demography according to our sample, but that does not explain "normal" times. Lo Cascio and Paine and I agree that there must have been a great deal of variability in the demographic regime of the city of Rome and the empire.

In chapter 4, part of Shaw's discussion applies to Africa, providing a valuable rural perspective for comparison with Bagnall's urban sample (chapter 7). Shaw's samples bridge the urban-rural continuum throughout more than a millennium as he takes us to the city of Rome during a period of its greatest growth during the late republic in the first century BC; the mixed urban-rural population of northern Italy in Parentium on the Adriatic starting from the sixth century AD; and ends up with rural monastic cemetery data from the Delta of Lower Egypt dating to the sixth to tenth centuries AD. The last data mentioned are analyzed in comparison with relevant nineteenth-century census data to suggest a common pattern for the last two thousand years. His main category of data is funerary inscriptions, but the inclusion of these data on media as disparate as graffiti on basilican walls, labels on unique types of funerary urns (so far unstudied in standard Roman funerary behavior analyses), mummy labels, and grave stelae indicates how epigraphic sources function as an important type of archaeological artifact. His work on the Republican funerary urns even has significance in gleaning information about the problems of the Roman calendar before the Julian reforms.

A key theme in Shaw's chapter is how climatic conditions interact with human disease vectors as the marked patterns of seasonal mortality in his data illustrate. The Parentium data are especially significant in that the sample represents a mix of urban and rural populations. Parentium was an "administrative agro-center" exhibiting a close association of the town population with the surrounding hinterland. The Republican Rome sample is particularly important because it comes from a period when the city of Rome was growing into the huge metropolis that it became in its heyday. Shaw's conclusion, that rural and urban populations are "strongly linked" in their common responses to environmental factors, compellingly confirms the volume's theme of treating city and hinterland as a unity in demographic terms.

Medieval Denmark, the topic of chapter 5, may seem like a far cry from the world of ancient Greece and Rome. However, the cases are not dissimilar because the focus is on a period in Scandinavia still at the threshold of urbanization. This chapter also represents a significant archaeological attempt to come to grips with the flow issue of demography and how it should be contextualized in the rural-urban continuum. It is a considerable advance that the authors can credibly discriminate among urban, migrant, and rural skeletal populations.

The authors separate townspeople and migrants along two dimensions: (1) infectious disease and (2) discrete genetic markers that allow for the tracking of physical secular trends. Regarding the former, they discern the effects of infectious epidemic disease and conclude, in support of the urban graveyard effect, that disease had a greater impact on urban populations than on rural ones. Their evidence reiterates the point that the effects of disease are density dependent because disease affected even the small agrarian as well as the market towns. Their data support the idea that towns and disease go together. Regarding the second dimension, the evidence illustrates how migrants are a self-selecting population element, frequently chiefly males (as Bagnall finds for Roman Egypt in chapter 7) in that here migrants were taller than townspeople and rural folk (stature has long been known to correlate with upward social mobility). The very act of moving to the urban setting may represent a statement of aspiring upward social mobility, expressed in the pursuit of economic betterment.

In chapter 6, we jump ahead to the most recent of the cities covered in this volume, one of the greatest cities of the modern world. For the period covered by Rothschild, however, New York was essentially a preindustrial city, showing great affinity with the earliest cities in this volume. For example, we learn that in 1851, the population in what would later become Central Park was distributed into scattered settlements, later joining the city population, as if a case of village coalescence. New York is a colonial city, like the colonial cities of ancient Greece (chapter 1). Of note, the commercial element was important in some cases of Greek colonization (Whitley 2001:124–127); Rothschild argues that New York's urbanization owed much to the economic changes of the colonial process, making it a "commercially driven urban entity."

Rothschild concentrates on artifact and land-use change analysis as her primary analytical tools. In this way, she provides the building blocks of population makeup analysis; New York proves to be an excellent case study of how a fully documented cultural context can be complemented by a vigorous historical archaeology in order to discriminate and thereby study the disparate groups that make up an urban population. The textual evidence on New York facilitates the identification of growing disparities in wealth and status between inhabitants within a single city block. The "theoretically neutral [street] grid" might give the impression of equality between the inhabitants. Such is the assumption of the highly standardized house plots and street blocks of the late Classical cities in Greece such as Priene and Olynthos (Whitley 2001:317). That assumption is wrong for New York; it might be wrong for those Greek cities.

In discussing New York's hinterland, Rothschild observes that the city had a "variety of hinterlands of differing sizes." She notes how Brooklyn evolved into the fourth largest U.S. city by its mixing of urbanites and primary farmers processing products for the New York market and how Long Island, Westchester, and Putnam counties and New Jersey (the immediate hinterland) served as the city's feeding zone. There was then an intermediate hinterland from which raw materials flowed to New York. And finally, there was the larger hinterland, more of a "sphere of influence," in which New York's long arm of commerce and culture reached west to Chicago and beyond and eastward directly to Europe. This discussion is evocative of the heady language of Cronon's *Nature's Metropolis* (1991) in which Chicago is set as the greatest city of the heartland of America with a hinterland that absorbs places such as Iowa totally and reaches far into the mountain west. Much of that story, however, is equally about how New York created Chicago (ultimately due to the opening of the Erie Canal in 1825, the influence of which, as Rothschild states, "cannot be overstated") by providing the chief end point of all commerce in the United States, and thus the entire continental United States came to play the role of New York's hinterland.

Rothschild also draws attention to the importance of transportation and how the definition of urban space and, more important, its perception in the eyes of the inhabitants directly affected the city's growth. New York was a walking city in its colonial phase but expanded beyond that in the postcolonial phase. Even the metropolis of Rome was basically a walking city, although a large one on the threshold of something beyond. At the beginning of the nineteenth century, New York was already too big for walking. This accounts for an important transition in urban evolution: New York, the walking city, was, as Rome before it, hetero-geneous (except for ethnicity and kin) in function and the social status of inhabi-tants, neighborhood by neighborhood. Rich and poor, and various forms of craft specialization and manufacture, resided side by side in the same neighborhoods. In early nineteenth-century New York, however, elite and middle-class residents began to separate home and workplace. Certainly the transport revolution trans-formed the density and landscape of cities. Equally useful are the results of arti-fact analysis of a mixed African-American–Irish neighborhood in what is now Central Park. Without the documentation, we would never have been able to discern the level of detail that is being extracted from these data. And in the case of actually matching artifacts with families and their known tax status, we have a remarkable nexus of knowledge of ethnicity, degree of wealth, and the artifacts themselves that allow us to define population makeup at a very deep "nuclear" level.

Last, Rothschild grapples with the more cognitive implications of the land use and artifact classes of study. She invokes the concept of "landscapes of power" to study how the inhabitants might have perceived the "social geography" of their neighborhood and city. As the city became more status and class conscious under the pressure of emerging industrial capitalism, the forms of expression on articles of daily use served as modes of material symbolism, flagging status in a city grow-ing so large that people could know another person's class not from individual and personal acquaintance but only through the symbols expressed on items of mate-rial culture. This is likely to be as true in the earliest towns as in the largest, most alienating, metropolis and reminds us that the issue of face-to-face interaction (Fletcher's I limits [Fletcher 1995]) is an important dimension of the definition of city life (cf. Wirth's "alienation" [Wirth 1938]). In a sense, activities become urban ones when it is impossible to have face-to-face acquaintance with all the members of the community. But here we can appreciate that the case of New York, barely "preindustrial," simply has a richness of data that can fill in missing pieces of the puzzle of emergent urbanization in cases where crucial aspects of the makeup of ancient cities cannot be filled in archaeologically. This is the best way that text and archaeology can work together to further our knowledge about any past community.

African Urbanization

In chapter 7, Roger Bagnall supplements his previous demographic work on cen-sus declarations from Roman Egypt (Bagnall and Frier 1994). Here he reviews a papyrus that has a fragment of an urban census from Upper Egypt (probably Lykopolis) that can be compared to the data from Middle Egypt already studied.

Bagnall is properly cautious about his interpretations due to the small size of the sample, but he offers tentative conclusions on this important flow data set. Of particular interest are the results that, compared to Middle Egypt, the Upper Egypt urban center is more dominated by conjugal families than extended ones and that the households are smaller than elsewhere. Bagnall interpreted this as a sign of lower wealth in Upper Egypt. The age structure also convinced him that mortality was higher here than elsewhere, perhaps lending support to the urban graveyard effect.

Also, the sex ratio, unusually high in favor of males here as in other urban contexts from the Roman Egyptian census data, suggests immigration of males in search of work in the urban centers, an indication of the self-selection of migrant populations previously noted in chapter 5 for medieval Denmark. Even with a small sample, important elements of the general urban character of Roman Egyptian cities are discernible: roughly similar age structure but with skewed sex ratios because of the pulling in of young males.

In closing, Bagnall hopes to be able to supplement his findings with a fresh papyrus find; "one may keep hoping." Bagnall is involved in a long-term project of excavation and recovery of papyri in Roman Egypt, thus excellently placed to find an important papyrus with good census information in the midst of a well-controlled modern archaeological excavation. Here is outstanding potential for achieving remarkable results from the natural interface between text and archaeology. And, unlike the case of Rome, where it is unlikely that the important documents of the Roman administration are ever to be found, Roman Egypt is yielding up new documents daily that might dramatically increase our data and thus enhance our demographic knowledge of this province.

In chapter 8, Chapurukha and Sibel Kusimba and Babatunde Agbaje-Williams note how African demography may be the "least understood" in the world, demonstrating how the study of African cities and demography has been hampered by the neglect of scholarship. This is tantamount to remnant European colonialism continuing its unrelenting assault on the cultures of Africa, creating a discourse of dependence that automatically relegates Africa to a secondary place. For the study of the demography of cities, past scholarship has tried to suggest that there are such intrinsic and inherent challenges to human nucleation posed by the conditions of the African continent that urbanization has been retarded. As the authors note, there is no evidence that Africa is so different; all environments that have produced urbanization have had their "own set of difficulties and constraints," and as they illustrate here, Africans met those challenges to produce urbanization broadly comparable to the process elsewhere (and in some ways notably unique).

The authors focus on sub-Saharan cities, especially on "low-density occupations of patchy and clumped settlements with an extensive skirt of low-density occupations," which are unfamiliar urban configurations they dub the *mbanza,* a

Kikongo word, meaning city or town to the Bakongo of Kongo and Angola. The type sites, among the Kongo kingdoms of central Africa, are of such low density that they do not at first appear to be urban at all, but their huge extent makes them too big to be reasonably called villages. The diversity of functions within and the degree of external trade direct us to call them urban (with recognizable urban activities [M. L. Smith 2003]), although they look like "giant villages." Fletcher (1993:741) characterized a similarly configured Great Zimbabwe in southern Africa as "dispersed palimpsest occupation." The fact that many of these cities have functioning agricultural zones within their (often hard to identify) boundaries should occasion no surprise, because we know that Roman cities (even Rome) possessed working agricultural fields within their walls, as seen for Pompeii (Jashemski 1979, 1993).

Furthermore, the dispersed giant village configuration was not confined to sub-Saharan Africa. The authors emphasize that the great cities of Egypt, Karnak, Luxor, and Memphis, were strung out along the Nile, with Memphis extending out a full 15 km (Wenke 1997). Regarding the Egyptian nomes, the smaller regional administrative centers, they suggest that the nomes developed from chiefly centers of redistribution. Chiefs needed to coordinate the gathering and then distribution of commodities, and towns grew up where chiefs lived and stored the tribute that could then be bulked and distributed. The process of village coalescence described here is provided a *mechanism* to explain why certain nucleated centers, a chief's compound and its surrounding residences of retainers and commoners, came into being.

The authors close with a case study of perhaps the largest *mbanza*, Old Oyo in the Yoruba Kingdom, a huge sprawl with as many as 100,000 people in 50 sq km. The population density of only 2,000 persons per sq km is perhaps unusually low for a preindustrial city, but quite normal for a modern urban density, which leads to an interesting consideration based on Fletcher's (1995) theoretical work. The authors think that the problems of limitations on communication (Fletcher's C limits) can be circumnavigated by increasing overall settlement size with dispersed (yet still visible and thus face-to-face communicable) occupation. The key consideration is the flexibility of this adaptation because it helps address the problem of providing subsistence for large nucleated populations. By dispersing population (yet not dispersing them totally into the hinterland), the pressure of providing for a single, centralized destination is taken off the traders and the suppliers. Consuming populations are moved closer to supply, cutting down on transport costs. It also cuts down on the density problem of interaction limits (Fletcher's I limits), lowering the stress level of humans in crowded contexts.

This modern adaptation is how all the transformations in Fletcher's (1995) history of urban growth are achieved; by increasing the size of cities, population density is decreased, because the relation between those two variables is inverse. The study of preindustrial *metropoleis* has perhaps misled us into thinking that very high nucleated densities are the natural human tendency for urban occupation—the norm. Maybe the distinctiveness of the various regional African urbanizations—the dispersion—is an equally attractive alternative for how cities can most comfortably be organized. In modern cities, this dispersion was achieved through the transport revolution, but African cities may have had it before that.

Far Eastern Urbanization

In chapter 9, Li Liu introduces us to the ongoing debate on the nature of the Xia-Shang transition in Chinese studies, especially whether it was a state-level society. Liu believes that the Erlitou evidence is compatible with a state polity, and she performs valuable service in discussing this case from a fully informed cross-cultural perspective (explicitly comparing China with Mesopotamia and Meso-america) and by summarizing data from past excavations that have not been available to an English-speaking audience previously.

Liu's approach is two-pronged: (1) she examines the internal organization of Erlitou itself to assess the nature of craft activity in that center—an investigation of functional differentiation within various zones of the urban site itself; and (2) she investigates hinterland communities to uncover their economic ties with Erlitou. She most explicitly articulates the emerging consensus of this volume that it is a question of "rural-urban *interaction*" not a "rural-urban *dichotomy*." Although Erlitou may have dominated the production and distribution of bronzes, Liu finds sufficient evidence to suggest that there was a great deal of utilitarian production sponsored by the Erlitou state and fostered in both the city itself and the hinterland communities. Furthermore, the prestige goods production network itself was multicentered, with thriving interaction between urban and rural zones of the region. That is clearly demonstrated by the kinds of tools produced at, and evidence of production in, the secondary centers investigated. The first traces of urbanization in this part of China still remain undetected, but as with later Shang cities, Erlitou's expansion into its regional hinterland seems primarily motivated by the search for key resources such as salt, copper, and prestige goods. The initial nucleation of Erlitou may have been a result of migration (perhaps coerced) from elsewhere or, as Liu suggests, a case of the now familiar village coalescence. Liu has painted a portrait of a complex landscape of urban-rural connections with an interdependent economy and an interesting mix of population elements living in each type of community.

In chapter 10, Sarah Nelson finds that "Korea has been understudied," so she introduces us to the ancient Korean metropolis of Kyongju, taking us from its modest beginning when six villages coalesced, seeking to provide for their common defense, to its sojourn as an imperial capital with perhaps 800,000 to 1 million inhabitants. There are fascinating glimpses of contacts with the Mediterranean world, reminding us that ancient Eastern and Western complex imperial systems were cognizant of each other and enjoyed some degree of communication for which we have only slight hints today. The long uninterrupted continuity of Kyongju's sojourn in the same location is unique for east Asia but similar to Rome. Kyongju exemplifies a healthy historical archaeology in which both documentary and archaeological sources can be studied as complementary data sets. For example, a fragment of an eighth century AD census pertains to three villages in the rural countryside, enumerating not only people but also animals and crops. There was a notable preponderance of females counted, perhaps indicating migration of males into the urban zone, as was concluded in chapters 5 and 7.

A notable feature of Kyongju is the number and ubiquity of shrines, defining a sacred landscape. These are evocative of the strong cult associations between city and rural sanctuaries in Greece. And as in the Andes (chapter 12), there are also very strong associations with sacred mountaintops, so that burial mounds, imitative of the surrounding sacred mountains, occur within the boundaries of the city. These burial mounds also provide useful data on patterns of early social stratification, regarding which the documentary data feature the bone ranks lineages and how they may have functioned in urban Silla.

The sacred landscape of Kyongju came to imitate the Chinese capital of Chang'An, modern Xian (Steinhardt 1990). Buddhist shrines, such as Hwangyonsa, increased the scale of monumentality, being "mini-cities" in and of themselves, and increased the degree of urbanization, showing here as elsewhere the importance of cult foundations for the enhancement and elaboration of city configurations. The growing population surrounding these shrines continued to remain mixed, with the houses of the nobles and the commoners juxtaposed. This is the pattern that we have seen characteristic of the ancient *metropoleis* and that only began to change as seen in New York on the verge of industrialization (chapter 6).

In chapter 11, Laura Junker takes us to another region of world urbanization that has been neglected: the cities of second millennium AD Southeast Asia. The study area provides evidence to the effect that rural population densities were very low, as with the Maya (Rice, chapter 13), but with the twist that the rural low densities do not prevent the region as a whole from showing a high (20 percent) percentage of urbanization (defined as the proportion of the population living in cities), as well as sporting some very large cities (supported by imported rice, very similar to the cases of Athens and Rome depending on outside imported grain). The key here is that we are dealing with a conglomeration of maritime trading cities, many on islands, arranged into primate centers with dendritically organized associated hinterlands focused on river routes into the interior. The fragmented nature of state society here, similar to that seen in ancient Greece and among the Maya, has driven theoretical ethnological work in the region, producing the notions of segmentary states, galactic polities, and theater states that have been liberally applied elsewhere.

As with Morris's "super-cities" (chapter 1), Junker refers to the largest cities in her sample as "hyperlarge." She reports urban densities of 20,000 persons per sq km—high but not remarkably so. However, the outskirts of these cities are fascinatingly similar to African *mbanzas*. A central densely packed core and precinct that seemed orderly and regularly configured was surrounded by a "dispersed and nebulous urban periphery with boundaries that were difficult to define." There were even "sprawling 'suburbs'" of walled compounds, gardens, and attached retainer houses that added to the impression of "massive urban scale," although the densities here seemed to be much lower than the cores of the cities. These zones confused foreign observers who were not even sure that these areas were urban.

Junker closes with a case study of the smaller city of Tanjay, in the Philippines, which seems to have functioned as a regional bulking center; that function may have been the chief reason for initial nucleation. Elites were connected by constant ritual feasting and other ceremonies, and the role of feasting in fostering and maintaining ties between communities critically dependent on maintaining well-disposed intercourse cannot be underestimated. Evidence here for feasting was widespread; this can be compared with the Andean institution as discussed by Janusek and Blom (chapter 12). For Southeast Asia, there is evidence that cult centers in the hinterland were present and important in linking to urban centers. Stelae, menhirs, dolmens, and other monumental markers with cult associations are found in the upriver secondary centers, along with prestige goods that provide explicit ties with the culture of the coastal *metropoleis*. So here, too, we find the association of city and hinterland cult center to be of major import.

Urbanization in the Precolumbian New World

In chapter 12, John Janusek and Deborah Blom provide a rich independent database of urbanization. Janusek and Blom set out to archaeologically identify different groups that make up the urban populations. As with Petersen, Boldsen, and Paine (chapter 5), they use human skeletal evidence, as well as artifact analysis, to achieve their end. These two chapters establish once and for all that archaeological analysis of constituent population groups, if carried out carefully and with discretion, can discriminate between the groups. That achievement alone bodes well for a future of significant work on the issue of population makeup.

Janusek and Blom believe that the most critical element in determining urban/rural social structure was the social matrix of identity at work. This social matrix, defined chiefly by the Andean concept of the *ayllu*, the term applied both to kinship and to community relations, determined that people in the city were inextricably tied to their surrounding hinterland, regional centers, and even entities farther off. The city served as a "magnet center of feasting and ceremony" anchoring the social matrix. This makes sense for the Andes because magnet settlements exist today, the *markas* that are centers of ceremony and gathering.

This concept of Andean urbanism recalls models of Chaco Canyon in New Mexico (Cameron and Toll 2001) and takes its cue that the organizational principle for a polity creating urban centers with an extreme degree of festival activity is the corporate political strategy as opposed to the network strategy (Blanton et al. 1996). A city starting out as a relatively empty ceremonial center, increasing density dramatically during high festivals, offers an alternative method and mechanism for urban origin, akin to village coalescence, but providing a rationale for the start of the process. Having an infrastructure of buildings and facilities without occupants makes nucleation much more feasible, a ready-made template for a densely packed urban center into which, periodically, a large gathering of people enters the city and spends a few days, driving up the density much higher than normal. This is precisely what happens in the modern metropolis (e.g., New York) with incoming commuting workers dramatically increasing the daytime (not seasonal) density. The massing of numbers for periodic visits to urban centers is thus not really a completely modern phenomenon. The corporate strategies may tend to produce smaller, less dominating urban centers than the network strategy. The corporate strategy facilitated a greater equilibrium between cities and their hinterlands. Small's (chapter 16) alternative foci of power in the countryside probably require the more fluid circulation of power between competing ruling elements that the corporate strategy permits.

Furthermore, ethnographically, serving vessels and decoration and modification of the human body correlate with the *ayllu*. Serving vessels give "clues" to identity in the social matrix, and body decoration and modification give "cues" to identity. The decorations on the serving vessels, the messages conveyed by the stylistic elements, were "turned on" during the social gatherings to indicate identity. That is the same basic process of the signifying elements of style on pottery in New York (chapter 6) and how they were meant to convey class and status. Perhaps this drive to "turn on" stylistic signifiers is a primary motivation for feasting.

Janusek and Blom further document how the membership of the *ayllus* transcended the urban-rural divisions, showing the intimate integration of city and hinterland. The multidirectionality of interaction and movement, migration in and out of the centers, lays down a principle for community maintenance and growth that will be equally dramatically demonstrated for Teotihuacan (chapter 15). City populations are ultimately creatures of some form of migration into a nucleated center, whether via a more ceremonial or more economic motivation, or a mix of the two, or whether via the establishing of a community de novo (even by coercion) or through the process of village coalescence.

In chapter 13 Don Rice notes that the Maya were the "Greeks of the New World" to Sylvanus Morley. At least in terms of urban life, the Maya were similar to the Greeks in having a culture characterized by small polities that had difficulty uniting into one overarching political-cultural system. We perceive here a relatively crowded countryside dotted with centers of moderately greater density, but so dispersed as to blur the boundary between city and hinterland as we saw for Africa (chapter 8). Indeed, the Maya centers look much like the African *mbanzas.* Tikal's core density of only 625 persons per sq km and outskirt density of 100 persons per sq km make for an unfamiliar cityscape.

Rice looks at subsistence regimes, asking whether the low-yielding swidden agriculture widespread in the Maya world could have supported the population densities encountered in both centers and their hinterlands. Rice's answer to this conundrum is the dispersal characteristic of both Maya city and hinterland, suggesting that the "garden city" view of Maya centers may hold the key. The degree to which the Maya resorted to this dispersed pattern may be a kind of modern "suburban" way of arranging population in urban centers, reminiscent of the African solution (chapter 8). The Maya cities seem to have a standard declining density gradient (Clark 1967:339–352), but with multiple "cores" or "nodes" (as with African cities [chapter 8] and Harappan cities [Kenoyer 1997]—the expected pattern within the declining density gradient [Crampton 1991]), as suggested by the temple and palace structures found in peripheral zones of centers. They are even linked by the *sacbeob* causeways, and, unlike the Chacoan road system, which seems to have linked the center with its agricultural supplying land (Earle 2001), the Maya roads seem to link nodes within the urban zone, strengthening their appearance as "suburban" cities. As with Greek cities, elites may have had second residences in both the core and the periphery of Maya centers. This dual residence may partly explain the apparent high densities that have been noted.

Rice explores whether the low population densities of Maya centers take them out of the realm of urbanism, as suggested by Webster (1997, 2002). Maya cities do not seem to be based on regular grids and thus show no "urban planning." But that is no objection because a regular grid is not a sine qua non of ancient urban places. The best examples are both Athens and Rome, which were not planned cities at all, but seem to betray their origins, with their aura of sloppy village coalescence. Besides, as Rice notes, there are some indications of urban planning in the largest Maya centers, especially with the interesting triangulation of orientation that may have been a mechanism for growth reasonably analogous to the laying of an orthogonal plat for a new street block seen today. This triangulation method seems to have applied to reworking agricultural fields and siting new structures. The Roman *centuriation* system laid out a regular grid in the center of town, but it continued far into the hinterland to impose regularity on the agricultural plots assigned to the town inhabitants. Rice also notes that there is little in the newly exploited corpus of Maya epigraphic material that discusses Maya cities and their layout, but much of the large corpus of ethnohistoric literature on Greco-Roman urbanism is focused on ideal philosophical considerations. Discussion of the city as a "physical plant" is not very prevalent. That the Maya were similarly silent, more focused on the details of cosmology, is not very different from the Greco-Roman approach.

Rice notes that the Maya centers were certainly "sacred landscapes" possessing a heavy focus on ceremonial activity. We have seen the same to be the case with Greece, Kyongju, the Southeast Asian cities, and Tiwanaku. Junker (chapter 11) noted that some of the theoretical models of "theater states" and such have been applied to the Maya. Whether or not such models overstate the ritual significance of polities in a landscape, there is no doubt that the ritual associations of either rural cult centers or cities as foci of cult activities in a number of cases in this volume bespeak ritual as a critically important variable in the integration of cities and their hinterlands. For the Maya, as with the denizens of Tiwanaku, ceremonial display allows the "turning on" of stylistic elements, even to the point of fostering intense polity competition for becoming the seat of the *may* turning (Rice 2004).

Inasmuch as Mesoamericanists have invoked Fox's (1977) model of urban types and argued that Maya centers fit Fox's type of "regal-ritual" center, Rice is surely right to suggest that the issue is not an either/or proposition. He concludes that, characteristically for the Maya, "even the largest sites were not disembedded from local and regional subsistence concerns in a manner that might be expected of an urban administrative city with broad trade and tribute networks." However, even the largest administrative cities were not divorced from their hinterlands, Rome being a prime example (Morley 1996). So, as with other cultural areas in this volume, the Maya urban type seems common to both preindustrial and modern worlds.

The other metropolis in this volume that has multiple treatments is Teotihuacan, discussed by both Rebecca Storey (chapter 14) and Larry Gorenflo (chapter 15). So dominant was it over its large hinterland (similar to Rome and New York) that the process of nucleation making it a "super-city" may have been one of coercion (Millon 1981). Coercion is a species of village coalescence rather than an alternative. What is critical to determine is why the elites in charge chose Teotihuacan's location for the effort of forced nucleation. Cowgill (2004, for references) touches on how nucleation into a large city is actually accomplished. He is right to suggest that there is something in the psychology of the city that possesses enough appeal to bring people out of the countryside and into an urbanizing settlement, which harks back to Morris's claim that urbanization was a lifestyle deliberately chosen in archaic Greece.

In this New World metropolis, the first true urban surface survey was applied, but there was little testing of the results by excavation. The Tlajinga 33 project of Rebecca Storey was intended to help fill in that gap and to capture something of the flow demography of Teotihuacan, via skeletal paleodemography, with excavation strategies directed to, and successful in, recovering a larger-than-usual sample of the normally underrepresented infant and child skeletons. The initial assumption was that the Teotihuacan data would address the question of the health of the urban inhabitants. Because infectious epidemic disease burdens were presumed lower in the Precolumbian New World, it was originally hypothesized the city's burial population would reflect that. However, individual skeletons showed a less-than-robust overall health, confirmed by full paleodemographic and paleopathological analysis (Storey 1992b). This was a surprise, but the explanation lay in the realization that tropical parasitical disease burdens had the same effect on urban populations in the New World as the epidemic diseases did in the Old.

Storey here refines and updates her previous work, attempting to take into account the effects of migration while demonstrating a declining quality of life through time so much so that the population of Tlajinga 33 was in crisis toward the end of the city's trajectory. In the late period, she finds an age distribution departing significantly from reference populations, a result Paine and I have found for second to third century AD Rome in our funerary inscription sample (chapter 3). Her skeletal sample is less subject to biases than our epigraphic sample, which we know has a challenging component of commemoration bias. As Paine and I note (Storey and Paine 2002), the convergences of results from both skeletal and epigraphic (independent) data sets are one important reason why we continue to work with epigraphic data that others have completely rejected (see Scheidel 2001b, 2003a). If two comparable preindustrial *metropoleis* such as Rome and Teotihuacan can show the same type of high mortality profiles in independent data sets, then there is good reason to suspect that the urban graveyard effect may be at work.

Storey's conclusion that many of the deaths were migrants coming into the compound is supported by the comparative data, via historical urban demography of the Old World showing how the higher mortality burden fell on the poorer sectors of the population—a factor she believes is also the case with the lower-status occupants of the Tlajinga 33 compound. The delicate balance of migration and mortality might have been so thoroughly disturbed that the population dynamics that kept Teotihuacan afloat were finally destabilized, and the city failed. The population of the compound was so stressed that migrants might have stopped moving to Tlajinga 33 because of the high mortality rate, which might partly explain the collapse of Teotihuacan as a viable city.

Gorenflo, however, sees no great demographic disturbances occurring in Teotihuacan's countryside. Without the crowding of the city of Teotihuacan, health risks from parasitical infection might well have been significantly reduced. One effect here is simply the shifting scales of analysis from within Teotihuacan to Gorenflo's 4 sq km grid squares in the hinterland. The general trends over the long periods for which the data were gathered would be smoothed out in generalized regional averages. So, the dramatic events in Tlajinga 33 disappear into the background continuum of population shifts.

Gorenflo's main contribution is to put estimated population numbers into visually enhanced format with his choropleth maps. The grid and its shading give immediate indication of small trends of population movement through time. This method of analysis represents a useful refinement and updating of the evidence. That he can demonstrate population shifts between adjacent areas represents another important innovation and a considerable contribution in the ability to map prehistoric migration patterns.

The theme that stands out so much is the constant movement and flux. The movement is not just from rural to urban but also from rural to rural and urban to urban. Perhaps here we have conclusive demonstration of the chief characteristic of the rural-urban continuum—its constant fluidity. Population parameters are constantly adjusting themselves. With the breakup of Teotihuacan and the greater village ruralization, the landscape of the Basin of Mexico became more like a modern "suburban" city configuration.

Cross-Cultural Synthesis

In chapter 16, David Small sets out a basic proposition about the relations of city and hinterland and an urban-rural continuum: the countryside can provide an alternative power base to the urban. He points out how we all pay lip service to the necessity of looking at both the city and the countryside but are hampered ultimately by our built-in modern assumption that the city is, in some fundamental way, always dominant. He asks us to adopt a "neutral analytical theoretical armature" that does not assume simple urban dominance. He begins with an amazing anecdote about how Julius Caesar, in the midst of his Gallic Wars, was unable to extract grain from his Gallic allies because those in the *oppida* (the proto-urban centers of Celtic Iron Age Europe) were unable to coerce the countryside elites into producing it. This is the *locus classicus* that the countryside could be an alternative power base, but the case is not merely an example from a culture with weak political centralization; Greece also represents an excellent example of rural alternative to the urban power base. Greek Pan-Hellenic sanctuaries wielded considerable sway over Greek *poleis* in religious, economic, and political spheres, illustrated by the long history of polis interactions with them (Small 1997).

Regarding the Maya city of Copán, Honduras, Small shows how the totality of work on both rural and urban components of this polity has advanced our understanding of urban-rural relations (Freter 1994; Gonlin 1994; Webster 2002). As with Janusek and Blom in chapter 12, there is a strong sense that the Copanec urban population was integrated by deep-seated lineage ties of organization. But Small zeroes in on Abrams's (1995) concept of "marginal product," which is an index of the amount production increases when additional labor is added to the production force. Small uses it as a rough index for measuring the degree of dominance of urban elements over rural ones in the evolution of early urbanization. When marginal productivity is low, the urban sector has greater power over the rural sector, but when the marginal product is high, the rural sector can resist urban dominance. Although there are challenges to operationalizing this index fully, Small deploys it effectively to ask questions about urban-rural relations in test cases: Uruk in Mesopotamia, Classical Greece, the Middle Bronze Age Levant, and the Maya at Colha.

Small speculates that specialized production can increase marginal product. For the Maya, for Erlitou China (chapter 9), and in other cases, production is often organized in the "attached craftsmen" mode where the craftsmen live with and produce directly for the elites. Does this mode artificially keep marginal product low (confined to low bulk and low numbers of luxury items) and enhance elite control? Where utilitarian goods are produced by craftsmen independently living in the rural countryside or at "secondary" centers, does the marginal product increase and counter urban dominance?

Nichols's chapter (chapter 17) is a closing summary, provided from the perspective of the original discussant at the conference, which ties together many of the cross-cultural themes of the volume.

Conclusion

Lessons from the Greek Polis

"It has always been stressed . . . that an ancient Greek city was inseparably connected with its countryside" (Hansen 1997:17). From the written sources defining the Greek polis, the term in Greek can be reduced to a binary concept; that is, a polis designated both a settlement (the nucleated population center and the inhabited territory) and a community (a multitude of humans). The way the two concepts are combined into one by Greek thought provides us a different way of thinking about the relation between city and countryside. Such an approach significantly empowers Small's viewpoint that the countryside can represent an alternative power base.

Just as in modern European languages there is a tension between the city and countryside and an antonymic relation between the words for both, so in Greek there was an opposition between the polis and the *chora*. However, whereas in modern languages the countryside defines the political community of the state (hence we have nation-states), in the Greek world the city defined the political community of the state. This difference probably explains why we impose a greater dichotomy on the city-hinterland distinction. To us, the nation is the unity, broken into units of city with "empty" countryside between, whereas to the Greeks, the city (plus its integrated territory) *was* the unity. The cities of the ancient Mediterranean world were much more completely integrated with their surrounding countryside (at times, almost on an equal footing of power) than we appreciate in the modern world. For our purposes in this volume, the city must be assessed within the context of its character as a unity across the urban-rural continuum. The concept of the polis as unity rightly counteracts our modern tendency to treat city and countryside differently.

A Rule-of-Thumb Urban Population Size Threshold

I have always thought that a true urban center needed to have a population density of at least 1,000 persons per sq km. However, I now think that the density need not be that high. A true city, one with the kinds of urban activities explored frequently in this volume, can have a population density even in the low hundreds of persons per square kilometer, as long as the overall site is in the tens of square kilometers, possessing a rough *continentia* (per the Roman definition of city boundaries—"where contiguous structures end" [*Digest* 50.16.2, 87, 139, 154, 239]), meaning that buildings and concentrations of habitational refuse are clustered very tightly together (in the standard densely nucleated city) or in agglomerations at least within sight of each other (as in the *mbanza* city).

Webster (2002:156) suggested that the low densities and small total populations of Maya centers would not produce the anonymity and alienation that seems characteristic of the "hyper-cities." Fletcher (1995) discussed settlement growth limits explicitly in terms of interaction limits, so the degree of face-to-face interaction is crucial to urbanism. But it seems doubtful that everyone knew everyone else even in small Maya centers or small Greek *poleis*. Cohen (2000) has exploded the myth that Greek *poleis* were face-to-face societies. The widespread belief that Athens was so extraordinary because all the citizens knew each other should have always raised doubt (Attika had 300,000 people), but Cohen shows that even the smaller divisions of Athens, the *demes,* were no more face-to-face than the city as a whole. When there are even hundreds in the population, everyone might recognize everyone else, but frequent face-to-face interaction is still limited to only tens of people. The compact size of Greek *poleis* may be one reason that consensual political systems were found in them (Morris 1997), because even simple recognition fosters memory and cooperation (M. L. Smith 2003:18). But that does not mean that these were face-to-face cultures, fostering mutual trust. With the Maya and the African *mbanzas,* populations in the hundreds were more dispersed, and face-to-face interactions with everyone were thus even less likely. Alienation does not require thousands of people, merely hundreds, and it starts in larger villages. When villages become "giant," it is just as real as in the most densely populated giant towns, the "super cities."

Thus, the overall population of the community should be in the range of five to ten thousand people or more. It is also perfectly acceptable to have open space and agricultural activity zones within the city proper, as we have seen were frequently the case (Roman: Jashemski 1979, 1993, Robinson 1992; Aztecs: Smith 1996:6; Maya: Tourtellot 1993; and Greece: Morgan and Coulton 1997:114).

We thus should abandon any notion that cities must be unrelieved landscapes of crowded human habitation.

What Are Cities For?

Gorenflo demonstrates high levels of population flux in the Basin of Mexico. For Copán, Small notes that the population must have been very mobile, given how easily it moved into alternative zones in the countryside after the collapse of the main group—the Copanecos were readily given to "population travel." The Greeks were also known to be great travelers. Several contributors strongly imply the constant mobility of populations in the city-hinterland continuum. Perhaps, ultimately, urbanization is a physiological mechanism for shifting human populations across a landscape, as if triggered by a human physiological response to allow rapid adjustments of species numbers across the landscape (without waiting for the biological processes of fertility and mortality). Urbanization is a settlement pattern type that easily accommodates, even fosters, this restless population flux. But that sounds like a group selection argument that has long been rejected by evolutionary biologists. However, if coerced mandated population movements (shifting of conquered populations was not at all uncommon in worldwide antiquity) do not count as a form of group selection, then nothing will. Human nucleation behavior into cities might be a form of group selection strategy that has proved eminently adaptable for humans and has fostered strong interspecific ties of cooperation. As Aristotle really remarked (not "Man is by nature a political animal"): "Humans by nature tend to live in cities."

The Western Urban Tradition

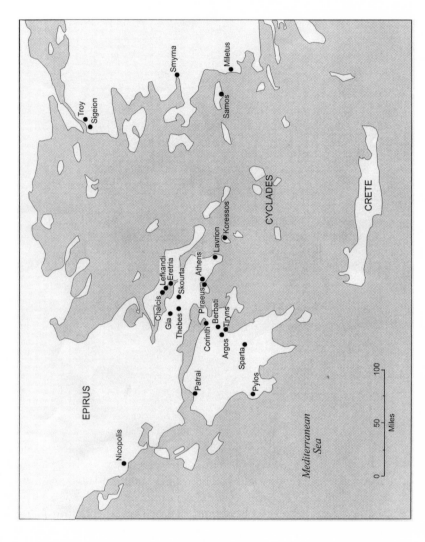

Figure 1-1. Aegean Greek cities.

I
The Growth of Greek Cities in the First Millennium BC

Ian Morris

Greece in 1000 BC was a world of villages. Most people lived in communities of just a few dozen souls; even the largest settlement, Athens (Figure 1-1), was probably just 3,000 to 4,000 strong. But at the millennium's end, the Greek east Mediterranean boasted some of the largest cities in preindustrial history. Alexandria, Antioch, and Seleucia-on-the-Tigris probably each had 250,000–500,000 inhabitants.

In this chapter I discuss the size of Greek cities and the implications of their growth. I identify three major transitions:

1. Archaic Greece (see table 1-1): The first transition, in the eighth century BC, was a response to Mediterranean-wide population growth. Greeks developed institutions that allowed larger groups to live together. By 700 BC, the largest towns probably had 10,000 people. Although Greeks elaborated their forms of urban life over the next millennium, the main outlines emerged in the Archaic period.

2. Classical Greece: Cities crossed a second threshold soon after 500 BC with the rise of imperial administrative centers. The control of empires provided enough wealth for Athens and Syracuse to grow beyond the carrying capacity of their hinterlands. By 431 BC Athens probably had 40,000 residents, and its harbor town Piraeus had another 25,000. Fifth-century Syracuse was roughly the same size as Athens and a century later had between 50,000 and 100,000 inhabitants.

3. Hellenistic Greece: The third breakthrough began at the end of the fourth century BC with the Macedonian conquest of the Persian Empire. The administrative centers this created controlled vastly greater revenues than Classical Athens or Syracuse. The growth of these cities paralleled Rome's emergence as an imperial center, and in the first two centuries AD these super-cities dominated the Mediterranean.

Understanding these transitions takes this chapter into larger theoretical issues.

Table 1-1. Conventional Periodization

Period	Dates BC
Late Bronze/Mycenaean Period	c. 1600–1200
Early Iron Age/Dark Age	c. 1200–700
Archaic	c. 700–480
Classical	480–323
Hellenistic	323–31

I suggest that two specific debates are particularly relevant. These models help organize the Greek data, but the Greek case also raises questions about the organizing frameworks.

The Interaction-Communication Transition

In a theoretical tour de force, Roland Fletcher (1995) has identified two independent variables in the history of settlement sizes. He calls the first *interaction limits* (I-limits), by which he means the maximum population densities people could tolerate. Members of tiny, mobile groups can live in great proximity, but sedentary communities of more than 50–100 rarely tolerate densities above 300 people per hectare (per ha). Fletcher (1995:81) suggests that I-limits are hardwired into humans by their "finite sensory capacity, [which] will produce universally constant parameter conditions."

Fletcher's second variable is the *communication limit,* or C-limit. Technology and culture limit the distance that messages can be effectively transmitted and therefore the size of community that can hold together within a particular technological system. A settlement may increase in density until it approaches the I-limit, when it begins expanding in space, or it may spread until it reaches its effective C-limit, when it begins increasing in density. Eventually, it presses against both I- and C-limits, and serious urban stresses develop. A settlement might then (1) fission into several smaller communities; (2) stagnate; (3) "bypass" the problem by dropping down to such low densities (fewer than 10 per ha) that extension is almost indefinitely possible; or (4) create what Fletcher (1995:106) calls "a new I-C assemblage [of cultural methods for dealing with interaction and communication] . . . enabling a transition."

Fletcher identifies three great I-C transitions in world history: (1) from tiny bands to sedentary villages of 1–2 ha; (2) from villages to agrarian cities of more than 100 ha, with populations in the range of 10,000–20,000; and (3) from agrarian cities to industrial super-cities of more than 100 sq km, with populations from 1 to 10 million. Each transition involved a revolution in material behavior.

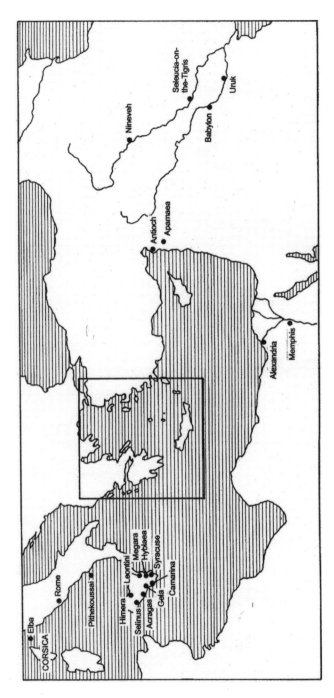

Figure 1-2. Cities of the greater Greek world. The area inside the square is shown in greater detail in Figure 1-1.

Greek cities in the eighth century BC are in many ways excellent illustrations of Fletcher's second transition, to agrarian cities of 100-plus ha. He argues that I-C assemblages enabling such growth typically involve "blocking" architecture restricting lines of sight; shifts from curvilinear to rectilinear buildings; creation of rectilinear monuments at least 30 m long; and the invention of writing and other information-storage technologies. These are all prominent features of the eighth-century archaeological record (Morris 2000:257–286; Snodgrass 1980:15–84), and Fletcher's model underwrites the importance of the eighth century in Greek history as a cultural revolution that created the frameworks of Classical civilization.

However, some features of the Greek case might challenge Fletcher's larger claims. First, settlement at Athens apparently covered some 200 ha for a full three centuries before the creation of the kind of I-C assemblage that Fletcher sees as necessary for a 100-ha city. Fletcher (1995:198–203) faces apparent exceptions to his generalizations. He (1995:90, 237 n. 11) notes that his 1–2 and 100-ha limits "are only conventions"; we can document I-C transitions in settlements ranging from 70 to 150 ha. Early Athens may have been an extreme case of a precocious sprawling town, suffering various forms of stress. However, given the weakness of our evidence, it may equally well be that Athens was in fact closer to 100 ha than 200 or that population fell below the critical 10 per ha threshold.

Fletcher suggests that breakthroughs from one I-C assemblage to another are best explained through Darwinian evolution: people constantly and randomly innovate within the limits imposed on them by social structures. When urban growth presses against the I-C limits, certain cultural traits, among those that happen to be in existence, will turn out to be adaptively advantageous and are reproduced more effectively. Other things being equal, the more culturally diverse a society is, the better chance it has of solving I-C pressures, and, usually, the traits that prove advantageous will have emerged before the transition. Fletcher (1995: 159) concludes that "each of the features takes some time to develop and the likelihood of their occurring together, very rapidly, after a community reaches the zone adjacent to both an I-limit and a C-limit is very small."

Here, too, eighth-century Greece raises questions. Some elements of the eighth-century cultural revolution can be traced back through the Iron Age, and others developed gradually across the Archaic period (Morris 1998a, 2000:195–256). But we are nevertheless dealing with traumatic, and transformative, cultural changes across just two generations: what Snodgrass (1980) called a "structural revolution." Population growth pushed up the size of the largest communities, creating revolutionary ferment and turning old ways of life upside down, and the new I-C assemblage then made possible further urban growth. I suggest that Fletcher downplays the importance of particular, local economic, and sociological changes to emphasize universal generalizations about material behavior.

The Consumer City

Fletcher (1995:151–153) sees the transition through the 70–150 ha threshold as the most important stage in urban history before the Industrial Revolution. He suggests that although cities must have resources to grow, economics matter less than I-C assemblages. But the Greek evidence suggests that in decoupling economic from "material/behavioral factors," Fletcher (1995:209–210) obscures other important phenomena. To understand the Classical and Hellenistic transitions that I describe below, we must return to an older sociological framework, developed by Max Weber.

Weber was less interested in settlement size than in the economic functions of cities. In his classic essay *The City* (1968 [1921]:1212–1372, summary at 1215–1217), Weber set up a three-part typology of urban economies:

> (1) Consumer cities: a rentier class of landowners or an administrative elite of office-holders sucked wealth into the city, either as rents or taxes. The elite then spent its wealth on retainers, artisans, etc., in the city, creating an urban market for food, and deriving further wealth from supplying it.
>
> (2) Producer cities: urban entrepreneurs set up factories, buying raw materials from the countryside and then selling finished products back to it, using profits from the value added by the workers' labor to buy food from the farmers.
>
> (3) Merchant cities: trading elites grew rich from selling local goods in distant markets and/or selling exotic imported goods at home.

Weber identified examples of each type in every period of European history but suggested that consumer cities were typical of the ancient Mediterranean, whereas producer cities dominated medieval Europe. Early modern merchant cities developed out of producer cities. The importance of this typology, he argued, was that merchant cities and incipient capitalism could not develop directly out of ancient consumer cities, which explains why Rome never experienced a capitalist take-off. Weber saw different sociological forces behind the Industrial Revolution and its breakthrough to super-cities than does Fletcher.

I argue that the second and third transitions in Greek city size, to Classical settlements of 40,000-plus and Hellenistic ones of 500,000-plus, require a Weberian explanation in terms of politics, economics, and power. Only with the creation of centralized empires could a rentier/administrative elite draw enough wealth into cities to support large populations. Urban growth was inseparable from administration and imperialism.

Through most of the twentieth century, professional ancient historians ignored Weber's frameworks, producing what Moses Finley (1985:61) called "a spate of pseudo-histories of ancient cities and regions in which every statement or calculation to be found in an ancient text, every artifact finds a place, creating a morass of unintelligible, meaningless, unrelated 'facts.'" The explanation is clear: few classicists were interested in grand, comparative history. Cities were important to classicists as physical containers for high culture, but urbanism as a process—and Weber's sweeping comparisons—were not. Finley (1977) revived Weber's ideas in a classic article, and following Leveau and Goudineau's (1983) response, Finley's use of Weber's categories became the starting point for most discussions of urbanism.

Most ancient historians continue to ask very particularistic questions and conclude that consumer, producer, and merchant cities are not sufficiently sharp analytical tools to answer them (e.g., Cornell and Lomas 1995; Engels 1990; Morley 1996; Parkins 1997; Parkins and Smith 1998; Wallace-Hadrill 1991). Others seem to misunderstand the issues, as when Mogens Hansen (2004:33) concludes that "the concept of the consumption city does not fit the great majority of Classical Greek *poleis.*" Hansen began from philology not sociology; noting that most of the settlements that Greeks called *poleis* had small populations, he concluded that Greek cities were self-sufficient. But the issue for urban history is not how Greeks used terminology (clearly, very loosely); it is the economic relationships that made possible the emergence of increasingly large cities, and Weber's categories are crucial for explaining these.

I make three arguments: (1) the most important ancient Greek cities were always consumer cities; (2) the size of Greek cities was a function of imperial power; and (3) until late in the first millennium BC, Greek cities were politically and militarily weak and consequently remained small. Only when the Greeks entered the framework of the Persian Empire did super-cities become possible. I begin with a brief review of the environmental parameters of Greek urbanism and then survey settlement growth across the first millennium BC.

The Parameters of Greek Urban Growth

Natural Environment

Ecologists define Mediterranean climates as having (1) sufficient rain for dry farming in most years, but not enough for dense forests; (2) mild winters; and (3) at least two-thirds of precipitation falling in the winter, with a hot, dry summer (Milliman et al. 1992). In ancient times as in modern, much of Greece met this definition, though the climate in the northwest is more Balkan, with cooler weather and higher, more evenly distributed precipitation. Generally speaking, the lower the precipitation, the higher its variability from year to year. Between 1930 and 1961, rainfall around Athens varied so much that barley failed one year in twenty, wheat one in four, and legumes three in four. Pollen samples, tree rings, and literary sources suggest that these figures are roughly applicable to antiquity (Garnsey 1988:8–16). According to a third-century BC proverb, "The year makes the crop, not the soil" (Theophrastus, *History of Plants* 8.7.6).

In southern Greece, ranges of hills and mountains divide up small plains, whereas farther north the plains are larger, and the northwest is mountainous and forested, with some fertile upland valleys. The geography, like the climate, is typically Mediterranean: traveling from the sea across agricultural plains and through semiarid foothills into rugged mountains often requires just a few miles, and fertile farmland can be an easy day's walk from high pastures. Between 750 and 500 BC tens of thousands of Greeks settled around the Mediterranean (Scheidel 2003b), and by 400 BC probably one-third of all Greeks lived outside the Aegean. They favored zones such as Sicily and southern Italy, ecologically similar to their homeland (cf. Braudel 1972[1949]:25–85; Horden and Purcell 2000), but with larger plains and more reliable rainfall (De Angelis 2000). But their massive emigration to Egypt and the Middle East between 330 and 250 BC took them into very different zones.

Agricultural Methods

Dry-grain farming was the rule. There was some irrigation (Hanson 1995:60–63), but it was not the norm. Manuring was intense, especially in Classical times; intensive surveys have revealed "haloes" of low-density sherd scatters around higher-density "sites" (Bintliff 2002; Snodgrass 1991, 1994).

Literary sources and archaeological remains suggest that by 750 BC (and probably before) the staple food was barley bread, with some wheat. People generally preferred wheat, but barley's resistance to fluctuations in rainfall made it the norm. Our evidence is poor, but the best guesses suggest that in good years the seed-yield to seed-sown ratio was around 4.8:1 for wheat and 6:1 for barley (Garnsey 1992:148). The amount of seed sown per unit of land varied. Garnsey estimates yields of 625 kg/ha for wheat and 770 kg/ha for barley as possible averages for good years, and Sallares (1991:79) suggests 400–600 kg/ha for wheat. Gallant (1991:77) provides figures for 1911–1950 showing that average yields varied from area to area, ranging from 470 (Arcadia) to 903 kg/ha (Kavala) for wheat and from 529 (Corfu) to 1,097 kg/ha (Thessaly) for barley.

A farmer's ability to produce beyond subsistence depended on skill, luck, and access to land and labor. In simulations, Gallant (1991:60–112) suggests that typical family farms in Classical Attica, working 5 or 6 ha with little extrafamilial labor, produced only small surpluses to sell in the city. He argues that sensible farmers stored as much grain as possible against the inevitable bad years.

There are too many unspecifiable variables for precise estimates of the costs of concentrating population. As a rough guide, though, farmers growing grain probably averaged production beyond subsistence, storage, and seed of around 10–20 percent. Some residents of ancient cities walked out to the fields and grew much of their own food, but to support 20,000 nonfarmers, urban markets needed to draw in surpluses from 100,000–200,000 country folk. The costs depended on transport technology, rural population density, forms of urban control over rural production, and farmers' assessments of the incentives for bringing grain to market. Laurence (1998:134) suggests that in the Roman Empire, the cost of wheat would increase by 40 percent for every 100 miles it was moved by road, as against 1.3 percent per 100 miles for sea transport. The scarcity of good roads within the Aegean (particularly earlier in the first millennium) and the often difficult terrain might have meant still higher costs for land transport.

Written sources suggest that Classical and Hellenistic Greeks had a strong preference for urban living. In well-populated countrysides, the costs of moving to a small city of fewer than 20,000 people were probably low. But as a city rose above that size, it needed to generate great wealth to pay prices high enough to attract food to its markets, or it had to use political and/or legal means to extract food from the countryside.

City Sizes

The Dark Age (ca. 1000–750 BC)

Evidence about the Dark Age is mainly archaeological. Writing disappeared after the destruction of the Bronze Age palaces around 1200 BC, returning only around 750 BC. Homer's *Iliad* and *Odyssey* probably date ca. 750–700 BC but purport to describe a heroic age, probably based on the pre-1200 Bronze Age. Homer imagined small towns, but we do not know how they related to real Dark Age settlements.

Dark Age houses were flimsy, and on long-lived urban sites survive poorly. Estimating populations depends on the distribution of settlement-type pottery, wells, and graves. This creates wide margins of error.

There were population movements and demographic decline after destructions around 1200 BC and again around 1100 BC. Barely one-tenth as many sites are known from the eleventh century as from the thirteenth. Many systematic surveys reveal no Dark Age sites. Visibility problems may exaggerate the decline, though there is evidence that surveys also underrepresent earlier Bronze Age sites (Bintliff et al. 1999). But the general pattern is clear: occupation contracted on a few centers, leaving much of Greece lightly settled or even abandoned (Morris 2000:195–207). Pollen data from Messenia even suggest that "during the Early Iron Age the landscape experienced the least intensive human impact of the last 4,000 years" (Zangger et al. 1997:593).

Bronze Age towns were quite small: just 8 ha at Tiryns, 20 to 30 at Pylos, Thebes, and Troy, and a little more at Gla (Davis et al. 1997:428–430; Dickinson 1994:78; Jablonka 1996). None of these sites necessarily had a population above 10,000. The largest town, Knossos on Crete, had perhaps 15,000 residents (Whitelaw 2001).

After these towns declined in the twelfth century BC, most people lived in hamlets of a few dozen inhabitants, often lasting only a few generations (Whitley 1991). The Dark Age was a time of "a tiny population, based in small, widely separated settlements, with broad tracts of country having no permanent population" (Snodgrass 1993:37). There may have been a shift toward mobile pastoralism after 1200 (Snodgrass 1987:189–199), but interregional variations outweigh diachronic in the limited first-millennium evidence (Legouilloux 2000).

But there were also larger sites. Finds cover 50 ha at Argos, 100 at Knossos, and 200 at Athens. As noted above, Athens and perhaps Knossos push the limits of Fletcher's model, but our evidence—scatters of find spots—may be misleading. Knossos may have been compact, but Athens and Argos probably consisted of clusters of villages separated by open spaces. On the mainland the few excavated houses are chiefly oval and apsidal, with open areas around them, although on Crete rectilinear houses were more tightly packed (Mazarakis Ainian 1997). Citywide densities were perhaps as low as 12.5–25 per ha, perhaps even falling below Fletcher's 10 per ha cutoff, but population probably never fell below 600–1,200 people at Argos, 1,250–2,500 at Knossos, and 2,500–5,000 at Athens (Morris 1991:29–34). Lefkandi may have been the biggest site in the tenth and ninth centuries, but we cannot yet even guess its population.

Snodgrass (1971, 1977) interpreted Dark Age burials as evidence for an egalitarian society, but I (Morris 1987) have argued that hidden selectivity masked a rank distinction between better-off peasants and a dependent lower class. The likely size of Athens, Argos, and Knossos and the scale of the Toumba building and mound at Lefkandi (Popham et al. 1993) also imply hierarchies. The distribution of Dark Age burial customs and pottery styles sometimes corresponds to later political boundaries, and similar (but weaker) political units possibly existed before 750 BC (Coldstream 1983; cf. Morgan and Whitelaw 1991). But there are no indications that Dark Age leaders wielded state-level political or military powers. Historians often interpret Homer's epics as evidence that by 800 BC Greece was dominated by loose social groups headed by chiefs who might muster warriors for raids and vendettas and monopolized some legal functions, but little more (e.g., Donlan 1989; Raaflaub 1997).

In most years, even Athens could support itself from its hinterland, but variations in rainfall would mean that local supplies sometimes failed. The same would be true for smaller villages. But farmers in other communities might have had bumper crops in the same year, and regional exchange systems must have developed. Already by ca. 700 BC the poet Hesiod (*Works and Days* 630–644) described seaborne trade, though he saw this more as a response to debt than a sound way to earn a living. His advice to "admire a small ship, but put your cargo in a large one" (643) implies an important role for the rich. Chiefs may have coordinated long-distance movement of goods through networks created by gift giving (Tandy 1997:93–111).

Archaic Greece (ca. 750–480 BC)

Around 750 BC, writing reappeared in Greece. Thousands of inscribed lines survive, usually on potsherds (Jeffrey 1990 [1961]), plus about 28,000 lines of Homer's *Iliad* and *Odyssey*, probably written down between 750 and 700 BC; 2,000 lines of Hesiod, recorded a little later; and another 25,000 lines of other poets across the seventh and sixth centuries. Van Wees (1992:269–271) estimates that Homer imagined Odysseus's Ithaca as having about 600 inhabitants and large cities (Troy, Pylos, Phaeacia) as having more like 4,000. But other than this guess, the texts are little help. Classical writers tell suggestive stories about the Archaic period, but it is hard to evaluate such anecdotes (Thomas 1989).

Archaic houses were more robust than Dark Age, and villages have been excavated in the Cyclades. But apart from their monumental architecture, the major Archaic centers, buried or destroyed by later activity, are poorly known. However, everything suggests that by 500 BC the major Greek cities were much larger than in 750.

There was rapid population growth in the late eighth century, particularly around the Aegean. Snodgrass (1977, 1980:23–24) argued that in Attica, the 2,400 sq km territory around Athens, population increased sevenfold in two generations—i.e., at a rate of 4 percent per annum, as fast as human populations have ever been known to grow. He suggested an almost equal rate for Argos. Because significant immigration was unlikely (population grew all round Greece; there are no signs of movements into Greece, and there was major emigration to new Greek cities in the west Mediterranean), this would require spectacular birthrates. Osborne (1996a:65) notes that if, as seems likely, life expectancy at birth (e_0) was between 25 and 30 years, even a stable population required 4–5 live births per woman. Only by raising e_0 to 37 years and hypothesizing 7 live births per woman can we reach 4 percent per annum growth.

Alternatively, death rates (especially infant mortality) may have fallen. But the burials do not support this. Between 900 and 725 BC, only 1 burial in 10 belongs to children, but after 725 BC, the adult:child ratio is roughly even. Fifty percent child mortality rates are normal in preindustrial societies, and there is no parallel for a rate of just 5–10 percent lasting nearly two centuries. The only plausible explanation is that before 725 BC the subadult burials had low archaeological visibility (Morris 1987, 1992:78–80, 1998b). The increase in child burials around 725 BC tells us more about beliefs than about demography. Concluding that the Dark Age record underrepresents the young roughly halves the rate of increase hypothesized by Snodgrass.

I (Morris 1987) have argued that class, as well as age, limited access to formal cemeteries in Dark Age Athens and that only the wealthier 25–33 percent of the adult population is represented before 750 BC, whereas after that date, all residents had access to the same cemeteries, causing the number of archaeologically visible burials to rise dramatically. This undermines using burial numbers as demographic data, although it opens up new ways to interpret social structure.

Even without the burials, however, there is clear evidence for larger settlements in Aegean Greece. Eretria went from a scattering of huts around 850 BC to interlinked villages covering 100 ha by 700 (Mazarakis Ainian 1987), with a population of perhaps 5,000. We cannot document density at other major centers, but I would guess that Athens reached 10,000 people by 700 BC. Corinth, Knossos, and Argos were surely at least as big as Eretria by 700, and there were probably dozens of communities like Smyrna, Thebes, and Miletus with populations over 1,000.

Later texts speak of *synoikismos,* population movements from villages to larger towns, but intensive surveys show that the number of minor sites also increased (e.g., Cherry et al. 1991:327–347; Ekroth 1996; Jameson et al. 1994:372–381, 547–559). Furthermore, digs in Cycladic villages show them blossoming from a dozen or two dozen houses around 800 BC into communities of hundreds by 700–650 (particularly Cambitoglou et al. 1988). Growth did not reach 4 percent per annum, but population probably doubled in the eighth century (Morris 2006; Scheidel 2003b) and affected all levels of the settlement hierarchy.

Large numbers of Greeks—particularly from Eretria, Chalcis, and Corinth—emigrated to new homes in Sicily and southern Italy. The first western *apoikia* ("home away from home"), Pithekoussai, probably had 4,000 to 5,000 residents in the late eighth century (Morris 1996:57). These may not all have been Greeks, and other settlements were smaller. De Angelis (2003:40–71) suggests that Megara Hyblaea, founded in 728 BC, began with just 240 to 320 settlers, growing to about 2,000 by 625 BC. But if we assume that the 23 or 24 *apoikiai* founded by ca. 700 BC (Graham 1982:160–162) averaged just 500 colonists each, that would still mean that more than 10,000 Greeks emigrated in roughly fifty years.

In the eighth century BC the Greek world changed from one of villages to one of towns. But the seventh-century evidence is confusing. In some areas, numbers of graves decline, and Camp (1979) argued from this and closures of wells in Athens that a drought wiped out much of the population, driving others to emigrate. Eretria seems almost abandoned between 700 and 550 BC, despite having strong fortifications and a flourishing sanctuary. Still more baffling is the disappearance of most evidence from Crete around 600 BC, even though sixth-century inscriptions are abundant (Morris 1998a:66–68). Meanwhile, Smyrna, Corinth, and other towns flourished (Akurgal 1983; Salmon 1984). The peculiar regional patterns and the prominence of certain kinds of evidence suggest that we are again dealing with problems of social change, archaeological dating, and new forms of deposits rather than with direct evidence for demography (Erickson 2006; Morris 1987:156–167, 1998a:77; Snodgrass 1983). These problems need closer study.

After the rapid late-eighth-century growth and the confusion of the seventh-century evidence, there are signs of another major change in the later sixth century. Snodgrass (1980:157–158) rightly observes that "whatever factors made possible the achievement of Archaic Greece, an advanced urban culture was not one of them," but by 550 BC more urban amenities were appearing, as were signs of clearer political and religious distinctions between town and country. Most late-sixth-century cities had a formal *agora* for political, commercial, and religious activity, bordered by temples and public buildings. At Athens, the Pisistratid tyrants (546–510 BC) built fountain houses and clay pipes to carry water across the city (Shapiro 1989; Thompson and Wycherley 1972). Athens probably had 20,000 residents by 500 BC, and Corinth was probably roughly the same size.

It seems that Greeks in towns such as Corinth, Argos, Athens, and Eretria rapidly created a new I-C assemblage between 750 and 700 BC. I have argued elsewhere (Morris 1987, 1998a, 2000:287–305) that this was a time of intense anxiety, competition, and experiment and that in some parts of central Greece (notably Athens) the shift toward a new cultural order was actually reversed in the seventh century. The cultural traits that proved adaptively advantageous in the eighth century—the alphabet, new artistic and symbolic systems, rectilinear houses, monumental temples, and a culture of egalitarian male citizenship—continued to evolve across the Archaic period, but the structural revolution of 750 to 700 BC nonetheless challenges Fletcher's Darwinian model of transitions to new levels of integration (Morris 1998a, 2000:155–191, 257–286; Snodgrass 1980).

Political organization changed massively between 800 and 500 BC. Controlling dependent labor in a largely empty landscape must have been a major issue for Dark Age elites, but by 700 Greece was getting crowded, and institutions forged in the tenth and ninth centuries were becoming unsuitable. Snodgrass (1980:15–84) suggests that the population pressure drove warfare, political centralization, greater hierarchy, and cultural innovations to justify the new order. There is some evidence that people started identifying more strongly with specific territories and frontiers (de Polignac 1995). Archaic Greek states generally lacked coercive power (Morris 1991:43–49; Snodgrass 1980:85–122), but by the late sixth century a powerful tyrant such as Polycrates of Samos could mobilize resources for substantial public works and a state navy (Herodotus 2.148, 3.39–40, 60).

The spending power of successful governments made their cities attractive places to settle, and trade networks to supply cities with food improved. Around 525 BC Athenian-painted pots for the first time show pictures of round, sail-driven merchant ships, as distinct from warships, which seem to have doubled as trading ships until this period (Casson 1971; cf. Herodotus 1.163). Plutarch (*Pericles* 26), writing around AD 100, adds that the Samians invented merchantmen (thereafter known as *samaina*) in the sixth century.

Around 525 to 500 BC, even major centers such as Athens and Corinth could still feed themselves from their hinterlands in good years. Garnsey (1988:104) suggests that Attica could feed 120,000 to 150,000 people, and Sallares (1991: 79) estimates 84,000 to 124,000. If their figures are roughly right, then by 500 BC Athens was reaching the point where food imports would be required in most years.

Plutarch (*Solon* 24) describes an Athenian law passed in 594 BC prohibiting all agricultural products except olive oil, which some historians take as evidence of early problems with food supply. However, as Garnsey (1988:111) notes, this law—assuming it is genuine—makes most sense as protection against exporting grain in poor agricultural years.

Other anecdotes may indicate increasing difficulty feeding Athens during the sixth century. A story in Aristotle's *Constitution of Athens* (16.6) mentions the tyrant Pisistratus meeting a farmer working particularly infertile soil, which some see as evidence for extension of cultivation into marginal land, and Herodotus (5.94–95) says that Pisistratus established a military base at Sigeion, not far from the route Black Sea grain ships would take regularly in Classical times. However, there are three problems with interpreting this as evidence for state interest in the food supply by 550 BC: (1) Herodotus was confused about chronology; (2) Sigeion is not directly on the trade route; and (3) there is no evidence for Black Sea connections with Athens so early (Tsetskhladze 1998). The story that Xerxes of Persia saw grain ships from the Black Sea bound for Greece in 480 BC (Herodotus 7.147) may be more relevant, but again there are three problems: (1) this may have been part of preparations to meet the Persian invasion; (2) it may have been part of a response to a poor agricultural year; and (3) Herodotus says the ships were bound for Aegina and the Peloponnese, not Athens.

These snippets are suggestive, but no more. *If* by 500 BC Athens had a population of about 20,000, and *if* the total population of Attica was approximately 150,000, and *if* Attica's carrying capacity was 120,000 to 150,000—all statements open to challenge—then late-sixth-century Athens was starting to depend on grain imports every year. At this period, Athens's ability to attract imports probably combined elements of Weber's producer and merchant cities. Athens was a center for certain manufactures, particularly ceramic tablewares. The number of artisans involved was small (Cook 1959) and prices low (Vickers and Gill 1994), but there are indications that the trade was profitable and market oriented (Osborne 1996b). Athenian olive oil was also widely traded. More important, silver mining intensified after 550 BC. By 483 BC, the mines were highly productive. There was a huge windfall that year, which the Athenians used to finance a state navy (Aristotle, *Constitution of Athens* 22.7; Herodotus 7.144). If, as in Classical times, rentiers living in Athens controlled most mines, this combination of income flows probably already made Athens the Aegean's richest city.

If Athens needed regular food imports by 500 BC, selling value-added goods paid for them. We simply do not know whether the city could have expanded further on this base because the Persian War of 480–479 BC transformed it into an imperial power.

The one Archaic community that could exploit a large agricultural hinterland through taxes and rents was Sparta. The Spartans conquered Laconia in the ninth century BC and neighboring Messenia in the eighth and seventh, reducing their populations to serfdom. These dependents (helots) worked the land as sharecroppers (Hodkinson 2000:113–151). Spartans fought wars of annexation until their military power reached its limits in the 560s (Herodotus 1.65–66), and then they changed strategy. By the 530s they had "subjugated most of the Peloponnese" (Herodotus 1.68), although more through diplomacy and bullying than direct warfare.

Sparta had an enormous supply zone, operating through coercion, not markets. Spartan ideology held that no full male citizen (Spartiate) engaged in manual labor. According to legend, there were originally 9,000 Spartiates (Plutarch, *Lycurgus* 8). The sources describe ritual systems that would require the Spartiates to live close together, and anecdotes imply that they and their families lived in the town of Sparta (e.g., Plutarch, *Cimon* 16). Sparta would then have had some 20,000–35,000 free residents around 500 BC, plus numerous helots and *perioikoi* ("dwellers around"). At 40,000-plus residents, it would have been by far the largest Greek city.

This is possible; we know almost nothing of the Archaic city's layout. Herodotus (1.56) says that Sparta and Athens were the major Greek states in the 540s, but no more than that. But Thucydides' famous comment (1.10) around 400 BC that if "the city of Sparta were to become deserted and only the temples and foundations of buildings remained, I think that future generations would, as time passed, find it very difficult to believe that the place had really been as powerful as it was represented to be" does not sound like Sparta was a major population center. Possibly the Spartiates and their families did not all live in Sparta. Transporting food for 40,000-plus people to Sparta would have been difficult; the social cost of dispersed settlement, closer to the sources of food, may have been lower than the physical cost of having helots move bulk commodities overland (particularly if the Spartiates still lived close enough to Sparta to participate in communal rituals).

Classical Greece (480–323 BC)

The Classical written sources are fuller than the Archaic. Much information comes from military figures, requiring untestable extrapolations to reach total populations, but the data do establish approximate scales. Beloch (1968[1886]) and Gomme (1933) scrupulously assessed these data. The archaeological record is also richer, including city walls, which sometimes give a rough sense of the settled area (Hansen 2004:33–40; Muggia 1997), and numerous excavated houses. The most important evidence comes from highly intensive surveys, which use sophisticated methods to deal with high-density urban sites (Alcock 1991; Bintliff and Snodgrass 1988).

As in Archaic times, population growth was uneven (Bintliff 1997). The Aegean grew fastest in the fifth century, though in the fourth century the north and west caught up. Growth was also concentrated in a few major centers. Ruschenbusch (1983, 1984, 1985) has argued that the typical city-state had fewer than 6,000 citizens in a territory of just a few hundred square kilometers. Some of his calculations are questionable (Nixon and Price 1990:158–162), but the general picture seems plausible. The "urban" centers of most city-states probably numbered just a thousand or two. These were large villages, not cities, feeding themselves in most years.

Surveys have revealed strong growth in rural settlement (Alcock [1993:33–49] summarizes the data; Davis et al. 1997; Jameson et al. 1994; Lohmann 1996; Wells 1996). In the southern Argolid, the ratio of third-order (probably farmstead) to second-order (village) sites rose from 3 to 1 in Archaic times to 6 to 1 in Classical (ca. 500–350 BC) to 10 to 1 in late Classical/early Hellenistic (ca. 350–250 BC; Jameson et al. 1994:383).

Everything about this development is disputed. Some scholars argue that few third-order sites were actual farms (e.g., Osborne 1992), but in southern Attica, where walls can be seen on the surface, many were definitely residential/production units (Lohmann 1993). There are also differences over chronology, which may reflect regional variations or dating problems. In southern Attica, dispersed settlement begins around 500 BC, lasting until 300, whereas in the southern Argolid, Berbati/Limnes in the northern Argolid, and on the Skourta plain, it begins around 350, lasting until 250 or 200 (Jameson et al. 1994:383–394; Lohmann 1993; Munn and Zimmermann-Munn 1989:100–110, 122–123; Pentinnen 1996:271–273, 278–281).

The shifts were partial. At Koressos, Cherry et al. (1991:337) estimate that at the height of dispersion, three-quarters of the population still lived in the main town (population 900–1,200). But even a shift of residence by 10–15 percent of the population could have serious consequences. A "new model" of Classical agriculture envisages farmers working contiguous fields, pasturing animals on them, and using manure to reduce fallow (e.g., Hodkinson 1988). Some historians argue that these agricultural changes shifted political power toward the middling citizens, fueling the rise of democratic institutions (Hanson 1995:41–89; Hodkinson 1992; Morris 1994:363–366).

The larger rural populations of the fourth and perhaps fifth centuries BC could support larger urban populations. At Sparta, the number of full citizens shrank during Classical times, largely because inheritance laws made it easy to concentrate property, and Spartiates whose estates could not support their mess contributions lost their citizen status (Hodkinson 2000). Five thousand Spartiates fought at Plataea in 479 BC (Herodotus 9.10), but by the battle of Leuctra in 371 there were only 1,200 Spartiates, 400 of whom died on the field (Xenophon, *Hellenica* 6.4.15). This decline may mean that the town of Sparta also shrank, though given the uncertainties discussed above, there is currently no way to know.

At Athens, by contrast, population increased sharply in the fifth century, definitely outgrowing local agricultural resources. Several texts provide military strengths (especially Thucydides 2.13, for 431 BC), and historians have extrapolated to total numbers of citizens, citizen families, resident aliens, and slaves. Estimates vary. For the likely high point, in 431 BC, Gomme (1933:26) suggested 315,500 people in Attica, whereas Hansen (1986) counted 350,000. The plague of 430–428 and heavy losses among poor rowers during the Peloponnesian War (431–404; Strauss 1986:70–86) reduced Athenian population. For 323 BC, at the death of Alexander, Gomme (1933) estimated 258,000. Garnsey (1988:90) suggested much lower figures, just 160,000 to 172,000 in 431 BC and 84,000–120,000 in the fourth century, but did not argue the case in detail. There is a wide margin of error in these guesses, but all agree that Attica was densely populated. Following Beloch (1968[1886]:56–57) in calculating the area of Attica at 2,527 sq km, Garnsey's figures give a density of 104 persons per sq km, Gomme's give 125, and Hansen's 139. Jardé (1925:142–143) estimated Attica's carrying capacity as 33 persons per sq km, and Garnsey estimated 42 per sq km. Sallares (1991:72) agrees on 35–42 per sq km. Even in the best years during the 430s, Attica imported two-thirds to three-quarters of its food.

Gomme (1933) estimated the combined urban population of Athens and Piraeus at 155,000 in 430 BC and 168,000 in 330. However, his only arguments were that "we may assume, I think, rather over a third of the citizen population . . . to have been living in the town-area by 430, [and] nearly a half, say 50,000[,] a hundred years later" (Gomme 1933:47). However, the walls of Athens only enclose 215 ha, of which 120 were used for domestic settlement. Travlos (1960:71–72) estimated 36,000 people, or 170 per ha. This is toward the high end of comparable figures (Fletcher 1995:73–81), but plausible. There is little evidence for houses outside the walls, and I (Morris 1987:100) estimate the population at Athens around 430 BC at 35,000–40,000. Piraeus was a distinct area and probably had at least another 25,000 people (Garland [1987:58] says "above the 30,000 mark," but without arguments).

These figures suggest that 10–25 percent of the Attic population lived at Athens, not the one-third Gomme suggested. The ancient texts are consistent with the lower figures. Thucydides (2.16) said that "most" Athenians lived in the countryside in 431 BC, and in the fourth century Xenophon (*Hellenica* 2.4.8–9, 2.26) and Demosthenes (57.10) used similar expressions. Xenophon (*Memora-*

bilia 3.6.14) even says there were 10,000 households, presumably about 40,000 people, in early fourth-century Athens, though this may be a purely conventional figure. Furthermore, fourth-century quotas for the representation of different regions on the civic council suggest that one citizen in nine came from the city of Athens.

Athens, then, probably peaked at around 40,000 inhabitants in the 430s. The Spartan siege in 404 caused severe famine, and the city probably had a smaller (though not dramatically smaller) fourth-century population. Throughout Classical times Athens depended not only on attracting grain from the Attic countryside but also on substantial imports from overseas, most famously from the Black Sea area.

In comparative terms, Athens was still small. So far as we know, the city never had the same health problems as Rome (Sallares 1991:257; but cf. Laurence 1997). Athens did employ *koprologoi* (dung collectors) to dispose of human waste (Aristotle, *Constitution of Athens* 50.2) and suffered a devastating epidemic in 430–427 BC (Thucydides 2.47–55; Sallares 1991:244–265). Thucydides comments that overcrowding exacerbated the epidemic, but this was unusual: beginning in 431, the city received an influx of refugees from Spartan invasions of the countryside. Emphasizing the peculiarity of the epidemic, Thucydides (2.53) observed that law and order broke down, and everyone acted as if each day was their last. But after 427 these urban ills are never mentioned again, even during the period 413–404 when the Spartans occupied Decelea and refugees settled in Athens year-round.

Athens's growth to 40,000 people was not a transformation from a large Archaic town into a sinkhole of mortality like Rome, but it nonetheless involved crossing a threshold. No Archaic city had played such an economic role or integrated the surpluses of such a large area. Even after 404 Athens's population probably never fell below 25,000, and it remained the major market.

The other example of major Classical urban growth is Syracuse on Sicily. Beginning in 485 BC, its tyrant Gelon forcibly moved the population of Camarina to Syracuse and then the richer citizens of Megara Hyblaea and Euboea, selling the poor into slavery (Herodotus 7.156). Around 475, Pindar (*Pythian* 2.1) already spoke of Syracuse's great size, and Diodorus of Sicily (11.72) commented that by 463 the population had grown greatly through imports of slaves. Thucydides (6.17) had Alcibiades refer to the swollen populations of Sicilian cities in a speech set in 415 BC, and speaking in his own voice he (7.28) observed that in 413 Syracuse was no smaller than Athens. Beloch (1968[1886]:281) estimated the population of Syracusan territory at 250,000 in 415, a density of 53–75 per sq km. The fifth-century walls encircled 120 ha, but by the 470s settlement had spread beyond them (Finley 1979:52). If the urban density was like that of Athens, the population of the city itself was also about 40,000.

Syracuse withstood an Athenian siege in 415–413, which must have reduced its population, and in 405 the citizens of Camarina and Gela who had been moved to Syracuse escaped to Leontini (Diodorus 13.113). But the new tyrant Dionysius I (405–367) took Syracuse from strength to strength. Plato (*Letters* 7.332c) could even say that he "united all Sicily into a single city." He incorporated freed slaves into the population and made new relocations (Diodorus 14.7, 14–15, 106–111). He substantially extended the city walls to protect his new community. We cannot make a precise estimate for Dionysius's city, but it was clearly larger than that of 415. It was probably the first Greek settlement to exceed 50,000 people and may indeed have reached Beloch's estimate (1968[1886]:281) of 100,000.

Most Sicilian cities had 10,000–20,000 residents (Muggia 1997:116–148). At least five had walls enclosing 100-plus ha, although normally only about half was used for housing (Muggia 1997). Diodorus (13.57) says that when Carthage sacked Selinus in 409 BC, there were 21,000 people within its walls. Many were probably rural refugees, and De Angelis (2003:146–149) estimates the normal urban population as 6,664–10,000.

The texts suggest that the fourth-century wars that swelled Syracuse's population brought ruin to the rest of Greek Sicily (Diodorus 14.66). Plutarch (*Timoleon* 1, 23) even calls Sicily *apolis,* "cityless," by 350. The causes, scale, and even historicity of this urban crisis are open to debate, and in any case, it was apparently short-lived. According to Plutarch (*Timoleon* 23) and Diodorus (16.82), drawing on the contemporary writer Athanis, by 337 BC Timoleon of Corinth had brought 60,000 colonists from Greece to Sicily and resettled the cities. Archaeological evidence shows flourishing cities in the late fourth century (Talbert 1974:146–160). Beloch (1968[1886]:281) suggested that Syracuse held 200,000 people by 300 BC.

Athens and Syracuse stand out from other Classical Greek cities: both were imperial administrative centers. In 478 BC, Athens took over the league that had been formed in 481 to resist Persia. By 441, it included 205 communities, nearly all paying tribute, which funded a league fleet. Most contributions were small, but the total, 407 talents of silver, was enough to feed 7,000–10,000 people at subsistence level for a year and supported the greatest navy in the Mediterranean. Most ships were Athenian, and most of the revenues flowed into the pockets of Athenians who rowed them (Gabrielsen 1994). Athens taxed movements of goods within the empire and diverted other economic benefits to the center (Morris 2001). According to Aristotle (*Constitution of Athens* 24.3; cf. Aristophanes, *Wasps* 656–663, 707–711), this produced enough wealth to support 20,000 people. Ancient figures are problematic, but the empire did inject major resources into Athens. More people than ever before earned or supplemented their income through industrial activity or state pay (Raaflaub 1998:22–26).

Athens drew in food because it could pay. It was a classic consumer city in the fifth century, extracting wealth from administering the empire and using it to buy agricultural goods. Thucydides (2.38) had Pericles say in a speech set in 430 that "the greatness of our city brings it about that all the good things from all over the world flow in to us, so that to us it seems just as natural to enjoy foreign goods as our own local products." The money in Athenian hands drew traders from all over the Mediterranean, and the city's large population made grain one of the most profitable commodities. At least in the fourth century, the Athenian assembly discussed the state of the grain supply every month (Aristotle, *Constitution of Athens* 43.4; cf. Xenophon, *Memorabilia* 3.6.13; Aristotle, *Rhetoric* 1.4.7, 11). Furthermore, Athenian law required any trader using Athenian shipping or finance to unload his entire grain shipment at Piraeus (Gauthier 1981), and although the Athenians did not directly use the fleet to bring grain to Athens, they regularly intervened against threats to the grain supply (Garnsey 1988:120–123). The Old Oligarch (2.11–12), probably writing in the 430s, recognized the fleet's role in guaranteeing that all the world's goods flowed through Athens. When Sparta captured the Athenian fleet in 405 and cut the Black Sea supply line, Athens rapidly succumbed.

The loss of empire in 404 BC interrupted but did not destroy Athens's trading relationships, and by 380 Isocrates (4.42) could once again celebrate Piraeus as "the market place in the middle of Greece." But shorn of its empire, Athens began to look less like Weber's model of a consumer city and more like his producer city. The Athenians increased silver production (particularly in the 350s) and organized state revenues more efficiently (particularly in the 330s). But these steps never fully compensated for the loss of imperial revenues. Population never returned to pre-431 levels, and state finances were in constant crisis. Most important, the loss of naval supremacy meant that supplies were constantly threatened (Garnsey 1988:134–164).

Syracuse's food supply has received less attention, although the city not only fed itself but also was a food exporter. Herodotus (7.158) says that in 480 BC Gelon offered grain for the entire Greek army fighting Persia, and according to Thucydides (3.27), one reason for Athenian intervention in Sicily in 427 was to cut off grain exports to the Peloponnese. In the late fourth century there is abundant evidence for Sicilian grain coming to Athens (Garnsey 1988:151–152; Habicht 1997:26–27, 69).

Like Athens, Syracuse drew wealth from its empire, paying much of it to poorer citizens working as wage laborers on vast building projects (e.g., Diodorus 15.13), although Syracuse never instituted pay for public office. Also like Athens, Syracuse was a major naval power. Asheri (1992:151) speaks of the Tyrrhenian Sea "becoming a Syracusan lake" in the 470s. In 453, Syracusan fleets ravaged Elba and Corsica, and in 439 Syracuse built 100 triremes (Diodorus 11.88, 12.30). This fleet defeated Athens in 413 (Thucydides 7.31–41, 59–71), and Dionysius I built 200 more ships in 385 (Diodorus 15.13).

But despite these similarities to Athens, Syracuse was probably supplied largely by land, despite the higher transport costs. Its territory covered 4,685 sq km, more than twice the area of Attica, and Diodorus (11.72) commented on Syracusan farms' wealth in 463. Plutarch (*Moralia* 551F) preserves a tradition that the tyrant Hiero (478–467 BC) promoted husbandry and that all the Syracusan tyrants redistributed land. Some of Syracuse's territory was worked by non-Greek serfs called *killyrioi* (Herodotus 7.155), recalling Sparta's helots. Di Vita (1956) suggested that these serfs farmed the territories of cities whose populations were relocated to Syracuse, sending part of the produce to the main city. The tyrants founded new cities, such as Aetna in 476 BC, for which Hieron confiscated native lands and divided them up into 10,000 properties (Diodorus 11.49). These new cities probably also supplied Syracuse. The tyrants placed Syracusan officials or puppet kings in other conquered cities, and Syracusan coins attest to trade with the Sicels of the interior (Ampolo 1984; Jenkins 1975).

Like fifth-century Athens, Syracuse was very much a consumer city. The wealth of empire flowed to a famously rich urban administrative elite (e.g., Plutarch, *Dion* 6, 15). They spent lavishly on retainers and public buildings, making money available to poorer citizens to buy food brought in from other parts of Sicily. Only Athens and Syracuse, the administrative centers of revenue-generating empires, broke through the carrying capacity of their immediate hinterlands to become cities of 40,000-plus. Other militarily strong cities, such as Sparta in the sixth and early fourth century or Thebes in the 360s, did not make this breakthrough, because they did not administer other cities so as to channel wealth back to the metropolis and into the pockets of urban consumers. The fifth-century wall at Thebes incorporates 328 ha, but Symeonoglou (1985:119) notes that only a quarter was settled. He (1985:203–206) estimates the population at 20,000 by 431 and nearly 25,000 in 362. He assumed densities of 300 per ha, which seems high, and 15,000–20,000, comfortably supportable by Thebes' hinterland in good years, may be more realistic.

Hellenistic Greece (323–31 BC)

Polybius and Diodorus provide narratives of parts of this period, and there are many inscriptions. As in Classical times, however, the sources rarely give population figures, and when writers such as Strabo and Pliny the Elder do so, they are rarely believable. Archaeology continues to be crucial, although Hellenistic levels typically receive less attention from excavators than earlier phases (particularly in Egypt and the Middle East).

A massive emigration of Greeks and Macedonians followed Alexander's conquest of the Persian Empire between 335 and 323 BC, only slowing after 250 BC (Billows 1995:146–182). Demographic trends in the Seleucid Empire varied from region to region (Alcock 1994), but on the whole there was population growth, urbanization, and more intensive agriculture (Aperghis 2001).

Survey data reveal a crowded and thriving countryside of small towns, villages, and farmsteads in the Aegean in the fourth and early third centuries, but by the later third century decline had set in, and many sites were abandoned (Alcock 1993:33–49, 1994:177–180). Alcock (1993:49–55) rightly warns against simply equating site numbers with population size, but the survey findings are consistent with textual accounts of decline. Around 150 BC, Polybius (36.17) wrote:

> In our time the whole of Greece has been subject to a low birth rate and a general decrease of the population, owing to which cities have become deserted and the land has ceased to yield fruit, although there have neither been continuous wars nor epidemics. . . . As men had fallen into such a state of pretentiousness, avarice, and indolence that they did not wish to marry, or if they married to rear the children born to them, or at most as a rule but one or two of them, so as to leave these in affluence and bring them up to waste their substance, the evil rapidly and insensibly grew. For in cases where of one or two children the one was carried off by war and the other by sickness, it is evident that the houses must have been left unoccupied, and as in the case of swarms of bees, so by small degrees cities became resourceless and feeble.

Small sites were particularly affected: in the southern Argolid, over half of the probable farmsteads used between 350 and 250 BC were abandoned by 200 (Jameson et al. 1994:394). This picture of an emptying countryside is consistent with texts such as Dio Chrysostom's *Euboean Discourse* (Dio Chrysostom, *Oration* 7.34–35), in which an imaginary local notable said that "almost two thirds of our land is a wilderness because of neglect and lack of population. I too own many acres, as I imagine some others do, not only in the mountains but also in the plains, and if anybody would till them, I should not only give him the chance for nothing but gladly pay money besides."

Despite Polybius's denial, internal wars and major conflicts with Rome in the second century BC probably did accelerate decline. One Roman raid in 167 carried off 150,000 people from Epirus (Livy 45.33–34), and in 146 Rome massacred or sold into slavery the entire population of Corinth (Pausanias 7.16.7–10). Roman absentee landlordism prevailed (e.g., Alcock 1993:72–92; Nepos, *Atticus* 14.2; Strabo 10.2.13), and Sulla's Greek wars in the 80s BC, including a sack of Athens in 86, exacerbated problems (Appian, *Roman History* 12.9.61–63).

Sicily suffered similarly. The First Punic War (264–246 BC) was fought mainly in western Sicily. Akragas and Selinous never recovered from their sacks, and there was a general population decline (Gallo 1994). Rome left many institutions untouched after Sicily became a province in 227, but much land was divided into vast slave-worked *latifundia* (plantations), supplying Rome's urban markets (Serrati 2000). The biggest slave revolts in history erupted on these estates in 133 and 104 BC (Diodorus 34). Syracuse had joined Rome in 263 and was rewarded, but defected to Hannibal in 216 and was brutally sacked in 212 (Polybius 7.14b, 8.3a, 37, 9.10; Livy 24.21–39, 25.23–31, 26.21; Plutarch, *Marcellus* 13–21). In the second and first century BC many coastal cities flourished while the older hill cities declined, but we know little about the countryside (Wilson 1990:17–32, 2000).

The Aegean cities declined. Some time after 294, Heraclides of Crete visited Athens, commenting that "the city itself is all dry and does not have a good water supply; the streets are narrow and winding, as they were built long ago. Most of the houses are cheaply built, and only a few reach a higher standard; a stranger would find it hard to believe at first sight that this was the famous city of Athens." He added that "the produce of the land is all priceless and delicious to taste, though in rather short supply" (Heraclides 1.1–2 [Austin 1981:no. 83]). Throughout the third and much of the second century, Athens faced regular food shortages (Garnsey 1988:163–164) and often depended on gifts from Hellenistic kings. After Sulla's sack in 86, it was nearly totally dependent on Roman largesse (Habicht 1997:328–337). By 150 BC, Athens probably had fewer than 10,000 residents, and there is no reason to think that other cities were any larger. Symeonoglou (1985:207) suggests that Hellenistic Thebes never surpassed 5,000 people.

Roman interventions transformed the urban system in the later first century BC. Julius Caesar founded a colony at Corinth in 44, and Augustus set up new cities at Nicopolis (soon after 31) and Patrai (by 14). Strabo (8.6.23, 7.7.5–6, 8.7.5) described all three as populous. Engels (1990:84) estimates the settled area of Corinth as 525 ha by AD 150 and extrapolates to a population of 80,000. Both figures can be questioned, but even if only half that size, Roman Corinth was one of the largest cities in mainland Greece's history.

Alexander established at least twenty new cities in the former Persian Empire (the number is disputed; see Fraser 1996) and settled them with his own soldiers and populations drawn from the local region. Most failed, but a few flourished, drawing immigrants from the old Graeco-Macedonian world. The most important were Alexandria in Egypt, founded in 331 BC, and Seleucus's foundations Seleucia-on-the-Tigris (305 BC; modern Tell Ubar) and Antioch (300 BC).

We have little literary or archaeological evidence for Alexandria's earliest history (Fraser 1972:I:3–7; Grimm 1996; Hoepfner 1990), although the situation is improving (Empereur 1998). Strabo (17.1.8) and Diodorus (17.52) both say Alexandria replaced Memphis as Egypt's capital in 331 BC, and commercial prospects drove Alexander's choice of site (Plutarch, *Alexander* 26; Arrian, *Anabasis* 3.1–2). Curtius (*History of Alexander* 4.8.5) says Alexander "provided the city with a large population" by forcibly emptying local cities. Public building boomed during the third century (Fraser 1972:I:12, 20, 21, 28, 36), and the city drew many Greek immigrants (Fraser 1972:I:63). Scheidel (2004) makes a strong case that population grew to 300,000 by 250 BC and then increased more slowly, to perhaps 400,000.

Ancient historians are normally skeptical about numbers reported in texts, but some believe that the Egyptian censuses were surprisingly accurate (Bagnall and Frier 1994), although others identify problems (Scheidel 2001a:118–162). For what the reports are worth, Diodorus (17.52) visited Alexandria in 60 BC and said that census returns put the free population at 300,000. Strabo (16.2.5) visited between 24 and 20 BC and estimated total population at 500,000. Both men called Alexandria the biggest city in the world, which would mean that its population surpassed Rome's. The *Gerousia Acts* papyrus speaks of 180,000 citizens at Alexandria voting in AD 37, which would mean a population close to a million (Rostovtzeff 1941:1138–1139), but few experts accept this figure.

Unlike earlier Greek cities, Alexandria was famous for urban problems, particularly street violence. Polybius (15.33) described especially gory murders around 200 BC, and Diodorus (1.83) mentioned a Roman being lynched for killing a sacred cat. Nearly a millennium after the city's foundation, Socrates (*History of the Church* 7.13) commented that Alexandria had always been more violent and anarchic than any other city (Barry 1993).

In western Asia the Macedonians took over the oldest and densest urban system in the ancient world. As early as 2800 BC, the walls of Uruk had enclosed 494 ha, and those of the seventh-century Assyrian capital Nineveh encircled 750 ha. According to the biblical book of Jonah, the city was "three days' walk across" (3.3), with a population of 120,000 (4.11). Modern estimates vary from 75,000 to 350,000 (van de Mieroop 1997:97 n. 19). Nineveh was destroyed in 612 BC, but fifth-century Babylon was even larger. Its outer wall enclosed 890 ha (George 1993; Wiseman 1985). Herodotus (1.178, 191) was astonished by Babylon's size, and according to Aristotle (*Politics* 1276a30), when Cyrus of Persia captured Babylon in 539 BC, it took three days for the news to reach some of its neighborhoods. The problems of estimating population are particularly acute in Mesopotamia (Postgate 1994; van de Mieroop 1997:97), but probably at least 100,000 people lived in Babylon on the eve of Alexander's conquest.

The Hellenistic cities created on this foundation were on a similar scale to Alexandria. Strabo (16.2.5) thought that Antioch, Seleucia, and Alexandria were roughly the same size, though Antioch was slightly smaller, and around AD 70, Pliny (*Natural History* 6.122) said that Seleucia had a population of 600,000. Seleucia's remains cover an enormous area, but little has so far been excavated (Hopkins 1972).

Pliny added that Seleucus created Seleucia in order to empty Babylon, just 40 miles away. Alexander certainly moved part of Babylon's population to Seleucia (Pausanias 1.16.3), and Antiochus I moved more in 273 (Austin 1981:no. 141). But Babylon (along with other nearby cities, including Uruk) remained a major center until the Parthian sack of 126 BC (Sherwin-White and Kuhrt 1993:149–161; van der Spek 1986). Most likely Seleucus created Seleucia to support his assumption of the title *basileus* or "king" (Sherwin-White 1987:18–20).

The original Antioch probably covered less than 90 ha (Will 2000), and its serious growth began only in the 230s, as wars with Ptolemy III undermined other Syrian cities. In the 180s Antiochus III settled mainland Greek refugees there (Libanius, *Oration* 11.205–207). Around 170 Antiochus IV expanded the city and built a new aqueduct, making Antioch for the first time a serious rival to Alexandria (Grainger 1990:124–126; Will 1990). By then it had eclipsed the other cities Seleucus founded in Syria, although a census in AD 6–7 nevertheless recorded 117,000 people at Apamea (Dessau 1892–1916:no. 2683).

The major Hellenistic phenomenon was the creation of larger Greek empires than ever before. The Macedonians and Greeks who took over Achaemenid Persia controlled far greater flows of wealth and resources than the Aegean had ever seen and took over established systems for supplying great cities with food. Van de Mieroop (1997:166–167) suggests that food was brought to Babylon along a network of canals extending 200 km north and south of the city, and documents describe merchants involved in this trade. According to Herodotus (1.192) fifth-century Babylonia fed not only its great city but also one-third of the Persian court and army, suggesting very high yields and efficient mobilization of surpluses. Over the next four centuries, the Greek-ruled *metropoleis* in the former Persian Empire outstripped their Achaemenid predecessors.

The Greek world's political center of gravity drifted irresistibly toward west Asia and Egypt. Alexandria, Seleucia, and Antioch were administrative centers controlling vast regional networks, with access to navigable rivers and the sea. Athens, Thebes, and other old Greek cities were increasingly marginal after the 330s. Cut off from the wealth flowing through imperial cities, they went into decline, accelerated by rural problems and ruinous wars with Rome. Only at the end of the first century BC did cities revive in Aegean Greece, and then it was under direct Roman sponsorship. Diodorus (46.22–24) could celebrate Roman Corinth as the market to the world.

At Alexandria, we have some evidence of food supply (Rostovtzeff 1941:909, 1273). At least in bad years, all grain exported from Egyptian estates had to come to the city, although as in Classical Athens, this operation was left in private hands (Rostovtzeff 1941:1551 n. 188). The Nile valley was densely settled. Diodorus (1.31) refers to 18,000 communities, with a population of 7,000,000; in the late first century AD Josephus (*Jewish War* 2.385) said that the population outside Alexandria was 7,500,000. Scheidel (2001a:181–250) defends these figures, though other historians (e.g., Bagnall and Frier 1994:56, 103; Rathbone 1990) lower the total to 4–5 million. In good years, this thriving agricultural zone not only fed Alexandria but also exported grain.

There were significant improvements in transportation between the third and first centuries BC, particularly in Roman-controlled areas (Hopkins 1980; Laurence 1998; Parker 1992). Bigger ships sailed more often and more safely, and better roads reached further inland. In combination with the jump in the wealth Greek cities could commandeer, these developments shattered the classical barriers to demographic growth. The first Greek super-cities took shape after 300 BC.

Conclusion

I draw seven conclusions from this review of the growth of Greek cities in the first millennium BC.

First, there were three major periods of transition in the growth of Greek cities, in the eighth, fifth, and late fourth/third centuries.

Second, the eighth-century transition created the cultural framework (Fletcher's I-C assemblage) that sustained Greek urban life for the next thousand years.

Third, the fifth-century transition permitted a few cities to capture imperial revenues, allowing them to grow well beyond the carrying capacity of their immediate hinterlands.

Fourth, the late fourth-/third-century transition allowed a few Greek cities in west Asia and Egypt to become large-scale administrative centers, capturing resources from large areas and supporting populations in the hundreds of thousands.

Fifth, once the cultural framework for urban life was in place, the growth of the largest Greek cities depended on imperial expansion and administration. Although there were always exceptions, Weber's consumer-city model remains the key to Greek urbanism.

Sixth, nothing in the history of Greek cities in the first millennium suggests they would have developed into producer or merchant cities. Stripped of its empire, fourth-century Athens resembled the producer-city model more than the consumer-city model, but its population never returned to its fifth-century level.

Seventh, and equally important, nothing suggests that further significant population growth was possible in the Greek cities after the first century BC, when Alexandria, Antioch, and Seleucia probably had 300,000–500,000 inhabitants. Absent a social, economic, and cultural transformation of the kind that happened in western Europe between AD 500 and 1500, the ancient city had reached its limits.

2

Did the Population of Imperial Rome Reproduce Itself?

Elio Lo Cascio

Recent contributions by several ancient historians take it for granted that the population of republican and imperial Rome did not reproduce itself due to the "appalling" living conditions of the *plebs urbana*. Pleket (1993:17), for example, speaks of the

> iron law that the population of large preindustrial megalopolises was incapable of reproducing itself sufficiently. In this respect Rome fully obeys the demographic law according to which big cities largely depended on immigration for keeping the population up to the mark. Life in such cities was far from healthy and as a result mortality rates vastly exceeded birthrates.

In the same vein Hopkins (1995–1996:60; see also Robinson 1992:1) holds that in Rome mortality must have been much higher than in small towns or the countryside and that therefore the city would have been "a huge death-trap." Scheidel (1994; cf. 1996, 2003a; see also Sallares 1999, 2002), studying the seasonality of death at Rome on the basis of the evidence of Christian epitaphs with the date of death, accepts the gloomy presentation by Scobie (1986) of the dreadful sanitary conditions of the city and again takes for granted an imbalance between the birthrate and the death rate, compensated only by continuous immigration. Jongman (1990, 2003) and Morley (1996:46–54; but see Morley 2001, a partial *retractatio* [recantation] of his most extreme conclusions) consider the substantial growth of the population of Rome in the late republic as responsible for the alleged demographic stagnation of the whole Italian peninsula in the same period, whereas Purcell (1999) builds his picture of the "populace" of late ancient Rome on this assumption. And a strong imbalance between birthrate and death rate is also the implicit conclusion of Paine and Storey's (1999; see also Storey and Paine 2002) characterization of the pattern of mortality in Rome as "catastrophic."

This chapter aims at checking these assumptions by testing the relevance of the comparative evidence put forward by these scholars, by challenging the picture given by Scobie, and by pointing out the effects that certain specific features of imperial Rome as a preindustrial city could have had on the mortality profile (a generous water supply, the grain distributions, and generally the careful organization of the supply of foodstuffs by the administration of the *annona* [grain supply]). The chapter then tries to draw some conclusions from what the literary and juridical sources say on the conditions of a specific sector of the urban population and in particular on the mechanisms at work in the distribution of the corn dole in order to see whether they imply that this sector, the so-called *plebs frumentaria* (people eligible for grain support)—a "closed" population—was in fact stationary or not.

In assuming that the level of population in Rome was always maintained only through a substantial and continuous influx of migrants, which would have lasted for many centuries, the ancient historians base themselves on comparative evidence, chiefly on the trend of population in London between the sixteenth and the nineteenth centuries as it was outlined in a famous and very influential article by Wrigley (1967) more than thirty years ago (see also Finlay 1981a, 1981b; Landers 1987, 1993; also de Vries 1974:109, 115–118, 1984:179–198). The foundation of the "iron law" is of course the imbalance between burials and baptisms as revealed by such documents as the bills of mortality or the parish registers.

More recently, however, both the traditional explanation of the surplus of deaths and the legitimacy of the generalization of this phenomenon have come under fire. The model of the "urban graveyard effect" or "urban natural decrease" has been severely criticized by Sharlin (1978:127), who proposes to replace this interpretation of the imbalance between births and deaths with a different interpretation, what he calls the model of "urban migration." Sharlin does not question that urban mortality must have been higher than rural mortality, but he thinks that the model of the urban natural decrease reverses the causal relationship between surplus of deaths and immigration. According to Sharlin, immigration is fed by people who not only live in more precarious conditions than stable residents but also marry and have children less easily. The inability to reproduce themselves would refer just to the "migrants," not to the stable residents. The features that distinguish stable residents from migrants are precisely the following: (1) better housing and less unhealthy environment; (2) greater resistance to infectious diseases due to greater acquired immunity; and (3) greater fertility because they represent occupational groups that are more likely to marry and among whom the sex ratio is more balanced. The model of urban migration is tested by Sharlin (1978; cf. Sharlin 1981 against Finlay 1981a; see also, e.g., Flinn 1981:22–24) on the basis of quantitative data referring to various European cities in the seventeenth and eighteenth centuries.

It seems to me that an even more general argument must be put forward. The documentary basis on which the two competing models are built is baptism and burial registration. When immigration to an urban center is strong, it is only natural that burials outnumber baptisms because many of the dead were not born in the urban center itself. To cause an increase in the death rate and a decrease in the birthrate, the simple change in the age structure of the urban population, which is in any event the result of a strong influx of immigrants, must be enough. In other words, strong immigration could give us a misleading idea of the difference in birthrate and mortality between the two areas involved. We tend to underestimate the death rate and therefore overestimate the natural increase in the area from which the migratory flux comes and, on the contrary, to overestimate the death rate and underestimate the natural increase in the area that receives the migratory flux (and the extent to which both this overestimation and this underestimation depend on what are the age classes chiefly involved in the migratory movement, inasmuch as the age structure of a population obviously also has an impact on the reproduction rate). Below is a quote from Jan de Vries (1984:181) that describes an example from the United States of today, a retirement community in St. Petersburg, Florida:

> The excess of deaths over births . . . is not a reflection of the city unhealthiness, for the demographic characteristics of the permanent residents is normal. It is the migrants to the city—in this case the old-age pensioners—who create the statistical illusion of a city unable to reproduce itself. This is because (1) their own births are, of course, registered elsewhere, (2) they give birth to no children in St. Petersburg (in this case because their children were born elsewhere), but (3) they do die in St. Petersburg.

The general character of the urban graveyard effect has also been called into question by van der Woude (1982) with reference to the demographic development of the northern Dutch cities between 1500 and 1800. This development seems to suggest that in these cities, which experienced a sustained population growth between the last decades of the sixteenth and the mid-seventeenth century, the birthrate would have been higher than the death rate. Van der Woude argues against the idea that the urban graveyard effect is a sort of law of nature. He considers it as the peculiar outcome of the general demographic stagnation of Europe between the seventeenth and the eighteenth century. He disputes that the allegedly poor sanitary conditions of the cities would explain the surplus of deaths when this is attested. Instead, he would suggest that the difference between births and deaths was the result of lower fertility, which was caused by a higher age at marriage, among other factors.

The evidence we possess on the demographic development of Rome between the seventeenth and the eighteenth century seems to corroborate both Sharlin's alternative model of the urban immigration and van der Woude's notion that the population of preindustrial cities could sometimes experience a measure of natural increase. This evidence is mainly composed of the so-called *Listae status animarum,* statistical tables that, after 1614, were regularly drawn up each year at Easter by the secretary to the cardinal vicar. These tables summarize all the data taken parish by parish: the whole population, the number of families and households, the number of people belonging to specific social groups, the number of men of all ages, the number of women of all ages, the number of the so-called *atti alla comunione* (males and females aged more than 12 or 13) and of the *non atti* (boys and girls under 12), and, finally, from 1702 onward, the number of the baptized and the number of the dead (Schiavoni 1982; Schiavoni and Sonnino 1982; Sonnino 1997).

We can draw significant conclusions from this evidence on the size of the population of Rome, on its age and sex structure, and on the natural trend, and we can easily calculate the migratory balance. The population of the city of Rome grew from ca. 100,000 to ca. 120,000 in the first half of the seventeenth century, and then, with the plague of 1656, it collapsed to the level seen at the beginning of the century. This sudden fall was also the consequence of the flight from the city of approximately 10,000 people. After the plague, the population began to grow again and attained the level of 135,000 by the end of the century and of 149,000 in the "holy year" of 1700. During the first quarter of the following century, the population was stationary around 130,000, and then it began to grow slowly, and afterward it fluctuated around 150,000–160,000 and then declined after 1798 (Schiavoni 1982:423–425, Appendix 1; Sonnino 1997:56–57, Table 1 and Graph 1). It must be pointed out that in the second half of the seventeenth century, when the population was growing, births (baptisms) outnumbered deaths, notwithstanding a very strong imbalance between males and females. In the following century, on the contrary, deaths outnumbered baptisms in almost every year, but the population at first remained stationary and then grew because of strong immigration (Schiavoni 1982:412–414, Table 2; Schiavoni and Sonnino 1982:102, Table II; see also Sonnino 1982:79–80, Table 28). These data seem to reveal, on the one hand, the impact of immigration on mortality (which rose from 23–28 per thousand in the second half of the seventeenth century to 38–46 in the following century); on the other hand, they seem to show that sanitary conditions were not responsible or exclusively responsible for the natural decrease in the eighteenth century inasmuch as they did not produce this effect in the previous century.

As a matter of fact, what the debate on the competing models of the urban natural decrease and of the urban migration has shown is that the demography of the early modern city can reveal different scenarios. In some cases, there seems to be no imbalance between births and deaths or births outnumber deaths; in some cases the imbalance seems to be the effect of a lower fertility and in others

of a higher mortality or of a combination of them; in some other cases the imbalance seems to be the effect of a higher mortality and/or a lower fertility of the
migrants. There is, therefore, no a priori reason why this imbalance (which is far
from generally attested in the cities of Europe) must be explained as the effect of
an "iron law." I endorse wholeheartedly what Jan de Vries (1984:183) said about
the critics of "this venerable orthodoxy of urban natural decrease," Sharlin and
van der Woude:

> The real service of the two critics is their insistence that the demography of
> the pre-industrial city be studied as a historical process rather than reduced
> to a mechanistic "law" based on assumed "natural" conditions. This requires
> that the historical process be specified and its operation demonstrated.

De Vries (1984:198) also said, "Sharlin and van der Woude must be credited with
exposing the inadequate foundations on which the conventional wisdom rests,
and pointing the way to forms of interpretation that are based on history and
demography rather than on dogma." It is perhaps appropriate to notice that
Wrigley (1990:110–111, n. 22) himself, in one of his last articles on these issues,
was much more careful concerning the importance of the urban graveyard effect
and its general validity.

In spite of the doubts among the modern historians, the notion of the *ville
tombeau*, or the idea that big cities were necessarily a "demographic sink," looms
large in descriptions of ancient urbanism, especially with reference to Rome.
Jongman (1990; cf. 2003) and Morley (1996:46–54), followed by Sallares (1999),
attribute to the graveyard effect in Rome the alleged stagnation or even decrease
of the Italian population at large between the last decades of the third and the
first century BC.

Morley starts from the guesstimates of the population of Italy and Rome in
225 and 28 BC advanced by Hopkins (1978a:64–72; see Table 1.2, 68–69) and
widely accepted. The free population of Italy would have shrunk from 4,500,000
to 4,000,000, whereas in the meantime the citizen population of Rome would
have risen from 150,000 to 650,000. Because this fourfold increase, which was
the result of continuous immigration, was attained notwithstanding a high rate
of natural decrease (estimated at 1 percent for the "core population" of stable
residents and at 2 percent for the "recent migrants"), it would have more than
compensated, and therefore neutralized, the natural increase of the population of
the rest of Italy (estimated at 3 per thousand) and changed the population increase into its opposite, a decline from 4,350,000 to 3,350,000. It is easy to show,
however, as I did elsewhere (Lo Cascio 1999b, 2001c), that these calculations do
not work because the proportion of the population of Italy constituted by the
population of Rome, although it increases from 225 to 28 BC, is never so large

as to neutralize the supposed population increase of 3 per thousand of the rest of Italy.

Just as the urban graveyard effect in London was not able to produce the stagnation or even the decline of the population of England (which on the contrary rose spectacularly from 3,010,000 to 8,660,000 in the period 1550–1800, whereas the population of London rose from 120,000 to 950,000 [Finlay and Shearer 1986:39, Table 1]), the alleged graveyard effect in Rome could not produce by itself the stagnation or the decline of the Italian population between 225 and 28 BC. We must suppose, then, either that the population of Italy at large was not increasing or that one of the estimates on which Morley bases his case, namely, that of the free citizen population of Italy in 28 BC, is wrong, built, as it is, on the (in my view [Lo Cascio 1994a]) mistaken idea that the Augustan census figures, quoted in the *Res gestae divi Augusti* (chapter 8), refer to the whole citizen population and not, as the republican ones did, to only the adult males.

If we interpret the Augustan census figures as referring to only the adult males, we will conclude that the free population of Italy in 28 BC was more or less 12 million rather than 4 million (Lo Cascio 1994b, against Beloch 1968[1886] and Brunt 1987[1971]) and that it had strongly increased since 225 BC (Lo Cascio 1999b, 1999c), notwithstanding the immigration to Rome of many hundreds of thousands of people and notwithstanding the urban graveyard effect, which must have been not so important as is commonly believed. (Indeed, Morley [2001] himself now seems to be much less skeptical on the plausibility of the scenario implied by this interpretation of the Augustan census figures.)

But a more serious problem is raised by the subsequent development of the population of Rome during the imperial times, for which we do not have such clear indications of very strong migratory movements into Rome. When immigration shrank, the population of Rome would have declined. But do we have evidence of such a shrinkage?

Our evidence on the size and structure of the population of Rome is almost nonexistent, even if we know that, for example, births and deaths were registered (Casarico 1985; Nicolet 1989:139–140; Schulz 1942, 1943; Virlouvet 1997; I do not share the doubts of Parkin [1992:35–38] on the existence of a regular registration of deaths). Because these data did not survive, we are reduced to estimating from plausibility and from the comparative evidence. First, we have to ask to what extent we are authorized to make mechanical comparisons between the early modern European cities and ancient Rome. We must single out similarities and differences on several grounds: (1) crowding and overcrowding; (2) sanitary conditions; (3) available food and therefore the conditions of supply and distribution of foodstuffs to the population at large; and (4) the natality regime and therefore fertility, along with the mortality regime and the sex ratio.

It seems to me that as far as these grounds are concerned we have no evidence that conditions in Rome were worse than or the same as in the early modern cities of Europe. On the contrary, the evidence we have would suggest that the stable population of Rome, constituted by the *plebs frumentaria,* was much better off and that its living conditions were comparable to the conditions of the stable populations of early modern cities in contrast with the conditions of the "migrants."

A traditional literature on the subject, the literature on daily life, gives a very negative view of overcrowding, promiscuity, and scarce hygiene of the population of imperial Rome, whose size is normally estimated at 1 million or more. Last, the gloomy picture of these conditions given by Scobie (1986) has won wide, although often uncritical, acceptance among Roman historians. Although Scobie (1986:404) recognizes that "the Romans achieved a remarkable level of standardization in the provision of certain basic facilities, such as public latrines and baths" and that "credit must be given to the Romans for some degree of progress in the sphere of public hygiene," he nonetheless takes as a term of comparison for his brief rereading of the literary and juridical sources on housing in Rome the levels of crowding and public hygiene that are thought unacceptable in some Western societies today. He refers therefore to parts of Rome as "slums," applying the definition of Townsend in his study of poverty in England, focusing on the issues of safety, housing facilities, and space. As Laurence (1997) has incisively observed, however, to put things in such a way is highly disputable. Scobie would have had to take as a term of comparison the big preindustrial cities, the only ones with which it is legitimate to compare Rome. According to Laurence, Scobie follows the lead of some contemporary theoreticians of urban planning, first of all Lewis Mumford (1961:Chapter 8), whose presentation of daily life in Rome in *The City in History* is perhaps the dimmest one ever written.

It is this ideological attitude toward the big city that suggested to the ancient historians themselves the image of Rome as "dystopia" in contrast to the image of orderly planning suggested by other Roman towns. Whether or not we are ready to accept this brilliant and original explanation of the attitudes of the ancient historians themselves, we must accept the urging to go beyond the shocking descriptions of Martial and Juvenal or the curious anecdotes of Suetonius (e.g., *Vespasian* 5.4) and return to the evidence provided by Vitruvius (Laurence 1997:12–13 on Vitruvius 2.8.17) in order to get a more objective view of living conditions in Rome. Above all, however, what we have to do first is to consider the impact that some features of the organization of Rome could have had on daily life, notwithstanding a level of crowding almost unparalleled in the history of the Western world; then we need to assess these peculiar features of imperial Rome through the comparison with other preindustrial cities, and only after this can we try to evaluate the relationship between the precarious housing and sanitary conditions and the level of mortality. The most eloquent and obvious comparison is seventeenth- and eighteenth-century Rome in terms of crowding, sanitary conditions, mortality, and birthrate. It is precisely the evidence we possess on early modern Rome that would forbid us to take it for granted that the population of imperial Rome would have never reproduced itself.

It seems unquestionable that crowding in Rome was almost unparalleled in Western history. Although the discussion on the size of the population of Rome is going on and will probably never cease, I think that it would be hard to deny that the density of population between the late republic and the late empire was in the region of 50,000 to 60,000 per sq km. I cannot discuss this question here, but I must say that the recent attempt by Storey (1997a, 1997b) to revive the lowest estimates given by Dureau de la Malle and Lot is not convincing; we possess too many convergent data from our ancient evidence that make it impossible to put the whole population of late republican and imperial Rome at less than, say, 800,000 and at a level just a bit lower in the third and fourth century. These data show the following: (1) the number of the recipients of the corn dole and of the *congiaria,* the money handouts, and later on of pork; (2) the amount of grain imported into Rome; and (3) the number of the *insulae,* that is, the buildings as cadastral units in Rome that we find in the so-called Regionary catalogues of the fourth century (Lo Cascio 1997, 2001a).

To reiterate the lowest estimates ever advanced is possible only if one neglects these data, which are, however, highly consistent. And in fact, apart from the comparison with housing in Ostia or Pompeii, which the contemporaries realized was completely different, the only argument advanced by Storey would be the intrinsic implausibility of the densities implied in the light of comparative evidence. However, anyone who takes into account the physical aspect of the historic centers in cities of Italy, such as Genoa, Naples, or Palermo, will not consider this argument very strong. There is no need to resort to the comparison with the "spot densities" (Storey 1997b:976) of some cities of the Third World today, such as Bombay, Hong Kong, or Calcutta (Stambaugh 1988, and the data referred to by him). It is enough to refer to the urban and demographic development of cities such as Naples or Rome itself to realize that densities of 500, 600, or even 700 per ha (that is, of 50,000, 60,000, or 70,000 per sq km) are far from implausible.

I will quote some figures at random (taken from Beloch 1968[1886]:409; De' Seta 1976:348; Lugli 1941–1942:198; Schiavoni 1982:404): the density of some *rioni* (regions) at Rome in 1881 was higher than 800 per ha, and the density of some of the districts of Naples during most of the nineteenth century was even higher than 1,500 per ha (and it is perhaps worth noticing that, according to De' Seta, even in the 1950s, in 16 out of 19 administrative districts of the city of Naples, the density was 45,000 per sq km, with peaks of 60,000–80,000!). The *città vecchia* (the historic town) of Trieste in 1931, which covered a total area of 37.56 ha of which just 10.5 were occupied by private buildings, had a population of a bit more than 18,000 and therefore 480 per ha if we take the whole area, but 1,700 per ha if we take only the built-up area. Rome in the mid-eighteenth century, as it is represented in the map of Nolli of 1748 with an area of perhaps one-quarter of the area of ancient Rome inside the Aurelian walls and therefore more or less 350 ha, had a population of more than 150,000, with a density of more than 430 per ha.

Two conclusions can be drawn from these data. First, levels of crowding like the one suggested by the most commonly accepted estimate of the population of Rome, one million, are by no means implausible in the light of the comparative evidence itself. Second, these levels are in any case very high and suggest an urban scenario at a very high risk. But was this risk surely higher for the whole course of the history of ancient Rome than the one experienced in other urban and rural scenarios of the Roman world? I would say no for the following reasons.

First, crowding was not the same in the various areas of the town for the whole urban history of Rome. The progressive extension of the imperial palaces, before and after the construction of the Neronian *Domus Aurea,* and the extension of the *horti* (gardens), emptied some of the central areas of the city, whereas the inhabited space grew well beyond the line of the *pomerium* (sacred city limits) of the Flavian age (which corresponded more or less to the line of the Aurelian walls), mostly in the Transtiberine region and toward the north and northeast surrounding areas. It is, moreover, virtually certain that the *suburbium* of Rome, especially after the second half of the first century, was very extensive and densely inhabited (Quilici 1974). And the population of Rome, as calculated from the data we have on the grain dole and the *congiaria,* did certainly include also the inhabitants of the area that Homo (1951:123–127) called the "commune" of Rome, the suburbs defined as the territory around the city as far as the borders of the territories of the towns surrounding Rome. (On the various ways in which one can conceptualize the borders of Rome, see Panciera 1999.) The reason for considering these people among the beneficiaries of the dole is that, since the introduction, probably with Caesar, of a new procedure of census taking in the towns of Italy (Lo Cascio 1997:3–14, 2001a:591ff.), they were "registered" at the census as "domiciled" in Rome (Lo Cascio 2000:27, 2001b:186–187). The recipients of the dole came therefore not only from the *continentia tecta,* that is, from the uninterrupted built area, but also from the countryside around the *continentia tecta.* In a famous passage, Dionysius (Dion. Hal iv 13, 4) of Halicarnassus pointed out that, in his age (the Augustan age), "if anyone wishes to estimate the size of Rome by looking at these suburbs he will necessarily be misled for want of a definite clue by which to determine up to what point it is still the city and where it ceases to be the city; so closely is the city connected with the country, giving the beholder the impression of a city stretching out indefinitely." The archaeological evidence confirms that these suburbs were thickly inhabited (see most recently Volpe 2000), and therefore it is on the whole probable that a substantial portion of the beneficiaries of the dole and of the citizen population of Rome would have lived in the suburbs.

On the other hand, the limits put on the height of the front of the buildings by Augustus, Nero, and Trajan and the rules that were followed in the reconstruction of the city after the great fire of AD 64, which had destroyed a substantial part of the city, are evidence of an attempt at urban planning: the enlargement and the alignment of the streets and the opening of new squares had the effect of reducing the crowding and of making safer the inhabited buildings (Sommella and Migliorati 1991:300–302). In addition, overcrowding was more tolerable because much of the time was spent either in the open air, as in most Mediterranean cities, or in places such as the public baths, as Pöhlmann (1884:73) noticed more than a century ago.

But, above all, what rendered life more tolerable in Rome were the quality and quantity of the services provided to the inhabitants, whatever their status and their economic conditions, especially after the urban and administrative reorganization of the city effected during the long Augustan age. First, an effective drainage system had been created very early on. The sewers were not intended to collect and dispose of human waste but to prevent the unhealthy stagnation of water and facilitate keeping the streets clean. The maintenance of the sewers was associated, in the imperial age, with the control of the bed and the banks of the Tiber in order to neutralize the flooding of the river or at least to make its effects less destructive (Robinson 1992:69–73, 85–94, 117–124). An impressive set of aqueducts, with numerous personnel to maintain them, provided a very generous supply of water. Even if its distribution was strongly imbalanced in favor of rich people and the emperor himself, water went to a network of public fountains, which increased in number during the imperial age.

The average quantity of water available to the individual inhabitant of Rome was unparalleled in other preindustrial cities and compares well even with nineteenth-century standards. To the water distributed through the *lacus* (reservoirs) and the *salientes* (fountains), one has to add the water that went to other public facilities, whose identification is uncertain, and, above all, to the public baths. Estimates have been advanced that put the whole amount of the water conducted to Rome at a level of 1,000 liters a head per day, which is double the quantity available to the inhabitant of Rome today (Coarelli 1989[1974]:36; also see the references in Bruun 1991:99–100; De Kleijn 2001:44–74). Other, more conservative estimates have been advanced for the water that went to the public fountains: 67 liters per head per day. It is worth noticing that in the nineteenth century, 25 liters was thought to be the necessary minimum (Bruun 1991:104, 1997:126–130). But Romans of every social condition, apart from the water they took at the public fountain for individual use, had at their disposal the enormous amount of water conducted to the baths, which became more numerous and larger during the first three centuries of the empire and were, moreover, free or almost free (Robinson 1992:113–116). One last "service" must be mentioned: the one pro-

vided by a paramilitary structure of several thousand firemen, who were distributed evenly in the various *regiones* (regions) of Rome. Apart from watching the
streets by night, their duty was to prevent and extinguish fires (Sablayrolles 1996).

Notwithstanding overcrowding in the city, therefore, hygienic and sanitary
conditions in Rome were apparently not worse than in other preindustrial cities
that experienced a modest rate of increase, like the same Rome in the seventeenth
century. Recently, however, it has been argued that what produced a much higher
mortality in Rome to cause the imbalance between births and deaths and therefore the "graveyard effect" would have been the incidence of malaria, which by
itself or in interaction with other diseases would have been responsible for a very
high percentage of deaths in Rome. To demonstrate this incidence, scholars have
invoked, apart from a couple of references by ancient authors who explicitly attest to the presence of the disease in the city itself and others who more generi-
cally refer to the unhealthiness of its lower areas, the epigraphic evidence of the
Christian epitaphs, ingeniously used to document the seasonality of death (Sallares 1999, 2002; Scheidel 1994, 1996; 2003a [the rather cavalier use made by
Scheidel of some literary references supposedly to malaria was commented on in
Lo Cascio 2001a]; Shaw 1996).

Christian epitaphs often declare the day and the month of death and therefore
allow us to quantify mortality in the different periods of the year. It is possible to
show that mortality was higher between August and October in late ancient
Rome, whereas early modern London and other preindustrial cities were characterized by a different seasonality, and in more recent times urban centers experienced much less pronounced seasonal peaks of mortality. However, a monocausal
explanation of the specific seasonality of death in Rome remains controversial:
Scheidel and Sallares think malaria is responsible, in interaction with other diseases whose gravity would have been enhanced by malaria itself, whereas Shaw is
inclined to look toward a more complex explanation.

I would make a preliminary observation: if the inability of the Roman population to reproduce itself depended, directly or indirectly, on malaria, then it did
not depend on the "iron law" that would apply to all the preindustrial cities because in most of them, and in any case in the cities of northern and central Europe, malaria cannot have played any role. If it is to be connected with seasonality,
as the epigraphic evidence would suggest, high mortality in Rome would have
depended on specific climatic and environmental features. In fact, exactly the
same seasonality of death can be observed in southern Italy in late antiquity, with
peaks almost as high as the peaks in Rome (Shaw 1996:115–118, Figure 5, and
115, 127:Figure 19). And even the comparative material (for example, from early
modern Apulia or Sicily) shows that seasonality of death is nothing specifically
"urban" (Shaw 1996:126). It is significant, moreover, that a different seasonality
is observed in northern Italy, not an absence of seasonality, so one can conclude
once more that, whatever the responsible pathogenic agents in the different cli-

matic and environmental conditions, seasonality of death appears to be a general feature of pretransitional populations, urban and rural.

The evidence of seventeenth- and eighteenth-century Rome confirms the presence of malaria in Rome, but it does not show a higher incidence than typhus, influenza, or enteric diseases. Moreover, malaria seems to have struck people from the countryside (the *agro romano*) who came to Rome to be doctored in the hospitals of the city, so it has been observed that, unlike the outbreaks of plague, these outbreaks "were often accompanied by a population increase as the hospital and the relief network operating in Rome attracted those in need of assistance from outside the walls" (Sonnino 1997:59). The early modern and modern evidence would suggest, then, that malaria was a serious problem in the countryside around Rome, rather than in the city itself. Moreover, it bears witness to the extremely variable incidence of the disease in time and space.

It should be enough to quote a datum that Sallares (1999, 2002) has drawn from the contributions of a famous Italian expert of malariology of the beginning of our century in referring to the small town of Sezze, on the hills above the Pontine Marshes, south of Rome. This scholar noticed that in the nineteenth century, the inhabitants of Sezze, whose houses faced the marshes, contracted the disease, whereas the inhabitants of the houses on the other slope did not. And the ancient evidence itself shows that, at least in some periods of the history of the city, the hills of Rome, which were inhabited, as one would expect, by the elite, were healthier than its low areas. What I mean is that the extreme variability of conditions even in very small areas does not allow us to generalize about the incidence of malaria on mortality in ancient Rome. It is possible that the material and administrative machinery devoted to the drainage of the lowlands in Rome was more effective in some periods and less in others. The very dense occupation and the intensive cultivation of the immediate hinterland of imperial Rome, which is documented by the sources and above all by archaeological evidence that is ever growing—an occupation that is unparalleled in the subsequent history of this area until the twentieth century—would suggest the presence of a very dense population between the late republic and the empire, which is not consistent with the widespread and continuous presence of malaria. Moreover, Sallares does not appear to have provided any *proof* of the presence, let alone of the incidence, of malaria in the Campagna Romana (countryside of Rome) in Roman times. (It is not by chance that Sallares [2002:236] uses expressions such as "balance of probability": "The balance of probability is that many of the low lying rural districts of Latium and southern Etruria were also affected by malaria during the time of the Roman Empire just as they were in more recent times.") Moreover, his attempt to explain the density of agricultural settlement does not carry conviction; but this is an argument I cannot pursue here.

It seems to me, in conclusion, that we do not have sufficient evidence that sanitary conditions in Rome were so bad as to produce a constant and marked imbalance between births and deaths. On the other hand, the nutritional conditions of at least a substantial part of the Roman population were presumably better than in most preindustrial cities, as I would conclude from what Garnsey (1998:226–252) has recently argued against Sippel (1988) on the diet of the poor in the city of Rome. There is no need to stress the importance of the *frumentationes,* the corn dole, in providing the basic calorific intake for this substantial part (Virlouvet 1995 and references there). The *frumentationes* were instituted as distributions at a fixed price of wheat to the male citizens aged more than 17. The individual allowance, however, was more or less enough to feed two people. The distributions soon became free, which means that the beneficiaries had more money to acquire more food (and other nonalimentary goods).

At the end of the republic and during the Augustan age, attempts were made to limit the number of the beneficiaries, but the dole went on to be distributed to the vast majority of the adult male citizens (that is, foreigners and slaves were excluded). Following one of these measures of limitation, the city was emptied of the recent migrants; many of them were transferred to colonies abroad, and others went back to their place of origin in Italy. On the other hand, Augustus created a complex and structured administration for the supply of the grain not only for the dole but also for general consumption. In due course, new infrastructures were built for this purpose, such as large granaries and, above all, two artificial harbors near the mouth of the Tiber. Furthermore, from the third century onward other foodstuffs were freely distributed, such as olive oil and pork, and the monthly allowance of wheat was changed into a daily allowance of bread, so one can legitimately say that the part of the Roman population to which the distributions were directed was almost completely fed by the state, whereas the remaining part could benefit from the regular supply of foodstuffs without the savage fluctuation of prices that was a familiar event in all preindustrial cities (Lo Cascio 1990, 1999a).

There is a final element to be considered in comparing Rome with the early modern European cities: birthrate and therefore nuptiality. We saw that some scholars attribute more importance, in determining the imbalance between births and deaths in the early modern cities, to a lower fertility than to a higher mortality among the recent migrants because nuptiality would remain very low especially as a consequence of a strongly imbalanced sex ratio. We do not possess any quantitative clue on the sex ratio in Rome (apart from the evidence of the epitaphs, which is strongly biased, as we will see in a moment), but it is a widely shared opinion that males strongly outnumbered females among the free population (for the servile population we cannot even make guesses [Scheidel 1999]). Males strongly outnumbered females in seventeenth- and eighteenth-century Rome: the sex ratio was as high as 163–175 males for 100 females in the period 1605–1630, declining slightly to 135–155 for 100 in 1631–1699 and to 120–

140 in the eighteenth century, with much lower values by the end of the century (Schiavoni and Sonnino 1982:103–104).

Notwithstanding this serious imbalance, the population experienced a natural increase, as we saw, in the second half of the seventeenth century. We must conclude, therefore, that even a strongly imbalanced sex ratio can allow a measure of natural increase. It must be observed, in any case, that the reproduction rate in a population characterized by a sex ratio favorable to males would tend to be higher than in a population characterized by a more balanced sex ratio, whereas it would be lower in a population characterized by a sex ratio favorable to females. If it is true that males strongly outnumbered females in Rome not only in the late republic but also during the early empire and in late antiquity, the birthrate must have been lower than in a population of identical size with a more balanced sex ratio, but higher than in a population where females outnumbered males (as in early modern London or in most of the other European cities).

In conclusion, we can say that there are no a priori reasons, on the basis of comparative evidence, to believe that deaths strongly outnumbered births in Rome for the whole of antiquity. But do we have indirect evidence that this was the case? Many scholars, since the end of the nineteenth century, have tried to build life tables of the population of the different regions of the empire on the basis of the age-at-death data, which can be drawn from the tens of thousands of epitaphs that survive from Roman times, especially for the areas for which this evidence is quantitatively more conspicuous, such as Italy and, above all, Rome.

These life tables, however, show peculiar features. They confirm that life expectancy at birth was low everywhere, perhaps between 20 and 30 years but similar to other pretransitional populations. They seem to reveal, however, enormous regional differences and, on the whole, a quite peculiar age and sex distribution: the age distribution is such as to be unparalleled by any certain and known distribution of a historical or contemporary population (see in general Parkin 1992:6–8). The African sample, in comparison with the Roman one, for example, would apparently suggest that life expectancy at 10 was much higher in Africa than in Rome (40 years or more against 20), and that could be taken to imply that sanitary conditions in Rome were much worse than in healthy Africa. But in fact it is the African data, unparalleled in all the other regions of the empire, that are abnormal; it must be pointed out that the alleged nonagenarians or centenarians constituted 7 percent of the whole sample in Africa but 1 percent in Rome. That is, it is possible to discover in this evidence the phenomenon of age exaggeration that is frequently found in societies with low literacy (Lo Cascio 1996 on Pliny *Natural History* 7.157, 7.159, 7.162–164).

As Keith Hopkins (1966–1967) showed many years ago in a seminal paper, the age and sex distribution as revealed by the funerary inscriptions all over the empire, a distribution that is absolutely unparalleled, seems to be due to the quality of the sample, which is so biased that it is useless to build plausible life tables. It is moreover significant that a similar conclusion was drawn by Louis Henry (1959) in the late 1950s, examining the nineteenth-century evidence of the epitaphs of a cemetery at Lyon. The bias could be the result of various factors. One is age rounding: the number of dead at an age that ends with the figure 0 or 5 is enormously higher than the number of dead at the intermediate ages. Another factor of bias is that parents tend to commemorate much more often if their children die very young, whence the very high representation in the sample of dead in ages 1 to 19. Similarly, the overrepresentation of males explains the apparently imbalanced sex ratio even in the countryside, as is proved by the much more reliable evidence of the Egyptian census returns where there is no such imbalance in the villages, unlike the towns (Bagnall and Frier 1994:Chapter 5).

Recently, Paine and Storey (1999) attempted to rescue some of the data we can draw from the funerary inscriptions of Rome; they took as their sample the inscriptions in which the age at death is given in terms of years, months, and days. They show that in these inscriptions, there is no bias caused by age rounding. In my view, this interesting phenomenon must be explained by supposing that age awareness in the city of Rome must have been greater than elsewhere due to a more precise and thorough registration of vital events. But this more limited sample does not give us a different age distribution in comparison with the whole sample, an age distribution, as we said, absolutely unparalleled in other pretransitional populations. According to Paine and Storey, this peculiar Roman age distribution would attest that, due to the dreadful sanitary conditions in Rome, the population of the city would have experienced a "catastrophic mortality," like the one that anthropologists and paleodemographers have found in some prehistoric human groups (Keckler 1997). This mortality would have been much less age specific and therefore would have struck young adults much more often than in normal conditions (and whatever the life expectancy at birth).

It seems to me that against this hypothesis the argument that a particular form of the so-called epigraphic habit (MacMullen 1982) could have biased (in an unrecoverable way) the sample of funerary inscriptions is still valid. What also emerges from the sample of the Christian epitaphs analyzed by Shaw indicates the kind of bias involved. The epitaphs set up by husbands to wives and by wives to husbands represent 45 percent of the sample, those set up by the parents to their children represent 43 percent of the sample, and those set up by the children to their parents are just 5 percent. Even more significant is that the epitaphs set up by husbands to wives are 30 percent, whereas those set up by wives to husbands are 14.5 percent (Shaw 1996:109, 137, Table 2).

But there is another reason why the conclusions of Paine and Storey do not seem to me to be acceptable: the sample is constituted by inscriptions whose time span is so long (more than two and one-half centuries) that large differences in mortality between different periods simply remain concealed. In particular, the distinction is concealed between periods of normal mortality and periods of crisis mortality (a notion that is much more familiar to the historian who studies the populations of the so-called demographic *ancien régime* than the notion of "catastrophic mortality"). It will be enough just to quote one example to show the problems posed by the use made by Paine and Storey of the Roman epigraphic evidence. In Tuscany in the period between 1580 and 1659, the years of crisis mortality (singled out as the years in which mortality was 50 percent higher than in normal years) are on average one every nine years (Del Panta 1980; cf. Del Panta et al. 1996:91–94 [by Sonnino]). If we had a single sample for 80 years instead of data for each year, we would build a life table sensibly different both from the life table of the normal years and from the life table of the years of crisis mortality. I wonder whether the peculiar profile of mortality discovered by Paine and Storey is also the result of the years of crisis mortality following outbreaks of infectious diseases, which were particularly severe as we know from other evidence, from the sixties of the second century AD onward and for the whole of the subsequent century (Duncan-Jones 1996; Lo Cascio 1991, 1994a). I note that now Paine and Storey (Paine and Storey, this volume; Storey and Paine 2002) seem to agree on the paramount importance of the epidemics of the Antonine years and of the third century in determining the mortality profile of the urban population of Rome.

In order to find some indirect clue to the problem regarding whether the population of Rome did reproduce itself or not, we can finally examine what we know about a specific sector of the Roman population, the *plebs frumentaria*. We know that in 2 BC, Augustus "closed" the *plebs frumentaria,* that is, he decided that the number of the adult male citizens over 17 regularly domiciled in Rome who were then the beneficiaries of the corn dole should not be exceeded in the future (Lo Cascio 1997:31–32, 47–58, on Cassius Dio 65.10.1). From that time, then, the citizen regularly domiciled in Rome who attained the age to get the dole would have had to wait until a vacancy was produced by the death (or the transfer outside Rome) of another beneficiary in order to be registered among the beneficiaries (the so-called *incisi*). We know, moreover, that the right to the dole was hereditary (Lo Cascio 1997:47–48 on Augustan History *Aurelianus* 35.1 and *Theodosian Code* 14.17.5); therefore, the immigrants were excluded, and the *liberti* were excluded as well.

In these conditions, one can say that the *plebs frumentaria* was really a "closed population" to which all adult male citizens domiciled in Rome and descendants of the beneficiaries could potentially belong. In order to be admitted to the dole it was necessary to attain the age of 17 and then wait until a vacancy was available to be filled. Several scenarios would have been possible: if the population does not reproduce itself, vacant places would be always available. If the population reproduces itself but is stationary, all the descendants of the beneficiaries will enjoy the benefit one day or another (unless they die before). If the population experiences a natural increase, it will be necessary to envisage a system by which to select the actual beneficiaries, and in fact we know that this system was the lot. The lot would have been necessary in any event in order to establish an order of priority in being registered. The presence of a system like this—the hereditary transmission of the potential right to the dole, accompanied by the lot to change this potential right into the actual enjoyment of the benefit—presupposes a scenario in which the *plebs frumentaria* is able to reproduce itself. This is the population of the stable residents at Rome, and it is possible that its demographic regime was more favorable than the demographic regime of the "migrants."

We know, however, that there was a different system by which vacancies were filled: some juridical sources mainly of the Severan age and some literary sources as well refer to the purchase of the *tessera* from the state, that is, the purchase of the right to enter the *plebs frumentaria* and to get the dole (Virlouvet 1995:205–216). Under this system, *liberti* could acquire the right to the monthly allowance. The purchase of the *tessera* obviously implies that sometimes the number of the dead among the beneficiaries surpassed the number of the young adults who could acquire by hereditary transmission the right to the dole. We can therefore deduce that when vacancies were filled through the sale of the *tesserae*, the *plebs frumentaria* failed to reproduce itself. And it could be significant that the references to the sale of the *tesserae* are particularly frequent in the sources of the Severan age, when the probable frequency of the years of crisis mortality must have produced a significant, even if probably a temporary, decrease of the population of the city.

That two different mechanisms were at work to keep fixed the number of the recipients of the dole—the lot and the purchase of the *tessera*—would suggest, in conclusion, that in the course of the imperial age there were periods in which the *plebs frumentaria* was able to reproduce itself and other periods in which it was not. This is the scenario that could explain how the whole population did not decline over the whole imperial period, although the age of the great immigration in the late republic was over by then.

3
Epidemics, Age at Death, and Mortality in Ancient Rome

Richard R. Paine and Glenn R. Storey

Discussions of preindustrial cities frequently focus on health issues. Scholars from many disciplines (e.g., Cohen 1989; de Vries 1984; McNeill 1976; Scheidel 2001b, 2003a; Storey 1992b; this volume) have long argued that ancient cities suffered high levels of epidemic disease and mortality. They relate these problems to population density, difficulties with public sanitation, and greater connections with outside populations. Although ancient Rome, on the basis of its size and connections, would be expected to display such early urban maladies on a large scale, Roman scholars have been divided on the health conditions of imperial Rome. Some scholars (e.g., Scobie 1986) believe that Rome was a nightmarish landscape of contagion and death, whereas others (e.g., Lo Cascio, this volume) question the pessimistic view. Others (e.g., Saller 1994; Scheidel 2001b, 2001c) dismiss both scenarios, arguing that we do not really have the ability to reconstruct the demographic characteristics of the city of Rome except in broad outlines. We would suggest broad outlines can be useful.

One data set that has generated especially strong debate is the record of funerary inscriptions from imperial Rome that contain ages at death. These inscriptions have been used to attempt to reconstruct the demography of the ancient city, beginning with Harkness (1896) and continuing to our own attempts to evaluate this data set (Paine and Storey 1999; Storey and Paine 2002). Many contemporary scholars of Roman demography (e.g., Duncan-Jones 1990:101–103; Hopkins 1966–1967, 1987; Parkin 1992:5–19; Scheidel 1996, 2001a, 2001b, 2001c; Shaw 1991) question any suggestion that the epigraphic age-at-death data can be used for demographic reconstruction.

This chapter examines one biological/demographic explanation for the age pattern found in the inscriptions. It tests our previous suggestion that catastrophic mortality could explain inscription age-at-death patterns by modeling and projecting the effects of a catastrophic episode on a theoretical mortality profile from a model population with demographic characteristics as might be expected for a preindustrial city such as Rome. Catastrophic mortality, caused by natural or human-based calamities, strikes populations without regard for age or sex. A large percentage of catastrophic mortality in a population leads to a death distribution that resembles the living distribution (Keckler 1997; Paine 2000). Roman history is filled with possible causes of catastrophic mortality (e.g., regular epidemics described by Livy, seasonal outbreaks [e.g., Salleres 2002; Scheidel 1996; Shaw 1996], and historically documented plagues). We decided to examine both the population implications of large plague events and questions of sample bias by modeling the possible effects of one important documented catastrophic event, the Antonine plague (AD 160–165 and again AD 189), on the living population of Rome and its distribution of death. We simulated the effects of the Antonine plague using a population projection including two episodes of catastrophic mortality in 91 years of normal mortality.

At the same time, our projection identifies, within broad limits, some of the possible long-term effects of the Antonine plague on the Roman population. This is a step toward understanding whether the Latin funerary inscription record might contain useable demographic data. Our work is not meant as a "straightforward reading of the extant sources as a faithful mirror of reality which lack[s] intellectual warranty" (contra Scheidel 2001b:2 n. 4) but as an exploration of whether some aspects of the funerary epigraphic data may enhance our understanding of the demographic structure of ancient Rome.

Issues

Accuracy of Ages

The accuracy of ages at death recorded in Latin funerary inscriptions (Duncan-Jones 1990; Scheidel 1996) has been questioned primarily on the basis of digit preference evidence from some inscription samples. Our previous work (Paine and Storey 1999; Storey and Paine 2002) shows little evidence of digit preference. Anthropologists perform meaningful demographic analysis based on approximate ages, both in ethnographic (e.g., Fix 1977; Howell 1979) and archaeological (e.g. Storey 1992b) contexts. We would suggest meaningful assessments of Roman demography are possible as long as inscription ages at death are within, on average, 10 percent of the actual ages at death and are not directionally biased (see Bocquet-Appel and Masset 1982 for a similar argument for paleodemography). We do not, currently, consider the accuracy of ages in the inscriptions to be a critical impediment to meaningful research.

Representation

Who are the individuals these inscriptions represent? They do not represent the entire population of the Roman Empire. Nor do they represent a cross section of the population of Rome itself. Quite possibly, they do represent an identifiable component of the Roman population, but, if so, they represent neither the highest nor the lowest strata of Roman society, but rather something in the middle. Parkin (1992:12) correctly characterized as exaggerated the argument that individuals commemorated on the tombstones were limited to the "respectable" classes. What is striking about the names of both the dedicatees and dedicators in the funerary inscriptions is how polyglot they appear to be. They are not chiefly the respectable classes of Roman society. They appear to be quite low on the social scale, though they clearly do not represent the poorest people, who ended up in common unmarked graves. Although specialist craftspeople are well represented in the funerary epigraphic record (Joshel 1992), we cannot simply assume that the population represented in that record is isomorphic to the pool of specialists. That consideration is of importance in assessing issues of migration taken up later in this chapter.

The inscriptions do not have to represent all the Roman population to be useful, but clearly we would like to know more about the population they do represent. Statistics from our sample tend to support a picture of a mixed lower-status representation in the epigraphic sample. The large majority (80 percent) of the inscriptions do not explicitly identify the status of the deceased. However, the character of the names of these individuals clearly suggests non-Roman, probably ex-servile status in the vast majority of cases. Only 0.89 percent of the dedicatees identify themselves as either senators or *equites* (knights), the two highest status elite levels. Only 3.4 percent note that they are freeborn; 2.2 percent are from the freeborn soldiery. Ordinary slaves constitute 5.1 percent of the sample. Only 1.6 percent come from the ranks of imperial slaves, the elite of the servile population.

Age/Sex Bias in Commemoration

Critiques of the funerary inscription data (e.g., Hopkins 1966–1967, 1987; Scheidel 2001b, 2001c) argue that representation in the funerary inscriptions is biased by societal patterns, specifically that the likelihood of being commemorated varies by age and sex. For example, young women are more likely to be commemorated than young men because their husbands are in a better position to pay for the memorial (Saller and Shaw 1984; Shaw 1984). Likewise, older individuals are less likely to enter the sample because they lack close living relatives to commemorate them. This is a potentially critical source of bias, but it cannot be addressed from the funerary epigraphy alone. Perhaps the mortality profiles can address it.

In typical human mortality profiles, the risk of death (seen in the hazard rate) is very high in the first years of life and then declines rapidly. The risk of death is very low in older children and young adults but then increases each year after about age 18 as people senesce. The hazard profile of the inscription sample is essentially flat. Young adults and old adults appear to have essentially the same risk of death. The age distribution of death (Figure 3-1) looks more like a living

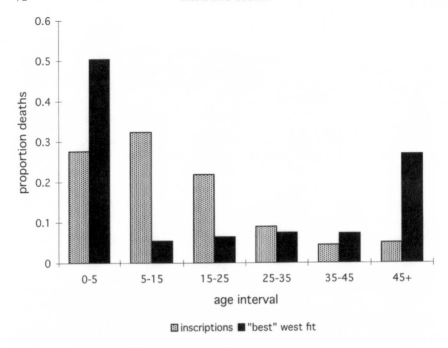

Figure 3-1. Comparison of distribution of death, by age, between the Latin funerary inscriptions and the best-fitting west model. Fit was determined by maximum likelihood estimation, using a procedure outlined by Paine (1989).

population than a typical death distribution (e.g., a distribution produced by the Brass [1971] or Coale and Demeny [1966, 1983] models). There are far more numerous older children and young adult deaths than would be expected in a stable population. This pattern could be produced in a cultural setting where increased age reduced an individual's probability of being commemorated. We see commemorative bias as the most important obstacle to retrieving ancient demographic patterns from the inscriptions. Addressing the question of the apparent flat hazard potentially brings us closer to understanding both the question of bias in the inscription sample and the health conditions in ancient Rome.

Methods

The Leslie Matrix

Leslie matrices (Leslie 1945) are used to project populations forward in time. They can project both population size and age structure and can be used to create full life tables and estimate vital rates for projected populations. One important feature of Leslie matrices is that they facilitate projections that incorporate short-

Table 3-1. Demographic Characteristics

Stable Model	α	β	TFR	CBR	CDR	r
1	0	1	3.1	22	22	.0001
2	0.65	0.95	6.15	45.2	44.5	.0007

Demographic characteristics of the stable model populations used in the two Leslie matrix projections. The α and β values presented are parameter values from the Brass relational model life tables used to generate the life tables. TFR = total fertility rate; CBR = crude birth rate; CDR = crude death rate.

term perturbations. Paine (2000) used Leslie matrix projections to study the possible implications of epidemic events for excavated skeletal series.

A Leslie matrix is a square matrix; the number of rows and columns in the matrix equals the number of age intervals. The top row of the matrix comprises age-specific fertility rates (ASFRs). Age-specific survival rates are found on the subdiagonal. When a Leslie matrix is postmultiplied by a vector representing an existing population, it yields a new vector representing the population at the end of the projection interval (for a good brief review of matrix algebra, see Caswell 1989; Leslie matrices are very clearly presented in Bradley and Meek [1986] and in Caswell).

Projecting any Leslie matrix produces a stable age distribution with stable demographic rates, given very weak preconditions. These conditions are set out in the theorem of Perron and Frobenius (summarized in Pollard 1973). The primary condition is that two consecutive F_j (the age-specific fertility rates represented in the top row of the Leslie matrix) be positive. This is true of virtually all models of human fertility. The number of intervals required to approach stability varies with the size of the matrix (the number of intervals of life span). The matrices used in our projections of the Antonine plague are for single-year intervals up to age 90.

We ran projections of two model populations on the basis of the Brass (1971) standard model life tables. The first was characterized by very low fertility and slow growth (Table 3-1). Low fertility has been widely cited (Parkin 1992) as a problem in imperial Rome. Following suggestions from Lo Cascio (personal communication 1998), we constructed a second model population, characterized by both higher fertility and higher mortality. This model is designed to conform to general estimates of preindustrial, agrarian populations. It has fertility consistent with a natural fertility population (Bentley, Jasienska, and Goldberg 1993; Campbell and Wood 1988) and life expectancy at birth conforming to levels suggested by paleodemographers (e.g., Storey 1992b). The second model population is also growing slowly, but at a significantly greater rate than the first model. The second model is the focus of discussion in this chapter.

We projected each model population for 100 years to generate a stable age distribution. This stable population would be used to initialize our projections simulating the Antonine plague. The initial model population size is approximately 2.4 million people. This is an enormously large population figure for Rome, but the scale could be moved up or down without affecting our interpretations. All projections were performed using Maple V for Macintosh. Maple is a computerized algebra program designed to perform complex operations without elaborate programming. Analyses and graphics were done on a spreadsheet.

The Plague Model

The Antonine plague consisted of two epidemic events, with apparently similar symptoms and impacts, separated by 25 to 30 years. The first wave of plague struck Rome between AD 160 and 165, and the second wave struck the city in AD 189. We represented each plague event with a unique Leslie matrix. To simulate the effects of the first round of plague, we constructed a second Leslie matrix characterized by catastrophic mortality. We began with the stable population matrix and subtracted 30 percent from the survival rate for every age category. For example, the survival rate for infants for a one-year interval decreases from 0.850 to 0.550, and the survival for 18-year-olds decreases from 0.994 to 0.694. We also reduced ASFRs by 30 percent. Realistically, the decline in fertility should probably be higher and should extend into the following year, but complex assumptions about fertility decline do not have a significant enough effect on the overall model to justify their inclusion. Assuming a higher or lower level of virulence would affect the outcome of the projection, but not the overall patterns.

The stable population matrix also forms the basis of the second model plague episode. In this model, we assumed persons who survived the first epidemic would have a higher probability of survival during the second. This higher survival could result from acquired immunities (a common outcome of surviving such diseases [McNeill 1976]) or from selection acting on a heterogeneous population weeding out those most frail and leaving a greater proportion of less-frail individuals among first-round survivors (see, for example, Vaupel and Yashin 1985a, 1985b; Wood et al. 1992). For present purposes, we kept the assumptions simple and gave individuals who survived the first epidemic (all those over age 27; the second epidemic episode strikes during year 28 of the projection) a 10 percent risk of dying of plague in the second episode. To show the effect of the second wave on births, we reduced ASFRs by 30 percent for ages under 27 years and by 15 percent for those over 27 years.

We simulated the effects of the Antonine plague using a 91-year population projection. Theoretically, the projection runs from AD 160 to AD 251. It is intended to show the effects of the plague on the living population and to provide an estimate of the plague's cumulative effect on the distribution of death. We cut the projection off after 91 years because another plague struck the Roman popu-

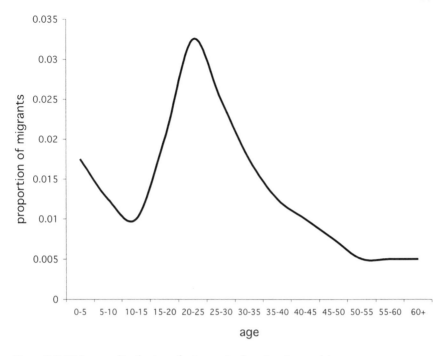

Figure 3-2. Living age distribution of migrants in the migration model.

lation in AD 251 (possibly measles—McNeill 1976:Chapter 3). We began with the stable population described above. In the second year of the projection we subjected the population to the first plague episode. For the next 26 years, fertility and mortality levels returned to those that created the original, stable population. During year 28 we subjected the population to the second plague episode. During the remaining years the population was subjected to the same fertility and survivorship probabilities that created the original stable population used to initialize the population. We tracked the size and shape of the living population, yearly crude birth rate (CBR), yearly crude death rate (CDR) and annual rate of population growth (r), yearly deaths, and cumulative deaths throughout projection.

Migration

At Lo Cascio's suggestion, we also modeled the possible effects of migration on age distribution at death and compared the model to the funerary epigraphic distribution (Storey and Paine 2002). We wanted to know two things: whether migration could be identified in the distribution of death and whether migration might have countered the effects of the Antonine plague as we had modeled them. Following Rogers and Castro (1984) we constructed a hypothetical model of the distribution of migrants (Figure 3-2). Our model shows the highest proportion

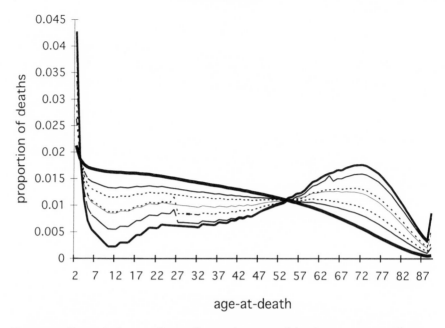

age-at-death

Figure 3-3. Change in the mortality profile over the course of the plague projection. The heaviest dark line (on top at age-at-death 12) represents the first plague year. The next-heaviest dark line (on the bottom at age-of-death 12) is the mortality profile for the stable model. The lighter lines represent the cumulative mortality profile taken at 5, 10, 25, 50, and 90 years into the projection.

of ages at migration as young adults between 15 and 30 (cf. Morley 1996:49). Bagnall and Frier (1994:160–169) found this age range to be that most represented in their Roman Egyptian census data. We modeled new migrants in 10-year segments, assuming a total fertility rate (TFR) of 6.1, and risk of death twice that of the host population. This yielded a CBR of 65.0 and a CDR of 96.3 for the migrant population.

Results and Discussion

The Plague Projection

Figure 3-3 compares the mortality profile of the stable population model with the catastrophic (wave 1) model. Adding 30 percent to the risk of death, regardless of age, dramatically increases the proportion of deaths between 3 and 50 years of age. At the same time there are significantly fewer deaths (proportionally) after age 50. It is important to note that the simulated plague year produces more than 10 times as many deaths as the stable population.

Over the course of time the projected cumulative death distribution will slowly converge with the stable age-at-death distribution. However, as Figure 3-3 dem-

Table 3-2. Goodness of Fit, Cumulative
Death Distributions

Projected year (end)	χ^2	α
1	—	—
2*	452.611	<.001
25	74.415	<.001
28**	136.452	<.001
70	43.127	<.001
91	31.235	<.001

Goodness of fit between cumulative death distributions generated by
Leslie matrix projection, at the end of the indicated projection year.
The χ^2 values presented are based on a sample size of 1,000 individuals.
* Following first wave of plague
** Following second wave

onstrates, this takes a long time. At the end of the 91-year projection, there are
still significantly greater early child and young adult deaths in the projected distribution (Table 3-2, Figure 3-3).

A recent update of our initial work provides further intriguing results suggesting that there were real measurable effects of the Antonine plague on the Roman
population that we have been able to identify in the record of the funerary inscriptions. At the suggestion of Lo Cascio (personal communication 1998), we
attempted to sort our current sample into two gross chronological categories, first
century AD and second century AD, on the basis of standard paleographical and
orthographical considerations (Gordon and Gordon 1957). We recently completed this phase of our project, distinguishing inscriptions from the late first
century AD from those of the second century AD and even late second and early
third centuries AD (Storey and Paine 2002).

The most striking result of this analysis is that the mean age at death increases
through time from the first century AD to the early third. The mean age at death
in the latter part of the first century AD in our sample was 14.1; in the first half
of the second century AD it increased to 17.6; at the end of the second century
AD and the beginning of the third, the mean age at death is 18.6. This trend is
interpreted as an inverse relation, a mean age-at-death decrease indicating population growth and an increase indicating population decline. If our scenario for
the mid-second-century to mid-third-century simulation has any merit at all, we
may possibly be seeing, in the increase in the mean age at death (and the statistics
generated from that variable), some reflection of the demographic problems associated with the Antonine plague. Although this result is tentative, we think it
warrants further investigation because it supports the demographic profile for the

city of Rome that we are in the process of exploring. Delineating the sample chronologically, as we have done, allays somewhat the problems that both Lo Cascio and Bagnall (this volume) identify: that the sample is of too long a temporal duration and thus might be distorting the demographic reality. We conclude (contra Scheidel 2001b, 2001c, 2003a and the conventional wisdom summarized by him) that it is still worth at least working with the epigraphic data to see whether it is possible to tease out demographically viable results.

Migration

Despite our construction of a model intended to maximize the impact of migrants on the distribution of death, the death distribution over a 100-year period (roughly the length of our simulation), including migrants, would not look very different from the distribution of death without migrants. However, as both Weiss (1973) and Paine (1989, 2000) point out, 100 years is more than enough time to reach a more or less stable age distribution. Perhaps the important distribution is that produced by migrants within the first 10 years of arrival. Here, the lion's share of mortality is in the 1–5 age group, as it is in the host population. Such early risk of death is common to all known human populations. The elderly were also stressed among the migrants, but there are secondary peaks of mortality among the young adults as well. The shape of the migrant pool is unknown, but the parameters set here are based on what seems standard for demographically studied migrants (Rogers and Castro 1984; Wrigley 1967). Morley (2003) has addressed the issue of migration, modeling ancient Rome on Wrigley's (1996:53) analysis for London. Starting with a CBR of 43 for Italy as a whole (life expectancy at birth of 25 and natural increase rate of 0.3 percent), the total numbers of births in Italy would have been about 172,000. Morley reckons that 15,000 of those births were "earmarked" for Rome, so one-tenth of the population of Italy has experience of life in the capital (compared to Wrigley's one-eighth estimate for London).

Implications for the Roman Population

The shocks to the Roman population would have been severe and long lasting. The first wave of catastrophic mortality reduces the population by just over 30 percent. It perturbs the stable growth rate but does not affect it in the long term. The second wave of plague kills fewer people but has serious effects on the population's ability to recover. This wave robs the population of reproductive-age females and older children who have survived the high-mortality early childhood years and are soon to begin their reproductive careers. This has long-term effects on crude birth rates, which prevent the population from recovering from the initial shock. After the second wave the population experiences 40 years of popula-

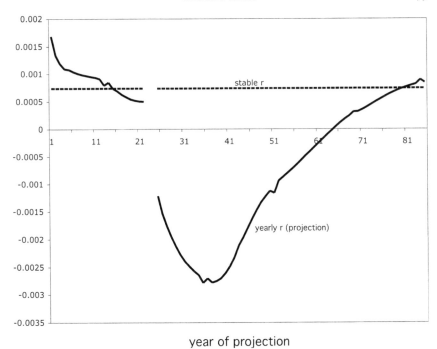

year of projection

Figure 3-4. The yearly intrinsic growth rate (r) of the projected population. The dashed line represents the r of the stable population. The catastrophic years have been omitted because they make distinguishing other yearly changes difficult.

tion decline before it begins to grow again (Figure 3-4). By the end of the projection the original growth rate has been reestablished.

The total population in year 91 (60 years later) is still smaller than the population that survived the second year of plague (Table 3-3). The long-term crisis produced by the projection fits Duncan-Jones's (1996) reconstructions of long-term productive declines in brickmaking, minting, construction, and other economic activities, although there has been serious challenge to Duncan-Jones's conclusions (Bruun 2003; Greenberg 2003). Our results are broadly in agreement with Scheidel's (2001c) views on the serious effects of epidemic disease on the age structure of the population of Rome.

Initially, we had also planned to examine the long-term effects of Livy's eight-year plague interval. Short intervals between disease events could have left the catastrophic profile we observe. However, given the severe, long-term population effects our projection attributes to Antonine plagues alone, we think we should examine our model more carefully first. Adding even minor disease events to the present model would yield a rapid population crash that is not justified by the

Table 3-3 Total Projected Population Size

Projected Year (end)	Total Population	Percentage of Year 1 Population
1	2,402,198	—
2*	1,651,967	68.77
25	1,681,902	70.02
28**	1,323,519	55.10
70	1,248,283	51.96
91	1,262,034	52.54

Total projected population size at various points in the Leslie matrix projection.
* Following first wave of plague
** Following second wave

historical record. The effects of migration also seem to have mitigated the serious consequences modeled here.

The conclusions for the migration analysis are as follows: (1) it would not take dramatic in-migration to bring Rome's population back up to preplague levels. This is almost certainly what happened. Population levels were restored quickly by in-migration, and the effects on the population were masked so that the catastrophic nature of the plague was somewhat mitigated. The migrants would not be recognizable in the age-at-death distribution, and the migrants are not responsible for the age-at-death distribution. The reasons for that distribution lie elsewhere.

How unhealthy was ancient Rome? The conditions of life in Rome have long been a topic of discussion, with the bulk of previous thought bordering on the panegyrical: that is, Rome had wonderful public amenities commensurate with its greatness as capital of an immense and wealthy empire. There were aqueducts conveying clean water into the heart of the city, magnificent public baths, and even a welfare system that provided free grain to some proportion of the city's nonelite population. There is now some disagreement as to whether Rome was a good provider of amenities. Mumford (1961:205–242) and Scobie (1986) are generally extremely negative on the question, suggesting that the Roman administration did little or nothing to improve the lot of its urban inhabitants. Russell (1985:25) painted the opposite picture, characterizing Rome as well governed, although noting that it was an unhealthy place to live.

Much of the argument boils down to how each investigator pictures the city. If the city is seen as one of "middle-class dwellings" (such as pictured by Armin Von Gerkan:1940, 1943, 1949), it was a pleasant place; if it appears to have been a "slummy metropolis" (Carcopino 1940 for example and Scobie 1986 par excellence), it was nasty (Hermansen 1978:167 for this contrast). Recently, the "slummy metropolis" picture of the city has been called into question by Laurence (1997) and Lo Cascio (this volume) on the grounds that (1) there is an inappropriate moralizing tone to Scobie's transference of Victorian urban reforming to the ancient Italian situation, and (2) the characterization is too biased toward the historical traditions of unhealthy conditions for northern European cities, which may now be undergoing some rethinking. Our own view is that we agree with (1) but not with (2), chiefly because the overall cross-cultural record of healthiness in preindustrial cities still points to a variety of serious health problems associated with the crowding of the human organism.

For example, on the question of dietary deficiency, the most sensible position is that of Garnsey (1998) who correctly, we think, stated that, on the basis of current available evidence, we cannot know what was the dietary state of most inhabitants of the city of Rome. Similarly, there is no way to tell what may have been the overall and long-term effects of the unpleasant aspects of Rome. We believe that is the only correct reply to the question of the health status of the ancient city. Our simulation, though suggestive, remains just that, a simulation with built-in assumptions. The catastrophic mortality (or the equivalent term favored by Lo Cascio, crisis mortality) possibility still remains only a possibility regarding the overall healthiness of the city. However, we believe it is sufficiently grounded in reasonable assumptions that we must take its implications seriously. There is also support for the kind of urban population crash we envision in the theoretical work of Fletcher (1995:203–207), whose simulations concerning population sizes for the largest preindustrial cities suggest that "the picture is somewhat ominous" (1995:207) in the resulting dramatic population decay curves.

Most of the reports we have on disease events in Rome do tend to suggest a rather gloomy picture. In the worst cases, we have reports of 2,000 dead per day (Jerome *Chronikon* 188, referring to AD 79 or 81; and Dio 73.14.3, events of AD 189, part of the Antonine plague, although that is specifically a tally of only one day) and 5,000 dead per day (*Augustan History,* the Two Gallieni 5.5, events of AD 251, the disease that closes our simulation). Constantinople allegedly suffered 10,000 deaths per day in AD 542 (Procopius 2.23.1–2). Nearly all the sources on serious disease episodes report figures in the tens of thousands. These could be inaccurate exaggerations. On the other hand, some of these figures might also be correct at least in terms of the scale of deaths occurring because the "Lists of Libitina" (Bodel 1994; Virlouvet 1997) were probably reasonably accurate death registers for the population of Rome. Even if the numbers are wildly exaggerated, the degree of shock to the population may not be. It is best to accept that we do not know the precise effects of disease episodes affecting Rome, but it is clear that a number were on a sufficient scale to cause possibly serious demographic harm, which is the tenor of Scheidel's (2001b, 2003a) review and Sallares's (2002) analysis of malaria in Rome.

We strongly recommend, however, that scholars cease to discuss the issue in terms of blame or praise of the Roman administration. Nor should we continue to indulge in idle speculation as to what the Roman administrators thought about these issues or to what degree they foresaw difficulties. It is not a question of how developed was the Roman (or any other ancient culture's) sense of foresight and urban planning skill. We reiterate that this is largely an environmental issue; disease vectors prosper best in conditions of crowding, and preindustrial cities have very high levels of crowding (often surpassing modern densities because high-volume mass transit was not available in the preindustrial context, thus keeping nucleated centers more densely packed than their modern counterparts).

We agree with the spirit of Lo Cascio's (this volume) conclusions that the demographics of the lower classes of the Roman population were variable. Sometimes the population was prospering and growing; at other times it was stagnant or in decline. The latter situation is discernible in the funerary epigraphy, though its severity may be exaggerated by the coarse chronologies we must currently employ to study it.

Implications for Roman Demographers

Even at the end of our projection, the two plague episodes have a clear impact on the age-at-death distribution. Many more deaths occur among older children and young adults than would occur in a stable population under either the Coale and Demeny (1966, 1983) or the Brass (1971) parameters (Table 3-3). At the same time there is a much smaller proportion of older adult deaths than in the model stable populations. The plague events clearly bring model death distributions closer to the inscription death distribution. The end of the projection is also the point in the projection furthest from any perturbation. At any other point in the projection, the effects are greater, but far from the inscription pattern. The year following the end of our projection (AD 251), Rome was visited by another powerful epidemic event that would serve to move the cumulative mortality profile back toward a catastrophic profile.

The plague model we have presented does not explain the inscription mortality profile. The year 91 cumulative death distribution is closer to the inscription death distribution but still contains a much lower proportion of older child and young adult deaths (Figure 3-5 top). The cumulative death distribution just five years after the second wave of plague (Figure 3-5 bottom) is still far from the inscription death distribution. We do not believe the Roman population could have survived levels of catastrophic mortality high enough to yield the age-at-death distribution in the inscription sample, though we intend to test the proposition.

Dedication bias (following Hopkins 1987, among others) remains the most viable explanation of certain features of the inscription mortality profile. The majority (61.1 percent) of our dedications are nuclear family relations, putting our results very much in line with the work of Saller and Shaw (1984) and Shaw

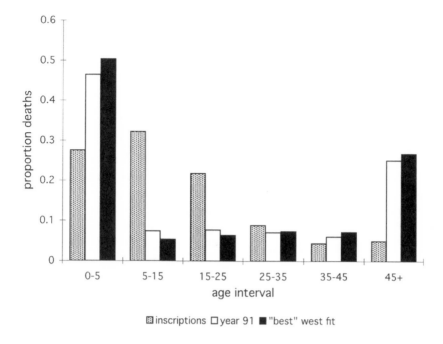

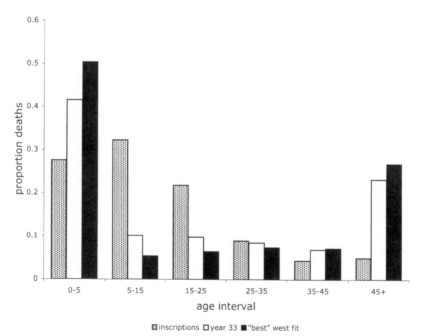

Figure 3-5. Comparison of age distribution of death between the inscription sample (checked bars), the projected cumulative age-at-death distribution (white), and the best-fitting west model age-at-death distribution (black): (*top*) at the end of the projection (year 91); (*bottom*) five years after the second catastrophic episode (year 33).

(1984) in which the vast majority of dedications in Roman funerary epigraphy of all periods (on the order of 75 percent) are nuclear family relations as that term is used today. Thus, the commemorative practices of funerary inscriptions introduce a bias when the majority of dedicators are nuclear family members, especially parents. We are testing this bias hypothesis with ongoing work by comparing the present sample to samples where deaths are not recorded with such precision and by examining patterns of dedication within those samples. We also are currently working on the Christian inscriptions from Rome that record age at death as accurately (generously provided by Brent Shaw, 1999).

The problems with the inscription sample are similar to those that plague archaeologists working with skeletal populations experience: evaluating the age data themselves and achieving a demonstrably representative sample. The solution is not necessarily to throw up our hands and give up working with these samples (Bocquet-Appel and Masset 1982). The challenge is to find a means to separate the demography from the noise (working with better current and historical living populations data and genetic techniques addressing questions of demographic history). Scheidel (2001b:11; see also Hopkins 1987) echoes the current historical bias against paleodemography without appreciating the work that has been done to address the deficiencies (e.g., Boldsen 1997a; Hoppa and Vaupel 2002; Konigsberg et al. 1997; Wittwer-Backoven and Buba 2002; Wood et al. 1992; see also Storey and Paine 2002:142–144). Our view is that, as with our exploration of the funerary age-at-death information, paleodemographic analysis can be fruitfully done if the work is carried out with proper appreciation of the challenges involved. We agree that "straightforward reading[s]" are not likely to be sufficiently sophisticated to avoid the biases and problems. But that does not mean that useful conclusions cannot be derived from more sophisticated attempts at analysis.

Current work with our sample demonstrates that the sample has some serious problems of representation in the older age categories that make it very difficult to achieve any kind of a reasonable fit with contemporary or more recent historical death patterns, for example the Coale and Demeny (1983) parameters. Some of the differences between the inscription sample and more recent patterns could have resulted from high levels of catastrophic mortality. Alternatively, the age distribution may be the result of commemorative bias in the current sample (the two hypotheses are not mutually exclusive). We have shown elsewhere (Paine and Storey 1999) that the data probably represent generally accurate age-awareness on the part of dedicators, as shown by the lack of digit preference. Previous studies, when demographic modeling with the Roman age-at-death data proved recalcitrant, tended to suggest that the information conveyed was not accurate. This was attributed either to innumeracy on the part of uneducated individuals or to culturally mandated distorting practices. That is not strictly correct; it is more a question of the mix of accurate age-at-death data coupled with the distorting effects of commemoration bias. It is not a problem of inaccurate ages recorded so much as a bias in who enters the inscriptional record. A revealing modern test is to ask people at random, as we have done, what day of the week they themselves and their children were born. Many people can state the latter but not the former. For one's own children, this information is easy to remember, but unless a parent has specifically informed one of what day of the week one was born, it is frequently unknown to everyone except the parent. A similar effect is probable with the cases from our sample. Parents dedicating to children more easily provided this kind of information than other dedicators. So, we suspect that the loss of parents served to prevent the recording of many older persons' deaths in the years-months-days form of our sample.

On the other hand, failure to conform to the Coale and Demeny parameters is not necessarily fatal. Our position is similar to that of Scheidel (2001b) and Sallares (1991:237, 2002 passim): the Coale-Demeny tables do not provide absolute parameters for preindustrial demography because they lack the broad range of high-mortality scenarios that were most likely prevalent in the ancient world. The tables were intended, above all, for fitting to samples. When samples such as our epigraphically derived sample cannot gainfully be fitted to modern patterns such as the Coale and Demeny parameters, we advocate neither discarding the data (contra Hopkins 1987) nor assuming that the modern patterns somehow do not apply (contra Lovejoy et al. 1977). Instead, we pursue a careful evaluation of the differences, considering both cultural and biological explanations. This chapter is a step in that evaluation.

4

Seasonal Mortality in Imperial Rome and the Mediterranean

Three Problem Cases

Brent D. Shaw

Seasonal fluctuations of death are a demographic fact of some considerable historical significance. Recurrent variations in the annual cycles of mortality formed by these seasonal clusters of deaths help the historian to define human populations in relation to their environments. These annual patterns of death suggest the fundamental underlying causes, including atmospheric conditions, temperature regimes, disease vectors, material sustenance, health resources, urban and rural discontinuities, and other such factors that produce the long periodic waves of mortality that are characteristic of any given population. Because of the lack of appropriate data, however, it is simply not possible to reconstitute these patterns with a great degree of confidence for most human populations of the Roman world. By means of the careful collation and analysis of large bodies of epigraphical data, however—principally tombstone epitaphs from the city of Rome and from other mixed urban and rural populations in Roman Italy—it has been possible to delineate the long annual rhythms of death that characterized the urban populations of the metropolis of Rome and the other centers of population in large parts of the Italian peninsula in late antiquity (Shaw 1996).

The conclusions that I reached concerning the annual oscillations of seasonal mortality that characterized the city of Rome have been confirmed by the parallel results obtained by Walter Scheidel (1994, 1996). Both sets of studies have revealed the recursive patterns of seasonal mortality that typified the populations of the city of Rome and of the outlying regions of Roman Italy in late antiquity. The temporal rhythms of mortality in the urban core of Rome and in town centers of central Italy rose and fell in an annual cycle with the incidence of deaths, reaching a peak in the period between August and October and then declining to lows in the months of December to March (Figure 4-1 top). This pattern was modified for both urban and rural populations living in regions farther to the north of the peninsula where high levels of mortality occurred in the midwinter months as well as those of late summer, thereby producing a typical bimodal summer-winter distribution of seasonal mortality (Figure 4-1 bottom). The prin-

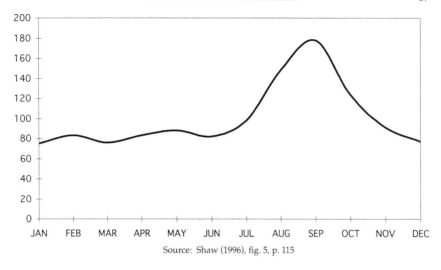

Source: Shaw (1996), fig. 5, p. 115

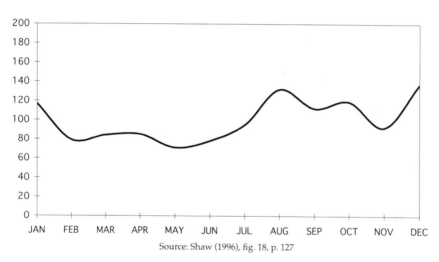

Source: Shaw (1996), fig. 18, p. 127

Figure 4-1. Seasonal mortality: (*top*) city of Rome (fourth to fifth centuries AD) *Source:* Shaw (1996:115, Figure 5); (*bottom*) northern Italy (fourth to fifth centuries AD) *Source:* Shaw (1996:127, Figure 18).

cipal physical factor in the environment that seems most closely correlated with these changing patterns is that of temperature. But temperature regimes themselves must only be supporting or repressing various kinds of disease vectors that are most evident in the population sample for the city of Rome. These surely varied from region to region. For the region of Latium, in which Rome was the large metropolitan center, it has been argued that malarial infection was the prin-

cipal disease responsible for the high mortality levels as well as for their seasonality (Sallares 2002).

The evidence that I used to compute these seasonal patterns was furnished
primarily by data provided by Christian burials from the city of Rome and from
other selected regions of Italy representing mixed rural-urban populations. In
general, the pre-Christian inhabitants of peninsular Italy and the city of Rome
did *not* record the times of their deaths in their funerary epitaphs, but instead
emphasized different quantitative aspects of their lives in the inscriptions on their
memorials, such as the length of their life or, if adults, the duration of their marriage. For peculiar religious and cultural reasons, Christians began to record the
actual day and month of their death and burial. It is therefore the Christian funerary epitaphs that are of particular use to the historical demographer. The data
collection that enables the computation of seasonal cycles is a difficult and pains-
taking process that requires the systematic collection of a sufficiently large number of funerary inscriptions from a specific representative cultural set of all funerary inscriptions to provide a sample for a given regional population. Any burials
from Mediterranean antiquity that might offer the possibility of extending or
increasing the numbers of this type of data are therefore a matter of some interest
to the historian of ancient populations.

In the process of collecting the evidence that produced the original database
for the study of seasonal mortality for Rome and Italy, I encountered a few other
intriguing groups of data relevant to the problem that reflected conditions in the
southern or eastern Mediterranean rather than those found in Italy. These cases
perhaps deserve brief mention in order to illustrate the nature of such data and
their limitations. Two typical examples of such isolated data sets are provided by
the rural cemeteries of 'Aïn Zára and En-Ngila in north Africa. Both of these
burial grounds are located in a hinterland region just south of Tripoli in what had
once been the Roman imperial province of Tripolitania. The burials in both cemeteries are characterized by the Christian practice of recording the precise day and
month of the death of the deceased person who is being commemorated. The
cemetery of 'Aïn Zára, dating to the tenth and eleventh centuries, is located about
14 km south-southeast of Tripoli (Aurigemma 1932). Of the 121 tombs, only 60
were sufficiently well preserved to provide usable epigraphical texts. Although
Aurigemma (1932:237–238) thought that the burial complex dated to the fifth
and sixth centuries AD, the coherence of the style and especially the specifics of
the orthography and the formulaic expression of the epitaphs would argue for a
date close to that of the En-Ngila cemetery. The cemetery of En-Ngila, which is
also located in Tripolitania, about 18 km south-southwest of Tripoli, contains a
large series of burials belonging to the tenth and eleventh centuries, with dated
epitaphs in the range between AD 945 and AD 1021 (Bartoccini and Mazzoleni
1977:157–198). There are not, however, a sufficient number of these burials that
record the month of decease (N = 12) to permit any serious analysis. The months

of death that were noted and can still be read are December (2), February (1), March (2), August (1), October (1), and November (1) (Gualandi 1973; Rizzardi 1973). These two Christian burial grounds, separated by only a small distance along the Gebel crest in the Tripolitanian hinterland not more than 15 km south of Tripoli, illustrate the problems of using such isolated cases for demographic analyses. The burial inscriptions date to a period far later than the epitaphs used for the model study that produced the seasonal mortality patterns for the city of Rome and peninsular Italy, where almost all of the Christian funerary inscriptions used for that reconstruction dated to the fourth and fifth centuries AD.

Despite the larger number of data from 'Ain Zára, the total is still below the number of individual cases required to produce a credible pattern of seasonal mortality. The one big problem that especially bedevils these, as other rural populations, is the paucity of the data. The deaths by month for 'Ain Zára are January (4), February (2), March (3), April and May (2 each), June and July (3 each), August (4), September (5), October (4), November (3), and December (4). The funerary inscriptions from a large urban center such as Rome have been preserved in sufficiently large numbers to permit valid general patterns to emerge. For most rural populations, this is not usually the case.

There are three other isolated groups of data on seasonal mortality, however, which, despite absolute dates that place them outside the temporal range of the data of the patterns of seasonal mortality established for Italy and Rome, might well be able to shed additional light on the problem of seasonal mortality and its relationship to peculiar environmental causes. Moreover, because they represent a range of environmental conditions different from those of Rome of the high empire, they might offer some chance for comparison.

The first of these discrete but problematic sets of data on seasonal mortality is provided by the large number of dated Christian funerary commemorations recorded in the basilica at Parenzo, Roman Parentium, in the Istrian Peninsula at the head of the Adriatic. These inscriptions record what was surely a mixed rural-urban population. Parentium was a Roman colonial settlement set at the center of a near-insular region that was the object of intensive agricultural development beginning in the first century BC and first century AD. There is every reason to believe that the modestly sized Roman town of Parentium was an administrative agrocenter for the region, and, as such, its population would have had a close relationship with the populations in its surrounding rural territory. Moreover, this "mixed" relationship probably remained substantially true of Parentium in late antiquity. Although the burial inscriptions in the basilica emphasize a typical Christian concern with recording the precise day of death of the deceased (or, as Christians put it, their "birthday," the *dies natalis* when they were "born" into their new eternal life), thus providing us an exact record of season of death, they are still difficult to interpret because of uncertainties concerning their temporal and cultural context.

The second of the three problem cases is provided by a substantial series of dated urban burials from the city of Rome, but ones that are of republican and not imperial date. The urban burials that are to be considered in this case date from a period in which the city of Rome was experiencing intense urban growth, a considerable part of this growth being fueled by large-scale in-migration from other town and village centers in Italy. The burials therefore catch the record of persons living in an urban environment that was "unstable," in the process of vertiginous change and growth, and in which the migrant population would have been especially exposed to the principal disease vectors of their new urban milieu. The particular Rome burials that are to be considered here are unusual, indeed perplexing, in their strangeness, and for reasons to be outlined below, it is even difficult to link the given dates of death recorded in them to the problem of seasonal mortality. But after some of the puzzles posed by these epitaphs have been resolved, it is possible that they might shed useful light on the problem of rural/urban demographic continuities and differences in Rome and central Italy of the time.

Finally, I shall consider a series of dated Christian funerary stelae provided by rural burials in Coptic cemeteries of the sixth to tenth centuries AD in Egypt. Although these burials date to a period after the end of Roman imperial authority in Egypt, the funerary commemorations might be able to confirm or to modify patterns of seasonal mortality that have been proposed for Roman Egypt of the high empire. Moreover, the context from which these burials are derived, the riverine environment of the Nile valley, is the best test provided of all three sets of data for rural-dwelling populations for which data are ordinarily exceedingly difficult to obtain. Even here, however, in the same general valley environment, there are local variations that must be noted and explained. One of the monastic communities is located in the region just south of the apex of the Delta, not far to the southwest of the modern conurbations of Cairo, near the site of Saqqara. The other site is much farther to the south in the Nile valley, in the hyperarid lands immediately adjacent to the Aswân in Upper Egypt. Although both populations were certainly "rural" by comparison with those of the late republican metropolis of Rome or those of late Roman Parentium, they still differed from each other in substantial ways.

Each of these problem cases will be considered in sequence. I shall then attempt to offer some general conclusions on what each set might contribute to an analysis of seasonal mortality in the ancient Mediterranean and on how these patterns might be related, in turn, to the problem of the relationship between rural and urban populations in Roman antiquity.

The Christian Dead of Parentium

The coastal city of Parentium, modern-day Parenzo in the Istrian Peninsula, where a Roman colony was established by the emperor Augustus, was the center of a wealthy and well-developed agricultural region in Regio X, the Tenth Region, of imperial Italy. In its last phases as a Roman city, a large Christian basilica was constructed under the aegis of the bishop Euphrasius in the years after AD 540 (Cuscito and Galli 1976:80ff. "Le costruzione eufrasiane: la basilica," with earlier bibliography, especially Malajoli 1940; for a plan of the basilica, see Degrassi 1934:102, Table iii). The Latin funerary epigraphy of Parentium that dates to the first centuries of rule by Roman emperors is characterized by a strong representation of imperial officials and local municipal worthies. The latter celebrate their status by the advertisement of their holding of offices in the government of the Roman colony (for the funerary epigraphy of the high empire from Parentium, see Degrassi 1934:numbers 1–46; for background, see Degrassi 1946:45–49 [1962:928–932]). The names of these men, as well as the names of slaves and freedmen of the local branch of the *familia Caesaris,* reflect a classic Romano-Italian nomenclature. The epigraphical records of their lives and careers are carved in impressive formal lettering on isolated stone blocks. The burials celebrated in the basilica built by Bishop Euphrasius, on the other hand, present a great contrast. The names of the Christian dead of late antique Parentium are found scrawled in the form of graffiti crudely inscribed on the walls of the apse of the basilica as a kind of popular memorial to those who had passed on to eternity.

The fundamental collection of these graffiti was edited by Degrassi (1934: numbers 95–178) and later reprised by Rugo (1975:numbers 91–135). As Degrassi (1934:45) makes clear, only a portion of the total number of the original graffiti now survive. Most of the existing inscriptions are located on the left side of the hemicycle formed by the apse of the church. Degrassi (1934:36) believed that the graffiti began to be inscribed toward the end of the sixth century and through the seventh. But precision dating eludes the researcher: dates as late as the eighth, and perhaps even the ninth, century have been suggested. Clearly, there were once many more of these crude graffiti than now exist. Many of them, indeed, have been lost by the cleaning and repair of the panels on which they were inscribed and by the normal wear of curious humans touching the exposed stone surfaces. The terse commemorative graffiti contain two simple pieces of information redacted in three statements: the month and the day of death, the term *obitum* or *obiit* ("he or she died"), followed by the name of the deceased.

As stated above, the time when these graffiti were inscribed on the church walls at Parentium is a matter of some dispute because there are no annual dates attached to any of the scrawlings. They must date to some time after the mid-sixth century, the period when the basilica was being constructed and on whose apsidal walls the funerary graffiti are preserved. Although many of the names of the deceased are recorded in the standard Latin nomenclature of the time, about a quarter of the whole reveal Germanic roots, which alone would seem to argue that they date to a period after the main influx of Lombards into the peninsula in the sixth century (Christie 1995:82f). As Degrassi (1934:46) notes, Germanic names

Table 4-1. Seasonal Distribution of Death at Parentium (N = 77)

	J	F	M	A	M	J	J	A	S	O	N	D
N=	7	2	9	8	5	9	9	8	2	5	6	7
IN=	108	36	139	128	80	142	139	124	32	77	96	108

N = actual number of cases; IN = Indexed Number = index of seasonal variation (for an explanation, see the appendix at the end of this chapter).

are already attested at Aquileia in the sixth century; on the other hand, some of the unusual *agnomina* (nickname) in the graffiti are attested in literary sources dating to the ninth century. The commemorations would *seem* to antedate the tenth century, when it became customary to maintain anniversary information on deaths in books and codices. In the graffiti, each of the deceased is marked by a precise date on which the individual died. Of the 84 graffiti that subsist, only 77 have an exact date of death to the day that is recorded or preserve a date that is sufficiently legible for us to specify at least the month in which the person died.

If we consider the simple elements of nomenclature and the occasional ecclesiastical title, the following basic facts about the population emerge: 44 males are commemorated as compared with 24 females (in 11 cases gender cannot be determined), and among the deceased there were 8 priests, 3 bishops, and 1 deacon. Not much more can be deduced about the social background of the commemorated. The annual distribution of death that the Parentium data suggest is found in Table 4-1. The figures are rather sparse. They cannot do anything more than suggest patterns in the data. They might indicate a bimodal distribution of death marked by two highs, one in the winter months of December to March/April and another in the mid-summer months of June to August (Figure 4-2).

This pattern matches the seasonal distribution of death typical of the more northerly regions that we have discerned in our data for northern Italy (Figure 4-1 bottom: calculated independently and exclusive of the data from Parentium; see Shaw 1996:126–128 and Figures 18 and 21). If so, the collected body of funerary epigraphy from Istria would then fit into a general pattern of seasonal mortality typical of the more northerly latitudes, and this for a time period about two and one-half to three centuries later than the main body of funerary inscriptions from the city of Rome and northern Italy that are otherwise available from the standard corpora of Latin inscriptions. Unfortunately, not much more can reasonably be argued from this unusual case. The numbers, although large for a coherent single body of such data, are still too sparse to permit anything but the most general of connections between them and other better-attested patterns of mortality.

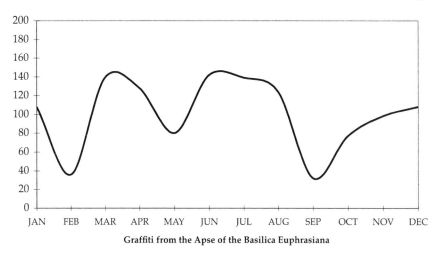

Graffiti from the Apse of the Basilica Euphrasiana

Figure 4-2. Seasonal mortality: Parentium, Italy (seventh to ninth centuries AD). *Source:* Graffiti from the apse of the Basilica Euphrasiana.

Some Unusual Burials from the City of Rome of the Late Republic

One of the stranger and more intriguing sets of data relevant to seasonal patterns of mortality in the past comes from the city of Rome of the republican period from a modern location just outside the Aurelian Wall known as the "Vineyard of San Cesario."[1] The data are fascinating precisely because they manifest a pre-Christian interest in recording the precise date of death of the deceased. The practice is known from a few isolated examples from other early contexts in Italy, but it was never part of a general pattern of "pagan" Roman funerary practices (Shaw 1996:102–104, on the Christian norms). In many ways, in their extreme brevity, these inscriptions mirror the same narrow concern with the day of one's death that is reflected in the Christian inscriptions from seventh- and eighth-century Parentium. They record nothing other than the name of the deceased along with the precise date on which the person died. The practice not only is unusual for pre-Christian funerary epigraphy but also stands in stark contrast to the general body of commemorative inscriptions from the city of Rome of the high empire. This is especially so because the funerary inscriptions from the vineyard of San Cesario are not just some "odd exceptions" to the rule. They are the reflection of a coherent practice engaged in by a not insignificant group of persons for perhaps two generations or so at this specific burial locale in the city of Rome.

It is perhaps best to begin with a description of the artifacts of the burials themselves. The earliest and indeed only detailed report of the discovery and of the site itself is found in an early eighteenth-century publication by Gianfrancesco Baldini (1738). (A brief passage from Baldini's report [1738:151] was quoted by Theodor Mommsen, *"Ollae effossae in Vinea S. Caesari"* ["Cinerary urns excavated in the Vineyard of San Cesario"], for the corpus of Latin inscriptions, *CIL* VI, 1103). According to Baldini's description, the discovery was made in July of the year 1732 in the vineyard of San Cesario located on the right-hand side of the Via Appia immediately as it exits the city of Rome. In excavations at this location, in what Baldini calls a *camera sepolcrale* (funerary chambers), there were found a surprisingly large number (*quantità straordinaria*) of small terracotta vases buried together, apparently purposefully placed there as part of a single large collection. Most of the vases were of the same general size and shape: all were about four inches in height, with small bases, fuller bodies, a narrow neck, and a wider mouth. Some of them were slightly glazed, some with a reddish veneer and others with blackish color, but most had no glazed finish. When the contents of these small urns were investigated, they proved to be a mixture of carbonized human remains: fragments of bone splinters that had survived the cremation of the body.

The deposits therefore represent a customary location where, within a relatively brief span of time (most of the vases look very similar, as if they were produced from the same workshop), there took place the burials of a group of people in Rome who shared a similar social background. The funerary practice that involved the collection of the bone fragments of the deceased following cremation seems to be the one referred to by the antiquarian and grammarian Festus.[2] The same practice is almost certainly noted in an inscription of late republican date, not from Rome, however, but from Puteoli on the Bay of Naples (of significance, as we shall later see) that records the burial of one Chrematinê, a slave woman and beautician (*ornatrix*) who was owned by a certain Numisia.[3]

For our purposes, the most important fact about the San Cesario burial vases is that they were inscribed in Latin letters either around the neck or around the main body of the vase. The inscriptions recorded the name of the deceased and the date of death. The saddest thing that Baldini reports is that he estimated that there once existed about 300 of these vases at the site, of which there survived only 125 by the time he made his report on the excavations in the vineyard. The loss of the remaining 175 is a great disappointment because to have more than double the data would have made conclusions drawn from them more reliable. By the time Mommsen came to record the inscriptions for the sixth volume of the *CIL*, he remarks that most of the 125 that Baldini and others had managed to record had also disappeared: they had either been dispersed from their original collections or had otherwise somehow been lost.

It is difficult to know precisely what the inscriptions and the vases represent, because they have few other known parallels. They were found in the general region in which large imperial columbaria were later located, and one might

Table 4-2. Social Status of the Deceased of the San Cesario Burials

	All	Slave	Freed	Free (+)	Free (?)
Male	108	1	21	9	74
Female	60	0	5	4	51

Slave: Only the one case with an explicit indication of such a status is included under this heading (he was, apparently, a public slave); Freed: Only those persons who are explicitly indicated as the l *(ibertus)* or the l *(iberta)* of a former master; Free (+): Only those persons bearing either the *tria nomina* or filiation; Free (?): A rather broad category that includes all other persons with single or double names, but with no explicit indication of slave or freed status; many freedpersons may well be hidden within this admittedly nebulous category.

imagine that they were a sort of republican precursor to similar burial practices later found at the same site. At very least, the San Cesario cemetery represents a place of collective burials of a socially homogeneous population (Table 4-2). The rituals of burying the dead, which are also stereotypically uniform, included both the cremation of the corpse and the marking of the day of decease by the location of a common type of ritualistic "death vase" that was added to the collection at the site. The large number of dates of death should therefore add to our knowledge of the general seasonal cycle of death in the city of Rome.

The more precise information provided by the similar burials at Puteoli make clear that the dates given on the urns must be either the actual date of death or the date on which the remains of the bones were collected to be placed in the cinerary jar. In either case, for the purpose of calculating gross seasonality of death, they amount to the same thing, because the latter date is usually only a few days after the former. In the case of Chrematinê the *ornatrix*, it is known that she died on the tenth of October and that her bones were collected for burial on the twelfth of the same month. In the case of one [Va?]leria Putiolana (Dessau 1892–1916:*ILS* number 7844), death occurred on the fourth of April (*pr. non. Apriles*), and the burial of her remains in a cinerary urn took place on the seventh day of the same month (*VII idus Apriles*). The data would therefore seem to offer a sure guide to dates of death and hence to the seasonal distribution of mortality, but this is just the point where the problems of interpretation begin. Indeed, it may ultimately be the case that the dates on the burial urns at the San Cesario vineyard will shed as much light on the history of the Roman calendar as they do on the problem of seasonal mortality. To begin our analysis, we might start with the social background of the deceased. One's social status is indicated by a wide range of personal names of republican type. As far as can be deduced from those inscriptions that are legible and that provide reliable evidence, the following general picture emerges.

The substantial presence of freedmen and the dominance of males in the sample seem to indicate that we are dealing with the burial of urban persons of lower social status who belonged to the *familiae* of the wealthy and powerful of the city. Almost without doubt, some of the single names disguise the presence of even more freedmen than are explicitly attested. The persons involved in the commemoration seem to include freedmen, slaves, and the general free population who were above the level of the kind of penury that would have assigned them to mass burials. The very poverty of the burial types, and the proletarian nature of the evidence, was a cause of some embarrassment to Baldini, who first reported the inscriptions.[4]

The names on our "humble vases," however, should contain valuable clues about the cultural, geographic, and social backgrounds of the deceased. From the body of inscriptions that have survived from the San Cesario burials, it is possible to rescue 181 names (there are 17 epitaphs where even this little is not possible). But their interpretation is still rather difficult. There are numbers of *gentilicial nomina* (clan names) that are more common than others, but none seem to point decisively to any general *terminus post quem*. The numbers of Aemilii (N = 5), for example, if they are dependents of the great political family, might well follow on the acme of their power in the late second and the early first century (Wiseman [1998] notes that they were a dominant family in the city from the end of the second century BC through the middle of the first). If the *gentilicial nomina* of those families whose freedmen are represented in the burials are taken as a group, however, and the student of them can form an estimate of those decades in which one would expect them to be well known or attested in the city of Rome *as a collective group,* then that student would tend to focus on the decades between the 90s and the 50s BC.

The *gentilicia* of the masters of families whose freedmen are represented in the burials include the following: the Caecilii, Celii [= Caelii], Cantinii, Apuleii, Baebii, Fulvii, Furii, Iunii, Larcii, Lutatii, Minatii [= Munatii], Paccii, Popillii, Sempronii, Sulpicii, and Valerii. Some of these *nomina* are well known in periods earlier than the decades specified, but *as a whole* the decades of the 90s to the 50s is when one would tend to expect all of them to reflect a contemporary collective representation. Greek background is indicated by faulty transcription to Latin, Greek usage in nomenclature, and the presence of Greek names in Greek script. And, as one commentator (Vetter 1953:70, cited in CIL I^2, vi, 1986:967) has already noted, some of the names also seem to indicate Oscan or Campanian origins. Although one need not go so far as to posit an immigrant community of such persons in Rome, it is rather interesting to note that there was only one other local society in Italy that produced a number of pre-Christian burials for which the date of death is consistently noted on their funerary epitaphs. This social group was the community of freedmen and persons of the same general status who lived in the town of Puteoli, and more widely in the Bay of Naples region, during the later republic.[5]

As in the burials at the San Cesario vineyard at Rome, most of those found in the Bay of Naples area, specifically those from Puteoli, also an urban population, seem to have been recovered from a place where the local population practiced the ritual of the cremation of the deceased, followed by the fragmentation of the bones and the placement of the ashes and bone splinters in burial urns.[6] The Puteoli burials bear all of the same hallmarks as the San Cesario burials at Rome: they are the burials of freedmen and persons of similar social status, and they are dated to the same general period of the late republic. As the words on Chrematinê's burial urn make clear, the funerals from the Puteoli and Bay of Naples region had a similar procedure of cremation followed by the later burial of the remnants of the ashes and bones. In the burials at Puteoli the remains of the deceased were also placed in smallish urns made either of lead or of terracotta, some of the latter being finished with a reddish glaze. The urns were then inscribed with the name of the deceased and, it seems, fairly often with the date of the person's death. The known (consular) dates at which these burials were attested (N = 6) cover the period of the last decades BC and the first decades AD: specifically, 13, 10, and 4 BC and AD 2, 32, and 38. As mentioned, however, some of the dates assigned to the early principate are questionable; they could just as well be dates of the late republican period. That is not the only coincidence.[7]

The San Cesario burials at Rome fit nicely within this same cultural and temporal context. They are definitely late republican in date; all of them antedate the Julian reforms of the calendar and the Caesarean and Augustan renaming of the months of July and August (Weinstock 1971:152–158, "Mensis Iulius"). For a study of seasonal mortality, however, the contorted problem of the reforms of the republican calendar needs to be discussed to help us to ascertain the precise months of death. The use of the calendar of the republican age in our inscriptions is indicated not only by the designations of the months of July and August, which in the inscriptions on the burial urns are still known by their traditional pre-Augustan names of Quin(c)tilis (N = 4) and Sextilis (N = 8), but also by the presence of intercalary months, which are noted five times.[8]

Given the peculiar nomenclature of the deceased, another possible indicator of date, Mommsen considered that the burial vases belonged to the earlier rather than to the latter half of the first century BC. He based his estimate mainly on the names of freedmen, drawing attention to the fact that those whose names are noted on the jars lack *cognomina* (familial personal name) and that such an absence of *cognomina* was very unusual after the age of Sulla. As the editors of the most recent edition of *CIL* I indicate, Cébeillac (1971:47–63) has attempted to push this diagnostic criterion back to the mid-80s BC. But they also point out that her claim is weak, because freedmen who lack *cognomina* are attested to the end of the republic and into the beginning of the principate (citing Solin 1972:404–407: 2, 405–407, 1974:125–130). Although there is a wider temporal spectrum in which this criterion applies, it is possible to say that the nomenclature of the deceased in the San Cesario cemetery can be used with caution to sustain a date in the first half of the first century (i.e., the data do not rule out such a hypothesis). All such guesses, however, are open to individual objections. Whereas the names of the months give a reasonable *terminus ante quem,* the orthography of some of the words (e.g., *idus, idibus* instead of *eidus* and *eidibus*) generally indicates a date that is post-Gracchan.[9] The sense that one gets from the main evidence bearing on dating, therefore, is that the San Cesario burials belong to the last century of the republic, probably to the generations just before and after Sulla—broadly speaking from the first half of the first century BC.

What can the data themselves tell us? First, they cannot, alas, provide a good independent countercheck on the seasonal pattern of mortality that is well attested for imperial Rome (Figure 4-1 top). The problems that prevent such a ready calculation are rooted in basic difficulties with the republican calendar. Unlike the imperial calendar after the reforms of Caesar and Augustus, in which months matched their intended seasons with reasonable exactitude, the republican calendar tended to wander off track. The pontiffs and other magistrates of the state repeatedly had to intervene to make the required adjustments by inserting an intercalary month to bring the calendar into agreement with the true solar year (Michels 1967:21–22, 145–172; Samuel 1972:160–164; the intercalary month was inserted at the end of February, sometimes with the deletion of some days from the end of the month of February itself). Any practical Roman, such as Cato the Elder, who wished to match times of the year with the seasons (for example, for agricultural purposes) sensibly avoided using the official state calendar for this very reason: "When Cato in the second century B.C. writes about farming in his *De Agricultura,* he uses the civil calendar only for the dates of business affairs, such as contracts. For other purposes he reckons mainly by the stars. . . . The Roman calendar of his day would have been useless for this purpose [i.e., the practice of agriculture], as it had no regular relation to the seasons" (Michels 1967:16 n. 19). The pattern that we have, therefore, is likely to be at variance with the actual year by some unknown quantity. Because our knowledge of the late republican calendar is so uncertain, however, we cannot be sure about the probable average variance from the true alignments between calendrical months and actual seasons of the year.

The problem of matching months of the republican calendar with seasonal points in the year is further exacerbated by the fact that we do not know precisely how often or in what years the intercalary month was added. "If there is any one thing on which the ancient evidence agrees, it is that the Roman intercalation was highly irregular; . . . [and], unless a flood of new evidence is forthcoming, it will not be possible to determine, in more than a few cases, which years of the Roman Republic were intercalary and which were not" (Michels 1967:168, 170). As topsy-turvy as it might seem, therefore, it is the annual seasonal pattern of death that is firmly established for the imperial city of Rome that is likely to provide our best check on the data from the burials in the vineyard of San Cesario from the late republic. In the large-scale mortality from the city of Rome, which can be measured with reasonable accuracy over long periods of time, there was a gradual rise in the toll of mortality until a pronounced high was reached in September, which was followed by a gradual decline in levels of mortality (Figure 4-3 top).

The same general annual pattern of mortality is in evidence in the data provided by the San Cesario burials, but it is decentered by about a month: the maximum in the republican burials appears in October rather than September. If two adjustments are made to the San Cesario data, however, they provide an annual cycle of mortality that is entirely concordant with that attested for Rome, and this despite the exiguous size of the data sample. The first adjustment is to add back in the deaths dated to the intercalary month (N = 4) on the assumption that most of these deaths would have been attached to the latter part of the calendrical month of February. The next adjustment is to calculate rolling averages for the months of June to September in the original data for the San Cesario burials in order to produce a smoothed data set for those months where the exiguous number of the data tends to produce erratic and unreal fluctuations in the mortality patterns. Once these two minor operations have been performed, the final step is to move the whole temporal location of the entire original set of annual data back in time by one month so that the late republican figures, for example, for October, now refer to the actual month of September. The San Cesario death dates for "September" now refer back to an actual month of August and so on. The resulting seasonal distribution of mortality (Figure 4-3 bottom), although displaying greater amplitudinal variation than that for the city of Rome of the later empire, follows much the same general pattern of movement. This reconfiguration of the data admittedly involves some speculation, but it is concordant with the control figures for the imperial metropolis that are unlikely to have changed very much from those produced by the population of Rome of the later republic.

In sum, the series of monthly death dates from the burials at San Cesario would indicate that the calendar of the later republic had wandered about a month off a true relationship to the actual seasonal months of the year. In one sense the San Cesario burials only serve to confirm that the general annual cycle of mortality in the city of Rome of the first century BC was much the same as that found in later centuries. But they also, rather inadvertently and fortuitously, provide a valuable insight into the Roman calendar of the late republic. The de-

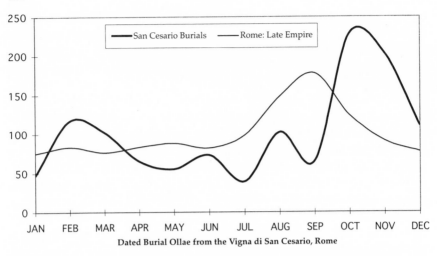

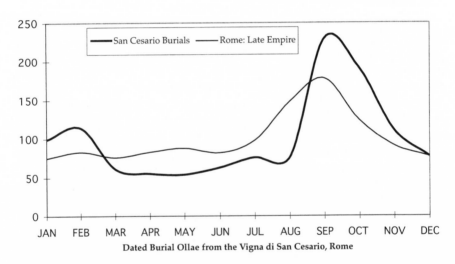

Figure 4-3. Seasonal mortality: (*top*) Rome, late republic (first century BC); (*bottom*) Rome, late republic (adjusted). *Source:* Dated burial *ollae* from the Vigna di San Cesario, Rome.

gree of disparity between the formal calendrical dates on the San Cesario burial urns and the actual seasons of the year is far from impossible. At two known points in the second century, for example, in 168 BC and in 190 BC, the republican calendar had advanced, respectively, two and one-half months and four months ahead of the seasonal year or "true" time.[10] If this adjustment is made (an adjustment that is not out of line either with our knowledge of the history of the calendar in the later republic or with the expected seasonal patterns of mortality), then the resulting distribution of seasonal mortality in the metropolis of the late republic is the same characteristic annual pattern that is well attested for the high empire. Some arguments have been proffered to claim that the calendar of the republic in the last quarter of the second century and the first quarter of the first century BC was close to the true solar year. But the arguments are weak and unpersuasive.[11] During this period, the official Roman calendar must have drifted off a true correlation with the tropical year by some unknown span of time. After a series of intercalations made in the 160s BC, the only subsequent interventions before the end of the republic that are well attested took place in 82 and 52 BC (Michels 1967:171–172). In the late 70s and early 60s, indeed, the calendar seems to have been about a month out of exact correspondence with solar time (Brind'Amour 1983:76–78). Our calculations would seem to indicate that, despite the best efforts of the pontiffs, the calendar of the republic at the time of the San Cesario burials had drifted about a month off course in advance of the "true" or solar time.

The Christian Burials of Coptic Egypt

For the human population of the province of Egypt of the high Roman Empire, the possibility of computing patterns of seasonal mortality has already been attempted several times, mainly on the basis of evidence provided by the so-called mummy labels. For these labels as standard types of data, the interested researcher can consult Quaegebeur (1978:232–259) and the corpus collected by Boyaval (1976). It is important to note that only a small proportion of all of the mummy labels (N = 127 of Total N = 2,195, or about 5 to 6 percent of the total) contain references to a month of the year. The scholarly dispute that has arisen over these "mummy labels" is over the significance of the "month" that is recorded on them. Despite the claims made by some scholars about the manifest and obvious significance of the data on these burial labels, I argued that there was something basically mistaken in any simple use of them as direct and unmediated indicators of seasonal mortality. Whatever the data on the mummy labels indicated, I held that they were *not* in any simple sense the date of death of the deceased (Shaw 1996:121–123, against the manner of their use by Boyaval). Since the time when I first lodged this objection, however, Walter Scheidel has resolved the main problem with the "mummy label" data by demonstrating that the dates on the labels must reflect the preparation for final burial *after* a 70-day waiting period set aside for completion of the process of mummification. The adjusted figures then produce a plausible annual cycle of seasonal mortality for the Nile valley (Scheidel 1998:285–292; see especially Figures 1–3). It would be beneficial, however, if some other data sets could be found that would offer a check on the evidence provided by the ancient mummy label data on the one hand and the evidence obtained by more recent demographic surveys that are available for "premodern" type rural populations of the Nile riverine environment on the other.

Bodies of evidence of this type are available for the Christian populations of Egypt, especially from epitaphs on the grave stelae set up by Coptic Christians to mark the burials of members of their rural monastic communities. These data are often disparate and difficult to collate because they are scattered in diverse, difficult-to-access publications and corpora of inscriptions (Lefebvre 1978 [1907]; for a general review of the evidence see Mallon 1914:Coll. 2821–2886, now updated by Krause 1991:1290–1299). There do exist, however, two specific coherent data sets provided by two cemetery complexes: one from the Coptic monastery of the Holy Simeon at Aswân in southern Upper Egypt and the other from the large monastery complex of the Holy Jeremiah, the Dayr Apa Jeremiah, at Saqqara to the north. The extensive church and monastic complex of Apa Jeremiah, located just to the southeast of the famous Step Pyramid of the Third Dynasty pharaoh Djoser at Gizeh, was constructed at the end of the fifth century AD and flourished until the mid-tenth century (Wietheger 1992, who offers comprehensive references to earlier archaeological, art-historical, and epigraphical studies). The epitaphs on the funerary stones of the Saqqara community were redacted according to a stereotypical formula that provided the person's name, occupation, and the precise day and month of death. Unlike the closed monastic community of Dayr Anbâ Hadrâ at Aswân, the one at Saqqara included both men and women. From the relatively large number of cases that can be collated (N = 120), a rather distinctive pattern of annual death emerges (Figure 4-4 top). After we make allowances for the unevenness produced by the smaller amount of data, we can see that there seems to be a single annual cycle with lows in the months from Thoth through Tybi (approximately from July through January), with the peak in death being reached in the months of Phamouthi through Pachon-Payni (approximately March through June).

The Coptic monastery of Dayr Anbâ Hadrâ or St. Simeon at Aswân has also yielded a rich harvest of Christian burial stelae. Dated examples are distributed over the period from the sixth to the ninth centuries AD and are marked by a formula beginning "Jesus Christ: day of the commemoration of the blessed X" that provides the person's name, rank in the monastic community, and the precise date of death. At the end of the eighth century this basic information about the deceased is followed by a stereotypical phrase: "May the Lord grant rest to X's soul in the bosom of Abraham, Isaac, and Jacob" (Meunier 1931:257–300, 433–484; Meunier not only collected and published the large number of texts recovered by Monneret de Villard's excavations but also collated all other known finds from the site). Because this is a monastic community, the population measured shares some peculiar characteristics. Almost all of the deceased are males; only 9 women are found among the cases that provide dates at death. The remaining 111

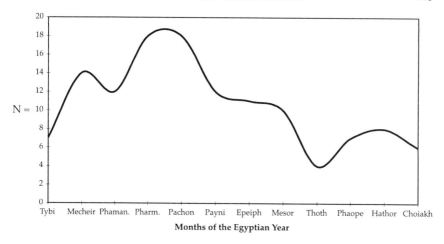

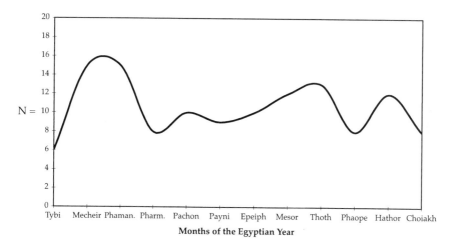

Figure 4-4. Seasonal mortality: (*top*) Coptic Saqqara, Egypt; (*bottom*) Coptic Aswân, Egypt.

are men. Although the total number of dated cases of death (N = 125) is substantial, no clear pattern emerges (Figure 4-4 bottom).

Part of the problem with the Aswân inscriptions is not their number, which is about the same as the number from Saqqara, but rather the fact that they are thinly distributed over a very long time span. The earliest of the Aswân epitaphs date to the beginning of the sixth century, and the latest date to the last decade of the tenth century. The majority of the Saqqara burial inscriptions, however,

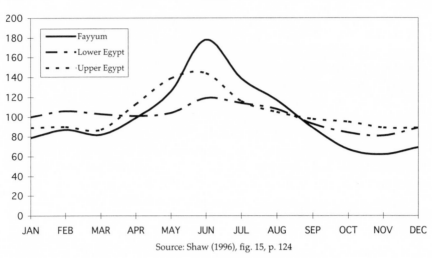

Source: Shaw (1996), fig. 15, p. 124

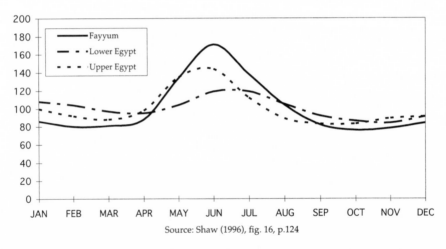

Source: Shaw (1996), fig. 16, p.124

Figure 4-5. Seasonal mortality: (*top*) Egypt, 1923; *Source:* Shaw (1996:124, Figure 15); (*bottom*) Egypt, 1926; *Source:* Shaw (1996:124, Figure 16).

seem to date to the last half of the eighth century AD. The inscriptions from Saqqara therefore constitute a coherent and compact series that is more likely to reflect the impact of seasonality on the mortality of the population, a characteristic that is absent in the Aswân series, which often does not record more than one burial in any given year.

The results on seasonal mortality that are deducible from the Saqqara epitaphs (the more coherent and therefore more reliable of the two Coptic burial series) can be compared with some standard patterns for premodern types of indigenous populations from rural Egypt in the period immediately after the First World War (Figure 4-5). By analyzing demographic statistics collected for the indigenous populations of Egypt in the 1920s for lands in Upper Egypt, we can see that there is a single annual cycle of death with lows in the months of October to January and highs in the April-to-June period. The modern series, in which the great upswing in annual mortality begins about a month later on average than the cycle indicated by the ancient data, is nevertheless very close in timing and sequence to the seasonal cycle of mortality that is deducible from the data provided by the cemeteries of the large monastic complex of St. Jeremiah at Saqqara. Given the problems and vagaries of the preservation of the small sample of data from antiquity, however, the correlation is close enough to confirm a typical Egyptian seasonal cycle of death that matches not only the best modern comparative data that we have but also the best reconstruction of the significance of the much vexed data provided by the mummy certificates. It is a pattern of seasonal mortality that is typically Egyptian and one that is significantly different in type from the northern Mediterranean types found in Rome and Italy.

Conclusions

The three different assemblages of funerary data, one provided by the urban San Cesario burials from the city of Rome of the late republic, another by the mixed rural/urban Christian burials from Parentium in northern Italy of late antiquity, and the third by the rural Coptic burials in Egypt, all share problematic aspects that make the interpretation of their significance for seasonal patterns of mortality a difficult and sometimes speculative undertaking. The sum of the arguments presented here is that once the vagaries of calendrical difficulties, dating, social context, and historical practice are taken into account, all three bodies of evidence broadly confirm the same general patterns of seasonal mortality found in these regions for their premodern populations. That is to say, in terms of the mixed rural/urban populations of Parentium in the Istrian Peninsula in northern Italy, the results, as vague as they are, tend to fall within the bimodal pattern of seasonality of death that seems to be generally true of rural and urban populations in "normal" conditions of mortality. That would further suggest that the rural and urban populations were so strongly interlinked that they responded in much the same way to the environmental factors that most condition patterns of mortality.

The urban sample provided by the San Cesario burials for late republican Rome, on the other hand, seems to reveal even for this earlier period the same monodal seasonal pattern of death attested in the tombstone epitaphs of the metropolis in the fourth to sixth centuries AD. Although the numbers are so small that too much emphasis should not be placed on the seasonal amplitudes of death displayed by this particular sample, it is notable that the intensity of seasonal mortality that is suggested by them is even greater than for the later period. It might well be that the conditions encountered and created by migrating populations in the conditions of intense urban development of late republican Rome exacerbated seasonal patterns of death. Regardless of intensity, it is still the typical urban pattern of death found in the urban and coastal regions of Latium and central Italy as opposed to that characteristic of northern Italian populations.

Finally, the two Egyptian samples could be categorized as "rural" in type but with the very strong qualification that they both reveal the peculiarities of the riverine environment of the Nile river valley much more than they do any general rural characteristics found among populations of the ancient Mediterranean outside Egypt. The Saqqara population seems to display the most pronounced seasonal variation that makes it, in effect, a strong "inversion" of normal patterns found elsewhere in the Mediterranean (e.g., urban Rome), whereas the Aswân population displays a much more modulated and even seasonal distribution of seasonal mortality that reflects the environmental conditions in the more arid and isolated regions of Upper Egypt. At this stage in our analysis, however, it should be emphasized that these data are resistant to any simple interpretation and that they are perhaps better understood in the context of the more numerous, coherent, and dependable data from other sources that will be used to resolve this particular problem of Roman demographic history.

Appendix: Indexes of Seasonality

The absolute quantitative data concerning a specific demographic factor for any given population group (for example, regional, temporal, or ethnic) will usually be very different from those for any other such group. One of the primary *desiderata* of historical demographers in tracking the seasonality of a specific demographic phenomenon (for example, birth, marriage, or death) in a given population is to be able to compare the results for that group with the seasonal cycles typical of other populations. To be able to effect such comparisons directly, historical demographers reduce the fixed and absolute numbers for any given data set to "indexes" of seasonality. The concept is relatively simple. The method reduces the aggregate demographic statistics for any given group to their annual average, which is then equated to the index number of "100." The extent to which the figures for any given month (for example, those on the frequency of births) exceed this average gives an index that is above 100 (e.g., 132). The extent to which they fall below this average gives them a negative index number (e.g., 78). The formula used to calculate the running index numbers for a given year is:

$$\text{Index number} = \frac{Ti \ / \ T}{Ni \ / \ 365.25} \times 100$$

Where:
Ti = the number of demographic events (births, marriages, deaths) in that month
T = the total number of such demographic events in that year
Ni = the number of days in the month for which the index is being calculated

Notes

1. The data were first commented on extensively in a major corpus of Latin inscriptions by Mommsen in the *Corpus Inscriptionum Latinarum* (henceforth *CIL*) I^1 (Berlin, 1862), nos. 822–1005; they were reedited by Ernst Lommatzsch in *CIL* I^2 (Berlin, 1918), nos. 1015–1198 (with the three suspected *falsae* [forged] at 1199–1201); the whole set was then reedited again in the light of inspection of the surviving vases by Mommsen, Bormann, and Mau by Mommsen in *CIL* VI.2, E. Bormann, W. Henzen and C. Huelsen, editors (Berlin, 1882), nos. 8211–8397, pp. 1103–1110. The most recent "incorporation" of them is to be found in *CIL* 1^2, fasc. iv, with the inscriptions themselves edited by Attilio Degrassi, third addendum text edited by Hans Kummrey (Berlin, 1986), nos. 1015–1201. Warmington (1940), 12–15, nos. 19–38, included a selection, with comments, as did Herman Dessau, *Inscriptiones Latinae Selectae* (1862–1916, henceforth *ILS*), 7839a–g, who offered a selection of seven of them. For facsimile drawings of some of the urns and inscriptions, see *CIL: Voluminis Primi: Tabulae Lithographae* (Berlin, 1862), plates xiii–xiv: "Ollae San Caesarianae," especially plate xiv, for some fine illustrations of the burial urns themselves. Despite their peculiar importance, they do not seem to have been made the object of any specific study in the last century; they have therefore not entered into general discussions of death culture in Roman society such as those offered by Toynbee (1971) or, more recently, by Morris (1992).

2. Festus, p. 148 (Lindsay 1965[1913]): s.v. "*Membrum*": "*Membrum abscidi mortuo dicebatur, cum digitus eius dicidebatur, ad quod servatum iusta fierent reliquo corpore conbusto*" ["Limb": "A limb was said to be cut off from the deceased, when his or her finger was cut off, on the grounds that, once it had been properly saved for this purpose, the proper funerary rituals could be performed after the rest of the body had been burnt"], as noted by Huelsen in his notes in *CIL* VI (1902), p. 3455.

3. *CIL* X 1935 = *ILS* 7841D (Puteoli): *Chrematine Numisiae ornatrix obieit VI eidus Octobr(ibus) Paullo Fabio Maximo Q. Aelio cos., ossua conlecta IV idus Oct. eisdem cos., Diaphrus conservae*. ["Chrematinê the (slave) beautician of Numisia, died on the sixth day before the Ides of October (10 October) in the consulships of Paullus Fabius Maximus and Quintus Aelius [Tubero] (11 BC); her bones were collected on the fourth day before the Ides of October (12 October) in the year of the same consuls. Diaphrus to his fellow (female) slave."]

4. In an age well before the legitimizing effects of social history, Baldini felt the need to close his perceptive analysis with an extended apology that reveals something of the changing aesthetics of scholarship: "I therefore end my presentation instead with a beautiful inscription recorded on a great marble plaque, with its text repeated on both sides of the stone, found just outside the lands of our Vineyard of San Cesario on the 7th of July of the year 1735. It is composed in the golden style which will sweeten the palate of one who has read, perhaps with a little disgust, the foul and foolish inscriptions on our vases" (Baldini 1738:161). Baldini obviously thought that his elevated tastes, and those of his readers, would be mollified by the presentation of the more formal epitaph of the career of the Roman centurion from the high empire with which he ended his report (Baldini 1738:161). In this "classier" inscription (subsequently catalogued as *CIL* VI 3580 = *ILS* 2641), the career of a centurion, M. Blossius Pudens, was commemorated and celebrated by his freedman, M. Blossius Olympicus. The centurion's marble monument was, unlike our poor and humble vases, carefully preserved in the collections of the Vatican Museum, where it can be seen today.

5. The epitaph of the *ornatrix* Chrematinê from this group has already been noted above in note 3. *CIL* X 1938 = *ILS* 7841C (Puteoli); *CIL* X 1985 = *ILS* 7842 (Naples); *CIL* X 2039A = *ILS* 7843 (Ager Puteolanus); *Notizie degli scavi* (henceforth, *NdS*) 1892, p. 479 =

ILS 7844 (Puteoli); others were noted by Dennison (1898:373–398), at p. 376, no. 7 = *ILS* 7845 (Puteoli): the last, an urn, cylindrical in shape, found in the Via Domiziana in Puteoli in 1896, was about 26 cm high and about 95 cm in circumference. The excavator, given the reference on the urn to Cn. Domitio cons(ule), dated it to AD 32, but a number of late republican dates are equally possible: Cn. Domitius Ahenobarbus (von Pauly and Wissowa 1894 on, *Real-Encyclopädie,* henceforth *RE,* "Domitius," no. 21), consul in 96 BC; Cn. Domitius Calvinus (*RE,* "Domitius," no. 43), who was consul in 53 BC, and another Cn. Domitius Ahenobarbus (*RE,* "Domitius," no. 23), who was consul in 32 BC.

6. *NdS* (1892), p. 479 = *ILS*SP7844 comes from the same place in Puteoli as does Dennison (1898:376), no. 7 (the burials in the Via Domiziana area); and Dennison (1898:378), no. 11: another such cinerary urn bearing the inscription "*M. Caecilius Clymeni l(ibertus) Felix*" was found in 1888 in the same region of Puteoli; Dennison (1898:385), no. 30, is another found in 1897 in the same general area of the Via Campana. The Via Domiziana and the Via Campana were prime locations for urban burials, located about 2 km north of the center of Puteoli.

7. "Barnaeus" is an unusual name borne by one of the persons buried at San Cesario. *CIL* I² 1175 = VI 8371: *C. Valeri(us) C. l. Barnaes,* a freedman of the Valerii; Solin (1996), vol. 3, 602, remarks of this particular case "2 Jh. v. Chr." ["second century before Christ"]. But there are only 10 examples known, and all of the rest, including one with rather similar background, are dated by Solin to the period between Sulla and Caesar. The name is one used for slaves and freedmen, particularly in the region of Campania in the last half century of the republic: *CIL* X, 3875, 4131, 4205 (Capua), *NdS* (1900), p. 103 (Nola), and *CIL* IV, 1865, 2430 (Pompeii). A recent publication of finds from the Bay of Naples area has revealed this same rare name recorded on a vase for a burial made in the same manner and place as the other Puteoli burials noted above. Moreover, the notice in the inscription on the new urn from Puteoli also states it was the location of three such burial vases or *ollae. L'Année épigraphique* (henceforth, *AE*) 1986:157 (Puteoli): originally published by A. Parma, *Puteoli* 7–8 (1983–1984), 301–303, no. 4: "*loca tria* olla / *L(uci) Audi Barnae[i]*" ["three burial places; the cinerary urn of Lucius Audius Barnaeus"].

8. Quintilis: *CIL* VI 8231 = *CIL* I² 1035, 8261 = 1065, 8342 = 1146, 8354 = 1158; Sextilis: *CIL* VI 8221 = *CIL* I² 1025, 8250 = 1054, 8256 = 1060, 8266 = 1070, 8314 = 1118, 8336 = 1140, 8337 = 1141, 8391 = 1195; intercalary months: *CIL* VI 8224 = *CIL* I² 1028, 8225 = 1029 (?), 8259 = 1063, 8295 = 1099, 8368 = 1172. The old republican names for these months, it is true, *could* continue in literary and other usage, sometimes well into the high principate. As late as the first decades of the second century AD, a writer such as Tacitus could continue to refer to the months by their old republican names (e.g., *Ann.,* 15.41)—although in his case the archaic usage is surely a deliberate anachronistic one, deployed by the historian for artistic and ideological purpose. The evidence of most epigraphical texts, on the other hand, suggests that there was a fairly uniform shift to the new names for these months and, with the Julian reform of the calendar, a concomitant abandonment of the archaic intercalary system.

9. The diagnostic test based on orthography and phonology is not airtight because the archaic forms are found later, although usually in contexts that were deliberately archaizing. And some of the inscriptions do still retain the more archaic "*ei*" for long "*i*" in *idus, idibus* (e.g., *CIL* VI 832 = *CIL* I² 1025, 835 = 1028, 844 = 1038, 846 = 1040, 860 = 1054).

10. Michels (1967:102, 169–170) and Samuel (1972:163): the evidence is Livy 44.37.38, which reports an eclipse just before the Battle of Pydna, which he dates *a. d. iii non. Sept.* (3 September) in 168 BC. The eclipse is dated to 21 June by our calendar; the Roman calen-

dar was therefore about two and one-half months in advance of "true" time: see Marchetti (1976:402–426). And there is Livy's report (37.4.4) on events of 190 BC: an eclipse dated to *a. d. v. id. Quinct.* (11 July), which actually took place on 14 March (Julian). For more detail on the reconstitution of the chronology of the period, see Derow (1973:345–356), but with the cautions of Warrior (1991:80–87): (i) "Derow's Hypothesis of Intercalation in Alternate Years," pp. 80–82. In 190 BC, the Roman calendar was therefore about four months in advance of solar time. By the later republic, the time to which the San Cesario inscriptions would seem to date, it appears that more care was given to the matter of intercalation. Although the calendar tended to be a month or even two off of "true" time, it did not tend to become as erratic as in the early second century. I suspect that the wide-ranging geographical operations of the Punic Wars might have placed intercalation "on hold" throughout those years, thereby producing the considerable discrepancy apparent in the 190s.

11. Samuel (1972:163f.), who argues that the reference to winter campaign seasons and true dates would seem to match for reports for the years 149 BC (Appian, *Punika*, 99), 109 BC (Sallust, *Bellum Iugurthinum*, 37.3), and 66 BC (Plutarch, *Pompeius*, 34). But all of the cases are open to serious objections; see, for example, Samuel (1972:68, 162–163, no. 5) on the case in Plutarch. Even so, they permit a divergence of a month or two from true concordance. Samuel does not lend much credibility to any of the arguments, rejecting most of the cases proffered by Ginzel (1906–1914), vol. 2, 268–273 and Holzapfel (1885:320–333).

5
Population Relationships in and around Medieval Danish Towns

Hans Christian Petersen, Jesper L. Boldsen, and Richard R. Paine

The urban segment formed a small minority of the population in medieval Scandinavia. However, during the Middle Ages (AD 1000–1536), towns became an essential part of the fabric of society. (As discussed below, Danish cities seem small in comparison to other preindustrial cities, so we shall use the term "towns," which to us does imply a substantial urban population.) Only four towns are clearly documented in the late Viking Age, before AD 1000 (Andrén 1985). A few more probably existed, but their existence is difficult to prove. During the Middle Ages, new towns were founded, and older towns were formally recognized as such through getting *købstadsrettigheder* (exclusive rights of trade within a specified area). At the end of the Middle Ages, 63 communities in present-day Denmark (excluding the island of Bornholm in the Baltic Sea) were towns in the sense of *købstad* (i.e., market town). The majority (50) of these towns were founded before AD 1300 (cf. Figure 5-1). Except for the sparsely populated areas in central and western Jutland, the number of towns remained more or less constant during the last two centuries of the Middle Ages, but the total size of the population was probably halved during that period (Johansen 1991). This means that urban communities throughout the Middle Ages played an ever-increasing part in the history of Denmark, although their number did not increase constantly.

Medieval Danish towns were small compared to other preindustrial urban centers and some notable urban communities discussed in this volume. This raises a question: just how urban were they? Discussions of preindustrial cities tend to focus on a number of issues. These include not only size and density but also the heterogeneity of their populations (in terms of social status, economic specialization, and genetic makeup) and their relationships to rural populations (as market centers and as destinations for migrants). In this chapter we consider some of these issues in an attempt to place medieval towns in the larger context of preindustrial cities. We focus on three types of data from the osteological record:

●: towns founded before AD 1000, ■: towns founded AD 1000-1099, ▲: towns founded AD 1100-1199, ▼: towns founded 1200-1299.

Figure 5-1. Maps of present-day Denmark (except Bornholm), illustrating the spread of urban communities from AD 1000 (left) to 1300. Based on data from Andrén (1985).

(1) the age pattern of mortality, (2) variation in adult stature, and (3) morphological variability in craniometric traits of adult males. We use these lines of evidence to characterize different segments of the medieval Danish population and to assess the urban character of medieval Danish towns.

Trade formed the points of contact between the rural majority of the population and the international network of exchange of goods, people, and germs. It was monopoly of trade rather than size of the local population that set urban communities apart from large rural villages. Just after the end of the Middle Ages some 8 percent of the population outside of the capital, Copenhagen, lived in the market towns. The average population of these market towns was less than 1,000 persons. However, the towns yielding skeletons for the analyses in this chapter were larger than average. Both Ribe and Viborg reached 4,000 inhabitants in the Middle Ages. From a population perspective it appears that two general segments were present in the medieval towns of Scandinavia: *townspeople—sensu stricto* and *migrants*. Townspeople *sensu stricto* were people who belonged to families that had been living in a particular town for several generations. The migrants were recent arrivals from the surrounding rural areas or from other urban communities.

The urban population had a large number of choices when deciding where to be buried (Kieffer-Olsen 1993). This makes it difficult to pinpoint the population segment from which a specific cemetery sample of skeletons was derived. Demographic patterns are hard to reconstruct on the basis of skeletons derived from partly or even fully excavated cemeteries, and the uncertainty of the social meaning of being buried in any given cemetery only adds to the confusion. Here we cautiously attempt to sort out this confusion and identify population characteristics along the interface of the rural-urban continuum.

Mortality

The cemetery at Sct. Mikkel, near Viborg in Jutland (an urban setting), is the only site in the present study that yielded a skeletal series suitable for demographic analysis. The cemetery was laid down in two phases: an eleventh-century phase that predates a stone church erected on the site and a phase associated with the period when the stone church was in use (ca. 1100 to 1529). The following analyses are based on the burial phase associated with the stone church; skeletons from the eleventh-century deposits were too poorly preserved to be in included in the demographic analysis presented here.

The mortality profiles in Figure 5-2a (after Boldsen 1984b) exhibit clear differences in survival for males and females. Males have higher survivorship than females through the young adult years, but this advantage disappears at older ages. The difference is statistically significant ($\chi2 = 11.07$, df = 2, p < 0.005). The reconstruction method used here is described in Boldsen (1984b) and in Paine and Boldsen (1995, 1997). The shape of the curve of sex-based differences in

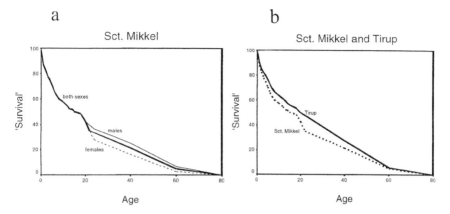

Figure 5-2. The distribution of age-at-death: (a) among the people buried in the Sct. Mikkel cemetery drawn in the shape of a survival curve; it is only possible to study the sexes separately for ages over 20 years; (b) for people buried in the Sct. Mikkel and the Tirup cemeteries drawn as survival functions. In these curves, the sexes have been combined.

adult mortality suggests that high levels of female mortality, at Sct. Mikkel and other medieval sites, were associated with childbearing (though see Walker 1995 for an alternative interpretation).

It is important to note that this is not a strictly medieval phenomenon; lower female survival throughout the reproductive years appears to be a characteristic of European agrarian populations from the Neolithic through the Middle Ages (Acsadi and Nemeskeri 1970; Paine and Boldsen 1995, 1997). Historical records (gathered from early parish registers) indicate that a similar pattern persisted in Denmark until at least the late seventeenth century (Paine and Boldsen 1995, 1997) and in England through much of the eighteenth century (Wrigley et al. 1997:303).

Given the assumption of high fertility levels, the maternal risk associated with childbirth need not have been high to create this pattern. In contemporary settings lacking effective modern medicine (Mace 2000), the maternal risk of death at childbirth outside a hospital is less than 1 percent. It follows a J-shaped function with high risk at first birth, which declines and then rises again in high-parity women (Mace 2000). However, because overall mortality tends to be low among reproductive-age adults, this can still have a significant effect. Mace and Sear (1996) have shown that even given a childbirth mortality under 1 percent (per birth), maternal mortality typically accounts for between 25 percent and 33 percent of all deaths of reproductive-age women in natural fertility populations. If fertility levels were sufficiently high, this could certainly account for male-female mortality differences at Sct. Mikkel.

Child mortality patterns from agrarian Europe (from the Neolithic through the Middle Ages) display a high degree of older-child loss and a high level of age-independent mortality (Paine and Boldsen 2002). Paine (2000) and Paine and Boldsen (2002) have suggested that the cause of these patterns was frequent epidemic cycles (for an illustration of this see Paine and Storey, this volume). In an environment where older children and young adults have a high risk of death, natural selection would be expected to favor early reproduction and short inter-birth intervals (Bentley et al. 2001; Paine 2000; Paine and Boldsen 2002).

Comparisons between Sct. Mikkel and the skeletal series from Tirup, a medie-val cemetery from a village parish in eastern Jutland (Boldsen 1997a, 1997b), suggest reduced survivorship among adolescents and young adults in the more ur-ban setting of Sct. Mikkel (Figure 5-2b). Large numbers of adolescent and young adult deaths are an outcome of catastrophic episodes (Keckler 1997; Paine 2000; Paine and Storey 1999, this volume, and R. Storey, this volume). Though the samples are small in both cases, and population growth is a potential confounding factor, differences in age at death between rural Tirup and "urban" Sct. Mikkel tend to support predictions (Boldsen 1984b) of a greater impact of epidemic disease on medieval Danish towns than on the surrounding countryside.

Together these patterns suggest some important characteristics of life in me-dieval Danish towns as well as in small agrarian and market towns generally. Epidemic diseases were probably a regular factor in community life. Medieval northern Europe experienced pandemic plague cycles in the sixth, seventh, and fourteenth centuries. Frequent outbreaks continued through the seventeenth cen-tury. Less historically notable epidemic events were probably regular occurrences. Such a pattern creates severe demographic stress. Epidemic events not only reduce population; they also suppress the population's ability to recover by dispropor-tionately reducing numbers of reproductive-age females (Paine 2000; Paine and Storey, this volume). High fertility and a significant mortality risk associated with childbearing are probable causes of the female survival disadvantage seen at Sct. Mikkel and similar sites.

Variation in Adult Stature

Stature is the most studied morphometric variable for humans. The dramatic increase of male adult stature over the last two centuries has puzzled human bi-ologists and been the subject of considerable public attention (e.g., Denmark Sta-tistics Department/Danmarks Statistik *Statistisk Årbog Statistical Yearbook* 1896–1990:Volumes 1–94). Furthermore, it has long been known that variation in stature is associated with social status (e.g., Mascie-Taylor and Boldsen 1985). It has been conventional wisdom to link these two phenomena and explain them as an association between conditions of living (well-being) and stature. However, the relationship between stature and health is complicated. Lasker and Mascie-Taylor (1989) have shown that at least part of the socially associated differences could be explained by selective social migration: tall people, on average, migrate up, and

Table 5-1. Descriptive Statistics for the Distribution of Height among the People Interred in Six Medieval Danish Parish Cemeteries

Site	Type	Sex	N	Mean	Variance	Standard Deviation
Sct. Mikkel	migrant	males	38	172.3	63.0	7.93
		females	34	158.3	39.4	6.28
Tirup	rural	males	65	166.6	50.5	7.11
		females	40	155.6	35.7	5.97
Ribe	urban	males	60	168.4	54.2	7.36
		females	39	155.6	22.8	4.78
Sct. Mathias	urban	males	3	162.2	53.6	7.32
		females	4	156.3	10.9	3.30
Svendborg	urban	males	20	164.9	68.1	8.25
		females	19	156.8	38.8	6.23
Nordby	rural	males	27	165.5	38.4	6.20
		females	12	152.4	51.8	7.20

short people migrate down, the social ladder. Boldsen and Søgaard (1998) have shown that there is absolutely no time-series association between mean stature and conditions of living during the twentieth century in Denmark. Although it is expected that better-situated people in the Middle Ages were taller than average (cf. Cinthio and Boldsen 1984), this relationship can in no way be taken for granted.

Since the nineteenth century scientists have taken considerable interest in the stature of people in the past (e.g., Pearson 1899). It has proven difficult to estimate stature from the length of long bones (Boldsen 1984a, 1990). However, during recent decades, Danish osteologists have routinely measured skeletal length in the grave, following a method developed by Boldsen (1984a), when excavating medieval cemeteries. This measure has been shown to reflect stature in a rather precise way (Petersen 2005). Therefore, we discuss measured stature (skeletal length recorded in the grave before taking the bones out of the ground) rather than height predicted from regression formulae.

Data on male and female stature from six different cemeteries were analyzed. The sites are all located in western Denmark—five in Jutland and one on Funen. All the stature measurements discussed here were taken using the method described by Boldsen (1984a). The descriptive statistics for measured heights are summarized in Table 5-1. Three of the sites were classified as burial places for townspeople *sensu stricto,* two sites are from rural communities, and one represents a migrant population in medieval Viborg. The data in Table 5-1 have previously

Table 5-2. Test Statistics for the Structure of Variance and Mean Height among Medieval Danish Communities

Effect	df	Variance χ^2	P	Mean χ^2	P
Among sites of same type and sex	6	4.21	p>0.05	7.79	p>0.05
Sex-type interaction	2	3.27	p>0.05	2.66	p>0.05
Type	2	0.96	p>0.05	24.68	p<0.001
Sex	1	9.41	p<0.01	266.16	p<0.001

been analyzed by Boldsen and Søgaard (1998), and the analysis here follows the same line of thought.

The data summarized in Table 5-1 were submitted to ANOVA (analysis of variance). The results are given in Table 5-2. Obviously, the sex difference was the single most important effect and, in fact, the only one acting on the variances. It appears that women in the Middle Ages on average were around 11.9 cm shorter than men from the same community and that males had a higher variance for stature than females. The sex effect on mean stature is so well known that it is almost trivial to report it. The population type effect, however, is quite surprising. It appears that people buried in the low-status Sct. Mikkel cemetery (the cemetery believed to represent a migrant population) were on average 4.8 cm taller than townspeople or the rural majority of Danes. In fact, this is an example of reversed polarity of a social gradient for height. The difference of stature between townspeople *sensu stricto* and villagers (1.0 cm) is statistically insignificant. Table 5-3 gives the estimates of stature for the two sexes of the three segments of the population in medieval Denmark.

The analysis of stature measured in the graves of medieval Danes indicates that there were clear, socially associated differences in the means. Of the three segments of society considered here, the migrant population was the tallest. Probably this segment of society formed less than 5 percent of the total population, so they would not influence the mean stature of the total population in any appreciable way. In this connection it is interesting that the mean height of townspeople *sensu stricto* and of the rural majority of the population do not differ significantly from the mean height of Danish men measured in the middle of the nineteenth century (Boldsen and Kronborg 1984).

Variability in Craniometric Traits among Adult Males

If medieval Danish towns were more heterogeneous economically, demographically, and socially than rural communities, as we assume of preindustrial cities

Table 5-3. Descriptive Statistics for the Distribution of Stature among Men and Women representing the Three Segments of the Population in Medieval Denmark

Type	Sex	n	Mean	s2	s.d.
Rural	males	92	166.3	47.0	6.9
	females	52	154.9	39.2	6.3
Migrant	males	38	172.3	63.0	7.9
	females	34	158.3	39.4	6.3
Urban	males	83	167.3	57.5	7.6
	females	62	156.0	27.1	5.2

generally, we expect them to contain more diverse populations than rural communities. Measuring morphological variability, here identified through craniometric traits, is one means of identifying relative population diversity, assuming that phenotypic variability is proportional to genetic variability

Dividing the medieval population into subgroups, we can predict patterns of variability. Villagers (the rural population) should be relatively homogeneous; they form small gene pools and are subject to common environmental influences. Townspeople should be relatively diverse. They tend to have multiple places of origin, form larger gene pools, and participate in a wider range of economic activities; thus they should be the most heterogeneous group, genetically and environmentally. Migrants may represent multiple origin points, but they are expected to have lower variability related to selective migration. We assume phenotypic variability is proportional to genetic variability.

In the present study, phenotypic variability was measured on the basis of variance-covariance matrices for five common frontal bone measurements (Table 5-4). These measurements were obtained from 282 adult male crania from 17 cemeteries in western Denmark (Jutland and Funen), covering the time period from AD 1100 to AD 1600. The cemeteries were divided into four categories, defined archaeologically: (1) village cemeteries; (2) town cemeteries; (3) town monastery cemeteries, which might be expected to differ from other town cemeteries; and (4) "migrant" cemeteries.

The variance-covariance matrices for cemeteries within each category were tested for homogeneity using Box's M, based on F-tests (Box 1949). No significant results were obtained, indicating that the within-category cemeteries could be pooled in order to obtain segmentwise matrices (Table 5-5). The pooled town and town monastery sample matrices were also compared. Again the result was not significant (F = 0.979, df = 15, 15031.5, p = 0.48), and so these two categories were also pooled. The resulting matrix was used to represent townspeople in general.

Table 5-4. Frontal Bone Measurements Employed

M9	Minimum frontal breadth
M10	Maximum frontal breadth
M26	Frontal sagittal arc
M29	Frontal sagittal chord
M43	Outer biorbital breadth

M#: Code according to Martin and Saller (1957).

Table 5-5. Frontal Bone Samples, Divided According to Type of Cemetery, and p-Values for Intratype Test of Variance-Covariance Homogeneity

Segment	No. cemeteries	No. crania	F	df1	df2	p-value
Town proper	2	34	1.647	15	3,124.6	0.055
Town monastery	5	95	1.065	60	15,832.3	0.341
Migrant	3	51	1.047	30	1,125.8	0.398
Village	7	102	1.114	90	4,644.3	0.218

On the basis of these results, and using the pooled segmentwise matrices with their respective degrees of freedom, the population segments (villagers, townspeople, and migrants) were compared using an approach similar to a discriminant analysis. In this approach, one matrix is employed as a reference matrix, representing baseline variability. The other matrix, the hypothesis matrix, is tested for surplus variability compared to this baseline variability. The reference matrix is thus assumed to represent the segment with the least variability. Key and Jantz (1990) originally presented the basic elements of this method for osteological studies (see Appendix).

If the F-test statistic is significant, the hypothesis matrix has more variability than the reference matrix. Nonsignificance does not imply the reference matrix has more variability than the hypothesis matrix. A separate test, reversing the reference matrix and the hypothesis matrix, must be performed.

The pooled village matrix was chosen as the reference matrix, representing baseline variability. The other matrices were compared to it. For comparisons within towns, the pooled migrant matrix was chosen as the reference matrix. Table 5-6 clearly demonstrates the greater craniometric variability of the townspeople compared to either villagers or migrants. This supports general reconstruc-

Table 5-6. Results of Intersegment Comparisons of Morphometric Variability

Comparison, baseline segment to the left	F	df1	df2	p-value
Village vs. town	1.219	610	460	0.012
Village vs. migrant	0.862	240	458.5	0.902
Migrant vs. town	1.392	610	225.4	0.002

tions of medieval Danish towns as genetically and environmentally diverse, i.e., increasingly "urban" places. Comparisons of craniometric variability also support strongly the archaeological identification of migrant cemeteries within towns. Migrants do appear to be a selected group (selective migration also appears to be a factor in stature differences; see above). It should be reemphasized that these patterns are currently demonstrated for males only. Similar studies of females are ongoing.

Conclusion

The overall conclusion is that it is indeed possible to identify different segments of the medieval Danish town population. The presence of two different segments and the lively traffic to and from towns is indicated by both stature and craniometric variability. This distinction indicates that the presumed migrant cemeteries have a special recruitment compared to other town cemeteries. Higher stature as well as reduced variability with regard to craniometric traits presumably reflects selective migration from villages to towns. The mortality pattern for the migrant segment indicates more severe conditions than for the village segment. On the basis of these indications it is possible to get insight into the palaeodemography of medieval society in general and the dynamic role played by the towns in particular. Consequently, when combined with archaeological results, the findings of the present study facilitate the identification of town population segments.

Appendix

Key and Jantz (1990) used a chi-square test to study intrasample variability. They erroneously based their test on N as degrees of freedom for a single cemetery matrix. In the present study an F-test was used because chi-square tests are prone to give liberal p-values with small sample sizes. The tests were based on N-1 degrees of freedom for single cemetery matrices. The number of degrees of freedom for pooled matrices is $\Sigma N_q - q$, where q is the number of samples pooled. The number of degrees of freedom for the reference matrix is called df_w, and the number of degrees of freedom for the hypothesis matrix is called df_h.

First, one calculates the sum-of-squares-and-cross-product matrices of the reference and hypothesis matrices, respectively: $SSCP_w$ and $SSCP_h$. Then calculate Λ:

$$\Lambda = \frac{|SSCP_w|}{|SSCP_w + SSCP_h|}$$

Then, the F-test statistic (one sided) is calculated as follows, in accordance with Rao (1973: 555f.):

$$F = \frac{(1 - \Lambda^{1/S})}{\Lambda^{1/S}} * \frac{df_2}{df_1}$$

where

$$df_1 = P*df_h \quad \text{and} \quad df_2 = M*S - \frac{P*df_h}{2} + 1 \text{ where}$$

df_1, and df_2 are the degrees of freedom,

$$M = df_w + df_h - \frac{(P + df_h + 1)}{2} \text{ and}$$

$$S = \sqrt{\frac{(P*df_h)^2 - 4}{P^2 + df_h^2 - 5}}$$

6

Colonial and Postcolonial New York

Issues of Size, Scale, and Structure

Nan A. Rothschild

A modern New Yorker transported back in time 300 or 350 years would not recognize the early city and would probably not even allow that it *was* a city. Much of the difference relates to size in its various manifestations—spatial area, numbers of residents, and density. However, the New York of 1700 as well as the New Amsterdam of 1650 was urban—"urban" being a relative rather than an absolute concept. (When I use the term "New York" here I mean Manhattan, because during the period in question, the other boroughs had not yet been incorporated into New York City.) It was a central place in its region, with dense settlement, specialized structures and services, and many other attributes that signal "city" (Blanton 1976). Cities are important and fascinating places and are also difficult to comprehend. They are by no means uniform from one to another or internally, and yet they have certain similarities that allow them to be seen as a group.

Anthropologists and other social scientists (geographers, sociologists, planners, and historians) have presented various models that explain urban differences and contribute to understanding how cities function. These models invoke a number of distinctive differences besides size and may be useful in evaluating New York in its earlier forms. Some scholars have suggested bimodal categories to characterize different urban types (such as preindustrial and industrial, Sjoberg 1960; Gemeinschaft-Gesellschaft, Tonnies 1974; Great and Little Traditions, Redfield and Singer 1954) or other schemes (Mumford 1961; Wirth 1938). Geography's central place theory is in some ways the most successful of these approaches. However, although many of these observations provide useful insights into important characteristics of urban life, such systems in general are too simple to allow for the range of complexity in urban forms and correlated behavior.

In this chapter I will discuss several aspects of early New York and its archaeological evaluation. Two relate to observable attributes, namely, size and social structure, whereas the others, applied by the archaeologist, concern the scale of analysis and type of data used to investigate the city. None of these is an independent variable. Size and structure are consequences of other processes, and analytic scale and data are chosen to illuminate specific research questions. Size and growth rate offer an easy way to monitor complex changes in the city, and given the nature of this volume, I begin with them.

Size and Growth Rate

Using criteria of population size and rate of growth as a basis, we can see that there were substantial differences in the community known as New York during the period between 1700 and 1870. I have chosen these dates because they mark watersheds in the city's population growth. Prior to this period, the seventeenth-century city of New Amsterdam was quite small (in 1628 it included 270 residents; when the British took control in 1664 it had 1,500). After the period, in 1880, Manhattan was home to more than one million people as the continuing influx of immigrants grew to new proportions. In examining the selected period of 1700–1870, we can see that around the turn of the century the population and especially the rate of population increase changed rather dramatically (Figure 6-1). Because size is a significant factor in community existence, it is worth considering the effects, if any, of this growth. Did these objective and striking changes in growth rate and population imply meaningful differences in the lives of early New Yorkers?

On the basis of these parameters, I suggest there were two different urban entities in New York, which I will call the "colonial" and "postcolonial" cities. These names not only are chronologically descriptive but also reflect meaningful differences in the communities described. At the same time, however, these changes are themselves the result of complex processes, and the possible explanations for this growth are the most crucial elements in the story. I will describe them briefly; a full account is beyond the scope of this chapter. The postcolonial and colonial cities were administered for different purposes, and with quite different visions, moving from periphery to core in Wallerstein's terms (1974), with the city becoming the focal point of its own history (Wolf 1982). A number of urban historians (notably Blackmar 1989; Burrows and Wallace 1998; Nash 1979) have suggested that specific economic changes were crucial in producing a new, commercially driven urban entity, the transition occurring sometime between the first third of the eighteenth and the early nineteenth century. They would view population change as a mirror of these other alterations—a perspective with which I agree.

Analytic Scale and Data

Urban anthropological archaeologists studying cities such as New York have available a range of investigative methods, depending on their interests and the nature

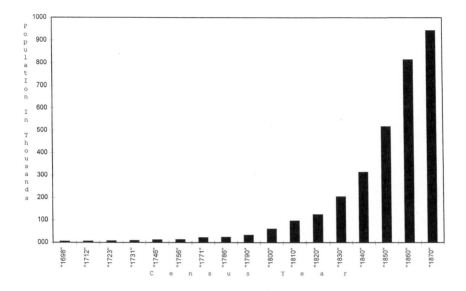

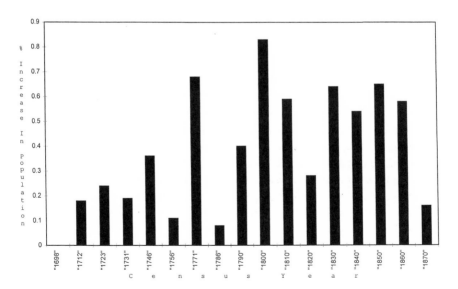

Figure 6-1. (*top*) Population of New York City, 1698–1870; (*bottom*) Rate of population increase in New York City, 1698–1870.

of the project. The most important choices concern the scale of analysis and the kind of data used. They have used information of two major kinds, one based on the analysis of artifacts and the other on land-use change, looking at urban layout and growth in a manner comparable to settlement pattern or space syntax analyses (Hillier and Hanson 1984). The scale of examination has ranged from small-scale projects (a household or subgroup within the city) to larger-scale studies of the whole city or its components. The most successful urban archaeological projects, in my opinion, have considered large-scale questions such as the following: How did a city develop? How was land use controlled? How did it organize its regional system? How did its various parts cohere? How did the landscape change as it grew?

At a small scale of analysis, one observes the ways in which the smallest urban social unit, the family or household, reflects, rejects, and makes personal the conditions and events in the wider sphere. Many of the small-scale kinds of questions have been addressed successfully in the postcolonial city when industrial capitalism was more fully developed, class structure was better defined, and New Yorkers used material markers of class to identify themselves to their neighbors. The choice of analytic scale and data type are selected according to the research questions of the project and are independent of parameters of urban size.

New York is different from many of the cities discussed in this volume in its history and the circumstances of its development. It was created de novo as a trading center by the Dutch and grew as the world economy expanded and forms of transportation changed. In considering its hinterland I suggest that it had a variety of hinterlands of differing sizes. It was fed by an area that includes portions of today's Long Island, New Jersey, and Westchester and Putnam counties. Farm produce and meat from domestic animals (sometimes the animals themselves on the hoof) were brought in to markets—initially periodic, but later permanent—along the East River and subsequently the Hudson shore (Rothschild 1990). The limits of this catchment relate to the ability to preserve the foods involved and the enlargement of the catchment with faster transportation and refrigeration. Other forms of hinterlands involve the city as a marketing, manufacturing, and shipping center. Raw materials were brought in from varying distances and exported as finished goods (e.g., leather hides were made into shoes, and wood was made into ships). European and other imports were also unloaded in New York's harbor and sent out to another form of hinterland, one that could perhaps be described as the area that fell under the city's sphere of influence, determining which technological innovations or new ceramic styles were worth having (Salwen et al. 1981). The relationship between city and hinterland is also complex in regard to the links connecting residents. New York City was the point of entry for thousands of European and other immigrants who stayed in the city only briefly and then emigrated to rural areas in other parts of the city and its environs or further inland. Some family members remained behind, however, and ethnic and kinship ties continued to exist between urban and rural folk.

Finding Sites

As archaeologists, we face a challenge comparable to that of blind people studying an elephant by feel. Fieldwork is slow and expensive; sampling is essential; but in order to design a sampling strategy, a great deal of information is needed to interpret the data from the sample. The benefit of doing research in the historic period is that there is extensive documentary information available, much of which must be examined before any fieldwork is conducted. Another factor that feeds into this complex picture is the way in which research sites are selected in a city such as New York. There have been two means by which sites have become available for excavation. Large blocks, mostly in lower Manhattan, have been chosen as project areas because the New York City Landmarks Preservation Commission has required developers to conduct archaeological evaluation of project areas in accordance with environmental protection laws; three of these blocks were excavated in compliance with similar federal legislation. Small sites, mostly backyard features such as privies or cisterns in residential areas such as Greenwich Village or sections of Brooklyn, where nineteenth-century buildings still stand, have sometimes been made available by landowners and excavated as field school sites or as other types of projects.

Thus, site selection is determined by a variety of factors, including the vagaries of development and the effectiveness with which environmental protection legislation is enforced, rather than by intellectual priorities. In order to utilize data generated by these projects effectively, we will ultimately need to impose a framework on the city as a site that will allow any project area to be incorporated. Geographic Information Systems (GIS) technology will be essential to this project. The framework would consist of a series of temporal layers providing information on land use and land ownership; the spatial distribution of inhabitants by ethnicity, social class, and occupation; and locations of major institutions of the time, among other factors. The framework would allow archaeologists working at any scale to propose meaningful research questions.

The Relationship between Size and Urban Life

In order to get a measure of the size of a community, observers use a variety of parameters, physical size and population being the most common. Both of these are relevant, as is the relationship between them, which yields another significant variable, density. Although these measurements are fairly easy to calculate and use, they are not sufficient to evaluate the changing conditions in the city and its hinterland, which, in some sense, they monitor. However, there are two ways in which size alone is important, with both applicable to the aspect of the whole city as community. One concerns the possibility of familiarity with one's fellow residents, which declines as their number increases. The other relates to physical access to the entire urban space. The area of a city, in combination with the available means of transport, will dictate whether residents are able to travel easily to all parts of the community.

Colonial New York was basically a walking city, although horses and horse-drawn coaches were available to some. Travel on foot was supplemented by cart men who, either alone or by horse, pulled wagons laden with goods (Burrows and Wallace 1998:188). From its southern tip to its northern extent, the grid of streets that had been laid out by 1797 stretched a bit over one and one-half miles, and the same distance measured its widest east-west dimension; the actual area that had been settled was considerably smaller (Figure 6-2 top; Rothschild 1990). Healthy adult residents went everywhere on foot.

The New York City in existence between 1800 and 1870 came to be a place that was not completely accessible on foot. The commissioners' plan extended the grid to 155th Street in 1811. Elite and middle-class residents began to acquire homes that were separate from their workplaces early in the nineteenth century (Wall 1994). The Dripps Map of 1851 shows scattered settlement (Stokes 1918:3:Plate 138) above 50th Street, and when Central Park was created in the mid-1850s, there were close to 60,000 people living in the three wards north of 40th Street (Rosenzweig and Blackmar 1992:60). By 1864, half of the city's residents lived north of 14th Street (Mackay 1987:20); Union Square was the city's geographic center (Scherzer 1992:27).

Horsecars were available for the privileged, but there was no mass transport until the 1830s, when the first of the "street railroads" was introduced. The New York and Harlem systems used horse-drawn cars running on tracks from 23rd Street to the Harlem River and had a branch that crossed Manhattan at 125th Street (Homberger 1994:77). Additional lines followed in the late 1840s and 1850s. The lack of public transportation (and its cost when it was introduced [Scherzer 1992:26]) meant that the elite had access to the entire city while most citizens were restricted to portions of it. The process of sorting urban space by wealth, homeownership, and occupation had begun.

The population ranged from almost 5,000 in 1698 to 33,131 in 1790, but the rate of population increase during this time was around 25–35 percent for what were mainly ten-year periods and was always less than 45 percent. The single exception for the pre-1790 period in Figure 6-1 bottom shows the increase between 1756 and 1771 as 68 percent, but when standardized to a ten-year interval, it is 45 percent. Beginning in 1800, population increase took place at a much faster rate; most intervals show a growth rate greater than 55 percent per decade. There are two exceptions: between 1860 and 1870 (the effects of the Civil War, no doubt) and 1810–1820 (perhaps because of the Panic of 1819 [Burrows and Wallace 1998:479]). The very large increase between 1790 and 1800 is related to the post–Revolutionary War repopulation of the city, to New York's prestige as temporary capital of the United States (Burrows and Wallace 1998:299), and especially to its development as the center of European imports; between the early 1790s and 1807, the value of imported goods funneled through New York in-

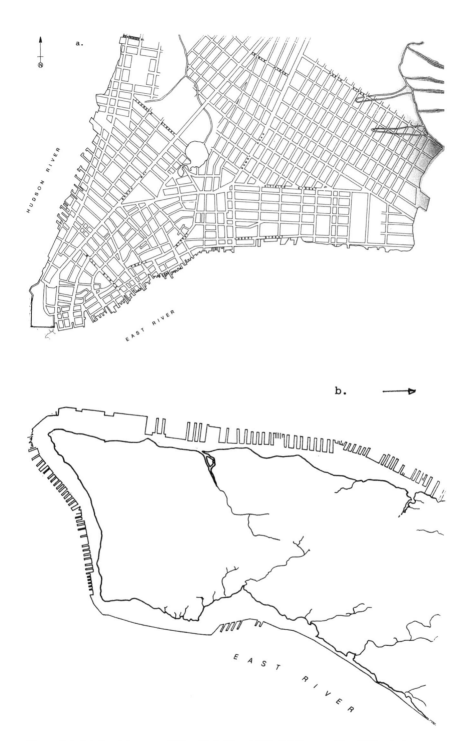

Figure 6-2. (a.) Spatial extent of New York City, 1797; (b.) Extent of landfilling in lower Manhattan. Direction of arrow indicates north.

creased from $1.4 million to $7.6 million (Burrows and Wallace 1998:333). By 1810, New York was the largest city in the United States (Jackson 1995:xi). The population densities for three dates in three different centuries of the city's history are 18,533 per sq km in 1695, 11,969 per sq km in 1756, and 26,255 per sq km in 1817. Both the seventeenth- and nineteenth-century figures are notably higher than average for a preindustrial city, and the eighteenth-century density is a respectable urban density for a city of any period (Storey 1997a, 1997b). These densities serve as a second indicator of the dramatic growth of New York throughout the period covered by this study.

The influence of the Erie Canal, which opened in 1825, cannot be overstated. As the cost of transport dropped (from $100 per ton to $9 per ton), the volume of transported goods increased radically, and the types of goods shipped also expanded (Burrows and Wallace 1998:431). New York became the hub of a greater proportion of all shipping in the United States, involving imports as well as local and midwestern products such as vegetables and timber. The huge number of ships moored in New York harbor required extensive dock construction on the Hudson and East rivers beginning in 1815 (Burrows and Wallace 1998:435); all this activity meant that jobs and population in the city increased, tripling in every ward between 1821 and 1835 (Burrows and Wallace 1998:576). Waves of immigrants from European countries—Germany, England, and Ireland— swamped the city. Three million arrived between 1840 and 1860, although many simply passed through on their way to other destinations. These immigrants were supplemented by thousands of rural Americans coming to the city to find a better life (Burrows and Wallace 1998:736).

As population expanded, the density and intensity of land use also increased. One measure of intensity can be seen in the ratio of "developed" land (covered by buildings or claimed in a formal way as part of a community's space—streets, sidewalks, and public parks) to "undeveloped" land (empty lots or portions of lots). A comparison of New York (Manhattan); Brooklyn, an independent town/ city consisting of a cluster of urbanites and farmers who produced food for New York and Providence, Rhode Island, shows that Manhattan land use was more intense than either of the other two early cities during the period studied (1650– 1920); it also grew at faster rate until the turn of the nineteenth century (Figure 6-3, Rothschild 1985). Brooklyn absorbed much of New York's overflow and by 1860 was the fourth-largest city in the United States (Fitts and Yamin 1996:2). Another aspect of this intensity is the pervasive and characteristic housing shortage in the city that resulted from the manipulation of land from a relatively early period (Blackmar 1989).

The process of landfilling, which had greatly enlarged lower Manhattan, had slowed down by 1800, but other attempts to regularize settlement (and make the sale of land easier) can be seen in the commissioners' plan completed in 1811 (Burrows and Wallace 1998:421), which firmly superimposed a rectangular grid

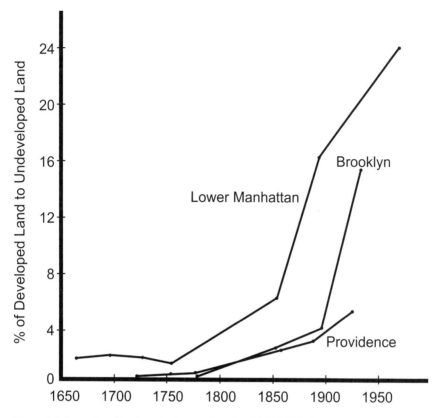

Figure 6-3. Intensity of land use in three early cities, 1650–1950.

on all but the already existing streets of lower Manhattan (and stubborn areas such as Greenwich Village, which refused to have its streets rearranged) and determined how growth would proceed. It laid out 12 south-to-north streets as far as 155th Street, following the long axis of the island, intersected at regular intervals by wide streets, and provided space for parks, a reservoir, and a marketplace. The rationality of this approach reflects the fact that by the mid-eighteenth century (Blackmar 1989:28) land had come to be a commodity, to be accumulated and sold in order to make money. Early in the nineteenth century, as the merchant elite (and then others in the upper and middle classes) separated their homes and workplaces (Wall 1994), there was a shift from areas of mixed land use to more specialized zones (Geismar 1985). For example, in colonial New York, the port area was the best place for merchants to have their homes/trading businesses, but the area was never exclusively an elite zone (Rothschild 1990). However, as merchants moved out, the area gradually became commercial, with a mixture of transient residents, maritime workers, prostitutes, and the poor. Developing residential areas began to be segregated by class into tenant neighborhoods and "respectable" areas (Blackmar 1989:104).

Social structural changes were driving some of these land-use changes, as wealth came to be increasingly concentrated in and controlled by a smaller segment of the city's residents (Rothschild 1990:111), and the class system was hardening while industrial capitalism progressed. The organization of labor shifted from a system in which apprentices learned trades from master craftsmen, hoping to advance to this status themselves, to a system characterized by a permanent laboring class with little chance of mobility. Apprentices and journeymen lost the ability to advance in their trades and no longer had the opportunity to live with the master's family (Burrows and Wallace 1998:635); they became tenants and workers. The union movement was born in the 1830s; by 1836 two-thirds of New York's workers had joined 52 unions (Burrows and Wallace 1998:605).

Archaeology's Contribution to Understanding New York

As noted earlier, archaeological analyses of the city have been conducted at different scales of analysis, using two primary kinds of information: land-use change and artifact analysis. Excavation and documentary information are required for all projects, but the research questions may be different for each.

Land-Use Analysis

Much of the research considering changes in land use has focused on the city's development, including leveling and filling. The methods of holding landfill in place are rarely documented; it is only through excavation that they have been revealed. Both the methods used and the labor needs required seem to have varied widely over time as filling moved out from the original shore and the river bottom depth increased. Archaeology on the first set of blocks to be filled along the East River, at the Seven Hanover Square block and 64 Pearl Street (which were filled between 1687 and 1697), showed that the fill was held by the stone foundations of the first structures. This was possible because the buildings were close to the shoreline, and depths were not great (Figure 6-2 bottom; Rothschild 1990). Later landfilling projects required greater capital and organization. A series of East Side sites filled during the eighteenth century, including the Telco and 175 Water Street blocks (both filled between 1730 and 1740 and 1755 and 1776; Geismar 1985; Sapan 1985) and the Assay Site (filled between 1789 and 1803), revealed the extensive technology of cribbing, cobb wharves, and bulkheads (Huey 1984). The 175 Water Street and the 207 Front Street sites uncovered another technique used to hold fill in place—the sinking of an old merchant ship (the Ronson ship was recovered at 175) across a series of house lots, presumably a cooperative effort. It can be assumed that those who incurred the costs of filling the land during this period did so because they expected to generate increased income through control of the waterfront, shipping, and merchant trade (Sapan 1985).

The material used for fill came from a number of sources. There are reports that some early fill used the labor of the poor (and perhaps the enslaved) who leveled hills in lower Manhattan (Geismar 1993), and the contents of the fill indicate that residents also deposited their domestic refuse and other debris and that some was brought by dirt carriers and butchers from nearby markets (Geismar 1987). The fill deposits are the equivalent of huge and valuable garbage middens, containing large quantities of organic materials that were better preserved in fill because of the more consistent moisture of the surrounding matrix. Close stratigraphic and content analysis of the landfill at Seven Hanover Square suggests "basket-loading" (constructing a fill with basketloads of earth) and the deposition of materials generated by the owners of some of the water lots (Rothschild and Pickman 1990).

Another form of large-scale analysis focuses on the changing urban landscape and considers how residents of the city navigated (Lynch 1960) and what their spatial cues would have been. This approach does not necessarily involve excavation, but imagines how landmarks, distinctive buildings, and the waterfront would have served as organizing factors. Early maps offer clues as to some of the spaces and structures that were considered important—the King's Farm, churches, and public buildings such as the City Tavern, the Exchange, or city hall. In its initial perspective, New Amsterdam and New York faced Europe; the waterfront was the important place in terms of both economy and orientation. By the end of the eighteenth century, after the Revolution, both the culture and the economy had shifted; the city faced inward, with Broadway, Wall and Broad streets, the Merchants' Coffee House, the Exchange, the Bank of New York, and Trinity Church at its core.

As the city grew larger and more stratified, somewhat separate landscapes of power and meaning would have been constructed according to class, ethnicity, gender, and age. This would have developed during the nineteenth century, when not all segments of the city were accessible to all. Space was beginning to be sorted by wealth and where one worked, determining where one lived and depending on what forms of transport were available (foot, ferry, or coach). Young, healthy, and motivated New Yorkers could and did cover much ground on foot. An analysis of the diary of a visitor to the city in 1854, Jeremiah O'Donovan, shows that he moved around through lower Manhattan and up the West Side as far as present-day Hell's Kitchen (the low 40s) on foot, selling his book to fellow Irish (Scherzer 1992:165). On the other hand, a carriage and coachman made life easier for the Robsons, an upper-middle-class family living on Washington Square in Greenwich Village around the same time. Perhaps Dr. Robson used it to go back and forth easily from his downtown office (Wall 1999:106). By the late nineteenth and early twentieth centuries, this sorting of occupants would have been well established, and zones with specific characteristics were imposed on the theoretically neutral grid plan (Scherzer 1992).

Landscape analysis at a somewhat smaller scale has been used to examine the social geography of neighborhoods. There are two different questions of interest at this level: first, to what degree were residents aware of a neighborhood as a meaningful place? Second, how coherently defined were neighborhoods, and how consistent were they in their composition?

The first question is difficult to answer. It is possible that the concept of neighborhood was late in developing, in part because of "Moving Day." A characteristic of the nineteenth century, "Moving Day," May 1, was the day each year when much of New York's population (tenants and, to a lesser degree, owners) could be ousted or choose to move (Blackmar 1989:213). One writer suggests that this practice may have furthered the separation of workers from emerging middle- and upper-class residents and that home ownership enhanced the increasing awareness (after 1830) that neighborhoods were distinctively different from one another (Scherzer 1992:27, 50, 52). It should be noted that some of the earliest characterizations of particular neighborhoods were negative ones assigned by outsiders (as dens of poverty and iniquity characterized by vice, disease, and prostitution), as was true of the Five Points area so maligned by such writers as Charles Dickens (1842).

Regardless of whether people were aware that the area they lived in was a distinctive (or even named) place, most city dwellers spent most of their time in a relatively small area, working and living there and frequenting local markets or merchants. It seems likely that these areas would have acquired identities, especially the newly formed more homogeneous ones uptown and those occupied by people at the extremes of the social spectrum. An interesting analysis of witnesses to marriages shows that a large proportion of these close ties were formed among local neighbors (Scherzer 1992:172–173).

The second question has been discussed by a number of social historians who have noted that prior to the nineteenth century, there were no relatively uniform neighborhoods in New York; most land use was quite mixed (Abbott 1974; Blackmar 1989:107; Wilkenfeld 1975) in terms of wealth and functional specialization or occupation. Residence and workplace were often housed in the same building, and rich, middling, and poor lived on the same streets. My research examined the degree of homogeneity within small spatial areas and suggests that the most significant basis of spatial clustering was that of ethnicity during the eighteenth century; early in the century, Dutch and English settlers lived separately from one another, whereas at the end of the period, the original settlers no longer lived separately from one another, but more recent immigrants (such as Scots and Germans) and those whose ethnicity was assigned to them (Jews and free blacks) were found in clustered locations on certain streets. This was presumably the same kind of adaptive strategy that urban migrants continue to use today in many parts of the world.

Further research revealed that when household location was evaluated, the closest residences in the early part of the eighteenth century were those of kin, who lived within a block or two of one another. This proximity did not persist late in the century, probably because housing choices were more constrained (Rothschild 1992). In 1789, although ethnic ties were spatially expressed among some groups, the beginnings of economic-based clusters were also apparent. Merchants were aggregated to a greater extent than other groups, and a second cluster appearing early in the nineteenth century consisted of artisans involved in ship-building (coopers, ship carpenters) and mariners working on ships.

A new project is investigating a fascinating community that appears to have been ethnically mixed, with African American and Irish immigrant residents. It existed for about 30 years (1825–1856) between 81st and 89th streets, close to Eighth Avenue, in what is now Central Park. African Americans bought land there because it was inexpensive, and after 1821, African American men who wished to vote had to own property worth $250. The Irish were tenants. The community had three churches and a school; its residents were evicted when the land was taken through laws of eminent domain so that the park could be built (Wall et al. 2001).

Artifact Analysis

The analysis of material remains has focused particularly on excavated kitchen and dining wares and food remains, supplemented by documentary research. Trash from household features and larger areas has produced a variety of interesting insights about the early city. The kinds of research questions posed, and to some degree their success, have varied between the colonial and postcolonial cities. A basic and useful form of information derived from deposits on the 175 Water Street block was reported by Geismar (1985), who observed that feature fill could be identified as dominated by either domestic or commercial materials and dated, providing a glimpse into the changing activities taking place on a single block over time. Given the right kinds of material, an archaeologist could presumably apply this technique to any large, multihouse lot site with time depth and get an internal view of how activities in the area were shifting.

Most analyses that make use of these artifact classes, however, have examined these data for manifestations of social status, especially class and ethnicity, to see how well these are represented in the archaeological record. Class has been more susceptible to identification than ethnicity, relying on the cost of assemblages. Class was relatively well defined in the postcolonial city, when capitalism was emerging strongly, but was less relevant in the colonial city, when ethnicity seems to have been more relevant. Meta Fayden Janowitz's study (1993) of the persistence of Dutch food ways (seen in ceramics and to some degree in faunal material) after 1664, when the British assumed control of the colony, allows us to look at the inner workings of the community and the way in which colonial power gradually permeates a society. According to her research, the shift from a dominant Dutch influence to a British one, seen in ceramic imports and the manufacture of local ceramics in the British style, did not happen for 60–80 years after the transfer of political power.

Another analysis of a series of later (eighteenth century) faunal assemblages from the Stadt Huys and Seven Hanover Square blocks (Rothschild 1990) linked the assemblages to individuals whose ethnicity was known and whose wealth was assessed by their tax rank (as a proxy for class). This study found greater variability than consistency in faunal remains linked to ethnicity, class, and rank, although the sample of identifiable deposits was small. European ethnicity is difficult to detect in faunal remains because it was expressed more clearly in spices and cooking style than in meat choices. One merchant family ate large quantities of expensive meats such as beef, whereas another similar family ate less meat but used only costly cuts such as sirloin and short loin. By the mid-eighteenth century, many New Yorkers had shifted to a more economical diet with substantial amounts of chicken and fish. The relationship between food and class seems to have been closer in the nineteenth century as class structure strengthened and there was more dining in public.

As the eighteenth century ended and the postcolonial period began, a number of factors had changed in New York, making urban life as well as the potential for archaeological analysis quite different. The most significant of these changes relates to the reformulation and hardening of class. Associated with this process is the increasing importance of material symbols used to express certain qualities as well as social rank. Much of the early archaeology in New York City had examined deposits from elite households, but a number of archaeologists began to examine middle- and working-class deposits in the 1990s. Diana Wall evaluated Bourdieu's (Bourdieu 1984:48, cited in Wall 1991) statement that the perception of class is as important as the actuality and is established by patterns of consumption by studying ceramic assemblages from a series of mostly middle-class nineteenth-century households in Greenwich Village. She found a remarkable consistency in the major ware types used in these homes. They were dominated by plain, paneled, Gothic-style ironstone everyday dishes, which signaled the home as a sacred space, a refuge from the commercial world. Tea sets showed more variation, ranging from plain to more elaborate porcelain versions.

The implications of this consistency in household ceramic usage are that a dominant set of ideas existed, defining what was appropriate for families who saw themselves as members of a particular class (Wall 1999). These perceptions led to standardized imports from England made for the American market. Consistent with Wall's analysis, other middle-class households in Brooklyn occupied in the mid-nineteenth century were analyzed by Fitts and Yamin (1996:78), who found the same kind of symbolic identification and the same ironstone. The choice of these wares was made in spite of the availability of less-expensive shell-edged or plain ceramics.

One of the most important recent archaeological projects in New York City is the Five Points block, excavated prior to the construction of a new federal court-house. The block housed a great variety of people, mostly working class and members of the lower ranks of society. Documentary information shows a great deal of ethnic heterogeneity among the residents (Irish, German, Polish and Russian Jews, and Africans), but the archaeology reveals a variability in lifestyle and aspiration that is even more dramatic and that contradicts the consistent and stereotypic accounts of the time that describe the area as a hellhole, occupied by the dregs of New York. The range of ceramics was large, but overlapped to a great degree those used by middle-class New Yorkers of the period. Some residents were using matched sets of shell-edged wares, some (Irish tenants especially) used the same molded granite Gothic wares observed in suburban Greenwich Village and Brooklyn, and a number of occupants had porcelain tea wares (Yamin 1998).

It is clear that many of the Five Pointers were involved in the same symbolic system as their better-off neighbors and were equally aware of the use of material culture to define themselves or their aspirations. A brothel excavated on the block had the most expensive and elite ceramics of all recovered, and its occupants or clients ate quite expensive cuts of meat and drank French wines. Again, the sur-prises found in a project such as this show how archaeology can offer a picture of the reality of life in city dwellers' homes that cannot be obtained through other means. (Note that this important archaeological collection was destroyed on Sep-tember 11, 2001; it had been stored in the subbasement of 6 World Trade Center, and one of the towers fell through this building.)

Conclusion

This chapter began with the premise that population size and growth rate are relevant factors in the examination of urban life. With the focus on New York City between 1700 and 1870, these data suggest that there were two different cities in existence during the period; they can be called colonial and postcolonial. Archaeologists examining the city have focused on different scales of analysis and have used two primary sources of information, land-use change and artifacts. In describing some of the projects conducted in New York, it seems that land-use and landscape analysis can be used successfully in both the colonial and post-colonial city; the fine-grained analysis of artifacts from individual features or house lots is particularly well suited to deposits from the postcolonial city for a number of reasons. After 1800, New York was gradually incorporated into the world economy as an industrial capitalist nation, characterized by a true class system. In this socioeconomic system, class is signaled by material symbols of a variety of types, including home furnishings. This form of expression becomes increasingly important in urban life as the population grows beyond the size where a resident will have personal knowledge of the class position of other residents. Many of these possessions can be, and are commonly, recovered through archaeological excavation. The dishes used in setting a table express the status or the aspirations of those eating from them. The archaeological analysis of these two New Yorks confirms the meaningful differences between them initially identified by population parameters and provides significant information that complements documentary information and can be obtained only through the arduous and sometimes tedious process of excavation.

Acknowledgments

A number of archaeologists have generously shared data with me for this chapter and throughout the period since the mid-1970s when urban archaeology began in New York. I am particularly grateful to Joan Geismar and Rebecca Yamin, and I thank Diana Wall for her thoughts as well as her data. Mobina Khan made Figure 6-1 quickly and efficiently. Michael Cooper has a special place in the pantheon for editing and other things. Any errors or misinterpretations are my own responsibility.

Urban Society on
the African Continent

7

An Urban Population from Roman Upper Egypt

Roger S. Bagnall

One of the most elusive aspects of the demography of Roman Egypt—the ancient society for which we have the best documentary data—has been the extent to which the results of the analysis of the census declarations from Middle Egypt (Bagnall and Frier 1994) can be considered typical of other parts of Egypt, let alone other provinces of the Roman Empire. The data explored in this chapter, coming from a papyrus edited after the appearance of Bagnall and Frier's (1994) work, may make a contribution to understanding some of the ways in which the population characteristics of Roman Egypt differed not only between urban and rural areas but also between different regions of Egypt, particularly different cities.

The study of the demography of the ancient Mediterranean world was long marked by a lack of methodological rigor, either in devising models or in assessing the ancient evidence. These deficiencies were scathingly catalogued in Tim Parkin's (1992) book on the subject. In recent years there have been substantial advances concerning both evidence and models. An excellent and detailed summary of this work can be found in Scheidel (2001b). There has been an enormous amount of critical work on the value of the ancient sources, the most salient element of which has been a more realistic valuation of the limits of our largest single body of evidence, the ages given on gravestones (see generally Parkin 1992:5–19). There is now a consensus that the ages in gravestones do not, in general, provide a pattern recognizable in any historical population and that commemoration therefore must be affected by one sort of bias or another. It has, to be sure, been argued that the patterns displayed by some bodies of inscriptions may be consistent with a population exhibiting catastrophic mortality (see Paine and Storey 1999, this volume). Although such catastrophes certainly occurred, most notably with the plague under Marcus Aurelius (Bagnall 2002; Duncan-Jones 1996; Scheidel 2002), this argument does not seem to me capable of explaining the persistence of distortion in population structures through a body of material extending over a long period of time. Nonetheless, it is certainly true that the various epigraphic data sets deserve individual valuation and examination. Scheidel (2001a), following up earlier work by Shaw (1996) and himself (1996, 1998), has used Egyptian funerary epigraphy to try to make the case for regional variation in the causes of death underlying seasonal patterns of mortality, although he rejects most other uses of the inscriptions for basic demographic questions.

Demographic modeling based on the more widespread and nuanced application of life tables to the ancient evidence has been even more central to the discussions of the last decade. In particular, it has been possible to show that the Egyptian census declarations on papyrus, which date to the period from Augustus to the mid-third century CE, reveal a population with mortality and fertility characteristics broadly consistent with those of the Coale-Demeny Model West tables with life expectancy at birth in the low twenties, probably between 22 and 25 (Bagnall and Frier 1994). Scheidel (2001a) has strongly reinforced the concerns expressed in our study of the census data about the extent to which any particular model life table derived from modern evidence is a fair representation of ancient (or even modern) high-mortality populations beset by endemic diseases. The problem is particularly acute in accounting for infant mortality, as very young children are poorly represented in both gravestones and the census data. Scheidel's work has, however, neither shown conclusively that the endemic diseases he discusses would collectively alter the models in a particular fashion nor provided a basis on which to construct a model more faithful to ancient realities.

The Egyptian census returns come partly from rural villages and partly from regional urban centers. There is thus an inherent possibility that these data can shed some light on the question of the demography of the rural/urban continuum. (This potential is, however, seriously limited in its range by the absence of any returns from Egypt's one very large city, Alexandria.) The data are not, however, so abundant as to allow for as much deepening of the analysis as one might wish. Because the number of published returns as of 1994, when Bruce Frier and I published our book on the demography of Roman Egypt, was only about 300, and the number of known individuals only about 1,100, the data become less and less robust the more one breaks them out into subsets. For this reason it was difficult for us either to distinguish between the demographic characteristics of the cities and those of the villages or to have a high level of confidence in those differences that could be discerned. In the case of mortality, it seemed from the data from Middle Egypt that there was, perhaps surprisingly, little if any difference between urban and rural rates (Bagnall and Frier 1994:164). Scheidel (2001a) has argued that our data do support such a difference.

The sex ratio, by contrast, seemed clearly higher in cities than in villages, a finding that stood up to examination from a variety of angles such as free versus slave or adults only, and we concluded that the normal metropolitan sex ratio was probably in the range of 125 to 130, compared to a ratio much closer to 100 in the villages (Bagnall and Frier 1994:95). Problems with both the census returns and the size of the database contributed to some diffidence in our treatment of these figures. Scheidel (2001a:160) has argued, with more confidence than the data warrant, that the city/village distinction and deficiencies in reporting males in villages explain all of the patterns in the data, without any need for recourse to positing a difference between male and female mortality, as Frier and I did. We would all agree, however, that the fact that the urban census returns in the database come from a period of more than two centuries and from more than one city made it impossible to have a clear idea of what a snapshot of a particular city at a given moment might look like.

An opportunity to remedy this deficiency has more recently been dangled before our eyes in the form of a papyrus roll found at Oxyrhynchos in Middle Egypt, excavated early in the twentieth century but only briefly described by the editors and not fully published until 1997 (Bagnall et al. 1997). This roll contained an enumeration of households, clearly extracted from census returns, for parts of a city. It was subsequently turned over and reused to copy the *Paeans* of the archaic Greek poet Pindar. Despite its archaeological provenance, it can be shown (by geographical and personal names used in it) to have been written in and to describe a city in Upper Egypt considerably to the south of the region from which most of our census declarations come. There are arguments in favor of both Ptolemais, a Greek city founded by Ptolemy I in the late fourth century BCE, and Lykopolis, an older regional center (or metropolis) in the same region. Because we have few published papyri from either city and little demographic information for the region where they were located, the register, even though very fragmentary, constitutes a substantial addition to our knowledge, and for our purposes here it does not matter greatly which city is in question. At the time of publication, we favored Ptolemais, but because recent study (especially Montevecchi 1998) and forthcoming new evidence (Clarysse and Thompson 2005) have strengthened the likelihood that the provenance is Lykopolis, I refer to it as Lykopolite in what follows.

The surviving fragments of the register record 63 households as they stood in the census of 89 CE. Of these, 36 are complete or nearly complete. We gain a total of 256 individuals for the database. As we examined the data, however, elation quickly turned to sobriety, for it became clear that these household listings were beset with numerous internal and external difficulties that render them less reliable than the Middle Egyptian returns. Because the right edges of fragments are often lost, the ages are preserved less often than in other documents, a problem exacerbated for males by the fact that their entries tended to be longer and extend farther to the right. The preserved ages, moreover, show a much higher degree of age rounding, coupled with an almost total absence of older ages, for which it is difficult to offer an explanation. It has been suggested (Storey and Paine 2002) that similar patterns in epigraphic evidence may point to catastrophic mortality, but it is difficult to see that such an explanation would make sense of a difference between Upper Egypt and Middle Egypt. The households listed are all headed by males of an age such as to subject them to the poll tax, i.e., between 14 and 62. This is probably the result of an official practice of grouping households by type in the records. With no female-headed households, the register is thus unlikely to be typical of the entire population (see Bagnall et al. 1997:89–94; cf. also Scheidel 2001a:188 n. 2).

For all these reasons, the data of the Lykopolis register demand caution. All the same, it remains our largest single body of census material for one place and for Upper Egypt as a whole, particularly at a given date; it is also earlier than the main corpus of the declarations, which come from the second and third centuries. There are two possible areas of significance to this point: first, the census had not yet achieved its mature form at this point, and the problems we see in the data may reflect deficiencies in the first-century census, particularly in the enumeration of women (who were not taxed and therefore less critical for the census); second, it is possible that the continued development of the Roman period brought real changes to the demography of Egypt. The body of data in the Lykopolis register is not large enough to settle these questions, but it allows us to raise them in a far more concrete form. (Scheidel 2001a unfortunately ignores this chronological problem in using this document.)

I shall summarize briefly the most salient findings. First, the Lykopolis register is, in comparison to Middle Egyptian cities, dominated by conjugal families and to a lesser degree by extended families. These gains come largely at the expense of the multiple-family category, and they do not disappear when Lykopolis is compared only to Middle Egyptian urban returns filed by males of taxpaying age. The results are smaller average households than elsewhere in Egypt. We have tentatively attributed this difference to disparities in wealth. The Lykopolis register shows less than half the percentage of slaves in the population that we find in the Middle Egyptian *metropoleis* (7 percent vs. 14.6 percent).

Second, the Lykopolis register shows a population with an age structure significantly different from that of Middle Egypt, with an even greater underreporting of juveniles and an increasing shortfall compared to the model for age groups after age 30. These discrepancies give rise to complex problems of interpretation. It is likely that some part of the problem—at least the juveniles—is a matter of poor reporting, for up to age 14, boys were not taxable. But there are good grounds to believe that the adult age structure of Lykopolis was in fact somewhat younger than that elsewhere in Egypt. If we are right about Lykopolis being poorer than Middle Egypt, it is perhaps more likely that this is the result of higher mortality than that it represents a higher growth rate.

Third, the Lykopolis register has a sex ratio for adults of 137, higher than the 120.8 found in the Middle Egyptian cities. For free adults, Lykopolis has a ratio of 148.3, compared to 128. We are inclined to attribute this sex ratio to the immigration of males from the villages in search of work. Scheidel (2001a:166–171) has argued against any role for immigration in explaining the shape of the data from the Lykopolis register and from other census declarations, although he believes that such immigration was substantial.

There are other aspects we might look at, but generally speaking the Lykopolis register does not significantly alter the picture of marriage and fertility found in the Middle Egyptian returns. In this regime, virtually all women marry eventually, the majority by age 20, but many are widowed or divorced at a relatively young age, and many of these do not remarry. Fertility is about 70 percent of the highest-known levels of natural fertility, well within a normal range for a pretransitional population. The distribution of births conforms to that found in populations that use no artificial means of birth control.

Now, from all these remarks, it will be evident that the Lykopolis register suffers from some significant limitations resulting in part from its early date, such as the haphazard registration of infants and children, and in part from its bureaucratic character, resulting in the omission of solitary females and families headed by widows. Because our data for children in the Middle Egyptian returns are also relatively poor, it is especially regrettable that the Lykopolis register does not help to fill this lacuna. But these deficiencies can to some degree be controlled, in part by focusing on adults and in part by using Middle Egyptian returns filed by male heads of household of taxpaying age as the control. This procedure has the evident drawback of reducing the size of the database and thus the statistical confidence level of the results, but it does allow us to rescue the Lykopolis data from the oblivion they might otherwise deserve.

In that light, Lykopolis appears to be a somewhat poorer cousin of the Middle Egyptian cities, with marriage and fertility patterns similar to those found elsewhere but probably a somewhat higher mortality rate, at least for females. The higher sex ratio in the free adult population also contributes to an overall impression of being like cities elsewhere in serving as a magnet for poor young males lacking opportunities in the villages, but the lower percentage of slaves suggests that when they got to the city they did not find as wealthy an economy as they may have hoped. These findings raise the question whether Upper Egypt was inherently poorer than areas farther north or just slower to develop economically under Roman rule than Middle Egypt—questions to which I can offer no answer at present. It is noteworthy, however, that a Demotic Egyptian population register from the Lykopolite *nome,* dating to the Ptolemaic period, shows similarities to some of the characteristics we find in the early Roman register I have been describing (Clarysse and Thompson 2005; Ptolemaic registers, unfortunately, lack ages, even though these were sometimes present in declarations [see Clarysse and Thompson 2002]). At least some of these patterns may thus have deep regional roots.

I venture one final speculation: the overall demographic regime of cities throughout Roman Egypt was probably roughly similar, with a common tendency to attract immigration and thus a skewed age and sex structure. Local and regional differences in the economy, however, most likely created variations within this underlying regime, mainly in mortality and slavery. Diachronic change in the economy may also have contributed to local diversity, but to measure that we would need another census register or two. The evidence found or published in the last decade, apart from the Lykopolis register, consists of more individual declarations rather than such registers, but as long as excavations in Egypt continue, one may keep hoping.

Acknowledgments

This chapter is in large measure based on work I have done jointly with Bruce Frier (Bagnall and Frier 1994; Bagnall et al. 1997), and I am deeply indebted to Frier's demographic analysis. He has also kindly read a draft of this chapter to prevent any serious misstatements, but he has no responsibility for the final outcome. The works I cite provide extensive bibliography on all the matters set forth here, and the reader is referred to them for details about what is only summarized in this chapter. I am grateful to Willy Clarysse and Dorothy Thompson for information about their forthcoming work on the Ptolemaic census registers, which lack ages but tell us a great deal about household size and structure.

8

Precolonial African Cities

Size and Density

Chapurukha Kusimba, Sibel Barut Kusimba,
and Babatunde Agbaje-Williams

African population and demography may be the least understood of any region in the world (Caldwell 1997). Nevertheless, numerous scholars have argued that patterns of population and urbanism in Africa are distinctive. In this chapter, we propose to explore the demography of African cities by first reviewing questions on African urbanization in general, including a review of the problems in estimating the population of African cities that are relevant to other regions. We will then examine the documentary and archaeological records that help elucidate the nature of African urban centers, noting their unusual dispersed settlement configurations. We will close with a case study of Yoruba urban centers to illustrate the unique challenges facing the study of urban populations in Africa.

African Urban Populations in Perspective

In a recent synthesis of African history, Reader (1997:254) argued that Africa's harsh environment, especially its endemic diseases, discouraged population growth and urbanism:

> While the out-of-Africa population soared from just hundreds (around 100,000 years ago) to 200 million (by 0 A.D.), and rose to just over 300 million in the next 1500 years, the African population increased from 1 million to no more than 20 million 100,000 years later (by 0 A.D.), and to only 47 million in A.D. 1500. . . . By leaving the tropical environments of the cradle-land in which humanity had evolved . . . [human groups who moved to Eurasia] also left behind the many parasites and disease organisms that had evolved in parallel with the human species. . . . Out of Africa, beyond the reach of the insects and organisms which had reinfected generation after generation, the multiplication of human numbers quickly assumed

Table 8-1. Estimates of African and World Population

	Time		
Population	100,000 years ago	0 AD	1500 AD
African population	1 million	20 million	47 million
Non-African population	hundreds	200 million	300 million
African population: percentage of world population	99% (of anatomically modern humans only)	10%	16%

Source: Reader (1997:254).

a hitherto unprecedented scale. . . . Meanwhile, contemporary populations in the tropical African cradle-land remained constrained by debility and disease. . . . It explains why the rise of indigenous cities and civilizations in Africa had hardly begun when the migrants returned with foreign ideas of how it should be done.

Reader's estimates compare African and non-African population at three times (Table 8-1). Storey (1992) has highlighted the unreliable nature of most population statistics from the ancient world on which Reader's figures are based. Furthermore, much of Reader's claim that European population in fact grows faster than African population is based on the first 100,000 years of his three-part comparison and on the questionable claim that the few hundred or so "modern humans" who supposedly left Africa 100,000 years ago did not encounter and interact with populations of more archaic humans, as accepted by many paleoanthropologists (Foley and Lahr 1992). In fact, by Reader's own estimates, African population grew relative to that of Eurasia from AD 1 to AD 1500.

A close corollary of Reader's argument is that the harsh environment, endemic diseases, and consequently small and slow-growing populations of Africa are a major reason why complex societies in Africa are rare and evolved later than in the rest of the world. He quotes Ki-Zerbo as saying:

The very vastness of the African continent, with a diluted and therefore readily itinerant population living in a nature at once generous with its fruits and minerals, but cruel with its endemic and epidemic diseases, prevented it from reaching the threshold of demographic concentration which has almost always been one of the preconditions of major qualitative changes in the social, political, and economic spheres (Ki-Zerbo, quoted in Reader 1997:266).

The idea that something intrinsic to Africa retarded the development of population and urbanism is a long-seated one in Western historiography, closely tied to the idea that Africa lacks history in general (Hegel 1965). Numerous factors have been isolated as the cause of Africa's lack of cities, including climate, soil, diet, and isolation:

> The African continent suffers, and has suffered in the past, from many privations and serious general weaknesses. It would be impossible to list them all or to describe how at different times they have been better or worse. . . . One was the shallowness of the red lateritic soil[;] . . . another was the climatic limit on the number of days when the land could be worked; a third was the regular shortage of meat in most people's diet (Braudel 1993[1963]: 124–125).

Rather than attributing a tendency against urbanism to an intrinsic feature of the African continent, others stress recent historical factors in the smaller population of Africa. Ki-Zerbo (1981:2), quoted selectively by Reader, thinks recent historical events, not the environment, caused Africa's low population densities:

> Moreover, the fact that Africa was underpopulated is one of the keys to its historical difficulties for, as F. Braudel has said, "Civilization is the daughter of number." Wars and endemic or epidemic diseases are not so much to blame, for the other continents have likewise suffered on those counts; however, the severe demographic drain of the slave trade and colonization certainly prevented the continent from attaining the particular threshold of concentration at which the critical economic and socio-political mutations take place. The harsh and monotonous climate also had its part to play.

According to Mabonguje (1981:135), in 1650, before much of the slave trade and colonization, Africa's population of 100 million represented more than 20 percent of the world total, although today it is only 10 percent. Inikori (1997:91) estimates that between 13 and 15.4 million slaves were exported in the Atlantic slave trade from 1650 to 1850. Because of the violence involved in slavery, the demographic effects go far beyond those captured. Although this chapter cannot claim to grapple fully with the debate over the effects of slavery and colonization on African population, it will use archaeological evidence to examine Reader's claim that precolonial African cities were smaller than those outside Africa.

The Environmental Factor

Reader's 1997 book of the history of Africa has as its overarching theme the human struggle to adapt to Africa's harsh and inhospitable climate. Indeed, much of Africa has fragile, vulnerable ecosystems, and most support relatively low population densities. Because the African continent straddles the equator, it has nearly horizontal vegetation bands. The moist equator is covered by lowland rainforest at the Congo Basin. Seasonally moist grasslands and woodlands lie north and south of the forests, and deserts, the Kalahari and Sahara, straddle the tropics of Capricorn and Cancer (Nyamweru 1998). In precolonial times, deserts of the Sahara and Botswana were inhabited by hunter-gatherers or itinerant pastoralists, although in early Holocene or Pleistocene times these areas were well watered and inhabited by stable agriculturalists (Grove 1993; Robbins et al. 1994). Grasslands are slightly more favorable to human groups, being seasonally wet and in most areas permitting successful agropastoralist economies, particularly in well-watered regions such as southeast Africa and highland East Africa. Opinion is sharply divided on the suitability of the equatorial rainforest as a human habitat. Some emphasize its lateritic soils and low plant and animal density (Bailey et al. 1989). Others argue that it in fact has a high density of edible plants and animals and would support agriculture well (Hladik and Hladik 1990; Vansina 1990).

In any case, it is true that areas of both quality soils and abundant rainfall are rare in Africa; these magnets of population include the Nile valley, the inland deltas of the Niger and Okavango, and areas of fertile volcanic soils in the East African highlands, northern Rwanda, or the slopes of Mount Cameroon. Seasonal grasslands and woodlands are prone to drought and have heavily leached or carbonate-loaded soils. Sleeping sickness is endemic over much of southern Africa and discourages the keeping of cattle or use of their fertilizer (Coquery-Vidrovitch 1972, 1997; Kusimba and Bronson 2000). Considering the continent as a whole, its relatively low population densities are a result of these often unfavorable ecological conditions. Adaptations to drought and poor soils stress mobility; shifting agriculture, pastoralism, and other peripatetic adaptations (Bollig 1987) are common in Africa.

Whether continents other than Africa are intrinsically more favorable for human settlement, however, is doubtful; each environment occupied by humans has its own set of difficulties and constraints. As on other continents, however, urban societies did arise in regions of high ecological and economic potential, including ancient Egypt; the middle Nile towns of Nubia, such as Kerma, Napata, and Meroe; the Ethiopian highlands; the East African coast; the Zimbabwean plateau; the Great Lakes region of East Africa; the Sahelian region of West Africa; and the West African forest zone. These areas all gave humans who possessed the right technologies the potential to produce a storable and transportable food surplus. In many areas of Africa, of course, cow and goat pastoralism is favorable to agriculture because of its greater flexibility in the face of environmental risks, especially drought. Such shifting economies are, of course, unlikely to develop urbanism even when socioeconomic stratification is present (Holl 1998a, 1998b).

Connah (1987) assigns great importance to the role of population pressure as a major impetus to the development of urbanism and states in Africa, such as the

Nile valley, where population pressure was created by circumscription of the arable land. Seasonal flooding of the Nile made agriculture possible using shaduf irrigation and supported surplus production and high population densities. Connah also links population pressure to the development of hierarchy in the Sahelian region, a steppe well suited for cereal cultivation and pastoralism bordering the Sahara desert, and in areas farther south where West African forest states developed, especially along the upper interfluves where soils were well drained and on forest fringes where land was easy to clear. In these areas, only three to four years of cultivation could produce food surpluses and stimulate population expansions. Ife and Oyo grew out of settlements in these areas. Three of Africa's most successful state societies, Ghana, Mali, and Songhai, and cities such as Timbuktu, Walata, Jenne-jeno, and Gao are found on or near the Inland Niger Delta and the upper and middle zones of the Niger (Vaum 1997). This region allowed the recessional cultivation of rice as well as a position on interregional trade routes and long-distance trade in gold and salt. In the Ethiopian highlands, Connah attributes the emergence of hierarchical society and cities such as Axum, Adulis, and many other regional centers of trade and ceremony to population pressure on the productive, volcanic soils of the area, which supported agriculture much better than the surroundings (Fattovich 2000).

In a similar way, the well-watered but narrow East African coast had numerous resources its arid hinterlands lacked, in spite of its poor soils. In Iron Age cities of the East African coast, competition for productive land and access to ocean resources are demonstrated by the presence of territorial markers such as mounds and burial tumuli, the system of land tenure in which clan leaders determined access and mediated land disputes, and the demarcation of clan land into sacred and ritual areas to ensure ownership through time (Chittick 1974, 1984; Horton 1996). In architecture, Swahili towns are closely built villages and towns with double-storied houses, which suggests competition for land (Connah 1987: 176–177).

Although the influence of environment has indeed been important in influencing the size and geographic location of African cities, environmental factors are not alone in fostering African urbanism. Historians of African precolonial cities have stressed nonenvironmental factors that have been just as important in encouraging the growth of cities. Internal, indigenous, creative adaptation and external demand stimulated urban development in favorable conjunctures where human, social, economic, or external resources were conducive to settlement. Other factors stimulating urban development included communications and channels of supply and demand (Southall 1997:326).

Indeed, numerous cities in the Sahelian region were linked primarily to trans-Saharan trade, including Kumbi Saleh and Awdahgust of the Ghana kingdom (eighth to twelfth centuries AD). Although most of these Saharan trade cities were located near oases, their primary purpose was as trade entrepôts.

Current State of Knowledge and Problems in Estimating Ancient African City Population Sizes

Caldwell (1997) argues that no reliable estimates of precolonial African population exist because of the absence of census data for this period. Even for historically documented settlements, the role of archaeology is vital for understanding African city size. However, both historical and archaeological estimates of city sizes may be unreliable for a variety of reasons.

Historical and traveler accounts of African city sizes suffer from errors of reporting (Fletcher 1993). First, copying of maps and other accounts tends to create error and over time can lead to several estimates of city size. Errors of estimation can be as profound as the observer's tendency to exaggerate, which is estimated as a factor of three. The tendency to round one's figures leads to exaggeration.

Sometimes site size estimates are given with incomplete information regarding what they mean. Does the estimate pertain to a site portion, such as the walled core, or to the entire site, or are neighboring mounds being described? Often insufficient survey and relative dating have not been carried out. In many areas, few ethnographic comparisons have been made for getting density factors. Sometimes, defining the edges of settlements can be difficult. Koumbi Sale is considered the sister city of an indigenous Soninke city, El-Ghaba, but the two towns are more than 1 km apart (Vaum 1997).

Archaeological evidence can suffer from similar problems. First, archaeological evidence of historically known towns is often patchy or lacking altogether. For example, Leo Africanus described Mbanza Kongo (DeMaret 2000) as a bustling city of more than 100,000 inhabitants, yet the site is unknown archaeologically (McIntosh 1997). The same is true of the Kanem city of Njimi east of Lake Chad (Connah 1987:17–18). On extensive sites, full surveys are lacking, and often only an undisclosed section of the site is being estimated. A focus on stone monuments as definitive of a "city" has often meant that only the monumental aspects of a site will be used to define its extent. Site excavations will often ignore the hinterland and even the mud-brick or wattle-and-daub remains that form the immediate surroundings of the walled portion of a site, especially in the case of African cities (see below).

Current Data and Basic Comparisons

Fletcher (1993) has provided size estimates for a variety of African cities (Tables 8-2 to 8-4). The majority are less than 5 sq km in size. Most date to the eighteenth and nineteenth centuries, although some were occupied earlier. Precolonial African towns rarely exceeded 30 sq km, with the majority being less than 5 sq km. However, such a size range is not appreciably smaller than that of European cities at the time (Storey 1992:119).

Table 8-2. African Precolonial Cities Less Than 0.5 sq km in Size

City	Age	Population Estimate
Meroe (core)	First -Third centuries B.C.	
Zinchera	First century	
Adulis	500 A.D.	21,000
Bigo (Core)	1400-1500	
Ain Farah	Sixteenth century	
Mgungudlovu	1828-1836	

Note: All ages are CE unless otherwise noted.
Source for Tables 8-2 to 8-5: Fletcher 1993, 2000.

Obviously, Tables 8-2 to 8-4 represent a highly selective overview of African cities. However, the compilation demonstrates that most African cities are a phenomenon of the second millennium CE, although some are precociously early, such as Jenne-jeno. To understand population and cities more fully, we must adopt a regional, demographic approach. The regional and historical scale of research required to glean this kind of data has been lacking in most of Africa, with the possible exception of Egypt (Hassan 1993).

Egypt is one of the few areas where extensive demographic archaeology has been carried out, especially by Hassan (1993), who provides a brief sketch of how urban population centers developed in Egypt. Town life began around 4000 BC in cities such as Merimde and Beni-Salama, which had populations around 1300–2000 persons. These types of settlements included rows of huts with dug floors and walls of plastered mud and workshop areas. Around 3500 BC, towns such as Heirakonpolis developed, with populations of around 1500–2000. These areas were also religious centers.

Butzer's (1976) studies of the Old Kingdom population centers included dispersed cities such as Memphis and Thebes, large and small centers (towns serving as nodes in a regional hierarchy of administration, economic, and religious activities), and nomes or administrative units (Upper Egypt, for example, had 22). Each nome had a nome capital connected to a number of smaller provincial towns, which were administrative nodes and local marketplaces. Nome capitals were political and religious centers, but they also collected taxes.

Why did nomes develop in Egypt? Hassan stresses that regional coordination among villages was advantageous due to periodic food shortages. Chiefs needed to coordinate such redistributions and used supernatural, juridical, and military power to do so. Cooperative units enlarged progressively, resulting in the appearance of regional chiefs, who kept part of the agricultural foodstuffs and goods and

Table 8-3. African Precolonial Cities Less Than 5 sq km in Size

City	Age	Population Estimate
Meroe (all)		
Aksum		
(75–100 ha)		
	500	20,000
Ain Farah (all)		
Mombasa	1400–1600	
Fez	Fourteenth century	37,700
Bono Namzo	Sixteenth century	4,000
Jenne-Jeno (main tell only - 33 ha)	500–1000	7,293–12,837
Jenne-Jeno (tell clusters of 25 sites – 98.7 ha)	500–1000	15,183–26,724
Great Zimbabwe (core – 50–70 ha)	1600–1700	
Agadez	Sixteenth century	50,000
Cairo	Seventeenth century	150,000
Kazargam	Seventeenth century	200,000
Zanzibar (60 ha)	Eighteenth century	
Sennar	Eighteenth century	30,000
Kilwa (47 ha)	Eighteenth century	
Kong	Nineteenth century	
Tripoli		
Timbuktu (1.5 sq km)	Nineteenth century	50,000
Sokoto	1830	120,000
Tananarivo (1.8 sq km)	1890	50,000
Birni N'gazargamo		
Ambohimasina		
Koumbi Saleh		15,000–20,000
Bigo (all - 2–3 sq km)	Fifteenth to sixteenth century	

All ages are CE unless otherwise noted.

sent part to the paramount chief, who was getting tribute from other petty chiefs, too. This accumulation by the regional chiefs encouraged city populations to grow.

Hassan's work in Egypt (1993, 1997a, 1997b) has demonstrated that every city must be seen in terms of its regional functions and relationships with other regional settlements, which form the very definition of a city (Trigger 1972). Unfortunately, work on a regional scale is still in its infancy in much of African archaeology.

Table 8-4. African Precolonial Cities less than 20 sq km in Size

City	Age	Population Estimate
Jebel Uri	Fifteenth to sixteenth century	
Zaria	Sixteenth century	40,000
Cairo (15–18 sq km)	Fifteenth to sixteenth century	
Cairo (15–18 km)	Eighteenth century	263,000
Marrakech	Sixteenth century	150,000 (Thirteenth century)
Begho	Sixteenth century	10,000
Awdaghoust	Seventeenth century	
Ougadougou	Nineteenth century	
Kano (18 sq km)	Nineteenth century	
Sokoto	Nineteenth century	120,000
Kumasi	Nineteenth century	
Masenya	Nineteenth century	30,000
Abomey	Nineteenth century	30,000
Ibadan	Nineteenth century	70,000
Kong (all)		
Fez (all)		
Zanzibar (all)		
Tananarive (all)		

All ages are CE unless otherwise noted.

Types of African Cities

Fletcher (2000) has recognized two types of African cities. The first are small, nucleated settlements of around 1 sq km or less that, according to Fletcher, are often part of literate societies. These include the nucleated settlements of the East African coast and Madagascar, such as Kilwa (47 ha), Zanzibar (60 ha), and Tananarivo (88 ha). In these cases, environmental conscription and island location or some other geographic factor has constrained city growth.

The second group of African cities consists of low-density occupations of patchy and clumped settlements with an extensive skirt of low-density occupations. Often these settlements do not have marked boundaries, and many times subsistence farming enclaves are important parts of the settlement. Any monuments they possess belong to a small walled section of the town. Often they lack stone buildings, and the chief's enclave is also made of wattle and daub. It is simply a much larger compound than the rest of the settlement. Often, these settlements are temporary or shifting. Given the importance of agricultural activities in these settlements, one might correctly call them, as DeMaret (2000) has, "giant villages."

Examples of giant villages include precolonial Addis Ababa, which included a mobile imperial capital and dispersed settlements around it. Addis and other Ethiopian cities often covered 30–40 sq km and included 30,000–40,000 people. Their Amharic rulers frequently relocated their capital cities when firewood became exhausted (McDow 1997:3). Settlements of the kings of the Kongo kingdom of central Africa, called *mbanza,* were large, low-density settlements of around four persons per square kilometer, which evolved as a result of trade, refugee settlement, or concentration of power. Mbanza Kongo is a famous example (DeMaret 2000). Areas of denser settlement were surrounded by cultivated fields. Often, the king's residence was an especially large compound of wattle and daub with more ornate decorations (DeMaret 2000). The lack of monumental or stone architecture of many African settlements and their often semipermanent nature lower their archaeological visibility (DeMaret 2000). It may indeed be more typical of African urban centers to lack stone buildings entirely or have them only as a city center.

Many of these dispersed settlements included walled areas for the king, such as Benin, Old Oyo, Awdaghoust, Begho, and Ouagoudougou. Fez had two walled areas and surrounding occupation, but the whole area covered 3.5 sq km. Jenne-Jeno's main mound of 33 ha is surrounded by 40 other mounds that were functionally differentiated and probably traded with each other. The full area covered 100 ha (McIntosh and McIntosh 1993:633). The stone "core" of Great Zimbabwe is about 1 sq km, and the total site area is more than 25 sq km and includes a palimpsest of dispersed settlements around it. The original inhabitants of these areas selected territories with high grazing potential for the practice of carnivorous pastoralism. Great Zimbabwe population estimates have ranged from 1,000 to 18,000 persons (Connah 1987; McIntosh 1997; Sinclair et al. 1993). The dispersed "giant village" is not limited to sub-Saharan Africa. In ancient Egypt, Karnak and Luxor (1500–2000 BC) and Memphis (500 BC), which was spread 15 km along the Nile, might be called dispersed (Fletcher 2000). Agglomerations of people often arose in acephalous societies for purposes of defense. South African defensive towns such as Molokwane (Whitelaw 1997) housed 10,000–16,000 people.

Dispersed Cities of Africa: Yoruba Case Study

Fletcher (1986, 2000) asserts that precolonial African cities were equivalent in size to those of the rest of the world (Table 8-5), with the exception of Chinese cities, which were unusually large (Storey 1992:120). Often, however, African cities are less dense than those in other areas of the world. Comparative data on city populations and densities from around the world support DeMaret's and Fletcher's studies. Using population, area, and density estimates for 425 cities, Storey (1992:120) found that African cities represent one of the lower average densities for its preindustrial cities (in persons per square kilometer, 12,724), measured by

Table 8-5. African Precolonial Cities Less Than 50 sq km in Size

City	Age	Population Estimate
Great Zimbabwe (all)	Fifteenth to sixteenth century	
Ife	Fifteenth century	
Gondar	Eighteenth century	80,000
Loango	Eighteenth century	30,000
Ibadan	Nineteenth century	
Ouagadougou	Nineteenth century	85,000
Benin (central area 30 sq km)	Nineteenth century	27,000
Zaria (all)	Nineteenth century	
Addis Ababa	Nineteenth century	
Kampala	Nineteenth century	

All ages are CE unless otherwise noted.

world region, but not significantly lower (cf. India, 12,600; West Asia, 16,817; Europe, 18,043; and East Asia, 21,027).

Old Oyo was perhaps the largest precolonial African city in terms of area. The full extent of the city was revealed only by systematic survey (Agbaje-Williams and Onyango-Abuje 1981). It is an excellent example of a "giant village," an area of more than 50 sq km with a very low population density.

Artifact distribution, site area, and modern inhabited settlements were used to estimate the population of Old Oyo, the capital of the former Oyo Yoruba empire of the eighteenth and nineteenth centuries. It is located 240 km north of Ibadan, within the Southern Guinea Savanna zone of Nigeria in the northeast section of the Oyo state. The site is now a national park, but historically it was the seat of an empire, which included most of Yorubaland, the Benin Republic, and part of Togo.

Oyo was founded in the fourteenth century AD by Oranmiyan, a prince of Ife. The kingdom expanded and consolidated in the seventeenth century, prospered from the Atlantic slave trade, and built a strong army. The emergent empire was plagued by slave and vassal revolts and finally abandoned in the 1830s in the face of a Fulani jihad (Johnson 1921). A few years before its abandonment, British explorers such as Clapperton (1829) and the Lander brothers (1832) visited the capital; their accounts show clearly that Old Oyo was a multiple-walled, large cosmopolitan city with ditches. According to Yoruba origin traditions, Old Oyo and other Yoruba towns were founded by people from Ife-Ife, the cradle of the Yoruba (Johnson 1921). Archaeological research in Yorubaland has confirmed the antiquity of a town at Ife.

The site of Old Oyo is surrounded by a 10×7 km perimeter wall. According to explorers, the population of Old Oyo was considerable, but no specific figures were offered. Lloyd (1972) gives a figure of 50,000, although without explanation. One of us (Agbaje-Williams 1978, 1983) conducted a systematic transect survey of 10 percent of Old Oyo in 1978. A total of 14 transects running from south to north were surveyed. The shortest was less than 2 km, and the longest was a bit over 10 km. The transects were placed at half-kilometer intervals with a constant width of 50 m. The objective was to sample the widest possible range of artifact types and their distribution. Among the materials and features found in this survey were a wall system, compound-courtyard complexes, pottery scatters, mounds, circular stone structures, grinding stones, grinding hollows on rock outcrops, and pits (David 1998). Nonresidential features such as mounds were not used in population estimates, but the pottery scatters were, which were found throughout the site, as well as the compound-courtyard complexes, which are square and rectangular building remains.

The total area of Old Oyo is 5,252.5 ha. Of this the built-up area is 1,870 ha, more than one-third of the total site area, and the area of compound courtyard complex is 884 ha. To understand what the population densities of Old Oyo may have been, we turned to nearby occupied towns such as Igbeti, Kishi, Saki, and Igboho. Of these, Igboho has the strongest affinity with the site. It has a similar ecology and was the seat of the Oyo state before Old Oyo itself, until the Nupe drove out the Aalafin (or king [Smith 1965]). Four kings reigned at Igboho before the reoccupation of Old Oyo, and their burial places are still there today. Igboho has similar artifacts to Old Oyo and multiple walls, as revealed by the 10-transect systematic survey carried out there in 1980.

We surveyed Igboho in 10 transects from 1 km to 4.5 km in length, 50 m apart. The survey revealed similar artifact types and features as at Old Oyo, including pottery, buildings, reservoirs, grinding stones and hollows, and circular stone structures. On the basis of a 10 percent sample, the town area is 1,505 ha. The built-up area was 4,367 ha, around one-third of the site, as at Old Oyo. Structurally, the buildings still share some elements of traditional Yoruba house type, the *elese meta* (three legs, that is, the three main walls—outer, inner, and innermost/courtyard walls) and the *impluvium* (courtyard pool), with slight modifications. Corrugated iron sheets for roofing instead of leaves and cement plastering of the walls are found.

Following transect survey at Igboho, a demographic study of the town was undertaken. Igboho is divided into 17 unequal zones on the basis of the street pattern. We selected five of these for a census of building type (bungalow, traditional house, and single story), number of rooms, people in each building type, and total area and the population of this area (Casselbery 1974:117–122; Frankfort 1950; Hassan 1978:55–58; LeBlanc 1971:210–211; Marcus 1975:79–90).

The five investigated zones had areas of 69.5 ha, including 324 houses and

2,470 rooms. The total population of the zones was 4,153. Ratios of land to persons based on these counts are 167 sq m per person. Dropping the zone without residential buildings or people from the calculation results in a density figure of 143 sq m per person. A third figure of 114 sq m per person is calculated from the average land per person figure in each of the five zones.

These three density figures, 167, 143, and 114 sq m, were used to compute the population of the unsurveyed zones of Igboho. Using the survey estimates from Old Oyo of 1,870 ha of total pottery scatter and area of the compound-courtyard complexes of 884 ha and then applying the density factors from above to the pottery scatter give population estimates of 111,976 (based on 167 ha per person), 130,769 (based on 143 ha per person), and 164,035 (based on 114 ha per person). The average of these three estimates is 135,593. Using the compound-courtyard spread figure of 884 ha and the same density estimates gives population estimates of 52,934 (167), 61,618 (143), and 77,544 (114). Its average is 64,099 (1,233 persons per sq km). The average of the pottery scatter estimates and the compound courtyard estimates is 99,846 (1,920 persons per sq km). This is not unexpected for the late eighteenth century, when the capital was at its zenith.

The same density estimates can be applied to another but slightly earlier Yoruba town, Ife. The site of Ife is considered to have three phases: Preclassic, Classic (fourteenth century AD, when the site covered 12 sq km), and Postclassic (Agbaje-Williams 1991; Eyo 1974; Willett 1967). Applying the Igboho density estimates to the Ile-Ife population gives us a range from 71,856 to 105,263 persons, similar to that at Old Oyo and not out of line with historical accounts.

Old Oyo and Ife have population sizes around 100,000 persons, near the limit of precolonial city population sizes (Fletcher 1986). Survey shows that up to one-third of their areas lacked structures of any kind because of the presence of agricultural pursuits within the city wall.

Conclusion

Storey's (1992) survey of preindustrial cities shows they have reasonably similar sizes and densities all around the ancient world. In a sample size of 59 African cities, Storey (1992:119) found that the mean population size was 12,724, the median 10,000, the maximum 57,735, and the minimum 1,250. These are similar to size estimates for cities in other parts of the world of the same period. He (Storey 1992:119) also concluded that "the phenomenon of preindustrial urbanism is uniform throughout the world. Similar numbers of people could be fed and housed given the existing technology, transport systems, hinterland productivity, and administrative structures available in the preindustrial era, which, despite local variations, were similar all over the world."

Hassan (1993) stresses similar limitations on all precolonial city sizes, especially on transport technology. Food and other goods from the hinterland are limited in size and amount when transport ability is also limited. The major limiting factor on city size, according to Hassan, is the resource base, the amount of food and tribute that can be transported, and the ability of a chief to control districts in his domain. Tribute exaction is a major factor in chiefly power and city size, as is transport capability. In the early city, the size depended primarily on the chief's power to exact tribute and command resources from the surrounding hinterland. Dominion over or connection with the countryside did not exceed a walking distance, usually around 5 km, even when donkeys or boats, for example on the Nile, could be used for transport (Hassan 1993:557). Hassan (1993:555) stresses resource base, transport capability of food and tribute, and ideological and military control of districts in supporting a city. As Hassan notes, large-scale urbanism only began in the European Renaissance with large-scale manufacture, trade, industry, and worldwide commerce.

Fletcher (1986, 1993, 2000) has also compared city sizes and densities but believes that communication methods and their efficiency are the more profound determinant of city size. The limitations on preindustrial city size were a result, he believes, of limits on communication systems of preliterate societies. He draws attention to the fact that all preindustrial towns have limits on the ease and ability of communication and interaction. For Fletcher, African towns are unusual because, in spite of a lack of writing, they reached the same sizes as other cities in the world at the same time. He believes that perhaps the limitations of communication on city size can be overcome and that city size can be increased by dispersed occupation, a common African pattern, or perhaps through external economic influence. One is tempted to believe, however, that transportation of hinterland surplus to the urban center is the main limiter of city size and that dispersion of settlement helps ease the need for single, centralized destinations for traders. In this way different parts of a city can be supplied with goods that they need in a decentralized pattern. In any case, the distinctiveness of the African city, if any, seems to be its dispersion. The especially dispersed nature of African urbanism results from the continuation of subsistence practices within the city walls. Yet, because these settlements perform a variety of trade, social, and religious functions for a broader hinterland, they are, in every sense of the word, cities in their own right.

Far Eastern Urbanization

9

Urbanization in China

Erlitou and Its Hinterland

Li Liu

In comparison to other regions in the world, there have been only limited studies on the archaeology of early urbanization in China, partly due to the lack of adequate information available for such studies. Issues on urbanism in China are also intertwined with questions concerning state formation, which have been controversial. Previous research has been focused primarily on the Shang Dynasty, particularly in its centers at Zhengzhou and Anyang in Henan. Several models have been proposed by these scholars to help to characterize the political contexts of early urbanism in China. These include models of city-states, segmentary states, territorial states, and village states (for a detailed discussion see Liu and Chen 2003). There is no consensus among scholars, however, regarding the nature of urbanization in China, and these two Shang cities, which have been the focus of discussion, may in fact not represent the earliest cities, but relatively mature stages of urban development. What we need to study are the processes during which the first urban centers emerged in China.

There are three traditions in the study of urban organization, all inherent in the writing of Childe (1950). First, there is the economic tradition, which characterizes urban organization as marked by specialization; this is exemplified by Wright's (1969) study of early Mesopotamian towns emphasizing the specialization of production and by Zeder's (1991) study of Mesopotamian cities, which develops the specialization of production and distribution in depth. Second, there is the sociological tradition in which elite groups in the central settlement underwrite an urban lifestyle, as demonstrated by Adams (1965, 1966, 1981). Third, there is the ideational tradition in which the central settlements are icons of the universe, as illustrated by Wheatley (1971). Although all these features co-occur in the processes of urban development, each scholar tends to emphasize one of these (Wright, personal communication 2004). My approach to urbanism follows the economic tradition, investigating production and distribution of material goods, which characterize the first cities in China.

There is little doubt in the minds of many scholars that the titles of the first city, the first state, and a capital of the first dynasty of the Xia are attributable to one site, that of Erlitou in Yanshi City, Henan Province (Figure 9-1). It is widely believed that the Erlitou site was the last capital city of the Xia Dynasty recorded in ancient texts. Since the Xia were conquered by the Shang people, who established the succeeding dynasty, according to textual records, the reconstructions of Xia-Shang relationships have dominated interpretations of the archaeological remains discovered at Erlitou and other sites in the Yiluo region. However, not all archaeologists and historians accept this view. Some have questioned the historic relation between Erlitou and Xia, and others have argued that the Erlitou polity was no more than a complex chiefdom (for more discussion and references see Liu and Chen 2003).

The lack of consensus concerning the time and location of the origins of urbanism in China may be attributed to the available archaeological data. Erlitou has been treated as a source of standard typological and chronological sequences, and excavations have paid more attention to individual palaces and burials than to the spatial layout of the site and the political-economic systems of the region. This situation has prevented us from understanding the processes of social transformation that occurred at a regional level.

Recent research on settlement patterns in the Yiluo River valley suggests that a rapid settlement nucleation may have taken place in the eastern hinterland of Erlitou during the Erlitou period, as indicated by a marked increase in site numbers, total occupation area, and size of the largest regional center (Liu et al. 2002/ 2004). Other studies on the relationships between core and peripheral settlements during the Erlitou period point to the development of a centralized sociopolitical organization, whose territorial expansion was primarily driven by the procurement of key resources (such as metal and salt) in the regions adjacent to the Yiluo basin (Liu and Chen 2001, 2003). The regional political-economic landscape of the Erlitou culture, therefore, indicates the emergence of a large monocentered polity. It may be characterized as a territorial state, the model proposed by Bruce Trigger (1993, 1999), which refers to a political entity with a single ruler who controlled a large area through a hierarchy of provincial and local administrators and administrative centers.

On the basis of this model, the urban centers of states were small and inhabited almost exclusively by administrators, elite specialists, and retainers, whereas farmers lived in dispersed homesteads and villages. According to Trigger (1993:10–11, 1999), territorial states tended to have a clearly separated two-tier economy. Whereas farmers manufactured what they needed from local raw materials on a part-time basis and exchanged these goods among themselves, elite craftsmen, living in cities or on royal estates, manufactured luxury goods for the king and upper classes, often from exotic materials. Food was obtained to support urban centers almost exclusively as rents or taxes from local communities.

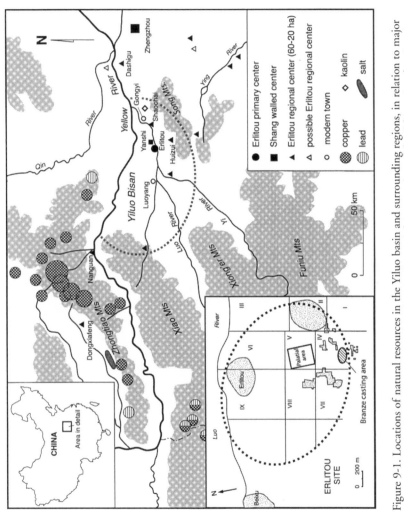

Figure 9-1. Locations of natural resources in the Yiluo basin and surrounding regions, in relation to major Erlitou and early Shang sites mentioned in the text. Lower left insert: plan of the Erlitou site, showing site sections excavated in 1959–2004.

Trigger's (1993:11) claim for "a clearly separated two-tier economy" in the Shang cities has not been supported by recent archaeological evidence, and many generalizations about the early urban morphology were perhaps influenced by Paul Wheatley's concept of the "ceremonial complex." This concept was used to describe Zhengzhou and Anyang as early urban centers (Wheatley 1971:30–47), each comprising a centrally situated ceremonial and administrative enclave occupied primarily by royalty, priests, and a few selected craftsmen, whereas the peasantry and majority of the artisans lived in villages dispersed through the surrounding countryside (Wheatley 1971:47). It is necessary to point out that Wheatley's propositions were largely derived from textual information and archaeological analysis undertaken prior to the 1970s. The new discoveries made in recent years, however, indicate that Zhengzhou's walls comprised two concentric systems. The inner walls, described by Wheatley as the ceremonial center, demarcated the palace-temple areas that were occupied by the elites, whereas the newly found outer walls defined the urban boundaries, within which all sorts of craft production for making prestige and utilitarian goods took place (Henan Institute 2001). Therefore, Wheatley's concept of the ceremonial complex as the early form of urbanism in China needs to be reevaluated.

In a similar vein, the characteristics of the territorial state in ancient China, as Trigger described, have not been evaluated or tested against recent archaeological data. We need to examine the evidence of excavations and surveys to see whether the early urban center at Erlitou was a place where the population did not engage in any agriculture, where all craftsmen in cities made only prestige items, and where all villages in the hinterland were agricultural communities with low levels of craft specialization.

Trigger's model portrays dichotomist situations in the sociopolitical context of production, often characterized as attached production versus independent production. As generally defined, attached full-time specialists worked under elite patrons to produce primarily luxury goods, whereas independent craftsmen made largely utilitarian items for an unspecified demand that varies according to economic, social, and political conditions (e.g., Brumfiel and Earle 1987:5–6; Costin 1991:3–11). However, it has also been pointed out that such a luxury/utilitarian dichotomy is too simplistic. Goods produced by attached craftsmen could also be utilitarian items, if these goods can be exploited by only a subset of the population (Costin 2001:297–300, for an overview). Furthermore, attached and independent are only idealized extremes of a continuum characterizing control and should not be taken as static categories; other parameters, such as concentration, scale, and intensity, should also be taken into consideration for understanding the organization of production (Costin 1991:Figure 1.4).

This study, therefore, looks at the very center of the early state in China and reexamines the Erlitou site and its hinterland in the Yiluo basin in order to gain more holistic insights into the relationship between production and the transitional processes of urbanization. There are two objectives in this research. The first is to analyze the changing spatial patterns of production activities through time at the Erlitou site in order to comprehend the internal socioeconomic relationships at an intrasite level. The second is to examine the economic relationships between Erlitou and its hinterland in order to understand the regional context of this first urban center. I will pay special attention to the patterns of production, examining the concepts and applications of attached versus independent craft specializations in both urban and rural settlements, with references to Trigger's two-tier economy model. By attached specialization/production I refer to the manufacture of prestige goods, especially bronze ritual objects, whereas by independent specialization I refer to those crafts for utilitarian purposes, including pottery, bone, and stone artifacts, although we do not know whether, and to what extent, the elite may have been involved in the production and distribution processes of these utilitarian items.

In this chapter, first I argue that overemphasis of the rural-urban economic dichotomy has been misleading and that, instead, urbanization in China needs to be understood from the perspective of rural-urban interactions at a regional level. Second, I argue that the morphology of the earliest urban center in China may have comprised not only a ceremonial and administrative center, as Wheatley (1971:47) rightly suggested, but also a craft production complex.

The Erlitou Urban Center

Erlitou is situated in the center of the Yiluo valley, a vast fertile alluvial basin surrounded by the Mangling hills and Yellow River to the north and mountain ranges on the other three sides. The Yi and Luo rivers flow from west to east through the basin and join one another, forming a single river channel before emptying into the Yellow River. The environmentally circumscribed condition of the basin apparently had advantages for its military defensibility, and the fertile alluvial land in the basin insured high yields of agricultural products, such as grains and domesticated animals, with great potential for supporting a high population density.

Various archaeologists who have excavated Erlitou have reported different site sizes for Erlitou, ranging from 300 ha to 900 ha, depending whether scattered remains to the north of the Luo River were included. On the basis of the latest survey, the site size of Erlitou is 300 ha (Erlitou 2001). Erlitou is now located on the south bank of the Luo River. Originally it was on the northern side of the ancient Luo River, which changed course to its present position during the Tang Dynasty (AD 618–907). Although small groups of people resided in the southeastern part of the site from the middle Yangshao to early Longshan periods (ca. 4000–2500 BC) (Zheng et al. 1987), Erlitou was primarily inhabited during the Erlitou (including Phases I–IV; ca. 1900–1500 BC) and Erligang (including

Table 9-1. Comparative Chronology among Three Cities and Association
with Ceramic Styles

Ca. BC	Phases	Erlitou	Yanshi	Zhengzhou
1400	Upper Erligang	ELG village	ELG walled city (200 ha)	ELG large walled city (25 sq. km)
1500	Late Lower Erligang	ELG village	ELG walled city (200 ha)	ELG large walled city (25 sq. km)
1560/1600	Erlitou IV / Early Lower Erligang	ELT city (<300 ha)	ELT & ELG small walled city (80 ha)	ELG large regional center (?)
1900	Erlitou III	ELT city (300 ha)		ELT village
	Erlitou II	ELT city		ELT village
	Erlitou I	ELT regional center (?)		ELT village

ELT = Erlitou ceramic assemblages; ELG = Erligang ceramic assemblages.

Lower and Upper phases; ca. 1600–1400 BC) periods (Institute of Archaeology
1999) (Table 9-1). Starting in 1959 the site has been continuously excavated for
more than 40 years, with only the results from the first 20 years of excavation in
a total area of 2 ha published in any detail (Institute of Archaeology 1999). This
provides the primary data for this study.

Previous excavations have focused on the eastern part of the site, which was
divided into nine sections for easy recording. Excavated areas are scattered over
all sections, but primarily concentrated in Sections II, III, IV, V, VI, VIII, and IX
(Figure 9-1). To date, a total area of less than 3 ha has been excavated, and a
wealth of material remains has been unearthed. These include houses; a rammed-
earth palatial enclosure and foundations; roads; ash pits; burials; hearths; remains
of bronze casting and bone workshops; kilns; and artifacts made of bronze, jade,
stone, bone, shell, and pottery.

Unfortunately, these data are not reported in a way that allows elaborate quantitative analyses, because a large part of the report was focused on ceramic typology rather than on numerical and spatial information. The following analyses
are the first attempt to address issues of spatial patterns of the site on the basis of
existing information; given the nature of the data available, the results are suggestive rather than conclusive.

In order to determine the functional components of the site and nature of its population, one must first establish the spatial distribution of different production activities, including construction, agriculture, and craft. Different production activities are determined by traces of workshops, waste products, and tools. Because no use-ware analysis on tools from Erlitou has been published, their functions can be only inferred primarily on the basis of tool forms. I categorize the tools into six groups for analysis as follows:

1. Construction tools (for digging and carpentry): stone spades, axes, wedges, and stone/bronze adzes and chisels. Spades may have been used for both agriculture and construction, as shovels are used today. As observed by the Erlitou excavators, some impressions of digging tools left on the walls of pits appear to match the sizes of spades (Institute of Archaeology 1999:39, 79–80). Therefore, I categorize spades as digging tools for construction. Small adzes and chisels were probably for small-scale carpentry such as boxes, bowls, handles, and so on.

2. Agricultural tools: stone and shell knives and sickles. Although stone and shell knives and sickles have usually been treated as agricultural implements (e.g., Pearson 1981; Yun 1997), they may also have been used as domestic cutting tools. However, because it is impossible to determine the functions of these tools without use-ware analysis, I treat these knives and sickles as agricultural tools here.

3. Fishing tools: bone/bronze fishhooks and pottery/stone net-sinkers.

4. Domestic craft tools: stone/pottery spindle whorls and bone/shell/bronze needles and awls. These were perhaps used for making textiles and clothing and for general maintenance.

5. Hunting or warfare weapons: stone/bone/shell/bronze arrowheads.

6. Tool-manufacture tools: whetstones. Most of them have grooves on the surface, indicating use in making or resharpening small tools such as awls and arrowheads.

Tools discovered from the first 20 years of excavations at Erlitou (Institute of Archaeology 1999) are analyzed in the current study. In the excavation report, numbers of features and artifacts from each phase were given in detail, but the locations where these features and artifacts were unearthed were not fully described, and in most cases, less than 60 percent of the tools were reported with spatial information.

In the following analyses, although the changing frequencies of tools through time are fairly reliable, the spatial distributions of tools present in site sections (shown in Figure 9-2) are only suggestive. By analyzing the temporal and spatial changes of features and artifacts on the basis of the available information, we better understand the political-economic organization at Erlitou.

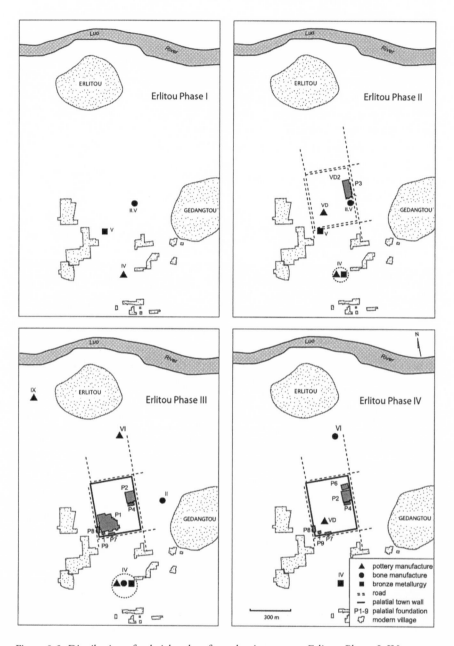

Figure 9-2. Distribution of palatial and craft production areas at Erlitou, Phases I–IV.

Spatial Order of Erlitou

Erlitou Phase I

When Erlitou was occupied during Phase I, it may have already been a large settlement, although material remains were scattered, and the deposits were relatively thin. Most excavated areas yielded remains dating to Phase I, but only 36 pits, 6 burials, and 54 tools were unearthed (Table 9-2).

With regard to craft specialization, Section V may have been a location of bronze casting, indicated by the finding of slag; Section II.V appears to have been a bone workshop, because bone and antler waste with traces of sawing and chopping were unearthed there. Ceramic production may have also been present in Section IV (Figure 9-2), suggested by the discovery of a potter's tool, *pai* (beater), which is the only such tool found at the site. Bronze objects appeared, but were limited to knives. Other tools made of stone, bone, shell, and pottery appear to belong to all functional categories described above. Agricultural tools were distributed in most excavated sections, whereas the tools for fishing, domestic craft, and hunting (mostly made of bone, shell, and antler) were concentrated in Section II.V (Figure 9-3). Because Section II.V was engaged in bone production, the high frequency of those tools and arrowheads unearthed there indicates that these artifacts may represent both production and consumption and that this bone workshop manufactured a variety of products for subsistence economic activities. Arrowheads were more likely used for hunting rather than for warfare, because little evidence of violence has been identified in the region. Given that other kinds of craft production, such as bronze casting and pottery making, were located in different sections, it is reasonable to argue that Erlitou was first developed as a large settlement with a number of discrete craft production workshops producing various products.

It is unclear whether the bronze knives were regarded as status markers, because they were not found in burials, and no elite burial has been dated to this phase. On the basis of archaeological remains in Phase I at Erlitou, the products from these workshops were primarily nonelite goods, and the population was most likely engaged in both craft and agricultural activities. No evidence for attached production has been identified, and no elite residence or administrative building of Phase I has been found to date.

Erlitou Phase II

Compared to Phase I, the Phase II occupation areas became larger, mainly concentrated in Sections II, IV, V, and VIII. The number of pits doubled, and the numbers of burials and tools tripled. Other features, such as houses, kilns, and hearths, which were absent in Phase I, have been found (Table 9-2). There was probably a considerable increase in population from Phase I to Phase II.

Some large rammed-earth foundations, probably the remains of a palatial

Table 9-2. Summary of Archaeological Features and Tools Found at Erlitou

Phases	Pit	Burial	House	Kiln	Hearth	Tools	Distribution areas (shown in Fig 10-2)	Thickness of deposits
Erlitou Phase I	36	6	0	0	0	54	II, II.V, IV, V, VD, VIII, IX	0.3–1.5 m
Erlitou Phase II	75	18	7	1	4	172	II, II.V, III, IV, V, VD, VD2, VIII, IX	0.7–2 m
Erlitou Phase III	138	47	12	5	4	823	II, II.V, III, IV, V, VD, VD2, VIII, IX	0.3–2.5 m
Erlitou Phase IV	129	36	4	1	6	1020	II, II.V, III, IV, V, VD, VD2, VIII, IX	1 m
Lower Erligang	14	3	0	0	0	94	II, II.V, III, IV, VD, VIII	0.4 m
Upper Erligang	8	1	0	0	0	76	II.V, VD	0.15 m

Data based on Institute of Archaeology (1999).

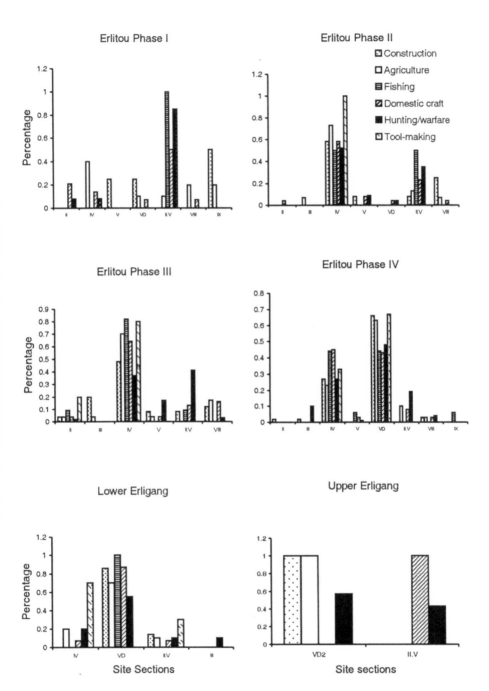

Figure 9-3. Histograms showing distribution of tool types at Erlitou, from Erlitou Phase I to Upper Erligang.

structure, were found in Section VD2. One of them was a palatial compound (Palace #3 built in Phase II), 0.75 ha in area (150 m long and 50 m wide), with five elite burials in its courtyard (Erlitou 2003). Four roads (10–20 m wide) extended on both north-south and east-west axes, demarcating the palatial area of about 10 ha (Xu and Zhao 2004) (Figure 9-2).

Although Section V may still have been a location for casting bronze, as indicated by fragments of crucibles, Section IV appears to have become the major craft production center including bronze casting and pottery making, suggested by the finding of a kiln, clay molds for casting bronze vessels, crucible fragments, and bronze waste from casting. It is possible that the pottery kiln located in this area was used for making clay molds and crucibles as a part of bronze production. A whetstone was also unearthed from Section IV (Institute of Archaeology 1999:85), indicating small tools were made or resharpened in this area. Large numbers of houses, pits, and burials have been excavated from Section IV; burials include children and adults, both male and female. Houses and burials were placed in proximity, indicating that this craft production center was densely populated by craftsmen and their families. However, no information is provided in the report for us to infer the social status of craftsmen. A ditch, up to 16 m wide, 3 m deep, and more than 100 m long, was found in the south of Section IV, but its complete shape is unclear (Zheng et al. 1984).

Bronze production areas surrounded by ditches have been found at two other Erlitou sites, Dongxiafeng and Nanguan near the Zhongtiao Mountains (Figure 9-1) (Liu and Chen 2001). At the Zhengzhou Shang city, a bronze foundry at Nanguanwai was also enclosed by ditches (Henan Institute 2001:307–367). It is possible, therefore, that Section IV at Erlitou was also ditched.

Material components found in Section IV are also similar to those in the craft production center enclosed with double ditches at Dongxiafeng, in which remains of bronze casting, pottery kilns, houses, pits, and burials were densely distributed (Institute of Archaeology et al. 1988). Craft production that focused on bronze metallurgy in such constrained areas may have been carried out by attached specialists under the control of the state (Liu and Chen 2001). If this were the case, Phase II would have witnessed the emergence of attached craft specialization at Erlitou, which was dominated by, but not limited to, bronze metallurgy. Such a pattern of production may have also been practiced in other Erlitou regional centers, such as Dongxiafeng and Nanguan.

In Section II.V, people continued to produce bone implements, indicated by bone and antler waste (Figure 9-2). Because the bone implements were primarily utilitarian items (such as needles, awls, hairpins, and arrowheads), it is possible that independent specialists operated the craft workshops in Section II.V. These two craft production centers (Sections IV and II.V) also yielded most of the food production tools (agricultural, fishing, and hunting) (Figure 9-3), suggesting that the craft-specialized communities probably produced their own food, at least to some extent.

Bronze items, mainly utilitarian tools, were still few in number. One well-furnished burial (81YLM4) contained a bronze plaque inlaid with turquoise and a bronze bell (Erlitou 1984), indicating that bronzes were now evidently used as status markers. Some clay molds appear to have been made for casting vessels, but the types of vessel are unclear, and archaeologists have not found bronze vessels dating to Phase II or earlier. White pottery ritual vessels made of kaolin have been regularly present as high-status markers in mortuary contexts. It is interesting to note that white pottery was not produced at Erlitou, but probably made in locations near the kaolin deposits, the closest of which are in the east of the Yiluo region (Figure 9-1) (Liu 2003). The fact that the bronze objects associated with elite burials occurred simultaneously with the development of attached craft production focusing on bronze metallurgy at Erlitou indicates the emergence of an institutionalized bronze metallurgy as a part of prestige-goods production networks. But because white pottery vessels, rather than bronzes, were a major status symbol circulated among elites, the prestige-goods production networks were most likely multicentered. This proposition needs to be tested in future archaeological investigation to locate the white pottery production areas.

Among all tool types, agricultural tools increased the most, making up 42 percent of the total Phase II tools analyzed (N = 172). This suggests a development of intensive agricultural activities to cope with the growing population. The number of arrowheads increased at a rate similar to other tools, indicating their primary function was the same as that in Phase I, that is, for hunting rather than for warfare (Figure 9-4).

Erlitou Phase III

Phase III witnessed the peak of development in all aspects at Erlitou. Material remains were uncovered from all excavated areas, the cultural deposits were the thickest among all phases, and the quantities of archaeological features multiplied. Compared to Phase II, the number of pits and houses nearly doubled, burials increased by more than 150 percent, kilns increased by 400 percent, and tools increased by 380 percent (Table 9-2).

At the end of Phase II and the beginning of Phase III, rammed-earth walls (2 m wide) were built on top of the existing roads in Section V, forming a palatial enclosure measured 10.8 ha in area. Within the enclosure there are two large rammed-earth foundations, Palace #1 and Palace #2, and many smaller structures (Figure 9-2) (Institute of Archaeology 1999:137; Xu and Zhao 2004; Xu et al. 2003). Palace #1 (9,600 sq m in size) comprised a single edifice with a large front courtyard, which was then enclosed by walls with roofed galleries. A layer of

Numbers of tools and pits from Erlitou

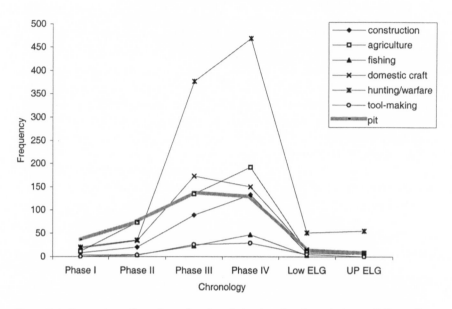

Figure 9-4. Comparison of numbers of tools and pits changing through time at Erlitou, all phases, illustrating the dramatic increase of arrowheads in Phases III and IV and the decreased numbers of pits in contrast to the increased numbers of production tools in Phase IV.

rammed-earth foundation, about 2 m thick, covered the entire compound. The main palatial structure (30 × 11 m in size), made of wattle and daub, consisted of one central large room and 11 small side rooms. It was built on top of a rammed-earth platform (900 sq m in size and more than 3 m in thickness), with three layers of pebbles (50 × 30 m in area and 60–65 cm thick) placed on its lower level (Institute of Archaeology 1999:138–144).

Palace #2 (4,200 sq m in size), superimposed on Palace #3 of Phase II, is located 150 m southwest of Palace #1. It was also built on top of a rammed-earth foundation up to 3 m thick. Within the compound, a rectangular-shaped platform made of rammed earth (about 1,070 sq m in size) supported the main structure, which was divided by wattle-and-daub walls into three rooms. The entire compound was then enclosed by walls with attached galleries on the eastern, southern, and western sides (Institute of Archaeology 1999:151–159; Thorp 1991). These two palatial compounds were different in size and form, suggesting that they may have served different functions, although the exact functions are still a matter of speculation.

The construction of these buildings and walls must have required large-scale earth moving. A ditch measuring 8–16 m wide, up to 4 m deep, and more than

350 m long has been found in the eastern border of the Erlitou site. It comprised numerous large pits dating from Phase II to Phase IV. Archaeologists have suggested that the soil was removed from these pits for constructing buildings or making pottery at the site (Erlitou 2001).

Judging from the large quantities of remains of kilns, slag, clay molds, crucibles, and bone wasters, the attached craft production center at Section IV continued to grow, producing bone artifacts, ceramics, and bronzes, including both utilitarian and ritual objects. Other craft workshops, perhaps continuously run by independent craftsmen, were also developing. Evidence for bone manufacture has been found in Section II, and more kilns for ceramics were found in Sections VI and IX (Figure 9-2) (Institute of Archaeology 1999; Zheng et al. 1987). The kiln in Section VI was dated to roughly Phase II or III (Xu, personal communication 2002). For the first time ritual bronzes, mostly drinking vessels, occurred in the archaeological record, but only from elite burials and residential areas at the Erlitou site. At the same time, white pottery ritual vessels were continuously distributed among elite individuals in both core and peripheral areas (Liu 2003). These phenomena suggest that bronze vessels were the privilege of individuals of the highest social status in the Erlitou polity.

Among the 823 tools dated to Phase III (Table 9-2), those for construction and food production have been found in most sections, with the highest concentration in the largest craft production center in Section IV (Figure 9-3). Whetstones were found in Sections II and IV, where evidence for bone manufacture was present. Agricultural tools decreased in proportion compared to previous phases, making up only 16 percent of the Phase III tools. This suggests that the Erlitou population may have become increasingly dependent on tribute for food as the level of craft specialization increased. It is notable that Phase III experienced the greatest growth in the number of arrowheads (377), which is more than 10 times the number in Phase II (35). This figure is in sharp contrast to other tool categories and features (e.g., pits), which show much less pronounced curves in growth (Figure 9-4). Such a dramatic increase in the number of arrowheads cannot be explained by the intensification of hunting activities alone; it was likely attributable to the expansion of the Erlitou territories toward the peripheral regions. The Erlitou expansion, probably military in nature, started in Phase II and reached the climax in Phase III. It was evidently driven by the procurement of key resources. Two regional centers, for example, may have been established at Dongxiafeng and Nanguan near the Zhongtiao Mountains, which are about 150 km northwest of Erlitou (Figure 9-1) for the purpose of obtaining and transporting salt and copper (Liu and Chen 2001, 2003).

In previous phases the palatial structures were few, and bronze metallurgy took place in more than one location at Erlitou. During Phase III the site seems to have experienced some significant changes in terms of urban planning. The palatial enclosure was built, more palaces were constructed, and the bronze casting was exclusively held in an area south of the palatial complex. Given the fact that Erlitou was the only site in China that yielded hard evidence for casting bronze ritual vessels during the Erlitou period (Liu 2003; Liu and Chen 2003), the centralized distribution of bronze-casting workshops near the palatial complex at the urban center suggests an increased state monopoly in producing high-status symbols. In contrast, bone and ceramic workshops were spread over more extended areas at the site, suggesting a continuous development of independent craft production. The attached craft production center seems to have also incorporated other materials and products, such as bone artifacts and pottery. It is not clear, however, on the basis of available data, if the bone and ceramic products made in the attached production area were different in function and type from those made in independent production areas, because it is also possible that these crafts may have also been operated as part of bronze production. Further study on the comparison of products from different workshops may provide information for understanding modes of production at Erlitou.

As in previous phases, the population of Erlitou Phase III included not only craft specialists but also farmers, and both elite and utilitarian goods were produced at the site.

Erlitou Phase IV

Phase IV experienced the initial decline of the settlement. Although material remains have been unearthed in most sections across the entire site, they are mostly in Sections III, IV, V, and VI. Compared to Phase III, the number of features is smaller, and cultural deposits are thinner. Pits decreased by 6 percent, burials by 30 percent, houses and hearths by 60 percent, and kilns by 400 percent in number (Table 9-2). These phenomena suggest that the population may have declined at Erlitou.

The palatial enclosure and Palace #2 were continuously in use (Xu and Zhao 2004), and another large structure (Palace #6, size unclear) was newly constructed to the north of Palace #2 (Erlitou 2003). However, Palace #1 was abandoned, indicated by burials, hearths, pits, and a kiln dating to Phase IV intruding into the palace foundations. Section IV was still the center for casting bronzes, including both ritual vessels and utilitarian items, and bronze ritual vessels continued to find their way into elite burials at Erlitou. But bone workshops seem to have been set up in the northern part of the site, indicated by a large quantity of bone waste, semifinished products, and whetstones found in several pits in Section VI. The bone products include awls, spades, arrowheads, and knives. Ceramic production may have taken place in Section VD, suggested by the remains of a kiln (Figure 9-2) (Institute of Archaeology 1999:260–267; Zheng 1996; Zheng et al. 1984). Taken together, although the bone and pottery production continued to flourish as independent productions, bronze casting was the only craft remaining as attached production in a centralized pattern.

Sections IV and VD also yielded most tool types, including whetstones, suggesting that various production activities continued in these craft centers (Figure 9-3). The bone-work area in Section VI was discovered in the 1980s, and no detailed report on the tools found there is available to date.

Contrary to the reduced numbers of all archaeological features, the quantities of tools in all categories increased, reaching a total of 1,020 (Table 9-2), except for those used in domestic craft production (Figure 9-4). These phenomena suggest that the Erlitou population engaged more intensively in food production and residential construction during this phase despite fewer people residing there. Arrowhead production increased markedly (from 377 to 469), indicating military conflict in the region.

In the Yiluo region a fortified settlement was established at Yanshi, 6 km northeast of Erlitou. Phase I at Yanshi (ca. 1600–1500 BC) overlaps with Erlitou Phase IV (ca. 1560–1500 BC) (Xia Shang Zhou 2000:65–68) (Table 9-1). However, the dates for Erlitou Phase IV reported by the Xia Shang Zhou Chronology Project are controversial (Liu 2001). On the basis of these dates, the Yanshi walled site would have developed during Erlitou Phase III, but only Phase IV ceramics have been identified there. Therefore, the beginning dates for Erlitou Phase IV may have been earlier than 1560 BC, or the initial occupation dates at Yanshi may have been later than 1600 BC. Ceramic assemblages from the earliest occupation at the Yanshi site include both Erlitou and Xiaqiyuan forms; the latter is believed to have been the predecessor of the Erligang ceramic assemblages of the early Shang, but it is unclear how long this Xiaqiyuan form of ceramics lasted at Yanshi. Shortly after the initial settlement at Yanshi, people constructed a group of palatial architectural structures surrounded by rammed-earth walls (4 ha), which were then surrounded by a second layer of rammed-earth enclosures (80 ha in area) (Table 9-1). Many Chinese archaeologists and historians believe that Yanshi was the first city built by the Shang people who conquered the Xia Dynasty, which was centered at Erlitou. Such arguments were primarily based on the differentiations in ceramic types and architectural styles between Erlitou and Yanshi, which are assumed to indicate cultures of two ethnic groups (e.g., Du et al. 1999:37; Gao et al. 1998; Wang 1999; Yang 2001). These assumptions, which relate archaeological cultures with ethnicities, are problematic and need to be further analyzed, but this subject is beyond the scope of the present study.

Although we have no archaeological evidence to link the Xia with Erlitou, the emergence of a fortification near Erlitou at the time of its decline raises interesting questions regarding the relationship between these two sites. The construction of the fortification at Yanshi coincides with an increase in the production of arrowheads at Erlitou. Because the two settlements are spaced such a short distance apart, it is difficult to imagine that they confronted each other with hostile relationships for a few decades. This phenomenon needs further study.

Although there are signs of decline at Erlitou during Phase IV, the urban cen-

ter was not taken over by a non-Erlitou population, because palatial structures
were still in use, ritual bronzes were being produced and distributed, and other
types of craft manufactures (such as bone and ceramic) also continued. Political
authorities may have continued in the urban center. The increased quantities of
food-production tools, however, suggest that the Erlitou population may have become more self-reliant in subsistence economy rather than depending on tribute.

Erligang Phases (ca. 1500–1400 BC)

The Erligang phase as a whole is also referred to as the early Shang period, representing the flourish of Shang material culture across a very large region, including
the middle Yellow River and middle Yangzi River. The primary center was located
at Zhengzhou (25 sq km in size), some 70 km east of Erlitou. This city included
a walled inner city for elite residents and a walled outer city occupied by houses
and craft workshops making bronze, pottery, and bone artifacts (Henan Institute
2001). Yanshi was enlarged to a fortified city of 200 ha in size and may have
become a regional center to extract tribute from the Yiluo region for Zhengzhou.
In a manner similar to the Erlitou expansion, the early Shang spread out to the
periphery in order to control key resources, especially salt, copper, and other prestige goods (Liu and Chen 2003).

The overall Erligang phase is dated to ca. 1600–1400 BC at Zhengzhou and
Yanshi, which overlapped with the Erlitou Phase IV (Xia Shang Zhou 2000:62–
65), as discussed above. When the Erligang assemblages appeared at Erlitou, they
date to the late Lower Erligang Phase (Table 9-1). Because archaeological cultures
are defined and based on ceramic typology in Chinese archaeology, this overlap
in chronology between Erlitou and Yanshi-Zhengzhou may indicate that the
Erlitou people continued to produce and use Erlitou-style pottery and that the
Yanshi-Zhengzhou people were making and consuming Erligang-style pottery.
The nature of the relationships and interactions between these three cities needs
to be investigated.

At Erlitou the Lower Erligang Phase witnessed the beginning of a total collapse
of this first urban center. The occupation area at the site declined considerably,
tools decreased sharply in number (N = 94), and the cultural deposits were thin
(Table 9-2). Material remains have been found mainly in Sections VD and II.V,
although scattered finds have been unearthed from other sections (Institute of
Archaeology 1999:347). Whetstones were found in Sections IV and V, indicating
that small tools may have been continuously made or resharpened at the site,
although evidence for craft specialization (such as a kiln, bronze casting, and bone
waste) was absent. Tool types were limited to those for agriculture, domestic craft
production, and construction, mainly uncovered in Section VD (Figure 9-3).
Only small numbers of pits and burials have been found, accounting for about
10 percent of the same categories in the previous phase (Table 9-2). The settlement was reduced to an ordinary farming village. The absence of pottery manu-

facture at Erlitou may account for the presence of Erligang ceramic assemblages at the site; perhaps the Erlitou people now obtained the pottery produced at Yanshi.

The number of archaeological features fell to a level below that of the initial occupation period (Phase I) at Erlitou (Table 9-2), suggesting an unprecedented decline of population. The number of arrowheads, however, is relatively high (Figure 9-4), indicating a prolonged hostile social environment.

The Upper Erligang Phase witnessed the final years of Erlitou occupation. People lived in a small area at the site (Sections II.V and VD), and no evidence for craft specialization was present. Few features have been found, and a small number of tools (N = 76) for construction, agriculture, domestic craft, and hunting were unearthed in Sections II.V and VD (Table 9-2, Figure 9-3). Apparently, a population even smaller than the previous phase lived there before abandoning the settlement completely.

During the Erligang phases, the disappearance of craft production at Erlitou coincided with the establishment of bronze foundries and other workshops at Zhengzhou (Table 9-1). The marked decline of population at Erlitou corresponded with the rapid growth of the Yanshi and Zhengzhou Shang cities and the Shang expansion to ever-greater territories. This territorial expansion was characterized by military conquests accompanied by population movement from the core to the periphery in order to occupy new lands and to obtain resources (Liu and Chen 2003). It is possible that the final collapse of Erlitou was a result of an urbanization process centered at Zhengzhou and the outward migrations from the Yiluo basin.

The Erlitou Hinterland

Besides the fertile alluvial land, the core area in the Yiluo basin offered a few nonagricultural natural resources that were crucial for the development of urbanism. These include timber for constructing palatial structures; pebbles for making thick layers of architectural foundations; lithic materials for making stone tools; kaolin clay for manufacturing elite ceramics; copper, tin, and lead for casting bronzes; charcoal as fuel for casting bronze alloys; firewood for firing pottery and household cooking; and salt for daily consumption for the entire population of the region. Most of these items were available from the surrounding regions within a radius of 20–200 km from Erlitou, and a number of Erlitou outposts have been found in the resource-rich areas on the periphery. A number of medium-sized Erlitou sites, probably regional centers, were distributed within and beyond the Yiluo basin, mostly located along major water transportation routes or resource-rich areas (Figure 9-1), suggesting that Erlitou's expansion was associated with political-economic motivations (Liu and Chen 2003).

Recent systematic regional surveys in the eastern part of the Yiluo basin suggest that the regional centers in this area were also developed for providing material goods to the urban center at Erlitou, as exemplified by Shaochai and Huizui in the east and south of Erlitou (Liu et al. 2002/2004).

Shaochai

Two subregional centers (20 ha and 13 ha in size) were found in the survey area (more than 180 sq km) from the late Longshan culture (ca. 2500–2000 BC) of the Neolithic period. Located in two small river valleys, each dominated a number of small villages, forming a two-tiered settlement hierarchy. The Erlitou period witnessed rapid settlement nucleation starting from Phase II, indicated by the emergence of a large subregional center at Shaochai (60 ha, 20 km east of Erlitou) (Figure 9-1). This change was accompanied by increased site numbers and occupation area, with a three-tiered settlement hierarchy in the survey area, and thus a four-tiered hierarchy in the Yiluo region (including the Erlitou site). Shaochai was located on the eastern bank of the Yiluo River, surrounded by fertile alluvial land, with easy access to mountainous areas rich in natural resources (such as stone, kaolin, timber, and so on). Given the fact that Shaochai was barely inhabited before the Erlitou period, its development into a subregional center may be the result not only of its production of agricultural products but also of its extraction of nonagricultural products from the surrounding areas, in combination with its function as a transportation node along the Yiluo River, controlling the flow of material goods into Erlitou. After Erlitou Phase IV, Shaochai first declined in size (ca. 18 ha) during the Upper Erligang period, probably abandoned before the late Shang phase, and then reinhabited by only a few small villages during the Zhou Dynasty (1045–771 BC). The process of development and decline at Shaochai was similar to that at Erlitou (Liu et al. 2002/2004).

Huizui

Another large settlement, perhaps a subregional center, has been identified at Huizui in Yanshi County, some 15 km south of Erlitou (Figure 9-1), dating primarily from Neolithic Yangshao and Longshan cultures to the Erlitou period (ca. 5000–1500 BC). This site appears to have been a location for producing stone tools and lime, indicated by the finding of large quantities of tool blanks, flakes, grinding slabs, semifinished and finished tools, and burnt limestone. The site in the Neolithic period was small in size, no more than 10 ha. Starting from the Longshan period (ca. 2500 BC) at the latest, it became specialized in making large quantities of stone tools and lime. During the Erlitou period the settlement increased to 25 ha in size, and the traces of tool manufacture, such as workshops and lithic wasters, have been found all over the settlement. The lithic products were predominantly limestone spades, and the limestone wasters were then burnt to make lime, which was commonly used as construction material during the late

Neolithic and Erlitou periods. After the Erlitou period Huizui went into decline, which continued during the Erligang period, a process also parallel to the collapse of the urban center at Erlitou (Institute of Archaeology 2003; Liu et al. 2002/ 2004).

Huizui is situated near the Songshan Mountains, which are rich in lithic deposits. Sandstones used as grinding slabs at Huizui were derived from quarries about 1 km from the site. Two types of lithics, oolitic limestone and dolomite limestone, were used for making spades at Huizui. A geological investigation suggests that the outcrops of these two types of limestone occur near the ridge of the Songshan range, at elevations of 650–700 m above sea level (Gorton 2003). The distance between limestone sources and Huizui is about 5 km as the crow flies, but the actual distance is greater, because the Songshan ridge is about 500 m higher than the surrounding alluvial plain. It is possible that there was a second tier of settlements located near the quarries, which supplied the lithic raw material to the stone-tool production site at Huizui. More archaeological surveys need to be done before reaching any conclusion.

Spades made of these two types of limestone have been identified at Erlitou (Institute of Archaeology 1999:400–404), suggesting that Huizui may have supplied stone spades to Erlitou (Ford 2001; Liu et al. 2002/2004). Given that Erlitou underwent considerable construction, which required large numbers of spades for digging, as well as many axes, adzes, and chisels for woodworking, it is possible that the increasing specialization in spade production at Huizui was related to the growing demand for them from Erlitou for its urban expansion.

The tools unearthed from the Erlitou strata at Huizui include agricultural implements, construction tools, domestic craft tools, and hunting/warfare tools. The components of Huizui tool types are similar to those from Erlitou. The Huizui community, therefore, appears to have practiced a mixed subsistence economy, combining food production and craft specialization. Huizui's economy was intertwined with the regional economy centered at Erlitou, and its development and decline reflected the sociopolitical changes in the region during the formation of early states.

It is notable that more lithic materials have been identified in the stone-tool assemblages from Erlitou than those in the Huizui tool blanks, suggesting that Huizui was not the sole supplier of stone products for Erlitou. This proposition is supported by recent surveys that located several other stone-tool manufacture sites near the Songshan Mountains. In contrast, little evidence for stone-tool manufacture has been identified at Erlitou, and what has been found was limited to reusing broken large tools to make small tools such as knives (e.g., Institute of Archaeology 1999:85, 179, 279). This urban center, therefore, may have obtained tools from a number of lithic-manufacture settlements, many of which are yet to be discovered by archaeologists.

Erlitou Demography: A Trial

There have been some attempts to reconstruct the urban population size during the Xia and Shang periods on the basis of ancient textual records and studies of Neolithic residential patterns, but the estimated population densities are extremely high and unrealistic. The most commonly cited ancient textual record is from the "Zhouce" in *Zhanguoce* (ca. 26–8 BC), which stated that "in ancient times the world within the four seas was divided into ten thousand states; the largest walled city was no bigger than 300 *zhang* [on each side], and the greatest population was no more than three thousand households." This hypothetical city, calculated as 4.761 ha in area with 15,000 residences, or as a habitation area of 160 sq m per household (five people), has been used as a model for estimating ancient urban population (Lin 1998; Song 1991), at a population density of 31,250 persons per sq km. However, this hypothetical city is merely a scholastic model without any archaeological support. Such a high density may have represented a "spot density," rather than the overall density, of a city (cf. Storey 1992:136–137).

The other source that was often used for estimating population density of early states in China (Song 1991) was derived from the settlement patterns of a Neolithic village at Jiangzhai in Shaanxi. On the basis of the number of houses distributed in the settlement, some archaeologists estimated that 500 persons lived in the village of 1.8 ha in an area surrounded by ditches at any point in time (Xi'an Banpo 1988), at a population density of 278 persons per ha. This estimate is problematic because the houses accounted for in the calculation were not all contemporary (Zhao 1998). Recent studies of the Jiangzhai population suggest 75–125 persons on the basis of settlement data and 85–100 persons on the basis of burial data (Zhao 1995, 1998); these account for an average population range of 80–112.5 persons, at a population density of 44–63 persons per ha.

The population sizes involved in the rise and fall of early cities in China are difficult to estimate, because these sites have only been partially excavated, and little research has been done concerning population density on the basis of archaeological data. To estimate the Erlitou population, we have to rely on information from other sites. The Erlitou regional center at Dongxiafeng near the Zhongtiao Mountains (Institute of Archaeology et al. 1988) provides a comparable case. Dongxiafeng (25 ha in area) comprised a craft production center surrounded by ditches (2.7 ha in area) and residential areas for the elite and commoners during the Erlitou Phase III. A total of 37 residential shelters (sizes vary from 3 to 13 sq m in area, with most of them 4 to 7 sq m) were found in the excavated area of 0.35 ha in this ditched craft production center. If 2–4 persons occupied each shelter, there would have been about 74–148 persons living in the residential shelters in the excavated area, with a density of 211–422 persons per ha. Thus the population of craftsmen living in the entire ditched enclosure may have been around 570–1,140 persons. Such a figure can be seen as a "spot density" because it is almost certain that the population densities in other parts of the site were much lower. Only one house (10.2 sq m), which may have hosted 4–6 persons, was found in an excavated area of 975 sq m at the north end of the site, where residents may have held higher social status (Liu and Chen 2001). This accounts for a population density range of 41–62 persons per ha, a figure similar to that of the Neolithic village at Jiangzhai (44–63 persons), as mentioned above. If this figure is applied to the rest of the site (22.3 ha), there may have been 914–1,383 persons who resided in the habitation areas outside of the ditched enclosure. Therefore, the total population during Erlitou Phase III at Dongxiafeng (25 ha) may have been around 1,484–2,523 persons, at a population density of 60–100 persons per ha (6,000–10,000 persons per sq km), and a mean of 8,000 persons per sq km. This figure falls into the lower range of urban population densities (with the mean of 14,542 persons per sq km and the median of 10,935 persons per sq km) on the basis of an analysis of 531 cities, including 425 preindustrial cities (Storey 1997b:974–975). The estimated population figure from Dong-xiafeng may represent the demography in an early stage of urban development in ancient China. Nevertheless, this estimate is hypothetical and needs to be tested when better population data become available.

Dongxiafeng may not be an ideal site to compare with Erlitou, but because we are limited by available archaeological data, this site still provides some useful information. Moreover, Dongxiafeng may have had a situation similar to Erlitou in that both settlements were not walled, and population densities in craft production areas were likely much higher than those in the rest of the site. If we apply the Dongxiafeng population density (60–100 persons per ha) to Erlitou (300 ha), we find that the maximum population size during its peak period (Phase III) may have reached 18,000–30,000 persons, with a mean of 24,000. This is comparable with that of Uruk in Mesopotamia during the Early Dynastic period, which covered more than 400 ha of land with 30,000–40,000 people, at a density of 75–100 persons per ha (Hassan 1981:237).

The population sizes in other phases are probably lower, as indicated by fewer features and artifacts discovered and smaller occupation areas (Table 9-2). Therefore, I have used the numbers of pits and burials in different phases to indicate the fluctuation of population size through time on the basis of the known population figure for Phase III (18,000–30,000). Table 9-3 illustrates the changing ratio of pits and burials during the six phases at Erlitou, and the mean ratio was used as the index for estimating the population range for each phase.

These calculations suggest that Erlitou may have started as a large settlement, perhaps a regional center, inhabited by about 3,500–5,800 people in Phase I (ca. 1900–1800 BC). Through the next 200 years (Phases II–III; ca. 1800–1600 BC), the population multiplied more than five times to about 18,000–30,000 people before beginning to decline to about 15,000–26,000 people in the next

Table 9-3. Estimates of Erlitou Population Range in Each Phase

Phases	Pits no.	Burials no.	Pits %	Burials %	Mean %	Population range	Mean population
ELT I	36	6	0.26	0.13	0.19	3,497–5,828	4,662
ELT II	75	18	0.54	0.38	0.46	8,338–13,897	11,117
ELT III	138	47	1.00	1.00	1.00	18,000–30,000	24,000
ELT IV	129	36	0.93	0.77	0.85	15,307–25,511	20,409
LW ELG	14	3	0.10	0.06	0.08	1,488–2,479	1,983
UP ELG	8	1	0.06	0.02	0.04	713–1,189	951

100 years (Phase IV; ca. 1600–1500 BC), and it finally was reduced to about 700–1,200 people by ca. 1400 BC (Erligang phases). These estimates are hypothetical, indicating a relative rate of population change through time.

It is very likely that during its heyday Erlitou's large urban population could not have been self-sufficient in terms of agricultural production, because a considerable portion of its population in the urban center was engaged in craft production and palatial construction. The relatively low proportion of agricultural tools particularly in Phase III, as discussed above, hints that Erlitou may have relied primarily on agricultural products extracted from the hinterland.

The amount of grain needed to sustain the Erlitou population may be estimated on the basis of ethnohistoric information from the Yiluo region. According to the 1959 data from Gongyi in the eastern part of the Yiluo basin, the average annual consumption of processed grain for each person (which is the average figure of 25 categories of grain ration for different age and professional groups) was about 191 kg (Gongxian 1991:479), or 240 kg of grain (including 20 percent husk). On the basis of this figure, the estimated Erlitou population of 18,000–30,000 persons would have consumed 4,320,000–7,200,000 kg of grain annually. Millet was the major staple crop in the Neolithic north China (Ren 1986). An average annual yield of millet in the Gongyi area in 1933 was recorded as 375 kg per ha (Gongxian 1991:260), which was based on a traditional dry-farming method with iron plow and cattle. Because Erlitou agriculture was based on stone/wooden tool technology, the productivity may have been lower. Another analysis based on ancient textual information suggests a yield of 300 kg per ha during the Xia and Shang periods (Yang 1988), which seems reasonable and is applied here. In addition, fallow was a common practice in ancient China, as recorded in the Shang oracle-bone inscriptions (Yang 1992:160–163). If fallow took place biannually, the average annual yield would have been 150 kg per ha. On the basis of this estimate, the Erlitou population during Phase III would have needed 288–480 sq km of farming land (Table 9-4). Furthermore, if we add the

Table 9-4. Estimating Land and Grain Needed for Sustaining the Urban and Rural Population in the Yiluo Region

Erlitou Urban Area	
Erlitou urban population range (persons)	18,000–30,000
Annual grain consumption per person (kg)	240
Annual grain consumption for ELT urban	
population (kg)	4,320,000–7,200,000
Grain yield (kg per ha)	150
Farming land needed for ELT urban population (sq km)	288–480
Gongyi Survey Area	
Gongyi survey area (sq km)	185
Settlement area in the survey region (ha)	113.45
Population density in settlement area, based on Jiangzhai	
(persons/ha)	44–63
Total population in the survey area	4,992–7,147
Regional population density in the survey area	
(persons/kg)	27–39
Yiluo Rural Region	
Yiluo region total arable land (sq km)	1330
Estimated grain produced in the Yiluo region (kg)	19,950,000
Estimated Yiluo region rural population (persons)	36,377–52,086
Estimated grain consumption of the rural	
population (kg)	8,730,551–12,500,562
Land needed for rural population (sq km)	582–833
Entire Yiluo Region	
Yiluo region total rural and urban population (persons)	54,377–82,085
Yiluo region total grain needed (kg)	13,050,551–19,700,562
Land needed to sustain total Yiluo population (sq km)	870–1,313
Yiluo region total area (sq km)	5,689
Yiluo regional population density (persons/sq km)	10–14

amount of land for sustaining the agricultural producers in the rural areas, the actual land for supporting the Erlitou urban population would have been even more.

The Yiluo region was densely populated with small and medium Erlitou settlements, which must have been providing agricultural products to the urban center. On the basis of the result of regional survey in the Gongyi region, 19 Erlitou Phase III sites with a total occupation area of 113.45 ha were defined in an area of 185 sq km (Liu et al. 2002/2004). If we adopt the population density of 44–63 persons/ha, derived from the Jiangzhai Neolithic village as mentioned above, for calculating the Erlitou rural population, this survey area may have been occupied by about 4,992–7,147 persons, with a regional population density of 27–39 persons per sq km in arable land areas. At the present, six counties/cities (Luoyang, Xin'an, Mengjin, Yanshi, Gongyi, and Yichuan) in the core area of the Yiluo basin cover a total area of 5,689 sq km, with the arable land of 2,463 sq km (Henan Bureau 1987) (Figure 9-1). However, the amount of cultivated land has been dramatically increased in recent decades due to intensive farming. In Gongyi, for example, the arable land in AD 1412 was about 200 sq km, which was only 54 percent of that (369 sq km) in 1985 (Gongxian 1989:254–255). If we apply this rate to the entire Yiluo region, the arable land in ancient times may have been about 1,330 sq km. If we use the regional population density derived from the Gongyi survey data (27–39 persons per sq km) to the Yiluo basin, the Erlitou rural population that resided in the arable land of the basin may have reached 36,377–52,086 persons. This population would have needed about 8,730,551–12,500,562 kg of grain annually, produced from 582–833 sq km of land (Table 9-4).

On the basis of the above estimates, the total Erlitou urban and rural population in the Yiluo basin may have reached 54,377–82,085 persons, who would have consumed 13,050,551–19,700,562 kg of grain annually, produced from 870–1,313 sq km of land. The regional population density is 10–14 persons per sq km for the entire Yiluo region. The estimated amount of arable land available in the Yiluo basin in ancient times (1,330 sq km) appears to have been sufficient to produce the surplus food for the growing urban population at Erlitou (Table 9-4). This result seems to confirm that the expansion of Erlitou to the periphery outside the Yiluo basin was not to obtain subsistence material such as food and tools but to procure elite goods and other key resources, especially salt and metal (Liu and Chen 2003). Furthermore, the Yiluo basin may have reached its full agricultural capacity in sustaining the rural and urban population during the heyday of the Erlitou period, and this situation in turn may have limited the further development of Erlitou urbanism. The development of a new urban site at Zhengzhou after the fall of Erlitou, therefore, may have been partially attributable to its geological setting, because Zhengzhou was situated in a much larger alluvial plain, the Huanghuai plain, which had greater agricultural potential for sustaining a larger population than the Yiluo basin.

The Erlitou urban population was about 33–37 percent of that in the entire core area of the early state (the Yiluo basin). The Erlitou polity expanded far beyond the Yiluo basin, but the current data do not allow us to determine the overall territory of the Erlitou polity. Therefore, it is difficult to estimate the total population size of this earliest state in China.

Discussion

More than fifty years ago, V. Gordon Childe articulated the concept of urban revolution and the development of full-time craft specialization as the foundation for urbanism (Childe 1950). Recently, archaeologists have achieved a much more comprehensive understanding of the relationships between social evolution and craft specialization to be able to evaluate and reassess Childe's model (Wailes 1996). Although Childe overemphasized elite-controlled craft specialization as an essential factor of urbanism, the strong correlation between political centralization and elite patronage of attached craft specialists has been observed in many early urban sites worldwide (e.g., Earle 1987; Stein 1996). Childe's proposition, however, did not foresee that independent craft production could also play an important role in the process of urbanism in Mesopotamia (Stein 1996). Many studies on city-states in Mesopotamia and Mesoamerica have also suggested that craft specialization increased simultaneously in both urban and rural areas during the formation of archaic states (e.g., Blanton et al. 1982; Johnson 1973, 1987; Schwartz and Falconer 1994a), and rural villages were closely involved in regional economic systems (Wright et al. 1989). Instead of being simple homogeneous food-producing sectors of state societies, rural areas often developed specialized craft productions, participated in long-distance trade systems, and formed hierarchical social organization (e.g., Hester and Shafer 1994; Smith 1994; Wattenmaker 1994). Current research demonstrates that the earliest urbanism in China shared many similarities with early cities in other parts of the world in terms of the functions of city and countryside and in rural-urban relationships.

The first urban center emergence at Erlitou was probably, in the first instance, on account of its fertile agriculture land, then because of its circumscribed natural environment for military defensibility (which may account for the lack of city walls at Erlitou), and finally on account of its easy access to surrounding regions via water channels for transportation of goods. Although the earliest stage of urbanization in the Yiluo basin remains elusive at the moment, Erlitou's initial development was unlikely to have been a natural indigenous population growth. There was a 500-year gap between the Neolithic and Erlitou occupations of the site, and in its Phase I, Erlitou appears to have become a sizeable settlement associated with several craft productions, probably already a regional center. The development of Erlitou, therefore, may have been the result of migration of population from elsewhere or an amalgamation of several villages from the region.

The process of urbanization that began in Phases I and II and then reached its peak in Phase III, during which political centralization (the development of the walled palace/temple complex in Section V) was accompanied by economic nucleation with the emergence of attached productions, especially focused on, although was not limited to, the manufacture of ritual bronzes. At the same time, we also see an increased scale in the production of nonprestige goods, such as pottery and bone artifacts, which may be characterized as independent craft specializations. At the height of the urbanization (Phase III), the attached production appears to comprise not only luxury goods but also utilitarian items. The patterns for distribution and consumption of these utilitarian craft products are poorly understood; it is possible that large quantities of ceramics and bone artifacts produced at Erlitou were to meet the demand from both the urban and its adjacent rural areas.

The ritual bronze casting appears to have been carried out at the same location (Section IV) near the palatial area throughout the entire period of the existence of this craft, whereas the locations for other types of crafts tended to have been farther away from the palatial area and moved around the settlement. These arrangements suggest that the ritual bronze production was the most tightly controlled by the state and that the residential segregation between the attached specialists and independent specialists was practiced. However, the residential patterns for independent craftsmen are unclear.

Increased nucleation in attached craft specializations along with the development of independent craft productions did not lead to a rural population alienated completely from agricultural activities, because there was no absolute division between agricultural and craft productions within the urban population. It is possible that members of craftsmen's families practiced a mixed economy and that urban communities engaged in craft and agricultural productions in varying proportions.

If we take all these factors into consideration, we can see that Erlitou was a political, economic, and ritual center, with a large population including elites, attached and independent craftsmen, and farmers. The ability to control the production and the distribution of sacred prestige goods was the essence of political power of the Erlitou ruling elite. On the basis of available data, however, it is not clear whether market systems had developed for exchanging utilitarian goods at Erlitou.

The hinterland played an active role in the formation of the early state. By producing and extracting both subsistence goods (e.g., food, stone tools, and construction materials) and elite goods (white pottery) for the urban center, subregional centers in rural areas constituted focal points in regional economic systems. Despite bronze metallurgy being the most important craft specialization, involving both core and periphery in the production processes, no bronze vessels have been found beyond the Erlitou site. Therefore, the economic relationship between urban and rural settlements may have been asymmetrical, suggesting a tributary system (cf. Wright 1977:381–382). Settlements in the entire core area of the early state were organized hierarchically, assuming different functions in the regional political-economic systems of early urbanism. On the basis of recent survey results, a four-tiered settlement hierarchy with Erlitou as the primary center developed during the Erlitou period in the Yiluo region, as discussed above. Such a settlement system resembles the archaic states identified by archaeologists in many other parts of the world (cf. Flannery 1998; Peebles and Kus 1977; Wright and Johnson 1975).

Some researchers have tended to focus primarily on ritual and political functions, with less emphasis on economic components, of early urban centers in China (e.g., Chang 1985; Wheatley 1971). On the basis of the above analysis, Erlitou, as the earliest urban site identified to date in China, was indeed a political and ritual center, but it was also associated with a dense population, who were engaged not only in various craft production activities for making both elite and utilitarian goods but also in agricultural activities. All these factors together formed the backbone of the political-economic system of the early state. In Mesopotamia, the early urbanism was characterized by the interdependence economically, politically, and spiritually between cities and their hinterlands. Cities depend on supplies of food and raw material coming from the rural areas, whereas the rural populations depend on goods and services (craft products and religious ceremonies) provided by cities (Pollock 1999:46–47). From the perspective of the regional political economy, therefore, the early urbanism in China was not much different from that in Mesopotamia. This seems contrary to what Trigger (1999) has proposed for the urban economy in early China, though.

Although the historical identity of Erlitou remains uncertain, the above analyses of urban-rural relationships in the Yiluo region clearly indicate the development of state-level political systems during the Erlitou period. These features, together with Erlitou territorial expansion on its periphery, reveal the nature of this earliest state and urbanism in China. The Erlitou polity was a monocentered territorial state characterized by growing political-economic centralization in the urban center and increasing rural-urban integration of its core and peripheral regions.

Acknowledgments

I wish to thank Henry Wright, Xingcan Chen, and Yun Kuen Lee, who read and commented on the draft of this chapter.

10

Population Growth and Change in the Ancient City of Kyongju

Sarah M. Nelson

The present city of Kyongju in southeastern Korea was the capital of the state of Silla from the beginnings of a polity known as Saro, by tradition founded in 57 BC, to a city of nearly one million people before the ultimate decline of United Silla in AD 935. Through time the city was known variously as Sorabol, Kumsong, and Kyongju. Each stage in the city's thousand-year history has left its imprint on the landscape. But the city did not simply grow larger or merely form accretions of one stage on another. The center of the city moved northward as Kyongju enlarged, and the flavor of the city shifted substantially. The experience of living in this city must have changed dramatically, because the landscape itself was altered by huge constructions. By the end of Kyongju's reign as capital, the increasing emulation of the Tang Dynasty of China had so altered even the contours of the city that the new center of the city would have been unrecognizable to earlier inhabitants. At present, Kyongju is a composite of all its previous configurations. However, it is important to note that much evidence is buried beneath later buildings, stones have been reutilized from previous buildings, and walls that were erected were torn down later. Only the general outlines of the earlier cities can be known, because Kyongju continues to be a living city.

The time period of the state of Old Silla is traditionally known as the "Three Kingdoms" period. The other two kingdoms were Koguryo in the north of the Korean peninsula and beyond and Paekche in the southwest. A loose grouping of autonomous cities, collectively known as Kaya, occupied the Naktong River valley and its delta in the earlier part of the Three Kingdoms period. Historical documents specify the beginnings of the Three Kingdoms period as the mid-first century BC, but most archaeologists consider the first three centuries to be merely formative. The era of mounded tombs, beginning in the early fourth century AD, is taken as the beginning of the Three Kingdoms proper. By AD 668, the Three Kingdoms period had come to a close, for Silla had conquered most of the Korean peninsula with the aid of Tang China. Following this event, Silla was known as Great Silla or United Silla.

Of the Three Kingdoms, the Silla state was the farthest from China and was the most remote from the Chinese influence. This remoteness has been used to explain its unique culture, but in reality Silla was closely connected to the other contemporaneous Korean kingdoms. Koguryo and Paekche both accepted many facets of Chinese culture much earlier than Silla did, so influence from China could have affected Silla through one or both of them had Silla been receptive to such influence. Polities formed in the southern areas of the Japanese islands were also in close contact with Silla, and they, too, had sporadic contact with China. Isolation from foreign ideas was not a characteristic of either the state of Silla or its capital city. Preservation of its unique culture must be attributed to other factors. It is fair to say, however, that the geographic location of the city was not propitious for interacting with other polities. Trade and other interaction occurred in spite of the naturally protected aspect of the city.

I have divided the changes in Kyongju into stages that correspond with its history. Before considering the details, let me offer a thumbnail sketch. In Stage I, the city of Sorabol had been formed from six villages located around the foot of the steep hills that protected the valley. Agricultural fields, workshops, and houses surrounded fortified hilltop castles. The castles follow the Korean pattern of meandering walls, rather than a square walled enclosure. The population must have been sparse, with no more than 10,000 inhabitants. Little evidence of interaction with China is apparent. In spite of this aspect, burials from Stage I show that, far from being isolated, the elite of Sorabol were connected to a vast trade network. Exotic items from both central Asia and the Mediterranean world were found in graves from this period. Stage II is characterized by large mounded tombs. During this time the city became known as Kumsong, "Gold Fortress." Whereas the Stage I buildings clustered near South Stream and South Mountain, in Stage II enormous new tombs were constructed in the middle of the plain, creating a "mountain range" of tombs north of the center. Artifacts in the tombs bespeak connections with northeastern Shamanism. Chinese artifacts are rare. A population of perhaps one hundred thousand people was necessary to support the elites' conspicuous consumption that is evident in the grave goods. Buddhism was accepted in Stage III. The effect on the landscape once again was striking, especially the building of massive Buddhist temples in the plain and countless smaller shrines throughout the hills and valleys on all sides but especially on Namsan, South Mountain. A new city was laid out in the style of Tang China, basically rectangular with a grid pattern of streets, which is still visible in the Kyongju of today. It is estimated that the city had nearly one million inhabitants. This estimate is derived from census data reported in *Samguk Yusa (Memorabilia of the Three Kingdoms)* (by the monk Ilyon in the thirteenth century [Ilyon 1972]), presumably gleaned from the Silla annals that are now lost. The custom of the time was to report households rather than individuals; 178,936 households were counted in Kumsong (Kyongju). The precise year is not reported. If households averaged five persons each (and they may well have been larger), this would amount to a population of 894,680. The city was said to be so rich that only tile-roofed houses (not the straw roofs of farmers) reached from the plain to the sea. The *Samguk Yusa* also enumerates 35 houses of nobles, with gold decoration on the exterior.

These changes in the city of Kyongju reflected growth in the population, but clearly are not merely larger versions of the same entity. The landscape alterations both reflected and caused changes in ideology. The expanding place of Silla in the east Asian world is another important variable in Kyongju's growth. Population expansion coincided with changes in the external relationships of Silla. I suggest that the very different regimes that are visible within the present city are a result of the interplay between internal and external change. Internally Silla experienced an expanding population, increasingly powerful elites, and more complex political organization. External influences included the intermittent expansion and power of China, as well as clashes with the growing polities within the Korean peninsula and on the nearby islands of Japan. But it is also important to note that, in spite of influences from China and elsewhere, the character of the city kept a distinctly "Korean" flavor. Even when Buddhist monuments were the dominating theme, the imposing tombs continued to attract the eye, as they do still. And the Buddhist art and architecture developed a local style, characterized by its monumentality. The derivation from China is clear, but local permutations are also evident.

Kyongju is unique among east Asian capitals for its continuity in one location without any hiatus. Its location was easily defended, with streams on three sides, the whole surrounded by rugged hills. It is easy to understand the selection of this place by a beleaguered, weak polity. But these same defensible characteristics made it an unlikely spot for an important center. Although the early success of Silla's expansion may have been attributable to the fortresslike situation of its capital and heartland, its continuation as capital is harder to understand. No obvious transportation route ran through it, although narrow roads along the rivers lead out of the valley. On the other hand, population could grow within the wide plain, where land and water for rice were plentiful. Rich sources of iron and gold must have also contributed to its prosperity, but exactly where those metals were mined is now unknown.

Not only the capital of Silla but also Korea itself has seemed "off the beaten track" for east Asia. This is a result of historical events, including the fact that Korea was the last country in the region to be "opened" to the West. Perhaps the fact that Korea has been understudied is more relevant to this interpretation than any intrinsic reasons for Korea to have been perceived as a backwater. Archaeological excavations have revealed constant connections between the peninsula and the wider world of Asia since well before the beginnings of the Three Kingdoms in the first century BC. The closest connections, demonstrated by bronze daggers and dolmens, were with northeastern China, at that time also considered "barbarian" territory by the Chinese.

During the Han Dynasty of China (206 BC to AD 220), the Korean peninsula was partly occupied, pacified, and exploited for sources of iron and other materials (Pearson 1978). A subsequent decline in the strength of China and its breakup into smaller states allowed the Three Kingdoms to struggle with each other for control of the Korean peninsula. Silla's place in the larger world of Asia was thus carved out of battles, diplomacy, and trade.

Methods: History and Archaeology

Interpreting growth and change in the population of Kyongju requires attention both to written documents and to archaeological discoveries. Two histories of this period in the Korean peninsula are *Samguk Sagi (History of the Three Kingdoms)* (written by Kim Pusik in 1145 [Kim and Yi 1997(1145)]) and *Samguk Yusa*. Many historians question the reliability of these documents on the grounds of their points of view (Confucian and Buddhist, respectively) and dependence on Chinese history (e.g., Gardiner 1969; Henderson 1959). Another difficulty with these documents is that they are replete with miraculous events (especially the Buddhist *Samguk Yusa*), which detract from the credibility of their narratives. Nevertheless, these histories are based on the now lost *Chronicles of Silla* and are probably reasonably reliable for descriptions of secular events, if not their precise dates. In addition, fragments of an eighth-century census pertaining to three villages give a rare view of the common people. People, animals, and fruit and nut trees were all counted periodically. It is notable that more females than males were counted in all age ranges of the population (Kim 1965), which suggests at least that boys were not preferred over girls. One document, which contains the sumptuary laws, and a few contemporary inscriptions add scraps of information that augment the histories.

Archaeological discoveries provide examples of material culture whose existence cannot be disputed, but interpretation of the archaeological record still plays an important part. In particular, the estimated dates, especially of tombs, are often contested because radiocarbon dates are rarely obtained for this period in Korea and because inscriptions in tombs are rare. Relative dating is often at the mercy of preconceived ideas about the time and place of origin of particular traits and the direction of stylistic changes (Pearson 1985). Thus the two types of sources, documentary and archaeological, are needed to complement and correct each other.

Stage I: The Formation of the State of Silla and the City of Sorabol (First Century BC to Third Century AD)

The legend of the beginning of Sorabol (Kyongju) as a city implies prior villages around the edges of the plain (Figure 10-1). Six tribes are said to have joined forces and created a polity called Saro (Kim 1976). The legend specifies that the

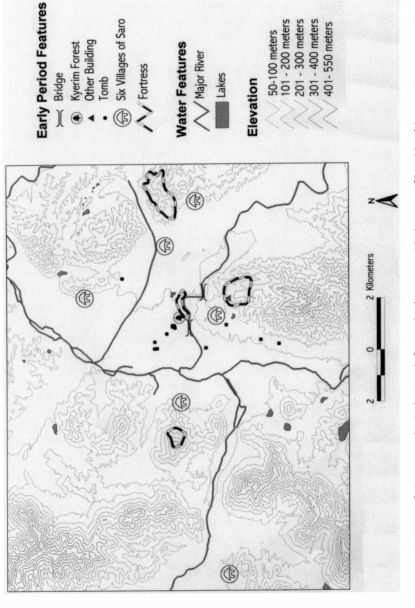

Early Period Features

)(Bridge
✹ Kyerim Forest
▲ Other Building
▪ Tomb
ⓒ Six Villages of Saro
∧∕ Fortress

Water Features

∧∕ Major River
▮ Lakes

Elevation

50-100 meters
101 - 200 meters
201 - 300 meters
301 - 400 meters
401 - 550 meters

N ⬥

2   0   2 Kilometers

Figure 10-1. Map of Kyongju in the Early Period, first to third centuries AD (*courtesy of Lisa Murphy*).

impetus to merge came from marauding enemies and from the additional strength that the six villages could mutually provide for each other (Ilyon 1972). The home base of these raiders was the northern part of the Korean peninsula. The Han Dynasty of China had established four commanderies north of the Han River in 108 BCE, and Chinese histories describe forays into the unconquered south (Gardiner 1969). Thus mutual protection from the Chinese outposts, as well as other expanding polities in the south of the peninsula, created the need for a government as a means of organizing defense. Sorabol, the center of the Saro villages, was born.

Other sections of the early histories refer to sacred mountains and streams and miraculous beginnings. Although they can be discounted as unlikely to be factual history, these legends reveal attitudes toward the landscape, especially the spiritual force of mountains and rocks, a theme that continues even at present. When representatives of the six original villages met, they rotated among the four sacred mountains surrounding the city (Ilyon 1972). Even today, people crossing a mountain pass add another stone to a stone pile for the mountain spirit. *Mudangs* (female shamans) are often associated with sacred stones, sacred mountains, or sacred trees. The legends also bespeak the desire for legitimization of later ruling families. Thus their first ancestors were kings discovered as children in miraculous circumstances or born from golden eggs, and queens descended from mountain goddesses (Nelson 1995).

Buildings from the city of Sorabol have not survived. The first ruler is said to have erected a castle on the eastern edge of the plain on Mt. Myonghwal. A crumbling wall in this location is attributed to a later period, but no excavations have been carried out to test the accuracy of this assumption or to attempt to locate an earlier castle. More substantial remains of a subsequent fortress can be identified. Known as Panwolsong, or Half Moon Castle, it was constructed on a crescent-shaped hill on the north bank of South Stream. It was probably both the domicile of the ruler and an early seat of government. Legend says that it was surrounded by a wall with 8 gates, with 21 buildings inside (Adams 1979). Excavations outside the wall and below it unearthed the foundations of several large buildings. Stone bridges, of which footings remain, led across the South River toward the foot of Namsan (South Mountain), demonstrating that south was the direction of other significant localities. Near Panwolsong, a forest called Kyerim, or Chicken Forest, was the location of several miraculous events relating to early rulers. It is still a park with trees and is remarkably preserved through its persistent association with these ancient traditions.

The excavated graves of this stage are north of Panwolsong beyond Kyerim, along a street called Wolsongno (Choi 1981, Choi 1979, 1980), and at the edge of the tomb park near King Michu's tomb (Kim and Lee 1975). Lying south of the center of the area between the three streams, the graves seem to claim this space for the ruling elite. In addition, each of the six tribes had a burial ground in the location of its original village near the foot of one of the surrounding hills (Kim 1976). An inscribed boulder discovered in 1995 describes six areas of the city, apparently reflecting the earlier positions of the original six villages.

Burials from this first stage have no mounds, but many have rich grave goods, indicating an already established hierarchy. Some of the elite graves contain horses and armor, as well as ornaments and objects of gold, jade, and glass. Although most glass beads may have been locally made (Lee Insook 1988), at least one glass bead shows connections with the Mediterranean world—a face bead probably made in Alexandria, Egypt. This bead is part of a necklace, which includes a characteristic native shape of bead, curved like a comma.

The juxtaposition of the distant and local beads in the necklace is particularly interesting, suggesting that beads were imported unstrung. The curved beads are found beginning in the Bronze Age. They later became prominent as pendants on the gold crowns, belts, and necklaces of the ruling class of Silla (Lee Insook 1987, 1988). They are clearly status markers, but probably had additional mythic significance. The most reasonable guess is that they began as a representation of an animal claw. Both tigers and bears were important in early Korean myth.

Stage II: The Mounded Tomb Period (Fourth to Sixth Centuries)—Expanding Power in the Southeast

As local expressions of power and control, giant tombs visually dominate the city in the Mounded Tomb Pperiod (Figure 10-2). They were erected north of the earlier tombs in what must have been uninhabited territory or perhaps agricultural fields. These enormous tombs constitute even today the most compelling sight in the city. The largest tomb overall is a double mound 123 m long and 23 m high (Kim and Pearson 1977), although the highest tomb reaches 25 m. The mounds are so large that after Kyongju ceased to be the capital, some of them were treated as natural hills, with houses and streets along their flanks and trees growing from their sides (Adams 1979). The houses and trees were only removed in the 1970s to create a tomb park as a tourist attraction. Of the few inscriptions that are found in the tombs, none name the occupant. Thus the exact order of the tombs is unknown, giving rise to speculation on the basis of stylistic differences (Pearson 1985).

The documents pertaining to this period mostly describe military conquests by Silla of nearby polities. Small city-states were gobbled up by Silla one by one. The population became divided into castelike strata, known as bone ranks because the Korean metaphor for kinship is bone rather than blood. The highest bone rank was Songgol, Holy Bone. Songgol were the only persons eligible to occupy the top positions in the society, including king and queen. Second in rank, but also high nobility, were the Chingol, the True Bone. Six lower ranks were named, down to the common people (Kim 1977). It is not known how (or

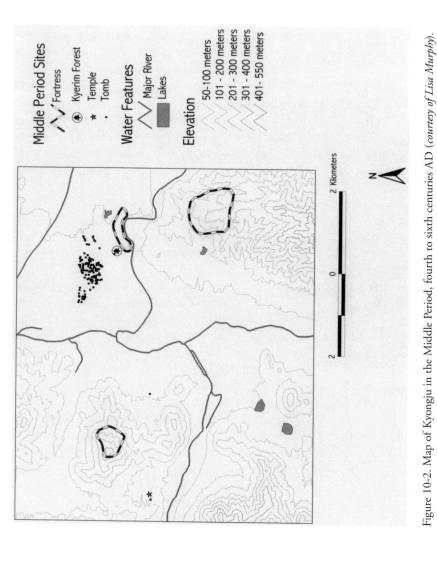

Middle Period Sites

⤳ Fortress

⊛ Kyerim Forest

★ Temple

• Tomb

Water Features

⤳ Major River

▮ Lakes

Elevation

⤳ 50-100 meters

⤳ 101 - 200 meters

⤳ 201 - 300 meters

⤳ 301 - 400 meters

⤳ 401- 550 meters

2 0 2 Kilometers

N

Figure 10-2. Map of Kyongju in the Middle Period, fourth to sixth centuries AD (*courtesy of Lisa Murphy*).

whether) these rankings were formed from the original six tribes, whose leaders seem to have been essentially equal. Some have suggested that the Holy Bone and True Bone derived from invaders from northeast China who brought with them the tradition of mounded tombs (e.g., Sohnet et al. 1970). It is also impossible to say how or whether the people of conquered cities figured into the system, but it seems likely that local hierarchies were left in place, although subject to Silla. Noble tombs found in burials in the expanding periphery of Silla tend to corroborate this view. They contain gold ornaments and smaller gilt-bronze crowns. It is at least clear that a large population was required for this kind of elaboration of both tombs and daily life. The city populace was divided into craft groups that made 22 different objects. People plied various crafts, both for daily consumption and for the elite (Choi 1971). Artisans worked at many kinds of textiles, pottery, metal and leather working, and so forth. The remains of a Silla kiln has been found northwest of the city, but locations of other workshops are unknown. Many artisans may have worked in their own villages, offering their productions as corveé labor.

Excavations of the tombs support the existence of bone ranks (Pearson et al. 1986). Gold crowns, belts, shoes, and other paraphernalia worn by rulers were found in the huge, elaborate tombs, and lesser objects were found in smaller tombs. These are obvious displays of wealth and power. Sumptuary laws also upheld the endogamous bone ranks (Kim 1965). From the kinds of hairpins to the number of horses and types of saddles allowed, conspicuous consumption was precisely defined by sex as well as by rank. For example, the lower ranks were forbidden fancy saddles and horse gear (both men and women, who are listed separately) and were limited in the number of horses they could own, but this demonstrates that all ranks did have riding horses, and both men and women were free to travel. No one was permitted, however, to rise above his or her station in life, which was determined by birth.

The placement of gold crowns and ceremonial belts with the queen in Tomb 98 suggests that she was the spiritual ruler, probably with shamanistic duties (Nelson 1991, 1993b). The crowns themselves furnish evidence of shamanic beliefs—trees and antlers are found on Manchurian and other shaman paraphernalia (Kim 1998). Dangling objects, especially the two long pendants that frame the face, are also found in Manchurian shaman costumes (Kim and Lee 1975). The amount of weapons and armor with the husband in Tomb 98 mark him as the war leader (Nelson 1991, 1993a). Thus king and queen corulers may have occurred in Silla as they did in early Japan (Piggott 2002). Gender differences seem to be marked only by the presence or absence of a sword (Ito 1971).

Some artifacts, however, demonstrate the continuance of trade with the Mediterranean world, either through central Asia and the Silk Road or by sea around India and Southeast Asia. One small glass pitcher from the Roman world was considered so precious that it was repaired with gold thread. A chased silver bowl, on the other hand, appears to derive from central Asia. Various objects made in China were also found in the tombs, including a small glazed bottle from southern China and bronze tripod vessels, but they are numerically rare. One lotus-pattern lacquer fragment is the only echo of Buddhist iconography. The ideology appears to be still dominated by local concepts in spite of the centuries of contact with other worlds implied by the exotic artifacts. Some of the sacredness of mountains, in fact, may be expressed in the shape and size of the tombs. The large tombs create a virtual range of hills across the center of Kyongju today, towering above the one-story houses.

The documents relate that the Silla court increasingly acquired Chinese characteristics. These included adoption of the Chinese calendar, posthumous reign names, and the use of the written Chinese language (Ilyon 1972). The earliest of the inscribed boulders describes a legal claim, which unfortunately does not describe the property itself. Later inscribed boulders mark the limits of Silla's territorial expansion. Four of these have been found. One was at North Fortress outside of Seoul, one is in the southeastern part of Korea, and two are far to the north in what is now North Korea (Kim 1979).

Stage III: Buddhist Monuments and a Rectangular City

The city of Kyongju began to take on a strongly Buddhist cast after Silla defeated its sister kingdoms of Paekche and Koguryo. Some Buddhist temples erected at that time are still in use today (for example, Pulguksa), and the hills around the city of Kyongju are full of Buddhist shrines large and small. The other notable change in the city was the creation of an entirely new gridded and walled city (Figure 10-3), reflecting the pattern of Chinese cities (Steinhardt 1990), especially the Tang Dynasty capital, Chang'an. But the rectangular grid of Chinese cities could not be completely imposed on the existing city. The irregular shape of Panwolsong in the south and the huge tomb mounds just north of it were impossible to move and too sacred to demolish, so this new city had to be erected yet farther north, bordering on the north stream. Some scholars have claimed that a palace area existed along that river, with a wide avenue leading south toward Panwolsong and South Mountain because that was the pattern of Chinese cities. Although this idea is compatible with existing patterns, it is unverified archaeologically. Indications of a city wall are found on earlier maps, but whether it was erected at the same time the gridded streets were laid out is uncertain.

As centralized power returned to China, Silla became more and more closely associated with the Tang Dynasty, as the imitation of Chang'an indicates. However, the adoption of Buddhism in Korea was related to both China and India. In the early days Silla was visited by Indian monks, and Korean monks are known to have made pilgrimages to India to bring back copies of the sutras (Ilyon 1972). Thus the power of China alone does not explain the adoption of Buddhism in Silla.

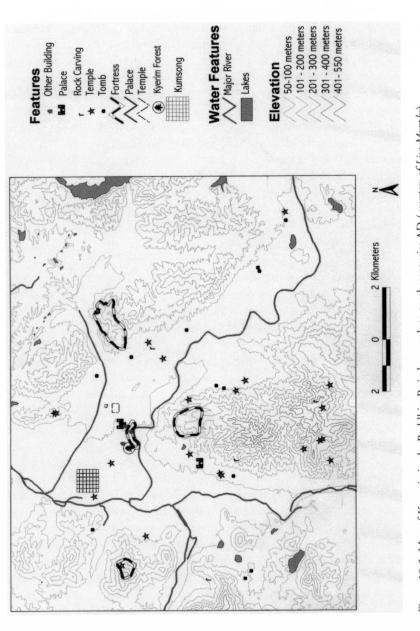

Features

- Other Building ⊟
- Palace ⊟
- Rock Carving r
- Temple ★
- Tomb ▪
- Fortress 〰
- Palace 〰
- Temple 〰
- Kyerim Forest ✺
- Kumsong ▦

Water Features

- Major River 〰
- Lakes ▪

Elevation

- 50-100 meters
- 101 - 200 meters
- 201 - 300 meters
- 301 - 400 meters
- 401 - 550 meters

N

2   0   2 Kilometers

Figure 10-3. Map of Kyongju in the Buddhist Period, seventh to tenth centuries AD (*courtesy of Lisa Murphy*).

Other factors, such as the fit of Buddhism with the aims of the elite, must have been influential. Whatever the causes, building related to Buddhism abounded.

For example, Hwangyongsa was an enormous temple covering an area of 9,000 sq m. It was built on the plain east of the new walled city. The twin stone pillars that flanked the flagpole are all that remain standing from this magnificent temple. With underground ceramic drains and wide streets, Hwangyongsa was something of a city in itself. Many buildings were erected within its walls, some of them immense. One dramatic roof end-tile is 1 m high. Altogether, 20,000 artifacts have been excavated from this site, showing the extent of activity in the temple.

Among the few remaining buildings are a stone pagoda made to appear to be constructed of bricks in the style of pagodas in Chang'an, various other stone pagodas, and a bottle-shaped building called Chomsongdae, "Star Gazing Pavilion," that is the oldest standing astronomical observatory in Asia. The remains of a pleasure palace on Namsan have also been excavated. Wine cups were floated along the curving canals in an early drinking game. The site of another palace is marked by Anapji Pond, which was excavated in 1975. Excavations demonstrated the rich life of the court, including five pavilions surrounding the artificial lake and rocks of unusual form outlining the garden. Four wooden boats were found on the bottom, along with inscribed wooden tablets, pottery, and roof tile. A 14-sided die was found, with various instructions for playing a drinking game.

Population growth is reflected in the city of Kyongju in very concrete ways. Silla became first a conqueror and then an imitator of China, leaving in the city the fossilized remnants of its earlier stages. In the present city, the past has been turned into tourist attractions, as the process of change continues. The mountains are still important; when high-rise apartment buildings cut off others' views of the mountains, lawsuits have been initiated. New stages have elements, as always, of both present and past.

Population growth over the thousand years that Kyongju served as the capital of Silla shows marked changes in the configuration of the city as well as an increase in population. When the six villages of Saro formed an alliance (Stage I), they also needed some of the trappings of government, which included a castle for the ruler's family and other governing officials and eventually government buildings. Because the purpose of the alliance in the first place was for defense, fortresses on the surrounding hills were erected. The fortresses would have needed provisions and at least some military personnel. In Stage II, enormous earth-mounded tombs were erected in the midst of the plain. They made a clear statement about the wealth and power of the ruling Kim family. The presence of the tombs also shifted the center of the city to the north. In the Buddhist period, Stage III, the city shifted even farther north. A gridded, walled city to emulate the capital of China was required, but the large tombs were in the way. Therefore, the area even farther to the north, right up against the north river, was used to create this imitation Chang'an. Large Buddhist temples arose in the plains and on the hills around the plain, filling the space available. Noble houses, along with those of ordinary people, crowded around the tombs and temples, and the population filled the corridor from Kyongju city down to the sea. More work, however, needs to be done on the rural population to complete the picture of the growth of the regional population. Kyongju is not unique in requiring the kind of systematic archaeological survey that would begin to fill in those gaps.

11

Population Dynamics and Urbanism in Premodern Island Southeast Asia

Laura Lee Junker

At the time of European contact, the Malay peninsula and island archipelagos of insular Southeast Asia were dotted with numerous maritime trading kingdoms of varying scale and complexity. These kingdoms lay at the intersection of sea routes linking China, mainland Southeast Asia, India, East Africa, and the Middle East in a vast network of spice and luxury goods trade (Figure 11-1).

In the fifteenth and sixteenth centuries, these maritime trading polities centered on coastal capitals such as Palembang, Melaka, Johor, Brunei, Manila, Ternate, Majapahit, Makassar, Kedah, and Jolo, impressively scaled cities that controlled the flow of tropical forest products and raw materials from the island interiors for export to China and other foreign lands in exchange for luxury goods. Some of the indigenous states and complex chiefdoms had trade interactions with the Chinese that date to at least the early to mid-first millennium AD, resulting in a substantial body of Chinese literature on specific polities. In addition, many of these Southeast Asian maritime trading kingdoms adopted Sanskrit-based writing systems (but in Malay script) from their Indic trade partners. Therefore, we have a substantial number of both contact-period European records and early non-European texts going back more than a millennium with information on polity location, scale, and trade relations in these island Southeast Asian complex societies. These historical sources provide quantitative and qualitative data relevant to issues of demography, population dynamics, and processes of urbanization in the early kingdoms and chiefdoms of the region.

Work by historians shows that the complex societies present in the island archipelagos of Southeast Asia at the time of European contact developed in a region with comparatively low population densities relative to land, with an average of fewer than six persons per sq km. Competition between political leaders focused on commanding labor rather than on commandeering land, which may explain the strong emphasis on alliance-building activities such as prestige-goods exchanges, ritualized feasting, and religious pageantry aimed at social cohesion in Southeast Asian complex societies. Cultural features related to environments, popu-

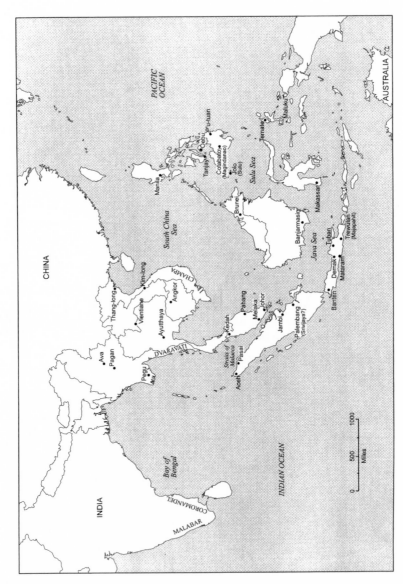

Figure 11-1. Location of historically known tenth- to sixteenth-century political centers in Southeast Asia and major maritime and overland trade routes.

lation distributions, and traditional economic modes tended to constrain inter-generational continuity in political leadership and to promote frequent fissioning of political factions, resulting in the notoriously unstable political units that are at the core of anthropological conceptualizations of these polities as "segmentary states" (Southall 1988), "galactic polities" (Tambiah 1976), and "theater states" (Geertz 1980b). Thus, demographic factors were key variables in how political systems and political economies were structured in island Southeast Asian states.

At the same time, historic sources also indicate that island Southeast Asian polities of the first millennium to mid-second millennium AD were highly urban-ized, with many coastal maritime trading ports housing 20 percent or more of the total population of the state. Chinese accounts of the first millennium AD de-scribed large-scale, cosmopolitan ports with extensive administrative and religious architecture, housing for both local nobility and foreign traders, craft production areas, and market locales. These "primate" centers controlled in various ways den-dritically organized networks of villages and towns radiating along rivers into the mountainous interior hinterlands of the island, often economically if not politi-cally integrating ethnically and linguistically diverse tribal swiddening popula-tions, hunter-gatherer groups, and lowland farmers into extensive trade webs. In this chapter, I will use historical and archaeological evidence to examine some of the factors that may have been significant in the maintenance of low population densities but high levels of urbanism in early island Southeast Asian complex societies, as well as how these demographic factors contributed to the unique forms of political structure and political economy found in these maritime trad-ing polities.

Unfortunately, archaeological research has not matched historical and ethno-graphic studies in addressing questions of complex society formation, population dynamics, and urbanism in Southeast Asia. Few premodern island Southeast Asian cities have received any systematic archaeological attention, and for many historically well-known polities, such as seventh- to eleventh-century Srivijaya, archaeologists have yet to even unequivocally locate the polity capital. In addi-tion, Southeast Asian archaeology has lagged behind that of other regions in the world in implementing programs of systematic regional-scale research, resulting in few settlement pattern studies to put archaeologically known cities within a larger regional context. However, I have provided a few examples of settlement pattern research in island Southeast Asia that has allowed us to document how "primate dendritic" settlement systems emerge over time, how their urban centers are formed, and what the dynamic connection is between urban centers and their hinterlands.

Population Densities and Ecology in Island Southeast Asia

Until the European colonial period, most of Southeast Asia (with the possible exception of Bali, Java, and parts of Vietnam) had exceedingly low population densities relative to land and resources (Reid 1988:11–18, 1992:460–463). In fact, complex societies in Southeast Asia can be said to be one of the least densely populated "civilizations" and "urban" societies in the premodern world. As shown in Table 11-1, a compilation of historically based population estimates for Southeast Asian islands and mainland countries in AD 1600 indicates an average density of 5.5 persons per sq km for the region. This overall density is less than one-fifth that of India and China, less than one-tenth that of Japan, less than one-third that of Polynesia, approximately two-thirds that of the mid-second millennium West African kingdoms such as Mali and Benin, and roughly half that of Europe of the same period. New World civilizations, such as those centered in Peru (the Inca) and the Valley of Mexico (the Aztec), also had significantly higher population densities than those of contact-period Southeast Asian chiefdoms and states.

The highest population densities in Southeast Asia were found in large coastal trading cities of the western archipelago and in limited areas of intensive farming, such as the Red River delta of Vietnam, central and eastern Java, Bali, and South Sulawesi (see Table 11-1). Most of these areas of higher density population are wide river valleys with thick volcanic soils allowing intensive, often hydraulically sustained, wet-rice agriculture (Miksic 2000). Yet, even these regions maintained pre-sixteenth-century populations that were well below those of most complex societies in human history. More typical of island Southeast Asia and many regions of mainland Southeast Asia are rugged mountainous interiors and steep-graded rivers that carry the less-fertile rain forest soils to relatively narrow coastal plains, sustaining only less-intensive forms of swidden agriculture (Shaffer 1996:9–10). Not surprisingly, the more rugged eastern archipelagos, including Maluku (the Moluccas or "Spice Islands"), the Philippines, and Borneo, were the least densely populated parts of Southeast Asia. However, even these regions of extreme low density supported complex societies on the level of chiefdoms or states and, in many cases, substantial-sized urban centers.

The reasons for these comparatively low population densities in the region prior to European colonization have continued to be debated among historians, anthropologists, and demographers. Although soil productivity and resources vary widely within the island archipelagos of insular Southeast Asia according to topography, geology, monsoonal conditions, and other factors, ecologists have generally described the region as resource rich for farmers, foragers, and exploiters of marine resources. The tropical rain forests of the interior yield abundant edible wild plants and potential domesticates (e.g., yams, taro, sago palm, banana, coconuts, breadfruit, and rice) and a variety of both wild and husbanded protein sources (e.g., pig, chicken, elephants, tigers, monkey, and deer), in addition to rich marine and coastal resources. Particularly after the initiation of rice farming, the region was capable of sustaining some of the largest populations in the world. Even using largely traditional unmechanized technologies, a hectare of rice yields almost 75 percent more calories than an equal-sized plot of wheat (Crosby

Table 11-1. Estimated Population Numbers and Population Densities for
Southeast Asia and Comparative Regions in Approximately AD 1600

Region	Estimated Population	Density in persons per sq km
Southeast Asia*	23,000,000	5.7
Burma	3,100,000	4.6
Laos (including northeast Thailand)	1,200,000	2.9
Siam (minus northeast)	1,800,000	5.3
Cambodia-Champa	1,230,000	4.5
Vietnam (north and central)	4,700,000	18.0
Malaya (including Patani)	500,000	3.4
Sumatra	2,400,000	3.4
Java	4,000,000	30.0
Borneo	670,000	0.9
Sulawesi	1,200,000	6.3
Bali	600,000	79.7
Lesser Sunda Islands	600,000	9.1
Maluku	275,000	3.7
Northern Philippines (Luzon and Visayas)	800,000	4.0
Southern Philippines (Mindinao and Sulu)	150,000	1.5
China**	150,000,000	37.5
India**	135,000,000	32.0
Japan**	22,000,000	59.5
Polynesia***	453,700	17.8
Europe**	100,000,000	10.4

*Population estimates for Southeast Asia were taken from Reid (1988:14), detailing original histori-
cal sources and methods of estimation.
** Population estimates for China (including China proper but not Inner Mongolia, Manchuria, and
Chinese Turkestan), India (including Pakistan and Bangladesh), Japan, and Europe were obtained
from McEvedy and Jones (1978). If population densities for Japan are corrected for inhabitable arable
land only, the figure is 366.7 persons per sq km. Europe includes all of continental Europe, Scandinavia, and the British Isles.
***Population estimates for Polynesia were obtained from Kirch (1984:19), combining West Polyne-
sia, East Polynesia, and the Polynesian Outliers for an overall regional density. New Zealand was
removed from the estimate due to its environmental differences and unique demographic characteristics in comparison to other Polynesian islands.

1972:175). In contrast to the precolonial period, in the late twentieth century the
tremendous productivity of rice allowed Southeast Asia and the tropical Indian
subcontinent combined to sustain around 26 percent of the world's population
(Indonesia, with around 179 million people, ranked as the fourth most populous
country in the world at the close of the millennium) (Shaffer 1996:10).

Given the relative bounty of arable agricultural land, the high potential productivity of both land resources and marine resources, and soaring postcolonial population levels sustained primarily through traditional agricultural practices, most researchers recognize that low precolonial population densities cannot be attributed in a broad sense to ecological limitations on subsistence. Other factors must be considered, such as health issues, social and cultural constraints on child-bearing, and mortality associated with warfare. Studies of health and nutrition show more than adequate diets at the period of contact (Owen 1987), suggesting that suppressed reproduction or high mortality due to poor nutrition was not a significant factor. Prolonged contact with West Asian, Arabian, and African (and indirectly European) peoples through maritime trade over several millennia meant that Southeast Asian peoples did not suffer the same catastrophic loss to disease at the time of European contact that befell Polynesians and New World populations. Reid (1992:461–462), using historical data, suggests a number of other factors that may have contributed to these relatively low population levels, including extended breast-feeding of children, high agricultural workloads of mothers and consequent depression of fertility, the widespread cultural practice of abortion, the ubiquity of fertility-reducing diseases such as malaria, and the high rate of warfare.

Certainly the intensive focus on swidden gardening for subsistence emphasized female labor in many parts of Southeast Asia (particularly island Southeast Asia), whereas men were often preoccupied with fishing, hunting, and trading activities (e.g., Geertz 1963; Schlegel 1979). The demographic effects of indigenous diseases such as malaria and imported diseases such as smallpox in the precolonial period are unclear due to a lack of historic documentation (Owen 1987). However, diseases readily transmitted through animals or people may have become more widespread as Southeast Asian populations expanded their maritime trade contacts in the late first millennium BC and first millennium AD to link once-isolated island archipelagos with populations on the East Asian mainland and with peoples as distant as India, the Arabian Peninsula, and the eastern coast of Africa (Hall 1985). This intensified contact may have had consequences for population growth in the initial period of state development in Southeast Asia, although this assertion remains speculative until more data from historical demographic studies and skeletal analyses of precolonial burial populations are available.

Warfare in Southeast Asia probably did not *directly* suppress population levels through high mortality rates, because historical and anthropological studies of precolonial warfare note that death tolls were generally low. Both intermittent local raiding and large-scale wars waged by Southeast Asian kings, chiefs, and tribal leaders were traditionally aimed at taking captive slaves and seizing portable resources rather than killing combatants and colonizing land (see Reid 1983b:27–33, 1992:461–462, and Junker 1999:336–369 for more extended discussions of Southeast Asian warfare). In fact, I suggest below that this style of warfare is primarily a *consequence* of low population densities, which placed a relatively high value on labor and engendered strategies such as massive slave raiding to expand the labor force under a local leader's control. However, Reid (1992:461) points out that sustained warfare could have a significant demographic impact on regions of Southeast Asia with already low-density populations that could not easily field a strong fighting force and faced further decimation by enforced migration or enslavement of their productive workforce.

Whatever the cause or causes of these remarkably low population densities, the demographic factor, combined with other features of the natural and cultural systems, had a profound effect on political formations and economic structures in these early Southeast Asian kingdoms and chiefdoms.

Implications of Ecology and Demography for Political Structure and Political Economy

Relatively low population levels, combined with an economic emphasis on swidden cropping rather than intensive permanent agriculture, an abundance of unoccupied fertile land, and a seemingly inexhaustible supply of wood and bamboo for easily rebuilding even large settlements, meant that many island Southeast Asian populations were inherently mobile and not particularly concerned with control of land as a political and economic commodity (Hall 1992:187; Reid 1983a:157; Winzeler 1981:462). Shortage of labor relative to land appears to have engendered a political system in which a ruler's power base was measured in terms of the size of the labor force bound to him through extensive alliance networks, rather than fixed geographic territories.

Alliance networks surrounding chiefs and kings were created and maintained through the charismatic attraction of individuals (e.g., Tambiah 1976), through the theatrical ceremonialism of the polity center (Geertz 1980b), and, most important, through voluminous gift exchanges between allied leaders and between elite patrons and their cadre of supporters (e.g., Wheatley 1983; Winzeler 1976). Unlike in strongly centralized polities, political relationships and hierarchies of authority had to be constantly reinforced through the strategic disbursement of wealth to cronies and clients. An elaborate series of bride wealth exchanges for polygamous marriages, the circulation of status-symboling goods as part of competitive feasting events, elite gift exchange associated with royal investitures, and other institutionalized forms of exchange were central to Southeast Asian political economies and were the very foundations of political power.

Much of the status-defining and alliance-cementing wealth in these societies was obtained through foreign trade. By the mid-first millennium AD (Tang period), and intensifying in the early second millennium AD (through the Sung, Yuan, and Ming periods), developing Southeast Asian kingdoms became involved in maritime luxury-good trade networks that stretched across the South China Sea and the Indian Ocean. These expanding trade networks eventually linked

India and Arab states to the west with Southeast Asian complex societies such as
Champa, Pegu, and Ayuddha (Ayutthaya) on the mainland; Srivijaya, Palembang, Majapahit, Brunei, Melaka, Maluku, Sulu, and various Philippine chiefdoms in the island archipelagos; and the Japanese kingdoms and Chinese empires
to the north and east (see Hall 1985, 1992; Hall and Whitmore 1976; Taylor
1992; Wheatley 1959; Wolters 1971 for detailed discussions of maritime trade in
precolonial Southeast Asia). Bornean gold and iron; Japanese silver and weap-
onry; Chinese porcelain, lacquerware, and silks; Indian silks and beads; Javanese
cotton textiles; Philippine tropical hardwoods and pearls; and Maluku spices and
aromatics were just some of the products circulated in these complex exchange
systems. With its vast wealth, labor resources, and complex bureaucratic structures, China was central to this trade, mass producing and exporting high-quality
luxury goods (e.g., porcelain, lacquerware, metal jewelry, bronzes, silks, and objects made of ivory and precious stones) in exchange for tropical raw materials to
manufactured elite goods (e.g., metal ores, tropical hardwoods, waxes and resins,
hemp, pearls, tortoise shells, animal pelts and ivory, and cotton) and medicinal or
food products consumed by Chinese elites (e.g., trepang and other marine delica-
cies, rare birds' nests for bird's nest soup, honey, nutmeg and other spices, and
rhino horns) (Wheatley 1959; Wu 1959). Southeast Asian kingdoms and chiefdoms competed for this wealth-generating foreign trade through lavishly equipped
trade missions to the Chinese court (where they could be ranked among the
"tributary states" and receive favored trade status) (see L. Andaya 1992:346; Junker 1999:212–218; and Smith 1979:445–451 for discussion of the significance
of tributary trade).

Thus, competition between political leaders (and between rulers and would-be
rulers) focused on commanding labor rather than commandeering land. Even
political expansion through militarism appears to have been primarily oriented
toward the capture of slave labor to augment local productive capacities, rather
than the seizure of land and territory (Andaya and Andaya 1982:61; Reid
1983b:27–33, 1992:461). The weakly integrated, leader-focused factions at the
core of Southeast Asian political structures meant that political leadership was
generally highly conflictive, unstable, and prone to relatively short cycles of expansion and collapse. That is, precolonial Southeast Asian kingdoms and chiefdoms were particularly illustrative of the phenomenon known as "political cycling," that is, repeated sequences of political coalescence and disintegration, with
rapid shifts in regional power centers.

Certain cultural features promoted political fissioning. One of these was the
widespread emphasis in Southeast Asian societies on bilateral descent rules in
inheritance and cognatic descent (Brown 1976). Fox (1977) has emphasized the
significance of corporate unilineal descent groups and particularly stratified lineages or "conical clans" in the development and maintenance of strongly centralized state structures in India, as well as China, Mesopotamia, and prehispanic

Mexico and Peru. Societies adhering to strong unilineal principles of descent can control the smooth flow of political authority from one generation to another with minimal disruption, and corporate descent groups can form the basis for state bureaucratic units ensuring the steady flow of resources from periphery to center. In most ethnographically or historically known complex societies of Southeast Asia, kinship is generally reckoned bilaterally, corporate descent groups are lacking, postmarital residence is bilocal or neolocal, and rank and wealth are inherited along both the maternal and paternal lines (Hall 1985:110–111; Reid 1988:147; Winzeler 1976:628). Even though imported Indian or Muslim law codes in some polities identified the eldest son as the legitimate heir, succession disputes were almost inevitable between the eldest son and younger sons, as well as both maternal and paternal uncles (B. Andaya 1992:419). In addition, in many Southeast Asian complex societies, polygamy was the cultural norm, at least among the rulers and other nobility (e.g., B. Andaya 1992:409, 419; Geertz 1980b:35; Reid 1988:152), producing multiple heirs and further exacerbating the conflict over succession.

Adding to the chaos of kingly and chiefly succession in some regions of Southeast Asia was a pronounced mythology of "folk heroism" in which ordinary individuals rise up and rebel against a tyrannical leader and usurp political power (B. Andaya 1992:421; Taylor 1992:178). Kingship in Southeast Asia depended strongly on the association with the inherited spiritual power of royal ancestors, which automatically set them above their followers, "reinforced by ideas and vocabulary of imported religions" (Andaya and Ishii 1992:546). However, the perception of ritual potency in rulers was vulnerable to any decline in general prosperity within their political sphere (B. Andaya 1992:420). Southeast Asian ideologies often left the door open for ordinary individuals, through revelation or the acquisition of sacred objects, to acquire spiritual power that could often lead to a kind of popular messianic rebellion (Andaya and Ishii 1992:551). Although the construction of a strong military was critical to protecting a ruler's economic activities (particularly for controlling trade and launching plunder-aimed raiding expeditions), warrior-elites were often able to garner significant wealth and establish independent power bases through their close association with elite patrons (Hall 1992:260) and ultimately threaten the latter's hegemony (Reid 1988:167).

Urbanism in Premodern Southeast Asia

Southeast Asia presents an interesting case for looking at population dynamics in premodern complex societies because it contradicts the notion that high population densities are generally necessary for a high degree of urbanism in early states. If we define "urbanism" as an index or ratio of concentrated "city"- or "town"-dwelling people versus the dispersed, rural component of the population (e.g., Fox 1977), then Southeast Asia is one of the most "urbanized" regions of the world in precolonial times, despite overall low population densities. As noted by Reid (1993:67), the first modern censuses of Southeast Asian colonial cities at around 1900 led to the mistaken notion that Southeast Asia was one of the *least* urbanized regions of the world prior to the twentieth century. However, Reid effectively demonstrates that it was the process of colonialism that progressively deurbanized Southeast Asia from the seventeenth to mid-twentieth centuries as once-flourishing indigenous maritime trade entrepôts foundered and indigenous populations were locked out of new European commercial centers. Reid notes that, until the seventeenth century, Asian cities tended to be larger than European ones (Reid 1993:68–73), with Thang-long (Vietnam), Ayutthaya (Thailand), Pegu (Burma), Melaka (Malay Peninsula), Makassar (Maluku), Mataram, and possibly other cities reaching populations in the 100,000–200,000 range in the sixteenth and early seventeenth centuries.

Table 11-2, a summary of some of Reid's sixteenth- and seventeenth-century population estimates and urban area estimates for Southeast Asian cities based on European contact-period accounts, shows a remarkable number of locales on both mainland Southeast Asia and in the island archipelagos that rivaled the most densely populated cities almost anywhere in the world in this period. Historically derived population estimates were almost certainly biased by the politics of European armaments and their interests in inflating native resistance to colonial rule, and urban area estimates were probably skewed by the common structure of Southeast Asian cities in which a densely packed and often walled royal center was surrounded by a more dispersed and nebulous urban periphery with boundaries that were difficult to define (Reid 1993:71, 73; see discussion below). Nonetheless, multiple sources are generally consistent in describing impressively scaled urban concentrations in the largest cities, with urban densities often averaging a remarkable 20,000 or more people per sq km. As evident in Table 11-2, populations varied markedly in Southeast Asian cities outside the largest tier, with a second tier of urban centers falling within the 50,000–100,000 range (e.g., Aceh [Sumatra], several northern Javanese ports including Tuban, and Kim-long [northern Vietnam]) and numerous cities in the 20,000–50,000 range (e.g., Pagan [Burma], Manila [Philippines], and Pahang [Malay Peninsula]).

More significant than the absolute size of Southeast Asian cities in the sixteenth and early seventeenth centuries is the percentage of the total indigenous populations living in the region's largest cities. Reid (1993:75) estimates that, over the region as a whole, about 5 percent of Southeast Asians inhabited the largest cities, a proportion that was significantly larger than most of contemporaneous Europe (McEvedy and Jones 1978), but somewhat lower than Mughal India or Late Ming/Early Ch'ing China of the same period (Raychaudhuri and Habib 1982:169). However, if we look at the percentage of urban dwellers for some of the most economically vibrant of the contact-period maritime trade ports in Southeast Asia, this urbanization index is even higher. For example, the narrow

Table 11-2. Estimates of the Population and Area of Selected Sixteenth and Seventeenth-Century Southeast Asian Cities from Historical Sources

Urban Center	Date	Range of Population Estimates	Range of Total Area Estimates (sq km)	Range of Walled Core or Citadel Area Estimates (sq km)
Ayutthaya (Thailand)	1545	>100,000	15	7.2
	1617-86	about 200,000		
Pegu (Burma)	1596	600,000	15	5.8
Thang-long (Vietnam)	Sixteenth century 1688	130,000	22	0.4
Makassar (Sulawesi)	1614-1660	>20,000 to >100,000	6	1.8
Melaka (Malay Peninsula)	1510	65,000–200,000	?	?
Pasai (Sumatra)	1512-1518	>12,000–20,000	?	?
Aceh (Sumatra)	1621-1688	>48,700–160,000	12	0.2
Brunei (Borneo)	1521, 1579	130,000–162,000	?	?
Manila (Philippines)	1565	40,000	?	?
Demak (Java)	1512	10,000–30,000	?	?
Mataram (Java)	1624	800,000	41	0.4

As compiled by Reid (1988:69, 71–72, 74).

Straits of Malacca that funneled trade traffic between the Indian Ocean and the South China Sea were dominated in the fifteenth and sixteenth centuries by the trade emporium of Melaka (Andaya and Andaya 1982:31–51; Gullick 1981:11–18; Thomaz 1993; Wheatley 1961:307–320). In 1511, Melaka was a city of 100,000–200,000, with a spectacular series of mosques and a walled royal core (with buildings for royal elephants, artillery, and the reception of foreign dignitaries) ruled by Muslim kings (Tome Pires 1944[1515]). Boasting trade volumes that nearly rivaled those of the wealthiest contemporaneous European ports such as Seville, and serving as the intersection of maritime trading networks stretching from the Red Sea and Persian Gulf to China and Japan, Melaka supported a bureaucratically complex port management system with harbor masters, warehouses, transporters, markets administrators, and support personnel for thousands of wealthy foreign traders semipermanently ensconced in urban estates. Most significant, an estimated 20 percent of the population of the entire Malayan Peninsula was concentrated in Melaka in about 1500 (Reid 1988; Thomaz 1993), a city that controlled no appreciable agricultural hinterland and relied almost exclusively on foreign trade to meet its basic subsistence needs. As reconstructed by Reid (1993:77), Melaka had no political hegemony or direct economic control over an extensive upriver hinterland, but instead relied almost wholly on foreign subsistence provisioning, including 45 rice ships each year from Burma, 30 from various ports in Thailand, an average of 50–60 annually from Java, and several from the Coromandel (eastern) coast of India. Reid estimates that these recorded ships would have provided a minimum of 7,000 tons of rice annually, more than enough to feed the 50,000-plus permanent residents of the city. Reid (1993:77) notes that Melaka was not alone as a coastal trading entrepôt with a comparatively high index of urbanism when examined in its regional context. The cities of Thang-long, Aceh, Banten, Brunei, and Makassar, at their respective peaks in the sixteenth and seventeenth centuries, all encompassed at least one-fifth of the population under their regional hegemony.

With the exception of a few cities such as Trowulan (Java), Ava (Burma), and Thang-long (Vietnam) located in rich rice-growing river valleys (what Hall [1985] refers to as "rice-plain states"), most Southeast Asian cities of the first and early second millennium AD (particularly those of island Southeast Asia) were port cities along the coast that were largely detached from interior agricultural bases for their basic subsistence (Hall 1985; Reid 1993:85). Maritime transport of staples was generally more efficient than moving tribute or trade goods along interior rivers, and it was considerably more effective than the land-based routes moving goods in complex societies such as the Aztec (e.g., Hassig 1985). Coastal port cities supported their burgeoning populations either by directly importing rice and other staple goods or by using their trade-obtained wealth to purchase foodstuffs in the free marketplace. Most premodern Southeast Asian complex societies had political economies that were strongly skewed toward D'Altroy and Earle's (1985) "wealth finance" rather than "tributary (or staple) finance" structures for mobilizing resources, because geography, environmental factors, demographic factors, a lack of manpower for large military forces, and decentralized, alliance-structured political relations all worked against the establishment of far-reaching hinterland tribute systems.

The overwhelming economic emphasis on maritime trade in most of these Southeast Asian cities also created the conditions for rapid growth in population, particularly at the height of their economic prosperity and regional political dominance. As described above for the fifteenth- to sixteenth-century port city of Melaka, a large number of artisans, traders, port administrators, transporters, and other commerce-related specialists were necessarily concentrated at the port cities (Geertz 1980b; Van Leur 1967; Wheatley 1961). In addition, many Southeast Asian port cities were literally operated on the backs of a foreign slave population who performed an astounding array of occupations, including farming; fishing; sailing; constructing public buildings; mining; craft production (including commercial-scale metallurgy and weaving); entertaining; serving as concubines or domestic servants in elite households; trading, interpreting, or writing for illiterate masters; fighting as warriors; raiding to acquire additional slaves; and even functioning as high-ranking port administrators (Reid 1983a, 1983b; Watson 1980). From the seventeenth to early nineteenth centuries, at the height of the maritime trading polity of Sulu in the southern Philippines, an estimated average of 2,000–3,000 captive slaves entered the workforce of Jolo and areas surrounding the port each year (Tarling 1963:146; Warren 1985:221–222). Warren (1985:221) suggests that this "slave mode of production" in agriculture and crafts freed up labor in the retinues of Sulu chiefs to support their trading and raiding interests full time.

In addition to these large imported workforces, Southeast Asian cities grew rapidly through the concentration of local nobility allied with the kings and paramount chiefs who controlled these trade centers, with local chiefs and elite kinsmen attracted by trade wealth and physical proximity to their generous patrons. Because political relations in Southeast Asia were based on personal ties of alliance, and portable wealth and labor rather than lands were the primary foundation for political power, lower-tier elites were not generally tethered to dispersed "territories" outside the capital to protect their economic interests (e.g., Hall 1992:187; Winzeler 1981:462). Instead, the nobility was commonly found clustered in the port cities in aristocratic compounds fanning out from the administrative center, which consisted of elaborate walled dwellings surrounded by the huts of their dependents (i.e., house servants, food producers, craft artisans, bodyguards, and other workers who included both "freemen" and "slaves") (Reid 1993:86–88).

Even in the smaller-scale Philippine maritime trading chiefdoms, *datus* or chiefs typically "owned" between 100 and several thousand slaves and controlled an equal number of nonslave household laborers (Junker 1999:128–137), so the establishment of residence by a single additional chief at a port city such as Jolo, Manila, or Cotabato could easily increase the urban population by hundreds and possibly thousands. The sprawling "suburbs" of walled elite compounds, gardens, and houses of attached vassals created an impression of massive urban scale among early European observers who were used to the compact European cities of the period (Reid 1993:88). The "segmentary" (Southall 1988) nature of political power relations meant that lower-tier elites had to maintain their own material base in the port city where opportunities for acquiring wealth were concentrated.

Otherwise, they could not accumulate sufficient prestige goods and slaves to support bride wealth payments, ritual feast exchanges, and other activities requiring political currency. In addition, the court ceremonialism and state pageantry that cemented the tenuous bonds between Southeast Asian rulers and their subordinates (Andaya and Ishii 1992; Geertz 1980a; Tambiah 1976) attracted aristocrats to these capitals for reasons beyond factors of political economy. As outlined in more detail below, large-scale Buddhist or Hindu temple complexes, Islamic mosques, and other "sacred landscapes" dominated the urban core of these cities, concentrating religious personnel and cosmologically connected elites.

As emphasized by Reid (1993:86), successful port cities in Southeast Asia were magnets for wealthy foreign traders, entrepreneurs, and aristocrats, as well as for dependent vassals of the ruler. It was the influx of foreigners connected with commerce or attracted by economic activities within the city itself that provided the diverse linguistic, social, and cultural character of Southeast Asia coastal capitals such as Palembang, Melaka, Majapahit, Johor, and Kedah (Geertz 1980b; Van Leur 1967; Wheatley 1961). Historic sources suggest that coastal trade ports operated in an economic mode that might be described as "mixed market" and "royal monopoly." At Melaka, harbor masters were assigned to administer trade with merchants of particular foreign nations, providing caravans of elephants to transport foreign cargoes from the vessels to large-scale underground warehouses where goods could be stored until the arrival of intended trade partners (Andaya and Andaya 1982:42–43; Thomaz 1993:73). Foreign merchants were allotted specific trade berths where the ruler's personal representative would inventory the goods, removing a percentage for port fees to be remanded to the port ruler (Miksic 1984:244; Thomaz 1993:73). In addition to these trade tariffs, gifts had to be presented to the Melakan ruler, to the ruler's "lord of the trading center," and to the various harbormasters in charge of the particular foreign trading groups (Andaya and Andaya 1982:43; Gullick 1981:13). These "gifts" often consisted of specific foreign luxury goods that were reserved as royal monopolies (including certain types of silks and porcelains). The remaining merchandise, including foodstuffs, mundane manufactured goods, raw materials, and luxury items, were then available for general trade. Because of the highly seasonal wind patterns in the South China Sea and Indian Ocean, most foreign traders had to remain in port for many months to complete their transactions, requiring additional personnel to house them and regulate their activities in the city. At any point in time, tens of thousands of foreign traders and their retinues occupied the city, living temporarily in specified areas assigned according to ethnic or linguistic affiliation and under the protection of specific Melakan administrators. There were also several thousand foreigners (including Persians, Gujaratis and Hindu Tamils from India, Borneans, Muslim Tagalogs and other ethnic groups of the Philippines, Burmese from Pegu, Javanese, Chams from the Vietnam coast, and Chinese) who lived semipermanently in the city in walled compounds like those of the local nobility (Andaya and Andaya 1982; Gullick 1981). Many of these foreigners, already of an aristocratic background in their lands of origin, accumulated wealth and power through their commercial activities, developed large retinues of slaves and dependent vassals, and in a few cases became high-ranked ministers in the local government (Reid 1993:114–123).

To return to the issue of why early Southeast Asian states are so highly urbanized, we can point to the concentrated population that can be supported by an affluent rice-based subsistence economy, the location of most Southeast Asian cities along the coast or on large navigable rivers that facilitate transport and population aggregation, and the strong emphasis placed on foreign trade in the economy of most Southeast Asian complex societies, which tends to funnel economic interactions and concentrate production activities within these coastal centers. In addition, the domination of portable wealth-based rather than land-based (tributary) forms of political economy, and a political structure bound together by networks of patron-vassal ties requiring significant face-to-face material exchanges and shared ceremonialism, tended to focus the critical political action and social matrix of the state in these port cities. All these factors appear to have created a landscape of hyperlarge, "primate" coastal centers that were either almost wholly economically and politically deactivated from more sparsely occupied interior hinterlands (thus consistent with the classic definition of "entrepôts" or "ports of trade" (e.g., Geertz 1980b) or that functioned as "gateways" to dendritic, river-based regional systems (e.g., Hirth 1978). We now turn to an examination of the historic record for how these cities are organized and constructed and the implications for their representation in the archaeological record.

The Archaeological Problem: Where Are the Cities?

Contact-period European documents and, in some cases, earlier Chinese texts and indigenous scripts provide significantly detailed descriptions of Southeast Asian cities of the early to mid-second millennium AD. The latter sources even refer to some very early urban centers of the late first millennium AD, such as the seventh- to eleventh-century maritime trading center of Srivijaya (eastern Sumatra), which continues to baffle archaeological attempts to locate what Chinese traders describe as a magnificent, but apparently all but archaeologically invisible, coastal capital (see discussion below).

Compared to other regions of complex society development, island Southeast Asia has received limited archaeological attention. Primarily the purview of historians, island Southeast Asia complex societies are rarely mentioned and almost never figure prominently in cross-culturally comparative studies of chiefdoms and states by anthropologists (Earle 1991; Service 1975; but see Flannery 1995). The reasons for this dearth of archaeological research are varied, but a major impediment to archaeological work is the perishable nature of urban architecture in the region and the generally low visibility of many key types of material remains.

As emphasized above, most of the major cities of premodern Southeast Asia were located either directly on the coast, at the mouth of often rapidly alluviating rivers with prograding coasts, or along large navigable rivers of the interior, as a function of problems of transport, agricultural production, and trade access. These ancient cities were almost invariably in geologically unstable areas, with the implication that they may have been frequently moved to deal with problems of flooding and too-rapid silting, processes that also make it difficult for archaeologists to locate them without relatively sophisticated geomorphological studies. Contact-period historic accounts indicate that the traditional structure of cities, both on the mainland and in island Southeast Asia, focused on a royal citadel at the center that was frequently walled and moated, with palaces, religious structures (Buddhist, Hindu, or Islamic), and administrative buildings laid out in an orderly fashion to reflect the "cosmic pretensions of its monarch" (Reid 1993:78). Outside this planned city center, meant to impress foreign merchants, diplomats, and other visitors, the rest of the city appeared chaotic, consisting of the fortified residential compounds of elites and their dependents and the urban sprawl of markets, workshops, and housing for foreigners.

In Buddhist and Hindu kingdoms of the mainland, the central planned area of the cities included large areas of several square kilometers, and stone masonry was used to construct durable religious edifices, leaving monumental archaeological traces of Burmese cities such as Pegu and Ava and Siamese cities such as Ayutthaya. However, most architectural features of mainland Asian cities and virtually the entirety of island Southeast Asian cities were made of perishable materials, with palaces, Buddhist monasteries and temples, Hindu religious structures, Islamic mosques, administrative buildings, markets, and residential compounds of all social classes constructed of wood, bamboo, and rattan (Reid 1993:83, 90; Wheatley 1983:242–243). In island Southeast Asian cities, these structures were often in the form of "pile-houses" in which daily activities took place literally off the ground. Because the structures lacked ground-level "floors," archaeologists have found it difficult even to locate buildings, and artifact patterns on the ground are unlikely to reflect any spatial concentration of past activities.

In island Southeast Asia, the only structures not constructed of timber would have been occasional clay-brick Buddhist stupas, the stone bases of Islamic mosques or Hindu temple complexes, and occasional stone megaliths. Megalithic monuments, including freestanding stone stelae, terraced platforms, stone-lined or stone-capped tombs, and large stone blocks carved into animal or human figurines, are associated with the emergence of early chiefdoms and states in limited regions of Sumatra, Java, and Bali between the late first millennium BC and the first millennium AD (Bellwood 1985:292–302; Christie 1979). In the Srivijaya example discussed in detail below, the inscribed stelae are clearly commemorative in nature and can sometimes be used to identify both capitals and secondary centers associated with a particular ruling lineage. The menhirs or dolmens are often found at upriver "secondary centers" and, along with prestige goods, tie interior settlements to the dominant elite culture of the coastal cities. In general, however, the most archaeologically visible traces of these urban concentrations would be high densities of habitation debris (pottery, metal goods, stone tools, nonperishable remnants of subsistence such as animal bone and shell), although many technologies of tropical Southeast Asia were of nonenduring materials that would leave no visible trace in the archaeological record (e.g., bamboo, wood, rattan, cordage, basketry, textiles, and so on).

Perhaps the best example of the problems of archaeological recognition of urban phenomena in Southeast Asia is the archaeological enigma of Srivijaya. More than two decades ago, Bennet Bronson expressed the frustration of many archaeologists working in the region when he noted the almost-astonishing fact that the historically well-documented seventh- to eleventh-century Srivijaya kingdom, the premier maritime trading power of the period described in Chinese texts as having an impressively large capital located somewhere along the eastern coast of Sumatra in the vicinity of the Musi River, still largely eludes archaeological documentation (Bronson 1979). In AD 671, the Chinese Buddhist monk Yi Jing traveled through island Southeast Asia as part of a sea pilgrimage to India, visiting a powerful maritime trading kingdom located somewhere along the southern islands bordering the South China Sea. Yi Jing spent six months at the Srivijaya capital, attracted by Buddhist scholars in the city, and then returned there for another ten-year sojourn between 685 and 695 (Wolters 1986:5). In this and other Chinese writings, the capital of the realm known as "Srivijaya" was described as a large, fortified international port exercising hegemony over most of the island coasts lining both the Strait of Malacca and the Strait of Sunda (including the coasts of the Malay Peninsula, Sumatra, western Borneo, and western Java), allowing almost exclusive control over the sea route between China and India. Yi Jing was most struck by the presence of a large Buddhist monastery in the center of the city where more than 1,000 monks studied Buddhist doctrine and wrote texts in Sanskrit. Although Yi Jing's text and writings of later Chinese monks who visited Srivijaya had little to say about the architecture of the capital that would help us to understand what archaeological traces might look like, they emphasized the grandeur and lavishness of court protocol, in which the elaborate regalia and symbols of sovereignty made of precious stones, fine textiles, gold, and silver were on continuous display (Wheatley 1983:243). Early Chinese writers also referred to Srivijaya as Jinzhou or "district of gold," impressed with the massive gold Buddha images within the city, the gold regalia of the king's court, and gold lotus-shaped vessels presented at ceremonial feasts that were filled with other valuable objects such as pearls (Hall 1985:272; Wolters 1986:21–22). Arab mer-

220   JUNKER

chants became frequent visitors to Srivijaya almost from its inception in the seventh century, but massively increased their numbers in the mid-eighth century
when a large Muslim trading community was established at the south China port
of Guangzhou, and Srivijaya became the primary transit point between the Persian Gulf and China. It is disappointing that Arab documents of the period do
not provide the detailed description of the physical layout and structures of the
city of value to archaeologists. However, they support the Chinese records in ex-
tolling the great wealth of the Srivijaya rulers and urban elite. Arab visitors of the
eighth century claimed that there was so much gold in the royal treasury that the
king's servants would ceremonially deposit gold bricks into an estuary on a daily
basis, and, on the death of the king, the gold would be dredged up for the suc-
cessor to redistribute to allies and retainers (Hall 1985:80–81).

    Before the seventh-century rise of the expansive Srivijaya state known to these
early Chinese and Arab writers, the eastern Sumatran coast appears to have been
occupied by a series of river-mouth chiefdoms vying to control maritime trade
along this strategic gateway to the Straits of Malacca and Indian Ocean (Andaya
and Andaya 1982:17–23; Hall 1992:196–202; Taylor 1992:173–176). Several
stone stelae with Malay inscriptions written in Sanskrit have been located in the
vicinity of the modern city of Palembang (Wheatley 1983:238; Wolters 1999:32).
These suggest that a Sumatran chief centered at Palembang in the Musi River
basin began a series of military campaigns between AD 671 and 685 that resulted
in the subjugation of the adjacent Batang Hari River and coastal chiefly center
of Jambi-Malayu and probably other polities of Sumatra's eastern coast (Hall
1992:200). Srivijaya's advantage in this regional power struggle is thought to have
lain in its location on an exceptionally large and fertile alluvial plain for surplus
rice production, coupled with an unusually wide and navigable Musi River, which
provided excellent access to interior products. The Srivijayan monarchs also successfully manipulated the Chinese tributary trade system to gain favored trade
status at the Chinese court, they developed a special relationship with numerous
maritime mercenary groups in the region to protect trade interests, and they
adopted the Sanskrit writing systems and Buddhist religion of their dominant
trade partners. The spectacular Buddhist monastery, golden Buddhas, and stupas,
as well as the impressive wooden palace structures and royal court described by
Chinese and Arab visitors undoubtedly also added to the image of Srivijaya as the
premier trading port of the region. Although no specific population estimates are
given by these early historic sources, a number of scholars suggest that the population of the capital could have reached 50,000 within a century of the city's
founding. Srivijaya continued its monopolistic control of commerce in the straits'
region from the mid-seventh to mid-eleventh centuries, but declined in the
twelfth century due to several factors, including a lapse in the formal Chinese
tributary trade that Srivijaya had so brilliantly exploited; the rising importance of
the spice trade, which shifted trade routes to the east; and militaristic expansion

by competing Siamese and Javanese states (Andaya and Andaya 1982:26–31; Hall 1985:209–214; Taylor 1992:174–175).

Given the scale and complexity of the capital of Srivijaya as described in Chinese texts, we would expect that locating the coastal port and systematically documenting it through archaeological investigations would be a simple matter. However, until the last decade, archaeologists working on the island of Sumatra had yet to discover substantial deposits of residential debris, enclosing walls (which are a visible feature of many mainland Asian cities of the period), early Buddhist architectural or artistic remains (such as temples or stone statuary), or other telltale evidence of the presence of a city of tens of thousands in the seventh through eleventh centuries (Bronson and Wisseman 1976; Wheatley 1983:240–243). Bennet Bronson and Jan Wisseman, after several frustrating field seasons of surface reconnaissance and excavations in the vicinity of Palembang, the most likely locus of the late first millennium polity, wryly concluded that "the entire vicinity . . . does not contain enough pre-fourteenth century domestic artifacts to make one small village" (1976:233), much less a bustling maritime trading port housing 1,000 Buddhist monks. Bronson and Wisseman recognized that a rethinking of problems of archaeological visibility in the tropical kingdoms of island Southeast Asia was necessary and that the logistical difficulties of regional survey had discouraged them as well as others from the regional approach necessary to gain an adequate archaeological picture of these kingdoms as regional-scale phenomena. Regional-scale work by Yves Manguin, Edward McKinnon, John Miksic, and others in this decade have in fact shown Bronson and Wisseman's assumption that Srivijaya could *not* have been centered at Palembang as premature.

A somewhat smaller-scale city of more recent date in premodern Southeast Asia further illustrates some of these problems of archaeological analysis. At the time of its conquest by the Spaniard Miguel de Legaspi's expedition in 1565, the maritime trading port of Manila was controlled by Raja Suleyman, an Islamic ruler who occupied an impressively scaled wooden pile-house palace within the fortified city of between 10,000 and 40,000 inhabitants (Junker 1999:145–146, 104–106). According to contact-period descriptions, Chinese-style iron cannons, which ringed the formidable wooden fortifications, were manufactured in large ironworks found in the administrative core of the settlement, along with public buildings, a foreign market, and housing areas for both local and foreign elite (primarily Chinese and Japanese). The entire city was apparently constructed of wooden pile-buildings, which, unfortunately, fueled a massive conflagration that virtually destroyed the site when the conquering Spaniards chose to burn the obstinate Raja Suleyman out of his fortifications. The lack of permanent architecture and many centuries of site destruction by the burgeoning populations of colonial and contemporary Manila have left us with an archaeological record that is almost devoid of interpretable remains that can illuminate the historic accounts of urban structure and processes of urbanization. The meager archaeological excavations have focused on burial areas (Peralta and Salazar 1974), although recent archaeological soundings in the colonial core of the city have yielded evidence for iron slag and other large-scale manufacturing activities, abundant Sung to Late Ming porcelain attesting to an economic emphasis on foreign trade, and probable elite residential zones (Junker 1999:106).

Partly because of these problems of archaeological visibility and preservation, archaeological work focused exclusively on locating and excavating core areas of historically known early urban centers in island Southeast Asia has been spectacularly unproductive. Archaeological excavations at smaller political centers located in what are presently more rural regions of island Southeast Asia have been more successful in generating data on the long-term formation of urban centers, their physical dimensions (population estimates, size, or both) at various points in time, and their internal organization. For example, in the Philippines, a long-term program of extensive surface survey, subsurface coring, and archaeological excavations at the coastal chiefly center of Tanjay on the island of Negros has documented the growth of this maritime trading port from a relatively small-scale pile-house town of about 3 to 5 ha at AD 500 to an approximately 30-ha settlement by the fifteenth and sixteenth centuries (Hutterer and Macdonald 1982; Junker 1990, 1999). These excavations revealed that the Visayan-speaking chiefs at Tanjay in the fifteenth and sixteenth centuries lived in walled compounds with large pile-houses spatially segregated from commoner housing; decorated their houses and burials with Chinese, Siamese, and Vietnamese porcelains; wore foreign beads from India and elsewhere; probably engaged in ritual feasting using foreign serving assemblages; manufactured metal goods and pottery for trade to interior populations; and obtained products from the island's interior for foreign export. With reference to possible stimuli for "urbanization," the Tanjay evidence shows a strong relationship between population growth at the coastal center and a political economy increasingly dependent on foreign luxury goods trade. The archaeological work at Tanjay suggests that, although larger urban centers of polities such as Srivijaya may always be better known through historical analysis, archaeological research at smaller centers may be more effective at revealing how and why towns and cities formed in Southeast Asia and how and why this region became one of the most "urbanized" in the precolonial world.

Another major impediment to archaeological analysis of the urbanization process in island Southeast Asia has been the lack of a regional approach that examines urban developments in their larger regional context. As noted above, areas of these urban centers distant from the "royal core" typically have a dispersed settlement pattern of widely scattered elite house compounds surrounded by sprawling, low-density dependent households. The urban character of these outlying areas, and even the city "boundaries," were not always evident to the contemporaneous observer. On a larger scale, it is only recently that archaeologists have turned to systematic regional survey techniques that allow them to place

what appear to be urban centers in the context of regional landscapes encompassing populations that, if not under the direct hegemony of coastal ports such as
Srivijaya, at least were strongly connected to them through exchange and other
forms of interaction. This larger regional picture helps us to approach the problem
of a high "urban" index from the perspective of "primate" settlement systems in
which the question is not only why capitals are so populous but also why settlements outside the hyperlarge urban center are so "undeveloped" and "small."

The Primate Center and Dendritic Settlement Systems

Most island Southeast Asian chiefdoms and kingdoms of the first millennium and
early second millennium A.D. fit what cultural geographers and anthropologists call a "dendritic" settlement system (e.g., Hirth 1978; Santley and Alexander
1992). Dendritic systems are characterized by the concentration of regional political and economic control within a single primate center, which exerts weakening
authority over a series of linearly radiating settlements. Most empirically observed
cases of strongly "dendritic" systems occur in situations where long-distance trade
plays a dominant role in the internal economy, concentrating economic advantage
and political power with those settlements located favorably for articulation with
external trade systems. In addition, Carol Smith (1976:345–353) suggests that
dendritic systems commonly develop in situations of marked intraregional ethnic
diversity in which a politically complex "core" occupied by the dominant ethnic
or cultural group controls trade into a less complexly organized periphery occupied by one or more politically subjugated ethnic groups. A third, and perhaps
most critical, feature characteristic of such systems is environmental or cultural
constraints on transport resulting in a linear convergence of trade networks on a
single, strategically located center. The result is a settlement system characterized
by the following: (1) the concentration of a sociopolitical elite in a single "primate" settlement; (2) a descending degree of economic and political hegemony
with increasing distance from the primate center; (3) more low-level centers than
are typical of a "central place" lattice system; (4) allegiance of each lower-level
center to only the center directly above it; and (5) a strongly unidirectional flow
of significant economic resources from periphery to center, reflecting pronounced
regional economic and political power differences (Kelley 1976:221). In a study
of dendritic settlement systems in ancient Mesoamerica, Hirth (1978:38) refers
to these strategically located centers as "gateway communities" that, because of
their strategic location at the intersection of riverine and sea routes, could simultaneously monitor the commodities flowing into the polity from external sources
and through the polity between distinct ecological zones. This single center at the
coast dominates the regional settlement system and exerts economic, political,
and ritual control through alliance-based exchanges over the interior hinterland
that serves as its agricultural base and source of exportable commodities for for-

eign trade. "Secondary" centers, "tertiary" centers, small agrarian villages, or some combination radiate out in a dendritic or branching pattern along the interior river course and its tributaries.

The "Rank-Size" analysis of geographers (e.g., Haggett 1965) has helped archaeologists to visualize how different spatial patterning in settlement might reflect distinct trajectories of urbanization and processes of political and economic centralization in complex societies (e.g., Blanton 1978; Crumley 1976; Johnson 1987; Kowalewski 1990; McIntosh and McIntosh 1993). In many complex societies, a plot of settlement size (i.e., population) versus site rank on dual logarithmic scales produces an approximately linear pattern with a few heavily populated cities and many smaller settlements. Geographers generally attribute this empirical regularity to economic factors favoring cost minimization and efficiency maximization in transporting goods, and this pattern is characteristic of "mature" urban systems with a stable political core and highly centralized economies. In contrast, a concave or "primate" rank-size pattern is one in which a single hyperlarge center dominates the settlement hierarchy and "secondary centers" are poorly developed. This settlement pattern may indicate an incipient stage in the development of an urban system that later conforms with a rank-size structure (Crumley 1976:65; Kowalewski 1990:51). However, in island Southeast Asian complex societies where foreign trade dominates the political economy, where water systems channel transport, and where the ceremonial grandeur of the royal center is fundamental to political alliance systems, we would expect primate settlement patterns and a dendritic regional settlement organization to characterize both emerging and "mature" polities (see Santley and Alexander's [1992:26–27] general discussion of "dendritic political economies").

Although few programs of systematic regional archaeological survey have been carried out in Southeast Asia, anthropologists and historians (e.g., Allen 1991; Andaya 1995; Bronson 1977; Hall 1985:1–20; Miksic 1984:241; Wolters 1967: 252, 341–342) have long recognized that the spatial organization of most historically known Southeast Asian maritime trading polities is "dendritic" and "primate" in patterning. Although Bennet Bronson was unable to document archaeologically such a regional system for the elusive Srivijaya kingdom of eastern Sumatra several decades ago, he did suggest an abstract model of what this type of settlement system would look like on the basis of historic and ethnographic evidence. His model depicts the coastal centers of two competing maritime trading polities occupying adjacent alluvial systems, both participating in long-distance trade interactions with a distant foreign power. Second-order and third-order upstream settlements are strategically located for the control of the interior movement of resources, and these in turn are connected by river with distant upriver settlements that serve as the initial concentration points for products originating in the more remote lowland areas of the drainage basin and in adjacent upland areas occupied by ethnically distinct, tribally organized, swidden-cultivating people and mobile hunter-gatherers.

The chiefly rulers at the coastal center maintain the flow of goods downriver through direct coercion of the adjacent lowland populations centered at the secondary riverbank towns and more distant villages under the latter's control. Ethnohistoric sources suggest that economic control by coastal rulers is achieved through a combination of gift-sealed alliances with local leaders, ideological sanctions by the ritually powerful lowland chiefs, and military threats (Andaya 1995: 545–547; Hall 1976:90–100; Wolters 1967:341–342). Due to the high level of mobility and geographic remoteness of upland groups, direct political domination by coastal chiefs and militarily or ritually enforced participation in the lowland economic system are generally not feasible. The lowland rulers at the coastal port are more likely to rely on individually transacted alliances with interior leaders, cemented by the interior flow of prestige goods and status-conferring titles (Miksic 1984:241). These rulers had to develop sufficiently stable and exclusive economic relations with interior populations to prevent any attempts by the foreign merchants with whom they habitually traded to circumvent the coastal center and trade directly with an interior source. In these systems, secondary and tertiary centers function primarily as "bulking centers" to concentrate goods for shipment downriver (Andaya and Andaya 1982:11; Reid 1993:53–61; also see Santley and Alexander 1992; Smith 1976). The strategic location of these bulking centers along river transport routes meant that any attempts to bypass them in delivering goods downstream would be difficult, if not impossible. Archaeologically, we would expect these upriver trade centers to be located at critical points of transport convergence within the river basin and to yield significantly greater quantities of both interior and coastal trade goods than the surrounding settlements.

In a recent archaeological study of the Musi River basin of Palembang, McKinnon (1993) has demonstrated that a regional approach, even if it is not based on wholly systematic recording techniques, provides more insight into processes of political centralization and urbanization in these maritime trading polities than haphazard searches for an elusive port center. McKinnon notes that large riverbank sites up to 80 km inland have megalithic architecture, in the form of limestone menhirs and dolmens, which mirror the style of stone monuments (but have no Sanskrit inscriptions) found at one of the probable locations of the Srivijaya capital at the mouth of the Musi River near modern Palembang. Burials in association with the limestone monuments at these interior sites, as well as scattered surface debris, include bronze jewelry and blades, glass beads, and imported Chinese stoneware and porcelains ranging from the ninth century to the thirteenth century in date that are stylistically and materially similar to luxury goods found along the coast and corresponding chronologically to the period of Srivijaya dominance (also see Manguin 1992:69–72).

Because the logistics of fieldwork in Sumatra precluded large-scale excavations, systematic surface collections, and even the preparation of accurate site maps, McKinnon is cautious in interpreting these interior sites as clear evidence for

Srivijaya-connected interior trade centers. However, I would argue that the significant investment in construction of stone ritual structures and tombs coupled with the significant quantities of foreign prestige goods at these riverine sites suggest the long-term presence of high-status individuals who may have controlled the flow of riverine trade supporting the coastal port. McKinnon (1993:236), in fact, suggests that iron, salt, and textiles might be added to these archaeologically visible coastal imports. These large inland centers may have been the concentration points for alluvial gold, ivory, rhino horns, resins, honey, birds' nests, and possibly pepper collected by upland groups for export to the coastal populations that may have been directly under Srivijaya hegemony. This archaeological work along the Musi River supports Manguin's (1992) assessment that the Srivijaya trade port is indeed near Palembang and that more systematic excavations will eventually reveal more about how this "primate" center functioned, particularly if those archaeological investigations focus on spatial patterns of artifacts rather than emphasizing monumental works. What is still missing from the Musi River survey, however, is any systematic consideration of the settlement system outside of centers containing elite monuments and status goods.

Similarly, Jane Allen (1991) has compiled archaeological data from the hinterlands of the seventeenth- to eighteenth-century Kedah maritime trading polity of the western coast of the Malay Peninsula. Her regionally focused work has demonstrated the presence of numerous large riverbank interior centers that probably functioned as intermediaries in the Kedah-centered regional trade, as evidenced in concentrations of Kedah-derived ceramics and Indian-style ritual structures. Historic sources suggest that leaders at these upriver centers were allied to the rulers at the polity center through the flow of prestige goods and that sometimes actual elite kinsmen of the ruler were sent to the hinterland as trade and tribute administrators (Hall 1985:92). These upriver secondary centers, particularly those inhabited by second-tier chiefs and located near the polity center, were significantly larger than the typical interior village and were often fortified for protection (although still considerably dwarfed by the primate coastal port) (Gullick 1988[1958]:28).

In addition, the presence of second-tier chiefs or local leaders whose close ties to the coastal rulers are cemented through the presentation of prestige goods (frequently of foreign derivation) would be manifested in similar status and wealth differences in the polity center, but on a smaller scale—that is, spatially discrete commoner and elite occupation areas, with trade wealth concentrated in the households of the latter. Unfortunately, extensive excavations have not been carried out at any of these riverbank trade centers, and these assumptions about site patterns and inferred functions have yet to be tested. However, through careful geological reconstruction of the Merbok and Muda rivers, Allen (1991) was able to demonstrate that the economic significance of various upriver settlements shifted according to rapidly changing alluvial configurations, i.e., inland centers that were well situated for efficiency of transport at one point in time were displaced when river shifts reduced their advantageous position as trade bulking centers. Again, poorly developed methodologies for locating and collecting the multitude of less-visible village sites has precluded the kinds of quantitative studies of site size differentials, rank-size patterns, and factors in population clustering that would provide a wider understanding of population dynamics in the regions surrounding growing port cities.

The Tanjay region of the Philippines is one locale where systematic archaeological survey has produced the detailed regional-scale settlement pattern data necessary to examine factors in the long-term growth of Southeast Asian maritime trading polities, their changing relationships with hinterland communities, the regional-level population dynamics, and the emergence of "primate" centers (Hutterer and Macdonald 1982; Junker 1990, 1994, 1996, 1999). A long-term program of archaeological surface survey in the 315 sq km Tanjay region resulted in mapping more than 500 settlement sites, many dated to the critical mid-first to mid-second millennium period of complex society development. Excavations were carried out not only at the coastal polity center of Tanjay (discussed above) but also at upriver secondary centers and at smaller lowland and upland villages that presumably provisioned the burgeoning population at the coastal capital, traded valuable interior export products critical to foreign maritime trade, or both. Prior to the advent of the foreign porcelain trade (the AD 500–1000 Aguilar phase), regional settlement showed a linear rank-size pattern indicative of limited population concentration at the coastal center of Tanjay relative to the hinterland settlements. In contrast, by the height of foreign trade in the fifteenth to sixteenth century (the AD 1400–1600 Osmena phase), the settlement system was extremely "primate" in form, with Tanjay expanding to a "hyper-large" maritime trade-focused center.

The regional settlement data from the Tanjay region support the suggestion of historians that the process of urbanization in island Southeast Asia and its relatively late occurrence are in some way tied to the expanding importance of maritime trade in the political economies of historic period polities such as Tanjay. At Tanjay, the rapid concentration of population at the coastal center by around AD 1400 is associated with massively increased volumes of Chinese, Annamese, and Siamese porcelain, bronze goods, exotic beads, and other foreign prestige goods in elite households and burials (Junker 1999). These foreign trade goods, simultaneously symbols of status and forms of political currency, proliferate throughout the region, drawing upland forager-traders and swidden farmers into the orbit of expanding riverbank trade centers and the coastal capital through the lure of exotic wealth (Junker 1994). Spatial analysis of sites in the region shows that settlement becomes more clustered around trade centers in the fifteenth to sixteenth century, as upland populations that collect forest products for foreign trade either seasonally or permanently migrate to trade centers (Junker 2002). At the height of foreign trade in the fifteenth to sixteenth century, interior products flow in greater volume to the coast (for example, botanical evidence reveals an influx of medicinal plants), and coastal populations increase production of manufactured goods such as iron weapons as trade exports. The expanding coastal port may also have served as an increasing ceremonial or ideological magnet for outlying populations connected through alliance and trade, shown empirically in more archaeological evidence for widespread ritual feasting at Tanjay in this period (Junker 2001).

Conclusion

The work of historians has revealed an interesting demographic paradox in the kingdoms and chiefdoms that dotted the coasts and river valleys of island Southeast Asia between the mid-first millennium AD and European contact: although overall population densities were generally low throughout the region in comparison to societies throughout the world of similar sociopolitical complexity, the degree of urbanization was surprisingly high, with 20 percent or more of the population inhabiting some large coastal cities in some states such as Melaka, Brunei, and Maluku. Research by historians and demographers has not satisfactorily answered the question of why population densities in general were so low in Southeast Asia, and particularly in island Southeast Asia, at the time of European contact. Reasoned argument, but with little concrete empirical data, has centered on the fertility-suppressing effects of indigenous communicable diseases such as malaria, the high agricultural workload of mothers in rice farming, cultural practices such as extended breast-feeding and abortion, and the high incidence of warfare in a complex political landscape. A significant problem in evaluating the population estimates and the various explanations for their low numbers is that the precolonial population data on which we rely is derived solely from sixteenth- and seventeenth-century European accounts and thus provides little insight into long-term population dynamics in the region. Investigations by archaeologists on complex society development in other parts of the world, such as the work presented in other chapters in this volume, illustrate what can be done to understand the long-term population dynamics of early states with systematically collected archaeological evidence. In island Southeast Asia, there have been no extensive excavations carried out at any historically known precolonial political center, and systematic regional settlement studies in areas of complex society development are almost nonexistent, making it difficult to evaluate any historically derived contact-period population estimates or to reconstruct long-term demographic trends.

We do know from historical accounts that shortages of labor relative to land are linked with contact-period political systems in which a ruler's power base was defined in terms of personal alliance networks rather than fixed geographic territories. These alliance networks were maintained through the charismatic attraction of individuals, through theatrical ceremonialism at the polity center, and through the strategic disbursement of portable wealth to cronies and clients as part of competitive feasting events, bride wealth exchanges, royal investiture, and other institutionalized forms of exchange. This wealth, which was the material glue of political formations in Southeast Asian complex societies in the historic period, was largely derived from foreign maritime luxury good trade. Here archaeological evidence is more compelling than for demographic issues, because archaeologists working in eastern Sumatra in areas associated with the Srivijaya kingdom and in the Philippines in areas associated with prehispanic chiefdoms such as Tanjay have documented extensive regional networks of foreign prestige goods exchange by the mid-first to early second millennia AD. If this heavy reliance on foreign prestige goods exchange and alliance-oriented forms of political economy are connected to labor limitations and low population levels, as they appear to be in historically well-known Southeast Asian kingdoms, then "low-density" complex societies may have been a long-term pattern in island Southeast Asia.

Methodological problems similar to those limiting our basic demographic inferences also plague our archaeological understanding of processes of urbanization in precolonial island Southeast Asia. Thus far, historians, particularly Anthony Reid, have been the main contributors to the discussion of why there is such a high degree of urbanism in this generally "underpopulated" region at the time of European contact. A number of ecological, geographic, and cultural factors are cited by historians as significant in the tendency for island Southeast Asian populations to concentrate into "primate centers" controlling dendritically organized hinterlands. These include the following: the fragmented geography of the Southeast Asian island world and the funneling effects of river-dominated landscapes; the efficiencies of maritime and river-based transport of staples to growing cities (vs. land-based transport); the tremendous surplus-producing potential of wet-rice; the overwhelming economic emphasis on maritime trade and its concentrating effects on various population segments engaged in commerce; the alliance-focused political relations that attracted lower-tiered elites to share the trade wealth of the capital while not tethering them to dispersed lands; the adoption of religions that associated kingship with centralized "sacred landscapes"; and the widespread practice of organized slave raiding that redistributed workers from rural hinterlands to growing urban centers.

Although historical analysis tells us a great deal about the end result of urbanization in such cities as Srivijaya, Mataram, Melaka, and Jolo and allows historians to make some inferences about possible causes for the growth of cities, we are presently lacking the archaeological data necessary to look at urbanization as a long-term process. We simply do not know very much about when and how rapidly urbanization occurred in various parts of Southeast Asia or about the connection between the emergence of cities and such factors as foreign maritime trade and the adoption of state religions associated with urbanism in western Asia, south Asia, and east Asia (e.g., Buddhism, Hinduism, and Islam). The very limited archaeological examples of regional settlement studies presented in this chapter suggest that, despite problems of poor preservation, lack of visible architectural remains, and difficult field conditions, archaeologists can make some headway in addressing these problems of complex society development. However, the discussion of the material evidence also underscores the pressing need for more regionally focused programs of archaeological investigation in Southeast Asia if we are to go beyond these vague generalities to more theoretically sophisticated modeling of population dynamics, complex society development, and processes of urbanization in Southeast Asia.

Urban Centers of the New World

12

Identifying Tiwanaku Urban Populations

Style, Identity, and Ceremony in Andean Cities

John Wayne Janusek and Deborah E. Blom

By their very nature, cities incorporate diversity. The emergence of pristine cities in any region transformed the character of human relations and manners of social organization in local societies. V. Gordon Childe (1936, 1950) considered the rise of cities an "urban revolution," a dramatic milestone on the road of cultural evolution that marked the emergence of civilization. Drawing on a conceptual arsenal steeped in nineteenth-century evolutionism, he argued that city life, the cornerstone of civilization, freed some people from mundane subsistence activities and fostered the rise of social diversity. In speaking of diversity, though, Childe had two specific forms in mind: difference in role, including specialized occupations, and difference in access to surplus resources, or social stratification. Other forms of social difference were not just insignificant but detrimental to the emergence of civilization, because in ancient cities, according to Childe (1950:16), there was "no room for skeptics and sectaries."

This idea of urbanism has a long history in social thought and was shaped by such influential sociologists as Emile Durkheim (1933[1893]) and Max Weber (1958). More important, it remains popular among archaeologists. All told, archaeology has not embraced a coherent concept of the preindustrial city that challenges Childe's vision. Central to his concept is an exaggerated focus on a city's integrative mechanisms and on the subversion of kin, clan, and other intimate identities, what Weber (1958:104-105) considered quaint "totemic" ties to new and increasingly important urban institutions. Urban institutions were fundamentally impersonal, political, and territorial. They arose sui generis as a thorough realignment of nonrational kin ties to more distant relations of inequality and "organic solidarity" (Durkheim 1933 {1893]). If "sectarian" or "totemic" ties remain—such as kinship, lineage, or ethnicity—they are primitive and potentially destructive survivals.

We examine conjoined evidence that encourages a reconsideration of such conventional ideas on the basis of recent research from Tiwanaku, a prehispanic state centered in the high south-central Andes (Figure 12-1). To address these issues we respond to the more pointed question of why highland Andean cities were relatively small. Two archaeologists, both of whose research focuses on Tiwanaku and the Lake Titicaca basin, propose intriguing answers. Kolata (1993:174) proposes that the considerable power and influence of ruling lineages placed structural limitations on the size of Andean cities such as Tiwanaku, which were dominated by a "singularity of purpose and higher degree of social control" than cities forged out of "riotous" market principles. Andean cities essentially were extended elite households, and residence was by right, fundamentally determined by one's relationship or role in elite lineages.

Stanish (1998), on the other hand, suggests that more than elite power and ideology, it was the nature of the Andean political economy that determined the size of Andean cities such as Tiwanaku. For him, cities are grounded primarily in economic rather than political or ideological principles, and in the highland Andes, the virtual absence of central markets (Earle 1985; Murra 1972, 1980[1956]) encouraged an alternative urban revolution. Stanish argues that such cities were small because most economic interaction was intimate rather than impersonal and centered on reciprocity and redistribution rather than laissez-faire market principles.

We offer evidence that expands the ideas proposed by Kolata and Stanish. As fundamental as ruling control or economic principles in shaping the Tiwanaku urban order, we suggest, was a particular social matrix that crystallized out of people's flexible and dynamic sense of community. This matrix, manifested as much in prominent elements of Tiwanaku state culture and ideology as in the daily practices of its urban residential groups, was critical in shaping the size and character of Andean cities such as Tiwanaku. In fact, we believe it shaped Tiwanaku ruling practices and economic relations. To develop this hypothesis, we recruit the combined results of our respective research in archaeology and bioanthropology in the Tiwanaku heartland, while drawing loosely on ethnohistorical analogy in the south-central Andes. Approaching Tiwanaku cities through the social matrix that defined boundaries and identities among their constituent populations, we find that they were "incomplete" communities tied inextricably to their surrounding hinterlands, regional centers, and far-off groups and polities. An important conclusion is that Tiwanaku cities, in particular Tiwanaku itself, were magnet centers of feasting and ceremony that anchored the coherence of far-reaching regional identities and, not least, the overarching political community of "the state." We believe the implications of our conjoined research go well beyond Tiwanaku and the Andes, for local social relations and institutions grounded in kin-based, sectarian, or totemistic ties, we argue, often were the very matrix out of which past cities and states were forged and developed.

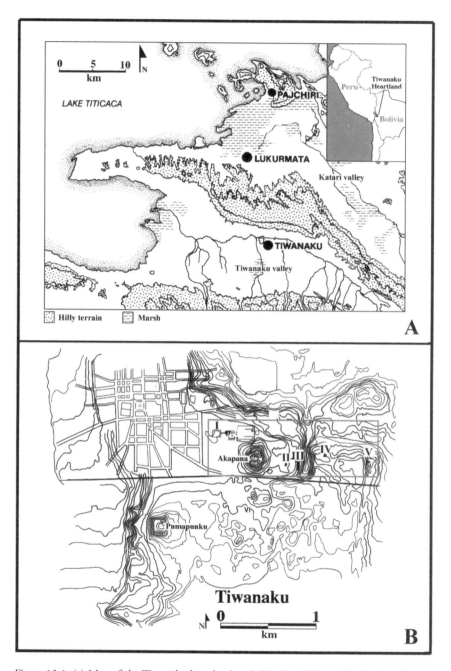

Figure 12-1. (a) Map of the Tiwanaku heartland, and (b) plan of Tiwanaku showing the relative location of some excavated residential areas: Putuni (I), Akapana East 1M (II), Akapana East 1 (III), Akapana East 2 (IV), Ch'iji Jawira (V), and Mollo Kontu (VI).

Social Identity and Urbanism in the Southern Andes

Archaeologists have begun to critique the strict correlation of city life and increasing differentiation in hierarchy and role. For example, a number of archaeologists are exploring the concept of heterarchy (Brumfiel 1994b; Crumley 1987b, 1995b; King and Potter 1994), a simple but effective idea that has encouraged a shift in focus toward elements of social organization that are neither necessarily ranked nor wholly integrative. Ongoing ethnohistorical and archaeological research in the Andes is establishing the foundation for an understanding of complexity as shifting relations of hierarchy and heterarchy rather than simply alternating periods of greater and lesser integration. Furthermore, it acknowledges that Andean communities were shifting, nested, or overlapping domains of identity more than they were static groups divided by rigid boundaries.

The flexible concept of *ayllu* is critical to understanding complexity and urbanism in the south-central Andes (e.g., Abercrombie 1986:24–101; Izko 1992:75–80; Martinez 1989; Platt 1982:50, 1987; Rasnake 1988:49–64; Rivera Cusicanqui 1992:102–122). *Ayllu* was in many instances a fundamental principle of social order, a general term for "community" that in its most specific sense referred to an intimate group of kin, what Abercrombie (1986:119) terms a "circulating *connubium*" of vital essences among people sharing corporate interests, resources, common ancestors, representative sacred places, and a common identity. Simultaneously, though, it was a slippery term that could refer to multiple nested or overlapping identities (Izko 1992:75–80; Platt 1987; Saignes 1985). For any individual, the meaning of the term could shift with context, day to day or region to region (Abercrombie 1986:74; Saignes 1985). In one instance it could designate what we term micro-*ayllus*, kin groups that acted as corporate groups, and in another it could refer to more-encompassing macro-*ayllus*, which, like modern ethnic groups, cohered largely during external conflicts and major community festivals and rituals (Abercrombie 1986; Izko 1992).

Ayllu even referred to an inclusive polity or hierarchy of encompassment that incorporated diverse communities dispersed over vast landscapes. At this level, unequal relations among *ayllus* were often described as intimate relations within the family, with political leaders as metaphorical "elder-brothers" or "fathers" (Abercrombie 1986:86; Platt 1987). For example, the Macha polity (or macro-*ayllu*) was divided into a "father" (upper) and a "mother" (lower) moiety or major *ayllu*, each of which comprised five minor or "child" *ayllus* and numerous micro or "baby" *ayllu* (Platt 1987:69–75). Parallel relations of family and generation characterized relations among the sacred places associated with such nested groups so that visually imposing *achachilas*, or snow-capped mountain peaks, embodied the most ancient ancestors of the entire polity. From one perspective, then, *ayllu* invoked an intricate and malleable sense of place, community, and identity for any individual. From another, *ayllu* defined complex relations in a hierarchical sociopolitical landscape, bestowing on them intimate or "totemistic" family terms. *Ayllu* provided social and personal coherence for constituent groups and individuals, but it also was the foundation for a hegemonic political ideology.

Corresponding to the social order was a dynamic form of urbanism in which salient social groups transcended urban-rural divisions. Major towns, known as *markas,* were, and to a great extent remain, important centers of political unity for an *ayllu* at any scale (Abercrombie 1986:94–95; Albó 1972; Choque Canqui 1993; Vellard 1963:127–148), anchoring inclusive identities in public rituals of social and ceremonial convergence. Each town maintained a relatively small permanent population, surrounded by smaller dispersed villages and hamlets where most members of constituent micro-*ayllus* maintained their permanent residences. Nevertheless, each micro-*ayllu* also maintained residences in the central town, the central symbol of the larger macro-*ayllu* community, in which houses pertaining to specific groups or hamlets tended to cluster as contiguous compounds or barrios. These temporary residences were filled during important ceremonies, especially large calendrical feasts when members of all micro-*ayllus* came to town in celebration. Surrounding the *marka* of Tiahuanaco today, for instance, are several outlying communities, most of which carry the same *ayllu* names that they maintained in the sixteenth century (Choque Canqui 1993:22). Tiwanaku's permanent population, which is relatively small (<500), literally explodes during important calendrical ceremonies. During these times the plaza, streets, and residential compounds are jammed with people from outlying communities, and everyday life is abandoned to music, feasting, dancing, and drinking.

In the past, such centers served as nodes of sociopolitical power, and periodic public rituals affirmed political unity and hierarchical social relations. Were Tiwanaku cities and towns also centers of feasting and social convergence? Did they also provide social coherence for the overarching hegemonic order and incorporated regional identities?

Ethnohistorical research in the southern Andes is helpful for interpreting Tiwanaku archaeology and bioarchaeology in two ways. First, Tiwanaku disappeared less than 400 years before European contact (ca. AD 1150), or some twelve to sixteen generations, making it likely that some documented principles of social order and urbanism may have originated much earlier, perhaps during phases of Tiwanaku hegemony (see Albarracín-Jordán 1992, 1996). Second, heterarchy and group identity, just like hierarchy and role, often leave visible if subtle traces in the ground and on human remains. Later in the southern Andes, an *ayllu* at any level established its identity through distinct styles of language, woven clothing, serving vessels, and burial patterns, as well as decorating and modifying the human body (Abercrombie 1986; Blom 1999; Cereceda et al. 1993; Gisbert et al. 1987; Hoshower et al. 1995). Style, as much a guide for action (Hodder 1990) as objectified action itself (Dietler and Herbich 1998), characterized things and actions on public display and in everyday domestic life. Nevertheless, highly visible expressions on clothing, the body, or feasting vessels were primary vehicles for establishing, negotiating, and reshaping identity in a dynamic and potentially volatile sociopolitical environment (Hebdige 1979; Hodder 1982; Pollock 1983: 364; M. E. Smith 1987; Wiessner 1983, 1990).

We examined serving-ceremonial vessels (Janusek 2002, 2003) and the human body (Blom 1999, 2005) as potentially significant vehicles of style in the Tiwanaku polity. As in other regions (DeBoer 1990; M. E. Smith 1987), vessels on display in the southern Andes were employed to consume food and fermented beer (of corn, *kusa,* or quinoa, *ch'ua*) in everyday life and in lively rituals of consumption. Ceramic vessels in recent Andean society have not been rigorously studied, but their role in Inca feasting is confirmed (Morris 1982; Morris and Thompson 1985). We argue that serving vessels played an important role in Tiwanaku urban life. As valued crafted goods, serving vessels embodied ideals and symbols that much of the time may have remained subliminal and unnoticed. Social gatherings "turned on" the communicative element of style. Certain elements were acknowledged while others remained unnoticed, and designs beautiful to some may have been considered distasteful to others. Taste was the domain of specific groups and individuals who participated in collective social festivities but also maintained unique identities and values.

Cranial modification was another significant vehicle for style in the Andes (Blom 1999, 2005; Cook 1997; Hoshower et al. 1995; Lozada 1998). Specific head shapes were created through any of a number of techniques—boards, straps, and pads—and head shape in many cases expressed group identity. In the Colca valley west of Lake Titicaca, for example, two macro-*ayllus* coexisted, Collaguas and Cabanas, each an ethnic group and polity comprised of smaller *ayllus* (Cook 1997). Members of each differentiated themselves from others in language, clothing, and head shape. The Collaguas shaped the heads of their children to emulate their principal sacred place or *huaca,* a nearby cone-shaped volcano. The resulting "tapered" head shape, produced by wearing tight woven bands, differed from that of the nearby Cabanas, who "flattened" their heads to emulate their own principal *huaca,* a nearby mountain that was low and wide. The Collaguas considered Cabanas heads ugly and disproportionate (Ulloa Mogollón 1965:40, in Cook 1997: 388). Cranial modification served to mark inclusive social identities, and its practical motivations were aesthetic and religious.

Bernabe Cobo (1956[1653]:Book 14, Chapter 6; also Blom 1999; Cook 1997:388) noted that the Aymara of the western Titicaca basin also practiced cranial modification and that like the Collaguas, with whom they maintained relations, they made their heads "long and pointed" to fit their pointed woolen hats (*chucos*). However, in an Aymara dictionary compiled in the basin in 1612, Bertonio (1984[1612]) included terms and phrases referring to three different head shapes, each produced via a different technique. A number of terms refer to tapered or conical heads (*cabeza ahusada*), but there are a few that refer to round heads (*cabeza redonda*) and flattened heads (*cabeza aplastada*). Apparently, tapered was the most common head shape in the western basin, where Bertonio resided. Both Cobo and Bertonio indicate that groups shaped their heads to fit their distinctive hats and to promote good health. Thus, cranial modification marked identity as both a final form and a technical process, and its motivation included health in addition to beauty and spirituality.

Serving vessels and head shape both served in part to embody style and mark social identity, but there is a fundamental difference between these media. Serving vessels offer "clues" to past social affiliations and identity. Serving vessels, like most material goods, are acquired, exchanged, and given away, so assemblages may change dramatically during an individual's lifetime or throughout the history of a social group. Thus, the relation between vessel style and social identity is complex, usually indirect, and always in flux. In contrast, head shape "cues" a person's identity (Blom 1999). It is imposed in early childhood (>5 years) and cannot be changed throughout the course of life. Whether or not a person changed one's social identity later in life, including one's china, clothing, dialect, or place of residence, the individual could not change the shape of the head. Cranial modification was permanent, an objective and inflexible mark of original social identity. By considering both permanent and impermanent aspects of identity, its clues and its cues, we can develop a powerful approach to social diversity in ancient cities such as Tiwanaku.

Populations in Tiwanaku and Its Heartland

Tiwanaku, located in the southern Lake Titicaca basin of South America, remained one of the most influential centers in the south-central Andes for some 650 years, throughout the Tiwanaku IV (AD 500–800) and V (AD 800–1150) phases of state hegemony. Located approximately 15 km in from the lakeshore, the site covers some 6 sq km in the Tiwanaku valley (Figure 12-1). Thirteen kilometers to the north, in the adjacent Katari Valley, was the lakeside settlement of Lukurmata. During the Late Formative period (100 BC–AD 500), Tiwanaku and Lukurmata emerged as major independent settlements at the head of interacting and loosely coalescing multicommunity polities (Janusek 2004). Toward the end of this period, in the face of shifting regional political, economic, and ritual conditions (Bandy 2002; Janusek 2004; Stanish 2003), Tiwanaku surfaced from this regional network of fluid, small-scale polities as the primary demographic, cultural, and political center in the Lake Titicaca basin. By AD 500, Lukurmata was incorporated into the expanding polity (Bermann 1994), and by AD 800, the end of the Tiwanaku IV phase, Lukurmata was an urban center of 1.2 sq km, surrounded by a cluster of settlements that together formed a metropolitan community of nearly 2 sq km (Janusek and Kolata 2003; Stanish 1989).

In the 1960s, archaeologists first began to consider the possibility that Tiwanaku

was an urban center (e.g., Rowe 1963:15) and on the basis of preliminary findings attempted to estimate its size and population. On the basis of a very brief
reconnaissance in 1966, Parsons (1968) estimated that the site covered 2.4 sq km
and housed a population of 5,200 to 10,500, possibly reaching a maximum of
20,000. Parsons arrived at this estimate by drawing on demographic profiles in
the central Basin of Mexico, which hypothesized population sizes on the basis of
surface scatter densities (Parsons 1968:245; Sanders et al. 1979). Tiwanaku would
represent a "high-density" settlement, with a population of 2,500–5,000 and possibly up to 10,000–12,000 people per sq km. Ponce Sanginés (1981) later revised
Tiwanaku's extent to 4.2 sq km. To estimate population, Ponce Sanginés multiplied this size by the same Mesoamerican data and came up with a range of 9,750
to 46,800 people (Ponce Sanginés 1981:62). On the basis of excavations in several residential areas of the site (Janusek 2003; Kolata 2003), we suggest adopting
the lower ranges of the Mesoamerican profiles and consider the fact that significant proportions of the site consisted of nonresidential places and activities. Sub-
tracting an estimated 45 percent of the site as either nonresidential or unoccupied
at any given time (including an estimated 25 percent of the site dedicated to
nonresidential constructions such as temples, cemeteries, middens, and water-
filled basins, or *qochas,* and another 20 percent of residential occupations unoccupied at any time), Tiwanaku, at 6 sq km during its peak extent from AD 700–
1000, could have housed an average population of approximately 10,000–20,000
people. As discussed below, we believe, nevertheless, that its population was cyclically in flux.

In AD 500 Tiwanaku emerged as the primary center at the head of dense
hierarchical networks of settlement stretching over a vast hinterland (Figure 12-2).
Unlike some pristine central cities such as Teotihuacan in Mexico's central basin
(Cowgill 1997; Sanders et al. 1979), Tiwanaku's emergence did not result in a
demographic implosion, but rather corresponded with a population surge in the
nearby hinterlands. The focus of the hinterland was a three-valley region consisting
of drainage basins for the Desaguadero, Tiwanaku, and Katari rivers. Tiwanaku-
period settlement in the Desaguadero region is currently under investigation
(Janusek et al. 2003), but the Tiwanaku and Katari valleys have been the subject
of much intensive regional research (Albarracín-Jordán 1996; Albarracín-Jordán
and Mathews 1990; Graffam 1992; Janusek and Kolata 2003; Kolata 1986, 1991;
Mathews 1992; Seddon 1994).

Survey in the Middle and Lower Tiwanaku valley revealed 100 sites dating to
the early (Tiwanaku IV) phase of the Tiwanaku period, a dramatic increase over
the Late Formative, which is represented by a maximum of nine sites (Albarracín-
Jordán and Mathews 1990:82; McAndrews et al. 1997:73). Settlement was fairly
well distributed across valley microzones and included 51 percent of sites on the
open pampa and 42 percent on the lower piedmont hill slopes. All sites but Tiwanaku were relatively small (<10 ha), most likely because Tiwanaku had come

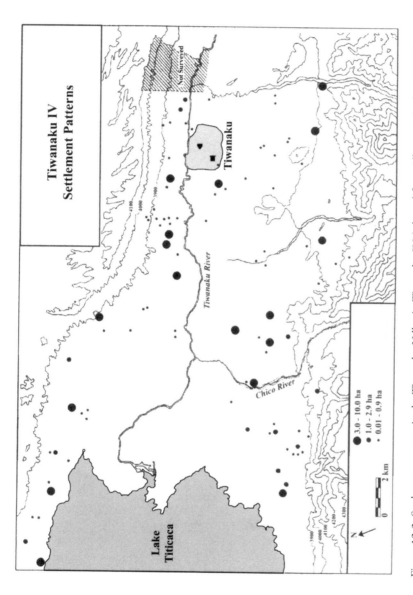

Figure 12-2. Settlement patterns in the Tiwanaku Valley in Tiwanaku IV (adapted from Albarracín-Jordán 2003:Figure 4.15).

to fill the roles of both primary local center and regional state center. Valley sites formed three tiers, including small towns (3–10 ha), villages (1–2.9 ha), and a range of smaller hamlets (0.01–0.9 ha) (Albarracín-Jordán 2003). The settlement distribution is collectively primo-convex and clearly hierarchical, but outside of Tiwanaku, settlement distribution presents striking rank-size complexity, tending to form local clusters centered on small towns. On the basis of these patterns, Albarracín-Jordán (1992) and others (McAndrews et al. 1997) argue that the Tiwanaku valley encompassed several semiautonomous communities, consisting of significant heterarchy in an overarching hierarchical system.

Survey in the southern Katari valley revealed 48 sites dating to the Tiwanaku period (Janusek and Kolata 2003). Unlike settlement in the Tiwanaku valley, settlement here favored the piedmont hill slopes at a decisive 96 percent of total occupation. The reasons were both environmental and cultural, for the Katari valley included a low and marshy floodplain known as the Koani Pampa, much of which (ca. 65 percent) was converted into extensive systems for raised field production in the Tiwanaku period (Kolata 1986, 1991; Seddon 1994). Lukurmata was a primary regional center that, if we again adopt the lower of the population estimates presented above, probably housed 2,500–5,000 people at its peak. Outside of Lukurmata, sites formed a graded hierarchy of towns (>10 ha), small towns and villages (3–10 ha), and hamlets (<3 ha). Settlement hugged the lower piedmont that bordered the productive floodplain and so displayed little overt clustering. Nevertheless, the largest sites incorporated monumental platforms and one or more causeways leading out into the Koani Pampa. In other words, the Katari valley housed a settlement network in which economic, ritual, and political power was distributed throughout the region and across distinct scales of settlement.

Because far fewer excavations have been conducted in rural settlements than in urban areas, estimating population for the hinterlands is somewhat trickier. If Mesoamerican rural demographic profiles hold for the Andes, then nonurban settlement may correspond with central Mexico's "low-density" settlement type (1,000–2,500 per sq km). By AD 800, total nonurban settlement in the Lower-Middle Tiwanaku valley (excluding Tiwanaku), and in the southern Katari valley (excluding Lukurmata), reached an estimated 317 ha, on average about 0.75 percent of the entire surveyed landscape. Population may have ranged from 3,000 to 8,000 people, complementing Tiwanaku's 5,000–10,000 and Lukurmata's 2,500–5,000 inhabitants.

Urban and rural domains of Tiwanaku society were inextricably bound together. Corresponding with the rise of urbanism, population density increased across all scales and types of settlement. Furthermore, there is solid evidence in the Tiwanaku and Katari valleys for the existence of semiautonomous sociopolitical communities that managed local productive resources, staged local rituals, and wielded some degree of political authority. Research at Tiwanaku and Lukurmata, described below, confirms that similar patterns characterized the urban centers themselves and suggests that life in nonurban settings was closely linked to social and ceremonial life in the cities.

Diversity and Identity in Tiwanaku Urban Centers

Our research in Tiwanaku and Lukurmata demonstrated that urban society in the Tiwanaku heartland comprised at least two levels of social difference and identity. One level, represented within the urban centers, appears to represent groups similar to later kin-based *ayllus,* and the second, represented between the centers, appears to represent regional macro-*ayllu.* This insight invites a new perspective on the number and character of Tiwanaku urban populations. Excavations in 10 areas of Tiwanaku (Figure 12-1b) revealed Tiwanaku IV–V phase occupations, ranging from ceremonial areas (e.g., Akapana, Putuni courtyard) to craft production barrios (e.g., Ch'iji Jawira), and eight of these revealed primary or secondary evidence of residential occupation (all but Mollo Kontu North and Akapana). Excavations in six major areas of Lukurmata revealed Tiwanaku IV–V phase occupations, and four of these included residential occupations.

Human remains recovered from residential, ceremonial, and cemetery contexts at both sites formed the basis for Blom's bioanthropological analysis. Blom (1999, 2005) analyzed 95 individuals from Tiwanaku, 78 from Lukurmata, and another 48 individuals from smaller sites in the Tiwanaku and Katari valleys.

Within each urban center, residential areas consisted of spatially bounded compounds and barrios (Janusek 2002, 2003). On the ground, each compound consisted of a large perimeter wall enclosing one or more domestic structures and various activity areas, as exemplified in the Akapana East 1M sector of Tiwanaku (see Janusek 2002, 2003). Such compound or barrio units, it appears, incorporated several minimal households, a fundamental activity unit represented by a dwelling and its associated ancillary structures, activity areas, and middens. Compounds differed greatly in size, spatial organization, and activities, suggesting that the nature of resident social groups varied accordingly.

In each center, walled compounds and barrios represented the most salient unit of social differentiation. Some compound groups in Tiwanaku and Lukurmata engaged in specialized craft production (Janusek 1999). Residents of Ch'iji Jawira produced certain types of vessels throughout the IV–V phases, including large storage vessels (65 percent of vessels) and serving *tazons* (bowls) (12.5 percent of vessels) (Rivera Casanovas 1994, 2003). Excavations here suggest that vessels were fired in open enclosures and small pit kilns (Franke 1991; Rivera Casanovas 1994), and they consistently revealed implements and by-products of manufacture, such as wasters and slumped vessels, that were rare or absent elsewhere. In Lukurmata, one small neighborhood at the south edge of the center, Misiton 1, produced llama bone panpipes during the Tiwanaku IV–Early V phases (Janusek

1999). Excavations revealed sections of two compounds with dwellings, open patios, long buildings, and middens that contained clusters of bone flutes, tools for making them (e.g., polishers, knives, and cutting surfaces), and production by-products (e.g., severed ends of long bones). At both sites craft production was a part of residential life, and it was the domain of compounds and barrios rather than entire urban settlements.

Mortuary ritual was an important element of life for residential compound groups. In Tiwanaku, humans were interred under a patio in Akapana East 2, in outdoor areas in Ch'iji Jawira, and in nearby mortuary clusters in both the Putuni area and Akapana East 1 (Couture and Sampeck 2003; Janusek 2003; Rivera Casanovas 1994). The presence of human burials inside of residential compounds indicates that mortuary ritual was not entirely relegated to discrete cemeteries. In Tiwanaku, at least, mortuary ritual was closely linked to domestic life, and it appears to have varied among residential groups. In the Putuni area alone, for example, some burial chambers contained scores of broken, elaborate ceremonial bowls termed *escudillas*. The desire to inter certain individuals near living spaces shared by intimate kindred emphasizes the importance of residential ancestor cults, perhaps similar to mortuary rituals documented at the time of European contact (Cobo 1956[1653]:73, 163–165; Rowe 1946:286, 298; Zuidema 1977/ 1978). In Akapana East 2, a stone marker had been set into the patio above a cyst burial containing three individuals. It appears that household or compound members apparently periodically remembered, made offerings to, and celebrated deceased relatives at auspicious times, reaffirming in ritually charged contexts local group coherence and identity.

The groups who practiced specialized activities and shared local mortuary rituals also used distinct artifact assemblages, most visibly serving wares (Janusek 2002, 2003). Within any compound, serving assemblages maintained surprising spatial and even historical continuity, whereas between them, assemblages varied significantly. For example, in Akapana East 1M, which revealed 12 superimposed occupations spanning the Tiwanaku IV phase, serving vessels adhered relatively strictly to Tiwanaku canons of form and iconography. Unlike other residential compounds, such as Akapana East 2, the inhabitants apparently used only vessels with stylistic affinity to orthodox Tiwanaku style. Most drinking chalices (*keros*) and bowls (*tazons*) displayed red, orange, or black slip, whereas iconography included a limited range of geometric, anthropomorphic, and mythical zoomorphic motifs. Assemblages included significant proportions of elaborate *escudillas* and consistent quantities of *sahumadors,* which were most likely used as lamps and ritual incense burners, respectively.

Serving assemblages were significantly distinct in other areas of Tiwanaku, including Putuni and Akapana East 2, but assemblages in Ch'iji Jawira, the ceramic production barrio at the east edge of Tiwanaku, were most unique (Alconini 1995; Janusek 1999; Rivera Casanovas 1994). Red slip here, the hallmark of

Tiwanaku style, was present on only 20–25 percent of serving wares. *Escudillas* were rare, and *sahumadors* were all but absent. On the other hand, llama motifs, rare in Akapana East and other areas, were common on *tazons* and on ceremonial vessels in local offerings. Also frequently represented were vessels associated with eastern Andean valleys, especially vessels representing the Tiwanaku "derived" style (ca. 20 percent of serving wares). Although their place of manufacture remains unclear, they were associated with the Cochabamba region some 200 km southeast of Tiwanaku (Bennett 1936:402; Ponce Sanginés 1981; Rydén 1957). The unusually high percentages of nonlocal serving wares suggest affiliations with one or more of these regions. It is possible, though speculative, that the inhabitants settled in Tiwanaku as an urban colony, a distinct ethnic barrio analogous to the Oaxaca or Merchants' barrios in Teotihuacan, central Mexico (Paddock 1983; Rattray 1987).

Other patterns of style differentiated Tiwanaku and Lukurmata as entire urban communities and local regional centers. Stylistic variation at this level involved both clues and cues, as represented, respectively, in serving wares and cranial forms. As in Tiwanaku, serving assemblages in Lukurmata varied significantly from one residential sector to the next (Janusek 1999:123, Figure 6), but all assemblages included a unique range of elaborate serving wares that were extremely rare in Tiwanaku. In most cases, these wares presented subtle twists on Tiwanaku style. They included modeled feline *incensarios* (incense burners), common in Lukurmata burials and offerings (Bermann 1994; Janusek and Earnest 1990), and they included tan wares, serving wares (typically *keros, tazons,* and *escudillas*) that instead of red or orange displayed a highly polished, unique beige paste. These vessels, like local red wares, usually displayed delicate volute motifs. The beige paste was unique to Lukurmata and other Katari valley sites, indicating that the region was served by local ceramic workshops and that style characterized the production process as much as the ceramic vessels themselves. The entire range of Lukurmata-style vessels consisted of varying proportions of assemblages in any area, ranging from 18 percent to 80 percent in excavated residential occupations (Janusek 1999). Their consistent presence indicates that Lukurmata maintained some community identity within the scope of Tiwanaku hegemony. The presence of Lukurmata-style vessels at nearby towns and villages indicates that this identity was to some extent regional in scope (Janusek and Kolata 2003).

Patterns of cranial modification apparently cued identity alongside serving and ceremonial vessels used in feasts and social gatherings (Blom 1999, 2005). Of all modified skulls from burials in Lukurmata and other Katari sites, more than two-thirds (70 percent) presented an annular form with an elongated cranial vault, achieved by tying turbanlike bands around the head (Figure 12-3).

This form of modification undoubtedly represents the "tapered" type documented in the Early Colonial period. Two other head shapes were present in smaller proportions, a flattened fronto-occipital form (6 percent), achieved by

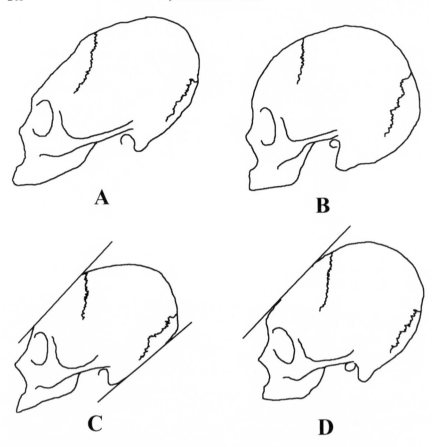

Figure 12-3. Types of cranial modification represented at Tiwanaku sites (adapted from Blom et al. 1998). Represented are (A) annular modification; (B) a normal skull; and two forms of fronto-occipital modification, (C) "flat"; and (D) "rounded."

tying a contraption of boards or stiff pads to the front and back of a child's head, and a higher proportion of normal or unmodified skulls (24 percent) (Figure 12-3). It is likely that Aymara terms for "flattened" and "round" heads refer to these cranial types. We found no correlation between either head shape and status or head shape and gender.

If the annular or tapered head shape predominated in Lukurmata and the Katari valley, the fronto-occipital or flattened type, very uncommon in Lukurmata, was most common in one far Tiwanaku colony. This style predominated at the regional center of Chen Chen, a large Tiwanaku regional site located in the middle Moquegua valley several days' journey from Tiwanaku (ca. 250 km).

Here, 82 percent of individuals displayed this head shape, and a smaller 18 percent displayed the natural "round" shape, whereas the tapered form so prevalent in Lukurmata was absent. If tapered heads predominated in Lukurmata, then flattened heads claimed Chen Chen, and in both, unmodified heads comprised minority populations.

In Tiwanaku, styles of head shape were more evenly represented. Unmodified "round" heads composed 19 percent of interred individuals, similar to their proportions in both Lukurmata (24 percent) and Chen Chen (18 percent). Flattened types predominated slightly, representing 48 percent of observable skulls, in relation to 31 percent represented by annular or tapered head types. Considering the consistent ethnohistorical observation that head shape corresponded with headwear, we are positive that these head shapes corresponded to different hat styles. Although woven garments quickly deteriorate in the altiplano, woven hats from other regions and from museum collections vary in shape and style. One study of Tiwanaku-style hats displays both woven, long, extended hats, what we argue are the *chucos* for tapered heads, and short, four-corner hats, most likely for flattened heads (Frame 1990). Supporting our correlation of head shape and hat style is that squat, four-cornered hats are common in Moquegua, where the flattened head shape predominated.

Social and Ceremonial Convergence in Tiwanaku

The convergence of diverse social groupings correlates well with growing evidence for massive public rituals and feasts in Tiwanaku. First, Tiwanaku centered around a prestigious and growing monumental core consisting of temples, palaces, and open courtyards and plazas as a major center of elite and ceremonial activity throughout the IV–V phases (Couture and Sampeck 2003; Kolata 1993; Kolata and Ponce Sanginés 1992; Manzanilla 1992). Second, residential areas, and particularly their open courtyards and patios, consistently yielded significant proportions of serving and ceremonial wares (all 19–25 percent), emphasizing the important role of local feasts and ceremonies. Third, Tiwanaku, more than any other excavated site in the region, yielded tremendous quantities of refuse, the product not just of everyday life but also of periodic local and public feasts, tossed into outdoor middens and massive adobe quarry pits.

Significant changes occurred at about AD 800 in two residential compounds near the monumental core, Akapana East 1 and 1M (Janusek 2003). One was converted into a massive compound (Akapana East 1) with a specialized kitchen structure, apparently a place to prepare food and drink for large-scale feasts that took place in a nearby open courtyard. This and another nearby compound, Akapana East 1M, incorporated small buildings with ephemeral floors, possibly indicating that they were inhabited only for the periodic special feasting occasions.

The transformations in Akapana East suggest that Tiwanaku, like a massive magnet settlement or *marka* in more recent Andean landscapes discussed above, was in part a center of ceremony and convergence, a role that increased through time.

Discussion: Unifying Diversity

Urban centers of the Tiwanaku core incorporated substantial diversity, and the form of urbanism they expressed helps us understand their dynamics and characterize their populations. Excavations at Tiwanaku and Lukurmata revealed two major domains of social differentiation, one within the cities and one between them and their respective regions. Both centers consisted of mutually differentiated compound groups who guarded, proclaimed, and negotiated their identities in serving-vessels assemblages, corporate economic activity, and intimate domestic rituals. Each compound housed a suprahousehold group, the coherence of which appears to have been grounded in an *ideal* of kinship and lineage, as it was in later micro-*ayllus*. Some groups, such as the inhabitants of Ch'iji Jawira, apparently maintained active ties and affiliations with nonlocal regions and polities and may have originally migrated from those regions. Rather than simple population growth and outward expansion, Tiwanaku urbanism involved multidirectional networks of interaction and movement, including movement into and colonization of the primary center itself.

Differentiation also characterized the relation between the two cities as urban communities. Stylistic clues and cues indicate that, at least in the Katari valley, people even in the core valleys maintained distinct regional identities within the broader ambit of Tiwanaku hegemony. Inhabitants of Lukurmata and local Katari settlements continually shaped their children's heads in one predominant way and employed in local feasts and ceremonies a unique range of elaborate vessels. Through both head shape and serving wares they marked their identity and expressed their unique social affiliations and exchange networks within the broader polity. Unlike social differentiation at the compound level, social differentiation among cities and regions did not involve clear corporate economic activity. It was loosely analogous and historically antecedent to the regional and ethnic identities maintained by macro-*ayllus* at the time of Spanish contact.

Among these scaled domains of identity, Tiwanaku was a center of social convergence and, thus, of state power. A ceremonial city in the conventional sense (Smith and Reynolds 1987; Wheatley 1971), Tiwanaku anchored the coherence of the overarching political community, in part through major feasts and rituals. In fact, the role of large-scale feasting apparently increased in Tiwanaku V (AD 800–1150) as the polity expanded and intensified its control in other regions (Goldstein 1989; Janusek 2003; Janusek and Kolata 2003; Seddon 1998). Major ceremonies and calendrical feasts would have been periodic reversals in the course of everyday life, lively times of intense human interaction in goods, news, gossip, politics, and fights. Like contemporary Aymara towns, it appears likely that for weeks at a time, plazas, courtyards, compounds, and feast preparation areas became nodes of bustling activity. People from settlements in the core valleys, and possibly from far-away regions such as Moquegua, would have come to visit, participate, and temporarily reside in the city. In the resulting diversity and festivity, the style inherent in items such as food containers, dormant or passive much of the time, would have been activated. Identification with various groupings, from compound groups to broader regional identities, involved elements of diversity in personal and material style, but the predominance of uniformity, of a clear Tiwanaku style or "state culture," emphasizes the great prestige inherent in identification with the state. As in the recent past, Tiwanaku leaders may have promoted the idea of Tiwanaku as a community or macro-*ayllu,* perhaps even bestowed on it intimate family terms. Fundamentally, though, state power resided in the local acceptance and internalization of state culture and ideology as a prestigious and convincing worldview.

The identities maintained by local populations, and the role of Tiwanaku as a major urban ceremonial center, help us understand the dynamics of Andean cities. As Stanish (1998) argues, Andean urbanism in part reflects Andean political economy. Without major markets, a great deal of human interaction was more intimate, and one potential mechanism of urban interaction and nucleation was all but absent. Economic interaction and exchange undoubtedly occurred in Lukurmata and especially Tiwanaku, but its most intense moments were facilitated by the periodic social and ceremonial events that occurred there. As Kolata (1993) notes, it was also partly the nature of ruling authority, as expressed in Tiwanaku urban order and material culture. We suggest, nevertheless, that it was not so much that leaders restricted settlement in cities but that they emphasized what Blanton and colleagues (1996) term a "corporate strategy" of rule in which direct political authority and control over resources was left in the hands of local groups and settlements. This is evident both in cities, where compound groups directly managed production, and in rural areas, where there is clear evidence for heterarchical settlement organization and the existence of vibrant local communities. Urban and nonurban domains of settlement maintained remarkable equilibrium, highlighting the fundamental point that no domain of power, whether political, economic, or ritual, was completely monopolized by state leaders.

Following these characteristics, Tiwanaku and its regional centers maintained relatively limited spatial extent. In part, this was because various domains of identity remained vibrant in the Tiwanaku core. The coherence of any local group, micro or macro, resided in a given place and sacred landscape, and as long as local identities remained significant, so did the places that gave them meaning. Most people remained in their communities, with their family and friends, fields and crafts, ancestors and sacred places. Tiwanaku remained relatively small in great part because it was not a stable demographic settlement as much as a pulsating center of ceremony and periodic convergence. To be sure, Tiwanaku incorporated substantial permanent populations, but throughout the year its population would have successively risen and fallen like waves, keyed to the course of major ritual events. We can imagine times of the year when Tiwanaku appeared relatively deserted, like more recent Andean *markas,* when perhaps population fell to less than 15 people per hectare, or 9,000 people. During major calendrical feasts or state-sponsored ceremonies, the population would have exploded for days or weeks at a time. We can imagine the population increasing to as much as 50 people per ha or more, or more than 30,000 in total. Tiwanaku was not a community complete in and of itself, but a central place of interaction and state ideology tying together vast networks of diverse groups and polities.

Our conclusions encourage an evaluation of conventional ideas about urbanism (e.g., Jacobs 1969; Sjoberg 1960), and we can isolate two key critiques. First, the traditional concept of the demographically stable preindustrial city, housing a permanent and ever-growing population, may not apply to many Andean cities. Tiwanaku was an urban ceremonial center, and as such it experienced cycles of influx and exodus. Ongoing archaeological and ethnohistorical research suggests that a similar model may apply to other major Andean cities, most notably Pachacamac (Patterson 1991; Rostworowski 1992; Shimada 1991) and perhaps the Inca center of Cuzco. Furthermore, social and ceremonial roles analogous to that of Tiwanaku may have been played by centers in other world regions, including Chaco in the southwest United States (Lekson 1999) and Classic Maya cities (Demarest 2003; Rice, this volume).

Second, Tiwanaku cities incorporated not only great diversity, which included differences in rank and role, but also differences that for some groups corresponded with status and occupation but that for others did not. Relations of inequality and institutions of integration developed as the urban capital expanded in Tiwanaku IV, but these materialized only in specific, if ultimately predominant, patterns of the urban order. More fundamental to diversity in Tiwanaku were the mutually differentiating relations of social identity out of which urban institutions developed. Parallel patterns of urban society are currently under examination in Teotihuacan, central Mexico (Headrick 1999; Manzanilla 1996) and hold much promise for understanding the dynamics of early Mesopotamian urbanism (Stone 1987).

Deep and enduring principles of social order shaped the contours of Tiwanaku economy and polity and helped determine the character of Tiwanaku urbanism. Despite Tiwanaku's far-reaching influence and prestige, local affiliations remained vibrant throughout the 650-year history of the polity. New social identities and types of groupings were created in the context of Tiwanaku hegemony while old ones were profoundly transformed. Still, the persistence and continual reproduction of group identity, in various social domains and at multiple social scales, is significant. Social differentiation and the power that resides in social identity and local corporate activities were key characteristics of Tiwanaku society, as expressed within cities and across rural landscapes. Childe (1950) argued that in preindustrial cities there is no room for the sectarian organization characteristic of nonurban societies. Tiwanaku reminds us that in some cases, relations rooted in sectarian and totemistic ties formed the very sociopolitical matrix of early cities and states.

Acknowledgments

Funding for this research was provided by Fulbright-Hays and the National Science Foundation (BNS# 9021098) (to Janusek) and the Wenner-Gren Foundation for Anthropological Research (#5863) (to Blom). Our projects benefited from logistical support provided by Alan Kolata, general director of the Proyecto Wila Jawira in Bolivia, of which our projects formed parts.

13
Late Classic Maya Population

Characteristics and Implications

Don S. Rice

[Survival is] the perpetual struggle for room and food.

—Thomas Malthus

Indigenous Maya speakers have an uninterrupted population history in the tropical lowlands of Mesoamerica spanning more than three millennia, and scholars of Maya culture have a long-standing interest in demographic characteristics of past Maya societies. In particular, population size and distribution have been implicated in the successes and failures of the Maya's "perpetual struggle for room and food." This chapter is an introduction to how and why archaeologists became interested in population issues in the Maya region, focusing on motivations and problems attendant to making population censuses from archaeological data. I review the natural and historical contexts for, and efforts to document, Late Classic (ca. AD 500–800) Maya population distribution and size in the southern Maya lowlands and close with brief comments on the implications of resulting population estimates for ongoing debates over agricultural practices and the urban nature of Classic Maya society.

The Lowland Maya

Landscape

The geographic focus of lowland Maya settlement and history lies south of the Tropic of Cancer and includes the Yucatán Peninsula and adjacent areas of Mesoamerica, a region that encompasses the modern political territories of Belize, eastern Mexico, northern Guatemala, and northern Honduras (Figure 13-1). The whole is a limestone platform approximately 175,000 sq km in area, bordered by water on the west, north, and east (López Ramos 1975; West 1964). Absolute elevation, geological age, and unevenness of the landform increase from northern Yucatán, Mexico, southward to northern Honduras.

The geology and topography of the Maya lowlands contribute to a mosaic of relatively thin, limestone-derived soils of variable structure and productivity. Water flow is equally variable but increasingly surficial from north to south (Back and Hanshaw 1978; Tamayo 1964). Subsurface drainage dominates in the north,

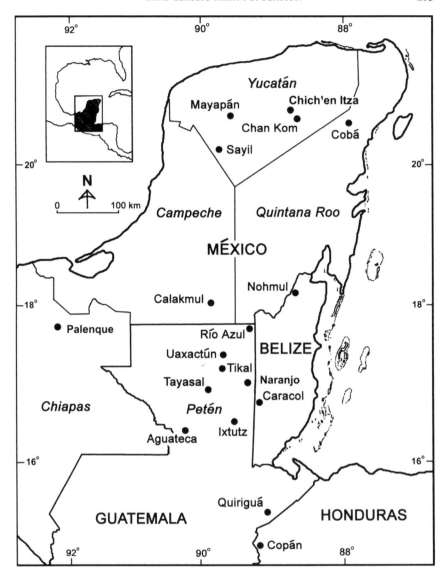

Figure 13-1. Map of the lowland Maya showing regions and sites referred to in the chapter.

with occasional sinkholes (or *cenotes*) giving access to subterranean aquifers; karsted regions to the south are marked by annual and perennial streams, and inland marsh or swamp wetland areas (*bajos*) form in broad floodplains or basins of residual clays, between the folded and eroded ridges of the upland terrain (Siemens 1978; Sweeting 1972). A north-south gradient of average total annual rainfall, as little as 500 mm in northwestern Yucatán to more than 3,000 mm in southern Department of Petén, Guatemala, adds to hydrographic variability, as do seasonal climatic fluctuations (Vivo Escoto 1964).

Extant tropical forest complexes in the Maya lowlands formed during the Pleistocene-Holocene transition (Leyden 1984) and the diversity of the resulting vegetation cover (Lundell 1937; Wagner 1964) and fauna that occupy the forest have long influenced the history of human extraction of resources in the region. Large numbers of potentially exploitable floral and faunal species have been identified, but concentration of biomass in forest canopies and the widely spaced distribution of useful species make procurement difficult (Voorhies 1982). Although natural plant and animal products were unquestionably harvested for food and industrial uses by the Maya, and the characteristics of natural forests undoubtedly influenced early economic and subsistence decisions, the history of Maya occupation in the lowlands is one of alteration of landscapes in the name of settlement and agriculture.

Culture History

It is projected that by at least 3,000 years ago ethnically distinct speakers of ancestral Maya languages began expanding east and south from the Gulf Coast and northward from the rugged highlands of Guatemala, moving along river valleys into the forested lowlands of Guatemala and Mexico. By 2,500 years ago the Maya lowlands were populated by small, dispersed communities of farming families who lived in wood-framed houses built on tamped earth floors or low plaster-surface rubble platforms, houses with few internal divisions, wattle and daubed exterior walls, and roofed in thatch (see Adams 1977).

Geochemical and pollen evidence of early Maya modification of terrain for house sites and farming has been reported from lake cores, at stratigraphic intervals radiocarbon dated as much as 500 years earlier than archaeologically confirmed occupation (Deevey 1978; Deevey et al. 1979; Islebe et al. 1996). The time lag attests to the dispersed and transitory nature of earliest settlement and the difficulty in recovering evidence for this occupation archaeologically. The ephemeral constitution and noncontiguous distribution of communities on the landscape, microbotanical evidence of burning and deforestation from lake cores, and macrobotanical remains of crop plants recovered in excavations together suggest that these early Maya grew corn and supplementary crops in the surrounding countryside using the techniques of slash-and-burn (or swidden) agriculture.

Slash-and-burn agriculture, practiced widely in the world's tropical forested regions, stereotypically entails farmers cutting and burning a patch of forest prior to a rainy season and sowing crops so that growth coincides with maximum soil moisture content (Norman 1979:86–136). After a field (or *milpa*) has been farmed for several years, nutrient leaching, soil compaction, increases in crop pests, and competition from grasses and weeds begin to reduce harvests dramatically. In response to this decline, farmers move to another forested location to begin the slash-and-burn process anew, and the former field is left to fallow, with vegetation recolonization and forest succession gradually rejuvenating the previously cropped soils.

The tropical soils of the Maya lowlands are fragile under forest and agriculture. Under conditions of high insolation, temperature, and rainfall, forest litter breaks down rapidly, and nutrients are either quickly recycled into vegetation or lost to soil water and moved out of rooting zones. Therefore, the relatively thin tropical soils do not act as nutrient "banks"; they do not store nutrients as effectively as deeper soils of temperate regions, and the majority of nutrients in the ecosystem are locked in vegetation. The longer ground surfaces are exposed to sun and rain by agriculture, the more severe are losses of fertility and structure, and longer periods of fallow are required for soils to regain some semblance of natural conditions. As a result of these factors, slash-and-burn agriculture is necessarily a land-extensive system; for fertile lands to be constantly available for cropping, a large portion of the landscape must remain at rest or undisturbed. This requirement has obvious implications for the size, distribution, and density of farming populations practicing slash-and-burn agriculture.

Because corn-based, rain-fed, slash-and-burn agriculture was commonplace among modern Maya observed by scholars in the first half of the twentieth century, the majority of those researchers believed the prehispanic Maya relied almost exclusively on similar practices (e.g., Gann 1918:53–55; Gann and Thompson 1937:66, 185; Morley 1946:158). Many assumed that slash and burn was the only sustainable agricultural technique practicable in the Maya lowlands (e.g., Cook 1909; Emerson 1935:12). Features of this agricultural system in turn conditioned expectations for ancient Maya communities to be widely dispersed and transitory, with low population numbers and densities and decentralized sociopolitical organizations.

A gloss on Maya cultural history is that once agricultural communities were established in the lowlands in the first millennium BC (Andrews V 1990; Andrews V and Hammond 1990), there was subsequent growth and expansion of Maya populations. The archaeological record for this dynamic consists of masonry residential platforms and superstructures of varying sizes and elaboration, arranged in groups situated variably across the landscape as deemed suitable by cosmological, economic, social, and topographic criteria (see Ashmore 1981). A plaza or plazas were invariably situated at the centers of communities of residential groups, formal spaces delimited by buildings dedicated to corporate activities.

During the Middle Preclassic (ca. 1000–300 BC) and Late Preclassic (ca. 300 BC–AD 250) periods, all regions of the Maya lowlands became colonized, and individual communities grew in size, density, and complexity. By AD 250 regional settlements were increasingly focused on large sites of monumental architecture thought to have housed Maya elites and governance. There is a history of Mayanists hypothesizing that these sites were complex cities in the Late Classic, with differentiated classes of occupants (see Becker 1979). In keeping with the assumed political parameters of slash-and-burn agriculture, however, most researchers have seen these sites as "vacant" (Thompson 1954:70) ceremonial centers, occupied by a restricted population of priest-astronomers and their retinue and surrounded by dispersed settlements of peasant farmers (Becker 1979; Thompson 1927, 1954). In the Late Classic period (ca. AD 600–950) centers were the loci of palaces and temples, architectural and freestanding sculpture (*stelae*), painted and sculpted hieroglyphic texts and iconographic programs celebrating elites and political events, production and consumption of labor-intensive crafts and exotic goods, and evidence for sophisticated astronomical and mathematical knowledge, which together are the defining cultural characteristics of Maya civilization.

The Classic Maya Collapse and Interest in Population Size

In the ninth and tenth centuries the architectural, artistic, and ceremonial and civic activities of centers ceased throughout much of the southern Maya lowlands, and there was a dramatic downturn in the sizes of regional populations, a phenomenon long known as the "Classic Maya collapse" (see Culbert 1973, 1988; Demarest et al. 2004; Webster 2002). After the final conquest of the region by Spaniards in the last decades of the seventeenth century and first years of the eighteenth century, tropical forest re-covered most of the lowlands of Belize and Guatemala and the northern margin of Honduras, and these regions remained relatively abandoned until in-migration of populations in the modern era. The northern lowlands, now comprising the Mexican states of Campeche, Yucatán, and Quintana Roo, did not suffer such collapse and abandonment, however. Rather, the period from approximately AD 800–1524 in this region has been characterized as one of cultural change, florescence, and population growth until the Spanish conquest (see Sabloff and Andrews V 1986), and descendants of the prehispanic Maya continued to occupy the region to the present day.

The early history of archaeology in the Maya lowlands was focused on the monumental centers and particularly on the sumptuous artifacts, calendrical inscriptions, hieroglyphic texts, and iconographic programs found therein (Sabloff 1990, 1991). As a result, well before the complexity, size, and variability of Maya settlements were known, archaeologists had identified the Classic Maya collapse in the south and begun to speculate on its causes. Prominent among the latter were failures of the agricultural system and failures of the political system (Sabloff 1973). In particular, the apparent abandonment of centers and their hinterlands begged questions of the ability of rain-fed, corn-based slash-and-burn agriculture to support Maya populations absent irreparable harm to the productive capacity of the landscape, of possible disjunctions between population size and the productive capacity of the cropping system, and of the compatibility between Maya populations and the system of governance manifest in center architecture. Concern for these questions prompted the earliest considerations of Maya population distribution and size.

As early as the 1920s archaeologists were aware of the ubiquity of small house sites in some regions of the forested Maya lowlands (Schufeldt 1950), with almost continuous settlement between some centers (Morley 1923:272). It was in the 1930s that a Carnegie Institution of Washington–sponsored project at the site of Uaxactún in the Department of Petén, Guatemala, initiated the first coordinated investigations of domestic and ceremonial remains to determine the numbers and living conditions of the population thought to have built and supported a large ceremonial complex (Ricketson and Ricketson 1937; Wauchope 1934).

In a cruciform survey area of approximately 2.27 sq km, a total of 78 "house mounds" were located in the 0.95 sq km considered "habitable" (arable land, calculated by removing land covered by center architecture and "uninhabitable" *bajo*) (Ricketson and Ricketson 1937:15–16), or 82 structures per sq km of habitable land (which equals the "economic density," or numbers of people per unit of arable land as opposed to numbers per total landscape area). Considering each structure a dwelling for a family of five persons, the investigators projected a density of 410 persons per sq km of habitable land and then reduced this total to 102 persons per sq km of habitable land under the unexplained assumption that only 25 percent of the house mounds were occupied at any one time. The investigators suggested that there would have been about 3 acres (approximately 1.25 ha) of arable land for each house mound mapped and that, given a modern yield of approximately 997 pounds of corn per acre, each house could have raised 2,991 pounds annually. If the family of five consumed approximately 3,650 pounds of corn annually, almost enough was raised per house if all houses were contemporaneous, and more than enough would have been produced for the projected 25 percent population (Ricketson and Ricketson 1937:18).

Although the Uaxactún project's director, Oliver Ricketson, accepted the dominance of corn-based agriculture in ancient Maya society, he rejected slash and burn as a destructive and unproductive system that never could have supported Maya populations at their peak (Ricketson and Ricketson 1937:12). Ricketson was not alone among contemporaries in his concerns over the productivity and sustainability of corn-based slash-and-burn agriculture and its ability to support "urbanization" (e.g., Cook 1909, 1921; Cooke 1931; Lundell 1933, 1937; Termer 1951), and these issues became hotly debated in the mid-1950s and early 1960s.

In her article "Environmental Limitation to the Development of Culture," Betty Meggers (1954) argued that the fragility of the lowland Maya environment, and resulting limited agricultural potential, established a ceiling for indigenous cultural development in the region and that the intellectual achievements and governmental system of the Classic Maya must have developed in more-productive landscapes elsewhere, then suffered "devolution" (the Classic Maya collapse) once introduced into the lowlands. Although Meggers was relatively ignorant of Maya culture history, others agreed that dispersed, low-density populations inherent to slash-and-burn agriculture were difficult to rationalize with Maya centers of monumental architecture and the demands of an "urban culture" (Altschuler 1958; Hester 1954; Palerm and Wolf 1957; Reina 1967). Supplementary systems of intensive agriculture were proposed that would have allowed the Maya "to maintain stable centers of control, while at the same time controlling an ever-shifting peasantry" (Wolf 1959:78).

Rebuttals took several tacks. There were more positive appraisals of the productive potential and stability of the Maya lowland environment and slash-and-burn agriculture (Cowgill 1960, 1961, 1962; Dumond 1961; Ferdon 1959) that suggested the latter could produce surpluses with no evidence of degradation that might have undermined the productivity of Maya agriculture. Data from the survey at Uaxactún were manipulated to reduce population sizes further, to levels easily supported by corn-based slash and burn (Brainerd 1954, 1956), and ethnographic sources and statistical experiments were marshaled to show that monumental structures built under political aegis could be constructed and maintained by a less-than-full-time corps of slash-and-burn agriculturalists (Erasmus 1965; Kaplan 1963).

Estimates of the carrying capacity of corn-based slash-and-burn or *milpa* agriculture from ethnographic studies of Maya populations have ranged from approximately 23 persons per sq km in the northern Yucatán Peninsula (Hester 1954; Kempton 1935) to approximately 77 persons per sq km in the Department of Petén, Guatemala (Cowgill 1961, 1962; Reina 1967), and the few settlement studies in the late 1950s and early 1960s produced mound counts implying population densities well above those limits (Bullard 1960; Sanders 1963; Willey et al. 1965). These surveys were limited in scale and intensity, however, and it was the exhaustive study of Maya settlement at the Petén site of Tikal that most influenced the ongoing debate about Maya agriculture and governance.

In 1961 a map of Tikal's central 9 sq km was published (Carr and Hazard 1961) that documented an average of 235 mounds per sq km; an additional 7 sq km were mapped with less-thorough techniques and yielded an average of 145 structures per sq km (Figure 13-2 bottom). On the basis of these survey data, a total population of nearly 11,000 people was projected for Late Classic Tikal, a large segment of which was assumed to be nonfarmers (Haviland 1963:521–524, 1965:19, 2003).

In 1965 additional settlement survey was initiated by the Tikal Sustaining Area Project in a cruciform arrangement of four survey arms, each 500 m wide and 12 km long (6 sq km), radiating out from the already surveyed central core of Tikal, under the assumption that settlement densities would eventually drop off in each arm and that sufficient arable land for slash-and-burn agriculture would be found to account for subsistence support for the center (Fry 1969,

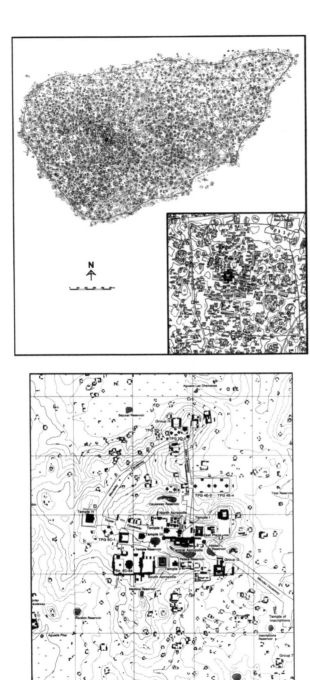

Figure 13-2. (*bottom*) Map of central portion of Tikal, Petén, Guatemala; visible rectangular units are 500 m on a side (modification of Ashmore 1992:Figure 14.4). (*top*) Map of the site of Mayapán, Yucatán, Mexico; reconstructed from Pollock et al. 1962: Map insert. A similar map is shown in Webster 2002:Figure 13, where he notes "the very dense concentrations of residential architecture within the wall that give this site an urban appearance."

2003; Puleston 1973:65–67, 1983). A fifth survey strip 500 m wide and 9.5 km long was mapped between the north boundary of the Tikal National Park and the site of Uaxactún. A total of 1,720 mounds were found within the five survey arms. *Bajos* imposed limits on settlement to the east and west, and settlement densities dropped off at 4.5 km north and 8 km south, with artificial ditches/earthworks associated with the drops in both cases (Puleston and Callender 1967; Webster et al. 2003). Nonetheless, in the mid-1960s the central and peripheral settlement zones of 63 sq km and 60 sq km, respectively, were defined within the bounds of the *bajos* and ditches/earthworks, with an estimated population of 40,000 for the "urban core," 635 persons per sq km, and a peripheral population density of approximately 100 persons per sq km (Haviland 1970:193, 1972:138).

The implications of the Tikal data for reconstructions of Maya agriculture are obvious. Estimated population densities in peripheral Tikal are above the highest proposed productive capacities of rain-fed, corn-based slash-and-burn farming in Petén, and the whole of Tikal's population could not have been supported by such a system. The estimated size and density of settlement in the Tikal site core and periphery also belied notions of vacant ceremonial centers surrounded by dispersed communities and made more suspect formerly proposed two-tiered social hierarchies of astronomer-priests and commoner farmers. The Tikal data did not settle arguments; studies of agriculture and the sociopolitical structure of society are necessarily comparative, and some considered the site of Tikal an anomaly. The surveys did, however, prompt numerous settlement studies grounded in serious consideration of the methodological problems attendant to reconstruction of population characteristics (Culbert and Rice 1990).

Estimating Late Classic Maya Populations

Although the past two decades have seen considerable advances in the reading of Maya hieroglyphic texts and the interpretation of Maya iconography, there are neither texts nor images that explicitly attest to the size and distribution of population at any site or in any region. Postconquest observations and ethnographic studies may suggest family and local population sizes at the time of conquest or in modern days, but the economic, social, and political fabric in which these families and communities were or are embedded is markedly different from the circumstances of the Late Classic Maya. Therefore, archaeologists interested in calculating population size, density, and complexity by necessity must work from settlement survey and site data. Some unit of culture—relative concentrations of artifacts, structures or rooms within structures, reservoirs or *aguadas*—is mapped and counted, ages of construction or use are determined for the counted sample, and numbers of contemporary units are converted to numbers of people. The process is fraught with problems and uncertainties.

In the southern lowlands it has been most common for the visible surface remains of structures, mounds found and mapped through survey beneath extant forest, to be counted as a basis for estimating population. In centers or noncenter zones where forest cover has been removed and preservation of superstructures may be unusually good, however, it may be possible to project population numbers using rooms as opposed to buildings as a basis for counts. The Maya had a propensity for refurbishing and building over structures, particularly in the Late Classic period, so surface remains represent only the last phase of occupation, and adjustments must be made to mound counts in order to estimate population for earlier periods. With the acknowledgment of this problem, the initial critical issue is whether the maps of surface remains adequately indicate the total number of structures that actually existed.

Archeologists must contend with the possibility of "invisible" structures, those small "minimally platformed" or ephemeral structures that left no surface indication or structures masked by debris from adjacent structures, and "hidden" structures that simply were not found or whose surface configuration was not considered a building (Johnston 1994, 2002, 2004). It is difficult to speculate on the number of unmapped structures in any given survey area, and testing a significant area of vacant terrain would be a monumental task. Although some experiments have been undertaken (Bronson 1968; Wilk and Wilhite 1991; Wilk et al. 1980), it is likely that the number of unmapped structures will vary in their spatial distribution and age within and between sites and regions and with the physiographic contexts of the settlements (Johnston 2002), so extrapolating from tests to other locations would be difficult. Despite the difficulties, some archaeologists working in the Maya area have considered upper adjustment of mapped mound remains to account for unmapped structures, adjustments anywhere from 35 percent to 100 percent, depending on the contexts (A. Chase 1990; D. Chase 1990; Webster and Freter 1990b).

Estimation of Maya populations from structural remains requires that the structures being counted are residential, structures in which people lived as opposed to structures housing adjunct domestic activities or civic or ceremonial functions. At the heart of the assignment of numbers of people to structures counted is the assumption that some determinable social unit, such as a family or household, resided in those structures (see Johnston and Gonlin 1998 for a review of perspectives on the nature of Maya residential units). Archaeologists working in the Maya lowlands acknowledge that even in groups of mounds that are primarily residential, some structures served auxiliary functions. In nucleated ceremonial centers the number of nonresidential buildings may be the majority. Determination of the number of nonresidential structures in a sample requires an extensive excavation program with careful analyses of artifacts and their contexts. Such projects have been few; the prototype was a small-structure excavation project at Tikal (Haviland 1965), and the most extensive has been carried out at the site of Copán, Honduras (Webster et al. 2000). The consensus is that a downward adjustment of between 5 percent and 30 percent must be made in small-structure counts to eliminate nonresidential loci.

Once a universe of structures is defined, their dates of construction and use must be determined and numbers of contemporaneous buildings calculated. Most archaeologists base age on ceramics recovered from buildings through excavation, but ceramic periods in the southern Maya lowlands are gross temporal units of anywhere from 200 to 500 years in length. Shorter ceramic phases keyed to particular types or wares may still be 100–200 years in length and encompass numerous Maya generations. Obsidian hydration dating of obsidian tools and debitage from structures at Copán offers the possibility of much tighter chronological reckoning, but the resulting dates there are debated, and the procedures have yet to be reliably extended elsewhere (Freter 1992, 1997; Webster et al. 2004; for a contrary view see Fash et al. 2004).

The issue of contemporaneity of structures goes beyond assigning building remains to a particular period or phase of construction. A continuing debate among archaeologists working in the Maya region is over the degree to which individual house locations, once established, were in continual residential use or fell into occasional disuse or abandonment during any given period. Under the assumption of slash and burn as the prevailing form of agriculture, large contemporaneity adjustments such as Ricketson's 25 percent at Uaxactún were implicitly justified. Other factors that could contribute to temporary disuse or permanent abandonment of particular structures include death of a family member or reduction in family size such that survivors are absorbed into other households, house foundations unused for periods after burning or collapse of a superstructure and before a new one is built, or the possibility of dual residence involving permanent residences and seasonal field houses. Adjustments for disuse and abandonment have ranged from 7 percent to 20 percent (Ringle and Andrews 1990; Sanders 1973; Webster and Freter 1990b).

Once the number of contemporaneous residential structures during a particular period is known, the last piece of the population equation is the number of people who occupied those buildings. Most archaeologists assume that the co-residential group was a nuclear or extended family, and it is likely that the makeup of such a household was variable over time and across space because of normal family cycles of member addition and subtraction (Haviland 1988). A common figure for the size of a Maya nuclear family is 5.6 individuals, a number based on ethnographic study of the village of Chan Kom in Yucatán (Redfield and Villa Rojas 1934:91). As few as 4 persons per family and as high as 6.07 people per house have been proposed from other ethnographic surveys (Puleston 1973:173–175; Sanders and Price 1968:163; Steggerda 1941:128), however, and descriptions from historic documents suggest that early postconquest residences held multiple families with coresidential group numbers anywhere from 10 to 25 individuals (Hellmuth 1977; Puleston 1973:177; Villagutierre 1933:136, 480).

Naroll's (1962) cross-culturally derived dictum of each individual requiring an average of 10 sq m of roofed space has also been applied to Tikal's small-structure data to arrive at average house occupancy of 5.4 individuals (Puleston 1973). Eliminating the immediate postconquest data from consideration because of the disrupted and subjugated circumstances of Maya residential life, most archaeologists use a residential figure between 4.0 and 5.6 individuals per structure.

Calculation of population sizes and densities requires all of the numbers and considerations noted above. Each researcher faces different problems collecting data, depending on the archaeological, environmental, and social contexts in which the person works in the field. Scholars also have differing opinions on appropriate adjustments to make, so there is expected variability in the formulae used to move from numbers of structures or rooms in structures to numbers of inhabitants.

Archaeologists also realize that in order to estimate populations, it is necessary to know the boundaries of sites and regions, and obtaining such knowledge is often not easy. In a similar way, traditional definitions of Maya sites as areas encompassing all major architectural groups lack the precision necessary for distinguishing center versus noncenter populations. In areas of high visibility and in zones where population was physiographically circumscribed, it may be possible to locate points of settlement decline and termination and to hypothesize cores and peripheries and bounded site territories. In heavily forested zones such delimitations are more problematic, because dense vegetation makes survey difficult and because settlement of varying densities may be situated over all high terrain. The Tikal sustaining area survey data made site territory definition less arbitrary; *bajos* and ditches/earthworks were thought to coincide with drop-offs in settlement, but in other areas construction of boundaries is necessarily subjective. Therefore, it has often been more productive to discuss population in terms of densities rather than in terms of absolute numbers.

Despite differing site characteristics and environmental contexts, differing research resources, and variable approaches to population calculation, there is a growing corpus of estimates of peak Late Classic population sizes and densities for center and noncenter zones in the southern Maya lowlands that are of the same order of magnitude and comparable (see Culbert and Rice 1990). A sampling of these data for selected centers and noncenter zones, including a reanalysis of data from Tikal, give a range of site- and region-specific estimates that have bearing on discussions of Maya subsistence and governance (Table 13-1).

Some Implications of the Numbers

Agriculture

There is variability in population estimates from one site to the next and one region to the next, as might be expected in a diverse tropical zone studied by way

Table 13-1. Late Classic Period Population Estimates from the Southern Maya Lowlands

TOTAL POPULATION			
Country and Location (Source)	Area (sq km)	Population	Density (per sq km)
Belize:			
Caracol (4) – whole site	177.0	155,000	88.0
Nohmul (9) – whole site	22.0	3,310	150.0
Belize/Guatemala:			
Three Rivers (11) – urban zones	242.0	198,610	821.0
Three Rivers (11) – rural zones	1,154.0	204,835	177.5
Guatemala:			
Aguateca (7) – monumental core	.98	1,480	1,510.0
Macanché-Salpetén (10) – combined lake basins	27.9	7,262	224.0
Quexil-Petenxil (10) – combined lake basins	23.5	3,836	163.0
Quirigua (2) – center	3.0	1,579	526.0
Rio Azul (1) – habitable urban zone	49.0	44,100	900.0
Tayasal (3) – central spine	8.0	10,400	1,300.0
Tayasal (3) – outer ring	18.0	11,000	611.0
Tayasal (3) – periphery	64.0	11,172	175.0
Tayasal (3) – whole site	90.0	32,272	359.0
Tikal (5) – central core	16.0	13,275	830.0
Tikal (5) – immediate periphery	104.0	45,720	440.0
Tikal (5) – total within site	120.0	62,000	517.0
Tikal (5) – rural within 10 km	194.0	29,696	153.0
Yaxhá-Sacnab (10) combined lake basins	29.5	6,253	211.0
Honduras:			
Copán (12) – urban core	.6	11,828	19,713.0
Copán (12) – rural Copán pocket	23.4	10,627	454.0
Copán Valley (12) – outside of Copán pocket	476.0	5,298	11.0
Copán Valley (12) – all zones	500.0	27,753	55.0
Mexico:			
Calakmul (6) –center	70.0	50,000	714.0
Mayapan (8) – whole site	4.0	12,000	3,000.0

[1]Adams 1999; [2]Ashmore 1990; [3]A. Chase 1990; [4]A. Chase and D. Chase 1996; [5]Culbert et al 1990; [6]Folan et al 1995; [7]Inomata 1995; [8]Pollock 1962; [9]Pyburn 1990; [10]D. Rice and P. Rice 1990; [11]Robichaux 1995; [12]Webster and Freter 1990b

of different research designs and with archaeologists choosing different solutions to their common problems in population estimation. Nonetheless, there is accumulating evidence that land availability per capita in the Late Classic period in many locales was below per capita land requirements under rain-fed, corn-based, full-fallow slash-and-burn agriculture. If "economic densities" are calculated, the situation is worse still. In the basins of Lakes Yaxhá and Sacnab in central Petén, Guatemala, for example, the ratio of land available to land needed by the estimated basin inhabitants is 38 percent if all terrain is considered arable, and the ratio drops to as low as 16 percent if only the most naturally fertile and well-drained soils are considered suitable for cropping (Rice 1978:Table 4.8, 1993: Table 2). The population estimates for sites and regions noted above suggest that land shortages under swidden agriculture elsewhere would have been more dramatic still.

One solution to land shortages under a full-fallow swidden system is to shorten the fallow period, to put more terrain in production for longer periods of time, but to do so requires investment in techniques to counter the deleterious effects of long-term cropping on soil fertility and structure, and even then there may not be enough cropland available. In the Yaxhá-Sacnab example, the Late Classic ratio of land availability to land needed for the extreme of perennial (no fallow) corn-based agriculture is 92 percent with the total landscape deemed arable. If all classes of terrain were not put into production, however, and this was undoubtedly the case, the ratio shrinks. More than intensification of land use is required, and the 35 years since the Tikal sustaining area surveys have been marked by scholarly projects searching for alternative crops and cropping strategies in an effort to resolve this dilemma of Maya subsistence (see Fedick 1996; Flannery 1982; Harrison and Turner 1978; Rice 1993).

These investigations have led to increased awareness that the Maya lowlands of Belize, Guatemala, Honduras, and Mexico are diverse in their inherent fertility, hydrography, physiography, and productive capacity. Likewise, there is growing consensus that this diversity must have been paralleled by a complex system of food production adapted to landscape variability, that the Maya practiced a multi-habitat and multitechnology system of agriculture (Chen 1987; Culbert et al. 1978). Strategies for which there is archaeological evidence include terraced-field cropping (Healy et al. 1983; Turner II 1974, 1979, 1983) and raised and drained or channelized field cropping in *bajos* and swampy margins of lakes and streams (Adams et al. 1981; Harrison 1978; Pohl 1990; Puleston 1977; Siemens 1982; Siemens and Puleston 1972; Turner II and Harrison 1983), both of which attest to labor-intensive, rain-fed cropping at varying fallow intensities (Fedick 1989; Ford 1986; Johnston 2003; Sanders 1973, 1979; Tourtellot 1993).

Paleoecological data confirm dramatic Late Classic deforestation throughout the lowlands, accelerated soil erosion, and nutrient sequestering (loss of soil nutrients to groundwater and alluvial and colluvial deposits) that were attendant to intensive field agriculture (e.g., Brenner 1983; Brenner et al. 1990; Dahlin et al. 1980; Deevey 1978; Deevey et al. 1979; Pohl et al. 1990; Pope 1986; Rice and Rice 1984; Rue 1987). Paleolimnological data also predict orbitally forced and/or human-induced drier climatic conditions in the northern lowlands in the Late Classic period that may have made raising field crops more precarious (Curtis et al. 1996, 1998; Gill 2000; Hodell et al. 1995; Leyden et al. 1998). Although consensus has emerged on the presence of prehispanic systems of rain-fed agriculture with higher productive potential than full-fallow swidden, the data documenting landscape impoverishment and possible climatic change fuel continued debate over the degree to which Maya impact on environment and agricultural failure, perhaps exacerbated by climate change, are causal variables in the cultural and demographic transformations that characterize the close of the Classic period (Culbert 1988; Gill 2000; Rice and Rice 1984).

Heightening concerns about potential Late Classic land and food shortfalls is the fact that the populous centers are often situated on the largest expanses of fertile, well-drained soils, with the density of nonresidential and domestic architecture precluding field agriculture altogether. There also exists the question of whether high population numbers and densities at centers reflect the possibility that a large percentage of inhabitants may have been nonproducers—both elites and their retainers and craft and service specialists and their families who were not engaged in raising their own food.

Two strategies that could have mitigated to a degree the support burden of field agriculture in more rural zones and that would have structured the character of the centers themselves are maintenance of stands of calorically important fruit and nut trees and integrated kitchen gardens focused on a diverse array of consumable and industrial plants. Historic records and ethnographic data provide ample evidence for Maya reliance in more recent times on orchards and gardens (Marcus 1982), but evidence for orchards and gardens in the Late Classic period is limited.

Extensive terracing within the centers of Caracol, Belize, and Ixtutz, Petén, situated between zones of monumental architecture and surrounding residential groups, implies horticultural production within these sites (Chase and Chase 1983, 1996:808, 1998), with the alignment and organization of the terraces at Caracol taken to indicate "direct . . . state involvement in agricultural management." Soil analyses in concert with settlement mapping at the site of Sayil, Yucatán, Mexico, suggest that inhabitants of that center also pursued intensive plant production on artificially enriched soils between residences (Dunning 1992). At Tikal, Petén, the ubiquity of *ramon* trees (*Brosimum alicastrum*) throughout the site's core, trees that produce large quantities of highly nutritious nuts, has led to the proposal that orchards dominated the center's open spaces and reduced considerably Late Classic Maya reliance on corn-based agriculture (Puleston 1968, 1973). Systematically conducted botanical surveys in the center of Cobá, Quin-

tana Roo, Mexico, have revealed a correlation between elite architecture and economically and nutritionally important species, which may result from the maintenance of gardens and orchards in the core of the site (Folan et al. 1979).

These architectural, agronomic, and botanical data, together with settlement
distributions and estimated Late Classic population densities, have prompted Gair
Tourtellot (1993:222) to suggest that Maya centers had a "garden city" appearance. The almost universal existence of open space around and separating architectural complexes is seen as indirect evidence for spatially restricted "infield"
systems, which consisted of intensively cultivated gardens and orchards, and open
fields within walking distance of residential groups. The spatial dispersion of elite
and nonelite settlement found in Maya centers, then, is considered the result of
producers living in the immediate vicinity of their zones of diversified subsistence
production (Drennan 1988).

Cities and Urbanism

It can be argued that implementation of highly intensive agricultural strategies
contributed to the "garden city" layout of Maya centers (Tourtellot 1993:222),
but how appropriate is the term "city," with its connotations of urban character
(where urbanization is the process by which central places exhibit increasingly
large and dense populations, increasingly differentiated workforces and the architecture that houses them, and increasingly centralized or incorporated administrative districts at their cores)? It is clear from accumulated settlement data that a
model of centers as inhabited by a small number of priests and surrounded by
dispersed communities of farmers lacks broad applicability. Wirth (1938) proposed that cities share large population size, dense population nucleation, and
high internal heterogeneity (where *heterogeneity* refers to differences in economic,
political, and sociological roles and statuses). As the population data presented
above suggest, some Late Classic centers yield evidence of relatively high population sizes and densities. These numbers should be put in perspective, however.

In a survey of 425 preindustrial cities worldwide, Storey (1992, 1997a:119–
120) found the mean population density for the sample to be 16,661 persons per
sq km, with a median population density of 12,897 people per sq km, reflecting
that the distribution is skewed toward low densities. More than 85 percent of the
preindustrial cities had population densities greater than 2,000 people per sq km,
whereas better than 75 percent of the cities had population densities greater than
5,000 persons per sq km. Given population estimates available to date, the largest
of Maya centers are at the lowest end of the continuum for this sample.

One Maya site, Mayapán, recently dubbed "the last great cosmopolitan city of
the pre-Columbian Maya world" (Masson et al. 2003), does fall in the top 85
percent of preindustrial cities, with population densities greater than 2,000 per sq
km, but it is Postclassic in date (occupied ca. AD 1250–1450) and the product
of unique circumstances. The site is defined by a stone defensive wall that encom-

passes more than 4 sq km and more than 4,000 structures (Figure 13-2 top), approximately half of which have been described as residential, and a peak population of about 12,000 has been projected for the site (Pollock 1962:15; Smith 1962:171). The traditional wisdom, based on historic sources, is that Mayapán became the capital of northern Yucatán after warfare brought about the decline of a polity centered on the site of Chich'en Itza. Placement of the new capital and the structure of governance there were said to be the result of an agreement between two antagonistic groups, the Itza (Cocom), former residents of Chich'en, and the Xiw (Roys 1962). A number of the major buildings at Mayapán were modeled on those at Chich'en Itza. The Itza and Xiw were to rule the site and its domain jointly (for an alternative view, see Boot 2001), and other regional lords were to send members of their families to Mayapán to ensure Itza/Xiw dominion over the peninsula. This forced collection of regional representatives is thought to have been responsible for the site's population density, as well as requiring its defensive posture.

Evidence of warfare can be found throughout the Maya historical record, and instances of conflict undoubtedly altered local demographies. Small-scale conflict was ubiquitous in the Late Classic period in the southern lowlands, and it is speculated that the central Belizean Classic center of Caracol experienced considerable population growth as a result of successful conclusions to warfare with Tikal in AD 562 and Naranjo in AD 626–636. Chase and Chase (1989) have argued that general populations benefited from warfare events, with postwar prosperity attracting population to "winners," and that "warfare can be seen as a catalyst for the site's development, and . . . the prosperity associated with successful warfare was used to integrate and organize Caracol's society." The centripetal force of waging successful wars did not move Caracol or other Classic sites out of the lower range of Storey's preindustrial cities, however.

Conflict had impacts on Maya centers other than attraction of population and raising settlement densities. In the late eighth century in the Petexbatun region of Petén, for example, the occupants of the site of Aguateca built defensive fortification walls around and between structures within the core of the site, and residential populations were consolidated therein in response to endemic warfare (Demarest et al. 1997; Inomata 1995, 1997). Conflicts in the Petexbatun region at the close of the Late Classic period also produced migrations of displaced Maya into the central Petén lakes region, particularly the vicinity of Lake Petén Itza, where new communities were founded on previously uninhabited lands and where migrants augmented the populations of previously established sites (Rice and Rice 2005).

Similarly, the decline of Chich'en Itza in the mid-thirteenth century and the fall of Mayapán to civil war in the mid-fifteenth century not only altered the demographic and political geographies in the north but also contributed to the migration of sociopolitical groups to central Petén (Pugh 2001, 2002; Rice and

Rice 2005; Rice et al. 1998). The presence of the Spaniards in the northern Yucatán peninsula in the sixteenth and seventeenth centuries also prompted considerable migration into the central Petén region and exacerbated local inter-Maya warfare between previous in-migrants, placing a premium on dense, fortified settlements, often situated in defensible locations such as islands and peninsulas (Pugh 2001, 2002; Rice and Rice 2005; Rice et al. 1998). None of these communities were, however, the size and density of Mayapán.

Although warfare and other processes, such as the political fortunes of rulers or ruling factions or the changing environmental conditions, undoubtedly affected distributions of Maya populations, particularly in the Postclassic period, they do not appear to have substantially influenced the structure and function of Classic period sites. What, if anything, then, does architectural patterning say about the nature of Maya sites as cities? Classic Maya centers have been described as largely "unplanned" in that they are not laid out on a grid pattern or based on cruciform or rectangular patterns of ingress and egress (Marcus 1983:196–197). Sites grew in area and construction volume by accretion over time, developing at their cores heavier concentrations of monumental architecture—palaces, temples, ball courts, and so on (see Morley et al. 1983:Table 11). These architectural complexes are most often situated on artificial or natural promontories. Many centers also have multiple focal points or "nuclei" around which patterns of settlement or land use evolved; variable numbers of "separate but equal" plaza groups were constructed sequentially or simultaneously and were often linked by elevated *sacbes,* paved avenues or causeways (Marcus 1983:198, 204–206).

Contrary to the unruly pattern that "growth by accretion" suggests for Classic period centers, it is increasingly apparent that site growth was "planned" with respect to the locations of core, monumental, or public structures relative to one another. Harrison (1989, 1999:190–191) has noted that at Tikal and other sites "there is a strong geometric relationship that binds the structures together." In some cases these relationships suggest that buildings were constructed simultaneously, but in many others they reflect city planning that takes into consideration locations of earlier structures, their viewsheds, and the genealogical and political structural relationships they mirrored (Grube, ed. 2000:230–231).

According to Harrison, at Tikal each structure had a single point in its plan that determined its location, a point representing the intersection at right angles of two lines formed by the front wall and the central axis of the structure. This location point was invariably established with reference to the location points of two earlier structures, with the three location points together creating a right triangle. Harrison (1999:187) suggests that "placement of a third building in alignment with the placement points of two earlier buildings demonstrated respect or honor of these earlier buildings." It is assumed that the most common basis for these triangular relationships between new buildings is ancestry, with new buildings honoring the ancestors who constructed earlier structures, in particular kings honoring their predecessors (Fash 1998; McAnany 1998; Miller 1985, 1998). Monumental structures at Tikal's core, then, might be viewed as a series of interconnected integral right triangles that reflect numerous important kinship and political relationships (Harrison 1999:173).

The exact origin of this right-triangle model for acknowledging and perpetuating ancestry and lineage power is unclear, but it is likely that triangulation as a measurement and placement system had long-standing use in agriculture for surveying and resurveying fields and was later adopted for locating architecture and art (Harrison 1999:190). The earliest right-triangle examples at Tikal are Early Classic (ca. AD 250–550) in date, but by the Late Classic period it was the basis of architectural planning at Tikal and other large Maya sites.

Although concerns for ancestry are demonstrable in architecture and art, there are no epigraphic or iconographic programs that explicitly state how the Maya viewed or interpreted their towns or cities. Nonetheless, elements of Maya cosmology do provide some insights (Ashmore 1989, 1992). The Maya conceived of their universe as consisting of a heaven and an underworld, each stratified in tiers and inhabited by hosts of supernaturals and, in the case of heaven, by deified ancestors. Between the upper and lower worlds was the earth, often portrayed as a saurian monster floating on a liquid underworld, which was horizontally divided into four cardinal (or intercardinal) quarters, each with a color designation and each inhabited by particular deities. Four supernaturals held up the corners of the sky, sacred mountains mediated between earth and heaven, and caves (portrayed as the mouths of saurians) allowed access to the world below. These three layers of reality were unified by the cyclical movements of the sun, moon, Venus, and deities identified with other elements of the observable cosmos. Maya astronomy included not only observations of the cyclical movement of celestial bodies but also the recording of the cycling of units of time, with the belief that events of history and conditions of humankind cycled with these periods.

It has been argued that Maya centers are cosmograms, replicating the structure and implications of the cosmos (Ashmore and Sabloff 2002; Carlson 1981; for a recent exchange of opinions on this issue, see Smith 2003 vs. Ashmore and Sabloff 2003). Ashmore (1992:173) has outlined the characteristics that provided cosmological infrastructure at the site of Tikal and elsewhere: emphasis on north-south axes, with the north representing the celestial realm and the south standing for the underworld; the common but not invariant presence of ball courts mediating north and south, where in mythology the ball game is a means of negotiation between celestial deities and the denizens of the underworld; the presence of subsidiary eastern and western architectural complexes that give form to the quadripartite earth and form right triangles with the north; and the frequent presence of *sacbes* linking various elements of often widely dispersed architectural groups and providing "symbolic coherence" to the whole. To these features should be added the presence of funerary temples of kings and nobles as mountains reaching to the heavens, counts of building tiers and steps of stairways that parallel the number of heavenly and netherworld levels, and architectural art portraying elements of the universe, supernaturals, and ancestors.

Maya towns and cities, then, were not only sites of civic authority but also sacred landscapes where cosmological issues are omnipresent, where architectural forms, facades, and placements invoked universal structures and relationships. Ancestors and myths and the nature of and divine mandates for secular authority are made clear, and centers became theaters in which sovereigns legitimized their rights to rule.

As Ashmore (1992:174) notes, the plans of sites were not simply static guides or informative maps; they were dynamic. Hierophanies, plays of light on architecture, cyclically repeated and kept alive celestial events of human significance. A wonderful example of such architectural planning and drama comes from the site of Palenque, where the placement of buildings was designed to repeat mythological images of death and accession events. The Temple of the Inscriptions was situated such that from any unobstructed location the sun on every winter solstice appears to set into the earth through the temple superstructure and into the tomb of a ruler named Pacal (Schele 1981:99).

At the same time, at the Temple of the Cross, the last rays of the sun first light a carved image of Chan-Bahlum, Pacal's son, on the west sanctuary jamb panel, holding in his hands an instrument of office. As shadows elongate, the sanctuary's inner panel with a carved image of Pacal holding a similar symbol of power is illuminated, and then finally, as the sun sets, the western jamb and a panel showing God L, the god of death, receiving the instrument of office (from Pacal) is lit just before the entire sanctuary goes dark. The Inscription and Cross temples were built to manipulate the solstice sunset to create a cyclical reenactment of Pacal's death and Chan-Bahlum's accession to Palenque's throne. The solstice hierophanies, their powerful characterizations and monumental scale, and public accessibility to them "argue for direct linkage between the perception of real events in the heavens and the mythology that explained the relationship of man to the cosmos and the function and identity of rulers" (Schele 1981:104).

Maya centers were dynamic in other ways. The architectural features that made up the civic core and perpetuated real and cosmological events and history were the sites of processions and performances of rites and ceremonies. City cores were public arenas in which the messages of the living were delivered, together with the messages of the ancestors and gods conveyed in architecture and art. As sites of divine and secular spectacle, Maya centers were thought to be foci of pilgrimage by surrounding populations, and public ceremony through pilgrimage was believed to be one means of integrating centers with their immediate peripheries.

Although the boundaries of civic/ceremonial cores of sites are very difficult to determine, it has long been suggested that Maya sites have an implicit concentric community structure. The size, formality, and density of nonresidential and residential buildings invariably decline as one moves from cores or nuclei to peripheries, although topography, hydrographic features, and settlement history would invariably distort any concentric pattern of zonation. Writing in the sixteenth century, Bishop Diego de Landa described the architectural pattern of northern Yucatecan Maya communities on which concentric ring models are based:

> Their dwelling place was as follows: in the middle of the town were their temples with beautiful plazas, and all around the temples stood the houses of the lords and the priests, and . . . the most important people. Thus came the houses of the richest and those who were held in the highest estimation nearest these, and at the outskirts of the town were the houses of the lower class [Tozzer 1941:62].

Implicit in this model is the sense that proximity to a site's core is positively correlated with status, wealth, and power, that this correlation existed at all residential levels, and that clusters of residences represent neighborhoods of related individuals or social groups (Stomper 2001:206). Coe (1965) has argued, on the basis of his reading of Landa's description of Maya *Uayeb* rites in sixteenth-century Yucatán (*Uayeb* is the period of five days leading up to the end of one year and the beginning of another, a time of transition and potential peril), that implicit quadripartite divisions were imposed on the concentric pattern of Maya settlements, with rituals, feasting and dancing, the movement of idols, and communal authority shifting from quadrant to quadrant at regular intervals and integrating the community.

In turn, communities were linked to the city center by causeways that "served as a symbolic unifier of disparate areas, in addition to being a means of transportation and communication" (Stomper 2001:207). Other means of articulation may have been less symbolic. Peripheral zones often contain complexes of buildings that include temples and palace structures, occasionally with architectural sculpture and free-standing monuments. These "minor" centers have variously been interpreted as more recent capitals of newer polities, residential sites of lesser regional lords, political "outposts" and extensions of centralized authority housed in cities, and "dower houses" or heritable estates of elites who reside primarily in site cores. There are few data by which to distinguish among such interpretations, but it is clear that there is a systemic relationship between these sites, less-conspicuous rural residences, and the residents and functions of site cores.

In a recent analysis of Classic Maya political structure, Rice (2004) has suggested that the Classic period Maya shared a unifying, multileveled, geopolitico-ritual organization similar to that observed among the Postclassic and early Colonial period lowland Maya, a proposal first made by Edmonson (1979). On the basis of direct historical analyses of multiple kinds of evidence, including hieroglyphic texts, iconography, and historic writings, she argues that Classic Maya political organization was based on the temporal *may*, a cycle of approximately 256 of our Gregorian years, with these 256-year cycles composed of thirteen *k'atuns*, the *k'atun* being a period of 20 *tuns*, or roughly 20 Gregorian years.

Classic period cities had the distinction, by analogy with Postclassic Mayapán, of seating the *may* and as such held the title *siyaj k'an*, "born of heaven" (Edmonson 1979, 1982, 1986). Large regional capitals such as Tikal, with "overlordship" (Martin and Grube 2000:21, 25–53) over smaller centers, were seats of the *may*. Smaller centers within the territories dominated by the *may* capitals were ritual seats of each of the thirteen constituent *k'atuns*. During the Postclassic and early Colonial periods, the *k'atun* seats not only were ritual centers but also controlled tribute rights, land titles, and appointments to public office within the realm for the 20-year duration. Communities within the territories of *may* and *k'atun* seats were integrated by their economic and political authority. They were also brought together by participation in the regional, ritually structured, and historico-mythological celebrations of the "turning" ("seating" or endings and beginnings) of the *may* and *k'atun* periods, as well as the several days of processions, speeches, feasting, drinking, and dancing that were carried out at the turning of every New Year. Because *may* and *k'atun* centers wielded considerable cosmological and political power, cities competed vigorously, sometimes violently, for the privilege of seating the *may* and *k'atun*, competition that Rice (2004) believes underlay much of Late Classic warfare.

The total of Maya sites participating in this cosmological system numbered in the hundreds (Morley et al. 1983:271). There are more than 75 centers with core monumental architecture reported in Petén alone (Rice and Puleston 1981:Figure 6.1, Table 6.1), and more than 275 known lowland sites possess sculpted inscriptions with calendrical dates (Wanyerka, personal communication 2001). Although each center or city shared similar architectural and constructional features, for reasons of history and location they varied in their physical size, composition, and layout, as well as in estimated populations.

Mayanists have long been aware of this variability, and efforts have been made to rank order centers on the basis of their numbers of carved monuments or *stelae* (Morley and Brainerd 1956:Table VII), by the distribution of "emblem glyphs" (Berlin 1958) referring to specific sites (Marcus 1973, 1974, 1976; cf. Mathews 1991), and by the number of discrete architectural plaza units (Adams and Jones 1981). More *stelae*, greater incidence of being named in inscriptions at other sites, or greater numbers of architectural complexes are all taken to imply greater ceremonial or civic importance, larger realms of control or influence, and larger supporting populations. These ranked hierarchies have contributed to debates over the nature of sovereignty and suzerainty in the Maya lowlands during the late Classic period, specifically over the number, size, and structure of Maya polities and the degree to which such polities were centralized or decentralized (e.g.,

Adams 1986; Culbert 1991; Demarest 1992; Fox et al. 1996; Houston 1993, 2000; Marcus 1976; Martin and Grube 2000; Mathews 1991).

Ranked hierarchies of sites on the basis of architecture or inscriptions also imply a potential continuum of center functions and relationships. Fox (1977) has suggested that variability in the aggregation and roles of cities is dependent on the degree to which economic, political, and religious institutions are specialized in the society in which sites are embedded and the degree to which society needs to centralize these activities in a central place or places. Fox (1977) has proposed a typology of cities that postulates a variety of urban forms and identifies a series of differentiated functions that define urban places and differentiate them. Regal-ritual cities, administrative cities, mercantile cities, colonial cities, and industrial cities are distinguished by their relative population size, socioeconomic heterogeneity, the primary locus of power (economics, politics, religion), and the historical contexts in which the city arises (for example, colonial and industrial cities appear only with the Industrial Revolution).

Sanders and Webster (1988) have recommended that the regal-ritual model can be of value to analyses of Maya centers, and Marcus (1983) believes the model is applicable to a number of highland Mesoamerican sites as well. The primary role of regal-ritual cities is ideological. All cities have ideological functions, but the regal-ritual type is distinctive in that its existence depends almost entirely on its ideological base. The centralizing process in such centers is political in nature, but control of ideology and ritual display is essential to governance. Whereas elites have political functions based in ideology and religious expression, regal-ritual centers have limited productive or distributive functions in an economic sense; there are specialists producing elite goods and rural part-time producers of goods living in the countryside. Fox (1977) links the regal-ritual city to decentralized political forms with relatively weak bases for authority and power. The permanent populations of ritual-regal centers tend to be small, the architectural forms found at the centers are often identical to those found in the more rural areas, and there is a lack of clear distinction between the urban population and those living in the peripheries.

Such a model fits scholarly perceptions of Maya central places, as shaped by competing needs for living space and food, and it is consistent with architectural, epigraphic, and iconographic evidence for elite rulers as royal dynasts whose rights to rule were based on lineal descent and whose intersite alliances were also kin based (see Christie 2003; Culbert 1991; Inomata and Houston 2001). Some scholars believe, however, that the regal-ritual model is inappropriate because it fails to acknowledge evidence for diversification of functions in Late Classic Maya centers, centralization of economic and political control in Maya elites, and the degree to which centers are capitals of city-states embedded in larger, stable political systems controlled by power hegemonic states (Chase and Chase 1996; Chase et al. 1990; Grube 2000; Martin and Grube 2000). In their view a more appropriate model would be Fox's administrative city, which is larger, heterogeneous, and bureaucratically structured and centralized, with primarily political function as the administrative capital of a state.

When identifying Classic period administrative centers in Mesoamerica, the primary comparative example is the site of Teotihuacan in the Teotihuacan Valley arm of the Valley of Mexico. At its peak, approximately AD 500, the epicenter of the site of Teotihuacan is thought to have had a population greater than 200,000 (Grube, ed. 2000:100–101; Sanders et al. 1979). The central part of the city was focused on a 2.5-km-long, north-south avenue called the Street of the Dead, lined with monumental architecture and elite residential compounds, surrounded on all sides by a rigidly gridded pattern of streets and residential compounds. As many as 2,000 of these compounds cover the approximately 22 sq km of the site, with each compound consisting of multiple courtyards surrounded by single-story, interconnected rooms that housed family and sleeping quarters, cooking and adjunct functions, storage, communal and family shrines, and industrial areas. The gridded pattern of the site, the size and density of its population, the presence of multiple workshops for manufacture of material items, and the presence of "barrios" of noncentral-Mexican residents (Zapotecs from Oaxaca, Maya from the lowlands, and so on) are offered as evidence of the urban nature of Teotihuacan, as well as the reasons why Maya sites are not considered urban (Sanders and Price 1968; Sanders and Webster 1988).

This chapter is not the place to explore the debate over the urban nature of Maya sites, except to say that proposed rank-order hierarchies of Late Classic centers suggest it is not an either-or argument and that extremes should not serve as models for characterizing all Maya sites. Site hierarchies can be based on economic, political, and/or religious functions, and only occasionally do the three converge in primate, urban central places (Marcus 1983:209). Given the range of projected population sizes of Maya centers, it is likely that those sites at the lower end of the continuum had limited bases for power and much more causal connection with ideological issues, whereas those at the upper end had broader political and socioeconomic purviews. It is unquestionable that processes of urbanization were contributing to the character of Late Classic Maya centers, but as Tourtellot (1993) has suggested, estimated population sizes and densities, settlement distributions, and the configuration of Maya centers imply that even the largest sites were not disembedded from local and regional subsistence concerns in a manner that might be expected of an urban administrative city with broad trade and tribute networks.

Closing

In 1990 Robert Santley (1990:325) wrote a closing chapter in a volume on prehispanic Maya population history (Culbert and Rice 1990) in which he took archaeologists to task for concentrating on descriptions of the distributions, sizes, and densities of populations rather than on relationships between demographic characteristics and political and socioeconomic structure, and subsistence management. Richard Paine (1997), an archaeologist and paleodemographer who works in the Maya region, picked up on Santley's admonishment in his introductory remarks for the edited proceedings of a 1994 conference on archaeological demography. He (Paine, ed. 1997:7, 12) noted that the exploration of such relationships first requires unification of settlement and osteological approaches in a "thicker" demography, one that can move beyond population numbers to investigation of demographic processes and structures. Only then can prehistoric demography inform and be informed by studies of environment, subsistence, and political and socioeconomic organization.

Both perspectives have merit, but a long history of concern for the character and dynamics of Maya populations gives them validity. As I hope this chapter confirms, efforts to project population sizes and densities for sites and regions have increasingly enlightened discussions of Maya subsistence and organizational issues. The stage is set for the kinds of theory building and understanding that Santley and Paine call for.

14

Mortality through Time in an Impoverished Residence of the Precolumbian City of Teotihuacan

A Paleodemographic View

Rebecca Storey

One of the reasons that Teotihuacan, located in the Basin of Mexico near present-day Mexico City, is such an important Precolumbian site is because it is the earliest in date in the New World to exemplify V. Gordon Childe's "urban revolution" (1950), a significant milestone of cultural evolution and human history. One of the dramatic impacts of urbanization on humans is a different lifestyle resulting directly from the higher densities and absolute numbers of people present in one settlement. It also creates an important dynamic between a city and the rural hinterland that supports it and creates most generally a contrast between conditions of life in the city versus that in rural settlements. The effect of the increase in density and numbers in the urban environment is to place humans in contact with a wide diversity of individuals having different economic specializations and levels of wealth, different ethnic backgrounds, and different social standings. These aspects of the "urban revolution" are all present at Teotihuacan (for the evidence, see Berlo 1992; Cowgill 1997; Millon 1981). In addition, the inability to know everyone in the settlement intimately, as is possible in village-based societies, makes urban living and interaction more impersonal in ways that must be adapted to by individuals and families. Studying the adaptation of humans to their social and physical environments is one of the basic problems of anthropology; Teotihuacan provides the opportunity to study it in an early urban society in the New World.

Teotihuacan is also the type of urban settlement called the preindustrial city, that is, an urban society dependent primarily on human and animal sources of energy (Sjoberg 1960) rather than on the inanimate sources and complex tools of more recent industrial societies. Before the eighteenth century in Europe, there were only preindustrial cities, and they have been the most common urban environments for humans. They obviously vary by geography; culture; and history of settlement, florescence, and decline. Cross-culturally, preindustrial cities can have several political and economic functions (Fox 1977; Sanders and Webster 1988). Therefore, they cannot be considered a uniform type of community.

Another aspect of urbanization that appears to have cross-cultural similarities is the complex relationship between a city and its sustaining area or hinterland (see van der Woude et al. 1990a). Cities typically are made up of nonagricultural specialists and laborers and thus must import food, fuel, and building supplies, mostly from nearby rural areas. Also, cities often dominate their hinterland socially and politically, but especially with preindustrial technologies, are quite dependent on them for necessities of life and migrants. Fortunately, the detailed Basin of Mexico settlement surveys make the study of the demography of the rural/urban continuum possible for Teotihuacan, especially given the high-quality rural survey data that can be compared to our urban population data for the city (Gorenflo, this volume). Teotihuacan is distinctive because, as Gorenflo discusses, the local population was definitely highly concentrated (up to 75 percent) in the urban area. Thus, Teotihuacan has always been thought to have contained significant numbers of farmers as residents, and because this is not the most convenient arrangement for agricultural production, this concentration has been thought to be somewhat coercive (see Millon 1981). As to how much territory was under Teotihuacan's direct control, there is debate, but probably it did not extend too far beyond the Basin of Mexico, perhaps over one-half million to one million people (Cowgill 2001). The transportation system based largely on human portage would have limited both the area of provisioning and the people who could be controlled. The city's prestige was far-flung in Mesoamerica and certainly exceeded its political control. However, the impression given by the settlement studies is how dominant Teotihuacan was in its hinterland.

Nevertheless, we can ask what kinds of similarities are present in most preindustrial cities, and, furthermore, what are the demographic and health patterns and risks to which the people must adjust among those similarities? Health and demography are informative about human adaptation, so similarities in health patterns and risks would indicate that urban living presented similar challenges everywhere. Teotihuacan provides a good cross-cultural test for preindustrial cities because of its evolution in a very different culture and environment than preindustrial cities in the Old World. The similarities in health and demography between Teotihuacan and preindustrial cities in Europe have been detailed elsewhere but will also be summarized here (see Storey 1992b). The specific aspect of the problem to be investigated here is whether there was any change through time in the health and demographic patterns and whether these might be informative as to why Teotihuacan ceased to be a dynamic preindustrial city by the seventh century AD.

Allied to the question of changes through time is the role played by migration (mentioned above as an important aspect of rural/urban relations) in the demography of a city such as Teotihuacan. Despite Lo Cascio's (this volume) challenge, to be further discussed below, the consensus among historical demographers remains that preindustrial cities were unable to maintain their numbers because of excess mortality over fertility, making them dependent on continuous migration to thrive (de Vries 1984). The reason that mortality is elevated in premodern cities is because of the effects of density and preindustrial public sanitation technology on health, which are well known (see Cohen 1989; Wrigley et al. 1997:201–206). Dense populations, as in urban situations, are susceptible to high disease burdens because of easy and continuous transmission of communicable infections. They are also more prone to mortality crises from periodic epidemics, whereas more rural areas are often untouched (Wrigley et al. 1997). Because they are dependent on rural hinterlands or long-distance transport for most food, they are also susceptible to malnutrition caused by vagaries of rural food production and delivery (McNeill 1976) and the economic cost of purchasing sufficient food. The buildup of garbage and its contamination of water supplies, which occur in preindustrial settlements because of a lack of sufficient controllable energy sources and the technology to efficiently remove garbage and clean the water, only perpetuate the bad health situation. All these situations lead to higher morbidity, which becomes evident in higher mortality, especially in vulnerable ages. However, it is possible that differences in the diseases that are present in the Old World versus the New World would make the situation less detrimental in the long run to a New World preindustrial city such as Teotihuacan.

The introduction of many infectious diseases to the natives of the New World at European contact starting in 1492 has been well documented (for example, Cook 1998). There have also been investigations into the kinds of diseases that would have been present in the Precolumbian New World. In a recent synthesis of this subject, Merbs (1992) agrees with previous research that the main difference is not a lack of infectious diseases, but a lack in the New World of the crowd type of diseases, such as smallpox, measles, malaria, and scarlet fever. These require very large, dense populations to survive, and they evolved after the ancestors of the Amerindians had left the Old World. Although the Precolumbian New World was certainly not devoid of infectious diseases, and people had health problems (see Verano and Ubelaker 1992), the number of diseases present seems to be fewer than in the Old World. A recent inventory of Precolumbian New World infectious diseases includes the staphylococci and streptococci bacteria, intestinal parasites, treponematoses, tuberculosis, some forms of leishmaniasis and trypanosomiasis, some fungal infections, some rickettsial infections, legionellosis, and hydatid disease (Merbs 1992). These diseases are notable in that they are often endemic in their appearance, that is, always present in low frequencies in a population, rather than severely epidemic like the crowd-type diseases of the Old World, although Old World cities surely possessed forms of these endemic diseases as well. Many of the enumerated syndromes, such as bacterial infections, treponematoses, and intestinal parasites, cause morbidity and potential chronic illness, but not necessarily high mortality. Although it is expected that a dense settlement such as Teotihuacan would experience a high disease burden of the infectious diseases present, is it likely that living conditions and the ability of people to adapt to that urban environment would fluctuate or deteriorate over time without the complications of crowd-type infections? Would not the disease burden and its effect on urban residents remain about the same? If conditions seem to deteriorate, what might have changed the ability of the residents to adapt? What would have been the effect on migration?

Although the health and demographic patterns of European preindustrial cities are studied primarily through written records, Teotihuacan lacks comparable sources of data and can be studied only through archaeological excavation and skeletal analysis. Although comparing European historical demographic analyses to Teotihuacan archaeological and skeletal analyses is not easy, it is nevertheless possible to gain similar insight into the Teotihuacan urban lifestyle from archaeology and human osteology. Not enough excavation has yet been carried out within the ancient city to provide a sufficient sample to answer all questions, but data from one extensively excavated compound that was occupied for perhaps 300–350 years are available to investigate chronological trends in demography and health at Teotihuacan.

The Tlajinga 33 Case Study

Teotihuacan was a city of around 125,000 to 200,000 that dominated the Basin of Mexico between circa 150 BC and AD 650 (Cowgill 1997; Millon 1981). It was one of the largest cities in the world during its heyday, and this population growth was quick; by 150 AD, it had most of its population and that of the Basin of Mexico within the urban area (see Cowgill 1997; Gorenflo, this volume). It grew to its maximum extent by around 300 AD and then remained stable, only declining slightly soon before the center was burned and the settlement mostly abandoned. By 300 AD, residents mostly lived in apartment compounds, large structures that housed multiple families. The city was also partly organized into neighborhoods or barrios, defined by clusters of apartment compounds spatially segregated from other parts of the city and often sharing similar craft specialties. The residents of a compound often seemed to cooperate in a craft specialty, and although probably containing a core of kin, the compounds were not occupied by simply one lineage (Storey 1992b). Individuals and families probably joined the compound under a variety of situations, including by marriage.

The excavation of one apartment compound, Tlajinga 33, yielded a skeletal population of 206 individuals. The compound was on the southern edge of the city and was definitely a part of the Tlajinga barrio of ceramic specialists during the Xolalpan phase, one of the best-defined neighborhoods in the city. The occupation of the compound dates from the Early Tlamimilolpa to Early Metepec phases (circa AD 250 to 550). By its peripheral location, use of earthen floors, adobe wall construction, less-massive outer walls, and so on, the Tlajinga 33 compound falls into the lower status of compounds so far excavated (see Millon

1976). The residents of Tlajinga 33 were craft specialists, first in lapidary of various expensive and inexpensive materials (Widmer 1991) and then adding to the lapidary specialization in later periods with the ceramic manufacture of San Martin Orange craters and amphoras (Sheehy 1992). Although the ceramic manufacture was perhaps part-time and on an as-needed basis (Sheehy 1992), the compound residents were not otherwise much involved in agriculture, as no evidence of agricultural implements was recovered during excavation. It is possible that the Tlajinga residents supported themselves economically through a combination of craft activities and hiring themselves out as laborers. Their overall status within the city in any case would have been as lower-class artisans and laborers.

A major objective of the Tlajinga 33 excavations was to recover a representative skeletal population for demographic and health analysis. Thus, burials and any human bone, whatever its context, were actively sought, and all burials were fine-screened to assure recovery of as many skeletal parts as possible. Although many of the skeletons were fragmentary, the excavation strategies did yield a large proportion of the infant and child skeletons that are often underrepresented in many archaeologically derived skeletal samples. Thus, equal proportions of adult males and females and all age groups were present for analysis (for further information on sexing and aging the skeletons, see Storey 1992b).

Because of the long period of occupation of the Tlajinga 33 compound, chronological changes can be studied, although the sample sizes available are small. The Tlajinga 33 skeletal sample can be divided into an Early Period—the Tlamimilolpa phase—and a Late Period—Xolalpan through Early Metepec phases—a division roughly corresponding to the two different craft specialties present in the compound. The Early Period corresponds to the purely lapidary specialization and the Late Period to ceramic production of San Martin Orange wares with lapidary craftwork still present. This division breaks the skeletal sample into two similar sizes and is different from previously published divisions (for example, Storey 1992b). It was accomplished by chronological reassignment of some deposits within the compound. The new dating and shorter occupation span suggested by the recent revision of the Teotihuacan chronology (see Cowgill 1997) also changes some of the interpretation of the demographic information available from the skeletal ages at death. The Tlajinga 33 compound should be representative of the majority of compounds of the city because of its lower-class status all through its history. It is the poorer sectors of preindustrial cities that tend to suffer the most from the characteristics of urban health and demography.

Poverty and Demography in European Preindustrial Cities

Preindustrial cities studied in Europe have demographic characteristics that apparently make sense in terms of the living conditions and health hazards present in dense populations lacking an extensive public health technology. The evidence has been that such European cities lost population internally, because deaths outnumbered births, and were dependent on migration from rural areas, where mortality was less, for maintaining population numbers and allowing the urban population to grow. The pattern is known as the "Law of Natural Urban Decrease" (de Vries 1984:179–198). Cities, as demographic sinks (Wrigley 1967), were then highly dependent on their rural hinterland for both resources and people and sometimes were powerful enough to take all or most of the natural increase of population of their rural area (de Vries 1984). Lo Cascio (this volume) has criticized this view of cities in the past in general being demographic sinks caused by unsanitary living conditions. He particularly quotes the views of Sharlin (1978) and van der Woude (1982). Sharlin's interesting hypothesis is that excess urban mortality was due to the mortality of immigrants, who would be in more precarious living conditions and less likely to marry, whereas stable residents would have had no trouble replacing themselves. Thus, the immigrants would only add to the deaths, but little to births. With regard to the other criticism, van der Woude (1982) determines that birth rates were likely to vary in urban situation and that at times cities would grow naturally, so cities are not necessarily sinks. That is, Lo Cascio argues, as if the sink model is built only on documentary evidence of baptism and burial registration without regard to the origin of the individuals. On the contrary, because one of the complicating factors in doing historical urban demography is the need to control for immigrants in demographic records, Finlay (1981a, 1981b) studied only children who had been born and died in a parish, because adults often tend to move and cannot be easily traced. It is on the mortality of these children that Finlay based his urban shortfall, the evidence that births were not enough to replace the population. In addition, de Vries (1984:182–197) provided documentary evidence to disprove Sharlin's hypothesis and counter van der Woude's argument. In fact, de Vries's evidence actually ends up revealing how important migration was to marriage opportunities in these cities, as revealed by the numbers of natives marrying nonnatives. The implication is that far from adding just to mortality, fertility in these cities would have been even lower without immigration.

Lo Cascio further argues that ancient Rome might have been able to maintain itself through natural increase and that it was not a particularly unsanitary place. His standard for comparison is early modern Rome, plus some information on the size of ancient Rome and its effect on the overall Italian population. As Wrigley (1990:104) points out, there is actually no contradiction between urban natural decrease and overall increase of population of a country, suggesting that the growth of London was responsible for the general population growth of England, in spite of the negative effect of the urban situation itself. Thus, Rome could have caused stagnation or growth in rural populations without necessarily changing anything about urban demography at the time. It would have all depended on the amount of migration to the city and the productivity of the rural sectors. Wrigley (1990:103; also Wrigley et al. 1997) also finds that data support the overall model that the greater the population density, the higher the mortality, making cities more unhealthy than rural areas, and that the greater the impact on mortality, the larger the city. Because disease probably has the greatest impact on urban mortality (Wrigley et al. 1997 for England), the availability of water, a sanitation system, or the presence of a grain dole do not in themselves indicate that water contamination and circulation of diseases were not present and harmful to urban dwellers.

Actually, historical demographic analysis has revealed that most of the mortality in urban areas fell on those in the poorer sectors and was especially dominated by the deaths of infants and young children. In preindustrial Geneva, differences in mortality by social class, as defined by occupation in the records, were marked, with the upper class having 35.9 years at birth, but the working class only 18.3 years (Perrenoud 1975:236). This is a gap of 16 years. In preindustrial London from 1580 to 1650, Finlay (1981b:Chapter 5) compared survivorships and life expectancies at birth for children under the age of 15 in two wealthy and two poor parishes. At least 60 percent of the children survived to age 15 in the wealthy parishes, with life expectancies of 30 to 36 years, whereas half or less survived in the poorer parishes, with life expectancies of 21 to 26 years. The gap between the worst parish and the best is fifteen years' life expectancy, very similar to the Geneva data. Work in eighteenth-century Amsterdam also provides evidence that in preindustrial cities, it was infant and child mortality that was high, not that of adults (de Vries 1984), and that these losses among the poor are what results in the net loss of population (Finlay 1981a). Two hundred years ago in his influential *Essay on the Principle of Population* (1970[1798]:93), Malthus noticed this feature of preindustrial cities, that is, that the burden of mortality was on the children of the poor.

The most common migrants to the preindustrial cities of Britain were lower-class unskilled young adults of both sexes (Clark and Souden 1987), who would be the exact labor replacements for the children lost to mortality. Thus, the dynamics of mortality and migration in the demography of these cities work to maintain the numbers and pool of labor represented by lower-class individuals, in spite of the costs in infant and child mortality. This allows cities to overcome in a real sense the drawbacks of urban health and lifestyle present in a preindustrial technology. In Europe, people would probably be attracted to the city in hopes of economic opportunity (Clark and Souden 1987), often only to have themselves and their children become the casualties of poverty in an urban environment. However, it becomes easy to understand how an urban center might be endangered if the mortality-migration cycle did not at least come out equal.

Chronological Trends at Tlajinga 33

The first problem to be faced in comparing Teotihuacan to the historical information from Europe is that the most salient demographic data available is the age distribution of deaths derived from the skeletons. Paleodemography, the aspect of anthropological demography that deals with age distributions of deaths derived from skeletal samples, is undergoing a revolution in interpreting its data, and there is still much discussion over the proper methods and analyses to use. There are basically two problems: one, estimating as accurately as possible the age at death of a skeleton, and two, how a skeletal sample reflects the living population from which it was derived. Skeletal estimations of age are bedeviled by problems of appropriate reference samples and a bias in current methods for adults, which overestimates the ages of young adults but tends to often severely underestimate the age of older individuals (see, for example, Aykroyd et al. 1999 and Saunders et al. 1992). Similar problems haunt at least some epigraphically derived death distributions (especially those for Rome; see Storey and Paine 2002). Currently there is work on better methods for age estimation, but the Tlajinga age estimations were derived using the traditional method of multiple indicators. Individuals were first seriated from youngest to oldest for an age indicator (see Lovejoy et al. 1985), and then age estimation for the indicator for each individual was made. Final age determinations were made by weighing various indicators, but some individuals could only be aged by one of these indicators. Although individuals were assigned to a general five-year range (and could be assigned to finer ages as infants and children), it must be accepted that there are errors in individual estimates, although estimates on younger individuals are likely to be more accurate (Aykroyd et al. 1999; Buikstra and Konigsberg 1985). For Tlajinga, I did all the age estimations, so any bias should be similar for the whole sample, and all skeletons were aged as one group, before any chronological distinctions were made. Thus, it was not known beforehand which individuals would be part of the Early or Late samples.

The distributions of ages at death are different for both periods (Table 14-1). The sexes are combined here, as is common practice in skeletal populations, because there is no statistical difference (tested by chi square) in the numbers of males versus females. Although both samples show uneven jumps in proportions of deaths from one age class to another, common in small samples, the main difference is that the Late Period is dominated by deaths from infancy to young adults, whereas the Early Period has more older adults over age 40. This difference is captured in a drop of 8 years in the mean age of death from 24 years in the Early Period to 16 years in the Late Period.

The difference between the two distributions is illustrated when the age distributions are converted to Kaplan-Meier survival curves. Kaplan-Meier curves are generally now favored by demographers and epidemiologists over actuarial methods of calculating survivorship and hazard (see Parmar and Machin 1995). For skeletons, the drawbacks of Kaplan-Meier are that the age estimates are not that exact and thus may compound errors in the calculation. A comparison of the results on Tlajinga 33 ages (calculated using SPSS for Windows) using actuarial life table methods and the Kaplan-Meier indicated virtually no difference in the

Table 14-1. Age Distributions of Death for the Tlajinga
Chronological Samples

Age Class	Early Period		Late Period	
	N	%	N	%
Infant	27	24.3	36	37.9
1–4	14	12.6	4	4.2
5–9	3	2.7	8	8.4
10–14	4	3.6	6	6.3
15–19	3	2.7	6	6.3
20–24	4	3.6	12	12.6
25–29	7	6.3	1	1.1
30–34	3	2.7	4	4.2
35–39	7	6.3	5	5.3
40–44	17	15.3	5	5.3
45–49	8	7.2	3	3.2
50–54	9	8.1	2	2.1
55 +	5	4.5	3	3.2
TOTAL	111		95	

results. Thus, Kaplan-Meier was retained, because it provides powerful statistical tests and calculation of the hazard throughout the lifespan. The Kaplan-Meier cumulative survival curves are given in Figure 14-1, where it is evident that the Late Period has proportionately fewer survivors at each estimated age than the Early Period.

The cumulative hazard function revealed that the hazard of mortality is higher for the Late Period at all ages until the oldest and that the differences are fairly dramatic for young and middle-aged adults. The difference between the two survival curves is statistically significant, using the Mantel-Cox (log-rank) test (p = 0.0035). This test is preferred for comparing two survival curves (Parmar and Machin 1995).

The differences, although statistically significant, could be due to chance sampling or aging errors, although it is in the proportion of younger individuals, where techniques are more accurate, where the two samples differ. Given the error in skeletal age estimation, Kaplan-Meier may be useful only when the differences are of this magnitude and type. Thus, I believe this difference is real, and the Late Period is a younger sample. The trend seems very suggestive of a deteriorating quality of life through time, especially considering that mortality among the young is where urban life is most likely to take its toll, because of the susceptibility of infants and children to disease and malnutrition (Goodman and Armelagos

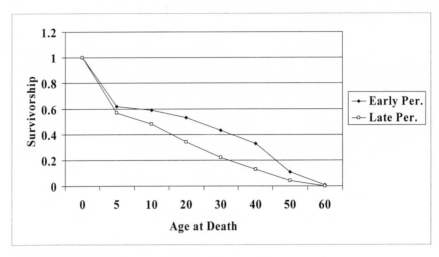

Figure 14-1. Kaplan-Meier survival curves of the estimated ages at death compared for the two chronological periods at Tlajinga 33.

1988). What is the implication of a difference in the pattern of deaths early versus late in the history of the compound?

However, just comparing the age distributions of deaths does not necessarily mean that different demographic situations are truly present. The other problem in paleodemography is interpreting how skeletons reflect their living population, because they are really only a sample of the deaths. Only in a stationary population, that is, a population neither growing nor declining, will the age distribution of deaths reflect the probabilities of dying during that age class (Sattenspiel and Harpending 1983). Otherwise, depending on the demographic patterns of the society from which the skeletal sample derives, the age distribution of deaths reflects strongly past fertility with generally smaller mortality effects (Johansson and Horowitz 1986). Thus, two age distributions can differ for a variety of reasons that do not necessarily reflect a worsening of health conditions and mortality, because two populations with similar mortality rates but very different fertility rates will have quite different age distributions of deaths (Johansson and Horowitz 1986). Stable population methods, which have been useful in anthropological demography, although they are now being superseded (Weiss 1989), can provide some simple models to investigate what might be the demographic differences between the two chronological periods at Tlajinga.

First, comparisons of the proportions of deaths at various ages can be compared with those from anthropological reference populations calculated using stable population methods. A stable population is one modeled such that mortality and fertility rates have been constant for 50 to 100 years and thus a stable age distribution is produced. The value of stable population theory is that if some demographic values are known, others can be calculated (Weiss 1989). The shape of the age distribution of deaths for a population is affected by its state of economic development, and there are characteristic shapes to this distribution (Waldron 1994). In premodern and current underdeveloped populations, mortality is high during infancy and childhood, low during adolescence and for young adults, and rises with increasing age. The result is a U-shaped distribution, because the great majority of deaths occur at both extremes of the ages (Waldron 1994). As populations develop, infant and childhood mortality drops dramatically, and almost all mortality is at the older ages, as it is in the United States and other developed nations. This produces a very skewed distribution. Anthropological populations, small and rather isolated groups that have only recently been affected by wider global economic and social processes, and skeletal populations from the past both share problems of accurate age estimation of individuals who do not know their chronological age. However, all should reveal a U-shaped age distribution at death. With the use of a method pioneered by Milner et al. (1989), age distributions of death can be calculated for anthropological and skeletal samples to look for the expected U-shaped distribution for premodern populations.

Milner et al. (1989) contrast the U-shaped distributions for two reference anthropological populations, the !Kung San, South African foragers, who are known to have low fertility as a population, and the Yanomamö, South American horticultural/foragers, a high-fertility population. The relative fertility of populations can be estimated by the ratio of deaths under age 5 to those over 45 years. High-fertility populations have around twice as many deaths in individuals under age 5, whereas low-fertility populations have equal or slightly more deaths over age 45. Both Tlajinga distributions can be compared to the Oneota, a North American skeletal population considered to closely resemble the Yanomamö case (Milner et al. 1989), and to a Yanomamö sample (Early and Peters 1990) on the basis of demographic information from 28 years of postcontact registration by missionaries. The information is considered by the authors to be the most accurate available for a population of this type, and the 130 deaths have been partitioned into the same age categories as the others (my calculations based on Early and Peters 1990:Chapter 7). This Yanomamö sample is from a high-fertility population, about eight births per female, and the group is definitely growing in size (Early and Peters 1990:Chapter 10).

For both Tlajinga age distributions, the proportion of deaths under age 5 is greater than over 45 years, indicating a high-fertility population, although the Late Period has the larger difference (5.0). The ratio of the Early Period (1.85 for the deaths under 5 to over 45) is very close to that of the Yanomamö (1.9) and the Oneota (1.8). This is not a surprising result, given that these skeletons were derived from a sedentary, natural fertility population dependent on intensive agriculture. It would be more notable if Teotihuacan residents were not part of a high-fertility population. What is more important is to determine whether there is any more demographic information present in the age distribution of deaths.

The underlying pattern in the Yanomamö reference population is that deaths are "heaped" at the youngest and oldest age categories, with proportionately few individuals dying between ages 5 and 44, the expected U-shaped distribution. Neither of the Tlajinga distributions has this pattern, although the Tlajinga Early Period distribution is the one that comes closest. The Early Period has low proportions of deaths between ages 5 and 34, but the proportions of adult deaths are almost equal at 35–45 and 45-plus. This may indicate that adult mortality is higher during middle age, perhaps as a result of the stresses of preindustrial urban life or the result simply of sampling, skeletal aging error, or a combination of all possibilities. Skeletal aging techniques for adults have often been criticized for underaging older individuals (see Aykroyd et al. 1999; Buikstra and Konigsberg 1985), so it is possible that some proportion of the individuals 35–45 have erroneous age estimations. However, recent experiments comparing skeletal aging techniques to individuals of known age reveal a somewhat complicated scenario for these ages. The age indicator combinations used at Spitalfields (Molleson et al. 1993:Figure 12.4) tended to overage this decade, whereas the age indicators singly and in combination at St. Thomas Belleville (Saunders et al. 1992:Table 2) overage those under 40 and underage those over 40. Thus, as I warned before, there will be errors in age estimation for the Tlajinga sample, but with the age indicators used here it is difficult to determine in what direction and by how much. It is just as likely that some 35–39 individuals would be in truth younger as that others should be older. Research is already under way on methods to improve age estimation (e.g., Bocquet-Appel and Masset 1996) and to provide better estimates of the magnitude of error (e.g., Aykroyd et al. 1999). In the future, different and more statistically precise age distributions of deaths for Tlajinga than those presently employed may be possible.

However, the Early Period distribution can be adjusted to bring it more in line with a U-shaped pattern by simply lowering the proportion of deaths 35–45, which is 0.22, to 0.11 (the same proportion as in ages 25–35 for the Yanomamö sample) and placing the difference in the 45-plus category. With a proportion of 0.11, the resulting age distribution is not significantly different from the original distribution (Kolmogorov-Smirnoff two-sample test, p > 0.05). Thus, it is possible that the Early Period adult deaths really do not diverge from a U-shaped pattern; skeletal aging errors just make it appear to do so. This adjusted age distribution, however, is distinctive from those populations because the 45-plus category proportion would be 0.31, close to the 0–5 category proportion of 0.37. The Early Period would then not be a high-fertility population but closer to a moderate to low one (Milner et al. 1989). In fact, the Early Period adjusted distribution is not significantly different from the !Kung reference population (Kolmogorov-

Smirnoff goodness-of-fit test, p > 0.05). The overall size of Teotihuacan seems to be fairly stationary during the Tlamimilolpa phase (Cowgill 1997; Millon 1988), so perhaps the moderate fertility indicated by the adjusted Early Period distribution, coupled with a moderate mortality, would be a reasonable model for the urban population at this time. However, as will be discussed later, paleopathological evidence could support a younger peak in adult mortality, as is present in the unadjusted Early Period distribution. The unadjusted Early Period age distribution of deaths is significantly different from the !Kung reference populations (Kolmogorov-Smirnoff goodness-of-fit test, p < 0.05), but not from the Yanomamö. This probably indicates that the Tlajinga Early Period is best treated as a high-fertility population and that the stationary population of the city of Teotihuacan is one caused by high fertility but also an offsetting high mortality. Even though the Tlajinga age distribution can obviously be brought more into line with other populations through fairly simple modeling, it does not mean that this provides a truer result.

As always with an urban population, the possibility that migrants to Tlajinga might be affecting the age distribution should be considered. If Teotihuacan's density is increasing mortality, as postulated for preindustrial cities, then migration might have been the only way the city maintained its size for much of its history (Storey 1992b). To be useful, any Early Period migrants should have contributed to fertility by marrying and surviving as adults for some years in the compound. Determining who is a migrant to Teotihuacan can be done from skeletons by traits of the mortuary treatment, because migrants often retain distinctive patterns from their homelands. Teotihuacan was host to several enclaves of foreigners (see Cowgill 1997; Spence 1992), which can be identified on mortuary grounds, as well as in other archaeological artifacts. However, Tlajinga 33 appears to be a Teotihuacan compound in its archaeological patterns and general mortuary treatments, and the evidence is that it always remained so. Thus, migrants probably entered as individuals and a few perhaps as families. The way to test for this is to use bone chemical analysis, which is being applied to the Tlajinga skeletons, to judge whether individuals might have moved during their lifetime (White et al. 2004). For example, oxygen isotopes reflect water supplies, and if these are different in teeth formed during childhood from the adult bone, then the individual moved some years before death. This type of information will allow refinement of the suppositions presented here. However, as Dumond (personal communication 2001) has calculated, postulating migrants to Tlajinga in the Early Period does remove some, although not all, of the anomalies of the age distribution of deaths. It also makes it most likely that, without migrants, the Early Period compound was a declining population.

The Late Period distribution, on the other hand, is quite different from that of any reference population because of its high number of deaths under age 25 and few older adults. It is a distribution that is definitely not characterized by concentrations of deaths under age 5 and over age 45. In this case, skeletal aging errors are not greatly distorting the distribution. Under age 25, skeletal aging methods have good accuracy (Buikstra and Konigsberg 1985), and if there are errors, it is likely that some individuals 25–35 are actually younger (see Molleson et al. 1993). The very young age distribution of deaths is a real pattern. Because of the strong effect of fertility on an age distribution of death, the impression is that the Late Period distribution would be characteristic of a high-fertility, high growth rate population, because the ratio of deaths under age 5 to those over 45 years is about 5. One way to measure mortality in paleodemography is to combine the mean age of death with estimates of rate of growth or decline independently determined from archaeological data (Johansson and Horowitz 1986). The archaeological data on the size and history of Teotihuacan, determined by the very methodical Teotihuacan Mapping Project (see, for example, Millon et al. 1973), most definitely does not support an interpretation of a rapidly growing population during the Late Period. In fact, Teotihuacan seems to have reached its maximum size early in its history and maintained it for several centuries until it began to decline late in its history, although the extent of decline during the last century is not clear (Cowgill 1997). Thus, during the Late Period at Tlajinga 33, which was probably about a century in length, Teotihuacan's population was most probably declining.

Figure 14-2 compares the Late Period age distribution of deaths with those of two models from the Coale and Demeny (1983) West family of model life tables for human populations. The Coale and Demeny tables are divided into four families, each with a slightly different mortality pattern, with 25 levels of mortality calculated separately for males and females. The West family is thought to be the most generally applicable to the ancient world, and Level 1 has the highest mortality. An advantage of the Coale and Demeny model life tables is that they have calculated the age distribution of deaths that would result from various rates of growth and decline compatible with stable-population theory. Thus, in Figure 14-2, the age distributions of death are from the model tables with the highest mortality and the highest rate of decline, −1 percent per year, providing the "worst-case" scenario available from the Coale and Demeny series. The differences of the Late Period from the comparison populations are dramatic, with more deaths from ages 5 to 25 and too few at 45-plus. Therefore, even with an archaeologically derived estimate of the population growth or decline, the Late Period does not resemble the stable population that would result from the worst-case scenario. Nor does the Late Period resemble the death distribution from a high growth rate population, the Male West Level 10 at greater than 3 percent per year (Figure 14-2), which has a mean age at death similar to the Late Period. The Late Period distribution is significantly different from both models presented (Kolmogorov-Smirnoff goodness-of-fit test, $p < 0.05$). The conclusion is that probably the Late Period age distribution is not from a stable population and most probably

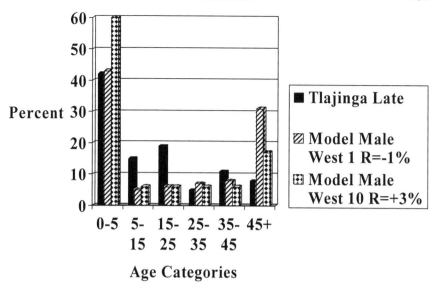

Figure 14-2. Age distribution of deaths of the Tlajinga Late Period compared to two model populations (models from Coale and Demeny 1983).

is one where mortality is causing more individuals to die younger than they should.

Again, migration might be affecting this age distribution of deaths. The bulk of deaths under age 25 might reflect the increasing presence of migrants who die, along with their recently born children, fairly soon after their arrival in the city and the compound. Dumond's (personal communication 2001) suggestion is that this pattern might also reflect nothing more than a change in burial location for older individuals. Because the whole compound was not excavated, this is always a possibility and certainly cannot be disproved here. However, similar numbers of burials were recovered for both periods, and both public and private space was excavated in similar proportions, which should yield a reasonably equal chance of recovering the range of individuals buried in the excavated portion for both periods. The difference with the Early Period is that during that time, there are perhaps not as many migrants, and most of them are surviving for a decade or more after arrival. Here, in the Late Period, migration rates are up (as was suggested in Storey 1992b), but the urban environment has become so unhealthy that children, ever vulnerable in an urban situation, and newly arrived migrants make up the bulk of deaths. The implication is that the compound had trouble maintaining numbers and was actually declining throughout the Late Period. This decline could be offset by migrants, but for Tlajinga 33, the reversals were only temporary. The very unstable pattern of deaths for a period of a century or slightly more is the best indicator of the demographic crisis that ultimately led to the abandonment of the compound. Is there evidence for deteriorating health through time?

Paleopathological information on stresses present during life, especially on stress severe enough to interfere with the normal growth processes of childhood, can be informative about health conditions and lifestyle in the past (see Storey 1992a, 1992b). The relationship between such paleopathological markers of stress on skeletons and their contribution to mortality is complex. For example, dental enamel hypoplasias, one of the indicators of childhood stress, can only be seen on those who survived the stress episode, so it is not at all certain that more individuals with hypoplasias indicate worse health. It may be that with better health conditions in the society, it is just that more individuals survive the stress episode to have hypoplasias on their teeth (Wood et al. 1992). There is evidence that the mean age of death of individuals with one occurrence of enamel hypoplasia is 4 years less than those with none and 10 years less in those with two or more occurrences (Goodman and Armelagos 1988) in the Dickson Mounds skeletal population from North America. It is possible that individuals with more hypoplasias are then more "hardy" and would then have a higher fertility, which would lower the mean age at death, than those who did not survive such severe stress as children (Wood et al. 1992). However, it is just as likely that the mean age at death is lower because the individuals died at younger ages because of greater "frailty" from accumulated stresses during life. There is plausible biological evidence for "immunological damage" resulting from severe childhood stress (Goodman and Armelagos 1988). Similarly, although specific mechanisms have not yet been determined, there is much empirical evidence that links poor health conditions in childhood with increased risks of mortality during adulthood (Elo and Preston 1992), specifically causing adults to die younger than they might otherwise have.

Wood et al. (1992) raise very important points about the difficulty of interpreting skeletal lesions of stress as simple reflections of poor health conditions. However, the cultural context at Tlajinga 33 does seem to make some interpretations more plausible. The Late Period age distribution of deaths does not appear to be one from a stable population. Various stresses that are present on bone are ubiquitous at Tlajinga 33, including dental enamel hypoplasias (Storey 1992b). It is possible that severe stress during childhood sufficient to impact growth shortens the lifespan of affected individuals, causing them to die younger during adulthood than if they had not been affected as children. Thus, the age distribution of deaths during the Late Period could be indicating an increasingly stressful health environment in the city and high mortality of infants, children, and young adults as a result. Given that the preindustrial urban population densities of the Old World were associated with high infant and juvenile mortality, especially among the poorer sectors of society, it is likely that similar processes of malnutrition and disease burdens were having the same effect at Teotihuacan for residents of poorer apartment compounds such as Tlajinga 33. Tlajinga 33 certainly does not represent a high-growth population, but it could be one with such exceptional mortality that the population is destabilized. A population in demographic collapse is not a stable population; the Late Period age distribution of deaths could come from a population losing young individuals far more quickly than could be replaced through either fertility or migration. In addition, even with the lack of crowd-type infections, the situation seems to have gotten worse through time, because the Early Period appears to be less divergent from a stable population. Research investigating the possibility that health indicators are more prevalent during the Late Period at Tlajinga is presently under way.

The Tlajinga 33 demographic situation serves to highlight the probable similarities of Teotihuacan to other preindustrial cities. Teotihuacan had a complex relationship with its rural sustaining area, including a probable dependence for some foodstuffs and for migrants. This is a problem because although there is archaeological evidence of migrants from various areas of Mesoamerica (for example, Spence 1992), there is no good archaeological estimate presently available of how much the population of Teotihuacan at any one period would have been composed of recent migrants to the city. Because migrants are overwhelmingly young adults in age historically and in contemporary populations (see Clark and Souden 1987), a proportion of migrants age 15 to 30 and the children under 5 years old who would have been born to them may be reflected in the age distributions of deaths, as discussed above. If Teotihuacan had control, or at least strong influence, over a rural area of a half-million to 1 million people (Cowgill 2001), then even at the slow growth rates postulated by Gorenflo (this volume) for the basin, the rural population would be growing on average by 1,000–2,000 people per year. This would probably provide enough migrants to keep the city's population stable. And if migrants did come in any numbers from farther places, there would be even less of a problem in maintaining population. Future research on skeletons and chemical signatures should clarify the question of Teotihuacan and migration.

However, the age distribution of deaths for the Late Period at Tlajinga indicates an untenable one for a living population, because a population dying young will lose too many productive adults for both economic health and reproductive replacement. Migrants probably would eventually stop moving to such residences and to a city that unhealthy. If in fact the Late Period is experiencing near-catastrophic mortality for both natives and migrants, the situation would eventually be beyond recovery for a compound such as Tlajinga 33. As population declined, compounds would be abandoned, and population would concentrate in fewer residences or leave for better conditions elsewhere. If similar conditions were present in many such poor compounds in the city, Teotihuacan would cease to be a thriving preindustrial city.

The Late Period age distribution of deaths indicates that the health situation in Teotihuacan may have drastically deteriorated by Late Xolalpan times and that poor nonagricultural specialists were declining in numbers much faster than migration could replace. If so, then the integrity of Teotihuacan as an economic and social power would have been severely compromised; other rival polities could have exploited and profited from Teotihuacan's demographic problems. By the time the Classic city "fell" during the sixth to seventh centuries AD (Cowgill 1997), Tlajinga 33 probably stood abandoned, for perhaps 50 to 100 years, apparently as part of the Metepec decline. At that time, Tlajinga 33 was an eloquent testament to the ultimate failure of Teotihuacan's urban lifestyle to mitigate the effects of maintaining a dense urban population in an arid highland environment with rudimentary sanitary technology, even with a lack of the crowd-type infections characteristic of the Old World. The important point is that preindustrial cities, whether in the Old or New World, faced similar health and demographic hazards, and the balance of mortality and migration, so necessary to the long-term vitality of such cities, could be destabilized. An important research question for Teotihuacan is, what might have been the cause of the Late Xolalpan problems? Is it just that nutritional and sanitary conditions became increasingly precarious as the city "aged"? Or was Teotihuacan the victim of a more short-term sociopolitical event or climatic perturbation, or both, that negatively impacted the city's economic and sanitary resources and caused a demographic decline that could not be quickly reversed? Teotihuacan continued to be a settlement of some size and importance, but never again was it of the size and influence it had been in the first centuries AD.

Acknowledgments

The Tlajinga 33 project was supported by the National Science Foundation (BNS 8005825, BNS 82-04862, and BNS 8005754). Permission for the project was granted by the Instituto Nacional de Antropología e Historía, Mexico. I am grateful to the Teotihuacan Center for Archaeological Research and its staff, which curates the Tlajinga 33 artifacts and skeletons. Many people have contributed to this project and have provided invaluable feedback for my work, but I would like to thank Randolph J. Widmer, William T. Sanders, George Cowgill, and René Millon for their long-term advice and help.

15

The Evolution of Regional Demography and Settlement in the Prehispanic Basin of Mexico

L. J. Gorenflo

Viewing archaeological problems in regional context has become so pervasive that it is easy to forget the relatively recent emergence of systematic regional inquiry in archaeology scarcely five decades ago (Willey 1953). Following this early lead, in 1960 William Sanders (1965; see Wolf 1976) embarked on a pioneering study of prehistoric regional settlement patterns and cultural ecology in the Teotihuacan Valley, located in the northeastern Basin of Mexico. Intensive archaeological surveys conducted in the valley between 1961 and 1966, designed to discover and map all sites in that area (see Evans et al. 2000; Kolb and Sanders 1996; Marino 1987; Sanders et al. 1975), were augmented by similar efforts in seven other portions of the Basin of Mexico between 1966 and 1975 (Blanton 1972; Gorenflo and Sanders 2006; Parsons 1971; Parsons et al. 1982; Sanders and Gorenflo 2006; see also Gorenflo and Sanders 2006; Parsons et al. 1983)—yielding data on more than 3,700 archaeological sites in that region dating between 1500 BC and 1519 AD.

In a synthesis published shortly after the completion of the final intensive archaeological survey in the basin (Sanders et al. 1979), researchers examined survey, excavation, and ethnohistoric data to explore sociocultural evolution in the region. One of the topics considered in that synthesis was the changing demography of the region and how population change related to sociocultural evolution. However, with the exception of two survey regions (Ixtapalapa and Texcoco) and selected occupations of a third (the Formative and Toltec occupations of the Teotihuacan Valley), the survey data providing the basis for the 1979 synthesis had not been finalized. Data from the remaining three regions surveyed by Jeffrey Parsons appeared in the early 1980s (Parsons et al. 1982, 1983), with much of the 1983 volume generated by a computerized database containing settlement data from the five survey regions examined by Parsons and colleagues at the University of Michigan. Data from the three regions surveyed by Sanders and his collaborators, in turn, have recently been finalized and computerized (see Gorenflo and Sanders 2006). Compiling these data, and organizing them in a form amenable to systematic analysis, introduces the possibility of revisiting many aspects of prehispanic settlement in the Basin of Mexico. One of these topics is the evolution of regional demography and associated settlement patterns and their mutual roles in the emergence of urbanization.

This chapter examines data on population and settlement in the Basin of Mexico dating between roughly 1500 BC and AD 1519, as documented primarily by intensive archaeological settlement surveys. The chapter begins by summarizing the methodological basis of settlement data in the basin, notably how they were collected and their reliability as a foundation for exploring demographic change and the evolution of settlement patterns. It then proceeds to an overview of Basin of Mexico demography, exploring total population change over time, tendencies in the regional organization of population by settlement type, and the spatial arrangement of population. An analysis of demographic change and the spatial arrangement of population provides insights on the demographic processes *likely* underlying documented settlement evolution, including the rise of urbanism in a regional context. The chapter closes by defining a series of problems associated with prehistoric demography and shifts in regional settlement in the basin that require further research.

The Study in Context

The Basin of Mexico consists of an elevated plain covering roughly 7,000 sq km, surrounded on its western, southern, and eastern sides by high mountain ranges and on its northern side by a series of low, discontinuous ranges of hills (see Sanders et al. 1979:81–89, Figure 15-1). Prior to the completion by the Spanish of a large drain in the northwestern part of the basin in the early seventeenth century to help control flooding in Mexico City (Gibson 1964:6), one of the most dominant features of the region was a system of shallow, interconnected lakes in its center, replenished by a combination of springs, rainfall, and seasonal streams fed by runoff from precipitation. Elevations in the basin range from as low as 2,235 m above sea level in the old lake bed to as high as 5,800 m in the massive snow-capped volcanoes in its southeastern corner. Rainfall occurs seasonally, on average ranging from 450 mm annually in the more arid northeastern portion to more than 1,500 mm annually in the southwestern mountains. Despite the risks associated with annual and spatial variation in precipitation and frosts from high elevations, prehispanic inhabitants in the Basin of Mexico succeeded in establishing a maize-based agricultural economy and a series of extremely complex sociocultural systems—including a pristine state centered at Teotihuacan and the heart of the Aztec Empire centered at Tenochtitlan. The region also came to support large populations prior to the Spanish conquest, with total inhabitants approaching 1,000,000 by the early sixteenth century (Sanders et al. 1979:162).

One of the most important types of data collected in the archaeological sur-

veys of the basin was information on the density of occupation over time, estimated primarily on the basis of surface remains. In cases where domestic architecture was preserved adequately, primarily in the form of residential mounds,
surveyors counted prehispanic houses and estimated population. Unfortunately,
in many cases architectural preservation was inadequate to serve as a basis for
population estimation, requiring an alternative method to estimate population on
the basis of subjective assignments of pottery density to one of several categories
equated with population density. Sanders's (1965:50; see also Parsons 1971:22–23)
study of rural settlements in modern central Mexico provided a basis for convert-
ing observed pottery densities to population densities.

This approach to estimating population is subject to several sources of possible
error—differences in qualitative density assessments between individuals, differences in the evaluation of pottery density due to varying surface conditions,
difficulty in assessing density on multicomponent sites, modifications of the density of surface remains due to erosion, subsequent land use and other processes,
and so on. The original researchers recognized the limitations of their method of
demographic estimation, acknowledging that it provides what generally should be
considered a reliable indicator of relative population density rather than absolute
demographic figures for the prehispanic basin (Sanders et al. 1979:39–40). Moreover, because the resulting estimates are derived from a common methodology,
they provide a basis for comparing population across space and time as well as for
a general understanding of prehispanic demographic change in this important
part of Mesoamerica.

A considerable amount of information was recorded for each site encountered
by the Basin of Mexico surveys. One of the more important for present purposes,
due to its association with a study of basin demographic and settlement evolution,
is *site type* (Table 15-1). In conjunction with demographic estimates, and within
limitations of the data, one can explore key questions of prehistoric settlement
and regional organization in the basin—notably the evolution of population and
its changing geographic distribution, along with the emergence of centers that
represent either early forms of urbanization or, in the case of Teotihuacan, indisputable urban settings (see Cowgill 1997; Robertson 2001).

Basin of Mexico Prehispanic Demography: Descriptive Reconstruction

A good starting point for the study of prehispanic regional demography and settlement in the Basin of Mexico is total population. Here and throughout this
study, rather than focus on the *entire* region, I rely exclusively on those portions
of the basin examined by intensive survey—the exception being the Late Aztec
period where provincial centers lying within the surveyed area, but not actually
surveyed due to modern overburden (see Gorenflo and Sanders 2004a; Parsons et
al. 1983:2), were incorporated in this study by estimating their population with

Table 15-1. Site Types Defined by Archaeological Surveys in the Basin of Mexico

Site Type	Description
Hamlet	Small communities, population less than 100 persons
Village	Small communities, population 100–1,000 persons, no civic-ceremonial-elite architecture
Center	Large nucleated communities; population (usually) 1,000–10,000 persons; civic, ceremonial, and elite architecture present; sub-types include local, provincial, regional, and supra-regional, depending on likely socio-political setting
Barrio of a Center	Large nucleated communities; population 1,000–5,000 persons; civic, ceremonial, and elite architecture present; located in proximity of provincial or regional center
Ceremonial Center	Sites often on isolated hilltops with ceremonial architecture and little evidence of domestic occupation; includes ceremonial caves
Salt-making Station	Communities lying on the edge or Lake Texcoco or Xaltocan and thought to represent the remains of settlements which manufactured salt from saline lake water
Questionable	Small sites, usually defined by very sparse surface remains, thought to represent temporary, special-purpose, or short-term occupation

Source: Sanders et al. 1979:52–60.

ethnohistoric sources (e.g., see Hodge 1984:117 for the case of Aztec Teotihuacan and Parsons 1971:117–120 for the case of Aztec Texcoco). Maintaining a geographic focus solely on surveyed sites excludes one section of the basin of considerable demographic importance at various points in the past—the southwestern portion covered by modern Mexico City and its closest suburbs—as well as an area on the northeastern fringe of the region that was never surveyed intensively (see Figure 15-1). Nevertheless, in the interest of ensuring comparability of data over space and time, one has little choice but to focus solely on those portions of the region examined with the same techniques. Note that for convenience, although I refer to the *Basin of Mexico* in discussing demographic issues below, I exclude the two portions of the region mentioned above throughout the remainder of this study.

· The total population estimated from archaeological survey for the Basin of Mexico varies widely over its prehistoric past (Figure 15-2). From relatively inauspicious beginnings in the Early Formative (1500–1150 BC) when the region contained a total population estimated at slightly fewer than 1,000 persons, by the

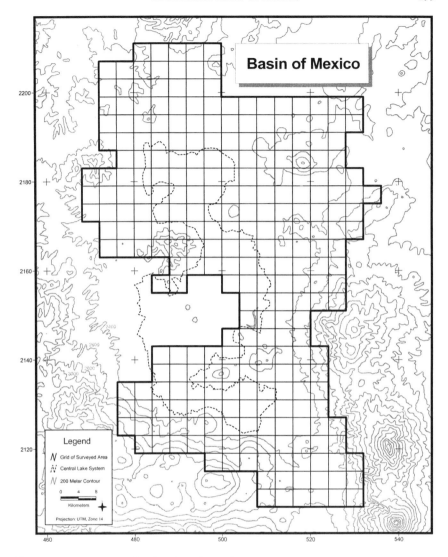

Figure 15-1. Area surveyed archaeologically in the Basin of Mexico.

Teotihuacan period estimated population in the basin exceeded 185,000. The demographic profile of the basin clearly reflects the rise of the Teotihuacan state, its collapse and following demographic decline through Early and Late Toltec times, and the marked increase in population accompanying the rise of the Aztec state within the basin proper—the latter yielding an estimated population of nearly 336,000 persons for the area surveyed.

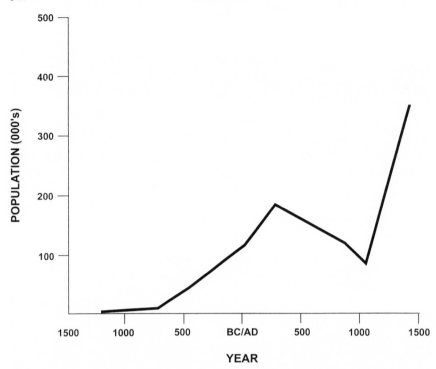

Figure 15-2. Change in total population in the Basin of Mexico (surveyed area) over time.

In examining the demographic profile of the prehispanic Basin of Mexico, it is tempting to conclude that the large populations that emerged at various times during its prehistory resulted from particularly rapid population growth. But cal-culating average annual rate of change reveals fairly modest increase between the median years for the main time periods examined—never greater than 0.53 percent (between Early and Middle Formative), with the remaining periods of population growth 0.44 percent or less per year. Such modest rates indicate populations where the vehicles of demographic change—fertility, mortality, and mobility—were in close balance. Unfortunately, they do not indicate the nature of this balance; for instance, fertility slightly exceeding mortality in a region closed to migration could yield results of the type documented, as could mortality in excess of fertility in an area experiencing sufficient net in-migration to com-pensate for the natural decline. What they do reveal is that dramatic demographic events were unnecessary for the demographic history observed. Because popula-tion totals for each period were aggregated and assigned to a single year (the median year of the major occupational period considered) for purposes of analy-sis, when the data clearly represent settlement remains accumulated over centuries (see Dewar 1991; Kintigh 1994), the rate of demographic change could be even less if the estimates are distributed over time.

Throughout the prehistory of the Basin of Mexico, there has always been a pyramidal distribution of the three main types of habitation sites, with hamlets by far the most prevalent, followed by villages and then centers (Table 15-2). Certain periods, such as the Late Toltec, were particularly dominated by hamlets, indicating regional organization dominated by dispersed, rural settlement. Indeed, a recent reanalysis of surface collections from Aztec sites in the Teotihuacan Valley indicates that survey crews may have missed several Late Toltec hamlets amid the vast rural Late Aztec settlement present in that part of the region—increasing the frequency of correspondence between the two periods to the point where it seems that Late Toltec hamlets almost always preceded Late Aztec occupations (Sanders 2000:65). Similarly, in a few periods, one finds slight surges in the relative importance of villages as site types in the regional settlement, notably the Late Formative, Early Toltec, and Late Aztec occupations.

When the assessment of settlement importance considers population per site type, the picture of Basin of Mexico settlement changes. In contrast to the frequency of site types, either villages or centers contained the greatest proportions of regional population for all occupations considered, depending on the time period examined (Table 15-3). In the Terminal Formative, one sees a dramatic shift from village- to center-dominated regional demography, with more than three-fourths of the total estimated population residing in centers (primarily Teotihuacan).

This tendency persists, though to a progressively lessened extent, into the Teotihuacan and Early Toltec period occupations. The Late Toltec occupation provides the first example of population in hamlets exceeding 10 percent (here more than 19 percent) since the Middle Formative, vivid testimony to the importance of this settlement type during the Late Toltec occupation. Although the greatest number of persons during the Late Aztec occupation of the Basin of Mexico resided in centers, this was just barely the case, pointing up the importance of rural settlement (particularly villages) during this time period. In the context of regional organization in the basin, such evaluations of demography in terms of community types reveal key differences that gave rise to urban and proto-urban settlement—with 29 to 77 percent of basin population residing in urban communities or centers beginning in the Late Formative. I discuss some implications of these very different forms of regional organization in the following section.

One of the more important perspectives on demography in the Basin of Mexico is the arrangement of population over space. The settlement maps previously published on prehispanic settlement in the basin (Sanders et al. 1979) provide a sense of this, but because they do not explicitly present numbers of people, the regional demographic perspective is lost. To convey a clearer sense of the spatial arrangement of population, I mapped estimated population by time period on a 4 × 4 km grid for the surveyed area, representing different population

Table 15-2. Percentages of Site Type by Period of Occupation

	Total	Hamlet	Village	Center	Barrio	Cerem.	Salt Station	Questionable	Other	Unknown
Total	3,702	64.6	18.6	2.2	0.5	2.5	1.6	5.6	0.3	4.2
Late Aztec	1,563	68.0	19.7	2.0	0.1	3.8	3.0	2.9	—	0.4
Late Toltec	835	70.1	15.4	1.1	0.1	1.0	0.7	3.5	—	8.1
Early Toltec	245	52.7	23.3	5.3	0.4	4.1	0.8	10.2	—	3.3
Teotihuacan	440	63.0	20.5	2.7	3.0	2.0	0.5	7.3	0.7	0.5
T. Formative	361	53.7	10.8	2.8	0.3	1.4	—	11.9	2.2	16.9
L. Formative	173	55.5	25.4	2.9	—	1.2	0.6	9.8	—	4.6
M. Formative	76	57.9	23.7	—	—	—	1.3	17.1	—	—
E. Formative	9	55.6	33.3	—	—	—	—	11.1	—	—

Notes: "Other" includes workshops and quarries (Teotihuacan Period) and elite districts (Terminal Formative Period); "—" denotes a percentage that rounds to zero.

Table 15-3. Percentages of Population by Period of Occupation and Site Type

	Total	Hamlet	Village	Center	Barrio	Cerem.	Salt Station	Questionable	Other	Unknown
Total	923,740	7.4	29.2	60.2	2.3	—	0.2	0.3	0.4	—
Late Aztec	336,040	8.4	33.2	55.6	1.8	—	0.4	0.6	—	—
Late Toltec	85,905	19.2	45.6	29.1	6.1	—	—	—	—	—
Early Toltec	121,836	3.8	20.8	72.5	2.9	—	0.1	—	—	—
Teotihuacan	185,370	5.3	17.9	73.8	2.9	—	0.1	—	—	—
T. Formative	133,075	3.5	15.6	76.8	1.1	—	—	0.2	2.8	—
L. Formative	48,726	5.5	59.2	35.3	—	—	—	—	—	—
M. Formative	11,829	12.3	87.3	—	—	—	0.5	—	—	—
E. Formative	959	29.6	70.4	—	—	—	—	—	—	—

Notes: "Other" includes workshops and quarries (Teotihuacan Period) and elite districts (Terminal Formative Period); "—" denotes a percentage that rounds to zero.

levels with varying shading densities (choropleth maps). Note that the shading densities employed are designed to promote an understanding of how population is arranged over space in individual time periods as well as support a comparison between time periods. That is to say, a particular shading density in one time period signifies the same thing as that density in another, enabling one to examine visually the spatial arrangement of population in a single time period as well as compare arrangements of population in different periods.

As documented elsewhere (Sanders et al. 1979:Map 5), settlement in the Basin of Mexico during prehispanic periods of occupation that featured ceramics began in the south. The map shown as Figure 15-3a clearly represents this, with only one cell outside of the southern half of the basin populated during the Early Formative period. The most densely populated cell, near the far southeastern corner of the region, reached just slightly more than 28 persons per sq km. Middle Formative regional demography in the basin reveals a continuation of the trend populating the region from the south, though in comparison to the Early Formative, population is both more dispersed and reaches greater densities (here 135 persons per sq km, again in the southeastern basin; Figure 15-3b). Although settlement tends to occur near the central lake system, another tendency seen in the Early Formative, Middle Formative occupations also occur some distance from the lakes (including the most densely populated unit mapped).

The Late Formative occupation in the Basin of Mexico reveals what appears in demographic terms to be a continuation of the main trends established in the Middle Formative—namely, an emphasis on the southern part of the region, a further geographic dispersal of people throughout the basin, and settlement that emphasizes proximity to the lake system but also occurs away from the lakeshore (Figure 15-3c). Population continued to increase, with the densest map unit containing an estimated 344 persons per sq km. For the first time, settlements interpreted as *centers* appear in the Basin of Mexico, representing the first hints of urbanization with an emerging administrative settlement hierarchy that would become so regionally important a few centuries later. All four Late Formative centers were fairly small, their location in the southern portion of the basin continuing the emphasis on that geographic part of the region.

With the arrival of the Terminal Formative, consistency in regional demographic trends established early in the Formative period ends. Population becomes much more concentrated in one place—the emerging urban center at Teotihuacan—amid a regionwide distribution that is much sparser by comparison (Figure 15-3d). Population is dispersed widely throughout all portions of the region save the far northern and far western peripheries, and a clear settlement preference for proximity to the lake system is absent. Maximum population density for a particular grid cell reached an estimated 5,000 persons per sq km, nearly 15 times that reached in the immediate preceding period. Nine other centers in the Basin of Mexico in addition to Teotihuacan dated to the Terminal Formative occupation,

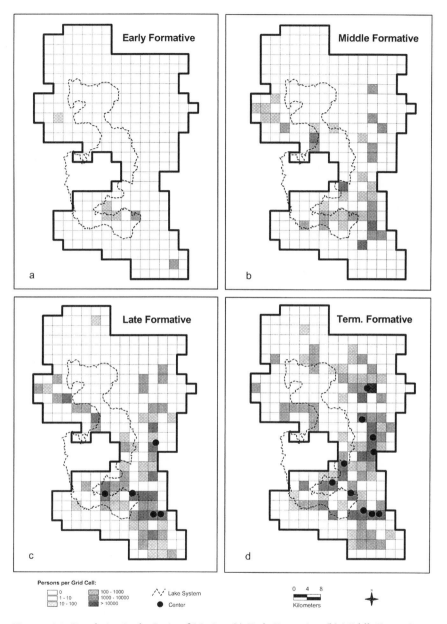

Figure 15-3. Population in the Basin of Mexico: (a) Early Formative; (b) Middle Formative; (c) Late Formative; (d) and Terminal Formative.

helping to account for many of the more densely occupied parts of the region. All nine occurred in the southern part of the basin, a vestige of the earlier regional organization of settlement. However, with more than half the population of the surveyed area residing at Teotihuacan, the emerging importance of the northern part of the region is indisputable.

The spatial distribution of Teotihuacan period population in the basin indicates a continuation of demographic concentration at the urban center of Teotihuacan, though the densest population occurred among five map units at and near the urban center (Figure 15-4a). Population density reached an estimated maximum 7,800 persons per sq km. The remainder of the region contained a relatively uniform, dispersed population, with more of the north and west showing low-density occupations than seen previously. Eleven other centers occurred in the Basin of Mexico during the Teotihuacan period in addition to the urban center, providing further evidence of demographic dispersal beyond Teotihuacan proper. All but three of the centers during the Teotihuacan occupation occur in the northern half of the Basin of Mexico, a tendency also reflected in the regional demography as that part of the basin assumed clear dominance. This heavy emphasis on the northern part of the basin, coupled with the enormous population of Teotihuacan and surrounding barrios, suggests precarious regional adaptation emphasizing an area with limited rainfall, concentrating population in one locality, and underutilizing the rich southern part of the region (Cowgill 1997:133).

Following the collapse of Teotihuacan, the Early Toltec population in the Basin of Mexico was arranged much differently in comparison to the preceding period. Population occurred in concentrations, but these concentrations were dispersed throughout much of the eastern and southern basin (Figure 15-4b). Many areas previously inhabited were abandoned, and those where population remained reached a maximum of 2,312 persons per sq km, well below the maximum achieved during the Teotihuacan period occupation. Of the 13 centers located in the Basin of Mexico during the Early Toltec occupation, 9 occurred in the northern half of the region—continuing the general geographic trend established in the Terminal Formative occupation. The urban center had declined considerably since its apex the preceding period. Probably as a consequence of this decline in overarching influence, the small Early Toltec centers likely represent the rise of small local polities to administer limited subsections of the region.

The regional demography in the Basin of Mexico during Late Toltec times marks yet another shift in the distribution of population. The geographic dispersal of population reached its greatest level to date during this time period (Figure 15-4c). Moreover, although population concentrations clearly occurred (reaching about 829 persons per sq km at Teotihuacan), people were much more evenly dispersed in what might be considered moderate densities for the time period in question. Although settlement clearly occurred near the lakeshore, the broad distribution of people during the Late Toltec suggests that many other components

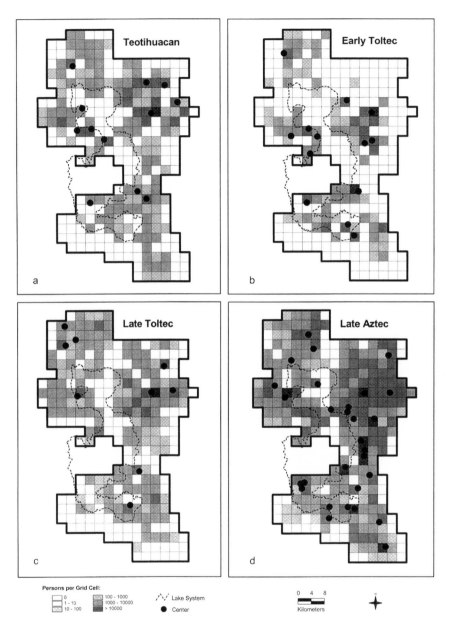

Figure 15-4. Population in the Basin of Mexico: (a) Teotihuacan; (b) Early Toltec; (c) Late Toltec; and (d) Late Aztec.

of the basin were also quite important. Archaeologists have identified 9 sites subsequently classified as centers, all but two in the northern part of the region. No one center appears particularly dominant within the basin, at least in terms of concentrated population, which is consistent with the emergence of the supraregional center of Tula to the north of the basin.

The Late Aztec occupation of the Basin of Mexico indicates the highest spatial dispersal attained during prehispanic times, with virtually every map unit containing at least some population (Figure 15-4d). Population tended to be distributed in relatively low densities with a few notable exceptions, the densest concentrations generally synonymous with the 29 *surveyed* provincial centers scattered throughout the surveyed area (see Gibson 1971; Hodge 1984). Despite the total population of the surveyed area approaching 340,000 people, the densest unit contained only about 1,560 persons per sq km. On the basis of available survey data, it is tempting to point toward what appears to be a continued demographic emphasis in the northern part of the basin in addition to the presence of about half the surveyed centers. However, we know that half or more of the population of the entire region resided in Tenochtitlan and surrounding environs—an area excluded from this study, as discussed above. Any consideration of urbanization would have to include an evaluation of this large urban center, the remaining city-state centers representing local concentrations of population, and associated economic and administrative influence.

Demographic Processes and Repercussions in the Basin of Mexico

Given the information on prehispanic settlement patterns in the Basin of Mexico, what do the data on regional population change over time reveal about demographic processes in the region? As discussed earlier, neither population growth nor population decline for the region as a whole would have required extraordinary events to yield the estimated populations for any of the time periods considered. That stated, certain events no doubt occurred and are lost in the broad temporal resolution employed in data collection and analysis. But in general the population change indicated in the Basin of Mexico *could* have occurred entirely through the process of natural increase or decrease, slightly modifying the balance between undoubtedly high mortality and fertility usually characteristic of preindustrial societies without access to modern health care. The ethnohistory of the basin is replete with claims of in-migration from points beyond its bounds (e.g., Gibson 1964:10–20), and such likely occurred throughout earlier periods in the region's prehistory. However, massive movements of people into (or out of) the basin would not have been necessary to produce the population change estimated—unless it served to compensate for other occurrences such as natural increase or decrease. In any event, all three potential sources of demographic change appear to have been largely in balance when considered as a whole, dampening the individual effect of each and reducing any overall net changes in population.

Demographic change affecting settlement patterns *within* the Basin of Mexico, in contrast, indicates the fundamental importance of mobility to restructure the geographic distribution of population from one period to another. One can gain an appreciation of this by focusing on population change between succeeding periods of occupation. Possible evidence of mobility appears in two instances. One is the trivial case where a grid cell is occupied during one period but unoccupied in the preceding period. Inhabitants of that spatial unit had to get there somehow, with the only possible explanation relocation from elsewhere—either another location within the Basin of Mexico or from beyond the boundary of the region. The second indication of likely mobility is when a grid cell was populated for two successive time periods but experienced population change in excess of the expected rate of growth. If one uses the average annual rate of change for the entire region as an indicator of expected growth between periods, then grid cells exhibiting average annual change in excess of this may have experienced the effects of net in-migration, once again from within the basin or beyond. The assumption that the average annual rate of change for the basin as a whole provides a good indicator of *expected* growth between two time periods is clearly a simplification. With the exception of Storey's (1992b) efforts, adequate site-specific work of a sort that would provide evidence on the spatial variability of prehispanic demography in the basin is lacking. Nevertheless, it is highly likely that population change varied locally without the influence of mobility—such that some of the grid units identified as experiencing net in-migration may have varied with the regionwide average purely due to fertility exceeding mortality. That stated, many of the differences in growth rate were striking and likely outside the range that could be accounted for by other demographic processes. These measures may be mapped to show the spatial pattern of possible migration between succeeding periods of occupation. In the interest of brevity I limit the number of maps presented here to two, one showing an instance of widespread in-migration where each inhabited unit would have involved mobility (Early–Middle Formative; Figure 15-5a) and one showing an instance where the regional distribution of population involved mobility in only some of the units mapped (Middle–Late Formative; Figure 15-5b). For these and other maps, indications of likely mobility are widespread, with no obvious indication of a particular spatial pattern.

Elsewhere, researchers have remarked on the singular nature of the Basin of Mexico in preindustrial demography (Harris 1977) and the likelihood that the resident population approached some sort of theoretical carrying capacity for intensive preindustrial maize agriculture during the Late Aztec occupation (Sanders et al. 1979:176–181; see also Gorenflo 1996; Williams 1989). Although by necessity a large and important portion of the basin has been excluded from this study, the demographic prehistory for the surveyed section of the basin examined

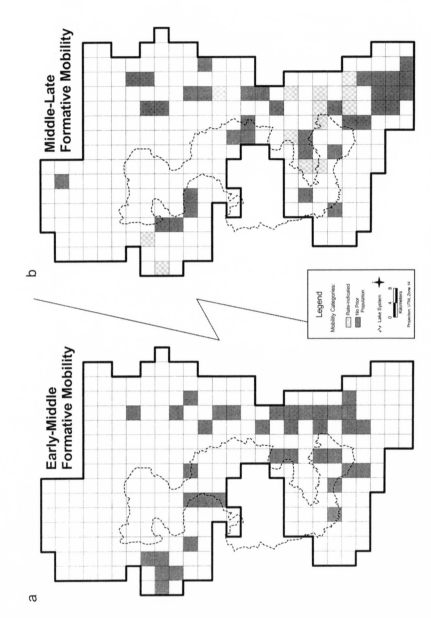

Figure 15-5. Geographic distribution of likely net in-migration: (a) Early–Middle Formative and (b) Middle–Late Formative.

does suggest some useful insights on regional evolution. Demographically, change apparently occurred at relatively slow rates over long periods of time—indicating that no one demographic process necessarily dominated another and that exceeding the bounds of economic support given the modest rates of population growth involved would have been unlikely in the absence of political upheaval or environmental calamity.

These conclusions about overall demographic change in the Basin of Mexico probably involving demographic processes of moderate magnitude contrast with the examination of evolving regional demography and the emerging settlement hierarchy. In general, mobility emerges as an apparently widespread means of adjusting the spatial arrangement of population for every period of prehispanic occupation considered. Indeed, the geographic arrangement of population for any period of occupation was largely a consequence of dramatic shifts in population that often can be explained only in terms of mobility. This process affected virtually all of the centers identified in Basin of Mexico surveys, thereby playing a central role in the emergence of settlement hierarchies and urban centers in the region. Mobility has long been seen as a key component of sociocultural change and regional organization in the basin at certain points in time. One example is the concentration of population at the site of Teotihuacan beginning toward the end of the Formative period, likely a result of some form of coercion in most cases (Millon 1981:221–222; Millon et al. 1973:59), but probably involving other reasons as well (e.g., Rattray 1993; Spence 1989), and ultimately yielding a city of 125,000 persons (Cowgill 1997; Millon 1976:212). Another is the maintenance of the urban Teotihuacan population, in the face of particularly high mortality in the preindustrial urban setting, through continuous replenishment via migration from the hinterland (Storey 1986, 1987, 1992b, this volume).

The evolution of Teotihuacan population between the beginning of the Common Era through 1519 provides a useful backdrop against which to consider this general process in regional context (Figure 15-6). The center emerged in Terminal Formative times, growing so rapidly that in-migration was certainly a key demographic process involved. The Teotihuacan period occupation of the urban center reveals continued rapid growth as well as the emergence of dispersed secondary centers. Regardless of the sociocultural processes involved, both the continued rapid evolution of the city and the populating of places previously uninhabited again involved people relocating from one place to another. The presence of urban Teotihuacan at the regional demographic *expense* of other centers in the Basin of Mexico declined considerably in succeeding periods, as both other centers and noncenters became increasingly important.

Mobility likely played an absolutely central role in expanded settlement during the Late Aztec occupation—certainly at Tenochtitlan. Founded on what probably was uninhabited swampland during the fourteenth century (Reyes Cortés and

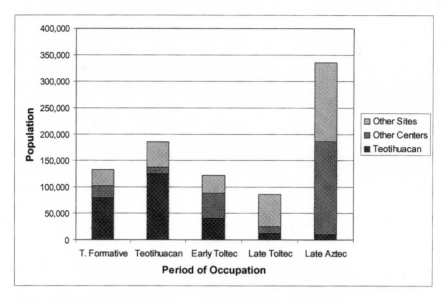

Figure 15-6. Population of Teotihuacan, other centers, and other surveyed sites over time.

García-Barcena 1979), Tenochtitlan grew very rapidly to 150,000–200,000 in-habitants over the ensuing two centuries (Calnek 1973:190). Many other places previously uninhabited, such as several of the more arid parts of the northern basin, also grew during the Late Aztec occupation of the basin, as people likely moved in response to growing population elsewhere and specialized in crops bet-ter suited to reduced rainfall (Evans 1990:125–127; see also Evans 1988; Parsons and Parsons 1990).

When one considers the demographic estimates examined above at a regional scale, evidence for widespread migration appears throughout Basin of Mexico prehistory. Mobility within the basin may have served as an important means of adjusting regional organization in response to ecological, economic, and socio-political changes, as well as responses to biological stress associated with life in prehispanic urban settings—capable of yielding (when necessary) much more im-mediate results than, say, changes resulting from shifts in mortality or fertility and the more slow-paced sociocultural shifts that often precede them (Zubrow 1976). Thus, although the prehispanic inhabitants of the Basin of Mexico may well have strained the capability of their surroundings, they demonstrated demographic characteristics that (in the form of relatively slow population change) would have been unlikely to exceed that capability and that (in the form of mobility) would have been capable of rapid adjustments in spatial organization when warranted. Researchers in the Valley of Oaxaca, using data and methods similar to those employed here, found evidence of widespread migration throughout much of the prehistoric past in that region (Blanton et al. 1996:31–35)—possibly indicating similar approaches to adaptation in two very different environmental and socio-cultural settings.

Conclusions

Archaeological data provide a means of examining the demography and settlement hierarchies of the prehispanic Basin of Mexico as they evolved over time. Although these data are not without their shortcomings, they provide a useful picture of broad trends in regional demography and regional organization. Evidence indicates slow-paced demographic change, either positive or negative, throughout the millennia examined, requiring no dramatic changes in the form of population increases or decreases and producing no demographic threat to the area that had not in essence been tested successfully in prior generations. Mobility emerges as a likely pervasive means of modifying the arrangement of population within the basin for all periods of occupation and a potentially important means of short-term adjustments in population distribution when such adjustments were necessary. Centers became established through mobility and appear to have grown through in-migration—from more modest administrative settlements to the great urban center of Teotihuacan.

At the risk of deferring potential insights of the study of Basin of Mexico demography to future inquiries, available data do not enable many questions to be answered definitively at this time. By design the chapter has avoided specific issues relevant to the emerging debate on the chronology of the Basin of Mexico, including both shifts in dates and the potential that certain types of material culture possibly represented simultaneous occupations of different cultures rather than chronologically different occupations (see Cowgill 1996b; Parsons et al. 1996). The reason for this avoidance rests in the persisting chronological uncertainty. The chapter also by design does not explore the complexities of change over time, which occurred over centuries and cannot be accounted for by simplistic explanations of one group of people and their material culture somehow replacing another (Parsons et al. 1996; see also Davies 1977, 1980; Dumond and Muller 1972; Vaillant 1938). The two most dramatic examples of mobility presented above, for example, would have demanded considerable shifts in adaptive strategy to support demographic rearrangement—the population concentration at Teotihuacan requiring a dependable food source, which likely involved large-scale irrigation (Nichols 1988; Nichols et al. 1991), and the concentration of population at Tenochtitlan requiring increased food production probably on the basis of chinampa agriculture in the nearby lake area (Armillas 1971; Parsons 1976). Finally, the chapter avoids any stronger statements regarding the relative importance of various demographic processes—ultimately posing more questions than answers. Certain insights have been gained from studies of other past settings with historical documentation—such as Storey's (1992b) consideration of other urban systems in her study of Teotihuacan paleodemography (e.g., Davis 1973; de Vries 1984; Russell 1958). The question of demographic processes, and their role in population change and the rise of urbanization in the prehispanic Basin of Mexico, will be resolved only through additional research, most likely through studies of paleodemography at particular sites and studies designed to reveal the presence of mobility patterns in the past.

Cross-Cultural Synthesis

16

Factoring the Countryside into Urban Populations

David B. Small

How do we characterize urban populations? Population study is more than simply a consideration of size. The character of a population is described as well by various components: its ethnic and economic makeup, its internal economic, social, and political articulation, and its religious organization, just to name some of the more obvious. In an urban environment many factors can affect these population characteristics. These factors range from subsistence systems to endemic diseases. But for this chapter, I would like to narrow the issue to looking at how city/rural relations affect the size and composition of urban populations. My interest is in beginning an investigation that should be able to facilitate our understanding of the effect that the relationship between urban and rural societies has not only on the size but also on the economic, political, and religious structure of archaeological urban populations.

My topic is not new. The issue of the impact of the countryside on urban populations has been one of concern both for archaeologists and for economic historians for several years. For the latter, mainly those working in Classical history, the question of the functional relationship between city and country has been polarized between advocates of a limited view of urban economics (Finley 1973; Hasebroek 1933; Hopkins 1978b; Jongman 1988; Polyani 1944; Weber 1958; Whittaker 1990) and those who view the city as more commercially advanced (Engels 1990; Hicks 1969; Laurence 1995). Advocates of a limited model of economics argue that the preindustrial city was essentially a consumer city, living off the agricultural produce of its hinterland. In a consumer city the population basically lives off agriculture. The population consisted of either farmers who lived in the city but traveled out to farm family holdings or nonfarmers who basically lived off of agricultural taxes from the countryside. Those who disagree with this view deny that the city was basically a nucleus of people who focused on the consumption of agricultural products, advocating instead that the population of cities was engaged in manufacturing or supplying services to the territory that it controlled.

In short, these differences in interpretation would have the city inhabited primarily either by nonspecialized agriculturalists or by specialized craftspeople. Each scenario is closely tied to the relationship that is seen between the city and its countryside.

Archaeology has not been so polemic. As archaeologists, we recognize that several factors of urban populations (size, complexity, hierarchy, and so on) are dependent on the nature of the flow of subsistence and other goods between cities and the countryside. In fact, the analysis of many urban sites is now often accompanied by the requisite rural survey (for example, Nicholas 1989). But even so, it is not easy to ascertain where archaeology stands on the effect of the hinterland on urban populations.

For example, the importance of the relationship between the city and the countryside has been highlighted by Yoffee (1995:284) in considering social change in Mesopotamia: "The countryside in early states, with its villages connected to cities and with its own specialized institutions of production and consumption, is utterly different than the countryside of prestate times." Few would object to this obvious conclusion. But it brings us no closer to understanding the relationship between urban and rural. What is the connection that would determine the nature of both the rural and urban populations? Although archaeologists have been quick to recognize the important relationship between city and country, that thinking has been only partially conceptualized. The dominant paradigms used in analyzing urban/rural relations have revolved around an assumed dominance of urban forces over rural populations.

The reason for this lack of development, I believe, is that our concepts of urban/rural connections have come to us from human geography. For the last 40 years archaeology has borrowed settlement concepts from geography—central place analysis, rank-size analysis, and others—where the centrality or hierarchical dominance of cities serves as an armature for urban/rural analysis (see overview in Ashmore and Knapp 1999). These concepts have formed the theoretical assumptions in most settlement survey research, such as Johnson's (1980) extremely influential Mesopotamian survey that framed the issue of urban/rural connections in archaeological landscapes in such terms as secondary and tertiary centers. This implied that urban sites themselves are not only politically but also economically dominant on a landscape.

This assumption has been so ingrained in archaeology that it features prominently in basic texts as well as in specialized studies. For example, this has become accepted dictum offered as a frame of reference in introductory regional overviews, such as Pollock's (1999) excellent *Ancient Mesopotamia*. In describing urbanization and settlement patterns, Pollock affirms that cities live off the food and raw materials of the countryside, leaving the employment of the urban population undetermined.

Given this theoretical bias, it is not surprising, then, that even in one of the most forward-thinking collections on the issue of the countryside in archaeological reconstruction, the editorial assumption is that "successful urban centers often maintained a parasitic or predatory relationship with their hinterlands, siphoning off as many assets as possible, while stopping short of undermining rural infrastructure" (Schwartz 1994:21).

It would be wrong to claim that there is not some truth to the views expressed above. Dominance, hierarchy, and urban control of rural populations and economies have certainly been true in some situations in the past, but to assume that there is always inequality between urban and rural is to miss some very important issues in understanding the nature of social power in the past. Rather than this assumption, I would argue here that we adopt a more robust analytical frame that can not only encompass urban dominance but also provide opportunity for alternative conclusions. I can best introduce this frame by reference to an event that took place in Gaul 2,000 ago (first pointed out by Crumley 1995a).

The year was 58 BC. Julius Caesar was the proconsul of Cisapline Gaul (northwesternmost Italy) and looking to conquer a great deal of the lands that lay just to the northwest of his province. The Aedui, a Celtic people who lived just to the west of the Saône River, had promised Caesar wheat to provision his army. But the wheat was not coming, and Caesar was impatient. He called in one of the leaders of the Aedui, Diviciacus, to find out why grain was not coming. When pressed on the subject, Liscus, another Aeduian leader, admitted that it was almost impossible for Diviciacus to collect grain because, as he put it, "certain persons, of paramount influence with the common folk, and of more power in their private capacity than the actual magistrates . . . by seditious and insolent language, were intimidating the population against the collection of corn as required" (Caesar 1936:27 [Gallic Wars I 16–17]). When we probe the situation further it becomes clear that what is happening in this case is that the leaders of the Aedui, who were located within the cities or *oppida* (fortified settlement) of the people (Wells 1995), did not have the power to tax the people living in the countryside. Furthermore, it is obvious that the countryside could and did here serve as an alternate base of political and economic power that could challenge that of the cities. Texts are always helpful in archaeological reconstruction, and without their assistance in this case, we would have assumed that the leaders in the cities could have obtained the needed wheat from their rural populations. Such an interpretation would have been wrong.

The relationship between urban and rural in Celtic Gaul was more complex and nuanced than indicated by a simple assumption of urban dominance. Archaeological investigations (summarized in Wells 1995) have shown that both urban and rural communities exhibited high degrees of hierarchical political status, economic specialization, and religious focus. The case of antique Gaul therefore calls to mind a framework for the analysis of urban populations on the basis of the relationship of cities to rural society. This analytical armature is more neutral than current paradigms of urban dominance. Rather than assuming dominance, we need to analyze the urban/rural relation as more open to either urban or rural dominance negotiated within multiple contexts—economic, political, social, religious, and so on. Dominance in one context does not necessarily carry over to another. In other words, a city could be dominant in its economic power (which would affect its population size), but subservient to rural religious authority (which would affect the religious composition of its population). It is only through this type of analysis that we will be able to judge the size, character, and complexity of any urban population. Although my example from Celtic society might have been predicted because the Celtic world was known for its weak centralization, best analyzed in a heterachical frame (Crumley 1987a, 1987b), I would argue that the Celtic case is really not that singular. Recent work on the Maya in Copán, Honduras (Abrams 1987, 1994, 1995; Andrews and Fash 1992; Braswell 1992; Fash 1983, 1991; Freter 1992, 1994, 1996, 2004; Hendon 1991; Johnston and Gonlin 1998; Paine and Freter 1996; Paine et al. 1995; Sanders 1989; Storey 1992a, 1999; Webster and Freter 1990a, 1990b; Webster and Gonlin 1988; Webster et al. 2000) has been robust enough to allow us to visualize some of the useable scales for studying urban/rural relations.

The Case of Copán

Located in northwest Honduras, the Copán polity appears to have been a peripheral outpost of past Mayan civilization. Work to date has identified limited occupation in the Preclassic period, starting as early as 1300 BCE. Political developments jump-started with the reign of K'inich Yax K'uk Mo', who might well have emigrated from a different Mayan polity (see Houston 1993). With his arrival Copán "takes off" with the construction of the Main Group, the architectural center of the polity. The end of royal succession at Copán occurs in the ninth century CE with the mysterious disappearance of the seventeenth king, U Cit Tok' (ca. 822 CE).

Spatially, the Copán community divides into three general regions of occupation. The urban core comprises the Main Group, the El Bosque and Las Sepulturas compounds. It is the most densely populated of the three regions, with a density of 1,425 structures per sq km. The Copán pocket lies outside the Main Group, with a density of 102 structures per sq km. The rural region incorporates the rest, with a density of 10 structures per sq km (Figure 16-1).

The basic units of social organization in the Copán polity were house compounds, which represented a continuum from small to larger and more complex and extended families. Fash (1983) and Freter (2004) both argue that these house compounds were organized into larger units similar to the *sian otot* noted by Wisdom (1940) in current Mayan societies. As Freter (2004) describes it, a *sian otot*

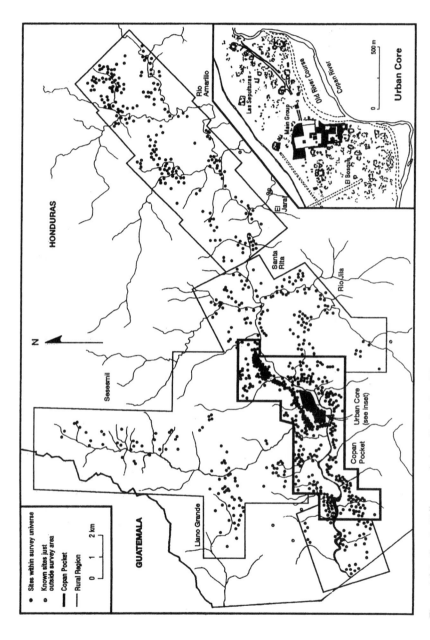

Figure 16-1. Copán Valley population distribution AD 700–850.

was a spatially discrete settlement cluster of 200 to 300 people composed of 60–80 households. Each *sian otot* occupied a specific territory composed of houselots, *milpas* . . . infield gardens, orchards and a great deal of unoccupied spaced which was either too rocky to cultivate or used as pasture land. . . . Boundaries between each *sian otot* were clearly recognized, but not formally marked. . . . Within *sian otot* related families often clustered into informal groups with small trails connecting households, thus the *sian otot* layout lacked a central plaza, streets, or grids. Families were composed of a "chief headman," his spouse, and unmarried children.

As Freter further demonstrates, the larger picture of Copán structure is probably best seen from the results of modern research into house compounds and regional distributions of population. According to Sanders (1989:102, quoted in Freter 2004:97):

The picture we have drawn of the Copán polity and society in the Coner phase [Late Classic] includes the following elements: (a) Extended family households varying considerably in social status, with polygyny closely related to this differentiation; (b) Households were incorporated into lineages of varying size and generational depth, closely integrated with a series of levels of ancestral cults; (c) The heads of maximal lineages formed a noble class and provided leadership in a number of separate but closely integrated spheres of activities—political, economic, religious. The immediate supporting households of these nobles included close kin, distant relatives, and unrelated clients; internal rank distinctions were significant. Some members of these expanded lineages had economically specialized roles, but the majority were probably cultivators; (d) At the top of the hierarchy was the king and the royal lineage who may have had several thousand people as direct economic and political dependents.

Enough good work has come out of research in Copán to identify three scales of analysis in the relationship between urban and rural populations: political/social, economic, and religious. Of course, all are closely intertwined, and aspects from one scale can be seen on several others. I will discuss three of these scales, with final considerations of the impact of rural population on urban along each axis.

The Political/Social Scale

In many ways the Copán polity was segmentary. The smallest social unit was the family. Groups of families with probable kin or dependent ties were further organized into *sian otots*. What separated urban populations from rural ones was a greater density of settlement of *sian otot* centers, as opposed to a wider distribution in the countryside, and greater architectural elaboration in the urban *sian otot*. As we saw, the ranking lineages were probably self-sufficient economically. Social integration on a political level was left up to the powers of the ruling lineage or *sian otot*. This required a great use of ideology to enforce and legitimate the dominance of the ruling lineage. The urban population settled around the main complex and within the urban pocket, not because of any economic integration, but one that was wholly ideological. This produced a rather fluid urban population that quickly and neatly migrated out of the pocket when the ruling lineage disappeared and established themselves in rural regions. My final observation is that a close resemblance between rural social structure, which is often kin aggregated, and urban social structure could indicate a fluid urban core given to population travel.

The Economic Scale

The economic relationship between urban and rural populations is one of the most interesting at Copán. Less is known in a definite way about the economics of the urban core. The size of the house compounds would indicate that they controlled large areas of agricultural land, but in addition to this base, Copán's urban population must have housed specialists, sometimes even the elite themselves, who engaged in the production of specialized marine shell ornament, palace-style pottery, and monumental architecture and decoration, as well as woodworkers and those who made ornamental lithics. Rural economics was somewhat different in that there were fewer large compounds and probably less land that was controlled by a limited number of people. House compounds were smaller and reflect more limited agricultural activity per family. However, there is evidence of nonagricultural production in plaster, manos and metates, utilitarian pottery, elite shell and bone working, and possible textiles. Freter (2004) argues that much of this production was performed by cooperatives on the *sian otot* level of organization.

What makes the investigation of Copán special is that the dating of many sites within the valley has given us the opportunity to view the dynamics of production over time and to look at the changing connection that this production would have had with urban elites in the polity.

In insightful analyses both Abrams and Freter have examined the changing nature of the relationship between the urban core and rural populations over time. Their key analytical concept is marginal product. According to Abrams (1995:198), "marginal product is a measure of efficiency with incremental additions of laborers, the difference between the total product with an added laborer from the previous total product. The marginal product is the direct consequence of the idealized law of diminishing returns." He (1995:197) sees the relationship between marginal product and social structure as closely linked and diachronic:

Marginal product, although a function of yield, may be a better reflection of each farmer's productivity relative to total yield, and thus may be a more sensitive indicator of political relations between the controllers and the workers of the land. A principal argument here is that as agricultural systems intensify with increasing amounts of labor input[,] . . . the productive and marginal values of the labor will fluctuate, and those stages of agricultural intensification that decrease the marginal value of labor provide the most probable economic contexts for the establishment and exercise of power.

Applying this model to Copán provides some windows into the relationship between urban elites and rural commoners over time:

Pre-400 CE—Presence of a long-term fallow swidden system; marginal labor value was positive, but modest; development of centralized political hierarchy was inhibited.

400–600 CE—Around 400, swidden system appears to have reached it limits, with temporary decline in marginal product; shortly after 400 we witness an intensification of the bottom lands in the Copán pocket and a subsequent immigration from rural areas; toward the end of the period large architectural projects—the Great Plaza and East Court in the main compound and Las Sepulturas in the urban core—take place (landowners are getting richer).

600–700 CE—Rural families profiting from intensification of Copán pocket as well as urban elite; bottomland labor is producing a high total product, but also a high marginal product; relationship between urban elite and rural commoners reflects hierarchy but is not so autocratic or exploitative.

700–800 CE—Capacity of intensive agriculture to absorb productive labor is reached, resulting in a sizeable nonproductive workforce; high productivity of intensification, but low marginal product create a great divide between rich and poor, urban and rural populations.

800–900 CE—Copán pocket witnesses decline in population, with resultant increase in marginal product; royal lineage collapses; out-migration from Copán pocket to rural zones with reestablishment of rural ceremonial centers.

As we might expect, the economic scale is sensitive to unequal relationships between urban and rural populations. Rural agricultural marginal product appears to be a sensitive indicator of predicting that relationship. Tied into this is the importance of rising rural nonagricultural production when marginal production is low. The effect on urban populations would include a dispersal of economic activity and an eventual organic economic integration of urban and rural populations.

The Religious Scale

Both urban and rural *sian otot* practiced rituals closely tied into ancestor worship. Places of ritual varied from civic/religious buildings located in the main compound and ritual installations in the royal compounds in urban zones to rural ceremonial centers in the rural territories. As noted by Freter (2004:97) and Sanders (1989), the Copán polity was not organically integrated economically, and a great amount of political power came from the manipulation of these rituals by elites throughout the polity. A measure of rural power that could have been challenging the dominance of the urban center can be seen in the establishment of the first rural ceremonial centers in the Middle Classic. We should note that at this time urban ideology and ritual purposefully extend into the rural territories, with the unprecedented placement of royal stelae in the countryside by the ruler Smoke Imix. One suspects that there might well have been some sort of competition between urban and rural power, with eventual urban dominance, because it appears that the ceremonial centers did not witness effective elaboration until the collapse of the urban center some 250 years later.

If we focus on the rural population's effect on the urban, we can see that the appearance of rural ceremonial centers could indicate an active religious competition between urban and rural populations. Tied to this scale is the issue of marginal production. Just when rural marginal production proves to be at its lowest, sectors of the urban population were displaying a great amount of religious ideology to add legitimacy to their extremely elevated position.

Where Do We Go from Here?

Copán represents the best context for initializing work on urban/rural populations, but four other cases do demonstrate that there are multiple approaches for this type of research. In each of these cases I will present the context and then suggest possible issues that could be addressed. In each of these cases, the evidence, either textual or archaeological, suggests that there was enough of a distinction that exploration of the relationship between urban and rural would be possible.

Uruk

The first example comes from the early state of Uruk in Mesopotamia. Our current understanding of textual evidence (Diakonoff 1969, 1982; Gelb 1969; Yoffee 1993) indicates that the dynamics of state development in this region, in their initial stages, saw the control of property divided between lands under the oversight of the temples and those held as independent estates by elites. It is thus possible that on an economic and social scale we have an active opposition between an urban-based control and one, that of the rural agricultural elite, that would be like the case in Gaul.

Several studies (most recently, Wright 1998) have shown that rural communities were engaged in the oversight of stored agricultural products, but I would argue that it is too soon to assume that the storage of these products was to supply subsistence to urban populations. The possibility that subsistence oversight and storage was correlated to rural population needs, which in turn were correlated with a high marginal production, needs to be explored.

With regard to the archaeological issue in the urban population, in the case of Uruk, evidence of rural economic independence would have direct bearing on the nature of its urban population. First, and very directly, to what degree could the urban populations count on the productivity of the private rural elite estates for subsistence? Could we have a situation similar to that witnessed in Gaul? If so, then what features produced by this subsistence risk might we expect to see in Uruk's urban population that increased connections between urban groups and other states? Would we see a heavy urban concentration on the use of ideology to win over agricultural goods from independent rural producers? Would we see a heavy concentration on the military for forcing independent rural populations to support the city?

Second, if there was high marginal production, then the political control that Uruk's urban population had over its hinterland was probably somewhat circumscribed. Taken diachronically, this might have fluctuated greatly. A hallmark of development in southern Mesopotamia is rapid early urbanization in the third millennium BCE, with a stability or even decrease in rural populations. Some have argued that the great increase in urban population stemmed from the influx of rural peoples into the cities. If so, why? Can we predict such rapidly forming urban populations from rural evidence? Was subsistence in the rural areas more risky than that for urban populations? Was there a decrease in marginal product in rural lands? What social structure would have produced so fluid a rural population?

Middle Bronze Age Levant

My second example comes from the Middle Bronze Age Levant. Falconer's (1994) analysis of village economy and society in the Jordan Valley in this period indicates strongly that villages, rather than becoming part of a larger urban-centered economic network dominated by Canaanite towns located along the coast, remained somewhat independent, offering a counterpart to the development of urban traditions located in the larger Canaanite cities. In looking at the relationship between urban and rural populations, the relationship was not what we would expect in an integrated territorial polity. Urban populations were smaller than normal.

With regard to the archaeological issue in urban populations, we could use both the social/political scale and the economic scale in this analysis. Does the relatively large size of the villages show a rural/social political formation that stood somewhat independently, both socially and economically, from urban centers? If so, then how can we use this information to highlight the urban populations? Were they also composed of loosely integrated social groups? Does that mean that there was less economic integration in the centers than supposed, with a consequent smaller urban population? The focus in the case of the Levantine settlements could also be that of marginal product. To what extent were populations in the countryside economically independent of the urban core? Can this be seen in different modes of production in the rural areas?

Ancient Greece

Recent work in Greek archaeology (de Polignac 1995; Morgan 1990; Small 1995, 1997) has stressed the importance of the urban/rural connection seen in the developmental relationship between urban centers and rural religious sanctuaries in ancient Greece. These studies have suggested that rural sanctuaries played an important role in shaping not only urban religious tradition but also an urban population's fundamental economic and political structure.

With regard to the archaeological issue in urban populations, the exciting dimension to the urban/rural spectrum in ancient Greece is that there was a wide range of rural sanctuary types, from small local sanctuaries to polis sanctuaries to interstate sanctuaries. Each type of rural context could be analyzed for its effect on urban populations, either alone or in conjunction with other sanctuary types. Already I (Small 1997) have argued that the effect of the interstate sanctuaries was first to make urban populations internally fluid and unstable in their political structures and then to create distinct relations of power within Greek urban populations. A very important scale in these relationships is temporal. The longevity and the rate of internal social and religious change in the sanctuaries varied greatly from slow in the interstate sanctuaries to more rapid in those that were smaller. How did this temporal scale fit into urban/rural dynamics when we can see that, internally, many Greek states were rapidly changing and that, externally, Greece was being politically and economically absorbed first into Hellenistic kingdoms and later into the Roman Empire?

The Maya at Colha

We return to the New World for our last example. Important work by King and Potter (1994; Potter and King 1995) at Colha in Belize follows earlier work by

Ball (1993) and Rice (1987) that identifies a general rural Mesoamerica that contains centers of production that are more often found in urban contexts, as well as exchange patterns that circumnavigate urban centers. Specifically, Colha was a large rural center for specialized lithic production. In addition it appears to have had lithic trade connections that circumnavigated any urban center.

We could explore the archaeological issue in the urban population from both the social/political scale and the economic scale. If the urban center for Colha was not the economic linchpin for the articulation of the population, as we suggest for Copán, then the urban population could be socially and economically integrated on more of a lineage model than one based on a market system (Sanders 1989, 1992; Webster et al. 2000). Compounding this issue is that of marginal production. How might we calculate rural marginal production in the case of such specialized production as that at Colha? Does specialized production, rather than part-time production, increase marginal production and thereby decrease the control of urban populations? If we have specialized rural production, does that mean that the urban population does not possess the greater share of specialized production and that whatever polity Colha belonged to was organically integrated economically in this territorial landscape?

Discussion

These five examples show, both directly and indirectly, that there is good cause to inject rural evidence into our considerations on the nature of urban populations. We cannot continue to simply assume that urban centers dominated their rural hinterlands to the point that these rural areas served to feed urban souls. We have to consider the distinct probability that the rural hinterlands, either as a whole or in part, represent alternative power bases sociopolitically, economically, and ideologically and can therefore impact urban populations in new ways. Although further investigation of this issue is bound to bring more points to the surface, there are some important issues that we should consider at this point in the formation of research designs. Simply put, we need to move beyond reliance on settlement survey for analysis of urban populations. Settlement studies have been very productive, but they can take us only so far, and, I would argue, a strict adherence only to the data from survey studies can be misleading as far as the relationship between urban and rural is concerned and its eventual effect on urban populations. The excellent work in the hinterland at Copán should serve as fair warning.

Close study of rural sites—and that means excavation—can hold some hope of testing concepts of urban/rural economic independence. Already, the contributors to Schwartz and Falconer's (1994a) volume on the countryside have suggested that we look at various forms of economic specialization and production to figure out whether urban populations were fully dependent on rural agricultural production. This could be extended to religious centers as well. We often assume that the religious center of a complex society was urban based, but several examples of rural religious centers in the Basin of Mexico (Townsend 1992:129–154) and much of the Mediterranean (Marinatos and Haag 1993) demonstrate that the connection between urban and rural populations can have rural religious foci, which affect the character of urban populations.

We need to consider identifying more thoroughly rural economic and political power. Although more excavation of rural communities is certainly needed, we should not overlook excavating rural sanctuaries, which were often arenas for the construction of rural political and economic power.

Conclusion

In short summary, then, there is much to indicate that we need to expand our conception of the relationship between urban populations and their rural hinterlands. Factoring the countryside into our understanding of urban populations allows us to analyze the growth, the size, and the very complexity of urban populations as a product of urban/rural negotiations, rather than simply the outcome of urban domination of country farmers.

17
Shining Stars and Black Holes

Population and Preindustrial Cities

Deborah L. Nichols

Today, more than one-half of the world's people live in a city, and the trend of increasing urbanization is expected to continue (Sanjek 1990:155). The roots of the urbanization of the modern world lie in the ancient past with the "urban revolution" (Childe 1950) that initiated a fundamental change in the size and organization of human communities and the larger societies of which cities are a part. The growth of urban populations throughout the world represents a marked departure from the small communities and kinship-based societies in which most of human biological and sociocultural evolution and history have taken place. The topic of population and preindustrial cities is wide ranging because the causes and consequences of human mortality, fertility, and migration are social, biological, and ecological. These processes are intricately connected, and their study necessitates a multifaceted or holistic approach (Trigger 1993:4–6, 25–26). The chapters in the volume respond to Paine's (1997:11–12) call to create a "thick demography" that balances the quantitative emphasis of paleodemography with a consideration of social processes as well as biological and ecological ones.

Well before agents and agency entered the vocabulary of most archaeologists, Cowgill (1975; see also 1996a) pointed out the importance of individual actors and their motives in population issues and social change. The basic unit of analysis in demography is the individual (Sanders 1997), and because preindustrial cities were large and heterogeneous, their skeletal remains (and associated mortuary goods and contexts) offer a rich body of information on individuals and social groups. The study of urban populations invites diverse theoretical perspectives, crosses subdisciplinary and disciplinary boundaries, and offers perhaps unique opportunities to wrestle with thorny theoretical issues of relations between micro- and macro-analysis and agency and structure (Drennan 2000) in the context of one of the most important long-term social and biological changes humans have experienced.

"Preindustrial" encompasses cities that are quite varied in their size, form, and cultural and historical contexts. Represented in this volume are some of the earliest cities in both chronological and developmental terms to some of the latest, largest, and most complex, for example, Kyongju, colonial New York City, and Rome. Cities are also dynamic, sometimes undergoing very rapid change, as when New York's population grew by 25 to 35 percent between 1698 and 1790 (Rothschild, chapter 6). In comparing preindustrial populations and cities, we need to bear in mind that the category "preindustrial" encompasses significant differences in terms of developmental trajectories.

Crosscutting the case studies in the volume are three major themes: "how to count," "shining stars and black holes," and "city and countryside."

How to Count: Estimating Population Size

Demographic data on preindustrial populations are obtained through two primary sources: written documents and archaeological remains. Where available, textual sources are likely to be given precedence over estimates derived from archaeological materials. No source or method, however, is unproblematic, even where systematic census data are available. Ongoing debates in the United States about how to conduct the national census and whether to use sampling methods to obtain an accurate head count illustrate the politics of under- and overnumeration. Although preindustrial cities were smaller, the politics of head counts were probably just as complicated. For most preindustrial cities, even those where writing was present, there are no complete census records, and population size and composition must be inferred or measured indirectly from other types of textual data, archaeological evidence, or both.

Written and archaeological records are both subject to the vagaries of preservation, and neither type of record was created to devise life tables. Archaeologists can take some small comfort from the fact that interpreting documentary data on preindustrial cities is neither simple nor straightforward, as attested to in the debates about the size of Classical Rome (Bagnall, chapter 7, Lo Cascio, chapter 2, Paine and Storey, chapter 3; see also Barber and Berdan 1998:178–186). The problem is even more complicated in the Americas because of the destruction of prehispanic texts in Mesoamerica and quipus in the Andes following the Spanish conquest and the effects of the Great Dying (Cook 1998). The catastrophic population decline that followed the footsteps of Europeans in the Americas complicates estimating the size and structure of precontact populations.

Archaeologists employ two general approaches to estimating ancient population parameters: osteological and settlement pattern, both regional and intrasite. The approaches to paleodemography are complementary, and I strongly concur with Paine (1997) that both should be pursued. Osteological research from a biosocial perspective on large skeletal populations from early cities lagged behind similar work in North America and Europe (Cohen 1990:71), but the research in this volume shows that this is now an active area of investigation in many world regions. There is a greater awareness that osteological analyses need to encompass the full spectrum of urban populations—from people who lived in a palace to the people who lived in a shanty—and rural communities (Buikstra 1997).

Settlement pattern studies provide data relevant to the size and the internal configuration and organization of cities and on the distribution of settlements at the regional level. Ideally, one wants to have both intrasite survey data on cities and regional data. For example, without regional settlement pattern studies in central Mexico and the detailed mapping of the ancient city of Teotihuacan, we would not have understood that the city's rapid growth between 100 BC and AD 200 involved the aggregation of 80 percent of the basin's population at Teotihuacan (Gorenflo, chapter 15; also Charlton and Nichols 1997b:184; Cowgill 1996b:329; Millon 1981:221–222; Sanders et al. 1979:114). Systematic surface survey of large regions is more feasible under some conditions than others, but even in areas where surface survey is highly productive, preindustrial cities may be overlain by dense modern construction, for example, Rome, New York, and Mexico City.

At the most basic level, we are interested in the size of preindustrial cities and tracing their population history. The archaeological answer to the question, How many people lived there? is anything but straightforward. Archaeologists usually begin with an archaeological "unit" of some kind (e.g., human skeleton, a mound, residential structure, artifact, and so on) that has some arguable relationship to population, and that relationship is assumed to remain constant. The units are dated (usually to an interval, period, or phase) and summed to obtain a relative population measure, assuming that increases or decreases are caused by changes in population numbers. To obtain an absolute estimate, either counts or densities, the archaeologist has to convert the measure using some kind of multiplier that is usually assumed to be constant (Nichols and Powell 1987:194; Rice and Culbert 1990:4–5). This multiplier may be based on a direct historical analogy, such as the relationship between dwellings and the number of occupants or refuse and population density, for example, or a more general formula may be employed, such as Naroll's (1962) figure of an average of 10 sq m of roofed space/person (Sanders 1999; Storey 1997a:121–123). The result should be an estimated range; however, all too frequently only the mean figure is cited, and this conveys a false sense of precision.

Archaeologists are aware that there are significant problems with these procedures (see Paine 1997:5–6; Rice and Culbert 1990:14–16; Wilson 1997:236). Rice (chapter 13) and Kusimba et al. (chapter 8) discuss the problems of contemporaneity and chronology and the relationship between archaeological units and population size and density. Archaeological phases and periods are usually of unequal duration and often encompass such long spans of time that shorter-term changes in growth and death rates and immigration are masked. The use of constants to characterize the relationship between some item of material culture and population and then to convert counts or densities of archaeological units into absolute estimates are clearly simplifying assumptions. Preindustrial urban households were stratified and differed in terms of wealth within, as well as between, classes and in the size of residences and amounts and types of household possessions (Smith 1987). The amount of refuse generated by a household also varied by occupation. A city with a large number of household-based craft workshops would have generated higher densities of refuse in domestic contexts than a city with few such workshops, even if both had the same number of residents and were occupied for the same amount of time, which is rarely the case. The situation becomes even more complicated if the intensity and organization of craft production changed over time in a city. How refuse was discarded and how subsequent site formation processes function are also important.

The Basin of Mexico regional settlement pattern survey has served as a model for reconstructing archaeological population histories in other regions (Nichols 1996; Sanders et al. 1979:34–40). The conversion from artifact to population densities was based on a direct historical analogy using a settlement typology derived from studies of twentieth-century rural settlements in the basin (Gorenflo, chapter 15). The archaeological estimates of the sixteenth-century contact-period population were compared against independently derived estimates from documentary sources. The same conversions have been applied to other parts of highland Mexico and the Andes, including Tiwanaku, discussed by Janusek and Blom (chapter 12; see also Parsons 1968). The population-artifact density conversions, however, have not been systematically reevaluated against subsequent excavation and intensive survey data from central Mexican sites, and their applicability to other regions also should be reexamined.

Another approach to urban paleodemography is often referred to as "ecological" and involves assessing the productive potential of a region in terms of the size of the urban population it can sustain with a particular system of technology. Rothshild's work on colonial New York illustrates how cities have multiple hinterlands. In the case of urban populations, both agricultural and nonagricultural resources need to be considered, as well as systems of supply and distribution and the long-term impact of urban populations on the landscape. Comparison of archaeological population estimates against the productivity of slash-and-burn rain-fed maize farming in the Late Classic southern Maya lowlands made clear that land must have been intensively cultivated, leading in some areas to environmental degradation. Garden plots around urban residences contributed to the dispersed character of most Maya cities. For the Classic Maya, but also elsewhere, Small (chapter 16) points out that most archaeological catchment's analyses simply assume that urban populations had unfettered access to resources of hinterlands.

Each approach to preindustrial urban populations, documentary, osteological, settlement pattern, and ecological, initially should be treated independently—each has strengths and weaknesses and its own theoretical and methodological issues to be addressed. Ideally, estimates derived from different approaches would be compared and cross-checked to establish a plausible minimum and maximum population size/density. Often when comparisons are made and they differ, as for example between documentary and archaeological population estimates, the tendency is to argue that one is methodologically flawed. This, of course, may be the case, but it is also possible that the differences reflect different segments of urban populations, a population at different points in time, or both.

Even though there are problems in archaeological estimates of urban population sizes, the effort is nonetheless important. Size and scale matter in human relations, as well as ecology and biology.

Shining Stars and Black Holes

The remains of ancient cities and the monumental architecture concentrated in them are among the most notable material manifestations of preindustrial states and civilization—the "shining stars" of ancient civilizations in the modern imagination. The covers of textbooks written to introduce students to archaeology commonly present images from ancient cities, especially monumental architecture, royal tombs, and elite sumptuary goods. The possibility that preindustrial cities might have been demographic "black holes" challenges modern-day romantic notions of life in ancient cities. Rebecca Storey (1992b) is one of the few anthropologists working on prehispanic cities in the Americas to study this issue, even though it has major implications for many aspects of ancient urban life and urban-rural social relations. One reason perhaps this issue has received less attention by archaeologists in the Americas is because of the lack of precontact censuses. Barrett and colleagues in their recent overview of infectious disease patterns discuss how the urban revolution intensified the increase in infectious disease mortality that was initiated with the shift from a mobile hunter-gatherer lifeway to a sedentary village–based one. These changes constitute the first epidemiological transition (Barrett et al. 1998:253):

> The severity of disease outbreaks during the first epidemiological transition intensified as regional populations increased and aggregated into urban centers. The crowded, unsanitary living conditions and poor nutrition characteristic of life in these early cities fostered rapid and devastating regional epidemics (Flinn 1974; McNeill 1976; McNeill 1978). The establishment of large cities increased problems of supplying clean water and removing human waste, while facilitating spread of even more virulent pathogens in enclosed and densely crowded habitations (McNeill 1976; Risse 1988).

This further intensified during the fifth century AD with expanded trade and population movements in Eurasia and then again beginning in the fifteenth century with the expansion of European states into the Americas, which introduced a whole suite of new diseases resulting in repeated epidemics (Cook 1998). Urban life played a role in disease spread from these encounters on both sides of the Atlantic. Moving in the opposite direction, some have suggested that frequent changes of sexual partners in the crowded European centers "favored a venereal form of transmission in the form of syphilis" of treponemal infections (Barrett et al. 1998:254).

Storey's (chapter 14) investigation of the Tlajinga 33 apartment compound in the ancient city of Teotihuacan offers an excellent model of paleodemographic research explicitly designed to research the urban graveyard effect. Her analysis indicates that at least for these relatively poor residents, Teotihuacan, the shining star of Mesoamerican Classic period cities, was an urban death trap in the Late Classic period. If the patterns identified for Tlajinga 33 reflect the general situation of the poor at Teotihuacan, then the inability of immigration to compensate for increased mortality in Late Teotihuacan times would have seriously challenged Teotihuacan's economic and political predominance. Storey's research needs to be expanded with data from other parts of the city and from sites in Teotihuacan's hinterlands.

Lo Cascio (chapter 2) also finds that conditions in Rome varied throughout its long history and that social class affected mortality rates. Shaw (chapter 4) documents how mortality in Rome fluctuated seasonally. Lo Cascio criticizes historians for overgeneralizing the urban graveyard effect, and he questions the view of Rome as a demographic sink in contrast to the recent research by Paine and Storey (chapter 3). The issue is an empirical one; however, it may not be resolved by analysis of the extant body of epigraphic data alone. Ideally, one ought to compare results of independently derived documentary, settlement, and osteological analyses of different segments of Rome's population at different points in time. I would expect to see temporal, as well as class, differences in the health (as related to both infectious diseases and nutrition) of Rome's population (Cohen 1989:68, 1990:72; Danforth 1999). The issue of preindustrial cities as demographic "black holes" for the poor extends beyond determining rates of urban mortality, fertility, and immigration to social relations, political economy, religion and ideology, and urban-rural relations.

City and Countryside: Polity, Economy, Ideology, and Population

Rome and the Korean city of Kyongju, whose population grew to an estimated one million persons before the decline of the United Silla state in AD 935 (Nelson, chapter 10), represent the upper size limit of preindustrial cities—most were much smaller. A comprehensive understanding of the dynamics of preindustrial urban populations also requires analysis of rural populations and communities and relations between city and countryside—*cities are part of larger societies* (Fox 1977; Schwartz and Falconer 1994a; Yoffee 1997:260–261). Preindustrial cities could not have existed without hinterlands that provided food, other resources, and immigrants, and this supply was not guaranteed (Garnsey 1990; Newman et al. 1990). The growth of southeast Asian port cities and maritime trade cannot be understood apart from the larger political economy (Junker, chapter 11). Control over hinterland resources and labor was not only a potential source of power but also a cause of competition and factionalism between urban and provincial elites and rural commoners (Small, chapter 16; see also Brumfiel 1994a, 1994b; Stone 1997:16).

In a major comparative study, Fletcher (1995) identifies three major transitions or thresholds in the size of human settlements related to what he theorizes as interaction limits (the maximum population density humans can deal with) and communication limits (the maximum distance over which information can be communicated with any particular technology). The first transition was from small mobile bands to sedentary villages of 1 to 2 ha, and the second transition involved the shift from villages to agrarian cities of more than 100 ha and populations on the order of 10,000 to 20,000. The change from agrarian to industrial cities of more than 100 sq km comprises Fletcher's third transition.

Morris (chapter 1) looks at the growth of Greek cities in terms of Fletcher's transitions. He argues, however, that Fletcher's emphasis on technological and material aspects of these structural revolutions fails to adequately consider socioeconomic relations and processes that Weber (1968[1921]) had previously called attention to in his early tripartite typology of urban economies, "consumer, producer, and mercantile." In the case of Greece the second transition, involving the development of cities with populations of approximately 40,000, and the third transition, when some cities exceeded 500,000 persons, are better explained by a Weberian framework that considers economics, politics, and power. Only with the creation of centralized empires could a mixed rentier/administrative elite draw sufficient wealth into cities to support such large populations. The history of urban growth, Morris concludes, is "inseparable from [the histories of] administration and imperialism," and Weber's model of the consumer city accords well with the nature of Greek urbanism.

Capital cities of expansionist states sometimes grew to exceptional sizes because of the flow of wealth into them (Sanders and Webster 1988, 1989; Trigger 1972:580–581)—wealth that was often carried on the currents of water transportation (see Rothschild, chapter 6; also see Sanders and Santley 1983). Stanish (1998) uses comparative data to show that despite their size, Andean empires were associated with a relatively low degree of urbanism. Even though Cuzco, the capital of the Inca Empire, was the largest city to have developed in the prehispanic Andes, it was relatively small compared to the total size of the Inca Empire or imperial cities in other parts of the world. Especially relevant is the comparison between prehispanic Andean and Mesoamerican cities of the Inca and the Aztecs because of their similar technology, isolation from the Old World, and the rapid development of both empires that were less than 100 years old when conquered by the Spanish in the sixteenth century.

Stanish (1998) argues that the absence of a market mechanism in the Andes imposed an upper limit on the size of cities (see also Kolata 1997). In contrast to the intensification of market exchange (along with tribute) in the Aztec political economy, the Inca state finance system relied heavily on administered trade and tribute within an ideology of reciprocity. Andean cities were largely administrative and ceremonial or ritual. The significant economic links between city and countryside occurred primarily through "appropriative rather than commercial mechanisms" (Trigger 1993:11, 2003:132). Similarly, the Egyptian state that was unified early in its development also exhibited a relatively low degree of urbanism and, like the Andes, had a politically centralized economy (Baines and Yoffee 1998:208–209; Charlton and Nichols 1997a; Trigger 1993, 2003; Wenke 1997).

Similar to Egypt and the Inca Empire, the early Chinese state discussed by Liu (chapter 9) does not seem to have been very urbanized, although her population estimates are probably the first systematic attempts because none are available for most Shang centers (Underhill et al. 1998; Wenke 1999:528; Yates 1997). Trigger (2003:107–111; cf. Yates 1997) considers early China, along with the early Egyptian and Inca states, as an example of a "territorial" state that encompassed a relatively large geographic area and had a hierarchy of administrative centers, but relatively small urban centers and limited commercial or market exchange between urban centers and rural communities. "Even national capitals, with a maximum population of probably no more than fifty thousand people, were no larger than those of a substantial city state. This was because these centers were inhabited almost exclusively by the ruling class and the administrators, craft specialists, and retainers who served them" (Trigger 1993:10–11, 2003:131–140). In these states, the economic connection between the city and rural villages tended to take the form of corvée labor, tribute, taxes, or rent (Stanish 1998, Trigger 1993:11).

Liu challenges the model that the "territorial state" in the Shang period was a traditional two-tier economy of elites exacting rent tax from commoner farmers, with the elites inhabiting ceremonial centers occupied by themselves and their attached craftsmen. Liu argues that the corollaries of this model—the ceremonial center must have a population that is not involved in any agricultural activity, that the craftsmen there make only prestige items, and that all the villages in the hinterland are purely agricultural and have virtually no craft specialization—have never been tested. The evidence from Erlitou indicates the production of both utilitarian and sumptuary goods and a mix of independent and attached specialists. The production of bronze ritual vessels (used as sacrificial offerings by elites in rituals of ancestor veneration) apparently came under state control, and this tends to support Trigger's territorial state model. Liu's work, however, also shows that not all craft production was elite controlled or restricted to urban centers. She sees similarities with Mesopotamia (southern Mesopotamia is devoid of many mineral resources). Mesopotamian core-periphery relations were largely based on trade (see chapters in Rothman 2001), and Liu sees early state expansion in China expressed in vigorous exchange between the Erlitou and secondary centers giving way to an emphasis on militarism and direct political control by the ruling lineage in the Xia-Shang transition.

Political economy was a significant aspect of the growth and composition of preindustrial cities. Why markets (or at least partial markets; see Hicks [1987]) and independent merchants were more important in some preindustrial state economies than others has not been satisfactorily explained. Complementing Junker's emphasis (chapter 11) on political economy, maritime trade, and urbanism in Southeast Asia, Janusek and Blom (chapter 12) focus on Andean cities, such as Tiwanaku, as centers of public ritual, feasting, and kin-based social relations. They point out that Childe's (1950) and Weber's (1968[1921]) concepts of urbanism emphasized the importance of stratification and class structure over kinship. Archaeologists and historians working in diverse geographical and historical contexts, including Mesopotamia, Shang China, Classical Greece, and the prehispanic Maya, have found that corporate groups grounded in an ideology or idiom of kinship continued to be important in early cities and states (see Charlton and Nichols 1997a:11–12 for a review). Tiwanaku was divided into residential compounds, and Janusek and Blom propose that each compound was occupied by a suprahousehold group integrated around an ideal of kinship and distinguished from other compounds by differences in material culture and household rituals. Some of these groups might have been founded by immigrants from outside the Tiwanku region who continued to maintain affiliations with their homelands. Janusek and Blom suggest that the convergence of people on the city for public rituals provided leaders an opportunity to promote a state ideology of Tiwanaku as a community writ large while at the same time people also expressed their local community affiliations.

Archaeologists have not given sufficient consideration to social relations between urban dwellers and rural communities and how they were sustained and to the processes of rural-urban migration—who migrated and under what conditions did people move from village to towns and cities and the reverse. Immigration was important not only in sustaining cities but in the creation of the earliest cities, for example, Uruk, that experienced rapid nucleation of populations from rural villages and smaller centers (Adams 1965, 1981; Adams and Nissen 1972). Isotopic and DNA studies are providing new data on immigration and the composition of early urban populations (e.g., Price et al. 2000; White et al. 2002).

Bagnall (chapter 7) suggests that differences in sex ratios among Middle Egyptian cities may reflect uneven economic conditions that influenced the migration of males from the countryside into cities. The pattern of late adolescent/young adult males migrating to cities from the countryside is a familiar one in the modern world, and it is interesting to see this pattern much earlier. Peterson et al.'s (chapter 5) research on Danish medieval towns suggests reduced survivorship among adolescent and young adults in more urban settings that they attribute to epidemic disease. Especially interesting is their documentation of selective migration of taller people moving to towns.

Gorenflo brings a geographer's perspective to the regional settlement pattern and population history of the Basin of Mexico, and his "mobility" maps offer a new way of looking at these data from an area that has been one of the most urbanized parts of the world for 2,000 years. There was considerable population relocation over time in the basin as a result of a number of factors, including the growth and decline of the large cities of Teotihuacan (ca. 100 BC–AD 650), Tula (ca. AD 900/950–1150/1200), and Tenochtitlan, the Aztec imperial capital conquered by the Spanish in 1519–1521. Native histories recorded after the Spanish conquest emphasize migrations of various ethnic groups from places outside the basin. Acknowledging the dating problem of the long archaeological periods, Gorenflo does not believe that *large-scale* population movements from outside the basin are necessary to account for the population changes indicated by the archaeological data. This is likely to refuel debates about interpreting native histories and material culture (e.g. ceramic styles) changes.

Diversity is a hallmark of urban life, and it was (and is) multidimensional. Ancient Andean people and others, such as the Classic period Maya, went to considerable lengths to express aspects of their social identities in bodily form through head shaping and the style of headgear and other clothing they wore. Janusek and Blom's discussion of patterns of Andean head shaping reflects an improving appreciation of the complexity of ethnicity by archaeologists (see Jones 1997; Spence 1992). Ethnicity has been a central theme of late-twentieth-century anthropology. The challenge for archaeologists is to develop middle-range theories linking material culture and the archeological record with more nuanced understandings of ethnicity and its situational aspects than the normative perspective that dominated both archaeologists' and historians' views of the past.

Conclusions

Preindustrial cities were both shining stars, places of innovation that brought together more diverse groups of people than had ever before resided in a single settlement, and black holes, places of tremendous hardship for some and at some times places of horrendous deaths. My comments have stressed social aspects of issues raised in this volume about preindustrial urban populations to emphasize that "population" is not just of interest in ecology, biology, and demography

(Southhall 1998:5). Scale matters in human social interactions in interesting and complex ways, as seen in the relationship between the size of preindustrial cities, state structures, and forms of political economy. Although the flow of wealth in large empires fostered the growth of capital cities, how large these urban centers became was also influenced by the form of the political economy and the development of market exchange. Good reconstructions of the size and structure of both urban and rural populations are essential for understanding social relations, yet for many preindustrial cities and states we do not even have reliable estimates of population size (e.g., Feinman 1998). The issue of the preindustrial urban death trap is important and deserves more attention from archaeologists outside of Europe than it has received. As at Teotihuacan, I expect that mortality and fertility varied among segments of the urban population and over time, and this raises many interesting questions, ranging from the organization of households to the politics, economics, and ideologies of urban-rural relations that encouraged or discouraged people moving into or out of cities.

A recent review of urban anthropology (Low 1996) makes little mention of archaeology, and demography does not fare much better. The exclusion of archaeology reflects disciplinary fragmentation but, perhaps, also an implicit assumption that archeological studies of cities are not relevant because urbanism in the modern world is so different from that of preindustrial cities. Rothschild's (chapter 6) discussion of New York City shows how the urban populations of colonial cities linked world systems, the development of capitalism and industrialization, and the formation of nation-states.

The chapters in this volume prompt archaeologists, historians, and demographers to continue to be critical about the development of methods and theories of preindustrial urban dynamics. At the same time, a comprehensive understanding of this important transformation in human societies cannot be accomplished without the long-term data of archaeology and history.

References

Abbott, C.
 1974 Neighborhoods of New York, 1760–1775. *New York History* 15:35–54.
Abercrombie, T.
 1986 The Politics of Sacrifice: An Aymara Cosmology in Action. Unpublished PhD dissertation, University of Chicago, Chicago.
Abrams, E.
 1987 Economic Specialization and Construction Personnel in Classic Period Copan, Honduras. *American Antiquity* 52:485–499.
 1994 *How the Maya Built Their World: Energetics and Ancient Architecture.* University of Texas Press, Austin.
 1995 A Model of Fluctuating Labor Value and the Establishment of State Power: An Application to the Prehispanic Maya. *Latin American Antiquity* 60:196–213.
Acsadi, G., and J. Nemeskeri
 1970 *History of Human Lifespan and Mortality.* Translated by K. Balas. Akademiai Kiado, Budapest.
Adams, E. B.
 1979 *Kyongju Guide: Cultural Spirit of Silla in Korea.* International Tourist, Seoul.
Adams, R. E. W.
 1986 Río Azul. *National Geographic* 169:420–451.
 1999 *Río Azul. An Ancient Maya City.* Oklahoma University Press, Norman.
Adams, R. E. W. (editor)
 1977 *The Origins of Maya Civilization.* School of American Research Advanced Seminar Series. University of New Mexico Press, Albuquerque.
Adams, R. E. W., W. E. Brown Jr., and T. P. Culbert
 1981 Radar Mapping, Archaeology, and Ancient Maya Land Use. *Science* 213:1457–1463.
Adams, R. E. W., and R. C. Jones
 1981 Spatial Patterns and Regional Growth among Maya Cities. *American Antiquity* 46:301–322.
Adams, R. McC.
 1965 *Land behind Baghdad: A History of Settlement on the Diyala Plains.* University of Chicago Press, Chicago.

1966   *The Evolution of Urban Society: Early Mesopotamia and Prehispanic Mexico.* Aldine, Chicago.

1981   *Heartland of Cities: Surveys of Ancient Settlement and Land Use on the Central Flood-plain of the Euphrates.* University of Chicago Press, Chicago.

Adams, R. McC., and H. Nissen
1972   *The Uruk Countryside: The Natural Setting of Urban Societies.* University of Chicago Press, Chicago.

Agbaje-Williams, B.
1978   Transect Survey of Old Oyo. Unpublished report. African Studies, University of Ibadan, Nigeria.

1983   A Contribution to the Archaeology of Old Oyo. Unpublished PhD dissertation, University of Ibadan, Nigeria.

1991   Archaeology and Yoruba Studies. In *Yoruba Historiography,* edited by T. Forola, pp. 5–29. African Studies Program, University of Wisconsin, Madison.

Agbaje-Williams, B., and J. C. Onyango-Abuje
1981   Archaeological Work at Old Oyo: 1978–81. *Nyame Akuma* 19:9–11.

Akurgal, E.
1983   *Alt-Smyrna,* Vol. 1. Türk Tarih Kurumu Basimevi, Ankara.

Albarracín-Jordán, J. V.
1992   Prehispanic and Early Colonial Settlement Patterns in the Lower Tiwanaku Valley, Bolivia. Unpublished PhD dissertation, Southern Methodist University.

1996   *Tiwanaku: Arqueología Regional y Dinámica Segmentaria.* Plural Editores, La Paz.

2003   Tiwanaku: A Pre-Inca, Segmentary State in the Andes. In *Tiwanaku and Its hinter-land: Archaeology and Paleoecology of an Andean Civilization,* edited by Alan L. Ko-lata, Vol. II, pp. 95–111. Smithsonian Institution Press,, Washington, DC.

Albarracín-Jordán, J. V., and J. E. Mathews
1990   *Asentamientos Prehispánicos del Valle de Tiwanaku, Vol. 1.* Producciones CIMA: La Paz.

Albó, X.
1972   Dinámica en la estructura intercomunitaria de Jesús de Machaca. *América Indígena* 32:773–816.

Alcock, S.
1991   Urban Survey and the Polis of Phlius. *Hesperia* 60:421–463.

1993   *Graecia Capta: The Landscapes of Roman Greece.* Cambridge University Press, New York.

1994   Breaking up the Hellenistic World. In *Classical Greece: Ancient Histories and Mod-ern Archaeologies,* edited by I. Morris, pp.171–190. Cambridge University Press, New York.

Alconini Mújica, S.
1995   *Rito, Símbolo e Historia en la Pirámide de Akapana, Tiwanaku: Un Análisis de Ce-rámica Ceremonial Prehispánica.* Editorial Acción, La Paz.

Allen, J.
1991   Trade and Site Distribution in Early Historic-Period Kedah: Geoarchaeological, His-toric and Locational Evidence. In *Indo-Pacific Prehistory 1990,* edited by P. Bellwood, Vol. 1, pp. 307–319. Bulletin of the Indo-Pacific Prehistory Association No. 10. Indo-Pacific Prehistory Association, Canberra, Australia.

Altschuler, M.
1958   On the environmental limitations of Maya cultural development. *Southwestern Jour-nal of Anthropology* 14:189–198.

Ampolo, C.
1984   Tributi e decime dei Siracusani. *Opus* 3:31–36.

Andaya, B. W.
1992   Political Development between the Sixteenth and Eighteenth Centuries. In *The Cambridge History of Southeast Asia*. Volume 1. *From Early Times to c. 1800*, edited by N. Tarling, pp. 402–459. Cambridge University Press, New York.
1995   Upstreams and Downstreams in Early Modern Sumatra. *Historian* 57:537–552.

Andaya, B. W., and L. Andaya
1982   *A History of Malaysia*. Macmillan, London.

Andaya, B. W., and Y. Ishii
1992   Religious Developments in Southeast Asia, c. 1500–1800. In *The Cambridge History of Southeast Asia*. Volume 1. *From Early Times to c. 1800*, edited by N. Tarling, pp. 508–571. Cambridge University Press, New York.

Andaya, L.
1992   Interactions with the Outside World and Adaptation in Southeast Asian Society, 1500–1800. In *The Cambridge History of Southeast Asia*. Volume 1. *From Early Times to c. 1800*, edited by N. Tarling, pp. 345–401. Cambridge University Press, New York.

Andrén, A.
1985   *Den urbana scenen: städer och samhälle i det medeltida Danmark*. CWK, Malmö.

Andrews, W., and B. Fash
1992   Continuity and Change in a Royal Maya Residential Complex at Copán. *Ancient Mesoamerica* 3:63–88.

Andrews V, E. W.
1990   The Early Ceramic History of the Lowland Maya. In *Vision and Revision in Maya Studies*, edited by F. S. Clancy and P. D. Harrison, pp. 1–20. University of New Mexico Press, Albuquerque.

Andrews V, E. W. and N. Hammond
1990   Redefinition of the Swasey Phase at Cuello, Belize. *American Antiquity* 54:570–584.

Aperghis, M.
2001   Population—Production—Taxation—Coinage: A Model for the Seleukid Economy. In *Hellenistic Economies*, edited by Z. Archibald, J. Davies, V. Gabrielsen, and G. Oliver, pp. 69–102. Routledge, London.

Armillas, P.
1971   Gardens in Swamps. *Science* 174:653–661.

Asheri, D.
1992   Sicily, 478–431 B.C. In *Cambridge Ancient History*, 2nd ed., Vol. 5, edited by D. Lewis, J. Boardman, J. Davies, and M. Ostwald, pp. 147–170. Cambridge University Press, New York.

Ashmore, W.
1989   Construction and Cosmology: Politics and Ideology in Lowland Maya Settlement Patterns. In *Word and Image in Maya Culture: Explorations in Language, Writing, and Representation*, edited by W. F. Hands and D. S. Rice, pp. 272–286. University of Utah Press, Salt Lake City.
1990   Ode to a Dragline: Demographic Reconstructions at Classic Quirigua. In *Precolumbian Population History in the Maya Lowlands*, edited by T. P. Culbert and D. S. Rice, pp. 63–82. University of New Mexico Press, Albuquerque.
1992   Deciphering Maya Architectural Plans. In *New Theories on the Ancient Maya*, ed-

ited by E. C. Danien and R. J. Sharer, pp. 173–184. The University Museum, Philadelphia.

Ashmore, W. (editor)
1981   *Lowland Maya Settlement Patterns.* University of New Mexico Press, Albuquerque.

Ashmore, W., and B. Knapp (editors)
1999   *Archaeologies of Landscape: Contemporary Perspectives.* Blackwell Publishers, New York.

Ashmore, W., and J. A. Sabloff
2002   Spatial Orders in Maya Civic Plans. *Latin American Antiquity* 13:201–215.
2003   Interpreting Ancient Maya Civic Plans: Reply to Smith. *Latin American Antiquity* 14:229–236.

Aurigemma, S.
1932   *L' "Area" cimiteriale cristiana di Aïn Zára presso Tripoli di Barberia.* Studi di Antichità Christiana No. 5. Pontifico Istituto di Archeologia Cristiana, Rome.

Austin, M.
1981   *The Hellenistic World from Alexander to the Roman Conquest.* Cambridge University Press, New York.

Aykroyd, R. G., D. Lucy, A. M. Pollard, and C. A. Roberts
1999   Nasty, Brutish, but Not Necessarily Short: A Reconsideration of the Statistical Methods Used to Calculate Age at Death from Adult Human Skeletal and Dental Age Indicators. *American Antiquity* 64:55–70.

Back W., and B. Hanshaw
1978   Hydrochemistry of the Northern Yucatan Peninsula, Mexico, with a Section on Mayan Water Practices. In *Geology and Hydrogeology of Northeastern Yucatan,* edited by W. C. Ward and A. E. Weidie, pp. 229–260. New Orleans Geological Survey, New Orleans.

Bagnall, R. S.
2002   The Effects of Plague: Model and Evidence. *Journal of Roman Archaeology* 15:114–120.

Bagnall, R. S., and B. W. Frier
1994   *The Demography of Roman Egypt.* Cambridge University Press, New York.

Bagnall, R. S., B. W. Frier, and I. C. Rutherford
1997   *The Census Register P. Oxy. 984: The Reverse of Pindar's Paeans.* Papyrologica Bruxellensia 29. Fondation Égyptologie Reine Élisabeth, Brussels.

Bailey, R., G. Head, M. Jenke, B. Owen, R. Rechten, and E. Zechentes
1989   Hunting and Gathering in the Tropical Rain Forest: Is it Possible? *American Anthropologist* 91:59–82.

Baines, John, and Norman Yoffee
1998   Order, Legitimacy, and Wealth in Ancient Egypt and Mesopotamia. In *Archaic States,* edited by G. M. Feinman, and J. Marcus, pp. 199–260. School of American Research Press, Santa Fe.

Baldini, G.
1738   Dissertazione VIII: Sopra certi Vasetti di creta in gran numero trovati in una Camera sepolcrale nella Vigna di S. Cesario in Roma. *Accademia Etrusca di Cortona: saggi e dissertazioni academiche* 2:151–161.

Ball, J. W.
1993   Pottery, Potters, Palaces, and Polities: Some Socioeconomic and Political Implications of Late Classic Maya Ceramic Industries. In *Lowland Maya Civilization in the Eighth Century A.D.,* edited by J. A. Sabloff and J. S. Henderson, pp. 243–272. Dumbarton Oaks, Washington, DC.

Bandy, M. S.
2002 Population and History in the Ancient Titicaca Basin. Unpublished PhD dissertation, Department of Anthropology, University of California, Berkeley.

Barber, R. J., and F. E. Berdan
1998 *The Emperor's Mirror: Understanding Cultures through Primary Sources.* University of Arizona Press, Tucson.

Barrett, R., C. W. Kuzawa, T. McDade, and G. J. Armelegos
1998 Emerging and Re-Emerging Infectious Diseases: The Third Epidemiologic Transition. *Annual Review of Anthropology* 27:247–271.

Barry, W.
1993 The Crowd of Ptolemaic Alexandria and the Riot of 203 BC. *Échos du monde classique/Classical Views* 37:415–431.

Bartoccini, R., and D. Mazzoleni
1977 Le iscrizioni del cimitero di En-Ngila. *Rivista di Archeologica Cristiana* 53:157–198.

Becker, M. J.
1979 Priests, Peasants, and Ceremonial centers: The Intellectual History of a Model. In *Maya Archaeology and Ethnohistory,* edited by N. Hammond and G. R. Willey, pp. 3–20. University of Texas Press, Austin.

Bellwood, P.
1985 *Prehistory of the Indo-Malaysian Archipelago.* Academic Press, New York.

Beloch, K. J.
1968 [1886] *Die Bevölkerung der Griechisch-Römischen Welt.* Studia Historica 60, L'erma di Bretschneider, Rome.

Bennett, W. C.
1936 Excavations in Bolivia. *Anthropological Papers of the American Museum of Natural History* 35:329–507.

Bentley, G. R., G. Jasienska, and T. Goldberg
1993 The Fertility in Agricultural Societies: Another Look at the Evidence. *Current Anthropology* 34:778–785.

Bentley, G. R., R. R. Paine, and J. L. Boldsen
2001 Reproductive Ecology and Early Agriculture. In *Reproductive Ecology and Human Evolution,* edited by P. T. Ellison. Aldine de Gruyter, New York.

Berlin, H.
1958 El glifo "emblema" en las inscripciones mayas. *Journal de la Société de Américanistes* 47:111–119.

Berlo, J. C. (editor)
1992 *Art, Ideology, and the City of Teotihuacan.* Dumbarton Oaks Research Library and Collection, Washington, D.C.

Bermann, M. P.
1994 *Lukurmata: Household Archaeology in Prehispanic Bolivia.* Princeton University Press, Princeton.

Bertonio, P. L.
1984 [1612] *Vocabulario de la Lengua Aymara.* CERES/IFEA/MUSEF, Cochabamba, Bolivia.

Billows, R.
1995 *Kings and Colonists.* E. J. Brill, New York.

Bintliff, J.
1997 Regional Survey, Demography, and the Rise of Complex Societies in the Ancient Aegean. *Journal of Field Archaeology* 24:1–38.

2002   Settlement Pattern Analysis and Demographic Modeling. In *New Developments in Italian Landscape Archaeology*, edited by P. Attema, pp. 28–35. BAR International Series 1091. Tempus Reparatum, Oxford.

Bintliff, J., P. Howard, and A. Snodgrass.
1999   The Hidden Landscape of Prehistoric Greece. *Journal of Mediterranean Archaeology* 12:139–168.

Bintliff, J., and A. Snodgrass
1988   Mediterranean Survey and the City. *Antiquity* 62:57–71.

Blackmar, E.
1989   *Manhattan for Rent, 1785–1850.* Cornell University Press, Ithaca.

Blanton, R. E.
1972   *Prehispanic Settlement Patterns of the Ixtapalapa Peninsula Region, Mexico.* Occasional Papers in Anthropology 6, Department of Anthropology, Pennsylvania State University, University Park.
1976   Anthropological Studies of Cities. *Annual Review of Anthropology* 5:249–264.
1978   *Monte Alban: Settlement Patterns at the Ancient Zapotec Capital.* Academic Press, New York.

Blanton, R. E., G. M. Feinman, S. A. Kowalewski, and P. N. Peregrine
1996   A Dual-Processual Theory for the Evolution of Mesoamerican Civilization. *Current Anthropology* 37:1–14.

Blanton, R., S. Kowalewski, G. Feinman, and J. Appel
1982   *Monte Alban's Hinterland. Part 1: The Prehispanic Settlement Patterns of the Central and Southern Parts of the Valley of Oaxaca, Mexico.* Memoir No. 15. University of Michigan Museum of Anthropology, Ann Arbor.

Blom, D. E.
1999   Tiwanaku Regional Interaction and Social Identity: A Bioarchaeological Approach. Unpublished PhD dissertation, University of Chicago, Chicago.
2005   Embodying Borders: Bioarchaeology and Diversity in Tiwanaku Society. *Journal of Anthropological Archaeology* 24:1–24.

Blom, D. E., B. Hallgrímsson, L. Keng, M. C. Lozada, and J. E. Buikstra
1998   Tiwanaku "Colonization": Bioarchaeological Implications for Migration in the Moquegua Valley, Peru. *World Archaeology* 30:238–261.

Bocquet-Appel, J. P., and C. Masset
1982   Farewell to Paleodemography. *Journal of Human Evolution* 11:321–333.
1996   Paleodemography: Expectancy and False Hope. *American Journal of Physical Anthropology* 99:571–584.

Bodel, J.
1994   Graveyards and Groves: A Study of the Lex Lucerina. *American Journal of Ancient History* 11:i–vii, 1–133.

Boldsen, J. L.
1984a   A Statistical Evaluation of the Basis for Predicting Stature from Lengths of Long Bones in European Population. *American Journal of Physical Anthropology* 65:305–311.
1984b   Paleodemography of Two Southern Scandinavian Medieval Communities. *Meddelanden från Lunds universitets historiska museum 1983–1984,* new series 5:107–115.
1990   Population Structure, Body Proportions and Height Prediction. *Journal of Forensic Medicine* (Istanbul) 6:157–165.
1997a   Estimating Patterns of Disease and Mortality in a Medieval Danish Village. In *Integrating Archaeological Demography: Multidisciplinary Approaches to Prehistoric Popula-*

tion. edited by R. R. Paine, pp. 232–241. Center for Archaeological Investigations, Occasional Papers 24, Southern Illinois University Press, Carbondale.

1997b   Patterns of Childhood Mortality in Medieval Scandinavia. *Revista di Antropologia* 74:147–159.

Boldsen, J. L., and D. Kronborg

1984   The Distribution of Stature among Danish Conscripts in 1852–1856. *Annals of Human Biology* 11:555–565.

Boldsen, J. L. and J. Søgaard

1998   A History of Height in Denmark. In *The Biological Standard of Living in Comparative Perspective,* edited by J. Komlos and J. Baten, pp. 467–482. Franz Steiner Verlag, Stuttgart.

Bollig, M.

1987   Ethnic Relations and Spatial Mobility in Africa: A Review of the Peripatetic Niche. In *The Other Nomads: Peripatetic Minorities in Cross-Cultural Perspective,* edited by A. Rao, pp. 179–228. Böhlau, Cologne.

Boot, E.

2001   Mul tepal—"Joint Rule or Government" at Chichen Itza, Yucatan, Mexico: Historic Reality, or Not? Paper presented at the Sixth European Maya Conference, European Association of Mayanists, Hamburg, December.

Boserup, E.

1965   *The Conditions of Agricultural Growth.* Aldine, Chicago.

Bourdieu, P.

1984   *A Social Critique of the Judgment of Taste.* Translated by Richard Nice. Harvard University Press, Cambridge.

Box, G. E. P.

1949   A General Distribution Theory for a Class of Likelihood Criteria. *Biometrika* 36: 317–346.

Boyaval, B.

1976   *Corpus des étiquettes de momies grecques.* L'Univerisité de Lille, Lille, France.

Bradley, I., and R. L. Meek

1986   *Matrices and Society: Matrix Algebra and Its Applications in the Social Sciences.* Princeton University Press, Princeton.

Brainerd, G. W.

1954   *The Maya Civilization.* Southwest Museum, Los Angeles.

1956   Changing Living Patterns of the Yucatan Maya. *American Antiquity* 22:162–164.

Brass, W.

1971   On the Scale of Mortality. In *Biological Aspects of Demography,* edited by William Brass. Taylor and Francis, London.

Braswell, G.

1992   Obsidian-Hydration Dating, the Coner Phase, and Revisionist Chronology at Copán, Honduras. *Latin American Antiquity* 3:130–147.

Braudel, F.

1972   [1949] *The Mediterranean and the Mediterranean World in the Age of Philip II.* Translated by Siân Reynolds. Collins, London. Originally published as *La Méditerranéen et le monde Méditerranéen à l'epoque de Philippe II.* Colin, Paris.

1993   [1963] *Grammaire des civilisations.* Flammarion, Paris. Originally published as part of *Le monde actrel, histoire et civilisations,* edited by S. Baile, F. Braudel, and R. Phillipe. Libraire Eugène Belin, Paris.

Brenner, M.

1983   *Paleolimnological Assessment of Human Disturbance in the Drainage Basins of Three Northern Guatemalan Lakes.* PhD dissertation, Department of Zoology, University of Florida, Gainesville.

Brenner, M., B. W. Leyden, and M. W. Binford

1990   Recent Sedimentary Histories of Shallow Lakes in the Guatemalan Savannas. *Journal of Paleolimnology* 86:1–14.

Brind'Amour, P.

1983   *Le calendrier romain: recherches chronologiques.* Editiones de l'Université d'Ottawa, Ottawa.

Bronson, B.

1968   Vacant terrain excavations at Tikal. Manuscript on file, Tikal Project, Museum, University of Pennsylvania, Philadelphia.

1977   Exchange at the Upstream and Downstream Ends: Notes toward a Functional Model of the Coastal State in Southeast Asia. In *Economic Exchange and Social Interaction in Southeast Asia,* edited by Karl Hutterer, pp. 39–52. University of Michigan Papers on South and Southeast Asia No. 13. Center for South and Southeast Asian Studies, Ann Arbor.

1979   The Archaeology of Sumatra and the Problem of Srivijaya. In *Early Southeast Asia: Essays in Archaeology, History and Historical Geography,* edited by R. B. Smith and W. Watson, pp. 393–405. Oxford University Press, New York.

Bronson, B., and J. Wisseman

1976   Palembang as Srivijaya: The Lateness of Early Cities in Southern Southeast Asia. *Asian Perspectives* 19:220–239.

Brown, D. E.

1976   *Principles of Social Structure: Southeast Asia.* Duckworth, London.

Brumfiel, E. M.

1994a   Ethnic Groups and Political Development in Ancient Mexico. In *Factional Competition and Political Development in the New World,* edited by E. M. Brumfiel and J. W. Fox, pp. 89–102. Cambridge University Press, New York.

1994b   Factional Competition and Political Development in the New World: An Introduction. In *Factional Competition and Political Development in the New Word,* edited by E. M. Brumfiel and J. W. Fox, pp. 3–13. Cambridge University Press, Cambridge.

Brumfiel, E. M., and T. K. Earle

1987   Specialization, Exchange, and Complex Societies: An Introduction. In *Specialization, Exchange, and Complex Societies,* edited by E. Brumfiel and T. Earle, pp. 1–9. Cambridge University Press, New York.

Brunt, P. A.

1987   [1971] *Italian Manpower 225 B.C.–A.D. 14,* 2nd ed. Oxford University Press, New York. Originally published 1971, Oxford University Press, New York.

Bruun, C.

1991   *The Water Supply of Ancient Rome: A Study of Roman Imperial Administration.* Societas Scientiarum Fennica, Helsinki.

1997   Acquedotti e condizioni sociali di Roma imperiale: immagini e realtà. In *La Rome impériale: démographie et logistique, École française de Rome, 25 March 1994,* Roma, 121–155.

2003   The Antonine Plague in Rome and Ostia. *Journal of Roman Archaeology* 16:426–434.

Buikstra, Jane E.
1997   Paleodemography: Context and Promise. In *Integrating Archaeological Demography: Multidisciplinary Approaches to Prehistoric Population,* edited by R. R. Paine, pp. 367–380. Center for Archaeological Investigations Occasional Paper No. 24. Southern Illinois University, Carbondale.

Buikstra, J. E., and L. W. Konigsberg
1985   Paleodemography: Critiques and Controversies. *American Anthropologist* 87:316–333.

Bullard, W. R.
1960   Maya Settlement Patterns in Northeastern Petén, Guatemala. *American Antiquity* 25:355–372.

Burrows, E. G., and M. Wallace
1998   *Gotham: A History of New York City to 1898.* Oxford University Press, New York.

Butzer, K. W.
1976   *Early Hydraulic Civilization in Egypt: A Study in Cultural Ecology.* University of Chicago Press, Chicago.

Caesar, G. J.
1936   *De Bello Gallico,* with an English translation by H. J. Edwards. Harvard University Press, Cambridge.

Caldwell, J. C.
1997   Population Data and Surveys. In *Encyclopaedia of Africa South of the Sahara,* Vol. 4, edited by J. Middleton, pp. 460–465. Charles Scribner's Sons, New York.

Calnek, E.
1973   The Localization of the Sixteenth Century Map Called the Maguey Plan. *American Antiquity* 38:190–195.

Cambitoglou, A., J. Coulton, J. Birmingham, and J. Green
1988   *Zagora II.* Athens Archaeological Society, Athens.

Cameron, C. M., and H. W. Toll
2001   Deciphering the Organization of Production in Chaco Canyon. *American Antiquity* 66:5–13.

Camp, J.
1979   A Drought in the Late Eighth Century BC. *Hesperia* 48:397–411.

Campbell, K. L., and J. W. Wood
1988   Fertility in Traditional Societies. In *Natural Human Fertility: Social and Biological Determinants,* edited by P. Diggory, M. Potts, and S. Teper, pp. 39–69. Macmillan, New York.

Carcopino, J.
1940   *Daily Life in Ancient Rome: The People and City at the Height of the Empire.* Translated from the French by E. O. Lorimer. Edited with bibliography and notes by H. T. Rowell. Yale University Press, New Haven.

Carlson, J.
1981   A Geomantic Model for the Interpretation of Mesoamerican Sites: An Essay in Cross-Cultural Comparison. In *Mesoamerican Sites and World-Views,* edited by E. P. Benson, pp. 143–216. Dumbarton Oaks Research Library and Collections, Washington, DC.

Carr, R. F., and J. E. Hazard
1961   *Map of the Ruins of Tikal, El Peten, Guatemala.* Tikal Report No. 11, University Museum, University of Pennsylvania, Philadelphia.

Casarico, L.

1985   Il controllo della popolazione nell'Egitto romano. 1. Le denunce di morte. Tipografia Tibeletti, Azzate, Italy.

Casselbery, S. E.

1974   Further Refinement of Formulae for Determining Population from Floor Area. *World Archaeology* 6:117–122.

Casson, L.

1971   *Ships and Seamanship in the Ancient World.* Princeton University Press, Princeton.

Caswell, H.

1989   *Matrix Population Models.* Sinauer Associates, Sunderland, MA.

Cébeillac, M.

1971   Quelques inscriptions inédites d'Ostie, de la république à l'empire. *Mélanges de l'École français de Rome: Antiquité* 82:39–125.

Cereceda, V., J. Dávalos, and J. Mejía

1993   *Una Diferencía, un Sentido: Los Diseños de los Textiles Tarabuco y Jalq'a.* Anthropólogos del Surandino (ASUR), Sucre, Bolivia.

Chang, K.

1985   Guanyu Zhongguo chuqi "chengshi" zhige gainian [On the Concept of Early "City" in China]. *Wenwu* [Cultural Relics] 2:61–67.

Charlton, T. H., and D. L. Nichols

1997a   The City-State Concept: Development and Applications. In *The Archaeology of City-States: Cross Cultural Approaches,* edited by D. L. Nichols and T. H. Charlton, pp. 1–14. Smithsonian Institution Press, Washington, DC.

1997b   Diachronic Studies of City-States: Permutations on a Theme—Central Mexico from 1700 B.C. to A.D. 1600. In *The Archaeology of City-States: Cross-Cultural Approaches,* edited by D. L. Nichols and T. H. Charlton, pp. 169–208. Smithsonian Institution Press, Washington, DC.

Chase, A. F.

1990   Maya Archaeology and Population Estimates in the Tayasal-Paxcaman Zone, Petén, Guatemala. In *Precolumbian Population History in the Maya Lowlands,* edited by T. P. Culbert and D. S. Rice, pp. 149–165. University of New Mexico Press, Albuquerque.

Chase, A. F., and D. Z. Chase

1983   Intensive Gardening among the Late Classic Maya: A Possible Example at Ixtutz. *Expedition* 25:2–11.

1989   The Investigation of Classic Period Warfare at Caracol, Belize. *Mayab* 5:5–18.

1996   More than Kin and King. *Current Anthropology* 37:803–830.

1998   Scale and Intensity in Classic Period Maya Agriculture: Terracing and Settlement at the "Garden City" of Caracol, Belize. *Culture and Agriculture* 20(2/3):60–77.

Chase, D. Z.

1990   The Invisible Maya: Population History and Archaeology at Santa Rita Corozal. In *Precolumbian Population History in the Maya Lowlands,* edited by T. P. Culbert and D. S. Rice, pp. 199–214. University of New Mexico Press, Albuquerque.

Chase, D. Z., A. F. Chase, and W. A. Haviland

1990   The Classic Maya City: Reconsidering "The Mesoamerican Urban Tradition." *American Anthropologist* 92:499–506.

Chen, A.

1987   Unraveling another Mayan mystery. *Discover* June:40–49.

Cherry, J., J. Davis, and E. Mantzourani (editors)
1991   *Landscape Archaeology as Long-Term History.* UCLA Institute of Archaeology, Los Angeles.

Childe, V. G.
1936   *Man Makes Himself.* Watts & Company: London.
1950   The Urban Revolution. *Town Planning Review* 21:3–17.

Chittick, H. N.
1974   *Kilwa: An Islamic Trading City on the East African Coast.* Memoir no. 5. British Institute in Eastern Africa, Nairobi.
1984   *Manda: Excavations at an Island Port on the Kenya Coast.* Memoir No. 9. British Institute in Eastern Africa, Nairobi.

Choi, B. H.
1981   The Evolution and Chronology of the Wooden-Chamber Tombs of the Old Silla Period. *Hanguk Kogo Hakbo* [*Korean Archaeology Journal*] 10/11:137–228 (in Korean).

Choi, H.
1971   *The Economic History of Korea.* Freedom Library: Seoul.

Choi, J. G.
1979   Report on Pit Burials in Choyangdong, Kyongju. *Hanguk Kogo Hakbo* [*Korean Archaeology Journal*] 9:35–39 (in Korean).
1980   Report of the Fourth Season at Choyangdong, Kyongju. *Archaeology in Korea* 9:35–39 (in Korean).

Choque Canqui, R.
1993   *Sociedad y Economía Colonial en el Sur Andino.* Hisbol, La Paz.

Christie, A. H.
1979   Lin-i, Funan, Java. In *Early Southeast Asia: Essays in Archaeology, History and Historical Geography,* edited by R. B. Smith and W. Watson, pp. 281–287. Oxford University Press, New York.

Christie, J. J.
2003   *Maya Palaces and Elite Residences: An Interdisciplinary Approach.* University of Texas Press, Austin.

Christie, N.
1995   *The Lombards.* Basil Blackwell, Cambridge, MA.

CIL (Corpus Inscriptionum Latinarum)
1862– *Corpus Inscriptionum Latinarum.* Walter de Gruyter, Berlin.

Cinthio, H., and J. L. Boldsen
1984   Patterns of Distribution in the Early Medieval Cemetery of Löddeköpinge. *Meddelanden från Lunds universitets historika museum,* new series 5:107–115.

Clapperton, H.
1829   *Journal of a Second Expedition into the Interior of Africa from the Bight of Benin to Soccatoo.* Translated by A. V. Salamé. John Murray, London.

Clark, C.
1967   *Population Growth and Land Use.* Macmillan, New York.

Clark, P., and D. Souden
1987   Introduction. In *Migration and Society in Early Modern England,* edited by P. Clark and D. Souden, pp. 11–48. Barnes and Noble Books, Totowa, NJ.

Clarysse, W., and D. J. Thompson
2002   A Ptolemaic Census Declaration from the Alexandria Museum. *Zeitschrift für Papyrologie und Epigraphik* 140:203–205.

2005   *Counting the People in Hellenistic Egypt.* Cambridge Classical Studies Vol. 2. Cambridge University Press, New York.

Coale, A., and P. Demeny
1966   *Regional Model Life Tables and Stable Populations.* Princeton University Press, Princeton.

Coale, A. J., and P. Demeny
1983   *Regional Model Life Tables and Stable Populations.* 2nd ed. Academic Press, New York.

Coarelli, F.
1989   [1974] *Guida archeologica di Roma.* 5th ed. A. Mondadori, Milan. Originally published 1974, A. Mondadori, Milan.

Cobo, F. B.
1956   [1653] *Historia del Nuevo Mundo,* Vol. II. Biblioteca de Autores Españoles 92. Ediciones Atlas, Madrid.

Coe, M. D.
1965   A Model of Ancient Maya Community Structure in the Maya Lowlands. *Southwestern Journal of Anthropology* 21:97–114.

Cohen, E. E.
2000   *The Athenian Nation.* Princeton University Press, Princeton.

Cohen, M. N.
1989   *Health and the Rise of Civilization.* Yale University Press, New Haven.
1990   Prehistoric Patterns of Hunger. In *Hunger in History,* edited by L. F. Newman, pp. 71–100. Basil Blackwell, Cambridge.

Coldstream, J. N.
1983   The Meaning of Regional Styles in the Eighth Century BC. In *The Greek Renaissance of the Eighth Century BC,* edited by R. Hägg, pp. 17–25. Svenska institutet i Athen, Stockholm.

Connah, G.
1987   *African Civilizations: Precolonial Cities and States in Tropical Africa: An Archaeological Perspective.* Cambridge University Press, New York.

Cook, N. D.
1997   Cabañas y collaguas en la era prehispánica. In *Arqueología, Antropología e Historia en los Andes: Homenaje a María Rostworowski,* edited by R. Varón Gabai and J. Flores Espinoza, pp. 379–396. Instituto de Estudios Peruanos and Banco Central de Reserva del Perú, Lima.
1998   *Born to Die: Disease and New World Conquest, 1492–1650.* Cambridge University Press, New York.

Cook, O. F.
1909   Vegetation Affected by Agriculture in Central America. *Bureau of Plant Industry Bulletin,* Vol. 145. U.S. Department of Agriculture, Washington, DC.
1921   Milpa Agriculture, a Primitive Tropical System. *Annual Report of the Smithsonian Institution,* Vol. 191, pp. 307– 326. Smithsonian Institution, Washington, DC.

Cook, R. M.
1959   Die Bedeutung der bemalten Keramik. *Jahrbuch des Deutschen Archäologischen Instituts* 74:114–123.

Cooke, C. W.
1931   Why the Mayan Cities of the Peten District, Guatemala, Were Abandoned. *Journal of the Washington Academy of Sciences* 21:283–287.

Coquery-Vidrovitch, C.
1972   Research on an African Mode of Production. In *Perspectives on the African Past,* edited by M. Klein and G. W. Johnson, pp. 33–51. Little, Brown and Co., Boston.

1997   Production Systems: An Overview. In *Encyclopedia of Africa South of the Sahara,* edited by J. Middleton, pp. 487–492. Charles Scribner's Sons, New York.

Cornell, T., and K. Lomas (editors)

1995   *Urban Society in Roman Italy.* University College London Press, London.

Costin, C. L.

1991   Craft Specialization: Issues in Defining, Documenting, and Explaining the Organization of Production. In *Archaeological Method and Theory,* edited by M. B. Schiffer, pp. 1–56. University of Arizona Press, Tucson.

2001   Craft Production Systems. In *Archaeology at the Millennium: A Sourcebook,* edited by G. M. Feinman and T. D. Price, pp. 273–328. Kluwer Academic/Plenum Publishers, New York.

Couture, N. C., and K. Sampeck

2003   Putuni: A History of Palace Architecture at Tiwanaku. In *Tiwanaku and Its Hinterland: Archaeology and Paleoecology of an Andean Civilization,* edited by A. L. Kolata, Vol. II, pp. 226–263. Smithsonian Institution Press, Washington, DC.

Cowgill, G. L.

1975   On Causes and Consequences of Ancient and Modern Population Changes. *American Anthropologist* 77:505–525.

1996a   Population, Human Nature, Knowing Actors, and Explaining the Onset of Complexity. In *Debating Complexity: Proceedings of the Twenty-sixth Annual Chacmool Conference,* edited by D. Meyer, P. Dawson, and D. T. Hanna, pp. 16–22. The Archaeological Association of the University of Calgary, Calgary.

1996b   A Reconsideration of the Postclassic Chronology of Central Mexico. *Ancient Mesoamerica* 7:325–331.

1997   State and Society in Teotihuacan. *Annual Review of Anthropology* 26:129–161.

2001   Teotihuacan. In *Archaeology of Ancient Mexico and Central America: An Encyclopedia,* edited by S. T. Evans and D. L. Webster, pp. 722–731. Garland Publishing, New York.

2004   Some Recent Data and Concepts about Ancient Urbanism. In *El Urbanismo en Mesoamerica (Urbanism in Mesoamerica),* Vol. 1, edited by W. T. Sanders, A. G. Mastache, and R. H. Cobean, pp. 1–20. Occasional Papers in Anthropology No. 28. Department of Anthropology, The Pennsylvania State University, University Park, PA.

Cowgill, U. M.

1960   Soil Fertility, Population, and the Ancient Maya. *Proceedings of the National Academy of Sciences* 46:1009–1011.

1961   Soil Fertility and the Ancient Maya. *Connecticut Academy of Arts and Sciences, Transactions* 42:1–56.

1962   An Agricultural Study of the Southern Maya Lowlands. *American Anthropologist* 64:273–286.

Crampton, G. R.

1991   Any Role Left for the Exponential Density Gradient? *Environment and Planning A* 23:1007–1024.

Cronon, W.

1991   *Nature's Metropolis: Chicago and the Great West.* W. W. Norton, New York.

Crosby, A. W.

1972   *The Columbian Exchange: Biological and Cultural Consequences of 1492.* Greenwood Publishing Co., Westport, CT.

Crumley, C. L.

1976   Towards a Locational Definition of State Systems of Settlement. *American Anthropologist* 78:59–73.

1987a   Celtic Settlement before the Conquest: The Dialectics of Landscape and Power. In
         Regional Dynamics: Burgundian Landscapes in Historical Perspective, edited by C. L.
         Crumley and W. H. Marquardt, pp. 403–29. Academic Press, New York.

1987b   A Dialectical Critique of Hierarchy. In *Power Relations and State Formation,* edited
         by T. C. Patterson and C. W. Gailey, pp. 155–159. American Anthropological As-
         sociation, Washington, DC.

1995a   Building a Historical Ecology of Gaulish Polities. In *Celtic Chiefdom, Celtic State,*
         edited by B. Arnold, pp. 37–56. Cambridge University Press, New York.

1995b   Heterarchy and the Analysis of Complex Societies. In *Heterarchy and the Analysis
         of Complex Societies,* edited by C. L. Crumley, R. M. Ehrenreich, and J. E. Levy,
         pp. 1–4. American Anthropological Association, Arlington, VA.

Culbert, T. P.
1988   The Collapse of Classic Maya Civilization. In *The Collapse of Ancient States and
         Civilizations,* edited by N. Yoffee and G. L. Cowgill, pp. 69–101. University of Ari-
         zona Press, Tucson.

Culbert, T. P. (editor)
1973   *The Classic Maya Collapse.* School of American Research Advanced Seminar Series.
         University of New Mexico Press, Albuquerque.

1991   *Classic Maya Political History. Hieroglyphic and Archaeological Evidence.* School of
         American Research Advanced Seminar Series. Cambridge University Press, Cam-
         bridge.

Culbert, T. P., L. J. Kosakowsky, R. E. Fry, and W. A. Haviland
1990   The Population of Tikal, Guatemala. In *Precolumbian Population History in the Maya
         Lowlands,* edited by T. P. Culbert and D. S. Rice, pp. 103–122. University of New
         Mexico Press, Albuquerque.

Culbert T. P., and D. S. Rice (editors)
1990   *Precolumbian Population History in the Maya Lowlands.* University of New Mexico
         Press, Albuquerque.

Culbert, T. P., M. Spencer, and P. C. Magers
1978   Regional Variability in Maya Lowland Agriculture. In *Pre-Hispanic Maya Agriculture,*
         edited by P. D. Harrison and B. L. Turner II, pp. 157–162. University of New
         Mexico Press, Albuquerque.

Curtis, J. H., M. Brenner, D. A. Hodell, R. A. Balser, G. A. Islebe, and H. Hooghiemstra
1998   A Multi-Proxy Study of Holocene Environmental Change in the Maya Lowlands of
         Petén, Guatemala. *Journal of Paleolimnology* 19:139–159.

Curtis, J. H., D. A. Hodell, and M. Brenner
1996   Climate Variability on the Yucatan Peninsula (Mexico) during the Past 3500 Years,
         and Implications for Maya Cultural Evolution. *Quaternary Research* 46:37–47.

Cuscito, G., and L. Galli
1976   *Parenzo.* Liviana, Padua.

Dahlin, B. H., J. E. Foss, and M. E. Chambers
1980   Project Acalches: Reconstructing the Natural and Cultural History of a Seasonal
         Swamp at El Mirador, Guatemala: Preliminary Results. In *El Mirador, Peten Guate-
         mala: An Interim Report,* edited by R. T. Matheny, pp. 37–57. Papers of the New
         World Archeological Foundation No. 45. Brigham Young University, Provo.

D'Altroy, T., and T. K. Earle
1985   State Finance, Wealth Finance, and Storage in the Inka Political Economy. *Current
         Anthropology* 26:187–206.

Danforth, M. E.
1999   Nutrition and Politics in Prehistory. *Annual Review of Anthropology* 28:1–25.
David, N.
1998   The Ethnoarchaeology and Field Archaeology of Grinding at Sukur, Adamawa State, Nigeria. *African Archaeological Review* 15:13–63.
Davies, N.
1977   *The Toltecs until the Fall of Tula.* University of Oklahoma Press, Norman.
1980   *The Toltec Heritage, from the Fall of Tula to the Rise of Tenochtitlan.* University of Oklahoma Press, Norman.
Davis, J., S. Alcock, J. Bennet, Y. Lolos, and C. Shelmerdine
1997   The Pylos Regional Archaeological Project, part 1. *Hesperia* 66:391–494.
Davis, K.
1973   *Cities and Mortality.* International Population and Urban Research, Reprint 33, University of California at Berkeley, Institute of International Studies, Berkeley.
De Angelis, F.
2000   Estimating the Agricultural Base of Greek Sicily. *Papers of the British School at Rome* 68:111–148.
2003   *Megara Hyblaia and Selinous.* Oxford University Press, New York.
DeBoer, W. R.
1990   Interaction, Imitation, and Communication as Expressed in Style: The Ucayali Experience. In *The Uses of Style in Archaeology,* edited by M. Conkey and C. Hastorf, pp. 82–104. New Directions in Archaeology. Cambridge University Press, New York.
Deevey, E. S.
1978   Holocene Forests and Maya Disturbance near Quexil Lake, Peten, Guatemala. *Polskie Archiwum Hydrobiologii* 25(1/2):117–129.
Deevey Jr., E. S., D. S. Rice, P. M. Rice, H. H. Vaughan, M. Brenner, and M. S. Flannery
1979   Mayan Urbanism: Impact on a Tropical Karst Environment. *Science* 206:298–306.
Degrassi, A.
1946   Parenzo, municipio Romano. *Athenaeum* 24:45–49.
Degrassi, A. (editor)
1934   *Inscriptiones Italiae,* Vol. 10. La Libreria dello stato, Rome.
De Kleijn G.
2001   *The Water Supply of Ancient Rome: City Area, Water and Population.* J. C. Gieben, Amsterdam.
Del Panta, L.
1980   *Le epidemie nella storia demografica italiana (secoli XIV–XIX).* Loescher, Torino, Italy.
Del Panta, L., M. Livi Bacci, G. Pinto, and E. Sonnino
1996   *La popolazione italiana dal medioevo a oggi.* Laterza, Rome.
Demarest, A. A.
1992   Ideology in Ancient Maya Cultural Evolution: The Dynamics of Galactic Polities. In *Ideology and Pre-Columbian Civilizations,* edited by A. A. Demarest and G. W. Conrad, pp. 135–157. School of American Research Advanced Seminar Series, School of American Research Press, Santa Fe.
2003   *Ancient Maya: The Rise and Fall of a Rain Forest Civilization.* Cambridge University Press, New York.
Demarest, A. A., M. O'Mansky, C. Wolley, D. Van Tuerenhout, T. Inomata, J. Palka, and H. Escobedo
1997   Classic Maya Defensive Systems and Warfare in the Petexbatún Region: Archaeological Evidence and Interpretations. *Ancient Mesoamerica* 8:229–253.

Demarest, A. A., P. M. Rice, and D. S. Rice (editors)
2004   *The Terminal Classic in the Maya Lowlands.* University Press of Colorado, Boulder.

DeMaret, P.
2000   Urban Origins in Central Africa—The Case of Kongo. In *The Development of Urbanism from a Global Perspective,* edited by P. J. J. Sinclair, http://www.arkeologi.uu.se/afr/projects/BOOK/DeMaretframe.htm. Department of Archaeology and Ancient History, University of Uppsala, Uppsala.

Denmark Statistiske Department/Danmarks Statistik
1896–   *Statistisk Årbog Statistical Yearbook.* Denmark Statistiske Department/Danmarks Statistik, Copenhagen.

Dennison, W.
1898   Some New Inscriptions from Puteoli, Baiae, Misenum, and Cumae. *American Journal of Archaeology* 2:373–398.

de Polignac, F.
1995   *Cults, Territory, and the Origins of the Greek City-State.* Translated by J. Lloyd. University of Chicago Press, Chicago.

Derow, P. S.
1973   The Roman Calendar, 190–168 B.C. *Phoenix* 27:345–356.

De' Seta, C.
1976   Napoli. In *Storia d'Italia,* Vol. 6, pp. 334–349. Atlante, Turin.

Dessau, H. (editor)
1892–   *Inscriptiones Latinae Selectae.* Weidmanns, Berlin.
1916

de Vries, J.
1974   *The Dutch Rural Economy in the Golden Age, 1500–1700.* Yale University Press, New Haven.
1984   *European Urbanization, 1500–1800.* Harvard University Press, Cambridge.

Dewar, R. E.
1991   Incorporating Variation in Occupation-Span into Settlement-Pattern Studies. *American Antiquity* 56:604–620.

Diakonoff, I. M.
1969   The Rise of the Despotic State in Mesopotamia. In *Ancient Mesopotamia,* edited by I. M. Diakonoff, pp. 173–197. Akademija Nauk SSSR, Moscow.
1982   The Structure of Near Eastern Society before the Middle of the Second Millennium B.C. *Oikumene* 3:7–100.

Dickens, C.
1842   *American Notes for General Circulation.* Harper and Brothers, New York.

Dickinson, O.
1994   *The Aegean Bronze Age.* Cambridge University Press, New York.

Dietler, M., and I. Herbich
1998   *Habitus,* Techniques, Style: An Integrated Approach to the Social Understanding of Material Culture and Boundaries. In *The Archaeology of Social Boundaries,* edited by M. T. Stark, pp. 232–263. Smithsonian Institution Press, Washington, DC.

Di Vita, A.
1956   La penetrazione siracusana nella Sicilia sudorientale alla luce delle più recenti scoperte archeologiche. *Kokalos* 2:177–205.

Donlan, W.
1989   The Pre-State Community of Greece. *Symbolae Osloenses* 64:5–29.

Drennan, R. D.

1988 Household Location and Compact versus Dispersed Settlement in Prehispanic Meso-america. In *House and Household in the Mesoamerican Past,* edited by R. Wilk and W. Ashmore, pp. 273–293. University of New Mexico Press, Albuquerque.

2000 Games, Players, Rules, and Circumstances: Looking for Understandings of Social Change at Different Levels. In *Cultural Evolution: Contemporary Viewpoints,* edited by G. M. Feinman and L. Manzanilla, pp. 177–196. Kluwer Academic/Plenum Publishers, New York.

Du, J., X. Wang, and L. Zhang

1999 Shilun Yanshi Shangcheng xiaocheng de jige wenti [On Several Issues Related to the Small City Inside the Yanshi Shang City]. *Kaogu [Archaeology]* 2:35–40.

Dumond, D. E.

1961 Swidden Agriculture and the Rise of Maya Civilization. *Southwestern Journal of Anthropology* 17:301–316.

Dumond, D., and F. Muller

1972 Classic to Postclassic in Highland Central Mexico. *Science* 175:1208–1215.

Duncan-Jones, R. P.

1990 *Structure and Scale in the Roman Economy.* Cambridge University Press, New York.

1996 The Impact of the Antonine Plague. *Journal of Roman Archaeology* 9:108–136.

Dunning, N. P.

1992 *Lords of the Hills: Ancient Maya Settlement in the Puuc Region, Yucatán, Mexico.* Prehistory Press, Madison.

Durkheim, E.

1933 [1893] *The Division of Labor in Society.* Macmillan, New York.

Earle, T. K.

1985 Commodity Exchange and Markets in the Inka State: Recent Archaeological Evidence. In *Markets and Marketing,* edited by S. Plattner, pp. 369–397. Society for Economic Anthropology Monograph No. 4. University Press of America, Lanham.

1987 Specialization and the Production of Wealth: Hawaiian Chiefdoms and the Inka Empire. In *Specialization, Exchange, and Complex Societies,* edited by E. M. Brumfiel and T. K. Earle, pp. 64–75. Cambridge University Press, New York.

1991 *Chiefdoms: Power, Economy and Ideology.* Cambridge University Press, New York.

2001 Economic Support of Chaco Canyon Society. *American Antiquity* 66:26–35.

Early, J. D., and J. F. Peters

1990 *The Population Dynamics of the Mucajai Yanomama.* Academic Press, New York.

Edmonson, M. S.

1979 Some Postclassic Questions about the Classic Maya. In *Tercera Mesa Redonda de Palenque, Vol. IV,* edited by M. G. Robertson and D. C. Jeffers, pp. 9–18. Pre-Columbian Art Research Center, Palenque, Chiapas, Mexico.

1982 *The Ancient Future of the Itza: The Book of the Chilam Balam of Tizimin.* University of Texas Press, Austin.

1986 *Heaven Born Merida and Its Destiny: The Book of Chilam Balam of Chumayel.* University of Texas Press, Austin.

Ekroth, G.

1996 The Late Geometric and Archaic periods. In *The Berbati-Limnes Archaeological Survey 1988–90,* edited by B. Wells, pp. 179–227. P. Åströms, Jonsered, Sweden.

Elo, I. F., and S. H. Preston

1992 Effects of Early-Life Conditions on Adult Mortality: A Review. *Population Index* 58:186–212.

Emerson, R. A.
1935   A Preliminary Survey of the Milpa System of Maize Culture as Practiced by the Maya Indians of the Northern Part of the Yucatan Peninsula. Manuscript on file, Cornell University, Ithaca.

Empereur, Jean-Yves
1998.   *Alexandria the Golden*. E. J. Brill, Leiden.

Engels, D.
1990   *Roman Corinth: An Alternative Model for the Classical City.* University of Chicago Press, Chicago.

Erasmus, C. J.
1965   Thoughts on Upward Collapse: An Essay on Explanation in Archaeology. *Southwestern Journal of Anthropology* 24:170–194.

Erickson, B.
2006   Archaic and Classical Crete. *Hesperia* (supplementary volume). Princeton UP, Princeton, NJ.

Erlitou Working Team, Institute of Archaeology CASS
1984   1981 nian Henan Yanshi Erlitou muzang fajue jianbao [Brief Report on the 1981 Excavation of Burials at the Erlitou Site in Yanshi, Henan]. *Kaogu [Archaeology]* 1:37–40.
2001   Erlitou yizhi tianye gongzuo de xinjinzhan [New Progress in the Fieldwork at the Erlitou Site]. *Zhongguo Shehui Kexueyuan Gudai Wenming Yanjiu Zhongxin Tongxun [Research Center for Ancient Civilizations Chinese Academy of Society Sciences]* 1:32–34.
2003   Erlitou yizhi gongdianqu kaogu qude zhongyao chengguo [Important Achievements in the Excavation of Palatial Area at Erlitou Site]. *Zhongguo Shehui Kexueyuan Gudai Wenming Yanjiu Zhongxin Tongxun [Research Center for Ancient Civilizations Chinese Academy of Society Sciences]* 5:50–53.

Evans, S. T.
1988   Cihuatecpan: The Village in Its Ecological and Historical Context. In *Excavations at Cihuatecpan, an Aztec Village in the Teotihuacan Valley,* edited by S. T. Evans, pp. 1–49. Publications in Anthropology No. 36, Vanderbilt University, Nashville.
1990   The Productivity of Maguey Terrace Agriculture in Central Mexico during the Aztec Period. *Latin American Antiquity* 1:117–132.

Evans, S. T., W. T. Sanders, and J. R. Parsons
2000   The Teothihacan Valley Project: Aztec Period Site Descriptions. In *The Aztec Occupation of the Valley. Part 1: Natural Environment 20th Century Occupation, Survey Methodology, and Site Descriptions, The Teotihuacan Valley Project, Final Report, Volume 5.* Occasional Papers in Anthropology 25. Edited by S. T. Evans and W. T. Sanders, pp. 85–499. Department of Anthropology, Pennsylvania State University, University Park.

Eyo, E.
1974   Recent Excavations at Ife and Owo, and Their Implications for Ife, Owo and Benin Studies. Unpublished PhD dissertation, University of Ibadan, Nigeria.

Falconer, S. E.
1994   Village Economy and Society in the Jordan Valley: A Study of Bronze Age Rural Complexity. In *Archaeological Views from the Countryside: Village Communities in Early Complex Societies,* edited by G. M. Schwartz and S. E. Falconer, pp. 121–42. Smithsonian Institution Press, Washington, DC.

Fash, W.
1983   Deducing Social Organization from Classic Maya Settlement Patterns: A Case Study

from the Copán Valley. In *Civilization in the Ancient Americas: Essays in Honor of Gordon R. Willey,* edited by R. Leventhal and A. Kolata, pp. 261–585. University of New Mexico Press, Albuquerque, and Peabody Museum of Archaeology, Harvard University, Cambridge.

1991   *Scribes, Warriors and Kings: The City of Copán and the Ancient Maya.* Thames and Hudson, New York.

1998   Dynastic Architectural Programs: Intention and Design in Classic Maya Buildings at Copán and Other Sites. In *Function and Meaning in Classic Maya Architecture,* edited by S. D. Houston, pp. 223–270. Dumbarton Oaks, Washington, DC.

Fash, W. L., E. W. Andrews, and T. K. Manahan

2004   Political Decentralization, Dynastic Collapse, and the Early Postclassic in the Urban Center of Copán, Honduras. In *The Terminal Classic in the Maya Lowlands,* edited by A. A. Demarest, P. M. Rice, and D. S. Rice, pp. 260–287. University Press of Colorado, Boulder.

Fattovich, R.

2000   *The Aksum Archaeological Area: A Preliminary Assessment.* Istituto Universitario Orientale, Centro Interdipartimentale de Servizi per l' Archeologia, Naples.

Fedick, S. L.

1989   The Economics of Agricultural Land Use and Settlement in the Upper Belize Valley. In *Prehistoric Maya Economies of Belize,* edited by P. A. McAnany and B. L. Issac, pp. 215–253. Research in Economic Anthropology, JAI Press, Greenwich, CT.

Fedick, S. L. (editor)

1996   *The Managed Mosaic. Ancient Maya Agriculture and Resource Use.* University of Utah Press, Salt Lake City.

Feinman, G. M.

1998   Scale and Social Organization: Perspectives on the Archaic State. In *Archaic States,* edited by G. M. Feinman and J. Marcus, pp. 95–134. School of American Research, Santa Fe.

Ferdon, E. N.

1959   Agricultural Potential and the Development of Cultures. *Southwestern Journal of Anthropology* 15:1–19.

Filion, P., T. E. Bunting, and K. Curtis (editors)

1996   *The Dynamics of the Dispersed City: Geographic and Planning Perspectives on Waterloo Region.* Department of Geography Publications Series No. 47. University of Waterloo, Waterloo, Ontario.

Finlay, R.

1981a   Natural Decrease in Early Modern Cities. *Past and Present* 92:169–174.

1981b   *Population and Metropolis: The Demography of London, 1580–1650.* Cambridge University Press, New York.

Finlay, R., and B. Shearer

1986   Population Growth and Suburban Expansion. In *London 1500–1700: The Making of the Metropolis,* edited by A. L. Beier and R. Finlay, pp. 37–59. Longman, New York.

Finley, M. I.

1973   *The Ancient Economy.* University of California Press, Berkeley.

1977   The Ancient City. *Comparative Studies in Society and History* 19:305–327.

1979   *Ancient Sicily.* Chatto and Windus, London.

1985   *Ancient History: Evidence and Models.* Chatto and Windus, London.

Fitts, R., and R. Yamin
1996   The Archaeology of Domesticity in Victorian Brooklyn: Exploratory Testing and Data Recovery at Block 2006 of the Atlantic Terminal Urban Renewal Area, Brooklyn, New York. Prepared for Atlantic Housing Corporation, c/o Hudson Companies, Inc., John Milner Associates, Inc., West Chester, Pennsylvania.

Fix, A. G.
1977   *Demography of the Semai Senoi.* Anthropological Papers No. 62, Museum of Anthropology, University of Michigan, Ann Arbor.

Flannery, Kent V.
1995   Prehistoric Social Evolution. In *Research Frontiers in Anthropology,* edited by C. R. Ember and M. Ember, pp. 3–25. Prentice-Hall, Englewood Cliffs, NJ.
1998   The Ground Plans of Archaic States. In *Archaic States,* edited by G. M. Feinman and J. Marcus, pp. 15–58. School of American Research Press, Santa Fe.

Flannery, K. V. (editor)
1982   *Maya Subsistence: Studies in Memory of Dennis E. Puleston.* Academic Press, New York.

Fletcher, R.
1986   Settlement Archaeology: World-wide Comparisons. *World Archaeology* 18:59–83.
1993   Settlement Area and Communication in African Towns and Cities. In *The Archaeology of Africa: Food, Metals, and Towns,* edited by T. Shaw, P. Sinclair, B. Andah, and A. Okpoko, pp. 732–749. Routledge, New York.
1995   *The Limits of Settlement Growth.* Cambridge University Press, New York.
2000   Diversity and Dispersal in African Urbanism: A Global Perspective. In *The Development of Urbanism from a Global Perspective,* edited by P. J. J. Sinclair, http://www.arkeologi.uu.se/afr/projects/BOOK/Fletcher/ Fletchframe.htm. Department of Archaeology and Ancient History, University of Uppsala, Uppsala.

Flinn, M. W.
1974   The Stabilization of Mortality in Preindustrial Western Europe. *Journal of European Economic History* 3:285–318.
1981   *The European Demographic System, 1500–1820.* Johns Hopkins University Press, Baltimore.

Folan, W. J., L. A. Fletcher, and E. R. Kintz
1979   Fruit, Fiber, Bark, and Resin: Social Organization of a Maya Urban Center. *Science* 204:697–701.

Folan, W. J., J. Marcus, S. Pincemin, M. del Rosario Domínguez Carrasco, L. Fletcher, and A. Morales López
1995   Calakmul: New Data from an Ancient Maya Capital in Campeche, Mexico. *Latin American Antiquity* 6:310–334.

Foley, R., and M. M. Lahr
1992   Beyond Out of Africa: Reassessing the Origins of Homo Sapiens. *Journal of Human Evolution* 22:523–529.

Ford, A.
1986   *Population Growth and Social Complexity: An Examination of Settlement and Environment in the Central Maya Lowlands.* Anthropological Research Paper No. 35. Department of Anthropology, Arizona State University, Tempe.

Ford, A.
2001   States and Stones: Ground Stone Tool Production at Huizui, China. Unpublished Honours thesis, La Trobe University, Melbourne.

Fox, J. W., G. W. Cook, A. F. Chase, and D. Z. Chase
1996   Questions of Political and Economic Integration: Segmentary versus Centralized States among the Ancient Maya. *Current Anthropology* 37:795–832.

Fox, R. G.
1977   *Urban Anthropology: Cities in Their Cultural Settings.* Prentice-Hall, Englewood Cliffs, NJ.

Frame, M.
1990   *Andean Four-Cornered Hats.* Metropolitan Museum of Art, New York.

Franke, E.
1991   Excavations at Chi'ji Jawira. Unpublished Master's thesis, University of Chicago, Chicago.

Frankfort, H. J.
1950   Town Planning in Ancient Mesoamerica. *Town Planning Review* 21:98–115.

Fraser, P.
1972   *Ptolemaic Alexandria.* 3 vols. Clarendon Press, Oxford.
1996   *The Cities of Alexander the Great.* Clarendon Press, Oxford.

Freter, A.
1992   Chronological Research at Copán: Methods and Implications. *Ancient Mesoamerica* 3:117–134.
1994   The Classic Maya Collapse at Copán, Honduras: An Analysis of Maya Rural Settlement. In *Archaeological Views from the Countryside: Village Communities in Early Complex Societies,* edited by G. M. Schwartz and S. E. Falconer, pp. 160–176. Smithsonian Institution Press, Washington, DC.
1996   Rural Utilitarian Ceramic Production in the Late Classic Period Copán Maya State. In *Arqueología Mesoamericana: Homenje a William T. Sanders II,* edited by A. G. Mastache, J. R. Parsons, R. S. Santley, and M. C. Serra Puche, pp. 209–230. Instituto Nacional de Anthropologia e Historia, Mexico City.
1997   The Question of Time: The Impact of Chronology on Copán Prehistoric Settlement Demography. In *Integrating Archaeological Demography,* edited by R. R. Paine, pp. 21–42. Occasional Papers Series, Vol. 24, Center for Archaeological Investigations, Southern Illinois University, Carbondale.
2004   A Multiscalar Model of Rural Households and Communities in Late Classic Copan Maya Society. *Ancient Mesoamerica* 15:93–106.

Fry, R. E.
1969   Ceramics and Settlement in the Periphery of Tikal, Guatemala. Unpublished PhD dissertation, Department of Anthropology, University of Arizona, Tucson.
2003   The Peripheries of Tikal. In *Tikal: Dynasties, Foreigners, and Affairs of State,* edited by J. A. Sabloff, pp. 143–170. School of American Research Press, Santa Fe.

Gabrielsen, V.
1994   *Financing the Athenian Fleet.* Johns Hopkins University Press, Baltimore.

Gallant, T.
1991   *Risk and Survival in Ancient Greece.* Stanford University Press, Stanford.

Gallo, L.
1994   Alcune considerazioni sulla demografia degli Elimi. *Annali della Scuola Normale di Pisa* 24:19–29.

Gann, T. W.
1918   *The Maya Indians of Southern Yucatán and Northern British Honduras.* Smithsonian Institution, Bureau of American Ethnology, Bulletin, Vol. 64, Washington, DC.

Gann, T. W., and J. E. S. Thompson
1937   *The History of the Maya: From the Earliest Times to the Present Day.* Scribner's, New York.

Gao, W., X. Yang, W. Wang, and J. Du
1998   Yanshi Shangcheng yu Xia Shang wenhua fenjie [The Yanshi Shang City and the Demarcation between the Xia and Shang Cultures]. *Kaogu* [*Archaeology*] 10:66–79.

Gardiner, K. H. J.
1969   *The Early History of Korea.* University of Hawaii Press, Honolulu.

Garland, R.
1987   *The Piraeus.* Cornell University Press, Ithaca.

Garnsey, P.
1988   *Famine and Food Supply in the Graeco-Roman World.* Cambridge University Press, New York.

1990   Responses to Food Crises in the Ancient Mediterranean World. In *Hunger in History,* edited by L. F. Newman, pp. 126–146. Basil Blackwell, Cambridge.

1992   Yield of the Land. In *Agriculture in Ancient Greece,* edited by B. Wells, pp. 147–153. The Institute, Stockholm.

1998   Mass Diet and Nutrition in the City of Rome. In *Cities, Peasants and Food in Classical Antiquity: Essays in Social and Economic History* (collected essays of P. Garnsey), edited with addenda by W. Scheidel, pp. 226–252. Cambridge University Press, New York.

Gauthier, P.
1981   De Lysias à Aristote (Ath. Pol. 51.4). *Revue historique des droits français et etrangers* 59:5–28.

Geertz, C.
1963   Agricultural Involution: The Process of Ecological Change in Indonesia. University of California Press, Berkeley.

1980a   Ports of Trade in Nineteenth-Century Bali. *Research in Economic Anthropology* 3:109–122.

1980b   *Negara: The Theatre State in Nineteenth-Century Bali.* Princeton University Press, Princeton.

Geismar, J. H.
1985   Patterns of Development in the Late-Eighteenth and Nineteenth Century American Seaport. *American Archeology* 5:175–184.

1987   Landfill and Health, a Municipal Concern, or Telling It Like It Was. *Council for Northeastern Historical Archaeology* 16:49–57.

1993   *Reconstruction of Foley Square History and Archaeology Research Report.* Office of Parks and Recreation, New York.

Gelb, I.
1969   On the Alleged Temple and State Economies in Ancient Mesopotamia. In *Studi in Onore de Edoardo Volterra* 6:137–154.

George, A. R.
1993   Babylon Revisited: Archaeology and Philology. *Antiquity* 67:734–746.

Gibson, C.
1964   *The Aztecs Under Spanish Rule.* Stanford University Press, Stanford.

1971   Structure of the Aztec Empire. In *Archaeology of Northern Mesoamerica,* edited by G. F. Ekholm and I. Bernal, pp. 376–393. Handbook of Middle American Indians, Vol. 10, R. Wauchope, general editor, University of Texas Press, Austin.

Gill, R. B.
2000   *The Great Maya Droughts: Water, Life, and Death.* University of New Mexico Press, Albuquerque.

Ginzel, F. K.
1906–   *Handbuch der mathematischen und technischen Chronologie.* 3 vols. J. C. Hinrichs,
1914   Leipzig.

Gisbert, T., S. Arze, and M. Cajías
1987   *Arte Textil y Mundo Andino.* Gisbert y Cía: La Paz.

Golden, M.
2000   A Decade of Demography: Recent Trends in the Study of Greek and Roman Populations. In *Polis and Politics: Studies in Ancient Greek History. Presented to Mogens Herman Hansen on his Sixtieth Birthday, August 20, 2000,* edited by P. Flensted-Jensen, T. H. Nielsen, and L. Rubinstein, pp. 23–40. Museum Tusculanum Press, University of Copenhagen, Copenhagen.

Goldstein, P. S.
1989   Omo, a Tiwanaku Provincial Center in Moquegua, Peru. Unpublished PhD dissertation, University of Chicago, Chicago.

Gomme, A.
1933   *The Population of Athens in the Fifth and Fourth Centuries B.C.* Blackwell, Oxford.

Gongxian County Chronicle Editorial Board
1989   *Gongxian zhi* [*Gongxian County Chronicle*]. Gongxian County Chronicle Editorial Board, Gongxian.
1991   *Gongxian zhi* [*Gongxian County Chronicle*]. Zhongzhou Guji Chubanshe [Zhongzhou Ancient Books Press], Zhengzhou.

Gonlin, N.
1994   Rural Household Diversity in Late Classic Copán, Honduras. In *Archaeological Views from the Countryside: Village Communities in Early Complex Societies,* edited by G. M. Schwartz and S. E. Falconer, pp. 177–197. Smithsonian Institution Press, Washington, DC.

Goodman, A. H., and G. J. Armelagos
1988   Childhood Stress and Decreased Longevity in a Prehistoric Population. *American Anthropologist* 90:936–944.

Gordon, J. S., and A. E. Gordon
1957   *Contributions to the Paleography of Latin Inscriptions.* University of California Press, Berkeley.

Gorenflo, L. J.
1996   Regional Efficiency in Prehispanic Central Mexico: Insights from Geographical Studies of Archaeological Settlement Patterns. In *Arqueología Mesoamericana. Homenaje a William T. Sanders,* edited by A. Guadalupe M., J. R. Parsons, R. S. Santley, and M. C. Serra Puche, pp. 135–159. Instituto Nacional de Anthropología e Historia, Mexico City.

Gorenflo, L. J., and W. T. Sanders
2006   *Archaeological Settlement Pattern Data from the Cuautitlán, Temascalapa, and Teotihuacán Regions, Mexico.* Occasional Papers in Anthropology, Department of Anthropology, Pennsylvania State University, University Park.
2006   *Prehispanic Settlement Pattern Data in the Temascalapa Region, Mexico.* Occasional Papers in Anthropology, Department of Anthropology, Pennsylvania State University, University Park.

Gorton, J.
   2003   Cambrian Sediments in the Songshan Range, Henan Province, China, and Their Archaeological Significance. Unpublished Honours Thesis, Department of Earth Sciences, La Trobe University, Melbourne.
Graffam, G. C.
   1992   Beyond State Collapse: Rural History, Raised Fields and Pastoralism in the South Andes. *American Anthropologist* 94:882–904.
Graham, A. J.
   1982   The Colonial Expansion of Greece. In *Cambridge Ancient History,* Vol. 3, edited by J. Boardman and N. Hammond, pp. 83–162. Cambridge University Press, New York.
Grainger, J.
   1990   *The Cities of Seleukid Syria.* Clarendon Press, Oxford.
Greenberg, J.
   2003   Plagued by Doubt: Reconsidering the Impact of a Mortality Crisis in the Second c. A.D. *Journal of Roman Archaeology* 16:413–425.
Grimm, G.
   1996   City Planning? In *Alexandria and Alexandrianism,* pp. 55–74. J. Paul Getty Museum, Malibu.
Grove, A. T.
   1993   *The Changing Geography of Africa.* 2nd ed. Oxford University Press, New York.
Grube, N.
   2000   The City-States of the Maya. In *A Comparative Study of Thirty City-State Cultures,* edited by M. H. Hansen, pp. 547–565. Historisk-filosofiske Skrifter 21, Det Kongelige Danske Videnskabernes Selskab, The Royal Danish Academy of Sciences and Letters, C. A. Reitzels Forlag, Copenhagen.
Grube, N. (editor)
   2000   *Maya: Divine Kings of the Rain Forest.* Könemann Verlagsgesellschaft mbH, Cologne.
Gualandi, G.
   1973   La presenza christiana nell'Ifriqiya: l'area cimiteriale di En-Ngila (Tripoli). *Felix Ravenna* 5–6:257–279.
Gullick, J. M.
   1981   *Malaysia: Economic Expansion and National Unity.* Ernest Benn, London.
   1988   [1958] *Indigenous Political Systems of Western Malaya.* Revised edition. London School of Economics Monographs on Social Anthropology No. 17. Athlone Press, Atlantic Highlands, NJ. Originally published by Athlone Press, London.
Habicht, C.
   1997   *Athens from Alexander to Antony.* Translated by D. L. Schneider. Harvard University Press, Cambridge.
Haggett, P.
   1965   *Locational Analysis in Human Geography.* St. Martin's Press, New York.
Hall, K.
   1976   State and Statecraft in Early Srivijaya. In *Explorations in Early Southeast Asian History: The Origins of Southeast Asian Statecraft,* edited by K. Hall and J. Whitmore, pp. 61–105. Michigan Papers on South and Southeast Asia No. 11. University of Michigan, Ann Arbor.
   1985   *Maritime Trade and State Development in Early Southeast Asia.* University of Hawaii Press, Honolulu.
   1992   Economic History of Early Southeast Asia. In *The Cambridge History of Southeast*

Asia. Volume 1. From Early Times to c. 1800, edited by N. Tarling, pp.183–275. Cambridge University Press, New York.

Hall, K., and J. Whitmore (editors)

1976   *Explorations in Early Southeast Asian History: The Origins of Southeast Asian Statecraft.* Center for South and Southeast Asian Studies, Paper No. 11. University of Michigan, Ann Arbor.

Hansen, M. H.

1986   *Demography and Democracy: The Number of Athenian Citizens in the Fourth Century B.C.* Systime, Herning, Denmark.

1997   The Polis as an Urban Centre: The Literary and Epigraphical Evidence. In *The Polis as an Urban Centre and as a Political Community,* edited by M. H. Hansen, pp. 9–86. Acts of the Copenhagen Polis Centre Vol. 4. Historisk-filosofiske Meddelelser 75. Royal Danish Academy of Sciences and Letters, Copenhagen.

2004   The Concept of the Consumption City Applied to the Greek Polis. In Thomas Nielsen, ed., *Once Again: Studies in the Ancient Greek Polis, pp.* 9–47. F. Steiner, Stuttgart.

Hanson, V. D.

1995   *The Other Greeks.* Free Press, New York.

Harkness, A. G.

1896   Age at Marriage and Death in the Roman Empire. *Transactions of the American Philological Association* 27:35–72.

Harris, M.

1977   *Cannibals and Kings: The Origins of Cultures.* Random House, New York.

Harrison, P. D.

1978   Bajos Revisited: Visual Evidence for One System of Agriculture. In *Pre-Hispanic Maya Agriculture,* edited by P. D. Harrison and B. L. Turner II, pp. 247–253. University of New Mexico Press, Albuquerque.

1989   Spatial Geometry and Logic in the Ancient Maya Mind, Part 2: Architecture. In *Seventh Palenque Round Table,* edited by V. M. Fields, pp. 243–252. Pre-Columbian Art Research Institute, San Francisco.

1999   *The Lords of Tikal: Rulers of an Ancient Maya City.* Thames and Hudson, New York.

Harrison, P. D., and B. L. Turner II (editors)

1978   *Pre-Hispanic Maya Agriculture.* University of New Mexico Press, Albuquerque.

Hasebroek, J.

1933   *Trade and Politics in Ancient Greece.* Bell, London.

Hassan, Fekri

1978   Demographic Archaeology. In *Advance in Archaeological Method and Theory,* Vol. 1, edited by M. B. Schiffer, pp. 49–103. Academic Press, New York.

1981   *Demographic Archaeology.* Academic Press, New York.

1993   Town and Village in Ancient Egypt: Ecology, Society, and Urbanization. In *The Archaeology of Africa: Food, Metals, and Towns,* edited by T. Shaw, P. Sinclair, B. Andah, and A. Okpoko, pp. 551–569. Routledge, New York.

1997a   Egypt: Beginnings of Agriculture. In *Encyclopedia of Precolonial Africa: Archaeology, History, Languages, Cultures, and Environments,* edited by J. O. Vogel, pp. 405–408. AltaMira Press, Walnut Creek, CA.

1997b   Egypt: Emergence of State Society. In *Encyclopedia of Precolonial Africa: Archaeology, History, Languages, Cultures, and Environments,* edited by J. O. Vogel, pp. 472–478. AltaMira Press, Walnut Creek, CA.

Hassig, R.

1985   *Trade, Tribute, and Transportation: The Sixteenth Century Political Economy of the Valley of Mexico.* University of Oklahoma Press, Norman.

Haviland, W. A.

1963   Excavation of Small Structures in the Northeast Quadrant of Tikal, Guatemala. Unpublished PhD dissertation, Department of Anthropology, University of Pennsylvania, Philadelphia.

1965   Prehistoric Settlement at Tikal. *Expedition* 7:14–23.

1970   Tikal, Guatemala, and Mesoamerican Urbanism. *World Archaeology* 2:186–197.

1972   Family Size, Prehistoric Population Estimates, and the Ancient Maya. *American Antiquity* 37:135–139.

1988   Musical Hammocks at Tikal: Problems with Reconstructing Household Composition. In *Household and Community in the Mesoamerican Past,* edited by R. R. Wilk and W. Ashmore, pp. 121–134. University of New Mexico Press, Albuquerque.

2003   Settlement, Society, and Demography at Tikal. In *Tikal: Dynasties, Foreigners, and Affairs of State,* edited by J. A. Sabloff, pp. 111–142. School of American Research Press, Santa Fe.

Headrick, A.

1999   The Street of the Dead . . . It Really Was. *Ancient Mesoamerica* 10:69–85.

Healy, P. F., J. D. H. Lambert, J. T. Arnason, and R. J. Hebda

1983   Caracol, Belize: Evidence on Ancient Maya Agricultural Terraces. *Journal of Field Archaeology* 10:397–410.

Hebdige, D.

1979   *Subculture: The Meaning of Style.* Routledge, New York.

Hegel, F.

1965   La Raison Dans l'Histoire: Introduction à la Philosophie de l'Histoire. Plon, Paris.

Hellmuth, N. M.

1977   Cholti-Lacandon (Chiapas) and Peten-Ytza Agriculture, Settlement Pattern and Population. In *Social Process in Maya Prehistory: Studies in Honour of Sir Eric Thompson,* edited by N. Hammond, pp. 421–448. Academic Press, New York.

Henan Bureau of Cartographic Survey

1987   *Henan Sheng Dituce* [*Atlas of Henan Province*]. Fujian Sheng Ditu Chubanshe [Fujian Province Atlas Press], Fuzhou.

Henan Institute of Cultural Relics

2001   *Zhengzhou Shangcheng* [*Zhengzhou Shang City*]. Wenwu Chubanshe [Cultural Relics Press], Beijing.

Henderson, G.

1959   Korea through the Fall of the Lolong Colony. *Koreana Quarterly* 131:147–168.

Hendon, J.

1991   Status and Power in Classic Maya Society: An Archaeological Study. *American Anthropologist* 93:894–918.

Henry, L.

1959   L'âge au décès d'après les inscriptions funéraires. *Population* 14:327–329.

Herlihy, D., and C. Klapisch-Zuber

1985   *Tuscans and Their Families: A Study of the Florentine Catasto of 1427.* Yale University Press, New Haven.

Hermansen, G.

1978   The Population of Imperial Rome: The Regionaries. *Historia* 27:129–168.

Hester Jr., J. A.
  1954   Natural and Cultural Bases of Ancient Maya Subsistence Economy. Unpublished
          PhD dissertation, Department of Anthropology, University of California, Los An-
          geles.
Hester, T., and H. Shafer
  1994   The Ancient Maya Craft Community at Colha, Belize, and Its External Relation-
          ships. In *Archaeological Views from the Countryside: Village Communities in Early
          Complex Societies,* edited by G. M. Schwartz and S. E. Falconer, pp. 48–63. Smith-
          sonian Institution Press, Washington, D.C.
Hicks, F.
  1987   First Steps toward a Market-Integrated Economy in Aztec Mexico. In *Early State
          Dynamics,* edited by H. J. M. Claessen and P. Van de Velde, pp. 91–107. E. J. Brill,
          Leiden.
Hicks, J.
  1969   *A Theory of Economic History.* Clarendon Press, Oxford.
Hillier, B., and J. Hanson.
  1984   *The Social Logic of Space.* Cambridge University Press, New York.
Hirth, K.
  1978   Interregional Trade and the Formation of Prehistoric Gateway Communities. *Ameri-
          can Antiquity* 43:35–45.
Hladik, C. M., and A. Hladik
  1990   Food Resources of the Rain Forest. In *Food and Nutrition in the African Rain Forest,*
          edited by C. M. Hladik, S. Bahuchet, and I. de Garine, pp. 14–18. UNESCO, Paris.
Hodder, I.
  1982   *Symbols in Action.* Cambridge University Press, New York.
  1990   Style as Historical Quality. In *The Uses of Style in Archaeology,* edited by M. W.
          Conkey and C. A. Hastorf, pp. 44–51. Cambridge University Press, New York.
Hodell, D. A., J. H. Curtis, and M. Brenner
  1995   Possible Role of Climate in the Collapse of Classic Maya Civilization. *Nature*
          375:391–394.
Hodge, M.
  1984   *Aztec City-States.* Memoirs No. 18 Museum of Anthropology, University of Michi-
          gan, Ann Arbor.
Hodkinson, S.
  1988   Animal Husbandry in the Greek Polis. In *Pastoral Economies in Classical Antiquity,*
          edited by C. R. Whittaker, pp. 35–74. Cambridge Philological Society, Cambridge.
  1992   Imperialist Democracy and Market-Oriented Pastoral Production in Classical Ath-
          ens. *Anthropozoologica* 16:53–60.
  2000   *Property and Wealth in Classical Sparta.* Duckworth, London.
Hoepfner, W.
  1990   Von Alexandria über Pergamon nach Nikopolis: Stadtbauten und Stadtbilder hel-
          lenistischer Zeit. In *Akten des XIII. Internationalen Kongresses für klassische Archäolo-
          gie, Berlin 1988,* pp. 275–278. P. von Zabern, Mainz.
Holl, A. F. C.
  1998a   The Dawn of African Pastoralisms: An Introductory Note. *Journal of Anthropological
          Archaeology* 17:81–96.
  1998b   Livestock Husbandry, Pastoralisms, and Territoriality: The West African Record.
          Journal of Anthropological Archaeology 17:143–165.

Holzapfel, L.
1885 *Römische Chronologie.* B. G. Teubner, Leipzig.
Homberger, E.
1994 *The Historical Atlas of New York City.* Henry Holt, New York.
Homo, L.
1951 *Rome Imperiale et L' Urbanisme dans L' Antiquité.* Editions Albin Michel, Paris.
Hopkins, C. (editor)
1972 *Topography and Architecture of Seleuceia-on-the-Tigris.* University of Michigan Press, Ann Arbor.
Hopkins, K.
1966– On the Probable Age Structure of the Roman Population. *Population Studies* 20:
1967   245–264.
1978a *Conquerors and Slaves.* Cambridge University Press, New York.
1978b Economic Growth and Towns in Classical Antiquity. In *Towns in Societies,* edited by P. Abrams and E. A. Wrigley, pp. 35–77. Cambridge University Press, New York.
1980   Taxes and Trade in the Roman Empire. *Journal of Roman Studies* 70:101–125.
1987   Graveyards for Historians. In *La mort, les morts, et l'au delà dans le monde romain: Actes du colloque de Caen, 20–22 novembre 1985,* edited by F. Hinard, pp. 113–126. Université de Caen, Caen.
1995– Rome, Taxes, Rents and Trade. *Kodai, Journal of Ancient History* 6/7:41–75.
1996
Hoppa, R., and J. Vaupel (editors)
2002 *Paleodemography: Age Distributions from Skeletal Samples.* Cambridge Studies in Biological and Evolutionary Anthropology 31. Cambridge University Press, New York.
Horden, P., and N. Purcell
2000 *The Corrupting Sea: A Study of Mediterranean History.* Blackwell, New York.
Horton, M.
1996 *Shanga: A Muslim Trading Community on the East African Coast.* British Institute in Eastern Africa, Nairobi.
Hoshower, L. M., J. E. Buikstra, P. S. Goldstein, and A. D. Webster
1995 Artificial Cranial Modification in the Omo M10 site: A Tiwanaku Complex from the Moquegua Valley, Peru. *Latin American Antiquity* 6:145–164.
Houston, S. D.
1993 *Hieroglyphs and History at Dos Pilas, Guatemala: Dynastic Politics of the Classic Maya.* University of Texas Press, Austin.
2000 Into the Minds of Ancients: Advances in Maya Glyph Studies. *Journal of World Prehistory* 14:121–201.
Howell, N.
1979 *Demography of the Dobe !Kung.* Academic Press, New York.
Huey, P.
1984 Old Slip and Cruger's Wharf at New York: An Archaeological Perspective of the Colonial American Waterfront. *Journal of the Society for Historical Archaeology* 18: 15–37.
Hutterer, K. L., and W. K. Macdonald (editors)
1982 *Houses Built on Scattered Poles: Prehistory and Ecology in Negros Oriental, Philippines.* University of San Carlos Press, Cebu City, Philippines.

Ilyon
1972   *Samguk Yusa: Legends and History of the Three Kingdoms of Ancient Korea.* Translated by Tao-Hung Ha and G. K. Mintz. Yonsei University Press, Seoul.

Inikori, J. E.
1997   Slave Trade, Western Africa. In *Encyclopaedia of Africa South of the Sahara*, Vol. 4, edited by J. Middleton, pp. 88–94. Charles Scribner's Sons, New York.

Inomata, T.
1995   Archaeological Investigations at the Fortified Center of Aguateca, El Peten, Guatemala: Implications for the Study of the Classic Maya Collapse. Unpublished PhD dissertation, Department of Anthropology, Vanderbilt University, Nashville.

1997   The Last Day of a Fortified Classic Maya Center: Archaeological Investigations at Aguateca, Guatemala. *Ancient Mesoamerica* 8:337–351.

Inomata, T., and S. D. Houston
2001   *Royal Courts of the Ancient Maya.* Westview Press, Boulder.

Institute of Archaeology, CASS
1999   *Yanshi Erlitou [Erlitou in Yanshi].* Zhongguo Dabaikequanshu Chubanshe [Chinese Encyclopedia Press], Beijing.

2003   Henan Yanshi Huizui yizhi fajue de xinshouhuo. *Zhongguo Shehui Kexueyuan Gudai Wenming Yanjiu Zhongxin Tongxun* 5:36–39.

Institute of Archaeology, CASS, National Museum of Chinese History, and Shanxi Institute of Archaeology
1988   *Xiaxian Dongxiafeng [Dongxiafeng in Xiaxian].* Wenwu Chubanshe [Cultural Relics Press], Beijing.

Islebe, G., H. Hooghiemstra, M. Brenner, J. H. Curtis, and D. A. Hodell
1996   A Holocene Vegetation History from Lowland Guatemala. *Holocene* 6:265–271.

Ito, A.
1971   Zur Chronologie der frühsillazeitichen Gräber in Südkorea. *Abhandlungen Bayerische Akademie der Wissenschaften, Philosophische—Historische Klass.* n. F. Heft 71. Verlag der Bayerische Akademie der Wissenschaften, Beck in Komm: Munich (in German with English Summary).

Izko, X.
1992   *La Doble Frontera: Ecología, Política y Ritual en el Altiplano Central.* Hisbol/Ceres, La Paz.

Jablonka, M.
1996   Ausgrabungen im Süden der Unterstadt von Troia: Grabungsbericht 1995. *Studia Troica* 6:65–96.

Jackson, K. T.
1995   *Encyclopedia of New York City.* Yale University Press, New Haven.

Jacobs, J.
1969   *The Economy of Cities.* Random House, New York.

Jameson, M., C. Runnels, and T. van Andel (editors)
1994   *A Greek Countryside.* Stanford University Press, Stanford.

Janowitz, M. F.
1993   Indian Corn and Dutch Pots: Seventeenth-Century Foodways in New Amsterdam/New York City. Unpublished PhD dissertation, City University of New York, New York.

Janusek, J. W.
1999   Craft and Local Power: Embedded Specialization in Tiwanaku Cities. *Latin American Antiquity* 10:107–131.

2002   Out of Many, One: Style and Social Boundaries in Tiwanaku. *Latin American Antiquity* 13:35–61.

2003   The Changing Face of Tiwanaku Residential Life: State and Local Identity in an Andean City. In *Tiwanaku and Its Hinterland: Archaeology and Paleoecology of an Andean Civilization,* edited by A. L. Kolata, Vol. II, pp. 264–295. Smithsonian Institution Press, Washington, DC.

2004   Tiwanaku and Its Precursors: Recent Research and Emerging Perspectives. *Journal of Archaeological Research* 12:121–183.

Janusek, J. W., and H. Earnest

1990   Urban Residence and Land Reclamation in Lukurmata: A View from the Core Area. In *Tiwanaku and Its Hinterland,* edited by A. L. Kolata, Vol. II, pp. 118–143. University of Chicago Press, Chicago.

Janusek, J. W., and A. L. Kolata

2003   Prehispanic Rural History in the Rio Katari Valley. In *Tiwanaku and Its Hinterland: Archaeology and Paleoecology of an Andean Civilization,* edited by A. L. Kolata, Vol. II, pp. 129–174. Smithsonian Institution Press, Washington, DC.

Janusek, J. W., A. T. Ohnstad, and A. P. Roddick

2003   Khonkho Wankane and the Rise of Tiwanaku. *Antiquity* 77(296). Electronic document, http://antiquity.ac.uk/projgall/janusek/janusek.html.

Jardé, A.

1925   *Les céréales dans l'antiquité grecque,* Vol. 1. E. de Boccard, Paris.

Jashemski, W. M. F.

1979   *The Gardens of Pompeii: Herculaneum and the Villas Destroyed by Vesuvius.* Caratzas, New Rochelle, NY.

1993   *The Gardens of Pompeii: Herculaneum and the Villas Destroyed by Vesuvius. Volume II.* Caratzas, New Rochelle, NY.

Jeffrey, L. H.

1990   [1961] *The Local Scripts of Archaic Greece.* 2nd ed., edited by A. Johnston. Clarendon Press, Oxford. Originally published by Clarendon Press, Oxford.

Jenkins, G. K.

1975   The Coinages of Enna, Galaria, Piakos, Imachara, Kephaloidion and Longane. In *Le emissioni dei centri siculi fino all'epoca di Timoleonte e i loro rapporti con la monetazione delle colonie greche di Sicilia,* edited by Centro internazionale de studi numimatici, pp. 77–103. Istituto italiano di numismatica, Rome.

Johansen, H. C.

1991   Danmark i Tal. In *Gylendal og Politikens Danmarkshistorie,* edited by O. Olsen, Vol. 16., pp. 9–167. Gyldendal and Politiken, Copenhagen.

Johansson, S. R., and S. Horowitz

1986   Estimating Mortality in Skeletal Populations: Influence of the Growth Rate on the Interpretation of Levels and Trends during the Transition to Agriculture. *American Journal of Physical Anthropology* 71:233–250.

Johnson, G. A.

1973   *Local Exchange and Early State Development in Southwestern Iran.* University of Michigan Museum of Anthropology Papers No. 51. University of Michigan Museum of Anthropology, Ann Arbor.

1980   Spatial Organization of Early Uruk Settlement Systems. In *L'Archéologies de l'Iraq du début de l'epoque Néolithique a 333 avant notre ere,* pp. 233–263. Colloques Internationaux 580. Centre National de la Recherche Scientifique, Paris.

1987   The Changing Organization of Uruk Administration on the Susiana Plain. In *The Archaeology of Western Iran: Settlement and Society from Prehistory to the Islamic Conquest,* edited by F. Hole, pp. 107–140. Smithsonian Institution Press, Washington, DC.

Johnson, S.

1921   *A History of the Yoruba from the Earliest Times to the Beginning of the British Protectorate.* Lagos, Nigeria.

Johnston, K. J.

1994   The "Invisible Maya": Late Classic Minimally-Platformed Residential Settlement at Itzán, Petén, Guatemala. Unpublished PhD dissertation, Department of Anthropology, Yale University, New Haven.

2002   Protrusion, Bioturbation, and Settlement Detection during Surface Survey: The Lowland Maya Case. *Journal of Archaeological Method and Theory* 9:1–67.

2003   The Intensification of Pre-Industrial Cereal Agriculture in the Tropics: Boserup, Cultivation Lengthening, and the Classic Maya. *Journal of Anthropological Archaeology* 22:126–161.

2004   The "Invisible" Maya: Minimally-Mounded Residential Settlement at Itzán, Petén, Guatemala. *Journal of Latin American Antiquity* 15:145–179.

Johnston, K. J., and N. Gonlin

1998   What Do Houses Mean? Approaches to the Analysis of Classic Maya Commoner Residences. *In Function and Meaning in Classic Maya Architecture,* edited by S. Houston, pp. 141–187. Dumbarton Oaks, Washington, DC.

Jones, S.

1997   *The Archaeology of Ethnicity: Constructing Identities in the Past and Present.* Routledge, London.

Jongman, W.

1988   *The Economy and Society of Pompeii.* J. C. Gieben, Amsterdam.

1990   Het Romeins imperialisme en de vertelijking van Italië. *Leidschrift* 7:43–58.

2003   Slavery and the Growth of Rome. In *Rome the Cosmopolis,* edited by C. Edwards and G. Woolf, pp. 100–122. Cambridge University Press, New York.

Joshel, S. R.

1992   *Work, Identity and Legal Status at Rome: A Study of the Occupational Inscriptions.* University of Oklahoma Press, Norman.

Junker, L. L.

1990   The Organization of Intra-Regional and Long-Distance Trade in Prehispanic Philippine Complex Societies. *Asian Perspectives* 29:167–209.

1994   Trade Competition, Conflict, and Political Transformations in Sixth- to Sixteenth-Century Philippine Chiefdoms. *Asian Perspectives* 33:229–260.

1996   Hunter-Gatherer Landscapes and Lowland Trade in the Prehispanic Philippines. *World Archaeology* 27:389–410.

1999   *Raiding, Trading, and Feasting: The Political Economy of Philippine Chiefdoms.* University of Hawaii Press, Honolulu.

2001   The Evolution of Ritual Feasting Systems in Prehispanic Philippine Chiefdoms. In *Feasts: Archaeological and Ethnographic Perspectives,* edited by M. Dietler and B. Hayden, pp. 267–310. Smithsonian Institution Press, Washington, D.C.

2002   Economic Specialization and Inter-Ethnic Trade between Foragers and Farmers in the Prehispanic Philippines. In *Forager-Traders in South and Southeast Asia,* edited by K. Morrison and L. Junker, pp. 203–241. Cambridge University Press, New York.

Kaplan, D.

1963   Men, Monuments and Political Systems. *Southwestern Journal of Anthropology* 19: 397–410.

Keckler, C. N. W.

1997   Catastrophic Mortality in Simulations of Forager Age-at-Death: Where Did All the Humans Go? In *Integrating Archaeological Demography: Multidisciplinary Approaches to Prehistoric Population,* edited by R. R. Paine, pp. 205–228. Center for Archaeological Investigations, Occasional Paper No. 24, Southern Illinois University Press, Carbondale.

Kelley, K. B.

1976   Dendritic Central-Place Systems and the Regional Organization of Navajo Trading Posts. In *Regional Analysis,* Vol. I: *Economic Systems,* edited by C. Smith, pp. 219–254. Academic Press, New York.

Kempton, J. H.

1935   Preliminary Report of the Agricultural Survey of Yucatan of 1935. Mimeographed paper. Carnegie Institution of Washington, Washington, DC.

Kenoyer, J. M.

1997   Early City-States in South Asia: Comparing the Harappan Phase and Early Historic Period. In *The Archaeology of City-States: Cross-Cultural Approaches,* edited by D. L. Nichols and T. H. Charlton, pp. 51–70. Smithsonian Institution Press, Washington, D.C.

Key, P. J., and R. L. Jantz

1990   Statistical Measures of Intrasample Variability. *Human Evolution* 5:457–469.

Kieffer-Olsen, J.

1993   Grav og gravskik i det middelalderlige Danmark. Unpublished thesis, Afdelingen for Middelalderarkæologi, Århus, Denmark.

Kim, C. S.

1965   The Emergence of Multi-Centered Despotism in the Silla Kingdom: A Study of Factional Struggles in Korea. Unpublished PhD dissertation, University of Washington, Seattle.

1977   The Kolpum System: Basis for Sillan Social Stratification. *Journal of Korean Studies* 1:43–69.

Kim, C. S., and U. C. Lee

1975   *A Report on the Excavation of Tombs at Hwangnamdong, Kyongju.* Jongnam University Museum Monograph No. 1. (In Korean, English summary.)

Kim, P. M.

1998   *Kumgwam ui pimil* [*Gold Crowns Decoded*]. P'urun Yoksa, Seoul.

Kim, P., and C. H. Yi

1997   [1145] *Samguk Sagi.* Sol, Seoul.

Kim, W. Y.

1976   The Six Villages of Saro and Kyongju Tombs. *Yoksa Hakbo* 70:1–14 (in Korean).

1979   Kyongju: The Homeland of Korean Culture. *Korean Journal* 22:25–32.

Kim, W. Y., and R. Pearson

1977   Three Royal Tombs: New Discoveries in Korean Archaeology. *Archaeology* 30:302–313.

King, E. M., and D. R. Potter

1994   Small Sites in Prehistoric Maya Socioeconomic Organization: A Perspective from Colha, Belize. In *Archaeological Views from the Countryside: Village Communities in*

Early Complex Societies, edited by G. M. Schwartz and S. E. Falconer, pp. 64–90. Smithsonian Institution Press, Washington, DC.

Kintigh, K. W.
1994   Contending with Contemporaneity in Settlement-Pattern Analysis. *American Antiquity* 59:143–148.

Kirch, P. V.
1984   *The Evolution of Polynesian Chiefdoms.* Cambridge University Press, New York.

Ki-Zerbo, J.
1981   General Introduction. In *General History of Africa, I, Methodology and African Prehistory,* edited by J. Ki-Zerbo, pp. 1–9. University of California Press, Berkeley and Los Angeles.

Kolata, A. L.
1986   The Agricultural Foundations of the Tiwanaku State: A View from the Heartland. *American Antiquity* 51:746–762.
1991   The Technology and Organization of Agricultural Production in the Tiwanaku State. *Latin American Antiquity* 2:99–125.
1993   *Tiwanaku: Portrait of an Andean Civilization.* Blackwell, New York.
1997   Of Kings and Capitals: Principles of Authority and the Nature of Cities in the Native Andean State. In *The Archaeology of City-States,* edited by D. L. Nichols and T. H. Charlton, pp. 245–254. Smithsonian Institution Press, Washington, DC.

Kolata, A. L. (editor)
2003   *Tiwanaku and Its Hinterland: Archaeology and Paleoecology of an Andean Civilization,* Vol. II. Smithsonian Institution Press, Washington, DC.

Kolata, A. L., and C. Ponce Sanginés
1992   Tiwanaku: The City at the Center. In *The Ancient Americas: Art from Sacred Landscapes,* edited by R. F. Townsend, pp. 317–334. Art Institute, Chicago.

Kolb, C. C., and W. T. Sanders
1996   The Surface Survey. In *The Teotihuacan Period Occupation of the Valley. The Teotihuacan Valley Project, Final Report,* Vol. 3, edited by W. T. Sanders, pp. 485–653. Occasional Papers in Anthropology No. 21, Part 3, Department of Anthropology, Pennsylvania State University, University Park.

Konigsberg, L. W., S. R. Frankenberg, and R. B. Walker
1997   Regress What on What? Paleodemographic Age Estimation As a Calibration Problem. In *Integrating Archaeology: Multidisciplinary Approaches to Prehistoric Population,* edited by R. R. Paine, pp. 64–88. Center for Archaeological Investigations, Occasional Paper No. 24, Southern Illinois University at Carbondale, Carbondale.

Kowalewski, S. A.
1990   The Evolution of Complexity in the Valley of Oaxaca. *Annual Review of Anthropology* 19:39–58.

Krause, M.
1991   Inscriptions. In *The Coptic Encyclopedia,* Vol. 4, edited by A. S. Atiya, pp. 1290–1299. Macmillan, New York.

Kusimba, C. M., and B. Bronson
2000   What Does Africa Mean to You? *In The Field* 71:6–7.

Lander, R., and J. Lander
1832   *Journal of an Expedition to Explore the Course and Termination of the Niger.* John Murray, London.

Landers, J.
1987   Mortality and Metropolis: The Case of London, 1675–1825. *Population Studies* 41:59–76.
1993   Death and the Metropolis: Studies in the Demographic History of London, 1670–1830. Cambridge University Press, New York.

Lasker, G. W., and C. G. N. Mascie-Taylor
1989   Effects of Social Class Differences and Social Mobility on Growth in Height, Weight and Body Mass Index in a British Cohort. *Annals of Human Biology* 16:1–8.

Laurence, R.
1995   *Roman Pompeii: Space and Society.* Routledge, New York.
1997   Writing the Roman Metropolis. In *Roman Urbanism: Beyond the Consumer City,* edited by H. M. Parkins, pp. 1–20. Routledge, New York.
1998   Land Transport in Roman Italy. In *Trade, Traders and the Ancient Sea,* edited by H. M. Parkins and C. Smith, pp. 129–148. Routledge, New York.

LeBlanc, S.
1971   An Addition to Narroll's Suggested Floor Area and Settlement, Population Relationship. *American Antiquity* 36:210–211.

Lee Insook
1987   Report Concerning Korean Prehistoric Gokok. In *Papers in Honor of the Retirement of Professor Kim Won-yong,* Vol. 1, edited by I. Hyo-jai, pp. 357–369. Seoul National University, Seoul (in Korean).
1988   A Study of Korean Ancient Glass. *Komunhwa* 34:79–95 (in Korean).

Lefebvre, G.
1978   [1907] *Recueil des inscriptions grecques-chrétiennes d'Egypte.* Ares, Chicago. Originally published by Imprimeri de L'Institut français d'archéologie orientale, Cairo.

Legouilloux, M.
2000   L'alimentation carnée au Ier millénaire avant J-C. en Grèce continentale et dans les Cyclades. *Pallas* 52:69–95.

Lekson, Stephen H.
1999   *The Chaco Meridian: Centers of Political Power in the Ancient Southwest.* AltaMira Press, Walnut Creek, CA.

Leslie, P. H.
1945   On the Uses of Matrices in Certain Population Mathematics. *Biometrika* 33:183–212.

Leveau, P., and C. Goudineau
1983   La ville antique: "ville de consommation"? *Études rurales* 89–91:275–289.

Leyden, B. W.
1984   Guatemalan Forest Synthesis after Pleistocene Aridity. *Proceedings of the National Academy of Sciences USA* 81:4856–4859.

Leyden, B. W., M. Brenner, and B. H. Dahlin
1998   Cultural and Climatic History of Cobá, a Lowland Maya City in Quintana Roo, Mexico. *Quaternary Research* 49:111–122.

Lin, Y.
1998   Guanyu Zhongguo zaoqi guojia xingshi de jige wenti [Issues on the Forms of Early States in China]. In *Lin Yun xueshu wenji* [*Selected Papers of Lin Yun*], edited by Y. Lin, pp. 85–99. Zhongguo Dabaikequanshu Chubanshe [Chinese Encyclopedia Press], Beijing.

Lindsay, W. M.
1965   [1913] *Sextus Pompeius Festus De Verborum Significatu Quae Supersunt Cum Pauli*

Epitome. Georg Olms Verlagsbuchhandlung, Hildesheim. Originally published by B. G. Teubner, Leipzig.

Liu, L.
2003 "The Products of Minds as Well as of Hands": Production of Prestige Goods in the Neolithic and Early State Periods of China. *Asian Perspectives* 2:1–40.

Liu, L., and X. Chen
2001 Cities and Towns: The Control of Natural Resources in Early States, China. *Bulletin of the Museum of Far Eastern Antiquities* 73:5–47.
2003 *State Formation in Early China*. Duckworth, London.

Liu, L., X. Chen, Y. K. Lee, H. Wright, and A. Rosen
2002/ Settlement Patterns and Development of Social Complexity in the Yiluo Region,
2004 North China. *Journal of Field Archaeology* 29:75–100.

Liu, X.
2001 Youguan Xiadai niandai he Xia wenhua cenian de jidian kanfa [Opinions on Dating the Xia Dynasty and Xia Culture]. *Zhongyuan wenwu* [*Central Plains Cultural Relics*] 2:32–33.

Lloyd, P. C.
1972 *The Political Development of Yoruba Kingdoms in the Eighteenth and Nineteenth Centuries*. Monograph of the Royal Anthropological Institute of Great Britain and Ireland, London.

Lo Cascio, E.
1990 L'organizzazione annonaria. In *Civiltà dei Romani, I, La città, il territorio, l'impero*, edited by S. Settis, pp. 229–248. Electa, Milan.
1991 Fra equilibrio e crisi. In *Storia di Roma*, Vol. II, edited by A. Schiavone, pp. 701–731. Einaudi, Turin.
1994a The Size of the Roman Population: Beloch and the Meaning of the Augustan Census Figures. *Journal of Roman Studies* 84:23–40.
1994b La dinamica della popolazione in Italia da Augusto al III secolo. In *L'Italie d'Auguste à Dioclétien, Atti del Colloquio Internazionale, École française de Rome, 25–28 marzo 1992*, pp. 91–125. Collection de l' École française de Rome n. 198. École française de Rome, Rome.
1996 Popolazione e risorse nel mondo antico. In *Storia dell'economia mondiale, I. Dall'antichità al medioevo*, edited by V. Castronovo, pp. 275–299. Bari, Rome.
1997 Le procedure di recensus dalla tarda Repubblica al tardoantico e il calcolo della popolazione di Roma. In *La Rome impériale: démographie et logistique, École française de Rome, 25 marzo 1994*, pp. 3–76. Collection de L'École Française de Rome No. 230. L'École Française de Rome, Rome.
1999a Canon frumentarius, suarius, vinarius: stato e privati nell'approvvigionamento dell'Vrbs. In *The Transformations of Vrbs Roma in Late Antiquity*, edited by W. H. Harris, pp. 163–182. Journal of Roman Archaeology Supplement. Ser. 33, Portsmouth, Rhode Island.
1999b Popolazione e risorse agricole nell'Italia del II secolo a.c. In *Demografia, sistemi agrari, regimi alimentari nel mondo antico*, edited by D. Vera, pp. 217–245. Bari, Rome.
1999c The Population of Roman Italy in Town and Country. In *Reconstructing Past Population Trends in Mediterranean Europe (3000 B.C.–A.D. 1800)*, edited by J. L. Bintliff and K. Sbonias, pp. 161–171. Oxbow Books, Oxford.
2000 La popolazione. In *Roma imperiale. Una metropoli antica*, edited by E. Lo Cascio, pp. 17–69. Carocci, Rome.

2001a   Il *census* a Roma e la sua evoluzione dall'età "serviana" alla prima età imperiale. *Mélanges de l'École française de Rome. Antiquité* 113:565–603.

2001b   La population. In *"La ville de Rome sous le Haut-Empire": nouvelles connaissances, nouvelles réflexions,* Colloque organisé par l'École française de Rome et la Société des Professeurs d'Histoire ancienne de l'Université, Rome 5–8 Mai 2001. *Pallas* 55:179–198.

2001c   Recruitment and the Size of the Roman Population from the Third to the First Century BCE. In *Debating Roman Demography,* edited by W. Scheidel, pp. 111–138. Mnemosyne Supplement 211. Brill, Boston.

Lohmann, H.

1993   *Atene.* Böhlau Verlag, Köln.

1996   Zur Siedlingsarchäologie der griechischen Polis. *Geographische Rundschau* 48:562–567.

López Ramos, E.

1975   Geological Summary of the Yucatan Peninsula. In *The Ocean Basins and Margins: The Gulf of Mexico and the Caribbean,* edited by A. E. M. Nairn and F. G. Stehi, pp. 257–282. Plenum Press, New York.

Lovejoy, C. O., R. S. Meindl, R. P. Mensforth, and T. J. Barton

1985   Multifactorial Determination of Skeletal Age at Death: A Method and Blind Tests of Its Accuracy. *American Journal of Physical Anthropology* 68:1–14.

Lovejoy, C. O., R. S. Meindl, T. R. Pryzbeck, T. S. Barton, K. G. Heople, and D. Kotting

1977   Paleodemography of the Libben Site, Ottawa County, Ohio. *Science* 198:291–293.

Low, S. M.

1996   The Anthropology of Cities: Imagining and Theorizing the City. *Annual Review of Anthropology* 25:383–409.

Lozada C., M. C.

1998   The Señorio of Chiribaya: A Bioarchaeological Study in the Osmore Drainage of Southern Peru. Unpublished PhD dissertation, University of Chicago, Chicago.

Lugli, G.

1941–   Il valore topografico e giuridico dell'"insula" in Roma antica. *Rendiconti della Pon-*
1942   *tifica Accademia Romana di Archeologia* 18:191–208.

Lundell, C. L.

1933   The Agriculture of the Maya. *Southwest Review* 19:65–77.

1937   *The Vegetation of Petén.* Carnegie Institution of Washington, Publication 478, Washington, DC.

Lynch, K.

1960   *The Image of the City.* MIT Press, Cambridge.

Mabogunje, A.

1981   Historical Geography: Economic Aspects. In *General History of Africa, I: Methodology and African Prehistory,* edited by J. Ki-Zerbo, pp. 1–9. University of California Press, Berkeley and Los Angeles.

Mace, R.

2000   Evolutionary Ecology of Human Life History. *Animal Behavior* 59:1–10.

Mace, R., and R. Sear

1996   Maternal Mortality in a Kenyan, Pastoralist Population. *International Journal of Gynecology and Obstetrics* 74:137–141.

Mackay, D. A.

1987   *The Building of Manhattan.* Harper and Row, New York.

MacMullen, R.
 1982   The Epigraphic Habit in the Roman Empire. *American Journal of Philology* 103: 233–246.
Malajoli, B.
 1940   *La basilica eufrasiana di Parenzo.* Le Te Venezie, Padua.
Mallon, A.
 1914   Copte: épigraphie. In *Dictionnaire d'Archaeologie Chretienne et de Liturgie,* edited by F. Cabrol, Vol. 3.2, cols. 2821–2886. Letouzey et Ané, Paris.
Malthus, T. R.
 1970   [1798] *Essay on the Principle of Population.* Pelican Books, Harmondsworth, UK.
Manguin, P-Y.
 1992   Excavations in South Sumatra, 1988–1990: New Evidence for Sriwijayan Sites. In *Southeast Asian Archaeology 1990,* edited by I. Glover, pp. 62–73. Centre for South-East Asian Studies, University of Hull, Hull, UK.
Manzanilla, L.
 1992   *Akapana: Una Pirámide en el Centro del Mundo.* Universidad Nacional Autónoma de México, Instituto de Investigaciones Antropológicas, Mexico City.
 1996   Corporate Groups and Domestic Activities at Teotihuacan. *Latin American Antiquity* 7:228–246.
Marchetti, P.
 1976   La marche du calendrier romain et la chronologie à l'époque de la bataille de Pydna. *Bulletin de Correspondance Hellénique* 100:401–426.
Marcus, J.
 1973   Territorial Organization of the Lowland Classic Maya. *Science* 180:911–916.
 1974   The Iconography of Power among the Classic Maya. *World Archaeology* 6:83–94.
 1975   The Size of the Early Mesoamerican Village. In *The Early Mesoamerican Village,* edited by K. V. Flannery, pp. 79–90. Academic Press, New York.
 1976   *Emblem and State in the Classic Maya Lowlands.* Dumbarton Oaks, Washington, DC.
 1982   The Plant World of the Sixteenth- and Seventeenth-Century Lowland Maya. In *Maya Subsistence: Studies in Memory of Dennis E. Puleston,* edited by K. V. Flannery, pp. 239–273. Academic Press, New York.
 1983   On the Nature of the Mesoamerican City. In *Prehistoric Settlement Patterns,* edited by E. Vogt and R. Leventhal, pp. 195–242. University of New Mexico Press, Albuquerque.
Marinatos, N., and R. Haag
 1993   *Greek Sanctuaries: New Approaches.* Routledge, New York.
Marino, J. D.
 1987   The Surface Survey. In *The Toltec Period Occupation of the Valley. The Teotihuacan Valley Project, Final Report, Vol. 4,* edited by W. T. Sanders. Occasional Papers in Anthropology No. 15, Part 2, Department of Anthropology, Pennsylvania State University, University Park.
Martin, S., and N. Grube
 2000   *Chronicle of the Maya Kings and Queens; Deciphering the Dynasties of the Ancient Maya.* Thames and Hudson, London.
Martinez, G.
 1989   *Espacio y Pensamiento I: Andes Meridionales.* Hisbol, La Paz.
Mascie-Taylor, C. G. N., and J. L. Boldsen
 1985   Regional and Social Analysis of Height Variation in a Contemporary British Sample. *Annals of Human Biology* 12:315–324.

Masson, M., C. Peraza Lope, and T. S. Hare

2003   The People of Mayapan: Multi-Level Perspective on the Last Great Cosmopolitan
        City of the Pre-Columbian Maya World. Paper presented at the Center for the His-
        tory of Ancient American Art and Culture's Maya Meetings at Texas, Austin.

Mathews, J. E.

1992   Prehispanic Settlement and Agriculture in the Middle Tiwanaku Valley, Bolivia. Un-
        published PhD dissertation, University of Chicago, Chicago.

Mathews, P.

1991   Classic Maya Emblem Glyphs. In *Classic Maya Political History: Hieroglyphic and
        Archaeological Evidence,* edited by T. P. Culbert, pp. 19–29. School of American Re-
        search Advanced Seminar Series, Cambridge University Press, New York.

Mazarakis Ainian, A.

1987   Geometric Eretria. *Antike Kunst* 30:3–24.

1997   *From Rulers' Dwellings to Temples.* Paul Aströms förlag, Jonsered, Sweden.

McAnany, P. A.

1998   Ancestors and the Classic Maya Built Environment. In *Function and Meaning in
        Classic Maya Architecture,* edited by S. D. Houston, pp. 271–298. Dumbarton Oaks,
        Washington, DC.

McAndrews, T. L., J. Albarracin-Jordan, and M. Bermann

1997   Regional Settlement Patterns in the Tiwanaku Valley of Bolivia. *Journal of Field Ar-
        chaeology* 24:67–84.

McDow, T.

1997   Addis Ababa. In *Encyclopaedia of Africa South of the Sahara,* Vol. 1, edited by J.
        Middleton, pp. 5–6. Charles Schribner's Sons, New York.

McEvedy, C., and R. Jones

1978   *Atlas of World Population History.* Penguin, Harmondsworth, New York.

McIntosh, R. J., and S. K. McIntosh

1993   Cities without Citadels: Understanding Urban Origins along the Middle Niger. In
        The Archaeology of Africa: Food, Metals, and Towns, edited by T. Shaw, P. Sinclair,
        B. Andah, and A. Okpoko, pp. 622–641. Routledge, London.

McIntosh, S. K.

1997   Urbanism in Sub-Saharan Africa. In *The Encyclopedia of Precolonial Africa: Archae-
        ology, History, Languages, Cultures, and Environments* edited by J. C. Vogel, pp. 461–
        465. AltaMira Press, Walnut Creek, CA.

McKinnon, E.

1993   A Note on Finds of Early Chinese Ceramics Associated with Megalithic Remains in
        Northwest Lampung. *Journal of Southeast Asian Studies* 24:227–238.

McNeill, W. H.

1976   *Plagues and People.* Anchor/Doubleday, Garden City, NY.

1978   Disease in History. *Society for Scientific Medicine* 12:79–81.

Meggers, B. J.

1954   Environmental Limitation(s) on the Development of Culture. *American Anthropolo-
        gist* 56:801–824.

Merbs, C. H.

1992   A New World of Infectious Disease. *Yearbook of Physical Anthropology* 35:3–42.

Meunier, H.

1931   Les stèles coptes du Monastère de Saint-Siméon à Assouan. *Aegyptus* 11:257–300,
        433–484.

Michels, A. K.
1967   *The Calendar of the Roman Republic.* Princeton University Press, Princeton.
Miksic, J. N.
1984   A Comparison between Some Long-Distance Trading Institutions of the Malacca Straits Area and of the Western Pacific. In *Southeast Asian Archaeology at the 15th Pacific Science Congress,* edited by D. Bayard, Studies in Prehistoric Archaeology, Vol. 1b., pp. 235–253. University of Otago, Dunedin, New Zealand.
2000   Heterogenetic Cities in Premodern Southeast Asia. *World Archaeology* 32:106–120.
Miller, M.
1985   Tikal, Guatemala: A Rationale for the Placement of the Funerary Pyramids. *Expedition* 27:6–15.
1998   A Design for Meaning in Maya Architecture. In *Function and Meaning in Classic Maya Architecture,* edited by S. D. Houston, pp. 187–222. Dumbarton Oaks, Washington, DC.
Milliman, J. D., L. Leftic, and G. Sestini (editors)
1992   The Mediterranean Sea and Climate Change: An Overview. In *Climatic Change and the Mediterranean: Environmental and Societal Impacts of Climatic Change and Sea-Level Rise in the Mediterranean Region,* edited by L. Jeftic, J. D. Milliman, and G. Sestini, pp. 1–14. Edward Arnold, New York.
Millon, R.
1976   Social Relations in Ancient Teotihuacan. In *The Valley of Mexico,* edited by E. R. Wolf, pp. 205–248. University of New Mexico Press, Albuquerque.
1981   Teotihuacan: City, State, and Civilization. In *Supplement,* edited by J. A. Sabloff, pp. 198–243. Handbook of Middle American Indians, Vol. 1, Archaeology. University of Texas Press, Austin, Texas.
1988   The Last Years of Teotihuacan Dominance. In *The Collapse of Ancient States and Civilizations,* edited by N. Yoffee and G. L. Cowgill, pp. 102–164. University of Arizona Press, Tucson.
Millon, R., B. Drewitt, and G. Cowgill
1973   Urbanization at Teotihuacan, Mexico: The Teotihuacan Map. University of Texas Press, Austin.
Milner, G. R., D. A. Humpf, and H. C. Harpending
1989   Pattern Matching of Age-at-Death Distributions in Paleodemographic Analysis. *American Journal of Physical Anthropology* 80:49–58.
Molleson, T., M. Cox, A. H. Waldron, and D. K. Whittaker
1993   *The Spitalfields Report.* Vol. 2. *The Anthropology: The Middling Sort.* Council for British Archaeology Research Report 86. Council for British Archaeology, York.
Montevecchi, O.
1998   La provenienza di P.Oxy. 984. *Aegyptus* 78:49–76.
Morgan, C.
1990   *Athletes and Oracles: The Transformation of Olympia and Delphi in the Eighth Century B.C.* Cambridge University Press, New York.
Morgan, C., and J. J. Coulton
1997   The Polis As a Physical Entity. In *The Polis As an Urban Centre and As a Political Community,* edited by M. H. Hansen, pp. 87–144. Acts of the Copenhagen Polis Centre, Vol. 4. Historisk-filosofiske Meddelelser 75. The Royal Danish Academy of Sciences and Letters, Copenhagen.

Morgan, C., and T. Whitelaw

1991   Pots and Politics: Ceramic Evidence for the Rise of the Argive State. *American Journal of Archaeology* 95:79–108.

Morley, N.

1996   *Metropolis and Hinterland: The City of Rome and the Italian Economy, 200 B.C.–A.D. 200.* Cambridge University Press, New York.

2001   The Transformation of Italy, 225–28 B.C. *Journal of Roman Studies* 91:50–62.

2003   Migration and the Metropolis. In *Rome the Cosmopolis,* edited by C. Edwards and G. Woolf, pp. 147–157. Cambridge University Press, New York.

Morley, S. G.

1923   Annual Report. *Carnegie Institution of Washington, Year Book* No. 22, pp. 267–272. Carnegie Institution, Washington, DC.

1946   *The Ancient Maya.* Stanford University Press, Stanford.

Morley, S. G., and G. W. Brainerd

1956   *The Ancient Maya.* 3rd ed., revised by G. W. Brainerd. Stanford University Press, Stanford.

Morley, S. G., G. W. Brainerd, and R. S. Sharer

1983   *The Ancient Maya.* 4th ed., revised by R. S. Sharer. Stanford University Press, Stanford.

Morris, C.

1982   The Infrastructure of Inka Control in the Peruvian Central Highlands. In *The Inca and Aztec States 1400–1800: Anthropology and History,* edited by G. A. Collier, R. I. Roslado, and J. D. Wirth, pp. 153–171. Academic Press, New York.

Morris, C., and D. E. Thompson

1985   *Huánuco Pampa: An Inca City and Its Hinterland.* Thames and Hudson, New York.

Morris, I.

1987   *Burial and Ancient Society.* Cambridge University Press, New York.

1991   The Early Polis as City and State. In *City and Country in the Ancient World,* edited by J. Rich and A. Wallace-Hadrill, pp. 24–57. Routledge, New York.

1992   *Death-Ritual and Social Structure in Classical Antiquity.* Cambridge University Press, New York.

1994   The Athenian Economy Twenty Years after The Ancient Economy. *Classical Philology* 89:351–366.

1996   The Absolute Chronology of the Greek Colonies in Sicily. *Acta Archaeologica* 67: 51–59.

1997   An Archaeology of Equalities? The Greek City-States. In *The Archaeology of City States,* edited by T. Charlton and D. Nichols, pp. 91–105. Smithsonian Institution Press, Washington, DC.

1998a   Archaeology and Archaic Greek History. In *Archaic Greece,* edited by N. Fisher and H. van Wees, pp. 1–91. Duckworth, London.

1998b   Burial and Ancient Society after Ten Years. In *Nécropoles et pouvoir,* edited by S. Marchegay, M. T. Le Dinahet, and J. F. Salles, pp. 21–36. Diffusion de Boccard, Paris.

2000   *Archaeology as Cultural History.* Blackwell, Malden, MA.

2001   The Athenian Empire (478–404 BC). http://www.stanford.edu/group/sshi/empires2.html.

2006   Early Iron Age Greece. In *Cambridge Economic History of the Greco-Roman World,* edited by I. Morris, R. Saller, and W. Scheidel. Cambridge University Press, New York.

Muggia, A.
1997   *L'area di rispetto nelle colonie Magno-Greche e Siceliote.* Sellerio, Palermo.

Mumford, L.
1961   *The City in History: Its Origins, Its Transformations, Its Prospects.* Harcourt, Brace, Jovanovich, San Diego.

Munn, M., and M. L. Zimmerman-Munn
1989   Studies on the Attic Boiotian Frontier. In *Boeotia Antiqua,* edited by J. Fossey, pp. 73–123. J. C. Gieben, Amsterdam.

Murra, J. V.
1972   El "control vertical" de un máximo de pisos ecológicos en la economía de las sociedades andinas. In *Visita de la Provincia de León de Huánuco en 1562,* edited by J. V. Murra, Vol. 2 pp. 429–476. Universidad Nacional Hermilio Valdizán: Huánuco.
1980   *The Economic Organization of the Inka State.* Research in Economic Anthropology Supplement 1. JAI Press, Greenwich, CT. [This is a reprint of The Economic Organization of the Inka State, 1956, Unpublished PhD dissertation, University of Chicago, Chicago.]

Naroll, R.
1962   Floor Area and Settlement Pattern. *American Antiquity* 27:587–589.

Nash, G. B.
1979   *The Urban Crucible: The Northern Seaports and the Origins of the American Revolution.* Harvard University Press, Cambridge.

Nelson, S. M.
1991   The Statuses of Women in Ko-Silla: Evidence from Archaeology and Historic Documents. *Korea Journal* 31:101–107.
1993a   *The Archaeology of Korea.* Cambridge University Press, New York.
1993b   Gender Hierarchy and the Queens of Silla. In *Sex and Gender Hierarchies,* edited by B. D. Miller, pp. 297–315. Cambridge University Press, New York.
1995   Roots of Animism in Korea, from the Earliest Inhabitants to the Silla Kingdom. In *Korean Cultural Roots: Religion and Social Thoughts,* edited by H. Kwon, pp. 19–30. Integrated Technical Resources, Chicago.

Newman, L., F. A. Boegehold, D. Herlihy, R. W. Kates, and K. Raaflab
1990   Agricultural Intensification, Urbanization, and Hierarchy. In *Hunger in History,* edited by L. F. Newman, pp. 101–125. Basil Blackwell, Cambridge.

Nicholas, L. M.
1989   Land Use in Prehispanic Oaxaca. In *Monte Albán's Hinterland, Part II: The Prehispanic Settlement Patterns in Tlacolula, Etla, and Ocotlán, the Valley of Oaxaca, Mexico,* by S. A. Kowalewski, G. M. Feinman, L. Finsten, R. E. Blanton, and L. M. Nicholas, pp. 449–505. Memoirs 23, Museum of Anthropology, University of Michigan, Ann Arbor.

Nichols, D. L.
1988   Infrared Aerial Photography and Prehispanic Irrigation at Teotihuacan: The Tlajinga Canals. *Journal of Field Archaeology* 15:17–27.
1996   An Overview of Regional Settlement Pattern Survey in Mesoamerica. In *Arquelogía Mesoamericana: Homenaje a William T. Sanders,* 2 vols., edited by A. G. Mastache, J. R. Parsons, M. C. Serra Puche, and R. S. Santley, Vol. 1:59–96. I. N. A. H., Mexico City.

Nichols, D. L., and S. Powell
    1987   Demographic Reconstructions in the American Southwest: Alternative Behavioral
            Means to the Same Archaeological Ends. *Kiva* 52:193–207.
Nichols, D. L., M. W. Spence, and M. D. Borland
    1991   Watering the Fields of Teotihuacan: Early Irrigation at the Ancient City. *Ancient
            Mesoamerica* 2:119–129.
Nicolet, C.
    1989   *L'inventario del mondo. Geografia e politica alle origini dell'impero romano.* Italian
            translation. Bari, Rome.
Nixon, L., and S. Price
    1990   The Size and Resources of Greek Cities. In *The Greek City,* edited by O. Murray and
            S. Price, pp. 137–170. Clarendon Press, Oxford.
Norman, M. J. T.
    1979   *Annual Cropping Systems in the Tropics.* University Presses of Florida, Gainesville.
Nyamweru, C.
    1998   *Sacred Groves and Environmental Conservation.* St. Lawrence University Press, Can-
            ton, NY.
Osborne, R.
    1992   Is It a Farm? In *Agriculture in Ancient Greece,* edited by B. Wells, pp. 21–27. The
            Institute, Stockholm.
    1996a   *Greece in the Making, 1200–479 B.C.* Routledge, New York.
    1996b   Pots, Trade, and the Archaic Greek Economy. *Antiquity* 70:31–44.
Owen, N. (editor)
    1987   *Death and Disease in Southeast Asia: Explorations in Social, Medical, and Demographic
            History.* Oxford University Press, New York.
Paddock, J.
    1983   The Oaxaca Barrio at Teotihuacan. In *The Cloud People: Divergent Evolution of the
            Zapotec and Mixtec Civilizations,* edited by K. V. Flannery and J. Marcus, pp. 170–
            175. Academic Press, New York.
Paine, R. R.
    1989   Model Life Table Fitting by Maximum Likelihood Estimation: A Procedure to Re-
            construct Paleodemographic Characteristics from Skeletal Age Distributions. *Ameri-
            can Journal of Physical Anthropology* 79:51–62.
    1997   The Need for a Multidisciplinary Approach to Prehistoric demography. In *Integrating
            Archaeological Demography,* edited by R. R. Paine, pp. 1–20. Occasional Papers Se-
            ries, Vol. 24, Center for Archaeological Investigations, Southern Illinois University,
            Carbondale.
    2000   If a Population Crashes in Prehistory, and There Is No Paleodemographer There
            to Hear It, Does It Make a Sound? *American Journal of Physical Anthropology* 112:
            181–190.
Paine, R. R. (editor)
    1997   *Integrating Archaeological Demography.* Occasional Papers Series, Vol. 24, Center for
            Archaeological Investigations, Southern Illinois University, Carbondale.
Paine, R. R., and J. L. Boldsen
    1995   Defining Extreme Longevity from the Mesolithic to the Middle Ages: Estimates
            Based on Skeletal Data. In *Exceptional Longevity: From Prehistory to the Present,* edited
            by B. Jeune and J. W. Vaupel, pp. 25–36. Odense Monographs on Population Aging
            No. 2. Odense University Press, Odense, Denmark.

1997   Long-Term Trends in Mortality Patters in Preindustrial Europe. (Abstract) *American Journal of Physical Anthropology, Supplement* 24:183.

2002   Linking Mortality and Population Dynamics. In *Paleodemography: Age Distributions from Skeletal Samples,* edited by Hoppa, R. D. and J. W. Vaupel. Cambridge Studies in Biological and Evolutionary Anthropology 31, pp. 169–80. Cambridge: Cambridge University Press.

Paine, R., and A. Freter
1996   Environmental Degradation and the Classic Maya Collapse at Copán, Honduras (A.D. 600–1250): Evidence from Studies of Household Survival. *Ancient Mesoamerica* 7:37–47.

Paine, R., A. Freter, and D. Webster
1995   A Mathematical Projection of Population Growth in the Copán Valley, Honduras, A.D. 400–800. *Latin American Antiquity* 7:51–60.

Paine, R. R., and G. R. Storey,
1999   Latin Funerary Inscriptions: Another Attempt at Demographic Analysis. In *Atti XI Congresso Internazionale di Epigrafia Greca e Latina, Roma 18–24 settembre 1997,* pp. 847–862. Edizioni Quasar, Rome.

Palerm, A., and E. R. Wolf
1957   Ecological Potential and Cultural Development in Mesoamerica. In *Studies in Human Ecology,* edited by the Anthropological Society of Washington, pp. 1–37. Pan American Union, Washington, DC.

Panciera, S.
1999   Dove finisce la città. In *La forma della città e del territorio. Esperienze metodologiche e risultati a confronto,* edited by S. Quilici Gigli, pp. 9–15. L' Erma di Bretschneider, Rome.

Parker, A. J.
1992   *Ancient Shipwrecks of the Mediterranean and Roman Provinces.* British Archaeological Reports International Series 80, Tempus Reparatum, Oxford.

Parkin, T. G.
1992   *Demography and Roman Society.* Johns Hopkins University Press, Baltimore.

Parkins, H. (editor)
1997   *Roman Urbanism.* Routledge, New York.

Parkins, H., and C. Smith (editors)
1998   *Trade, Traders and the Ancient City.* Routledge, New York.

Parmar, M. K. B., and D. Machin
1995   *Survival Analysis: A Practical Approach.* John Wiley and Sons, New York.

Parsons, J. R.
1968   An Estimate of Size and Population for Middle Horizon Tiahuanaco, Bolivia. *American Antiquity* 33:243–245.

1971   *Prehistoric Settlement Patterns in the Texcoco Region, Mexico.* Memoirs No. 3. Museum of Anthropology, University of Michigan, Ann Arbor.

1976   The Role of Chinampa Agriculture in the Food Supply of Aztec Tenochtitlan. In *Culture Change and Continuity,* edited by C. Cleland, pp. 233–257. Academic Press, New York.

Parsons, J. R., E. Brumfiel, and M. Hodge
1996   Developmental Implications of Earlier Dates for Early Aztec in the Basin of Mexico. *Ancient Mesoamerica* 7:217–230.

Parsons, J. R., E. Brumfiel, M. Parsons, and D. Wilson
  1982   *Prehispanic Settlement Patterns in the Southern Valley of Mexico: The Chalco-Xochimilco Region.* Memoirs No. 14. Museum of Anthropology, University of Michigan, Ann Arbor.
Parsons, J. R., K. Kintigh, and S. A. Gregg
  1983   Archaeological Settlement Pattern Data from the Chalco, Xochimilco, Ixtapalapa, Texcoco, and Zumpango Regions, Mexico. Technical Reports No. 14, Museum of Anthropology, University of Michigan, Ann Arbor.
Parsons, J. R., and M. H. Parsons
  1990   *Maguey Utilization in Highland Central Mexico.* Anthropological Papers No. 82, Museum of Anthropology, University of Michigan, Ann Arbor.
Patterson, T. C.
  1991   *The Inca Empire: The Formation and Disintegration of a Pre-Capitalist State.* Berg Press, New York.
Pearson, K.
  1899   Mathematical Contributions to the Theory of Evolution. V. On the Reconstruction of the Stature of Prehistoric Races. *Philosophical Transactions of the Royal Society of London,* Series A, 192:169–244.
Pearson, R. J.
  1978   Lolang and the Rise of Korean States and Chiefdoms. *Journal of the Hong Kong Archaeological Society* 7:77–90.
  1981   Social Complexity in Chinese Coastal Neolithic Sites. *Science* 213:1078–1086.
  1985   Some Recent Studies in the Chronology and Social Development of Old Silla. In *Essays in Honor of Professor Dr. Tsugio Mikami on his 77th Birthday: Archaeology,* edited by the Editorial Committee for the Essays. Heibonsha, Tokyo. Pre-publication manuscript in the possession of S. Nelson.
Pearson, R. J., J-W. Lee, W. Koh, and A. Underhill
  1986   Social Ranking and the Kingdom of Old Silla, Korea: Analysis of Burials. *Journal of Anthropological Archaeology* 8:1–50.
Peebles, C., and S. Kus
  1977   Some Archaeological Correlates of Ranked Societies. *American Antiquity* 42:421–448.
Pentinnen, A.
  1996   The Classical and Hellenistic Periods. In *Agriculture in Ancient Greece,* edited by B. Wells, pp. 229–283. The Institute, Stockholm.
Peralta, J., and L. A. Salazar
  1974   *Pre-Spanish Manila: A Reconstruction of the Pre-History of Manila.* National Historical Commission, Manila.
Perrenoud, A.
  1975   L'inégalité sociale devant la mort à Genéve au XVIIe siècle. *Population* 30 (numéro spécial):221–243.
Petersen, H. C.
  2005   On the Accuracy of Estimating Living Stature from Skeletal Length in the Grave and by Linear Regression. *International Journal of Osteoarchaeology* 15:106–114.
Piggott, J. R.
  2002   The Last Classical Female Sovereign, Koken-Shotoku Tenno. In *Women and Confucian Cultures in Premodern China, Korea, and Japan,* edited by D. Ko, J. Habousch, and J. Piggott. University of California Press, Berkeley.

Platt, T.
1982   The Role of the Andean Ayllu in the Reproduction of the Petty Commodity Re-
        gime in Northern Potosi (Bolivia). In *Ecology and Exchange in the Andes,* edited by
        D. Lehman, pp. 27–69. Cambridge University Press, New York.
1987   Entre Ch'axwa y Muxsa: Para una Historia del Pensamiento Político Aymara. In *Tres
        Reflexiones Sobre el Pensamiento Andino,* edited by T. Bouysse-Cassagne, O. Harris,
        T. Platt, and V. Careceda, pp. 61–132. Hisbol, La Paz.

Pleket, H. W.
1993   Rome: A Pre-industrial Megalopolis. In *Megalopolis: The Giant City in History,* edited
        by T. Barker and A. Sutcliffe, pp. 14–35. St. Martin's Press, New York.

Pohl, M. D. (editor)
1990   *Ancient Maya Wetland Agriculture: Excavations on Albion Island, Northern Belize.*
        Westview Press, Boulder.

Pohl, M. D., P. R. Bloom, and K. O. Pope
1990   Interpretation of Wetland Farming in Northern Belize: Excavations at San Antonio,
        Rio Hondo. In *Ancient Maya Wetland Agriculture: Excavations on Albion Island,
        Northern Belize,* edited by M. D. Pohl, pp. 187–278. Westview Press, Boulder.

Pollard, J. H.
1973   *Mathematical Models for the Growth of Human Populations.* Cambridge University
        Press, New York.

Pollock, H. E. D.
1962   Introduction. In *Mayapán, Yucatan, Mexico,* edited by H. E. D. Pollock, R. Roys,
        T. Proskouriakoff, and A. L. Smith, pp. 1–24. Publication 619, Carnegie Institution
        of Washington, Washington, DC.

Pollock, H. E. D., R. Roys, T. Proskouriakoff, and A. L. Smith (editors)
1962   *Mayapán, Yucatan, Mexico.* Publication 619, Carnegie Institution of Washington,
        Washington, DC.

Pollock, S.
1983   Style and Information: An Analysis of Susiana Ceramics. *Journal of Anthropological
        Archaeology* 2:354–390.
1999   *Ancient Mesopotamia.* Cambridge University Press, New York.

Polanyi, K.
1944   *The Great Transformation.* Farrar and Rinehart, New York.

Ponce Sanginés, C.
1981   *Tiwanaku: Espacio, Tiempo, Cultura: Ensayo de síntesis arqueológica.* Los Amigos del
        Libro (originally published 1972, Academia Nacional de Ciencias de Bolivia), La Paz.

Pope, K. O.
1986   Paleoecology of the Ulua Valley, Honduras: An Archaeological Perspective. Unpub-
        lished PhD dissertation, Department of Geology, Stanford University, Stanford.

Popham, M., P. Calligas, and L. H. Sackett
1993   *Lefkandi II,* Vol. I. Thames and Hudson, London.

Postgate, N.
1994   How Many Sumerians per Hectare? Probing the Anatomy of an Early City. *Cam-
        bridge Archaeological Journal* 4:47–65.

Potter, D. R., and E. M. King
1995   Socioeconomies. In *Heterarchy and the Analysis of Complex Societies,* edited by R. M.
        Ehrenreich, C. L. Crumley, and J. E. Levy, pp. 17–32. American Anthropological
        Association, Washington, DC.

Price, T. Douglas, L. Manzanilla, and W. H. Middleton
    2000   Immigration and the Ancient City of Teotihuacan in Mexico: A Study Using Strontium Isotope Ratios in Human Bone and Teeth. *Journal of Archaeological Science* 27:903–913.

Pugh, T. W.
    2001   Architecture, Ritual, and Social Identity at Late Postclassic Zacpetén, Petén, Guatemala: Identification of the Kowoj. Unpublished PhD dissertation, Department of Anthropology, Southern Illinois University, Carbondale.
    2002   Remembering Mayapán: Kowoj Domestic Architecture As Social Metaphor and Power. In *The Dynamics of Power,* edited by M. O'Donovan, pp. 301–323. Center for Archaeological Investigations Occasional Paper No. 30. Southern Illinois University, Carbondale.

Puleston, D. E.
    1968   Brosimum Alicastrum As a Subsistence Alternative for the Classic Maya of the Central Southern Lowlands. Unpublished Master's thesis, Department of Anthropology, University of Pennsylvania, Philadelphia.
    1973   Ancient Maya Settlement and Environment at Tikal, Guatemala: Implications for Subsistence Models. Unpublished PhD dissertation, Department of Anthropology, University of Pennsylvania, Philadelphia.
    1977   The Art and Archaeology of Hydraulic Agriculture in the Maya Lowlands. In *Social Process in Maya Prehistory: Studies in Honour of Sir Eric Thompson,* edited by N. D. C. Hammond, pp. 449–469. Academic Press, New York.
    1983   *The Settlement Survey of Tikal.* Tikal Reports No. 13. University Museum Monograph 48, University of Pennsylvania, Philadelphia.

Puleston, D. E., and D. W. Callender Jr.
    1967   Defensive Earthworks at Tikal. *Expedition* 9:40–48.

Purcell, N.
    1999   The Populace of Rome in Late Antiquity. In *The Transformations of Vrbs Roma in Late Antiquity,* edited by W. V. Harris, pp. 135–161. Journal of Roman Archaeology Supplement. Ser. 33, Portsmouth, Rhode Island.

Pyburn, K. A.
    1990   Settlement Patterns at Nohmul: Preliminary Results of Four Excavation Seasons. In *Precolumbian Population History in the Maya Lowlands,* edited by T. P. Culbert and D. S. Rice, pp. 183–198. University of New Mexico Press, Albuquerque.

Quaegebeur, J.
    1978   Mummy Labels: An Orientation. In *Textes grecques, démotiques et bilingues,* edited by E. Bostwell and P. W. Pestman, pp. 232–259. E. J. Brill, Leiden.

Quilici, L.
    1974   La campagna romana come suburbio di Roma antica. *La parola del passato* 29:410–438.

Raaflaub, K.
    1997   Homeric Society. In *A New Companion to Homer,* edited by I. Morris and B. Powell, pp. 624–648. E. J. Brill, Leiden.
    1998   The Transformation of Athens in the Fifth Century. In *Democracy, Empire, and the Arts in Fifth-Century Athens,* edited by K. Raaflaub and D. Boedeker, pp. 15–41. Harvard University Press, Cambridge.

Rao, C. R.
    1973   *Linear Statistical Inference and Its Applications.* Second edition, John Wiley, New York.

Rasnake, R. N.
  1988   *Domination and Cultural Resistance: Authority and Power among Andean People.* Duke
          University Press, Durham.
Rathbone, D.
  1990   Villages, land and population in Graeco-Roman Egypt. *Proceedings of the Cambridge
          Philological Society* 36:103– 142.
Rattray, E. C.
  1987   Los Barrios Foráneos de Teotihuacan. In *Teotihuacan: Nuevos Datos, Nuevas Síntesis,
          Nuevos Problemas,* edited by E. M. d. Tapia and E. C. Rattray, pp. 243–274. Univer-
          sidad Nacional Autónoma de Mexico, Mexico City.
  1993   *The Oaxaca Barrio at Teotihuacan.* Monografías Mesoamericanas No. 1. Instituto de
          Estudios Avanzados, Universidad de las Américas, Puebla, Mexico.
Raychaudhuri, T., and I. Habib
  1982   *The Cambridge Economic History of India.* Vol. I. Cambridge University Press, New
          York.
Reader, J
  1997   *Africa: A Biography of the Continent.* Hamish Hamilton, London.
Redfield, R., and M. Singer
  1954   The Cultural Role of Cities. *Economic Development and Cultural Change* 3:53–73.
Redfield, R., and A. Villa Rojas
  1934   *Chan Kom: A Maya Village.* Carnegie Institution of Washington, Washington, DC.
Reid, A.
  1983a   "Closed" and "Open" Slave Systems in Pre-Colonial Southeast Asia. In *Slavery,
          Bondage and Dependency in Southeast Asia,* edited by A. Reid, pp. 156–181. St. Mar-
          tin's Press, New York.
  1983b   Introduction: Slavery and Bondage in Southeast Asian History. In *Slavery, Bondage
          and Dependency in Southeast Asia,* edited by A. Reid, pp. 1–43. St. Martin's Press,
          New York.
  1988   Southeast Asia in the Age of Commerce 1450–1680, Vol. 1: *The Lands below the
          Winds.* Yale University Press, New Haven.
  1992   Economic and Social Change, c. 1400–1800. In *The Cambridge History of Southeast
          Asia.* Vol. 1. *From Early Times to c. 1800,* edited by N. Tarling, pp. 460–507. Cam-
          bridge University Press, New York.
  1993   *Southeast Asia in the Early Modern Era.* Cornell University Press, Ithaca.
Reina, R.
  1967   Milpas and Milperos: Implications for Prehistoric Times. *American Anthropologist*
          69:1–20.
Ren, S.
  1986   Woguo xinshiqi-tongshiqi bingyong shidai nongzuowu he qita shiyong zhiwu yicun
          [Remains of Agricultural Products and Other Food in Neolithic and Chalcolithic
          China]. *Shiqian yanjiu* [*Prehistoric Studies*] 2:77–94.
Reyes Cortés, M., and J. Garcia-Barcena
  1979   Estratificación en el Area de la Catedral. In *El Recinto Sagrado de México,* edited by
          C. Bega Sosa, pp. 16–28. Secretaria de Educación Pública—Instituto Nacional de
          Anthropología e Historia, Mexico City.
Rice, D. S.
  1978   Population Growth and Subsistence Alternatives in a Tropical Lacustrine Environ-

ment. In *Pre-Hispanic Maya Agriculture,* edited by P. D. Harrison and B. L. Turner II, pp. 35–62. University of New Mexico Press, Albuquerque.

1993   Eighth-Century Physical Geography, Environment, and Natural Resources in the Maya Lowlands. In *Lowland Maya Civilization in the Eighth Century A.D.,* edited by J. A. Sabloff and J. S. Henderson, pp. 11–64. Dumbarton Oaks, Washington, DC.

Rice, D. S., and T. P. Culbert

1990   Historical Contexts for Population Reconstruction in the Maya Lowlands. In *Precolumbian Population History in the Maya Lowlands,* edited by T. P. Culbert and D. S. Rice, pp. 1–36. University of New Mexico Press, Albuquerque.

Rice, D. S., and D. E. Puleston

1981   Ancient Maya Settlement Patterns in the Peten, Guatemala. In *Lowland Maya Settlement Patterns,* edited by W. Ashmore, pp. 121–156. School of American Research Advanced Seminar Series, University of New Mexico Press, Albuquerque.

Rice, D. S., and P. M. Rice

1984   Lessons from the Maya. *Latin American Research Review* 19:7–34.

1990   Population Size and Population Change in the Central Peten Lakes Region, Guatemala. In *Precolumbian Population History in the Maya Lowlands,* edited by T. P. Culbert and D. S. Rice, pp. 123–148. University of New Mexico Press, Albuquerque.

2005   Seventeenth-Century Maya Political Geography and Resistance in Central Petén, Guatemala. In *The Postclassic- to Spanish-Era Transition in Mesoamerica: Archaeological Perspectives,* edited by R. Alexander and S. Kepecs. University of New Mexico Press, Albuquerque.

Rice, D. S., P. M. Rice, and T. W. Pugh

1998   Settlement Continuity and Change in the Central Petén Lakes Region: The Case of Zacpetén. In *Anatomía de una civilización. Aproximaciones interdisciplinarias a la cultura maya,* edited by A. Ciudad Ruíz, Y. Fernández Marquínez, J. M. García Campillo, M.ª J. Iglesias Ponce de León, A. Lacadena García-Gallo, and L. T. Sanz Castro, pp. 208–252. Pub. 4, Sociedad Española de Estudios Mayas, Madrid.

Rice, P. M.

1987   Economic Change in the Lowland Maya Late Classic period. In *Specialization, Exchange, and Complex Societies,* edited by E. M. Brumfiel and T. K. Earle, pp. 76–85. Cambridge University Press, New York.

2004   *Maya Political Science.* University of Texas Press, Austin.

Rice, P. M., and D. S. Rice

2006   The Final Frontier of the Maya: Central Petén, Guatemala, A.D. 1450–1700. In *Frontiers through Space and Time: Interdisciplinary Perspectives on Frontier Studies,* edited by B. J. Parker and L. Rodseth. University of Utah Press, Salt Lake City.

Ricketson Jr., O. G., and E. B. Ricketson

1937   *Uaxactun, Guatemala, Group E, 1926–1931.* Carnegie Institution of Washington, Publication No. 477, Washington, DC.

Ringle III, W. M., and E. W. Andrews V

1990   The Demography of Komchen, an Early Maya Town in Northern Yucatan. In *Precolumbian Population History in the Maya Lowlands,* edited by T. P. Culbert and D. S. Rice, pp. 215–244. University of New Mexico Press, Albuquerque.

Risse, G. B.

1988   Epidemics and History: Ecological Perspectives and Social Responses. In *AIDS: The Burdens of History,* edited by E. Fee and D. M. Fox, pp. 33–66. University of California Press, Berkeley.

Rivera Casanovas, C. S.

1994 Ch'iji Jawira: Evidencias sobre la Producción de Cerámica en Tiwanaku. Unpublished Licentiatura thesis, Universidad Mayor de San Andrés, Bolivia.

2003 Ch'iji Jawira; A Case of Ceramic Specialization in the Tiwanaku Urban Periphery. In *Tiwanaku and Its Hinterland: Archaeology and Paleoecology of an Andean Civilization,* edited by A. L. Kolata. Vol. II, pp. 296–315. Smithsonian Institution Press, Washington, DC.

Rivera Cusicanqui, S.

1992 *Ayllus y Proyectos de Desarrollo en el Norte de Potosi.* Aruwiyiri, La Paz.

Rizzardi, C.

1973 Recenti rinvenimenti epigrafici nell'area cimiteriale di En-Ngila (Tripoli). *Felix Ravenna* 5–6:257–279.

Robbins, L., M. Murphy, K. Stewart, A. Campbell, and G. Brook.

1994 Barbed Bone Points, Paleoenvironment, and the Antiquity of Fish Exploitation in the Kalahari Desert, Botswana. *Journal of Field Archaeology* 21:257–264.

Robertson, I. G.

2001 Mapping the Social Landscape of an Early Urban Center: Socio-Spatial Variation at Teotihuacan. Unpublished PhD dissertation, Arizona State University, Tempe.

Robichaux, H. R.

1995 Survey in Regions of La Milpa and Dos Hombres, Programme for Belize Conservation Area, Belize. Unpublished PhD dissertation, Department of Anthropology, University of Texas at Austin, Austin.

Robinson, O. F.

1992 *Ancient Rome: City Planning and Administration.* Routledge, New York.

Rogers, A., and L. J. Castro

1984 Model Migration Schedules. In *Migration, Urbanization, and Spatial Population Dynamics,* edited by A. Rogers, pp. 41–88. Westview Press, Boulder, Colorado.

Rosenzweig, R., and E. Blackmar

1992 *The Park and the People: A History of Central Park.* Henry Holt, New York.

Rostovtzeff, M.

1941 *Social and Economic History of the Hellenistic World,* 3 vols. Clarendon Press, Oxford.

Rostworowski de Diez Canseco, M.

1992 *Pachacamac y el Señor de los Milagros: Una Trayectoria Milenaria.* Instituto de Estudios Peruanos, Lima.

Rothman, M. (editor)

2001 *Uruk Mesopotamia and Its Neighbors: Cross Cultural Interactions in the Era of State Formation.* School of American Research, Santa Fe.

Rothschild, N. A.

1985 Spatial Aspects of Urbanization. *American Archeology* 5:163–170.

1990 *New York City Neighborhoods: The Eighteenth Century.* Academic Press, San Diego.

1992 Spatial and Social Proximity in Early New York City. *Journal of Anthropological Archaeology* 11:202–218.

Rothschild, N. A., and A. Pickman

1990 *The Archaeological Excavations on the Seven Hanover Square Block.* City Landmarks Preservation Commission, New York.

Rowe, J. H.

1946 Inca Culture at the Time of the Spanish Conquest. In *The Andean Civilizations, Handbook of South American Indians,* Volume 2. Bureau of American Ethnology

Bulletin 143, edited by J. H. Steward, pp. 183–330. Smithsonian Institution, Washington, DC.

1963 Urban Settlements in Ancient Peru. *Ñawpa Pacha* 1:1–28.

Roys, R.

1962 Literary Sources for the History of Mayapán. In *Mayapan, Yucatan, Mexico,* edited by H. E. D. Pollock, R. Roys, T. Proskouriakoff, and A. L. Smith, pp. 27–86. Publication 619, Carnegie Institution of Washington, Washington, DC.

Rue, D. J.

1987 Early Agriculture and Early Postclassic Occupation in Western Honduras. *Nature* 326(6110):285–286.

Rugo, P.

1975 *Le iscrizione dei sec. VI-VII-VIII esistenti in Italia,* Vol. II. Tipografia Bertoncello, Cittadella.

Ruschenbusch, E.

1983 Tribut und Bürgerzahl im ersten athenischen Seebund. *Zeitschrift für Papyrologie und Epigraphik* 53:125–143.

1984 Die Bevölkerungszahl Griechenlands im 5. und 4. Jh. v. Chr. *Zeitschrift für Papyrologie und Epigraphik* 56:55–57.

1985 Die Zahl der griechischen Staaten und Arealgrösse und Bürgerzahl der 'Normalpolis'. *Zeitschrift für Papyrologie und Epigraphik* 59:253–263.

Russell, J. C.

1958 Late Ancient and Medieval Population. *Transactions of the American Philosophical Society* 48(3):1–101.

1985 *The Control of Late Ancient and Medieval Population.* American Philosophical Society Memoirs 60. American Philosophical Society, Philadelphia.

Rydén, S.

1957 *Andean Excavations 1: The Tiahuanaco Era East of Lake Titicaca.* Ethnographical Museum of Sweden, Monograph Series, no 4. Ethnographical Museum of Sweden, Stockholm.

Sablayrolles, R.

1996 *Libertinus miles. Les cohortes de vigiles.* Collection de l'École française de Rome n. 224. École française de Rome, Rome.

Sabloff, J. A.

1973 Major Themes in the Past Hypotheses of the Maya Collapse. In *The Classic Maya Collapse,* edited by T. P. Culbert, pp. 35–40. University of New Mexico Press, Albuquerque.

1990 *The New Archaeology and the Ancient Maya.* W. H. Freeman, New York.

1991 Turning points: Maya Archaeology Comes of Age. *Natural History* 1/91:6–11.

Sabloff, J., and E. W. Andrews V (editors)

1986 *Late Lowland Maya Civilization: Classic to Postclassic.* School of American Research Advanced Seminar Series. University of New Mexico Press, Albuquerque.

Saignes, T.

1985 *Los Andes Orientales: Historia de un Olvido.* IFEA/CERES: Cochabamba, Bolivia.

Sallares, R.

1991 *The Ecology of the Ancient Greek World.* Cornell University Press, Ithaca.

1999 Malattie e demografia nel Lazio e in Toscana nell'antichità. In *Demografia, sistemi agrari, regimi alimentari nel mondo antico,* edited by D. Vera, pp. 131–188. Bari, Rome.

2002   *Rome and Malaria.* Oxford University Press, New York

Saller, R. P.
  1994   *Patriarchy, Property and Death in the Roman Family.* Cambridge University Press, New York.

Saller, R. P., and B. D. Shaw
  1984   Tombstones and Roman Family Relations in the Principate: Civilians, Soldiers and Slaves. *Journal of Roman Studies* 74:124–156.

Salmon, J.
  1984   *Wealthy Corinth.* Clarendon Press, Oxford.

Salwen, B., S. T. Bridges, N. A. Rothschild
  1981   The Utility of Small Samples from Historic Sites: Onderdonk, Clinton Avenue and Van Campen. *Historical Archaeology* 15:79–94.

Samuel, A. E.
  1972   *Greek and Roman Chronology.* Beck, Munich.

Sanders, W. T.
  1963   Cultural Ecology of the Maya Lowlands, Part II. *Estudios de Cultura Maya* 3:203–241.
  1965   *Cultural Ecology of the Teotihuacán Valley: A Preliminary Report of the Results of the Teotihuacán Valley Project,* Department of Anthropology, Pennsylvania State University: University Park.
  1973   The Cultural Ecology of the Lowland Maya: A Reevaluation. In *The Classic Maya Collapse,* edited by T. P. Culbert, pp. 325–365. University of New Mexico Press, Albuquerque.
  1979   The Jolly Green Giant in Tenth Century Yucatan, or Fact and Fancy in Classic Maya Agriculture. *Reviews in Anthropology* 6:493–506.
  1989   Household, Lineage, and State at Eighth-Century Copán, Honduras. In *The House of the Bacabs,* edited by D. Webster, pp. 89–105. Studies in Precolumbian Art and Archaeology 92. Dumbarton Oaks, Washington, DC.
  1992   Ranking and Stratification in Prehispanic Mesoamerica. In *Mesoamerican Elites,* edited by D. Z. Chase and A. F. Chase, pp. 278–91. University of Oklahoma Press, Norman.
  1997   Prehistoric Population Studies and Anthropology's Future. In *Integrating Archaeological Demography: Multidisciplinary Approaches to Prehistoric Population,* edited by R. R. Paine, pp. 381–386. Center for Archaeological Investigations Occasional Paper No. 24. Southern Illinois University, Carbondale.
  1999   Three Valleys: Twenty-Five Years of Settlement Archaeology in Mesoamerica. In *Settlement Pattern Studies in the Americas,* edited by B. R. Billman and G. M. Feinman, pp. 12–21. Smithsonian Institution Press, Washington, D.C.
  2000   Methodology. In *The Aztec Occupation of the Valley. Part 1: Natural Environment 20th Century Occupation, Survey Methodology, and Site Descriptions, The Teotihuacan Valley Project, Final Report, Volume 5.* Occasional Papers in Anthropology 25. Edited by S. T. Evans and W. T. Sanders, pp. 59–65. Department of Anthropology, Pennsylvania State University, University Park.

Sanders, W. T., J. R. Parsons, and R. S. Santley
  1979   *The Basin of Mexico: Ecological Processes in the Evolution of a Civilization.* Academic Press, New York.

Sanders, W. T., and B. A. Price
  1968   *Mesoamerica: The Evolution of a Civilization.* Random House, New York.

Sanders, W. T., and R. S. Santley

1983   A Tale of Three Cities: Energetics and Urbanization in Pre-Hispanic Central Mexico. In *Prehispanic Settlement Patterns: Essays in Honor of Gordon R. Willey,* edited by E. Z. Vogt and R. M. Levanthal, pp. 243–291. University of New Mexico Press, Albuquerque, and Peabody Museum of Archaeology and Ethnology, Cambridge.

Sanders, W. T. and L. J. Gorenflo

2006   *Prehispanic Settlement Pattern Data in the Cuautitlán Region, Mexico.* Occasional Papers in Anthropology, Department of Anthropology, Pennsylvania State University, University Park.

Sanders, W. T., and D. L. Webster

1988   The Mesoamerican Urban Tradition. *American Anthropologist* 90:521–546.

1989   The Mesoamerican Urban Tradition: A Reply to Smith. *American Anthropologist* 90:460–461.

Sanders, W. T., M. West, J. Marino, and C. Fletcher

1975   *The Formative Period Occupation of the Valley. The Teotihuacan Valley Project, Final Report,* Vol. II. Occasional Papers in Anthropology No. 10. Department of Anthropology, Pennsylvania State University, University Park.

Sanjek, Roger

1990   Urban Anthropology in the 1980s: A World View. *Annual Review of Anthropology* 19:151–186.

Santley, R. S.

1990   Demographic Archaeology in the Maya Lowlands. In *Precolumbian Population History in the Maya Lowlands,* edited by T. P. Culbert and D. S. Rice, pp. 325–343. University of New Mexico Press, Albuquerque.

Santley, R. S., and R. Alexander

1992   The Political Economy of Core-Periphery Systems. In *Resources, Power, and Interregional Interaction,* edited by E. Schortman and P. Urban, pp. 23–49. Plenum Press, New York.

Sapan, W. H.

1985   Landfilling at the Telco Block. *American Archaeology* 5:170–174.

Sattenspiel, L., and H. Harpending

1983   Stable Population and Skeletal Age. *American Antiquity* 48:489–498.

Saunders, S. R., C. Fitzgerald, T. Rogers, C. Dudar, and H. McKillop

1992   A Test of Several Methods of Skeletal Age Estimation Using a Documented Archaeological Sample. *Canadian Society of Forensic Science Journal* 25:97–118.

Scheidel, W.

1994   Libitina's Bitter Gains: Seasonal Mortality and Endemic Disease in the Ancient City of Rome. *Ancient Society* 25:151–175.

1996   *Measuring Sex, Age and Death in the Roman Empire: Explorations in Ancient Demography.* Journal of Roman Archaeology, Supplement No. 21, Ann Arbor.

1998   The Meaning of Dates on Mummy Labels: Seasonal Mortality and Mortuary Practice in Roman Egypt. *Journal of Roman Archaeology* 11:285–292.

1999   The Slave Population of Roman Italy: Speculation and Constraints. *Topoi* 9:129–144.

2001a   *Death on the Nile: Disease and the Demography of Roman Egypt.* Leiden, E. J. Brill.

2001b   Progress and Problems in Roman Demography. In *Debating Roman Demography,* edited by W. Scheidel, pp. 1–81. Mnemosyne Supplement 211. E. J. Brill, Boston.

2001c   Roman Age Structure: Evidence and Models. *Journal of Roman Studies* 91:1–26.

2002   A Model of Demographic and Economic Change in Roman Egypt after the Antonine Plague. *Journal of Roman Archaeology* 15:97–114.

2003a   Germs for Rome. In *Rome the Cosmopolis,* edited by C. Edwards and G. Woolf, pp. 158–176. Cambridge University Press, New York.

2003b   The Greek Demographic Expansion: Models and Comparisons. *Journal of Hellenic Studies* 123:120–140.

2004   Creating a Metropolis: A Comparative Demographic Perspective. In *Ancient Alexandria between Egypt and Greece,* edited by W. Harris and G. Ruffini, pp. 1–31. E. J. Brill, Leiden.

Schele, L.
1981   Sacred Site and World-View at Palenque. In *Mesoamerican Sites and World-Views,* edited by E. P. Benson, pp. 87–118. Dumbarton Oaks Research Library and Collections, Washington, DC.

Scherzer, K. A.
1992   The Unbounded Community: Neighborhood Life and Social Structure in New York City, 1830–1875. Duke University Press, Durham.

Schiavoni, C.
1982   Brevi cenni sullo sviluppo della popolazione romana dal 1700 al 1824. In *La demografia storica delle città italiane (Relazioni e comunicazioni presentate al Convegno tenuto ad Assisi nei giorni 27–29 ottobre 1980),* pp. 401–431. CLUEB, Bologna.

Schiavoni, C., and E. Sonnino
1982   Aspects généraux de l'évolution démographique à Rome: 1598–1824. *Annales de démographie historique,* pp. 91–109.

Schlegel, S. A.
1979   *Tiruray Subsistence: From Shifting Cultivation to Plow Agriculture.* Ateneo de Manila University Press, Quezon City.

Schufeldt, P. W.
1950   Reminiscences of a Chiclero. In *Morleyana,* edited by A. J. O. Anderson, pp. 224–229. School of American Research and Museum of New Mexico, Santa Fe.

Schulz, F.
1942   Roman Registers of Birth and Birth Certificates. *Journal of Roman Studies* 32:78–91.

1943   Roman Registers of Birth and Birth Certificates. *Journal of Roman Studies* 33:55–64.

Schwartz, G. M.
1994   Rural Economic Specialization and Early Urbanization in the Khabur Valley, Syria. In *Archaeological Views from the Countryside: Village Communities in Early Complex Societies,* edited by G. M. Schwarz and S. E. Falconer, pp. 19–36. Smithsonian Institution Press, Washington, DC.

Schwartz, G. M., and S. E. Falconer
1994a   *Archaeological Views from the Countryside: Village Communities in Early Complex Societies.* Smithsonian Institution Press, Washington, DC.

1994b   Rural Approaches to Social Complexity. In *Archaeological Views from the Countryside: Village Communities in Early Complex Societies,* edited by G. M. Schwartz and S. E. Falconer, pp. 1–9. Smithsonian Institution Press, Washington, DC.

Scobie, A.
1986   Slums, Sanitation and Mortality in the Roman World. *Klio* 68:399–433.

Seddon, M. T.
1994   Excavations in the Raised Fields of the Río Catari Sub-Basin, Bolivia. Unpublished Master's thesis, University of Chicago, Chicago.

1998   Ritual, Power, and the Development of a Complex Society: The Island of the Sun and the Tiwanaku State. Unpublished PhD dissertation, University of Chicago, Chicago.

Serrati, J.

2000   Garrisons and Grain: Sicily between the Punic Wars. In *Sicily from Aeneas to Augustus,* edited by C. Smith and J. Serrati, pp. 115–33. Edinburgh University Press, Edinburgh.

Service, E. R.

1975   *Origins of the State and Civilization.* W. W. Norton, New York.

Shaffer, L.

1996   *Maritime Southeast Asia to 1500.* M. E. Sharpe, Armonk, NY.

Shapiro, H. A.

1989   *Art and Cult under the Tyrants.* P. von Zabern, Mainz.

Sharlin, A.

1978   Natural Decrease in Early Modern Cities: A Reconsideration. *Past and Present* 79: 126–138.

1981   A Rejoinder. *Past and Present* 92:175–180.

Shaw, B. D.

1984   Latin Funerary Epigraphy and Family Life in the Later Roman Empire. *Historia* 33:457–497.

1991   The Cultural Meaning of Death: Age and Gender in the Roman Family. In *The Family in Italy from Antiquity to the Present,* edited by D. I. Kertzer and R. P. Saller, pp. 66–90. Yale University Press, New Haven.

1996   Seasons of Death: Aspects of Mortality in Imperial Rome. *Journal of Roman Studies* 86:100–138.

Sheehy, J. J.

1992   Ceramic Production in Ancient Teotihuacan, Mexico: A Case Study of Tlajinga 33. Unpublished PhD dissertation, Department of Anthropology, Pennsylvania State University, University Park.

Sherwin-White, S.

1987   Seleucid Babylonia. In *Hellenism in the East,* edited by S. Sherwin-White and A. Kuhrt, pp. 1–31. Duckworth, London.

Sherwin-White, S., and A. Kuhrt

1993   *From Samarkhand to Sardis.* Duckworth, London.

Sherwin-White, S., and A. Kuhrt (editors)

1987   *Hellenism in the East.* Duckworth, London.

Shimada, I.

1991   Pachacamac Archaeology: Retrospect and Prospect. In *Pachacamac,* edited by M. Uhle, pp. xv–lxvi. University of Pennsylvania Press, Philadelphia.

Siemens, A. H.

1978   Karst and the Pre-Hispanic Maya in the Southern Lowlands. In *Pre-Hispanic Maya Agriculture,* edited by P. D. Harrison and B. L. Turner II, pp. 117–144. University of New Mexico Press, Albuquerque.

1982   Prehispanic Agricultural Use of the Wetlands of Northern Belize. In *Maya Subsistence: Studies in Memory of Dennis E. Puleston,* edited by K. V. Flannery, pp. 205–225. Academic Press, New York.

Siemens, A. H., and D. E. Puleston

1972   Ridged Fields and Associated Features in Southern Campeche: New Perspectives on the Lowland Maya. *American Antiquity* 37:228–240.

Sinclair, P. J. J. I. Pikirayi, G. Pwiti, and R. C. Soper.
    1993   Urban Trajectories on the Zimbabwean Plateau. In *The Archaeology of Africa: Food, Metals and Towns* edited by T. Shaw, P. Sinclair, B. Andah, and A. Okpoko, pp. 705–731. Routledge, New York.

Sippel, D. V.
    1988   Dietary Deficiency among the Lower Classes of the Late Republican and Early Imperial Rome. *Ancient World* 16:47–54.

Sjoberg, Gideon
    1960   *The Preindustrial City, Past and Present.* Free Press, Glencoe, IL.

Small, D. B.
    1995   A Different Distinction: The Case of the Greek State. In *The Economic Anthropology of the State,* edited by E. Brumfiel, pp. 287–314. Monographs in Economic Anthropology. No. 11, University Press of America, Lanham, MD.
    1997   City-State Dynamics through a Greek Lens. In *The Archaeology of City States,* edited by T. Charlton and D. Nichols, pp. 107–118. Smithsonian Institution Press, Washington, DC.

Smith, A. L.
    1962   Residential and Associated Structures at Mayapán. In *Mayapan, Yucatan, Mexico,* edited by H. E. D. Pollock, R. Roys, T. Proskouriakoff, and A. L. Smith, pp. 165–320. Publication 619, Carnegie Institution of Washington, Washington, DC.

Smith, B., and H. B. Reynolds
    1987   *The City As a Sacred Center.* E. J. Brill, Boston.

Smith, C. A.
    1976   Exchange Systems and the Spatial Distribution of Elites: The Organization of Stratification in Agrarian Societies. In *Regional Analysis,* Vol. II: *Social Systems,* edited by C. A. Smith, pp. 339–374. Academic Press, New York.

Smith, M. E.
    1987   Household Possessions and Wealth in Agrarian States: Implications for Archaeology. *Journal of Anthropological Archaeology* 6:297–335.
    1994   Social Complexity in the Aztec Countryside. In *Archaeological Views from the Countryside: Village Communities in Early Complex Societies,* edited by G. M. Schwartz and S. E. Falconer, pp. 143–159. Smithsonian Institution Press, Washington, DC.
    1996   *The Aztecs.* Basil Blackwell, New York.
    2003   Can We Read Cosmology in Ancient Maya City Plans? Comment on Ashmore and Sabloff. *Latin American Antiquity* 14:221–228.

Smith, M. L.
    2003   Introduction. In *The Social Construction of Ancient Cities,* edited by M. L. Smith, pp. 1–36. Smithsonian Books, Washington DC.

Smith, R.
    1965   The Alafin in Exile: A Study of the Igboho Period in Oyo History. *Journal of African History* 6:57–77.

Smith, R. B.
    1979   Mainland South East Asia in the Seventh and Eighth Centuries. In *Early South East Asia,* edited by R. B. Smith and W. Watson, pp. 443–456. Oxford University Press, New York.

Snodgrass, A.
    1971   *The Dark Age of Greece.* Edinburgh University Press, Edinburgh.
    1977   *Archaeology and the Rise of the Greek State.* Cambridge University Press, New York.

1980   *Archaic Greece.* J. M. Dent, London.

1983   Two Demographic Notes. In *The Greek Renaissance of the Eighth Century B.C.,* edited by R. Hägg, pp. 167–171. Svenska institutet i Athen, Stockholm.

1987   *An Archaeology of Greece.* University of California Press, Berkeley.

1991   Archaeology and the Study of the Greek City. In *City and Country in the Ancient World,* edited by J. Rich and A. Wallace-Hadrill, pp. 1–24. Routledge, New York.

1993   The Rise of the Polis. In *The Ancient Greek City-State,* edited by M. Hansen, pp. 30–40. Royal Danish Academy of Science and Letters, Copenhagen.

1994   Response: The Archaeological Aspect. In *Classical Greece: Ancient Histories and Modern Archaeologies,* edited by I. Morris, pp. 197–200. Cambridge University Press, New York.

Sohn P., C. C. Kim, and Y. S. Hong
1970   *The History of Korea.* Korean National Commission for UNESCO: Seoul.

Solin, H.
1972   Namengebung und Epigraphik: Betrachtung zur onomastischen Exegese römischer Inschriften. In *Akten des VI. Internationalen Kongresses für Griechische und Lateinische Epigraphik.* Beck, Munich.

1974   Onomastica ed epigrafia. Riflessioni sull'esegesi onomastica delle iscrizioni romane. *Quaderni Urbinati di Cultura Classica* 18:105–132.

1996   *Die stadtrömischen Sklavennamen: ein Namenbuch,* Vol. 3. Franz Steiner Verlag, Stuttgart.

Sommella, P., and L. Migliorati
1991   Il segno urbano. In I principi e il mondo. In *Storia di Roma,* 2.2, edited by A. Schiavone, pp. 287–309. Einaudi, Turin.

Song, Z.
1991   Xia Shang renkou chutan [Preliminary Investigations on the Xia and Shang Population]. *Lishi yanjiu* [*Historic Studies*] 4:92–106.

Sonnino, E.
1982   Bilanci demografici di cittè italiane: problemi di ricerca e risultat. In *La demografia storica delle cittè italiane (Relazioni e comunicazioni presentate al Convegno tenuto ad Assisi nei giorni 27–29 ottobre 1980),* Bologna, 47–108. CLUEB, Bologna.

1997   The Population in Baroque Rome. In *Rome-Amsterdam: Two Growing Cities in Seventeenth-Century Europe,* edited by P. van Kessel and E. Schulte, pp. 50–70. Amsterdam University Press, Amsterdam.

Southall, A.
1988   The Segmentary State in Africa and Asia. *Comparative Studies in Society and History* 30:52–82.

1997   Precolonial Era. In *Encyclopaedia of Africa South of the Sahara,* Vol. 4. Edited by J. Middleton, pp. 326–328. Charles Scribner's Sons, New York.

1998   *The City in Time and Space.* Cambridge University Press, New York.

Spence, M. W.
1989   Excavaciones Recientes en Tlailotlacan, el Barrio Oaxaqueño de Teotihuacan. *Arquelogía* 5:81–104.

1992   Tlailotlacan, a Zapotec Enclave in Teotihuacan. In *Art, Ideology, and the City of Teotihuacan,* edited by J. C. Berlo, pp. 59–88. Dumbarton Oaks Research Library and Collection, Washington, D.C.

Stambaugh, J. E.
1988   *The Ancient Roman City.* Johns Hopkins University Press, Baltimore.

Stanish, C.

1989   Tamaño y Complejidad de los Asentamientos Nucleares de Tiwanaku. In *Arqueología de Lukurmata* Volume 2, edited by A. L. Kolata, pp. 41–57. Instituto Nacional de Arqueología and Ediciones Puma Punku: La Paz.

1998   Urbanization in the Ancient Andes. Conference paper presented at the 95th Annual Conference of the American Anthropological Association, Philadelphia.

2003   *Ancient Titicaca: The Evolution of Complex Society in Southern Peru and Northern Bolivia.* University of California Press, Berkeley.

Steggerda, M.

1941   *Maya Indians of Yucatan.* Carnegie Institution of Washington, Publication 531, Washington, DC.

Stein, G. J.

1996   Producers, Patrons, and Prestige: Craft Specialists and Emergent Elites in Mesopotamia from 5500–3100 B.C. In *Craft Specialization and Social Evolution: In Memory of V. Gordon Childe,* edited by B. Wailes, pp. 26–38. University of Pennsylvania Press, Philadelphia.

Steinhardt, N. S.

1990   *Chinese Imperial City Planning.* University of Hawaii Press, Honolulu.

Stokes, I. N. P.

1918   *The Iconography of Manhattan Island, 1498–1909.* 6 vols. Robert H. Dodd, New York.

Stomper, J. A.

2001   Model for Late Classic Community Structure. In *Landscape and Power in Ancient Mesoamerica,* edited by R. Koontz, K. Reese-Taylor, and A. Headrick, pp. 197–230. Westview Press, Boulder.

Stone, E. C.

1987   *Nippur Neighborhoods.* Oriental Institute, Chicago.

1997   City-States and Their Centers: The Mesopotamian Data. In *The Archaeology of City-States: Cross Cultural Approaches,* edited by D. L. Nichols and T. H. Charlton, pp. 15–26. Smithsonian Institution Press, Washington, DC.

Storey, G. R.

1992   Preindustrial Urban Demography: The Ancient Roman Evidence. Unpublished anthropology PhD dissertation, Pennsylvania State University, University Park.

1997a   Estimating the Population of Ancient Roman Cities. In *Integrating Archaeology: Multidisciplinary Approaches to Prehistoric Population,* edited by R. R. Paine, pp. 101–130. Center for Archaeological Investigations, Occasional Paper No. 24, Southern Illinois University at Carbondale, Carbondale.

1997b   The Population of Ancient Rome. *Antiquity* 71:966–978.

Storey, G. R., and R. R. Paine

2002   Age at Death in Roman Funerary Inscriptions: New Samples, Analyses and Demographic Implications. *Antiquitas 26: Études de Démographie de Monde Gréco-Romain (Acta Universitatis Wratislaviensis 245),* edited by W. Suder, pp. 127–149. Wydawnistwo Uniwersytetu Wroclawskiego, Wroclaw, Poland.

Storey, R.

1986   Perinatal Mortality at Pre-Colombian Teotihuacan. *American Journal of Physical Anthropology* 69:541–548.

1987   A First Look at the Paleodemography of the Ancient City of Teotihuacan. In *Teotihuacan. Nuevos Datos, Nuevas Sintesis, Nuevos Problemas,* edited by E. McClung de

Tapia and E. C. Rattray, pp. 91–114. Arqueología, Serie Anthropología 72. Universidad Nacional Autónoma de México, Mexico City.

1992a The Children of Copan: Issues in Paleopathology and Paleodemography. *Ancient Mesoamerica* 3:161–167.

1992b *Life and Death in the Ancient City of Teotihuacan: A Modern Paleodemographic Synthesis.* University of Alabama Press, Tuscaloosa.

1999 Late Classic Nutrition and Skeletal Indicators at Copan, Honduras. In *Reconstructing Ancient Maya Diet,* edited by C. White, pp. 169–182. University of Utah Press, Salt Lake City.

Strauss, B.
1986 *Athens after the Peloponnesian War.* Cornell University Press, Ithaca.

Sweeting, M. J.
1972 *Karst Landforms.* Macmillan, London.

Symeonoglou, S.
1985 *The Topography of Thebes from the Bronze Age to Modern Times.* Princeton University Press, Princeton.

Talbert, R.
1974 *Timoleon and the Revival of Greek Sicily.* Cambridge University Press, New York.

Tamayo, J. L.
1964 The Hydrography of Middle America. In *Natural Environment and Early Culture,* edited by R. C. West, pp. 84–121. Handbook of Middle American Indians, R. Wauchope, general editor. University of Texas Press, Austin.

Tambiah, S.
1976 *World Conqueror and World Renouncer: A Study in Religion and Polity in Thailand against a Historical Background.* Cambridge University Press, New York.

Tandy, D.
1997 *Warriors into Traders.* University of California Press, Berkeley.

Tarling, N.
1963 *Piracy and Politics in the Malay World.* F. W. Chesire, Melbourne.

Taylor, K.
1992 The Early Kingdoms. In *The Cambridge History of Southeast Asia. Volume 1. From Early Times to c. 1800,* edited by N. Tarling, pp. 137–182. Cambridge University Press, New York.

Termer, F.
1951 The Density of Population in the Southern and Northern Maya Empires As an Archaeological and Geographical Problem. In *The Civilizations of Ancient America. Proceedings of the 29th International Congress of Americanists,* edited by S. Tax, pp. 101–107. University of Chicago Press, Chicago.

Thomas, R.
1989 *Oral Tradition and Written Record in Classical Athens.* Cambridge University Press, New York.

Thomaz, L. F. F. R.
1993 The Malay Sultanate of Melaka. In *Southeast Asia in the Early Modern Era,* edited by A. Reid, pp. 69–90. Cornell University Press, Ithaca.

Thompson, H. A., and R. E. Wycherley
1972 *The Agora of Athens.* Athenian Agora, Vol. 14. American School of Classical Studies at Athens, Princeton, New Jersey.

Thompson, J. E. S.

1927   *The Civilization of the Mayas.* Anthropology leaflet 25, Field Museum of Natural History, Chicago.

1954   *The Rise and Fall of Maya Civilization.* University of Oklahoma Press, Norman.

Thorp, R.

1991   Erlitou and the Search for the Xia. *Early China* 16:1–38.

Tome Pires

1944   [1515] *The Suma Oriental of Tome Pires.* Translated by A. Cortasao. Hakluyt Society, London.

Tonnies, F.

1974   *On Social Ideas and Ideologies.* Translated by E. G. Jacoby. Harper and Row, New York.

Tourtellot, G.

1993   A View of Ancient Maya Settlements in the Eighth Century. In *Lowland Maya Civilization in the Eighth Century A.D.,* edited by J. A. Sabloff and J. S. Henderson, pp. 219–242. Dumbarton Oaks, Washington, DC.

Townsend, R. F.

1992   *The Aztecs.* Thames and Hudson, New York.

Toynbee, J. M. C.

1971   *Death and Burial in the Roman World.* Thames and Hudson, London.

Tozzer, A. M.

1941   *Landa's Relación de las Cosas de Yucatán: A Translation.* Papers of the Peabody Museum of American Archaeology and Ethnology, Volume XVIII, Harvard University, Cambridge.

Travlos, J.

1960   Poleodomiki Exeleixis ton Athinon. Vivliothiki tiz en Athinais Etaireias, Athens.

1971   *A Pictorial Dictionary of Ancient Athens.* Praeger, New York.

Trigger, B.

1972   Determinants of Urban Growth in pre-Industrial Societies. In *Man, Settlement, and Urbanism,* edited by P. J. Ucko, R. Tringham, and G. W. Dimbley, pp. 575–599. Duckworth, London.

1993   *Early Civilizations: Ancient Egypt in Context.* American University in Cairo Press, Cairo.

1999   Shang Political Organization: A Comparative Approach. *Journal of East Asian Archaeology* 1:43–62.

2003   *Artifacts and Ideas: Essays in Archaeology.* Transactions Publishers, New Brunswick, NJ.

Tsetskhladze, G.

1998   Trade on the Black Sea in the Archaic and Classical Periods. In *Trade, Traders and the Ancient City,* edited by H. Parkins and C. Smith, pp. 52–74. Routledge, New York.

Turner II, B. L.

1974   Prehistoric Intensive Agriculture in the Mayan Lowlands: New Evidence from the Rio Bec Region. Unpublished PhD dissertation, Department of Geography, University of Wisconsin, Madison.

1979   Prehispanic Terracing in the Central Maya Lowlands: Problems of Agricultural Intensification. In *Maya Archaeology and Ethnohistory,* edited by N. D. C. Hammond and G. R. Willey, pp. 103–115. University of Texas Press, Austin.

1983   *Once beneath the Forest: Prehistoric Terracing in the Río Bec Region of the Maya Low-lands.* Westview Press, Boulder.

Turner II, B. L., and P. D. Harrison (editors)

1983   *Pulltrouser Swamp: Ancient Maya Habitat, Agriculture, and Settlement in Northern Belize.* University of Texas Press, Austin.

Ulloa Mogollón, J.

1965   Relación de la provincia de los collaguas para la discripción de las Indias que su magestad manda hacer. In *Relaciones geograficas de Indias-Peru,* edited by M. J. d. l. Espada. Vol. I. Ediciones Atlas, Madrid.

Underhill, A. P., G. M. Feinman, L. Nicholas, G. Bennett, F. Cai, H. Yu, F. Luan, and H. Fang

1998   Systematic, Regional Survey in SE Shandong Province, China. *Journal of Field Archaeology* 25:453–474.

Vaillant, G.

1938   Correlation of Archaeological and Historical Sequences in the Valley of Mexico. *American Anthropologist* 40:535–573.

Van de Mieroop, M.

1997   *The Ancient Mesopotamian City.* Clarendon Press, Oxford.

van der Spek, R. J.

1986   *Grondbezit in het seleucidische rijk.* Amsterdam Free University, Amsterdam.

van der Woude, A. M.

1982   Population Developments in the Northern Netherlands (1500–1800) and the Validity of the "Urban Graveyard" Effect. *Annales de démographie historique* 1982:55–75.

van der Woude, A. M., J. de Vries, and A. Hayami

1990   Introduction: The Hierarchies, Provisioning, and Demographic Patterns of Cities. In *Urbanization in History: A Process of Dynamic Interaction,* edited by A. M. van der Woude, A. Hayami, and J. de Vries, pp. 1–19. Clarendon Press, Oxford.

Van Leur, J. C.

1967   *Indonesian Trade and Society.* Van Hoeve Publications, The Hague.

Van Liere, W. J.

1980   Traditional Water Management in the Lower Mekong Basin. *World Archaeology* 11:265–280.

Van Setten van der Meer, N. C.

1979   Sawah Cultivation in Ancient Java: Aspects of Development during the Indo-Javanese Period, Fifth to Fifteenth Century. Faculty of Asian Studies, University of Canberra, Canberra, Australia.

Vansina, J.

1990   *Paths in the Rainforests.* University of Wisconsin Press, Madison.

Van Wees, H.

1992   *Status Warriors.* J. C. Gieben, Amsterdam.

Vaum, P. A.

1997   Western African States. In *Encyclopedia of Precolonial Africa: Archaeology, History, Languages, Cultures, and Environments,* edited by J. O. Vogel, pp. 489–495. AltaMira Press, Walnut Creek, CA.

Vaupel, J., and A. Yashin

1985a   Heterogeneity's Ruses: Some Surprising Effects of Selection on Population Dynamics. *American Statistician* 39:176–185.

1985b   The Deviant Dynamics of Death in Heterogeneous Populations. In *Sociological Methodology,* edited by N. B. Tuma, pp. 179–211. Jossey-Bass, San Francisco.

Vellard, J.
1963   *Civilisations des Andes: Evolution des Populations du Haut-Plateau Bolivien.* Galli-
        mard, Paris.
Verano, J. W., and D. H. Ubelaker (editors)
1992   *Disease and Demography in the Americas.* Smithsonian Institution Press, Washing-
        ton, D.C.
Vetter, E.
1953   *Handbuch der italischen Dialekte, Band 1.* Texte mit Erklärung, Glossen, Wörterrer-
        zeichnis. C. Winter, Heidelberg.
Vickers, M., and D. Gill
1994   *Artful Crafts.* Clarendon Press, Oxford.
Villagutierre Soto-Mayor, J. de
1933   *Historia de la conquista de la Provincia de el Itzá, reducción y progresos de la del
        Lacandón.* Biblioteca "Goathemala" de la Sociedad de Geográfia e Historia, Vol. 9,
        Tipografía Nacional, Guatemala.
Virlouvet, C.
1995   *Tessera frumentaria. Les procédures de la distribution du blé public à Rome à la fin de
        la République et au début de l'Empire.* École française de Rome and De Boccard, Paris.
1997   Existait-Il des Registres de Décès à Rome au Ier Siècle ap. J.-C.? In *La Rome impériale:
        démographie et logistique, École française de Rome, 25 marzo 1994,* pp. 77–88. Col-
        lection de L'École Française de Rome No. 230. L'École Française de Rome, Rome.
Vivo Escoto, J. A.
1964   Weather and Climate of Mexico and Central America. In *Natural Environment and
        Early Cultures,* edited by R. C. West, pp. 187–215. Handbook of Middle American
        Indians, R. Wauchope, general editor. University of Texas Press, Austin.
Volpe, R.
2000   Il suburbio. In *Roma antica,* edited by A. Giardina, pp. 183–210. Bari, Rome.
von Gerkan, A.
1940   Die Einwohnerzahl Roms in Der Kaiserzeit. *Mitteilungen des Deutschen Archaeolo-
        gischen Instituts: Roemische Abteilung* 55:149–195.
1943   Weiteres zur Einwohnerzahl Roms in Der Kaiserzeit. *Mitteilungen des Deutschen Ar-
        chaeologischen Instituts: Roemische Abteilung* 58:213–243.
1949   Grenzen und Grossen der vierzehn Regionen Roms. *Bonner Jahrbuch* 149:5–65.
Von Pauly, A. F., and G. Wissowa (editors)
1894–   *Real-Encyclopädie der classischen Altertumswissenschaft.* J. B. Metzler, Stuttgart.
von Pöhlmann, R.
1884   *Die Übervölkerung der antiken Großstädten.* S. Hirzel, Leipzig.
Voorhies, B. L.
1982   An Ecological Model of the Early Maya of the Central Lowlands. In *Maya Subsis-
        tence: Studies in Memory of Dennis E. Puleston,* edited by Kent V. Flannery, pp. 65–
        95. Academic Press, New York.
Wagner, P. L.
1964   Natural Vegetation of Middle America. In *Natural Environment and Early Cul-
        tures,* edited by R. C. West, pp. 187–215. Handbook of Middle American Indians,
        R. Wauchope, general editor. University of Texas Press, Austin.
Wailes, B. (editor)
1996   *Craft Specialization and Social Evolution: In Memory of V. Gordon Childe.* University
        of Pennsylvania Press, Philadelphia.

Waldron, T.
1994   *Counting the Dead: The Epidemiology of Skeletal Populations.* John Wiley and Sons, New York.

Walker, P. L.
1995   Problems of Preservation and Sexism in Sexing: Some Lessons from Historical Collections for Paleodemographers. In *Grave Reflections: Portraying the Past through Cemetery Studies,* edited by S. R. Saunders and A. Herring, pp. 31–47. Canadian Scholars Press, Toronto.

Wall, D. diZ.
1991   Sacred Dinners and Secular Teas: Constructing Domesticity in Mid-19th Century New York. *Historical Archaeology* 25:69–81.
1994   *The Archaeology of Gender.* Plenum Press, New York.
1999   Examining Gender, Class and Ethnicity in Nineteenth-Century New York City. *Historical Archaeology* 33:102–117.

Wall, D. diZ., N. A. Rothschild, C. Copeland, and H. Seignoret
2001   The Seneca Village Project: Working with Modern Communities in Creating the Past. Paper presented at Society for American Archaeology meetings, New Orleans.

Wallace-Hadrill, A.
1991   Elites and Trade in the Roman Town. In *City and Country in the Ancient World,* edited by J. Rich and A. Wallace-Hadrill, pp. 241–272. Routledge, New York.

Wallerstein, I.
1974   *The Modern World-System: Capitalist Agriculture and the Origins of the European World Economy in the 16th Century.* Academic Press, New York.

Wang, X.
1999   Yanshi Shangcheng buju de tansuo he sikao [Inquiry into the Plan of the Yanshi Shang City]. *Kaogu [Archaeology]* 2:24–34.

Warmington, E. H. (editor and translator)
1940   *Remains of Old Latin.* W. Heinemann, London.

Warren, J. F.
1985   *The Sulu Zone, 1768–1898: The Dynamics of External Trade, Slavery and Ethnicity in the Transformation of a Southeast Asian Maritime State.* 2nd ed. New Day Publications, Quezon City.

Warrior, V. M.
1991   Notes on Intercalation. *Latomus* 50:80–87.

Watson, J. L. (editor)
1980   *Asian and African Systems of Slavery.* University of California Press, Berkeley.

Wattenmaker, P.
1994   State Formation and the Organization of Domestic Craft Production at Third- Millennium B.C. Kurban Hoyuk, Southeast Turkey. In *Archaeological Views from the Countryside: Village Communities in Early Complex Societies,* edited by G. M. Schwartz and S. E. Falconer, pp. 109–120. Smithsonian Institution Press, Washington D. C.

Wauchope, R.
1934   *House Mounds of Uaxactun, Guatemala.* Carnegie Institution of Washington, Washington, DC.

Weber, M.
1958   *The City.* Translated by D. Martindale and G. Neuwirth. Free Press, Glencoe, IL.
1968   [1921] The City (Non-Legislative Domination). In *Economy and Society: An Outline of Interpretive Sociology,* edited by G. Roth and C. Wittich, Vol. 3, pp. 1212–1372.

Bedminster Press, New York. Originally published in *Archiv für Sozialwizsenschaft und Sozialpolitik* 47:621–772.

Webster, D. L.

1997   City-State of the Maya. In *The Archaeology of City States,* edited by T. Charlton and D. Nichols, pp. 135–154. Smithsonian Institution Press, Washington, DC.

2002   *The Fall of the Ancient Maya. Solving the Mystery of the Maya Collapse.* Thames and Hudson, New York.

Webster, D. L., and A. Freter

1990a   Settlement History and the Classic Collapse at Copán: A Refined Chronological Perspective. *Latin American Antiquity* 1:66–85.

1990b   The Demography of Late Classic Copán. In *Precolumbian Population History in the Maya Lowlands,* edited by T. P. Culbert and D. S. Rice, pp. 37–62. University of New Mexico Press, Albuquerque.

Webster, D. L., A. Freter, and N. Gonlin

2000   *Copan: The Rise and Fall of an Ancient Maya Kingdom.* Harcourt College Publishers, Fort Worth, TX.

Webster, D. L., A. Freter, and R. Storey

2004   Dating Copán Culture-History: Implications for the Terminal Classic and the Collapse. In *The Terminal Classic in the Maya Lowlands,* edited by A. A. Demarest, P. M. Rice, and D. S. Rice, pp. 231–259. University Press of Colorado, Boulder.

Webster, D. L., and N. Gonlin

1988   Household Remains of the Humblest Maya. *Journal of Field Archaeology* 15:169–190.

Webster, D. L., J. Silverstein, T. Murtha, and H. Martinez

2003   Re-Evaluation of the Earthworks at Tikal, Guatemala. Annual Report to the National Science Foundation. Project BSC 02–11579, Department of Anthropology, Pennsylvania State University, University Park.

Weinstock, S.

1971   *Divus Iulius.* Clarendon Press, Oxford.

Weiss, K. M.

1973   *Demographic Models for Anthropology.* Society for American Archaeology Monograph No. 27. Society for American Archaeology, Washington, DC.

1989   A Survey of Human Biodemography. *Journal of Quantitative Anthropology* 1:79–151.

Wells, B. (editor)

1996   *The Berbati-Limnes Archaeological Survey 1988–90.* Paul Åströms Förlag, Jonsered, Sweden.

Wells, P. S.

1995   Settlement and Social Systems at the End of the Iron Age. In *Celtic Chiefdom, Celtic State.* edited by B. Arnold and D. B. Gibson, pp. 88–96. Cambridge University Press, New York.

Wenke, Robert J.

1997   City-States, Nation-States, and Territorial States: The Problem of Egypt. In *The Archaeology of City-States: Cross-Cultural Approaches,* edited by D. L. Nichols and T. H. Charlton, pp. 51–71. Smithsonian Institution Press, Washington, DC.

1999   *Patterns in Prehistory.* 4th ed. Oxford University Press, New York.

West, R. C.

1964   The Natural Regions of Middle America. In *Natural Environment and Early Cultures,* edited by R. C. West, pp. 363–383. Handbook of Middle American Indians, R. Wauchope, general editor. University of Texas Press, Austin.

Wheatley, Paul

1959   Geographical Notes on Some Commodities Involved in the Sung Maritime Trade. *Journal of the Malaysian Branch of the Royal Asiatic Society* 32:7–143.

1961   The Golden Khersonese: Studies in the Historical Geography of the Malay Peninsula before A.D. 1500. 1st ed. University of Malaya Press, Kuala Lumpur.

1971   *The Pivot of the Four Quarters: A Preliminary Enquiry into the Origins and Character of the Ancient Chinese City.* Aldine Publishing, Chicago.

1983   *Nagara and Commandery: Origins of Southeast Asian Urban Traditions.* Department of Geography Research Paper No. 207–208. University of Chicago, Chicago.

White, C., M. W. Spence, F. J. Longstaffe, H. Stuart-Williams, and L. R. Law

2002   Geographic Identities of the Sacrificial Victims from the Feathered Serpent Pyramid, Teotihuacan: Implications for the Nature of State Power. *Latin American Antiquity* 12:217–236.

White, C. D., R. Storey, M. Spence, and F. Longstaffe

2004   Immigration, Assimilation, and Status in the Ancient City of Teotihuacan: Isotopic Evidence from Tlajinga 33. *Latin American Antiquity* 15:176–198.

Whitelaw, G.

1997   Southern African Iron Age. In *Encyclopedia of Precolonial Africa: Archaeology, History, Languages, Cultures, and Environments,* edited by J. O. Vogel, pp. 444–455. AltaMira Press, Walnut Creek, CA.

Whitelaw, T.

2001   From Sites to Communities: Defining the Human Dimensions on Minoan Urbanism. In *Urbanism in the Aegean Bronze Age,* edited by K. Branigan, pp. 15–37. Sheffield Studies in Aegean Archaeology, Sheffield, UK.

Whitley, J.

1991   Social Diversity in Dark Age Greece. *Annual of the British School at Athens* 86: 341–365.

2001   *The Archaeology of Ancient Greece.* Cambridge University Press, New York.

Whittaker, C. R.

1990   The Consumer City Revisited: The *Vicus* and the City. *Journal of Roman Archaeology* 3:110–18.

Widmer, R. J.

1991   Lapidary Craft Specialization at Teotihuacan: Implications for Community Structure at 33:S3W1 and Economic Organization in the City. *Ancient Mesoamerica* 2:131–147.

Wiessner, P.

1983   Style and Social Information in Kalahari San Projectile Points. *American Antiquity* 48:253–276.

1990   Is There a Unity to Style? *In The Uses of Style in Archaeology,* edited by M. Conkey and C. Hastorf, pp. 105–112. New Directions in Archaeology. Cambridge University Press, New York.

Wietheger, C.

1992   Das Jeremias Kloster zu Saqqara unter besonderer Berücksichtigung der Inschriften. Oros, Altenberge, Germany.

Wilk, R. R., and H. Wilhite

1991   Patterns of Household and Settlement Change at Cuello. In *Cuello: An Early Maya Community in Belize,* edited by N. Hammond, pp. 118–133. Cambridge University Press, New York.

Wilk, R. R., H. Wilhite, and L. Reynolds

1980   The Settlement Area Sampling Project at Cuello, 1980. Paper presented at the 45th Annual Meeting of the Society for American Archaeology, Philadelphia.

Wilkenfeld, B. M.

1975   *The Social and Economic Structure of the City of New York, 1695–1796.* Arno Press, New York.

Will, E.

1990   La capitale de Séleucides. *Akten des XIII Internationalen Kongresses für klassiches Archäologie, Berlin 1988,* pp. 259–265. P. von Zabern, Mainz.

2000   Antioche, la métropole de l'Asie. In *Mégapoles méditerranéenes,* edited by C. Nicolet, R. Ilbert, and J-C. Depaule, pp. 482–491. Collection del L'École française de Rome 261. École française de Rome, Rome.

Willett, F.

1967   *Ife in the History of West African Sculpture.* McGraw-Hill, New York.

Willey, G. R.

1953   *Prehistoric Settlement Patterns in the Viru Valley, Peru.* Bureau of American Ethnology Bulletin No. 155. Government Printing Office, Washington, D.C.

Willey, G. R., W. R. Bullard Jr., J. B. Glass, and J. C. Gifford

1965   *Prehistoric Maya Settlements in the Belize Valley.* Peabody Museum of Archaeology and Ethnology, Papers 54, Harvard University Press, Cambridge.

Williams, B. J.

1989   Contact Period Rural Overpopulation in the Basin of Mexico: Carrying-Capacity Models Tested with Documentary Data. *American Antiquity* 54:715–732.

Wilson, D. J.

1997   Early State Formation on the North Coast of Peru: A Critique of the City-State Model. In *The Archaeology of City-States: Cross-Cultural Approaches,* edited by D. L. Nichols and T. H. Charlton, pp. 229–244. Smithsonian Institution Press, Washington, DC.

Wilson, R.

1990   *Sicily under the Roman Empire: The Archaeology of a Roman Province, 36 B.C.–A.D. 535.* Aris and Phillips, Warminster, UK.

2000   Ciceronian Sicily: An Archaeological Perspective. In *Sicily from Aeneas to Augustus,* edited by C. Smith and J. Serrati, pp. 134–60. Edinburgh University Press, Edinburgh.

Winzeler, R.

1976   Ecology, Culture, Social Organization and State Formation in Southeast Asia. *Current Anthropology* 17:623–640.

1981   The Study of the Southeast Asian State. In *The Study of the State,* edited by H. Claessen and P. Skalnik, pp. 455–467. Mouton, The Hague.

Wirth, L.

1938   Urbanism As a Way of Life. *American Journal of Sociology* 44:3–24.

Wisdom, C.

1940   *The Chorti Indians of Guatemala.* University of Chicago Press, Chicago.

Wiseman, D. J.

1985   *Nebuchadnezzar and Babylon.* Oxford University Press, New York.

Wiseman, T. P.

1998   *Roman Drama and Roman History.* University of Exeter Press, Exeter, UK.

Wittmer-Backoven, U., and H. Buba

   2002   Age Estimation by Tooth Cementum Annulation: Perspectives of a New Validation Study. In *Paleodemography: Age Distributions from Skeletal Samples,* edited by R. D. Hoppa and J. W. Vaupel, pp. 107–128. Cambridge University Press, New York.

Wolf, E. R.

   1959   *Sons of the Shaking Earth.* University of Chicago Press, Chicago.

   1976   Introduction. In *The Valley of Mexico,* edited by E. R. Wolf, pp. 1–10. University of New Mexico Press, Albuquerque.

   1982   *Europe and the People without History.* University of California Press, Berkeley.

Wolters, O. W.

   1967   *Early Indonesian Commerce.* Cornell University Press, Ithaca.

   1971   *The Fall of Srivijaya in Malay History.* Cornell University Press, Ithaca.

   1986   Restudying Some Chinese Writings on Srivijaya. *Indonesia* 42:1–41.

   1999   *History, Culture and Region in Southeast Asian Perspectives.* University of Hawaii Press, Honolulu.

Wood, J. W., G. R. Milner, H. C. Harpending, and K. M. Weiss

   1992   The Osteological Paradox: Problems of Inferring Health from Skeletal Samples. *Current Anthropology* 33:343–370.

Woods, R.

   2003   Urban-Rural Mortality Differentials: An Unresolved Debate. *Population and Development Review* 29:29–46.

Wright, H. T.

   1969   *The Administration of Rural Production in an Early Mesopotamian Town.* University of Michigan Museum of Anthropology, Ann Arbor.

   1977   Recent Research on the Origin of the State. *Annual Review of Anthropology* 6:379–397.

   1998   Uruk States in Southwestern Iran. In *Archaic States,* edited by G. M. Feinman and J. Marcus, pp. 173–198. School of American Research Press, Santa Fe.

Wright, H. T., and G. A. Johnson

   1975   Population, Exchange, and Early State Formation in Southwestern Iran. *American Anthropologist* 77:267–289.

Wright, H. T., R. Redding, and S. Pollock

   1989   Monitoring Interannual Variability: An Example from the Period of Early State Development in Southwestern Iran. In *Bad Year Economics: Cultural Responses to Risk and Uncertainty,* edited by P. Halstead and J. O'Shea. Cambridge University Press, New York.

Wrigley, E. A.

   1967   A Simple Model of London's Importance in Changing English Society and Economy 1650–1750. *Past and Present* 37:44–70.

   1990   Brake or Accelerator? Urban Growth and Population Growth before the Industrial Revolution. In *Urbanization in History: A Process of Dynamic Interactions,* edited by A. van der Woude, A. Hayami, and J. de Vries, pp. 101–112. Oxford University Press, New York.

Wrigley, E. A., R. S. Davies, J. E. Oeppen, and R. S. Schofield

   1997   *English Population History from Family Reconstruction, 1580–1837.* Cambridge University Press, New York.

Wu, C. H.

   1959   A Study of References to the Philippines in Chinese Sources from Earliest Times to the Ming Dynasty. *Philippine Social Sciences and Humanities Review* 24:1–182.

Xi'an Banpo Museum

1988   *Jiangzhai: Xinshiqi shidai yizhi fajue baogao* [*Jianzhai: Excavation Report of a Neolithic Site*]. Wenwu Chubanshe [Cultural Relics Press], Beijing.

Xia Shang Zhou Chronology Project Team (editor)

2000   *Xia Shang Zhou duandai gongcheng 1996–2000 nian jieduan chengguo baogao* [*Xia-Shang-Zhou Chronology Project: Report of Research in 1996–2000*]. Shijie Tushu [World Books Press], Beijing.

Xu, H., G. Chen, and H. Zhao

2003   Erlitou yizhi gongdianqu kaogu youyou zhongyao faxian [*New Discoveries in the Palatial Area at the Erlitou Site*]. *Zhongguo Wenwubao* [China Cultural Relics News]. 17 Jan. Beijing.

Xu, H., and H. Zhao

2004   Erlitou yizhi faxian gongcheng chengqiang deng zhongyao yicun [*Discovery of Palatial Walls at the Erlitou Site*]. *Zhongguo Wenwubao* [China Cultural Relics News]. 18 June. Beijing.

Yamin, R. (editor)

1998   *Tales of Five Points: Working Class Life in Nineteenth-Century New York,* Vol. 1. John Milner Associates, West Chester, NY.

Yang, G.

1988   Dui Xia Shang Zhou muchanliang de tuice [Estimating Agricultural Yields in the Xia, Shang, and Zhou Periods]. *Zhonguo Nongshi* [*Chinese Agriculture*] 2:24–26.

Yang, H.

2001   *Gongdian Kaogu Tonglun* [*Archaeology of Palaces*]. Zijincheng Chubanshe [Forbidden Palace Press], Beijing.

Yang, S.

1992   *Shangdai jingjishi* [*Economic History of Shang Dynasty*]. Guizhou Renmin Chubanshe [Guizhou People Press], Guiyang.

Yates, R. D. S.

1997   The City-State in Ancient China. In *The Archaeology of City States,* edited by D. L. Nichols and T. H. Charlton, pp. 71–90. Smithsonian Institution Press, Washington, DC.

Yoffee, N.

1993   Too Many Chiefs? (or Safe Texts for the 90s). In *Archaeological Theory: Who Sets the Agenda?* edited by N. Yoffee and A. Sherratt, pp. 60–78. Cambridge University Press, New York.

1995   Political Economy in Early Mesopotamian States. *Annual Review of Anthropology* 24:281–311.

1997   The Obvious and Chimerical: City-States in Archaeological Perspective. In *The Archaeology of City-States: Cross-Cultural Approaches,* edited by D. L. Nichols and T. H. Charlton, pp. 255–264. Smithsonian Institution Press, Washington, DC.

Yun, X.

1997   Xinshiqi shidai muzang zhong suizang laodong gongju de kaocha [Investigation of Production Tools in Neolithic Burials]. In *Kaogu Qiuzhij* [*Seeking the Truth in the Field of Archaeology*], edited by Institute of Archaeology CASS, pp. 83–113. Zhongguo Shehui Kexue Chubanshe [Chinese Social Sciences Press], Beijing.

Zangger, E., M. Timpson, S. Yazvenko, E. Kuhnke, and J. Knauss.

1997   The Pylos Regional Archaeological Project, Part II: Landscape Evolution and Site Preservation. *Hesperia* 66:549–641.

Zeder, M. A.
1991   *Feeding Cities.* Smithsonian Institution Press, Washington, DC.

Zhao, C.
1995   Jiangzhai yiqi mudi zaitan [More Investigation of the Jiangzhai Cemetery]. *Huaxia kaogu [Huaxia Archaeology]* 4:26–46.

1998   Yetan Jiangzhai yiqi cunluozhong de fangwu yu renkou [On the Houses and Population in the Village during Phase I at Jiangzhai]. *Kaogu yu wenwu [Archaeology and Cultural Relics]* 5:49–55.

Zheng, G.
1996   Yanshixian Erlitou yizhi [The Erlitou Site at Yanshi County]. In *Zhongguo Kaoguxue Nianjian [Yearbook of Chinese Archaeology]*, edited by the Chinese Archaeology Association, pp. 167–168. Wenwu Chubanshe [Cultural Relics Press], Beijing.

Zheng, G., G. Yang, G. Zhang, and J. Du
1984   Yanshixian Erlitou yizhi [The Erlitou Site at Yanshi County]. In *Zhongguo Kaoguxue Nianjian [Yearbook of Chinese Archaeology]*, edited by the Chinese Archaeology Association, pp. 128–129. Wenwu Chubanshe [Cultural Relics Press], Beijing.

1987   Yanshixian Erlitou yizhi [The Erlitou Site at Yanshi County]. In *Zhongguo Kaoguxue Nianjian [Yearbook of Chinese Archaeology]*, edited by the Chinese Archaeology Association, pp. 178–180. Wenwu Chubanshe [Cultural Relics Press], Beijing.

Zubrow, E. B. W.
1976   Demographic Anthropology: An Introductory Analysis. In *Demographic Anthropology*, edited by E. B. W. Zubrow, pp. 1–25. University of New Mexico Press, Albuquerque.

Zuidema, R. T.
1977–   Shafttombs and the Inca Empire. *Steward Journal of Anthropology* 9:133–178.
78

Contributors

Babatunde Agbaje-Williams (PhD, University of Ibadan) is at the Institute of African Studies, University of Ibadan, Ibadan, Nigeria. His work focuses on Yoruba historical archaeology and cultural resource management. His books include *Cultural Resources in Ijesaland Western Nigeria* (with A. O. Ogundiran, 1992) and *Archaeological Investigation of Itagunmodi Potsherd Pavement Site in Ijesaland, Osun State, Nigeria* (1995). Articles include "Archaeology and Yoruba Studies," *Yoruba Historiography* (1991); "Potsherd Pavements and Early Urban Sites in Yorubaland, Nigeria: An Interim Report" (2001); and "Yoruba Urbanism: The Archaeology and Historical Ethnography of Ile-Ife and Old Oyo" (2004).

Roger S. Bagnall is Professor of Classics and History at Columbia University. Among his books are *Egypt in Late Antiquity* (1993), *The Demography of Roman Egypt* (with Bruce Frier, 1994), and *Reading Papyri, Writing Ancient History* (1995). He will be Sather Professor of Classical Literature at the University of California, Berkeley, in the fall of 2005.

Deborah E. Blom is Associate Professor of Anthropology at the University of Vermont. She has been working in the Andean region of Bolivia and Peru since 1993. Her areas of specialties include human osteology, paleopathology, mortuary practices, migration, and ethnicity and identity. Articles she has published on these topics include "Tiwanaku 'Colonization': Bioarchaeological Implications for Migration in the Moquegua Valley, Peru," with others, *World Archaeology* (1998); "Making Place: Humans as Objects of Dedication in Tiwanaku Society," with John W. Janusek, *World Archaeology* (2004); and "Embodying Borders: Human Body Modification and Diversity in Tiwanaku Society," *Journal of Anthropological Archaeology* (2005). She is currently codirecting a project at the site of Tiwanaku, Bolivia, with Nicole Couture of McGill University.

Jesper L. Boldsen is Head of the Department of Anthropology, Institute of Forensic Medicine, University of Southern Denmark, Odense. He has studied the Danish population during the Middle Ages for nearly 30 years on the basis of excavated skeletons. His main research interests are paleodemography, paleo-epidemiology, medieval population structure, and the evolution of patterns of mortality in Holocene Europe. He has published more than 100 scientific papers. Recent examples include "Estimating Patterns of Disease and Mortality in a Medieval Danish Village," in R. R. Paine, ed., *Integrating Archaeological Demography: Multi-Disciplinary Approaches to Prehistoric Population* (1997); "Patterns of Childhood Mortality in Medieval Scandinavia," *Revista di Antropologia* (1997); "Epidemiological Approaches to the Paleopathological Diagnosis of Leprosy," *American Journal of Physical Anthropology* (2001); and "Transition Analysis: A New Method for Estimating Age from Skeletons," with G. R. Milner, L. W. Konigsberg, and J. W. Wood, in R. D. Hoppa and J. W. Vaupel, eds., *Paleodemography: Age Distributions from Skeletal Samples* (2002).

L. J. Gorenflo holds the position of Director in the Center for Applied Biodiversity Science's Human Dimensions Program at Conservation International. With advanced degrees in anthropology (MA) and geography (PhD), Gorenflo focuses on issues involving regional adaptation in prehistoric, historic, and modern contexts. He has conducted research and published on a range of topics associated with human settlement and demographics, including studies of settlement patterns in the prehispanic Basin of Mexico, regional settlement and historical demography throughout Micronesia, and the impacts of human settlement and land use on biodiversity conservation at both regional and global scales.

John Wayne Janusek is Assistant Professor of Anthropology at Vanderbilt University. He has conducted archaeological research in the Bolivian Andes since 1987, investigating urban and rural dimensions of complex societies in the region. He is author of *Identity and Power in the Ancient Andes: Tiwanaku Cities through Time* (2004) and *Ancient Tiwanaku: Civilization in the High Andes* (2006).

Laura Lee Junker is Associate Professor, Department of Anthropology, University of Illinois at Chicago. She specializes in the political economy of prehispanic chiefdoms in the Philippines. Her publications include *Raiding, Trading, and Feasting: The Political Economy of Philippine Chiefdoms* (1999) and *Forager-Traders in South and Southeast Asia: Long-Term Histories* (edited, 2002).

Chapurukha Kusimba is Associate Curator of African Archaeology and Ethnology at the Field Museum of Natural History, Chicago, and Adjunct Associate Professor at Northwestern University and the University of Illinois at Chicago. He received his doctorate in anthropology from Bryn Mawr College, Pennsylvania, in 1993. He has published extensively on African archaeology and anthropology. His research has been supported by the National Science Foundation, the National Geographic Society, the Fulbright Fellowship, and the Field Museum. His most recent books are *East African Archaeology: Foragers, Potters, Smiths, and Traders* (edited with Sibel Kusimba, 2003) and *Unwrapping a Little Known Textile Tradition: Malagasy Textiles* (edited with Bennet Bronson and J. Claire Odland, 2004). His current research is in Kenya and the Czech Republic.

Sibel Barut Kusimba is Assistant Professor of Anthropology at Northern Illinois University. She conducts fieldwork in Kenya and has conducted research on Stone Age foragers and Iron Age regional interactions. She is the author of *African Foragers: Technology, Environment, Interactions* (2003), which was named an "Outstanding Title" by *Choice*.

Li Liu (PhD, 1994, Harvard University) currently teaches at La Trobe University and codirects the Yiluo River Archaeological Project in central China. Her research interests include settlement archaeology, zooarchaeology, Neolithic China, and state formation in China. Her two most recent publications on China are *The Chinese Neolithic: Trajectories to Early States* (2004) and *State Formation in Early China* (coedited with Xingcan Chen, 2003).

Elio Lo Cascio is Professor of Roman History at the University Federico II of Naples. He spent several terms conducting research at the University of Cambridge (1976–1978) and at the Institute for Advanced Study, Princeton, where he was a member of the School of Historical Studies (1993 and 2001). His published work primarily focuses on three topics: the administrative history of the principate and of the late empire; the economic and social history of Rome, with particular emphasis on monetary history from the late republic to the late empire; and Roman population history and the impact of demographic change on the economic and social history of Rome. His most recent publications include *Il princeps e il suo impero: Studi di storia amministrativa e finanziaria romana* (2000) and the edited volumes *Roma imperiale: Una metropoli antica* (2000); *Mercati permanenti e mercati periodici nel mondo romano* (2000); *Production and Public Powers in Antiquity* (with D. W. Rathbone, 2000); *Modalità insediative e strutture agrarie nell'Italia meridionale in età romana* (with A. Storchi Marino, 2001); and *Credito e moneta nel mondo romano* (2003). He is the editor of the series *Pragmateiai: Texts and Studies in the Economic, Social and Administrative History of the Ancient World*.

Ian Morris is the Jean and Rebecca Willard Professor of Classics and Professor of History at Stanford University and Director of the Stanford Archaeology Center. His most recent books are *Archaeology as Cultural History: Words and Things in*

Iron Age Greece (2000), *The Greeks: History, Culture, and Society* (with Barry Powell, 2005), and *The Ancient Economy: Evidence and Models* (edited with Joe Manning, 2005). He directs a major excavation at Monte Polizzo in Sicily and is currently completing editorial work on *The Cambridge Economic History of the Greco-Roman World.*

Sarah M. Nelson is a John Evans Professor at the University of Denver. Her most recent books are *Ancient Queens* (2003), *Gender in Archaeology* (second edition, 2004), *Korean Social Archaeology* (2004), and a novel, *Jade Dragon* (2004).

Deborah L. Nichols is the William J. Bryant Professor of Anthropology at Dartmouth College. She has conducted archaeological research on the development of ancient cities and states in Mesoamerica, and she has also worked in the U.S. Southwest. Her recent publications include "Neutrons, Markets, Cities, and Empires," with Elizabeth Brumfiel, Hector Neff, Thomas H Charlton, Michael D. Glascock, and Mary Hodge, *Journal of Anthropological Archaeology* (2002); *Archeology Is Anthropology,* Archeological Papers of the American Anthropological Association No. 13 (coedited with Susan D. Gillespie, 2003); and "Rural and Urban Landscapes of the Aztec State," in Rosemary Joyce and Julia Hendon, eds., *Mesoamerican Archaeology: Theory and Practice* (2004).

Richard R. Paine (PhD Anthropology and Demography, Penn State University) is Associate Professor of Anthropology at the University of Utah. His research interests include prehistoric demography, the impact of epidemic disease on ancient populations, and the evolution of mortality patterns in Holocene Europe. Among his recent publications are "If a Population Crashes in Prehistory and There Is No Paleodemographer to Hear It, Does It Make a Sound?" *American Journal of Physical Anthropology* (2000) and "Linking Mortality and Population Dynamics," with Jesper L. Boldsen, in R. D. Hoppa and J. W. Vaupel, eds., *Paleodemography: Age Distributions from Skeletal Samples* (2002), which examines the impact of epidemic disease on the distribution of mortality. He is currently editing *The Evolution of Human Life History* with Kristen Hawkes.

Hans Christian Petersen is Associate Professor (Biostatistics), Department of Statistics, University of Southern Denmark in Odense. He received his PhD in Biology (Palaeoanthropology and Population Biology) at the Institute of Genetics and Ecology, Aarhus University, Denmark, in 1992. He was Head of the Osteological Unit, Museum of National Antiquities, Stockholm, Sweden, 1991–1992; the Invited Maître de Conférences (associate professor), Laboratoire d'Anthropologie, Université de Bordeaux I, France, Spring 1994; Research Fellow at the National Institute of Public Health, Copenhagen, Denmark, 1995–1996, and Assistant Research Professor at the Anthropological DataBase and Institute of

Public Health, University of Southern Denmark, 1997–2001. Publications include "A Discriminant Analysis Approach to Morphological Regionalization in the European Late Mesolithic," *Anthropologischer Anzeiger* (1997); "On Statistical Methods for Comparison of Intrasample Morphometric Variability: Zalavár Revisited," *American Journal of Physical Anthropology* (2000); "Reproduction Life History and Hip Fractures," with B. Jeune, J. W. Vaupel, and K. Christensen, *Annals of Epidemiology* (2002); and "On the Accuracy of Estimating Living Stature from Skeletal Length in the Grave and by Linear Regression," *International Journal of Osteoarchaeology* (2005).

Don S. Rice completed his PhD degree in Anthropology at the Pennsylvania State University in 1976, specializing in archaeology and cultural ecology. He then took two years of postdoctoral training in paleoecology and tropical ecology at the University of Florida on a Social Science Research Council fellowship. Rice taught at the University of Chicago (1976–1987) and the University of Virginia (1987–1991) before moving to Southern Illinois University, Carbondale, where he is currently the Associate Provost for Academic Administration and a Professor of Anthropology. His most recent publications include *The Terminal Classic in the Maya Lowlands: Collapse, Transition, and Transformation,* edited with Arthur A. Demarest and Prudence M. Rice (2004), and "History in the Future: Historical Data and Investigations in Lowland Maya Studies," with Prudence M. Rice, in Greg Borgstede and Charles Golden, eds., *Continuities and Contentions in Maya Archaeology: A Perspective at the New Millennium* (2004). Don and Pru Rice are currently directing a multiyear project investigating the sixteenth-century Maya political geography in the central lakes region of the Department of Petén, Guatemala.

Nan A. Rothschild is the Ann Whitney Olin Professor of Anthropology at Barnard College, Columbia University. She has conducted field research in New York City and in New Mexico. Her publications include *New York City Neighborhoods: The Eighteenth Century* (1990, but soon to be published in paperback from Eliot Werner Publications) and *Colonial Encounters in a Native American Landscape* (2003). She received her PhD from New York University.

Brent D. Shaw is the Andrew Fleming West Professor of Classics at Princeton University. He has published on the history of Roman North Africa, and he is currently working on projects that are specifically directed to the understanding of civil and sectarian violence in the fourth- and fifth-century empire in what might be called the Age of Augustine. More relevant to the current volume, he has published on the history of the Roman family and on the subject of demography of the Roman world, specifically its urban-centered populations in the western empire.

David B. Small obtained his PhD in Classical Archaeology from Cambridge University, but he has transformed himself into an "old-fashioned" generalist. An original member of the early heterarchy group, his interests center on past complexity. His current work takes him to Crete, where he is studying the evolution of rural complexity, and to Honduras, where he is excavating a large rural site, in efforts to understand the many facets of rural production, exchange, and power.

Glenn R. Storey is Associate Professor of Classics and Anthropology at the University of Iowa (PhD, Penn State). He has published on issues of Roman demography; the archaeology, history, and literature of domestic residences in Roman cities; and issues of the Roman economy. His fieldwork includes Mesoamerica at Teotihuacan in Mexico and Copán, Honduras; the American Midatlantic; the American Southwest; the American Midwest; Roman Italy (especially Rome and Ostia); Nijmegen, The Netherlands; and Gangivecchio, Sicily, where he has experimented with ground-penetrating radar applications to archaeology. He is currently editing a beginning classical Greek textbook and a grammar primer by the Nigerian scholar James Eezuduemhoi.

Rebecca Storey, Department of Anthropology, University of Houston (PhD, Penn State), is a bioarchaeologist specializing in the Pre-Columbian Peoples of Mesoamerica from Teotihuacan and the Maya area. Publications include *Life and Death in the Ancient City of Teotihuacan* (1992), "Social Disruption and the Maya Civilization of Mesoamerica" and "Health and Nutrition in Pre-Hispanic Mesoamerica," in R. Steckel and J. Rose, eds., *The Backbone of History* (2002), and "The Ancestors," in P. A. McAnany, ed., *K'axob: Ritual, Work, and Family* (2004).

Index

abortion, 208, 228

administrative city (Fox): as appropriate model for Maya, 274–275; trade and tribute networks, 275

age: awareness, 84; classes, 54; distribution, 19, 74, 75, 78; distribution, peculiar, and sex, 65; given on gravestones, 139; exaggeration, 65; inaccurate, 85; older, absence of, 141; rounding, 66, 141; and sex distribution, peculiar, 65; and sex structure, 144; structure, 11, 54, 79, 142, 144

age at death: and frailty, 292; distributions, 76, 80, 82, 83, 284–286; epigraphic, 69, 70; estimating accurately, of a skeleton, 284; mean, 77; skeletal, 281

age distribution of death: anomalies in, 289; and demographic information, 288; derived from skeletons, 283; and migrants, 293; effect on fertility, 290; and healthiness of environment, 292; similarity to a living population, 71–72. *See also* age at death

age estimation: accuracy of younger estimates, 284; errors, 285, 288; and unknown chronological age, 287

agglomeration. *See* coalescence, village (or amalgamation)

agriculture: cereal cultivation, 149; chinampa, 313; Classical, 41; emergence of Erlitou, 187; failure and Maya collapse, 256; high yields, 165; intensive, 173, 186, 258, 324; intensive, capacity to absorb labor, 324; limited potential, 257; lowland farmers,

205; maize, 309; shifting, 148; taxes, 317; within city walls, 157; zones, 12. *See also* slash-and-burn agriculture

agro-center, administrative, 8, 89

Alexander the Great, 46, 48, 49

Alexandria (Egypt), 48, 49, 50, 51, 140, 196

alienation, 10, 22

alliance: building activities, 203; exchange, 223; gift-sealed, 225; networks, 209, 228–229; personal ties of, 215; trade, 228

amalgamation. *See* coalescence, village (or amalgamation)

amenities: public, 80; urban, 38

ancestors: ancient, 236; and communities, 249; cults, 321; and secular authority, 271; worship and *sian otot*, 325

Andes, 1, 14, 233–251, 331, 333, 336, 337

ANOVA (analysis of variance), 116

Antioch (Asia Minor), 27, 48, 49, 50, 51

Antonine plague (epidemic under Marcus Aurelius), 5, 7, 67, 70, 73, 74, 75, 77, 79, 81, 139

aqueducts, 61, 80

archaeological remains, 175; of bronze casting, 166; low visibility of, 218; material and cultural deposits, 178. *See also* archaeology

archaeology (archaeological): attention, limited, 217; and bioanthropology (bioarchaeology), 234, 237; city size, 150; cultures defined by ceramic typology, 178; and ethnohistorical research, 250; historical, 9, 14, 121–136, 193, 205, 340; investiga-

terial, rural areas, 189; dispersed, 5; and diversity, 233; as dynamic, 331; emergence, and maritime foreign trade, 230; function, 121; growth of, 149, 229; high culture, 32; hyper, definition of, 22; hyperlarge, 2, 15; hypo-urban, definition of, 4; industrialization, 1; influx (in-migration) of rural peoples into, 326; innovation, 339; males, attractor for, 143; maritime trading, 14; merchant (Weber), 31, 32, 51; Mesopotamian, 161; mini, 14; as *oppida,* definition of, 319; as part of larger societies, 336; port, 214–17; pristine, 233; producer (Weber), 31, 32, 45, 51; scale, 203; shift from agrarian to industrial, 336; suburban, 5, 17, 20; super, 2, 15, 18, 22, 27, 28, 31, 32, 51; trading, large coastal, 206; typology of (Fox), 274; unhealthier than rural areas, 282–83

cities, African: Egypt, 12; Iron Age of East African coast, 149; lack of, 147; less dense, 154; Middle Egyptian, 142, 143, 339; patterns, 145; Roman Egyptian, 11, 143; Saharan trade, 149; sub-Saharan, 11; and towns, precolonial, 145–58; types, 153

cities, Andean: as administrative, ceremonial or ritual, 337; dynamics of, 249; as extended elite households, 234; and Mesoamerican, comparison of, 337; size, 234; Tiwanaku, 234, 250

cities, Asian: autonomous, Kaya (Korea), 190; Chinese, pattern of, 199; Chinese, unusually large, 154; Harappan, 17; Shang, 164; southeast Asian port, 336

cities, European: Aegean, 48; Classical, 1; Dutch, 54; early modern, 57, 58, 64; and malaria, 62; quantitative data of seventeenth and eighteenth centuries, 53; size range, 150

cities, Mayan: complex, Maya sites as, 255; dispersed character of, 333; and town, 270

citizenship, egalitarian male, culture of, 38

city: area of, 125–26; attributes, 121; center, planned, 218; communication methods and efficiency, 158; as community, 125; core, 271; and country, 60; definition of, 2, 152; dwellers, 132; features, 2; flavor of, 190; gridded and walled, 199; growth,

153; hypothetical, 182; inhabitants, 318; inner, walled, 178; integrating mechanisms, 233; life, 10, 233, 236; population of, engaged in manufacturing, 317; physical plant of, 18; planning, 269; preindustrial, 250, 277; psychology of, 18; segment, accessible to all, 131; stretching out indefinitely, 60; walking, 9–10; walls, 41, 43, 44, 178, 182, 199

city and countryside: alternative power base to urban, 20; flow of subsistence and other goods between, 318; functions, 187; as major theme, 331; relations, 21. *See also* city and hinterland

city and hinterland: characteristic dispersal of, 17; condition of, 125; cult activities for integration of, 15, 18; interdependence, 189; intimate integration of, 16; relationship, 124; unity of, 2, 8. *See also* hinterland

cityscapes, 1

city-state: capitals, Maya centers as, 274; Greek concept of polis, 2; gobbled up by Silla, 196; as hypo-urban, 4; as model for early urbanism in China, 161; nature of Greek, 21–22; not self-sufficient, 32; Pan-Hellenic sanctuaries and sway over, 20; population of typical Greek, 4; and preference for urban living, 5; sanctuaries, 327; size, 41; territorial state model, 337

civic council of Athens, 43

Civil War, effects of, 126

civil war, fall of Mayapán, 268

clan: land, demarcation of, 149; subversion of, 233

class: and artifacts as manifestations of social status, 133; consciousness, 10; and ethnicity, 133; and landscapes of power and meaning, 131; permanent laboring, 130; reformulation and hardening of, 134; social, 125; structure, 124, 134, 338; system, 130, 135; working, 135

clients, 135, 321

climate: African, 147; Balkan, 32; change, 266; conditions, 8; Mediterranean, 32, 33; perturbation, and Teotihuacan, 294; seasonal fluctuations, 254

clues to past social affiliations and identity, 239

Coale and Demeny, 72, 82, 84, 85, 140, 290